Principles of International Economic Law

Second Edition

MATTHIAS HERDEGEN

University of Nottingham
Hallward Library

OXFORD

UNIVERSITY PRESS

OXFORD
UNIVERSITY PRESS

Great Clarendon Street, Oxford, OX2 6DP,
United Kingdom

Oxford University Press is a department of the University of Oxford.
It furthers the University's objective of excellence in research, scholarship,
and education by publishing worldwide. Oxford is a registered trade mark of
Oxford University Press in the UK and in certain other countries

© Matthias Herdegen 2016

The moral rights of the author have been asserted

First Edition published in 2013
Second Edition published in 2016
Impression: 1

All rights reserved. No part of this publication may be reproduced, stored in
a retrieval system, or transmitted, in any form or by any means, without the
prior permission in writing of Oxford University Press, or as expressly permitted
by law, by licence or under terms agreed with the appropriate reprographics
rights organization. Enquiries concerning reproduction outside the scope of the
above should be sent to the Rights Department, Oxford University Press, at the
address above

You must not circulate this work in any other form
and you must impose this same condition on any acquirer

Crown copyright material is reproduced under Class Licence
Number C01P0000148 with the permission of OPSI
and the Queen's Printer for Scotland

Published in the United States of America by Oxford University Press
198 Madison Avenue, New York, NY 10016, United States of America

British Library Cataloguing in Publication Data
Data available

Library of Congress Control Number: 2016936068

ISBN 978–0–19–879056–3 (hbk.)
ISBN 978–0–19–879057–0 (pbk.)

Printed and bound by
CPI Group (UK) Ltd, Croydon, CR0 4YY

Links to third party websites are provided by Oxford in good faith and
for information only. Oxford disclaims any responsibility for the materials
contained in any third party website referenced in this work.

UNIVERSITY LIBRARY NOTTINGHAM	
100762753 3	
Askews & Holts	

Acknowledgements

This book owes much insight, stimulus, and encouragement to many, in all the years of research, teaching, and advisory practice in international economic law. Colleagues and students alike on both sides of the Atlantic broadened and deepened the author's sensitivity to the interplay between international economic law in the traditional sense and other legal regimes, especially human rights and environmental law as well as for the balance between universal or regional standards and proper deference to local or national values in all their diversity.

The same holds true for a *leitmotif* of the book, the contribution of modern international economic law to rationality, to the rule of law, and other aspects of 'good governance'. The new edition reflects recent developments in many fields. In particular, world trade law, (mega-)regional agreements, corporate social responsibility, and environmental law are areas of considerable and persistent dynamics. On the global and regional levels we see tectonic changes in the architecture of monetary law and the financial system.

My particular thanks go to present or former research assistants at my chair at the University of Bonn, in particular to Carsten Kalla LLM (Columbia).

M.H.

Table of Contents

PART II. INTERNATIONAL ECONOMIC LAW AS
AN ORDER OF RULES AND PRINCIPLES

PART V. THE INTERNATIONAL LAW
OF FOREIGN INVESTMENT

PART VI. INTERNATIONAL MONETARY LAW AND
THE INTERNATIONAL FINANCIAL ARCHITECTURE

Table of International Cases

Cases are listed alphabetically under the relevant court or tribunal.

IV. CASES BROUGHT BEFORE THE EUROPEAN COURT OF FIRST INSTANCE

V. CASES BROUGHT BEFORE THE EUROPEAN COURT OF HUMAN RIGHTS (ECTHR)

VI. CASES BROUGHT BEFORE THE INTER-AMERICAN COURT OF HUMAN RIGHTS (IACTHR)

VII. CASES BROUGHT BEFORE THE AFRICAN COURT ON HUMAN AND PEOPLES' RIGHTS (AFCHPR)

VIII. CASES BROUGHT BEFORE THE SOUTHERN AFRICAN DEVELOPMENT COMMUNITY TRIBUNAL (SADC)

IX. CASES BROUGHT BEFORE THE WTO'S APPELLATE BODY

X. CASES BROUGHT BEFORE THE WTO'S PANELS

XI. IRAN–US CLAIMS TRIBUNAL

XII. ICSID CASES

XIII. UNCITRAL CASES

XIV. CASES BROUGHT BEFORE THE US SUPREME COURT

XV. CASES BROUGHT BEFORE THE HOUSE OF LORDS

XVI. CASES BROUGHT BEFORE THE GERMAN FEDERAL CONSTITUTIONAL COURT (BUNDESVERFASSUNGSGERICHT)

XVII. CASES BROUGHT BEFORE THE GERMAN FEDERAL COURT OF JUSTICE (BUNDESGERICHTSHOF—BGH)

XVIII. MISCELLANEOUS CASES BROUGHT BEFORE VARIOUS NATIONAL COURTS

1. Germany

2. USA

XIX. MISCELLANEOUS CASES

Table of International Treaties and Conventions

Table of National Legislation

Legislation is listed alphabetically under the relevant country.

List of Abbreviations

AC	Law Reports, Appeal Cases (Third Series)
AfCHPR	African Court on Human and People's Rights
AFDI	Annuaire Français de Droit International
AIDI	Annuaire de l'Institut de Droit International (Yearbook of the Institute of International Law)
AJIL	American Journal of International Law
All ER	All England Law Reports
Am Rev Int'l Arb	American Review of International Arbitration
Am U Int'l L Rev	American University International Law Review
Am UJ Int'l L & Pol'y	American University Journal of International Law and Policy
Antitrust LJ	Antitrust Law Journal
Arb Int'l	Arbitration International
Ariz J Int'l & Comp L	Arizona Journal of International and Comparative Law
ASEAN	Association of Southeast Asian Nations
ASIL	American Society of International Law
AVR	Archiv des Völkerrechts
BCCI	Bank of Credit and Commerce International
BCSC	British Columbia Supreme Court
Berk J Int'l L	Berkeley Journal of International Law
BGH	Federal Court of Justice, Germany (Bundesgerichtshof)
BGHZ	Entscheidungen des Bundesgerichtshofes in Zivilsachen (Decisions of the German Federal Court of Justice for civil matters)
BIS	Bank for International Settlements
BLCR	Boston College Law Review
Brooklyn J Int'l L	Brooklyn Journal of International Law
BTLJ	Berkley Technology Law Journal
BU Int'l LJ	Boston University International Law Journal
BULR	Boston University Law Review
BVerfGE	Entscheidungen des Bundesverfassungsgerichts (decisions of the German Federal Constitutional Court)
BYIL	British Yearbook of International Law
CBLR	Columbia Business Law Review
CCJ	Caribbean Court of Justice
CETA	Comprehensive Economic and Trade Agreement
Ch	Chapter
Chi J Int'l L	Chicago Journal of International Law
CML Rev	Common Market Law Review
Colo. J. Int'l Envt'l. L.& Pol'y	Colorado Journal of International Environmental Law and Policy
Colum J Transnat'l L	Columbia Journal of Transnational Law
Colum L Rev	Columbia Law Review

Cornell Int'l LJ	Cornell International Law Journal
Cornell L Rev	Cornell Law Review
CUP	Cambridge University Press
ECFR	European Company and Financial Law Review
ECLI	European Case Law Identifier
ECJ	European Court of Justice
ECOWAS	Economic Community of West African States
ECR	European Court Report
ECtHR	European Court of Human Rights
edn	edition
EITI	Extractive Industries Transparency Initiative
EJIL	European Journal of International Law
EMU	European Monetary Union
EPIL	Encyclopedia of Public International Law
EU	European Union
Eur Bus L Rev	European Business Law Review
Eur Competition J	European Competition Journal
Eur Competition L Ann	European Competition Law Annual
Eur St Aid LQ	European State Aid Law Quarterly
EuZW	Europäische Zeitschrift für Wirtschaftsrecht
EYIEL	European Yearbook of International Economic Law
f/ff	and following
F.2d	Federal Reporter, Second Series
F.3d	Federal Reporter, Third Series
F.Appx.	Federal Appendix
F.Supp	Federal Supplement
Fordham Int'l LJ	Fordham International Law Journal
Foreign Pol'y	Foreign Policy
FORUM	International Law FORUM du droit international
FSB	Financial Stability Board
Ga J Int'l & Comp L	Georgia Journal of International and Comparative Law
GA Res	Resolution of United Nations General Assembly
German LJ	German Law Journal
GJIL	Georgetown Journal of International Law
GRUR	Gewerblicher Rechtschutz und Urheberrecht
GYIL	German Yearbook of International Law
Harv Int'l LJ	Harvard International Law Journal
Hastings Int'l & Comp L Rev	Hastings International and Comparative Law Review
HLR	Harvard Law Review
HRLJ	Human Rights Law Journal
Hum Rts & Int'l Legal Discourse	Human Rights and International Legal Discourse
Hum Rts Q	Human Rights Quarterly
HWWA	Hamburgisches Welt-Wirtschafts-Archiv

IACtHR	Inter-American Court of Human Rights
IBLJ	International Business Law Journal
IBRD	International Bank for Reconstruction and Development
ICANN	Internet Corporation for Assigned Names and Numbers
ICC	International Chamber of Commerce
ICJ	International Court of Justice
ICLQ	International and Comparative Law Quarterly
ICLR	International Construction Law Review
ICSID	International Centre for Settlement of Investment Disputes
ICSID Rev	ICSID Review
IIC	International Review of Intellectual Property and Competition Law
ILM	International Legal Materials
ILR	International Law Reports
IMF	International Monetary Fund
Ind J Global Legal Stud	Indiana Journal of Global Legal Studies
Int'l L & Pol	International Law and Politics
Int'l Law	International Lawyer
Int'l Org	International Organization
Int'l Trade & Bus L Rev	International Trade and Business Law Review
ITLOS	International Tribunal for the Law of the Sea
JAL	Journal of African Law
JCLS	Journal of Corporate Law Studies
J Droit Int'l	Journal du Droit International
JEL	Journal of Environmental Law
J Energy Nat Resources L	Journal of Energy & Natural Resources Law
JIBL	Journal of International Banking Law
JIB Law	Journal of International Biotechnology Law
JICJ	Journal of International Criminal Justice
J Int'l Arbit	Journal of International Arbitration
J Int'l Dispute Settlement	Journal of International Dispute Settlement
J Int'l Econ L	Journal of International Economic Law
JL & Com	Journal of Law and Commerce
JL & Econ Dev	Journal of Law and Economic Development
JLTP	University of Illinois Journal of Law, Technology & Policy
J Priv Int'l L	Journal of Private International Law
J Transnat'l L & Pol'y	Journal of Transnational Law and Policy
JWI	Journal of World Investment (now JWIT)
JWIT	Journal of World Investment and Trade
JWT	Journal of World Trade
JWTL	Journal of World Trade Law
JZ	Juristenzeitung
Law Bus Rev	Law Business Review
Law & Prac Int'l Cts & Tribunals	Law and Practice of International Courts and Tribunals
LCIA	London Court of International Arbitration

Loy LA Int'l & Comp L Rev	Loyola of Los Angeles International and Comparative Law Review
LIEI	Legal Issues of Economic Integration
LQR	Law Quarterly Review
Max Planck YB UN L	Max Planck Yearbook of United Nations Law
McGill LJ	Mc Gill Law Journal
Melb J Int'l L	Melbourne Journal of International Law
Mich J Int'l L	Michigan Journal of International Law
Minn J Global Trade	Minnesota Journal of Global Trade
Minn L Rev	Minnesota Law Review
MJIEL	Manchester Journal of International Economic Law
NAFTA	North American Free Trade Agreement
Nat Resources J	Natural Resources Journal
NCJ Int'l L & Com Reg	North Carolina Journal of International Law and Commercial Regulation
NE 2d	North Eastern Reporter, Second Series
New England Econ Rev	New England Economic Review
NILR	Netherlands International Law Review
NJW	Neue Juristische Wochenschrift
Nordic J Int'l L	Nordic Journal of International Law
Northwest J Int'l Law Bus	Northwestern Journal of International Law and Business
Notre Dame L Rev	Notre Dame Law Review
NQHR	Netherlands Quarterly of Human Rights
NYIL	Netherlands Yearbook of International Law
NY2d	New York Reports, Second Series
NYS 2d	New York Supplement, Second Series
NYU Envt'l LJ	New York University Environmental Law Journal
NYU J Int'l L & Pol	New York University Journal of International Law and Politics
Nw J Int'l L & Bus	Northwestern Journal of International Law and Business
OJ	Official Journal of the European Communities
OUP	Oxford University Press
para/paras	paragraph/paragraphs
PCA	Permanent Court of Arbitration
PCIJ	Permanent Court of International Justice
QJ Econ	Quarterly Journal of Economics
RAE	Review of Agricultural Economics
RablesZ	Rabels Zeitschrift für ausländisches und internationals Privatrecht
RdC Rep	Recueil des Cours de l'Académie de Droit International de la Haye, Reports of Judgments, Advisory Opinions and Orders

Rev Arb	Revue de l'arbitrage
Rev Banking & Fin L	Review of Banking and Finance Law Privé
Rev Crit Dr Intern Priv	Revue Critique de Droit International
RGDIP	Revue générale de droit international public
RIAA	Reports of International Arbitral Awards
RIW	Recht der Internationalen Wirtschaft
SADC	Southern African Development Community
Schw Z Int & Eu R	Schweizerische Zeitschrift für Internationales und Europäisches Recht
SDILJ	San Diego International Law Journal
SDNY	Southern District Court of New York
Stan L Rev	Stanford Law Review
Stockholm Int'l Arb Rev	Stockholm International Arbitration Review
Stud Int'l Fin Econ & Tech L	Studies in International Financial, Economic, and Technology Law
Stud Transnat'l Legal Pol'y	Studies in Transnational Legal Policy
Suffolk U L Rev	Suffolk University Law Reform
Sup Ct	Supreme Court
TEU	Treaty on European Union
Texas Int'l LJ	Texas International Law Journal
TFEU	Treaty of the Functioning of the European Union
TJICL	Tulane Journal of International and Comparative Law
TPP	Trans-Pacific Partnership
TTIP	Transatlantic Trade and Investment Partnership
UC Davis J Int'l L & Pol'y	UC Davis Journal of International Law and Policy
ULR	Utrecht Law Review
U Miami Bus L Rev	University of Miami Business Law Review
UN	United Nations
UN Doc	United Nations Documents
UNHCR	United Nations High Commissioner for Refugees
UNHRC	United Nations Human Rights Committee
UNTS	United Nations Treaty Series
UNYB	Yearbook of the United Nations
UP	University Press
U Pa J Int'l Econ L	University of Pennsylvania Journal of International Economic Law
U Rich L Rev	University of Richmond Law Review
USCTR	Iran–United States Claims Tribunal
USPQ	United States Patents Quarterly
Va J Int'l L	Virginia Journal of International Law
Va L & Bus Rev	Virginia Law and Business Review
Vand J Transnat'l L	Vanderbilt Journal of Transnational Law
Villanova L Rev	Villanova Law Review
VRÜ	Verfassung und Recht in Übersee

WBRO   World Bank Research Observer
W Comp   World Competition
WLR   Weekly Law Reports
WM   Wertpapier-Mitteilungen (Zeitschrift für Wirtschafts-und Bankrecht)

Yale J Int'l L   Yale Journal of International Law
Yale LJ   Yale Law Journal
YBCA   Yearbook of Commercial Arbitration
YIEL   Yearbook of International Environmental Law

ZaöRV   Zeitschrift für ausländisches öffentliches Recht und Völkerrecht
ZGR   Zeitschrift für Unternehmens- und Gesellschaftsrecht

PART I

CONTENTS, HISTORY, AND STRUCTURE OF INTERNATIONAL ECONOMIC LAW

I

The Law of International Economic Relations: Contents and Structure

1. Understanding and Contents of International Economic Law

The notion 'International Economic Law' encompasses a complex architecture of rules governing international economic relations and transboundary economic conduct by States, international organizations, and private actors. The term essentially refers to the regulation of cross-border transactions in goods, services, and capital, monetary relations and the international protection of intellectual property. To some extent, it also addresses the movement of companies and natural persons as well as aspects of international competition.

Although there is consensus on the core subjects, the content of 'international economic law' remains controversial and leaves room for subjectively coloured choices.[1] A narrow concept of 'international economic law' only refers to the segment of public international law directly governing economic relations between States or international organizations, focusing on world trade law, international investment law, and international monetary law.[2] A broader understanding also reflects the role of private actors or hybrid entities administering public goods of major relevance to the international community, like ICANN (Internet Corporation for Assigned Names and Numbers) and more adequately pays tribute to the interplay between international and domestic law in a transboundary economic context. This understanding of international economic law includes the norms of public international law addressing cross-border activities of private undertakings by international agreements as well as issues of jurisdiction of States and the hotly debated 'extraterritorial' legislation.

---

[1] See S Charnovitz, 'What is International Economic Law?' (2011) 14 J Int'l Econ L 3.
[2] D Carreau and B Juillard, *Droit international économique* (5th edn, Librairie générale de droit et de jurisprudence 2013); WJ Davey and JH Jackson, 'The Future of International Economic Law' (2007) 10 J Int'l Econ L 439; R Dolzer, 'Die Wirtschaft im Völkerrecht' in W Graf Vitzthum (ed), *Völkerrecht* (6th edn, De Gruyter 2013) 491; AT Guzman and JHB Pauwelyn, *International Trade Law* (2nd edn, Aspen Publishers 2012); M Herdegen, 'International Economic Law' in R Wolfrum (ed), *The Max Planck Encyclopedia of Public International Law* (OUP 2012) vol V, 777; JH Jackson, *The World Trading System* (2nd edn, MIT Press 1997); AF Lowenfeld, *International Economic Law* (2nd edn, OUP 2008); I Seidl-Hohenveldern, *International Economic Law* (3rd edn, Kluwer Law International 1999).

This book follows a broad understanding of 'international economic law',[3] that is an understanding not just as the part of public international law addressing the economic order, but rather as the law of international economic relations. Thus, the book also covers the basic elements of what is termed 'international (transnational) business law'[4] or 'international commercial law'.[5] It includes legal standards for international undertakings and activities as to human rights, transparency (ban on corruption), environmental protection, labour conditions, or the prohibition on trade with certain arms or other potentially harmful goods.

Several reasons support the inclusion of rules addressing private undertakings and individuals. A concept restricted to the rules governing the relations between States would provide a most fragmentary understanding of the modern order of economic relations and would fully ignore many sets of rules essential to the status of private actors engaged in transnational activities. International law itself pays more and more attention to economic rights and freedoms of individuals and other private actors, in treaties on human rights or in agreements on investment protection. The Convention on the Settlement of Investment Disputes between States and Nationals of Other States (ICSID Convention) provides for arbitration and conciliation between States and foreign investors. For the purposes of dispute settlement, the Convention places a foreign investor and the host State on the same footing, once both parties have accepted the jurisdiction of ICSID. From this perspective, ICSID is a most innovative step in the field of investment protection similar to the individual complaint created by the European Convention on Human Rights.

Many rules for international transactions or the settlement of commercial disputes are laid down in international treaties such as the UN Convention on Contracts for the International Sale of Goods (CISG) or the New York Convention on the Recognition and Enforcement of Foreign Arbitral Awards. Often cooperation among administrative authorities results in international rules for companies which become law by harmonized legislation in many or even most States. Thus, the Basel Committee on Banking Supervision, an important forum of G20 members and some other countries on banking supervision, has adopted non-binding standards for the resilience of the banking sector, in particular for the adequate capital of internationally active banks and liquidity risk management ('Basel Accords'),[6] which are implemented by domestic laws. Some kind of soft convergence is being reached in the area of accounting standards.

Economic realities should also be considered. Quite a number of multinational corporations have an economic (and often political) weight comparable, if not

[3] H Kronke, W Melis, and AK Schnyder (eds), *Handbuch Internationales Wirtschaftsrecht* (Schmidt 2005).
[4] R Folsom, M Gordon, JA Spanogle, P Fitzgerald, and MP Van Alstine, *International Business Transactions* (11th edn, Aspen Publishers 2012).
[5] R Goode, H Kronke, E McKendrick, and J Wool, *Transnational Commercial Law* (2nd edn, OUP 2012).
[6] For an analysis see S Rutova and T Volkheimer, 'Revisiting the Basel Accords: Lessons Learned from the Credit Crisis' (2011) 19 U Miami Bus L Rev 83.

superior, to many States.[7] The quest of developing countries for foreign investment and access to technology often places multinational corporations on a negotiating level *vis-à-vis* States in context with conditions for investment and the grant of concessions. Some companies even succeeded in having contracts with foreign States 'internationalized' (ie governed by international law instead of national law), thus placing the contract out of reach of unilateral intervention by their State counterpart.

International law also develops binding standards and 'soft law' (codes of conduct) for multilateral corporations. From the view of multinational corporations and other private actors with transboundary economic activities, international rules and national law must be read together.

2. The Interaction between International and Domestic Law

The interplay between national and international law shapes the international economic order in many ways. Public international law conditions the exercise of regulatory powers in the domestic sphere. Fundamental principles common to most municipal systems like the principle of good faith or the ban on corruption may give rise to 'general principles of law recognized by civilized nations' in terms of Article 38(1)(c) of the Statute of the International Court of Justice and thus emerge as principles of public international law.

In *World Duty Free Ltd v Kenya*, the arbitral tribunal held that:

> In light of domestic laws and international conventions relating to corruption, and in light of the decisions taken in this matter by courts and arbitral tribunals, this Tribunal is convinced that bribery is contrary to the international public policy of most, if not all, States or, to use another formula, to transnational public policy. Thus, claims based on contracts of corruption or on contracts obtained by corruption cannot be upheld by this Arbitral Tribunal.[8]

Resolutions of the UN Security Council under Chapter VII of the Charter of the United Nations (UN Charter) like a trade embargo under Article 41 of the UN Charter or individual sanctions against persons or entities supposedly implicated in international terrorism must be implemented by national legislation.

Article 48 of the UN Charter provides:

1. The action required to carry out the decisions of the Security Council for the maintenance of international peace and security shall be taken by all the Members of the United Nations or by some of them, as the Security Council may determine.
2. Such decisions shall be carried out by the Members of the United Nations directly and through their action in the appropriate international agencies of which they are members.

---

[7] See Ch III.8.
[8] *World Duty Free Co Ltd v Kenya*, ICSID Case No ARB/00/7 (Award) (2007) 46 ILM 339 para 157.

Thus, it is only through national legislation (or EU legislation) that UN measures evoke individual rights and obligations.

The implementation of resolutions of the UN Security Council shows how different layers of international and national legal rules may interact, giving rise to certain complexity. In the European Union, the competent EU organs decide within the Common Foreign and Security Policy (Article 28 TEU), and then within the Common Commercial Policy (Article 215 TFEU) or within the framework of the rules on the freedom of capital movements (Article 75 TFEU) on the implementation of UN sanctions. In addition, EU Member States may enact parallel restrictions and sanction violations under their criminal law. Finally, human rights standards guaranteeing individual freedoms, for example the European Convention on Human Rights, may call for consideration. Thus in *Bosphorus v Ireland*, the European Court of Human Rights ruled on the conformity with the European Human Rights Convention of an embargo measure against a Serbian aircraft, leased by a Turkish airline and seized by the Irish authorities under an EU regulation which, in turn, implemented sanctions imposed by the UN Security Council.[9] Persons targeted by individual or 'smart' sanctions under anti-terror resolutions of the Security Council repeatedly brought complaints against implementing measures before the European Court of Human Rights.[10] In the case of *Kadi and Al Barakaat*, the European Court of Justice examined restrictions of property against supposed accomplices of international terrorism based on resolutions of the UN Security Council in the light of EU fundamental rights (which are strongly inspired by the European Convention on Human Rights).[11]

In international investment law, arbitral tribunals will apply relevant agreements and the national law of the host State as far as appropriate. Under the ICSID Convention, for example, arbitral tribunals will apply national law (usually the law of the host State) and 'such rules of international law as may be applicable' (Article 42(1)).

National law often refers to international standards. Under the US Alien Tort Claims Act of 1789 (ATCA or ATS),[12] 'the district courts shall have original jurisdiction of any civil action by an alien for a tort only, committed in violation of the law of nations or a treaty of the United States'. Many actions brought in the United States against multinational corporations for violations of human rights committed abroad were based on the ATCA. The recent decision of the US Supreme Court in *Kiobel* has dramatically reduced the scope of claims covered by jurisdiction under the ATCA.[13]

---

[9] ECtHR *Bosphorus Hava Yollari Turizm v Ireland* App no 45036/98 (30 June 2005).
[10] ECtHR *Al-Dulimi and Management Inc v Switzerland* App no 5809/08 (26 November 2013), confirmed by the Grand Chamber judgment of 21 June 2016.
[11] ECJ Joined Cases C-402/05 P and C-415/05 P *Yassin Abdullah Kadi and Al Barakaat International Foundation v Council of the EU and Commission of the EC* (ECJ Judgment) [2008] ECR I-6351 paras 280ff.
[12] See Ch VII and Ch X.3(d).
[13] US Supreme Court *Kiobel v Royal Dutch Petroleum Co* 133 S.Ct. 1659 (2013) 13; see Ch VII.

National law may provide that courts have to refuse the application or recognition of acts of foreign States, for example expropriations, if they are inconsistent with international law. Some States incorporate international law or at least parts of it into domestic law.[14] On the other hand, international law in many ways supports domestic law. Thus, treaties on investment protection may require foreign investors to comply with the law of the host States ('conformity clause').[15]

In the *Fraport* case,[16] an international arbitral tribunal denied investment protection to a German enterprise on the grounds that it had blatantly disrespected the limitation on the foreign share in domestic companies in the airport sector under the laws of the Philippines. Conversely, 'umbrella clauses' in investment treaties oblige host States to honour commitments under their own national laws.[17]

3. The Interaction of Different National Laws

In many disputes it is decisive which national law a court chooses to apply (eg on a contract between a US citizen and a British corporation to be performed in Panama), its own domestic law or foreign law. This choice is governed by the forum State's rules on the conflict of laws.

The 'extraterritorial' reach of national legislation is one of the controversial issues of international economic law.[18] It refers to the application of one State's rules to activities undertaken abroad or to the status of persons or things situated in another State.

In the *Sensor* case,[19] the Dutch subsidiary of a US firm relied on an export prohibition of the US administration (directed against a gas-pipeline deal between European States and the Soviet Union) in order to refuse compliance with a contract on the delivery of certain material finally destined for the Soviet Union. A Dutch court refused to apply the US regulation and enforced the contract under Dutch law.

In principle, States are free to apply or not the laws of other countries which serve the respective country's economic and/or political interests, like the prohibition of the export of goods attributed to a State's cultural heritage or of its natural resources (such as the exportation of archaeological materials, tribal masks, or species of animals and plants). However, under the Articles of Agreement of the International

---

[14] See MN Shaw, *International Law* (7th edn, CUP 2014) 99.
[15] See Ch XXXIV.3(b).
[16] *Fraport AG Frankfurt Airport Services Worldwide v Republic of the Philippines*, ICSID Case No ARB/03/25 (Award 2007) paras 300ff; the award was annulled in 2010 for procedural reasons; nevertheless, the award may still be considered an important contribution to international investment law.
[17] See Ch XXXIV.4(f).   [18] See Ch VI.6–8.
[19] District Court at The Hague *Compagnie Européenne des Pétroles SA v Sensor Nederland BV* (1983) 22 ILM 66; see AV Lowe, 'International Law Issues Arising in the "Pipeline Dispute": The British Position' (1984) 27 GYIL 54; DF Vagts, 'The Pipeline Controversy: An American Viewpoint' (1984) 27 GYIL 38.

Monetary Fund, States must give effect to currency exchange restrictions of other members:

> Exchange contracts which involve the currency of any member and which are contrary to the exchange control regulations of that member maintained or imposed consistently with this Agreement shall be unenforceable in the territories of any member. In addition, members may, by mutual accord, cooperate in measures for the purpose of making the exchange control regulations of either member more effective, provided that such measures and regulations are consistent with this Agreement.[20]

4. Main Areas of International Economic Law

The core areas of international economic law are international trade law, the law of regional economic integration, and other bi- or multilateral trade agreements, international investment law and international monetary law. It also comprises areas related to trade and investment such as international commercial arbitration, double taxation agreements, and international intellectual or industrial property law as well as international competition law. Advanced integration of economies as achieved in the European Union will require a regime for the movement of persons, including free establishment, and finally, common antitrust rules.

(a) International trade law

The international agreements on the exchange of goods and services across borders are based on the reciprocal character of the respective rights and obligations of the parties and aim at achieving mutual benefits for all of them.[21] The World Trade Organization (WTO) provides the institutional basis for global trade relations and is built on pre-existing structures under the General Agreement on Tariffs and Trade (GATT 1947). Its principal objectives are to reduce existing trade barriers and to expand international trade, raise the standard of living, attain sustainable development, and secure an adequate share in the growth of international trade for developing countries (WTO Agreement, preamble). The institutional system of the WTO administers a number of trade agreements. The GATT (1947 and 1994) is the basic legal instrument for substantially reducing tariffs and other barriers to trade in goods and for eliminating discriminatory treatment. General exceptions allow for restrictive measures for the protection of enumerated public interests such as public morals or health. Specific exceptions, inter alia, relate to the protection of domestic producers against unforeseen serious harm arising from imports and trade concessions (safeguards). The WTO Agreement on the Application of Sanitary and

---

[20] Article VIII(2)(b) Articles of Agreement of the International Monetary Fund.
[21] D Bethlehem et al, *The Oxford Handbook of International Trade Law* (OUP 2009); AT Guzman and JHB Pauwelyn, *International Trade Law* (2nd edn, Aspen Publishers 2012); AF Lowenfeld, *International Economic Law* (2nd edn, OUP 2008).

Phytosanitary Measures (SPS Agreement) and the Agreement on Technical Barriers to Trade (TBT Agreement) complement the GATT rules. Other WTO agreements establish a special regime for the agricultural sector (Agreement on Agriculture) or address subsidies, antidumping measures, trade-related aspects of intellectual property (TRIPS), trade-related investment measures (TRIMs), and government procurement. The General Agreement on Trade in Services (GATS) integrates services into the WTO system.

(b) Regional economic law and free trade agreements

Bi- and multilateral free trade agreements and other forms of regional economic law overlap with WTO law. These agreements range from free trade areas over custom unions to more ambitious forms of regional economic integration.[22] Among them, the system of the European Union has reached a unique level of economic and political integration. WTO law permits preferential trade agreements, if covering 'substantially all the trade' (see Article XXIV: 4 and 8 of the GATT). The North American Free Trade Area (NAFTA), the Association of South East Asian Nations (ASEAN), the Asia-Pacific Economic Cooperation (APEC), the Andean Community of Nations (CAN), and the Common Market of the South (MERCOSUR) stand out as examples of regional economic agreements. The European Union has negotiated the Comprehensive Economic and Trade Agreement with Canada (CETA). In 2016, twelve States of the Pacific Rim, among them the United States, Canada, Australia, and Mexico, signed the Trans-Pacific Partnership Agreement (TPP). Amid much controversy, the negotiations of the Transatlantic Trade and Investment Partnership (TTIP) between the United States and the European Union are still ongoing.

(c) International antitrust and competition law

International antitrust and competition law governs the interplay of domestic competition and antitrust rules concerning the issue of transboundary undertakings.[23] WTO law (GATS) contains rudimentary rules sanctioning the abuse of regulatory powers and practices restraining competition.[24] In the absence of a truly international regime for competition, the establishment and application of competition rules lie with the individual domestic bodies. International agreements,

---

[22] S Norberg, 'The Agreement on a European Economic Area' (1992) 29 CML Rev 1171; TA O'Keefe, *Latin American and Caribbean Trade Agreements* (Brill Academic Publishers 2009); A Toledano Laredo, 'The EEA Agreement: An Overall View' (1992) 29 CML Rev 1199; M Toscano Franca Filho, L Lixinski, and M Belen Olmos Giupponi (eds), *The Law of Mercosur* (Hart Publishing 2010); J Vervaele, 'Mercosur and Regional Integration in South America' (2005) 54 ICLQ 387.

[23] EM Fox, 'Towards World Antitrust and Market Access' (1997) 91 AJIL 1; C Noonan, *The Emerging Principles of International Competition Law* (OUP 2008).

[24] See WTO, *Mexico: Measures Affecting Telecommunication Services—Report of the Panel* (2004) WT/DS204/R paras 7.224ff.

for example between the European Union and the United States, provide for mutual assistance and cooperation among competition authorities.

(d) International investment law

International investment law covers the promotion of foreign investments and their protection against undue interferences by the host State.[25] Establishing a favourable investment climate is now recognized as a cornerstone of economic development.[26] The main sources of international investment law are bilateral investment treaties and, rising in number, preferential trade agreements or treaties for specific sectors with an investment protection regime like the Energy Charter Treaty. By establishing standards for legal stability, predictability of State action, adequate protection, and due process, particularly through the guarantees of 'fair and equitable treatment' and 'full protection and security', international investment law has intense repercussions on the legal system of the host State and enhances the rule of law. Arbitral decisions nowadays consider respect for the integrity of the law of the host State as 'a critical part of development and a concern of international investment law'.[27] Recent treaty practice tends to defer widely to legitimate political choices, leaving considerably more room for national standards concerning environment, health, or labour conditions.

(e) International monetary law

An important sector of international economic law covers monetary relations.[28] The Statute of the International Monetary Fund (IMF) provides rules for the surveillance of currency arrangements and assistance to Member States in case of balance of payment deficits. Among monetary unions and monetary zones, the European Economic and Monetary Union with its European System of Central Banks has reached an unparalleled degree of monetary and fiscal integration for

---

[25] See Ch XXXIV.4.

[26] See RD Bishop, J Crawford, and WM Reisman, *Foreign Investment Disputes* (Aspen Publishers 2005); R Dolzer, M Herdegen, and B Vogel, *Foreign Investment* (Konrad Adenauer Stiftung 2006); R Dolzer and C Schreuer, *Principles of International Investment Law* (2nd edn, OUP 2012); C Dugan et al, *Investor-State Arbitration* (Oceana Publications Inc 2008); C McLachlan, L Shore, and M Weiniger, *International Investment Arbitration* (OUP 2007); P Muchlinsky, F Ortino, and C Schreuer, *The Oxford Handbook of International Investment Law* (OUP 2008); A Reinisch, *Standards of Investment Protection* (OUP 2008); M Sornarajah, *The International Law of Foreign Investment* (3rd edn, CUP 2010).

[27] *Fraport AG Frankfurt Airport Services Worldwide v Republic of the Philippines*, ICSID Case No ARB/03/25 (Award 2007) para 402.

[28] MS Copelovitch, *The International Monetary Fund in the Global Economy: Banks, Bonds, and Bailouts* (CUP 2010); M Giovanoli (ed), *International Monetary Law* (OUP 2000); M Giovanoli, 'The Reform of the International Financial Architecture after the Global Crisis' (2009) 42 Int'l L & Pol 81; M Giovanoli, *International Monetary Law and Financial Law, The Global Crisis* (OUP 2011); H Hahn and U Häde, *Währungsrecht* (2nd edn, CH Beck 2010); C Proctor, *Mann on the Legal Aspect of Money* (7th edn, OUP 2012).

the Members of the Eurozone.[29] Nevertheless, the insufficient convergence of economic and excessive fiscal deficits has caused a rift within the Eurozone.

(f) Intellectual property law

A number of treaties address the protection of intellectual property (copyright, design protection, patents including for example bio-patents on DNA-sequences, new trademarks, topographies of integrated circuits).[30] In WTO law, the Agreement on Trade Related Aspects of Intellectual Property Rights (TRIPS) marks a significant step towards universal standards of efficient protection. Salient issues are the protection of 'bio-patents' (eg newly 'designed' varieties of Broccoli[31]) and restraints on the exercise of patents and similar rights under competition law.[32]

(g) International commercial law

The international law governing commercial transactions between private actors is traditionally placed on the periphery of international economic law. It is, however, of considerable relevance for today's international economic relations.[33] International agreements like the United Nations Convention on Contracts for the International Sale of Goods (CISG)[34] are directed at the harmonization of substantive law. Transboundary e-commerce increases the need for uniform rules. Another area of international commercial law covers the settlement of disputes, in particular international arbitration,[35] which often extends to disputes between States and foreign corporations (eg arbitration under the UNCITRAL Rules).

5. The Relationship between International Economic Law and Economic Rationality

To some extent, any legal order will refer to rationality, in economic as well as in other contexts.[36] The modern international economic order aims at activating

---

[29] See Part VI.   [30] See Ch XVIII.4(b).

[31] See the decisions G2/07 and G1/08 ('Broccoli/Tomatoes', 9 December 2010) as well as most recently the decisions G2/12 and G2/13 ('Broccoli/Tomatoes', 25 March 2015) of the Enlarged Board of Appeal of the European Patent Office.

[32] F Abbott, T Cottier, and F Gurry, *The International Intellectual Property System* (Aspen Publishers 1999); T Cottier and P Véron, *Concise International and European IP Law* (2nd edn, Kluwer Law International 2011); C Correa, *Trade Related Aspects of Intellectual Property Rights* (Alphascript Publishing 2007); D Gervais, *Intellectual Property, Trade and Development* (2nd edn, OUP 2014); PW Grubb and PR Thomsen, *Patents for Chemicals, Pharmaceuticals and Biotechnology* (5th edn, OUP 2010); LR Helfer, KJ Alter, and MF Guerzovich, 'Islands of Effective International Adjudication: Constructing an Intellectual Property Rule of Law in the Andean Community' (2009) 103 AJIL 1.

[33] For an overview of the topic see M Bridge, *The International Sale of Goods* (3rd edn, OUP 2013); R Goode, H Kronke, E McKendrick, and J Wool, *Transnational Commercial Law* (2nd edn, OUP 2012); C Murray, *Schmitthoff's Export Trade* (12th edn, Sweet & Maxwell 2011).

[34] See Ch XXIV.3.   [35] See Ch X.2.

[36] M Herdegen, *Staat und Rationalität* (Ferdinand Schöningh 2010).

market forces and private initiative by eliminating barriers to trade and to the flow of capital. It also fosters a positive investment climate.

Still, the whole international law focuses less on economic rationality and economic incentives, but on the respect for the human person and its autonomy as well as on States' responsibility for welfare and social balance. The basic tenets of international law do not allow to subordinate the individual to economic priorities and to regulate rights and duties of individuals according to economic efficiency. Human rights, internationally recognized social standards, and the constitutional underpinnings of the human person in the modern *Rechtsstaat* do not allow an understanding of the legal order as an instrument merely serving economic rationality. On the contrary, the concept of the human person underlying and characterizing the legal order directs the normative framework for economic relations. This primacy of the normative vision of the individual also conditions the relation between economic analysis and the legal order.[37] Thus, it is not the idea of the *homo economicus*, but rather the legal rules for individual freedom and social standards, as well as the control of economic power that establish the framework for the economic order, on the domestic as well as on the international level. In the same vein, it is not the agenda for liberalization or investment protection that conditions human rights and their enjoyment. Quite the contrary, human rights standards establish the framework for economic choices.

Select Bibliography

D Carreau and B Juillard, *Droit international économique* (5th edn, Librairie générale de droit et de jurisprudence 2013).

S Charnovitz, 'What is International Economic Law?' (2011) 14 J Int'l Econ L 3.

T Cottier, 'Challenges Ahead in International Economic Law' (2009) 12 J Int'l Econ L 3.

WJ Davey and JH Jackson, 'The Future of International Economic Law' (2007) 10 J Int'l Econ L 439.

M Herdegen, 'International Economic Law' in R Wolfrum (ed), *The Max Planck Encyclopedia of Public International Law* (OUP 2012) vol V, 777.

JH Jackson, W Davey, and A Sykes, *Legal Problems of International Economic Relations* (6th edn, West Group 2014).

JH Jackson, 'International Economic Law: Complexity and Puzzles' (2007) 10 J Int'l Econ L 3.

R Jennings and A Watts, *Oppenheim's International Law* (9th edn, OUP 1992).

F Lachenmann and R Wolfrum (eds), *The Max Planck Encyclopedia of Public International Law, International Economic Law* (OUP 2016).

---

[37] K Mathis, *Efficiency Instead of Justice?: Searching for the Philosophical Foundations of the Economic Analysis of Law* (Springer 2011); EJ Mestmäcker, *A Legal Theory without Law: Posner v Hayek on Economic Analysis of Law* (Mohr Siebeck 2007); RA Posner, *Economic Analysis of Law* (9th edn, Aspen Publishers 2014); SAB Schropp, *Trade Policy Flexibility and Enforcement in the WTO: A Law and Economics Analysis* (CUP 2014); S Shavell, *Foundations of Economic Analysis of Law* (Harvard University Press 2004).

G Loible, 'International Economic Law' in MD Evans (ed), *International Law* (3rd edn, OUP 2010) 722.

AF Lowenfeld, *International Economic Law* (2nd edn, OUP 2008).

E-U Petersmann, *Constitutional Functions and Constitutional Problems of International Economic Law* (Westview Press 1991).

CB Picker, ID Bunn, and DW Arner (eds), *International Economic Law: The State and Future of the Discipline* (Hart Publishing 2008).

AH Qureshi and A Ziegler, *International Economic Law* (3rd edn, Sweet & Maxwell 2011).

G Schwarzenberger, 'The Principles and Standards of International Economic Law' (1966 I) 117 RdC 1.

I Seidl-Hohenveldern, *International Economic Law* (3rd edn, Kluwer Law International 1999).

II

Past and Present of the International Economic Order

1. The Historical Foundations of International Economic Law

In general international law, few principles directly affect international economic relations. Under customary law, States may freely determine economic relations with other countries. The International Court of Justice succinctly describes this freedom in the *Nicaragua* case:

A State is not bound to continue particular trade relations longer than it sees fit to do so, in the absence of a treaty commitment or other specific legal obligation.[1]

In the modern world, most States have opted for limiting their freedom of economic choices in favour of trade liberalization on the global, regional, or bilateral level. The network of free trade agreements nowadays consists of hundreds of treaties.[2]

In medieval times, the German Hanseatic League (Hanse), a confederation of commercial cities on or near the North and the Baltic Sea, established in the 13th century, granted to the merchants of its members freedom of trade and establishment as well as the protection of life and property.[3]

The writings of Adam Smith and David Hume laid the conceptual underpinnings for the free trade movement in the later 18th century. Adam Smith relied on market mechanisms and the adequate allocation of resources driven by self-interest as the most suitable force of productivity not only for the national market but also for international trade:

If a foreign country can supply us with a commodity cheaper than we ourselves can make it, better buy it off with some part of the produce of our own industry, employed in a way in which we have some advantage.[4]

---

[1] ICJ, *Military and Paramilitary Activities in and against Nicaragua (Nicaragua v United States)* (Merits) [1986] ICJ Rep 14 para 275.

[2] For an historical account of the historical development see GR Winham, *The Evolution of International Trade Agreements* (University of Toronto Press 1992).

[3] See E Reibstein, 'Das Völkerrecht der deutschen Hanse' (1956) 17 ZaöRV 38.

[4] A Smith, *An Inquiry into the Nature and Causes of the Wealth of Nations*, ed K Sutherland (OUP 2008) 293.

Later, David Ricardo[5] and John Stuart Mill[6] developed the theory of 'comparative advantage',[7] placing Adam Smith's argument for free trade on a broader conceptual basis. According to this theory, countries should avail themselves of their disposable resources (factors of production) for their maximum welfare by specializing and exporting relatively low-cost products and in turn receiving higher-cost products in imports. Thus, an industrialized country and an agricultural country might realize cost advantages by trading clothes and wine. Adam Smith and the advocates of the 'comparative advantage' did not campaign for any international (and even less global) interest in integrated markets and eliminating barriers to trade as an end in itself. They rather relied on the domestic interest of each country and its industry as the driving force behind the opening of markets.[8]

The credo of welfare-accumulation and mutual benefits flowing from free trade characterizes the classical period of economic liberalism as highlighted by the Cobden-Chevalier Treaty of 1860 and as practised notably by the United Kingdom and other countries in the second half of the 19th century and the period before the First World War. By contrast, the United States, a country with a long protectionist tradition, relied on tariffs, first as an important source of revenue and later, until the Second World War, for the protection of domestic industries. In the last decade of the 19th century, a number of European States such as Austria-Hungary, Italy, Germany, and France also opted for a protectionist policy. With the outbreak of the First World War, the liberal approach to world trade, always competing with high tariff policies in several countries, disintegrated. Protectionist tendencies and the instability of currencies barred the return to a liberal international economic order in the inter-war period.

The relatively high degree of integration of capital markets prevailing in the late 19th century[9] until the First World War rested essentially on the gold standard,[10] which was adopted by central banks as the common policy in terms of a 'socially constructed institution'.[11] This regime, with currencies pegged against gold, meant fixed exchange rates and allowed the free flow of money across borders. This insured reliable exchange rates according to their convertibility into gold.

Since the turn of the 19th century, the concept of a universal minimum standard[12] arose as the relevant parameter for protection and for an adequate treatment of foreigners by the host State. This concept primarily aims at protection by the

[5] D Ricardo, *On the Principles of Political Economy and Taxation*, ed P Sraffa, The Works and Correspondence of David Ricardo vol. 1 (CUP 1953).

[6] JS Mill, *The Principles of Political Economy: with some of their applications to social philosophy*, ed JM Robson, Collected Works of John Stuart Mill vols. I–II (University of Toronto Press, Routledge & Kegan Paul 1965) in particular book III.

[7] D Irwin, *Against the Tide: An Intellectual History of Free Trade* (Princeton University Press 1996) 78, 218.

[8] See D Rodrik, *The Globalization Paradox: Why Global Markets, States and Democracy Can't Coexist* (OUP 2011) 9–13.

[9] M Wolf, *Why Globalization Works* (2nd edn, Yale University Press 2005) 113.

[10] See Ch XXXVIII.2.

[11] B Eichengreen, *Globalizing Capital: A History of the International Monetary System* (2nd edn, Princeton University Press 2008) ch 2.

[12] See Ch VI.4(a).

exercise of police powers and calls for a 'decent' and non-arbitrary treatment. The minimum standard continues to be relevant for foreign investors and often dominates the interpretation of investment treaties (particularly of clauses on 'fair and equitable treatment' and 'full protection and security'). As opposed to the minimum standard, the so-called 'Calvo doctrine' (named after the Argentinean diplomat and international lawyer Carlos Calvo (1824–1906)) advocated national treatment for foreigners and judicial protection only by national courts. After losing influence in the Latin American countries in the last decades, the Calvo doctrine experienced a renaissance in recent years (notably in Venezuela, Ecuador, and Bolivia).[13]

Between and after the two World Wars, the emergence of State economies and waves of nationalizations in communist countries challenged established rules on full compensation for the expropriation of foreign property. At the London Economic Conference in 1933, multilateral endeavours to revive the world economy, through currency stabilization by settling intergovernmental debts and by the reduction of tariffs, met with failure.

The contours of modern international economic law emerged towards the end of the Second World War. The Conference of Bretton Woods (1944) led to the establishment of the International Monetary Fund (IMF) and the World Bank Group. Loans to countries with softer currencies or suffering from payment deficits (flowing from imports exceeding exports) have become a crucial mechanism in the stabilization of international trade relations. The Havana Charter of 1948 which provided the establishment of an International Trade Organization (ITO), provoking criticism in the United States, never entered into force. However, a pivotal element of the Charter was realized in 1948: the General Agreement on Tariffs and Trade (GATT) of 1947. The GATT aims to liberalize world trade through the reduction of tariffs and the elimination or restriction of non-tariff barriers to trade. The post-war bilateral treaties on friendship, commerce, and navigation operated as a precursor to the modern types of investment treaties and preferential trade agreements.[14]

John Maynard Keynes, Harry Dexter White, and the other drafters of the Bretton Woods Agreements as well as the subsequent practice of Member States under these agreements and the GATT were far from supporting an unbridled flow of capital and goods or an unfettered integration of markets.[15] In the immediate post-war period the philosophy that the domestic economies require constant gardening in the interest of employment and adequate economic growth prevailed. The control of capital movements was conceived to be a legitimate and permanent instrument of governments.

---

[13] See Ch VI.4(b).

[14] See AL Paulus, 'Treaties of Friendship Commerce and Navigation' in R Wolfrum (ed), *The Max Planck Encyclopedia of Public International Law* (OUP 2012) vol IX, 1140.

[15] See D Rodrik, *The Globalization Paradox: Why Global Markets, States and Democracy Can't Coexist* (OUP 2011) 69.

2. The Concerns of Developing Countries and the Call for a 'New Economic Order'

The gap between industrialized and developing countries catalysed the demand for a new equilibrium in the international economic system and enhanced the consideration of the needs and interests of developing countries. In the 1960s and 1970s, many developing countries, supported by other non-aligned or communist countries, called for a 'New International Economic Order'.[16] The concept focuses on national sovereignty over a State's resources, underlines sovereign equality of States irrespective of their economic and social choices, and emphasizes the discretion of States as to the admission of foreign investments. It claims better conditions for the economic and social development of poorer countries in international trade and investment and requires that profits are shared equally between the host State and the investors. It also lowers the standard for compensation of expropriated foreign companies ('appropriate' rather than 'adequate' compensation). The call for a New International Economic Order is closely linked to the push for a 'right to development'. The right to development[17] implies certain forms of solidarity of wealthy States with developing countries, but has never reached a clear definition.[18]

The movement towards a New International Economic Order found its expression in the Resolution 1803 (1962) of the UN General Assembly on Permanent Sovereignty over Natural Resources[19] and, more prominently, in the Charter of Economic Rights and Duties of States[20] adopted by the UN General Assembly's

---

[16] R Caldera, 'The Juridical Basis of a New International Order' (1986 I) RdC 196, 387; D Carreau, 'Le nouvel ordre économique international' (1977) 104 J Droit Int'l 595; DC Dicke (ed), *Foreign Debts in the Present and a New International Economic Order* (Westview Press 1986); J Makarczyk, *Principles of a New International Economic Order* (Martinus Nijhoff Publishers 1988); T Oppermann, 'Neue Weltwirtschaftsordnung und internationales Wirtschaftsrecht' in B Börner, H Jahrreiss, and K Stern (eds), *Festschrift für Karl Carstens zum 70. Geburtstag* (Carl Heymann 1984) vol I, 449; T Oppermann and E-U Petersmann (eds), *Reforming the International Economic Order* (CH Beck 1987); G Sacerdoti, 'New International Economic Order (NIEO)' in R Wolfrum (ed), *The Max Planck Encyclopedia of Public International Law* (OUP 2012) vol VII, 659; TW Wälde, 'A Requiem for the "New International Economic Order"' in E Hafner et al (eds), *Liber Amicorum Professor Seidl-Hohenveldern* (Brill Academic Publishers 1998) 771; a recent appraisal can be found in AH Qureshi, 'Critical Concepts in the New International Economic Order and its Impact on the Development of International Economic Law' (2010) 7 MJIEL 3.

[17] Cf International Law Association, *Report of the Sixty-Second Conference in Seoul* (1986) Part I No 6; K M'Baye, 'Le droit au développement comme un droit de l'homme' (1972) 5 Revue des droits de l'homme 505; H Petersmann, 'The Right to Development in the United Nations: An Opportunity for Strengthening Popular Participation in Development' in J Jekewitz (ed), *Festschrift für Karl Josef Partsch zum 75. Geburtstag* (Duncker & Humblot 1989) 125; Ch Tomuschat, 'Das Recht auf Entwicklung' (1982) 25 GYIL 85.

[18] For a general outline of the idea of solidarity in international law see R Wolfrum and C Kojima (eds), *Solidarity: A Structural Principle of International Law* (Springer 2010).

[19] See S Hobe, 'Evolution of the Principle on Permanent Sovereignty Over Natural Resources' in M Bungenberg and S Hobe (eds), *Permanent Sovereignty Over Natural Resources* (Springer 2015).

[20] K Boon, 'Charter of Economic Rights and Duties of States (1974)' in R Wolfrum (ed), *The Max Planck Encyclopedia of Public International Law* (OUP 2012) vol II, 87; J Castañeda, 'La Charte

Resolution 3281 (XXIX), with the most important industrialized Western States either voting against[21] or abstaining.[22]

The Charter of Economic Rights and Duties of States proclaims the unfettered sovereignty of every State over its resources and economic life in Article 2:

1. Every State has and shall freely exercise full permanent sovereignty, including possession, use and disposal, over all its wealth, natural resources and economic activities.
2. Each State has the right:
   (a) To regulate and exercise authority over foreign investment within its national jurisdiction in accordance with its laws and regulations and in conformity with its national objectives and priorities. No State shall be compelled to grant preferential treatment to foreign investment;
   (b) To regulate and supervise the activities of transnational corporations within its national jurisdiction and take measures to ensure that such activities comply with its laws, rules and regulations and conform with its economic and social policies. Transnational corporations shall not intervene in the internal affairs of a host State. Every State should, with full regard for its sovereign rights, cooperate with other States in the exercise of the right set forth in this subparagraph;
   (c) To nationalize, expropriate or transfer ownership of foreign property, in which case appropriate compensation should be paid by the State adopting such measures, taking into account its relevant laws and regulations and all circumstances that the State considers pertinent. In any case where the question of compensation gives rise to a controversy, it shall be settled under the domestic law of the nationalizing State and by its tribunals, unless it is freely and mutually agreed by all States concerned that other peaceful means be sought on the basis of the sovereign equality of States and in accordance with the principle of free choice of means.

The Charter requires the interests of developing countries to be taken into account in context with the development of international economic relations (Articles 5ff). It recommends that developed countries grant generalized preferences in trade (Article 18) and other areas of economic cooperation to developing countries (Article 19). The Charter calls for stable, remunerative, and equitable prices for commodities and primary products (Article 14; see also Article 5) and stresses the importance of technology transfer (Article 13(2)). The authority of the Charter of Economic Rights and Duties suffers from the rejection or non-approval of many important Western States.

---

des droits et devoirs économiques des États' (1974) 20 AFDI 31; DC Dicke (ed), *Foreign Debts in the Present and a New International Economic Order* (Westview Press 1986); RR Ferrer (ed), *Exégesis de la Carta de derechos y deberes económicos de los Estados* (Editorial Porrúa 1976); Ch Tomuschat, 'Die Charta der wirtschaftlichen Rechte und Pflichten der Staaten' (1976) 36 ZaöRV 444; M Virally, 'La Charte des droits et devoirs économiques des États' (1974) 20 AFDI 57.

[21] Belgium, Denmark, the Federal Republic of Germany, Luxembourg, the United Kingdom, and the United States.

[22] Austria, Canada, France, Ireland, Israel, Italy, Japan, the Netherlands, Norway, and Spain.

In 1986, the International Law Association adopted a declaration on the international order (Declaration on the Progressive Development of Principles of Public International Law Relating to a New International Economic Order),[23] which strives for the reconciliation of traditional positions as to full compensation for the expropriation of foreign property and the loyal fulfilment of States' contractual obligations towards foreign investors (including agreed mechanisms of dispute settlement) with legitimate claims of developing countries.

In the meantime, the quest for private foreign investment (which the Charter of Economic Rights and Duties treats less as a chance than as a concern to be controlled by the host States) as a vital factor for economic and social development as well as the collapse of most communist systems radically changed the terms of the discourse on the international economic order in the last decades of the 20th century. An ever-increasing number of bi- and multilateral investment treaties provides comprehensive protection of foreign investments.[24]

The so-called 'Monterrey Consensus', adopted at the International Conference on Financing for Development (2002), underlines the role of private investment:

> Private international capital flows, particularly foreign direct investment, along with international financial stability, are vital complements to national and international development efforts. Foreign direct investment contributes toward financing sustained economic growth over the long term. It is especially important for its potential to transfer knowledge and technology, create jobs, boost overall productivity, enhance competitiveness and entrepreneurship, and ultimately eradicate poverty through economic growth and development. A central challenge, therefore, is to create the necessary domestic and international conditions to facilitate direct investment flows, conducive to achieving national development priorities particularly Africa, least developed countries, small island developing States, and landlocked developing countries, and also to countries with economies in transition.[25]

Despite the set-back for the 'New International Economic Order' as formulated some decades ago, the obvious legitimacy of many concerns of developing countries has considerably influenced the evolution of international economic law. Tariff preferences and other custom-made rules for developing countries form part of the WTO system and of the commercial policy of the European Union and of other important States or international organizations. Technology transfer and financial assistance to facilitate the access of developing countries to science and technology remain on the agenda of international economic law.

---

[23] See International Law Association, *Report of the Sixty-Second Conference* (1986) 2; see also T Oppermann, 'Die Seoul-Erklärung der International Law Association vom 29.–30. August 1986 über die fortschreitende Entwicklung von Völkerrechtsprinzipien einer neuen Weltwirtschaftsordnung' in K-H Böckstiegel, H-E Folz, JM Mössner, and K Zemanek (eds), *Festschrift für Ignaz Seidl-Hohenveldern* (Carl Heymanns 1988) 449.

[24] See Ch XXXIV.1.

[25] United Nations, *Report of the International Conference of the Financing for Development* (2002) para 20.

3. The System of the World Trade Organization (WTO)

The 'Uruguay reform' (1994) of the world trading system led to the establishment of the WTO, the revised GATT 1994, and several other agreements such as the General Agreement on Trade in Services (GATS) or the Agreement on Trade-Related Aspects of Intellectual Property Rights (TRIPS). The Dispute Settlement Understanding (DSU) provides the establishment of the WTO's Dispute Settlement Body with independent panels and an Appellate Body. On this basis, the settlement of disputes among WTO members is much more judicial than political in character.

In a broad sense, the WTO regime may be considered as the 'constitutional framework' for world trade. However, the WTO system does not lend itself to be conceptualized in terms of fundamental individual rights and values that underlie or even supersede explicit rules. Rather than generating complex balancing processes and a large margin of interpretation the WTO system operates as a finely tuned interplay of principles and exceptions.

4. The Regional Integration of Markets

Under the umbrella of the GATT 1947 and the new WTO system (and to some extent besides it) regional integration of economies within free trade areas (as the one established by the North American Free Trade Agreement (NAFTA)), customs unions (such as the Mercado Común del Sur (MERCOSUR) and the South African Customs Union (SACU)), and economic communities flourishes. Free trade areas are characterized by the elimination of internal tariffs for trade between Member States, whilst customs unions additionally have common external tariffs.[26] Economic communities pursue an even more intense integration of markets, for example with the extensive freedom of the movement of workers or common competition rules. Beyond realizing a comprehensive internal market, the European Union has acquired many features usually associated with a federal State. The wide range of bilateral and multilateral regional agreements on trade and economic integration supplement and, to some extent, erode the WTO rules ('spaghetti bowl').[27] New 'mega-regional' agreements like the Comprehensive Economic and Trade Agreement with Canada (CETA), the Trans-Pacific Partnership Agreement (TPP), and the Transatlantic Trade and Investment Partnership (TTIP) have further nurtured these concerns.

---

[26] For a definition of a customs union see eg Article XXIV(8) GATT.

[27] The term was first used by J Bhagwati, 'U.S. Trade Policy: The Infatuation with Free Trade Agreements' in J Bhagwati and AO Krueger (eds), *The Dangerous Drift to Preferential Trade Agreements* (AEI Press 1995); see on the 'spaghetti-bowl'-effect JHB Pauwelyn, 'Adding Sweeteners to Softwood Lumber: The WTO-NAFTA "Spaghetti Bowl" is Cooking' (2006) 9 J Int'l Econ L 197; so also R Leal-Arcas, 'Proliferation of Regional Trade Agreements: Complementing or Supplanting Multilateralism?' (2010–11) 11 Chi J Int'l L 597.

5. Globalization of Economic Relations: Chances, Risks, and Asymmetries

Public debate often refers to the intense interconnection of national economies as 'globalization'.[28] This term focuses primarily on the sophisticated integration of capital markets and the international trade in goods. The global integration of markets in services lags behind. Even less elaborated is the permeability of labour markets (with exceptions such as the European Union with its comprehensive freedom of movement for employees).

In the current debate, many 'critics' of globalization often ignore that the interconnection of economies is by no means a recent phenomenon and that there are quite different degrees of market integration as to capital, services, and persons. The integration of capital markets had reached a very high level in the period before the First World War which was attained again only a number of decades later.[29] Many industrial States still jealously restrain access to their labour markets for foreign workers.

Economic globalization reaches well back into the early era of great colonial empires.[30] In the epoch of colonization, private actors with a hybrid status and semi-sovereign powers were among the driving forces of globalization. Prominent examples of those actors are the Hudson's Bay Company (founded in 1670), the British East India Company (founded in 1600), and the Dutch East India Company (founded in 1602). The British East India Company exercised truly governmental functions until 1858. In the long run, the development of modern means of transportation and communication provided an important stimulus for further expansion.

It has taken a long time for economic globalization to find a normative basis in treaties on the liberalization of international trade (especially the GATT 1947 and WTO treaties of 1994) and in the agreements on an international monetary system. The elimination of barriers to foreign investments and the control of distortions of competition are also important elements of globalization.

---

[28] See S Alam, N Klein, and J Overland, *Globalisation and the Quest for Social and Environmental Justice* (Routledge 2010); U Beck, *Was ist Globalisierung?* (3rd edn, Suhrkamp 2007); W Benedek, K De Feyter, and F Marrella, *Economic Globalisation and Human Rights* (CUP 2011); J Bhagwati, *In Defense of Globalisation* (OUP 2007); JB Donges and A Freytag (eds), *Die Rolle des Staates in einer globalisierten Wirtschaft* (Lucius & Lucius 1998); PR Krugman, M Obstfeld, and M Melitz, *International Economics: Theory and Policy* (10th edn, Prentice Hall 2014); WH Reinicke, *Global Public Policy: Governing Without Government?* (Brookings Institution Press 1998); H Siebert, *Weltwirtschaft* (UTB 1997); H Siebert and O Lorz, *Außenwirtschaft* (9th edn, UTB 2014); J Spero and J Hart, *Politics of International Economic Relations* (7th edn, Wadsworth Publishing 2006); J Stiglitz, *Globalisation and Its Discontents* (WW Norton & Co 2002); T Vollmöller, *Die Globalisierung des öffentlichen Wirtschaftsrechts* (Carl Heymanns 2000); Ch von Weizsäcker, *Logik der Globalisierung* (Vandenhoeck & Ruprecht 2003); M Wolf, *Why Globalisation Works* (Yale University Press 2004).

[29] M Wolf, *Why Globalisation Works* (Yale University Press 2004).

[30] For an historical overview on international economic law see G Schwarzenberger, 'The Principles and Standards of International Economic Law' (1966) 117 RdC 1.

Perhaps even more important are developments within States and their constitutional structures. In a political context, the triumph of the model of a government based on democracy and the rule of law as well as the transformation of many economies with central planning into market systems catalysed the process of globalization. In many countries, this transformation dramatically reduced the public sector.

Globalization with a high mobility of money and other forms of capital fosters competition among States to attract domestic and foreign investors. This competition also refers to legal parameters of the investment climate such as rules on establishment of undertakings, taxation, labour law, and social security as well as other conditions for the production and marketing of goods. From this perspective, globalization enhances competition among legal systems.[31]

The widespread liberalization of markets for services brought about the removal of State monopolies and privatization of public services, in particular in the sectors of post and telecommunication.

Economic globalization is associated with treaties and other international instruments for the protection of certain goods of paramount importance for the entire international community. Among these 'global commons' ('global public goods') rank the protection of the ozone layer and other aspects of climate protection, clean water, and clean air as well as the protection of the cultural heritage and of biological diversity. In a legal context the most attractive facet of globalization is related to universal standards of human rights, which increasingly influence the economic order. Human rights may reinforce and support the economic freedoms associated with liberalization (freedom of communication or guarantee of property).

The welfare gains flowing from interconnection of economies have been highlighted since the late 18th century. In particular, Adam Smith (An Enquiry into the Nature and the Causes of the Wealth of Nations, 1876) and David Ricardo (On the Principles of Political Economies and Taxation, 1870) provided lasting insights into the comparative advantages of free trade and the international division of labour.[32] The French economist and publicist Frederic Bastiat (1801–50) coined the famous phrase on the pacifying role of international trading relations: 'Where goods do not cross borders, soldiers will.'

On the other hand, for many poor countries the welfare gains of globalization did not materialize as expected.[33] There are great imbalances between world

---

[31] See J Gerber, *Global Competition: Law, Markets and Globalisation* (OUP 2010).

[32] H Siebert and O Lorz, *Außenwirtschaft* (9th edn, UTB 2014) 27; PR Krugman, M Obstfeld, and M Melitz, *International Economics: Theory and Policy* (10th edn, Prentice Hall 2014) 27; V Smith, 'Human Betterment Through Globalization' <http://www.flowidealism.org/Downloads/V-Smith.pdf> (accessed 23 June 2016).

[33] See P Collier, *The Bottom Billion: Why the Poorest Countries Are Failing and What Can Be Done About It* (OUP 2008) 79; TL Roe, AL Somwaru, and X Diao, 'Globalization: Welfare Distribution and Costs among Developed and Developing Countries' (2006) 28 RAE 399; SL Schmukler, 'Financial Globalization: Gain and Pain for Developing Countries' (2004) Federal Reserve Bank of Atlante Economic Review <http://siteresources.worldbank.org/DEC/Resources/SCHMUKLER-EconomicReview.pdf> (accessed 23 June 2016).

regions as to their share in international trade with goods and services and the flow of investments. The European Union and its Member States, the United States, China, and Japan are the most important actors, with respect to import as well as to export. The integration of markets presents undeniable burdens and risks for countries suffering from global standards of education and technology, lack of natural resources, and non-competitive industries. Although WTO law and other agreements provide preferential treatment for developing countries in a selective way, it cannot adequately respond to pre-existing inequalities. Despite globalization, gross imbalances and asymmetries in the allocation of wealth and the distribution of welfare gains persist. However, many of these asymmetries are rooted in inequalities among States and within States which have preceded economic globalization. All too often, the chances of globalization bypass countries with highly deficient internal structures, lack of transparency, inadequate control of public administration, and other characteristics associated with 'bad governance'.

In recent years, for different reasons, growing criticism of economic globalization has taken force in developing as well as in industrialized countries.[34] This criticism draws on fears about the domination by the great trading blocks and a marginalization of developing countries. The competition catalysed by globalization is seen as a threat not only from the perspective of poor countries. Even in prosperous countries benefiting from globalization, international competition is often seen as a danger for social and cultural 'biotopes' and for values deeply rooted in the collective conscience.[35] These anxieties are often associated with a preoccupation with the economic and political power of international corporations and with legitimate, but often fuzzy, concerns about the risks of 'modern technologies' and the international marketing of high-tech products (like genetically modified food, animal feed, and seed). The criticism of globalization often distorts perception of the chances which the globalization of economic relations also presents for poorer States, especially in context with foreign investment.

The integration of economies has generated a mechanism of 'global' governance. However, this governance is limited to specific sectors and is often characterized by mere informal cooperation. In any case, this governance is far from any sort of global economic governance. International governance is not the exclusive domain of States and international organizations. Non-governmental organizations and private undertakings set standards and incentives for compliance. Thus, private rating agencies strongly influence the standing of cooperation and even of States as debtors.

Not only the development of the world economy, the international division of labour, and international competition but also the legal framework for the

---

[34] M Doucet, *Global Justice and Democracy: The Anti-globalisation Movement* (Routledge 2010).
[35] JP Paul, 'Cultural Resistance to Global Governance' (2001) 22 Mich J Int'l L 1.

international economic order present demands on the internal structure of States. The WTO system and the standards developed by the International Monetary Fund and the World Bank embody a number of parameters both for the institutional system as for social and economic choices.

The so-called 'Washington Consensus' relates to a broad spectrum of political and economic reforms as to conditions for a successful development. This term, coined by the American economist John Williamson, in its original meaning refers to a development strategy pursued by the World Bank, the US Department of Treasury, the International Monetary Fund, and other institutions based in Washington DC[36] with respect to crisis-ridden countries of Latin America. The 'Washington Consensus' in its original meaning contained ten elements (recommendations):

1. fiscal policy discipline;
2. redirection of public spending from subsidies towards promotion of growth, education, health care, and infrastructure investments;
3. tax reform (inter alia, broadening the basis for taxation);
4. market-determined, positive interest rates;
5. competitive exchange rates;
6. trade liberalization;
7. liberalization of foreign direct investment;
8. privatization of State enterprises;
9. deregulation facilitating market access subject to the protection of specific public interests such as safety, environmental and consumer protection, and prudential supervision of financial institutions;
10. protection of property rights.[37]

Recently, the 'Washington Consensus' has become a target for allegedly being a 'neo-liberal' development policy and for allegedly focusing more on economic growth than on sustainable improvement of social conditions. Simplistic criticism even holds the 'neo-liberal' agenda of the 'Washington Consensus' responsible for the financial crisis shaking western industrialized countries since 2008.[38] On the other hand, the economic counter-movement with an agenda diametrically opposed to the 'Washington Consensus', characterized by protectionism, heavy restrictions of foreign direct investment, and a strong dose of legal instability (as practised in certain countries of Latin America and elsewhere), hardly improved the living conditions of the population at large.

---

[36] J Williamson, 'What Should the World Bank Think About the Washington Consensus?' (2000) 15 The World Bank Research Observer 251.

[37] J Williamson, 'What Washington Means By Policy Reform' in J Williamson (ed), *Latin American Adjustment: How Much Has Happened?* (Institute for International Economics 1990) 7.

[38] For a critical view of the 'neo-liberal agenda', see JD Ostry, P Loungani, and D Furceri, 'Neoliberalism: Oversold?' (2016) Finance & Development, 38.

6. Economic Interdependence and International Security: A Complex Relationship

The exchange of goods and services as well as international capital flows stand in a complex and controversial relationship with international security. 'Liberal' theorists emphasize the contribution of commercial ties to peace as well as the economic incentive to avoid military conflicts with trade partners.[39] By contrast, 'realist' theorists underline the vulnerability which may flow from economic interdependence.[40] From the 'realist' perspective, the focus of domestic leaders on maximizing security pulls them towards widening the territorial scope of control to reduce economic dependence.[41] A new approach associates the lower or higher likelihood of conflict with higher or lower expectations of profitable future trade.[42] Empirical analysis tends to support this trade expectations theory.

Select Bibliography

M Bungenberg and S Hobe (eds), *Permanent Sovereignty Over Natural Resources* (Springer 2015).

DC Copeland, *Economic Interdependence and War* (Princeton University Press 2014).

RW Cox, 'Ideologies and the New International Economic Order: Reflections on some Recent Literature' (1979) 33 Int'l Org 257.

J Gerber, *Global Competition: Law, Markets and Globalisation* (OUP 2010).

JN Gordon, 'The Shaping Force of Corporate Law in the New Economic Order' (1997) 31 U Rich L Rev 1473.

D Irwin, *Against the Tide: An Intellectual History of Free Trade* (Princeton University Press 1998).

JH Jackson, *The World Trading System* (2nd edn, MIT Press 1997).

PFJ Macrory, AE Appleton, and MG Plummer (eds), *The World Trade Organization: Legal, Economic and Political Analysis* (Springer New York 2005) vols 1–3.

J Makarczyk, *Principles of a New International Economic Order* (Martinus Nijhoff Publishers 1988).

M Matsushita, TJ Schoenbaum, PC Mavroidis, and M Hahn, *The World Trade Organization: Law, Practice and Policy* (3rd edn, OUP 2015).

D Rodrik, *The Globalization Paradox: Why Global Markets, States and Democracy Can't Coexist* (OUP 2011).

---

[39] M Gasiorowski and S Polachek, 'Conflict and Interdependence: East-West Linkages in the Era of Détente' (1982) 26 J Conflict Resolution 709; P McDonald, *The Invisible Hand of Peace: Capitalism, the War Machine, and International Relations Theory* (CUP 2009).

[40] J Mearsheimer, 'The False Promise of International Institutions' (1994–95), 19 International Security 5.

[41] K Waltz, *Theory of International Politics* (Random House 1979) 106.

[42] DC Copeland, *Economic Interdependence and War* (Princeton University Press 2014) 27.

J Stiglitz, *Globalisation and Its Discontents* (WW Norton & Co 2002).
P-T Stoll and F Schorkopf, *WTO: World Economic Order, World Trade Law* (Nijhoff Leiden 2006).
RCA White, 'A New International Economic Order' (1975) 24 ICLQ 542.
M Wolf, *Why Globalization Works* (Yale University Press 2004).

III

The Actors of International Economic Law

1. Subjects of International Law and Actors in International Economic Relations

Traditional international law recognizes only a limited number of entities capable of possessing international rights or duties and of bringing international claims.[1] The primary legal subjects in international law have always been States.[2] Other traditional subjects of international law are insurgents recognized as belligerents and entities *sui generis*, for example the Holy See, the Sovereign Order of Malta, and the International Committee of the Red Cross.[3] International (intergovernmental) organizations are also recognized as having international legal personality, the most prominent of them being the United Nations.[4] Since the end of the Second World War, the number and importance of international organizations with an economic mission such as the IMF, the World Bank Group, and the WTO, has increased steadily.

The scope of actors in international economic relations reaches well beyond international legal subjects in the strict sense.[5] International non-governmental organizations (NGOs), transnational corporations, non-formal governmental forums, and inter-agency cooperations shape today's international economic scene and influence the formulation of rules and standards. In addition, the development of human rights standards and the possibility of investors to bring claims against a State before the International Centre for Settlement of Investment Disputes (ICSID) have strengthened the role and the legal standing of companies and individuals in international economic relations.

---

[1] See generally, C Walter, 'Subjects of International Law' in R Wolfrum (ed), *The Max Planck Encyclopedia of Public International Law* (OUP 2012) vol IX, 634.

[2] A Cassese, *International Law* (2nd edn, OUP 2005) 71; R Jennings and A Watts (eds), *Oppenheim's International Law* (OUP 1992) vol I, para 6; MN Shaw, *International Law* (7th edn, CUP 2014) 143.

[3] See MN Shaw, *International Law* (7th edn, CUP 2014) 162ff, 178ff.

[4] See Advisory Opinion of the ICJ on *Reparation of Injuries Suffered in the Service of the United Nations* (Advisory Opinion) [1949] ICJ Rep 174; J Crawford, *Brownlie's Principles of Public International Law* (8th edn, OUP 2012) 166ff.

[5] See generally on actors in international economic diplomacy, N Bayne and S Woolcock, 'What is Economic Diplomacy?' in N Bayne and S Woolcock (eds), *The New Economic Diplomacy* (3rd edn, Ashgate 2011) 3f; R Hofmann (ed), *Non-State Actors as New Subjects of International Law—From the Traditional State Order Towards the Law of Global Community* (Duncker & Humblot 2000).

2. States

Despite the increasing variety of actors on the international plane, the world economic order is essentially still a system of coordination among States. States, in all their diversity, continue to be the most important subjects in international law and in international economic relations. States exercise regulatory power over economic activities in several ways. Within their own jurisdiction, they act through legislation and administrative supervision. On the international plane, they also influence international economic relations through the creation of new international rules and through their membership in international organizations and other forums of intergovernmental cooperation. Finally, States also participate directly in economic transactions, for example in trade in commodities or with regard to financial operations as central banks without legal personality of their own.

In principle, each State is free to choose its own economic system. The principle of non-intervention protects this freedom of States under customary international law.[6] However, a broad range of international agreements restrict economic choices. By defining 'strategic sectors', States control industrial and other economic activities considered as particularly sensitive. Their sovereign rights include the power to administer natural resources such as commodities or genetic resources. States also control the supply of energy via transport infrastructures. Another unique feature concerning the economic activities of States resides in the fact that they are in many cases subject to different rules than their (private) competitors. For instance, international rules on State immunity prevent States and their subdivisions from being subjected to foreign jurisdiction in the case of *acta iure imperii*.[7]

3. State Enterprises

States do not only participate in economic transactions directly but also through governmental agencies such as State enterprises. Such separate entities owe their creation mainly to reasons of specialization and efficiency.[8] Many State enterprises exploit and market natural resources like oil and gas. In recent years, several sovereign wealth funds (SWF) are ranking among the most potent investors and allow their governments to implement an 'ethical' or otherwise selective investment policy. State enterprises are usually legally and organizationally independent of the

---

[6] See ICJ *Military and Paramilitary Activities in and against Nicaragua (Nicaragua v United States)* [1986] ICJ Rep 14 para 108.

[7] J Kokott, 'States, Sovereign Equality' in R Wolfrum (ed), *The Max Planck Encyclopedia of Public International Law* (OUP 2012) vol IX, 571.

[8] See generally on organisational structures, Organization of Economic Cooperation and Development (OECD), 'Public Sector Modernisation: Changing Organisational Structures' (2004) OECD Observer, Policy Brief.

State, thus having the capacity of having rights and obligations of all kinds in their own name.

Despite their legal autonomy, State enterprises acting as an extension of the State and exercising public power[9] or possessing assets serving sovereign purposes (eg legally independent central banks) like the State itself enjoy immunity from legal proceedings. Separate treatment between State enterprises and States is also inappropriate if the corporate veil has been established for purposes of fraud and malfeasance.[10] As a rule, actions of State enterprises and corporate obligations do not engage the responsibility of the State.[11] Conversely, State enterprises may only be held liable for obligations of the State if a rigid divide between the two would lead to inequitable results.[12]

The Articles of the International Law Commission (ILC) on State Responsibility (2001) provide an exception from the general rule that actions of legally independent entities are not attributable to the State. Article 8 of the ILC Articles reads as follows:

Conduct directed or controlled by a State
The conduct of a person or group of persons shall be considered an act of a State under international law if the person or group of persons is in fact acting on the instructions of, or under the direction or control of that State in carrying out the conduct.

The term 'person' in Article 8 of the ILC Articles includes natural persons as well as legal entities like companies, which are controlled by the State.[13] State responsibility may also be established when the State is 'using its ownership interest in or control of a corporation specifically in order to achieve a particular result'.[14] Occasionally, State enterprises seek release from their corporate liability arguing that the State defeated the fulfilment of their obligations by imposing legal or administrative restrictions (eg export bans). This is a valid reason as long as the enterprise, like a private entity, operates in full autonomy from the State. If, however, the State deliberately intervenes by releasing its own enterprise from its contractual obligations, the enterprise cannot rely on such collusive intervention.[15]

WTO law and regional trade agreements also deal with State-owned enterprises, (eg Article XVII GATT 1994 and Article 1503 NAFTA).

---

[9] R Dolzer and C Schreuer, *Principles of International Investment Law* (2nd edn, OUP 2012) 219f; *Phillips Petroleum Co v Islamic Republic of Iran* [1989] 21 Iran-USCTR 79.

[10] See ICJ *Barcelona Traction, Light and Power Company* (*Belgium v Spain*) (Judgment) [1970] ICJ Rep 3, 39.

[11] R Dolzer and C Schreuer, *Principles of International Investment Law* (2nd edn, OUP 2012) 219. In the case of the Chernobyl disaster, German courts have denied a direct liability of the Soviet Union for damages due to the legal independency of the operator of the nuclear power plant, see Amtsgericht Bonn (district court) NJW 1988, 1393; Landgericht Bonn (county court) NJW 1989, 1225.

[12] *First National Bank v Banco Para El Comercio Exterior de Cuba* 462 US 611 (1983).

[13] See J Crawford, *The International Law Commission's Articles on State Responsibility* (CUP 2002) 110.

[14] J Crawford, *The International Law Commission's Articles on State Responsibility* (CUP 2002) 112.

[15] See I Seidl-Hohenveldern, *Corporations in and under International Law* (CUP 1987) 55; see also House of Lords *Czarnikow Ltd v Rolimpex* 1979 AC 351.

4. International Organizations

(a) Role and history

Next to States, international (intergovernmental) organizations (IGOs) are the most relevant actors in today's international law.[16] Even though some of them have existed since the 19th century,[17] the majority of international organizations have been established in the second half of the 20th century.[18] After the end of the Second World War, the limited influence of the single State and the need for enhanced international cooperation as well as the complexity of economic relations and the activities of transnational corporations have fostered the creation of international economic organizations and other forms of intergovernmental cooperation. Quite a number of international organizations (eg the European Union) are members of other international organizations.

International organizations play a vital regulatory role both by creating legally binding rules for their Member States and by formulating non-binding standards and recommendations. They also provide forums for intergovernmental cooperation, consultation, and support. By now, direct involvement of international organizations in the market of commodities (eg by purchasing and selling commodities in order to stabilize prices) has given way to softer mechanisms of influencing trade.

(b) International organizations as legal entities and the liability of members

The founding agreements usually provide for legal personality of international organizations both under international and municipal law. In principle, the status of international organizations as a legal entity separated from their Member States protects the Member State from liability for the organization's obligations. There are, however, exceptional situations in which the 'piercing of the corporate veil'

---

[16] See ICJ *Reparation for Injuries Suffered in the Service of the United Nations* (Advisory Opinion) [1949] ICJ Rep 174; ICJ *Legality of the Threat or Use of Nuclear Weapons* (Advisory Opinion) [1996] ICJ Rep 226; A Cassese, *International Law* (2nd edn, OUP 2005); see on the history of international organizations, CF Amerasinghe, *Principles of the Institutional Law of International Organizations* (2nd edn, CUP 2005) 1–6.

[17] AA Stein, 'Incentive Compatibility and Global Governance: Existential Multilateralism, a Weakly Confederal World, and Hegemony' in AS Alexandroff (ed), *Can the World Be Governed?* (The Center for International Governance Innovation and Wilfrid Laurier University Press 2008) 17. The first international organizations were the international river commissions managing the rivers Rhine (1815), Elbe (1821), Douro (1835), Po (1849), and Danube (1856); K Schmalenbach, 'International Organizations or Institutions, General Aspects' in R Wolfrum (ed), *The Max Planck Encyclopedia of Public International Law* (OUP 2012) vol V, 1126 para 2.

[18] According to the Union of International Associations, in 1909 the number of IGOs amounted to 37, while in 2012 this number had increased to 7,710. see <http://www.uia.org/sites/uia.org/files/misc_pdfs/stats/Historical_overview_of_number_of_international_organizations_by_type_1909–2013.pdf> (accessed 23 June 2016).

seems appropriate, thus extending obligations of the international organization to its members.

The collapse of the International Tin Council catalysed a controversy over members' liability for the financial commitments of the organization.[19] In this case, the managers of the Council's buffer stock, over time, had engaged in highly speculative deals with tin, without the members of the International Tin Council or its representative organs interfering. After the organization went insolvent, private creditors sought relief with the members and brought actions against the Member States and the then European Community.

The extension of the liability of an international organization to its members, as a general principle of international law, can be based on common features of the company laws of most States.[20] Members' liability seems justified if

- the founding Member States failed to provide the organization with enough capital resources;[21]
- the organization's activities evidently did not keep within its object and purpose as defined in the founding agreement; and
- the members seeking cover behind the autonomy of the organization as a separate legal entity would amount to an abuse of law or bad faith.

However, it is important to draw a distinction between liability under international law and the liability towards private creditors. The criteria for a piercing of the corporate veil can only create liability of Member States with a view to their international obligations. As for the members' liability for obligations under municipal law, for example out of sales or loan agreements, international law only sets the conditions for the possibility of a piercing of the corporate veil, that is the criteria for allowing a national court to pass over the legal personality of the organization. As a lesson drawn from the debacle involving the International Tin Council, a growing number of constituent agreements of international organizations exclude the liability of members for the obligations of the organization.[22] Hence, the International Natural Rubber Agreement explicitly limited the liability of the Members of the International Natural Rubber Organization to their contributions under the Agreement.[23]

---

[19] See M Herdegen, 'The Insolvency of International Organizations and the Legal Position of Creditors: Some Observations in the Light of the International Tin Council Crisis' (1988) 35 NILR 135; EJ McFadden, 'The Collapse of Tin: Restructuring a Failed Commodity Agreement' (1986) 80 AJIL 811.

[20] See M Hartwig, *Die Haftung der Mitgliedstaaten für internationale Organisationen* (Responsibility of Member States for International Organizations) (Springer 1993).

[21] See M Hartwig, *Die Haftung der Mitgliedstaaten für internationale Organisationen* (Responsibility of Member States for International Organizations) (Springer 1993).

[22] See M Hartwig, *Die Haftung der Mitgliedstaaten für internationale Organisationen* (Responsibility of Member States for International Organizations) (Springer 1993) para 1589.

[23] Article 48(4) of the International Natural Rubber Agreement (1995); see also Articles 7(2) and 23 of the International Cocoa Agreement (2010) and Article 22(2) of the International Coffee Agreement (2007).

(c) The United Nations and its 'specialized agencies'

Some important forums of cooperation in international economic law have been established within the framework of the United Nations. In 1964, the UN General Assembly established the United Nations Conference on Trade and Development (UNCTAD)[24] to promote the integration of poorer countries into the world economy with due regard for their development. The United Nations Commission on International Trade Law (UNCITRAL),[25] set up in 1966, has the task of elaborating an improved legal framework for the facilitation of international trade and investment.[26]

The Economic and Social Council of the United Nations (ECOSOC) has entered into agreements with so-called 'specialized agencies', thus bringing them into relationship with the United Nations (Articles 57 and 63 UN Charter). Among the 'specialized agencies' (currently 15)[27] rank a number of international organizations whose activities, directly or indirectly, relate to international economic relations:

- International Labour Organization (ILO);
- Food and Agriculture Organization (FAO)[28] which fights hunger and fosters the agricultural development of developing countries and countries in transition;
- United Nations Educational, Scientific and Cultural Organization (UNESCO);
- World Health Organization (WHO);
- World Bank Group
  - International Bank for Reconstruction and Development (IBRD)
  - International Development Association (IDA)
  - International Finance Corporation (IFC)
  - Multilateral Investment Guarantee Agency (MIGA)
  - International Centre for Settlement of Investment Disputes (ICSID);
- International Monetary Fund (IMF);
- International Civil Aviation Organization (ICAO);
- International Maritime Organization (IMO);
- International Telecommunication Union (ITU);

[24] See <http://www.unctad.org> (accessed 23 June 2016).
[25] See <http://www.uncitral.org> (accessed 23 June 2016).
[26] In the past decades, UNCITRAL has presented several model laws, eg the Model Law on International Commercial Arbitration (1985/2006), the Model Law on International Credit Transfer (1992), the Model Law on Cross Border Insolvencies (1997), the Model Law on Electronic Commerce (1996/98), the Model Law on Electronic Signatures (2001), and the Model Law on International Commercial Conciliation (2002).
[27] See <http://www.un.org/en/sections/about-un/funds-programmes-specialized-agencies-and-others/index.html> (accessed 23 June 2016).
[28] See <http://www.fao.org> (accessed 23 June 2016).

- Universal Postal Union (UPU);
- World Meteorological Organization (WMO);
- World Intellectual Property Organization (WIPO);
- International Fund for Agricultural Development (IFAD);
- United Nations Industrial Development Organization (UNIDO);[29] and
- World Tourism Organization (UNWTO).

Moreover, several other organizations, on the basis of their cooperation with the UN, are classified as 'related organizations'. These include:

- the International Atomic Energy Agency (IAEA);
- the Preparatory Commission for the Nuclear-Test-Ban Treaty Organization (CTBTO);
- the Organisation for the Prohibition of Chemical Weapons (OPCW); and
- the World Trade Organization (WTO).

(d) International organizations as actors in international economic relations

In institutional terms, the international economic order rests on three pillars:

- the International Monetary Fund (IMF);
- the World Bank (International Bank for Reconstruction and Development— IBRD) with all its siblings; and
- the World Trade Organization (WTO).

The IMF and the IBRD are fruits of the 1944 Bretton Woods Conference.[30] The IMF plays a key role in international monetary relations. Today, the IMF's main task is to monitor fluctuations in exchange rates and to provide assistance to Member States with serious financial problems (balance of payments deficit).

The main purpose of the IBRD is to assist in the reconstruction and economic development of its Member States. The IBRD's mission was to finance specific development projects of developing States. However, in the last decades the Bank became engaged more and more in programme-based lending.[31] Closely associated with the IBRD, the International Development Association (IDA), established in 1960, aims at reducing poverty by providing interest-free loans and grants.

---

[29] See <http://www.unido.org> (accessed 23 June 2016).

[30] Both organizations were founded in 1944 at the Bretton Woods Conference; see on the History of IMF and IBRD, ES Mason and RE Asher, *The World Bank Since Bretton Woods* (The Brookings Institution 1973); S Schlemmer-Schulte, 'International Monetary Fund (IMF)' in R Wolfrum (ed), *The Max Planck Encyclopedia of Public International Law* (OUP 2012) vol V, 1037; see generally on international financial institutions, M Ragazzi, 'Financial Institutions, International' in R Wolfrum (ed), *The Max Planck Encyclopedia of Public International Law* (OUP 2012) vol IV, 21.

[31] See IF Shihata, *The World Bank in a Changing World* (Martinus Nijhoff Publishers 1991) vol I, 26.

Another agency of the World Bank Group, the International Finance Corporation (IFC) assists private investment in borrower countries. The International Centre for Settlement of Investment Disputes (ICSID) and the Multilateral Investment Guarantee Agency (MIGA) also belong to the World Bank Group.

The Havana Charter for an International Trade Organization (1948) provided for the establishment of the International Trade Organization (ITO)[32] as the third institutional pillar of the international economic order. However, because of strong US opposition to the comprehensive approach of the ITO only the General Agreement on Tariffs and Trade (GATT) entered into force in 1947. Though being a provisional arrangement in the first place, the GATT with its evolving organizational structure operated more and more as a de facto international organization. Finally, the establishment of the World Trade Organization (WTO), in 1994, vested the world trade order with a new and solid institutional basis.[33] The International Labour Organization (ILO, created in 1919)[34] sets international labour standards and supervises their implementation. The ILO, in particular, combats discrimination and contributes to improved labour conditions as well as to adequate social security for workers. At the same time, the ILO labour standards counteract 'social dumping' and other forms of 'races to the bottom'.

A number of commodity organisations comprising producer as well as consumer countries like the International Natural Rubber Organization (INRO) or the International Tin Council were established with the objective to ensure stable price levels, for example through market operations or the regulation of production. As this model of directly influencing supply and prices fell short of expectations, most international commodity organizations have been reduced to forums for international communication and consultation. Only few organizations like the Organization of the Petroleum Exporting Countries (OPEC) coordinate the marketing of products or even operate as a cartel.

Apart from the universal international organizations, there is a variety of regional international economic organizations. The Organization for Economic Co-operation and Development (OECD) was established as a forum of cooperation for Western industrialized countries and now includes important emerging countries (such as Mexico, Chile, and Turkey).[35] In light of the Ukrainian crisis the OECD postponed the process of Russia's accession to the organization.[36] By coordinating the economic and monetary policies of its members, the OECD

---

[32] See JH Jackson, *The World Trading System* (3rd edn, MIT Press 1999) 31.
[33] See Ch XI.2.   [34] See <http://www.ilo.org> (accessed 23 June 2016).
[35] See <http://www.oecd.org> (accessed 23 June 2016); C Trüe, 'Organization for Economic Cooperation and Development, Nuclear Energy Agency' in R Wolfrum (ed), The Max Planck Encyclopedia of Public International Law (OUP 2012) vol VII, 1036; the OECD currently consists of 35 Member States: Australia, Austria, Belgium, Canada, Chile, the Czech Republic, Denmark, Estonia, Finland, France, Germany, Greece, Hungary, Iceland, Ireland, Israel, Italy, Japan, Korea, Latvia, Luxembourg, Mexico, the Netherlands, New Zealand, Norway, Poland, Portugal, Slovakia, Slovenia, Spain, Sweden, Switzerland, Turkey, the United Kingdom, and the United States.
[36] See for the statement made by the OECD <http://www.oecd.org/russia/statement-by-the-oecd-regarding-the-status-of-the-accession-process-with-russia-and-co-operation-with-ukraine.htm> (accessed 23 June 2016).

has gained significant importance. Additionally, the OECD supports the economic development of developing countries through its Development Assistance Committee (DAC), which currently comprises 28 OECD Member States as well as the European Union.[37] The World Bank, the IMF, and the United Nations Development Programme (UNDP) participate as observers.

Regional development banks make important contributions to the promotion of development as well as to the assistance in economic and political transformation processes. Nowadays, there are three major regional development banks: the Inter-American Development Bank, the Asian Development Bank, and the European Bank for Reconstruction and Development. Some South American countries established the Banco del Sur in 2007 as a counterweight to the Washington-based Inter-American Development Bank.

Within the European Union, the European Investment Bank[38] assists development in the weaker economies of the Union. The European Investment Bank also provides assistance to projects in developing countries, for example in the African, Caribbean and Pacific (ACP) regions. The new Asian Infrastructure Investment Bank (AIIB) was launched by China as an interstate development bank.[39]

The BRIC States established a Development Bank and a Monetary Fund, parallel to the World Bank and the IMF. The creation of these new institutions means a significant power shift in monetary politics away from the dominating influence of North America and Western Europe.

Traditionally, regional cooperation is carried out within free trade areas and customs unions. Some but not all of these regional arrangements have taken the form of legally independent organizations as for example the European Free Trade Association (EFTA). A hitherto unparalleled level of economic and political integration has been achieved by the European Union, thanks to the high degree of industrialization and the far-reaching homogeneity concerning social, cultural, and economic values on the one hand, and the unprecedented disposition to transfer national sovereignty to supranational bodies on the other hand. The broad and still expanding competences of the European Union and its organs which directly affect the Member States and the 'EU nationals' individually accord the European Union a status in the international order which has no counterpart anywhere else in the world. There is no similar international organization with such a far-reaching influence on its Member States. Inspired by the European model of integration, Latin American countries have established some institutionally consolidated forms of economic cooperation as, for instance, the Andean Pact and the MERCOSUR. In the African region, the African Union, created in 2001, is inspired by the European model.[40] For parts of the Asian region, the Association of Southeast Asian Nations (ASEAN) was initially established as a forum for economic cooperation. Particularly in the past decades, ASEAN has evolved rapidly, introducing an Asian Free Trade

---

[37] See for all the 29 DAC members <http://www.oecd.org/dac/dacmembers.htm> (accessed 23 June 2016).
[38] See Articles 308ff of the TFEU.   [39] See Ch XL.2.
[40] Constitutive Act of the African Union of 11 July 2000, OAU Doc CAB/LEG/23.15.

Area, creating an Asian Investment Area, and adopting the ASEAN Charter in 2007, which goes far beyond pure economic integration and introduces democracy, good governance, the rule of law, and human rights into ASEAN's purposes and principles.[41]

A recent phenomenon with a massive impact on trade and development are 'mega-regional' agreements like the Comprehensive Economic and Trade Agreement (CETA) between Canada and the European Union, the Trans-Pacific Partnership Agreement (TPP) among twelve States of the Pacific Rim, and the currently negotiated Transatlantic Trade and Investment Partnership (TTIP) between the United States and the European Union.

5. Non-institutionalized Forums of Cooperation in Economic Relations

Alongside international organizations, new forms of inter-State cooperation have emerged as a response to the ever-increasing economic globalization. These forums coordinate monetary and other economic policies, formulate standards (eg for the financial sector) or channel common interests without a firm institutional structure and without strictly binding mechanisms.

The most important of these non-formal platforms of cooperation is the Group of Twenty (G20).[42] The G20 is *the* forum for global economic 'governance'. The G20 emerged from the Group of Seven (G7) which unites the seven most important industrialized Western States: the United States, Canada, France, Germany, Italy, Japan, and the United Kingdom. In 1997, the G7 became the Group of Eight (G8) when Russia joined. Representatives of the European Union also take part in the meetings of the G7/G8. In response to Russia's actions in the Crimea crisis, the G7 suspended the participation of Russia.[43]

The G20 was established in 1999 at the G7 Cologne Summit in order to enable a joint discussion of both industrialized and developing countries on key global economy issues, ensuring more representation in economic, demographic, and regional terms.[44] The G20 integrates the 19 most important industrial countries and emerging economies plus the European Union, representing around 85 per

---

[41] Articles 1(7) and 2(2) of the ASEAN Charter. Article 14 even provides for the establishment of an ASEAN human rights body.

[42] See AS Alexandroff and J Kirton, 'The "Great Recession" and the Emergence of the G-20 Leaders' Summit' in AS Alexandroff and AF Cooper (eds), *Rising States, Rising Institutions: Challenges for Global Governance* (Brookings Institution Press 2010); L Delabie, 'Les modes de cooperation interétatique informels: G8 et G20' (2009) 55 AFDI 629.

[43] European Council, *G7 The Hague declaration* EUCO 73/14 (24 March 2014) para 6.

[44] See on the background of the G20, AS Alexandroff and J Kirton, 'The "Great Recession" and the Emergence of the G-20 Leaders' Summit' in AS Alexandroff and AF Cooper (eds), *Rising States, Rising Institutions: Challenges for Global Governance* (Brookings Institution Press 2010); JH Freis, 'The G-20 Emphasis on Promoting Integrity in Financial Markets' in M Giovanoli and D Devos (eds), *International Monetary and Financial Law* (OUP 2010); C Schmucker and K Gnath, 'From the G8 to the G20: Reforming the Global Economic Governance System' (2011) 2 EYIEL 389.

cent of global gross domestic product, over 75 per cent of world trade (including EU intra-trade) as well as about two-thirds of the world's population.[45] It comprises Argentina, Australia, Brazil, Canada, China, France, Germany, India, Indonesia, Italy, Japan, Mexico, Russia, Saudi Arabia, South Africa, South Korea, Turkey, the United Kingdom, the United States, and the European Union. At the Pittsburgh Summit in 2009, the G20 was designated to be the leading forum for international economic cooperation.[46] This change reflects the growing importance of emerging economies, especially the so-called 'BRIC'-countries (Brazil, Russia, India, and China) which—together with the G7—represent the major political actors in shaping the framework for global economic relations. The aggregated voting power represented in the G20 dominates the International Monetary Fund. Thus, the G20 has turned into a kind of steering body for the world economy.[47] At its regular meetings (World Economic Summits) the G20 discusses aspects of international economic and monetary policies.

Especially with regard to financial and monetary cooperation, the Group of 10 (G10), including the most important Western industrialized States, was established in 1962 in order to provide the IMF with special credits in case of cash-flow difficulties.

The G10 initially included Belgium, Canada, France, Germany, Italy, Japan, the Netherlands, Sweden, the United Kingdom, and the United States. Switzerland joined the G10 in 1984.

Within the United Nations Conference for Trade and Development (UNCTAD), a Group of originally 77 developing countries emerged in 1964 to combine their economic interests vis-à-vis the industrialized States. Today, the G77 has more than 130 members.[48] The Cairns Group[49] was established in 1986 as an interest group of agricultural countries. Within the WTO, the most influential interest group is the G21, a group of developing countries formed in 2003 under the leadership of Brazil, India, China, and South Africa, pursuing the agricultural interests of its members by calling for the opening of the markets for agricultural products, in particular through the elimination of import duties and subsidies, and for a reduction of internal subsidies distorting international competition.[50] Comparable to

---

[45] See <http://www.oecd.org/g20/g20-members.htm> (accessed 23 June 2016).

[46] See Leader's Statement: The Pittsburgh Summit (24–25 September 2009), available at <http://ec.europa.eu/commission_2010-2014/president/pdf/statement_20090826_en_2.pdf> (accessed 23 June 2016).

[47] For a further analysis of the international legal status of the G8 and G20, see L Delabie, 'Les modes de coopération interétatique informels: G8 et G20' (2009) 55 AFDI 629, 651.

[48] There are currently 134 Member States, see <http://www.g77.org/doc/members.html> (accessed 23 June 2016).

[49] Members of the Cairns Group are, among others: Argentina, Australia, Brazil, Canada, Colombia, India, and New Zealand.

[50] Additionally, a major group of developing countries led by India and China (G33) has joined together, not only claiming the opening of markets, but also aiming to protect their national agriculture. On the contrary, the G90, established by the majority of the poorest countries, rejects certain liberalization measures concerning trade in services or investments.

the development of the G20, the creation of the G21 within the WTO marks a considerable shift of power towards the emerging economies.

6. International Inter-Agency Cooperation

Inter-agency cooperation—understood as the cooperation between national authorities of participating States[51]—has an ever-increasing impact on domestic legislation and administrative practice.[52] The process of mutual information and cooperation between national authorities contributes to a soft harmonization of administrative practices beyond legally binding standards. The concept of 'global administrative law'[53] essentially refers to such international cooperation between executive or administrative authorities. This form of international cooperation provides national authorities with a sort of institutional independence, thus 'dis-aggregating' the State in its monolithic appearance. The executive-sided coop-eration of the State raises questions both of democratic legitimacy and political control.[54]

Under the roof of the Bank for International Settlements (BIS), the Basel Committee on Banking Supervision provides a forum for cooperation on bank-ing supervisory matters.[55] The members represented in the Committee comprise the G10 countries and Argentina, Australia, Brazil, China, the European Union, Hong Kong, India, Indonesia, Luxembourg, Mexico, Russia, Saudi Arabia, Singapore, South Africa, South Korea, Spain, and Turkey. The Committee is com-posed of the heads of the central banks and of the authorities for banking supervi-sion of the participating States. By consensus, it establishes banking standards to be implemented by domestic legislation. The Basel standards serve as a model for the supervisory regime in a great number of States. They have an immense practi-cal significance for the financial sector, even though they are not legally binding under international law.

---

[51] On cooperation between international organizations, see C Tietje, 'Global Governance and Inter-Agency Co-operation in International Economic Law' (2002) 36 JWT 501.

[52] See generally, K Raustiala, 'The Architecture of International Cooperation: Transgovernmental Networks and the Future of International Law' (2002) 43 Va J Int'l L 1; A-M Slaughter, 'Governing Through Government Networks' in M Byers (ed), *The Role of Law in International Politics* (OUP 2000) 177.

[53] N Krisch and B Kingsbury, 'Introduction: Global Governance and Global Administrative Law in the International Legal Order' (2006) 17 EJIL 1; S Cassese, 'Administrative Law Without the State? The Challenge of Global Regulation' (2005) 37 NYU J Int'l L & Pol 663; RB Stewart, 'The Global Regulatory Challenge to U.S. Administrative Law ' (2005) 37 NYU J Int'l L & Pol 695.

[54] See eg A-M Slaughter, 'Governing Through Government Networks' in M Byers (ed), *The Role of Law in International Politics* (OUP 2000) 177 (193ff); K Raustiala, 'The Architecture of International Cooperation: Transgovernmental Networks and the Future of International Law' (2002) 43 Va J Int'l L 1 (70ff).

[55] See <http://www.bis.org/bcbs> (accessed 23 June 2016); MS Barr and GP Miller, 'Global Administrative Law: The View from Basel' (2006) 17 EJIL 15; KP Follak, 'The Basel Committee and EU Banking Regulation in the Aftermath of the Credit Crisis' in M Giovanoli and D Devos (eds), *International Monetary and Financial Law* (OUP 2010) 177, 181.

The Financial Stability Board (FSB) operates as a forum for cooperation in the interest of global financial stability between the financial authorities of G20 Member States (in particular central banks, ministries of economics and finance, and financial supervision authorities) as well as institutions like the European Central Bank, the European Commission, the Bank for International Settlements, the International Monetary Fund, the OECD, the World Bank, and other standard setting bodies.[56] The FSB formulates standards and recommendations for regulatory, supervisory, and other financial sector policies, addressing vulnerabilities which may affect the stability of the financial systems and fostering a level playing field through coherent legislative and administrative implementation.

The International Organization of Securities Commissions (IOSCO) is a private non-profit organization founded under the law of Quebec. It is composed of representatives of securities commissions of more than 100 countries.[57] The Technical Committee of IOSCO develops standards for supervision. The International Association of Insurance Supervisors (IAIS) coordinates the formulation of standards by national insurance authorities. Various forms of inter-agency cooperation (on a regional and global level) exist in the field of postal services and telecommunication as well as in the sector of energy regulation.

The International Competition Network (ICN) provides a forum for more than 80 national competition authorities to exchange experiences and perspectives, thereby promoting convergence of administrative practices. Agreements between the European Union and the United States establish a framework for the cooperation of European and US competition authorities—the Department of Justice and the Federal Trade Commission.[58]

7. Non-governmental Organizations

Non-governmental international organizations (NGOs) are established by private actors (a group of individuals or corporate entities) under national law to pursue a particular agenda.[59] Early NGOs had the mission to promote and protect basic human rights or humanitarian standards in wartime.[60] Today, NGOs operate in almost all fields of international law, including international economic law. NGOs

---

[56] See on the FSB, KP Follak, 'The Basel Committee and EU Banking Regulation in the Aftermath of the Credit Crisis' in M Giovanoli and D Devos (eds), *International Monetary and Financial Law* (OUP 2010) 177, 181.

[57] See <http://www.iosco.org> (accessed 23 June 2016).

[58] The framework is based primarily on the 1991 Competition Cooperation Agreement [1995] OJ L 95/47 and the 1998 Positive Comity Agreement [1998] OJ L 173/28

[59] JL Dunoff, SR Ratner and D Wippman, *International Law, Norms, Actors, Process* (2nd edn, Aspen Publishers 2006) 192; on the different notions of NGOs see S Hobe, 'Non-Governmental Organizations' in R Wolfrum (ed), *The Max Planck Encyclopedia of Public International Law* (OUP 2012) vol VII, 716 paras 1ff.

[60] Examples of such NGOs are the associations established in the 17th and 18th centuries to promote the abolitions of slave trade and slavery itself, and the Red Cross Movement in the 19th century.

are a significant feature of modern international life.[61] Though NGOs (with the exception of the International Committee of the Red Cross) do not have international legal personality, a considerable number of them are highly visible and often influential actors on the international scene.[62]

NGOs working in the field of international economic law include established economic NGOs such as the International Chamber of Commerce (ICC), the International Air Transport Association (IATA), the International Federation of Consulting Engineers (FIDIC), and international trade unions and employers' associations. Beyond these 'genuine' economic organizations, NGOs working in the context of environmental protection, human rights, and the fight against corruption (eg Greenpeace, Amnesty International, and Transparency International) address more and more economic issues.

NGOs also fulfil a most important function in fact-finding. Many cases of human rights violations or environmental damage were brought to light or made the focus of broad discussion by the intense investigations of NGOs. National and international courts or dispute settlement bodies, in varying degrees, give consideration to the opinion of NGOs, especially in human rights and environmental issues.[63]

Many NGOs have proven their ability to exert a considerable international pressure and to influence both State and non-State actors. This role often makes NGOs compete with State organs and parliamentary control, and raises issues of accountability and legitimacy.[64]

In the course of the energetic campaign of Greenpeace against the oil company Shell and its plan to dispose of the oil storage facility Brent Spar at the North Sea in 1995,[65] many (including the German Government) responded to Greenpeace's fierce criticism and its call to boycott Shell. In the end, Shell, giving in to Greenpeace's pressure, disposed of the platform on shore. As was revealed afterwards, the form of the disposal finally chosen caused greater environmental damage than Shell's initial plan. Greenpeace (to its own credit) confessed that its worldwide campaign rested on a deficient risk assessment. On repeated occasions, Greenpeace and other

---

[61] D Thürer, 'The Emergence of Non-Governmental Organizations and Transnational Enterprises in International Law and the Changing Role of the State' in R Hofman and N Geissler (eds), *Non-State Actors as New Subjects of International Law* (Duncker & Humblot 2000) 37, 41.

[62] MN Shaw, *International Law* (7th edn, CUP 2014) 190ff; JL Dunoff, SR Ratner and D Wippman, *International Law, Norms, Actors, Process* (2nd edn, Aspen Publishers 2006) 192. The importance of NGOs in today's international community is reflected among others in the Committee on NGOs established within the Economic and Social Council (ECOSOC) of the United Nations.

[63] See eg JP Trachtman and PM Moremen, 'Costs and Benefits of Private Participation in WTO Dispute Settlement: Whose Right Is It Anyway?' (2003) 44 Harv Int'l LJ 221. For NGOs as Amici Curiae see L van den Eynde, 'An Empirical Look at the Amicus Curiae Practice of Human Rights NGOs Before the European Court of Human Rights' (2013) 31 NQHR 271.

[64] See M Herdegen, 'Nichtregierungsorganisationen: rechtlicher Status, Einfluss und Legitimität' in S Hieble, N Kassebohm, and H Lilie (eds), *Festschrift für Volkmar Mehle* (Nomos 2009) 261; A Reinisch, 'Governance Through Accountability' (2001) 44 GYIL 270; DC Thomas, 'International NGOs, State Sovereignty and Democratic Values' (2001) 2 Chi J Int'l L 389.

[65] See <http://www.greenpeace.org/international/en/about/history/the-brent-spar/> (accessed 23 June 2016).

(European and African) NGOs have campaigned against US American food aid involving genetically modified products to famine-ridden African countries. Like their object, these actions have stirred great controversy.[66] Another, more recent environmental activity of high visibility is the 'Detox campaign' launched by Greenpeace which calls for toxic-free fashion and clean water.

NGOs like Attac have joined the ranks of globalization critics. A number of these organizations are very actively engaged in the controversies surrounding the TTIP or the negotiation of the Trade in Services Agreement (TISA). Thanks to these activities, large sectors of European societies are far more sensitive to propagated risks for environmental and health standards resulting from trade liberalization or investment protection than to likely benefits for economic growth and employment.

NGOs also participate as observers in intergovernmental conferences as well as environmental proceedings and human rights litigation, often in context with economic activities.[67] In particular with regard to environmental standards, NGOs have become internationally recognized actors. Thus, the Aarhus Convention on Access to Information in Environmental Matters[68] was elaborated upon the instigation of NGOs. NGOs also cooperate with private enterprises, trade unions, and other institutions in the 'Global Reporting Initiative' which promotes voluntary reporting on the sustainability of business activities.[69]

8. Private Enterprises and Standards for Transnational Corporations

(a) The role of private enterprises in international economic law

The international exchange of goods, services, and payments mainly rests on transactions by private companies. They have the nationality of the State in which they are incorporated or in which they have their registered office (seat of management).[70]

---

[66] See P Driessen, *Eco-Imperialism* (Free Enterprise Press 2003) 19.

[67] See U Beyerlin, 'The Role of NGOs in Environmental Litigation' (2001) 61 ZaöRV 357; SW Burgiel, 'Non-state Actors and the Cartagena Protocol on Biosafety' in MM Betsill and E Corell (eds), *NGO Diplomacy: The Influence of Nongovernmental Organizations in International Environmental Negotiations* (MIT Press 2008) 67; MT Kamminga, 'The Evolving Status of NGOs under International Law: A Threat to the Inter-State System?' in P Alston (ed), *Non-State Actors and Human Rights* (OUP 2005) 93.

[68] UNECE Convention on Access to Information, Public Participation in Decision-making and Access to Justice in Environmental Matters of 25 June 1998.

[69] HS Brown, M de Jong, and T Lessidrenska, 'The Rise of the Global Reporting Initiative: a Case of Institutional Entrepreneurship' (2009) 18 Environmental Politics 182; S Benn, D Dunphy, and A Griffiths, *Organizational Change for Corporate Sustainability* (3rd edn, Routledge 2014) 79; C Adams and V Narayanan, 'The "Standardization" of Sustainability Reporting' in J Unerman, J Bebbington, and B O'Dwyer (eds), *Sustainability Accounting and Accountability* (2nd edn, Routledge 2014) 72f.

[70] MN Shaw, *International Law* (7th edn, CUP 2014) 588ff; R Dolzer and C Schreuer, *Principles of International Investment Law* (2nd edn, OUP 2012) 47ff; a differentiated approach is taken by the ILC Draft Articles on Diplomatic Protection (2006) in Art 9.

US or British company laws follow the doctrine of incorporation.[71] Other systems (like in Germany and Austria)[72] principally refer to the seat of management. However, European Union law catalysed certain flexibility with respect to the seat of management. The right of establishment (Articles 49ff TFEU) allows companies lawfully established in one EU country to operate essentially or even entirely in other EU States without conforming to the rules of incorporation applying in the country of establishment (subject to possible exceptions, eg with respect to the protection of creditors).[73] German company law has been modified so as to enable German companies to establish their effective administrative headquarters in a country other than their that of registered office.[74] Germany now also recognizes the legal personality of a company incorporated under the law of another EU Member State.[75]

Private companies are subject to national jurisdiction, be it in their home State or in the host State in which they carry out their activities. The home State may grant diplomatic protection to its corporate nationals against their host State.[76]

Private 'transnational corporations' (TNCs)—or 'multinational enterprises' (MNEs)—participate in transboundary commercial activities.[77] TNCs play a vital role in international trade and investment. They account for a large share of the most capital-rich business entities worldwide.

The revenues of a number of corporations surpass the GDP of many or even most States. According to the Forbes Global 2000 list in 2015, Wal-Mart's revenues amounted to USD 485.7 billion, Sinopec reachedUSD 427.6 billion, Royal Dutch Shell USD 420.4 billion, and Exxon Mobil USD 376.2 billion.[78] In comparison, South Africa achieved in 2015 a GDP of USD 317.3[79] billion, Peru USD 179.9 billion, and Romania USD 174.9 billion.[80]

---

[71] See §§ 14ff of the UK Companies Act (2006) which refers to incorporation or the registration of a company. The United States follow the incorporation doctrine since a Supreme Court ruling in 1868: *Paul v Virginia* [1868] 75 US 168.

[72] See § 10 of the Austrian IPRG (International Private Law Act) of 1978.

[73] O Mörsdorf, 'The Legal Mobility of Companies within the European Union through Cross-border Conversion' (2012) 49 CML Rev. 629.

[74] See § 4a of the German Act on Companies with Limited Liability (GmbH-Gesetz); § 5 of the German Shares Act (Aktiengesetz).

[75] BGHZ 178, 192. With regard to third countries, the German Federal Court of Justice continues to refer to the seat of management, BGHZ 153, 353.

[76] See on diplomatic protection, ICJ *Barcelona Traction, Light and Power Company (Belgium v Spain)* [1970] ICJ Rep 3, 42. Under customary law, diplomatic protection based on the nationality of the shareholders of a company may only be exercised in exceptional cases. See on a treaty explicitly protecting nationals of one of the contracting States holding shares in companies of the other contracting States, ICJ *Elettronica Sicula SpA (ELSI) (United States of America v Italy)* [1989] ICJ Rep 15.

[77] D Thürer, 'The Emergence of Non-Governmental Organizations and Transnational Enterprises in International Law and the Changing Role of the State' in R Hofmann and N Geissler (eds), *Non-State Actors as New Subjects of International Law* (Duncker & Humblot 2000) 37 (46).

[78] <http://www.forbes.com/global2000/list/> (accessed 23 June 2016).

[79] Gross domestic product (GDP) can be measured on the basis of purchasing power parity (PPP) (which reflects living conditions) or just of exchange rates (nominal). To ensure a greater comparability, reference is made to the nominal GDP.

[80] For the World Economic Outlook of the International Monetary Fund launched in October 2015, see <https://www.imf.org/external/pubs/ft/weo/2015/02/weodata/index.aspx> (accessed 23 June 2016).

Their network of operative bases in different countries and regions of the world provides TNCs—especially the very large ones—with the opportunity to take advantage of the regulatory, economic, and political differences between countries and regions on the one hand, and to respond flexibly to new challenges by shifting resources and operations within their operative system on the other hand.[81] Their economic strength and international fields of operation make it easier for TNCs to escape the regulatory reach of national authorities. At the same time, these advantages often enable them to influence domestic politics more effectively than other private business entities with a more limited reach.

Some States, in particular developing countries, often take a critical view on TNCs activities on their territory. Among the concerns of host countries (especially those with weak authorities) are: true or apparent imbalances of power, undue political influence of TNCs in host countries, and insufficient regard of TNCs for environmental interests or labour and human rights standards. However, TNCs contribute significantly to the economic and technological development of host countries, providing employment and improving the balance of payments. The sometimes conflicting interests of developing and industrialised countries, especially with regard to foreign direct investment (FDI), were central aspects in the discussion on a 'New International Economic Order'[82] and remain a contentious issue.

(b) Corporate social responsibility: codes of conduct and other international standards

i. *The concept of 'corporate social responsibility'*

As a response to widespread concerns about the role of TNCs, several codes of conduct or other soft law instruments have been established. These instruments are committed to internationally convergent standards of 'corporate social responsibility'.[83] This responsibility has several dimensions. It refers to the corporation's employees, local communities affected by the corporation's operations and broader public interests. Corporate social responsibility aims at respect for human rights, labour standards, and sustainable development as well as transparency and it bans undue political interference in the host State.

---

[81] See D Thürer, 'The Emergence of Non-Governmental Organizations and Transnational Enterprises in International Law and the Changing Role of the State' in R Hofmann and N Geissler (eds), *Non-State Actors as New Subjects of International Law* (Duncker & Humblot 2000) 37 (47); CF Hillemanns, 'UN Norms on the Responsibilities of Transnational Corporations and Other Business Enterprises with regard to Human Rights' (2003) 4 German LJ 1065 (1067).

[82] See Ch II.2.

[83] See J Dillard, K Haynes, and A Murray (eds) *Corporate Social Responsibility: A Research Handbook* (Routledge 2012); A Crane, A McWilliams, D Matten, J Moon, and DS Siegel (eds) *The Oxford Handbook of Corporate Social Responsibility* (OUP 2009); TE Lambooy, *Corporate Social Responsibility. Legal and Semi-legal Frameworks Supporting CSR* (Kluwer 2010); P Muchlinski, 'Corporations in International Law' in R Wolfrum (ed), *The Max Planck Encyclopedia of Public International Law* (OUP 2012) vol II, 797 para 16.

ii.   Instruments of the United Nations and its 'specialized agencies'

Within the United Nations, there were several attempts to lay down standards of corporate social responsibility.[84] The 'Draft Code of Conduct on Transnational Corporations'[85] was presented to the General Assembly in 1990, but was never fully adopted.[86] The 'Global Compact'[87] is an initiative of former UN Secretary-General Kofi Annan and aims at voluntary compliance by TNCs. It rests on ten principles which refer to

- human rights (businesses should support and respect the protection of inter-nationally proclaimed human rights and ensure that they are not complicit in human rights abuses);
- labour standards (businesses should uphold the freedom of association and the effective recognition of the right to collective bargaining; the elimination of all forms of forced and compulsory labour; the effective abolition of child labour; and the elimination of discrimination in respect of employment and occupation);
- environmental protection (businesses should support a precautionary approach to environmental challenges; undertake initiatives to promote greater environmental responsibility; and encourage the development and diffusion of environmentally friendly technologies); and
- fight against corruption (businesses should work against corruption in all its forms, including extortion and bribery).

After the project of the former UN Sub-Commission on the Promotion and Protection of Human Rights to establish a framework of 'Norms on the Responsibility of Transnational Corporations and Other Business Enterprises with Regard to Human Rights' had failed,[88] the UN Secretary-General appointed John Ruggie as his Special Representative on Human Rights and Transnational Corporations and other Business Enterprises. In his final report, the Special Representative presented the 'UN Guiding Principles on Business and Human Rights' which were endorsed by the UN Human Rights Council.[89] The 'UN Guiding Principles on Business and Human Rights' enhance the relevance of human rights standards for corporate social responsibility on a global level.

---

[84] See for a contemporary account, JH Knox, 'The Human Rights Council Endorses "Guiding Principles" for Corporations' (2011) 15 ASIL Insights No 21; J Rubin, 'Transnational Corporations and International Codes of Conduct: A Study of the Relationship Between International Legal Cooperation and Economic Development' (1995) 10 Am U J Int'l L & Pol'y 1275.

[85] (1990) UN Doc E/1990/94.

[86] See JL Dunoff, SR Ratner, and D Wippman, *International Law, Norms, Actors, Process* (2nd edn, Aspen Publishers 2006) 211.

[87] For the Global Compact Initiative launched in July 2000 see <http://www.unglobalcompact.org> (accessed 23 June 2016); A Rasche and G Kell (eds), *The United Nations Global Compact: Achievements, Trends and Challenges* (CUP 2010).

[88] See Ch.VII.3.   [89] See Ch.VII.3(a).

The International Labour Organization (ILO), a specialized agency of the United Nations, issued the 'Tripartite Declaration of Principles on Multinational Enterprises and Social Policy' for the first time in 1977.[90] The declaration focuses on the protection of individual and collective interests of workers as enshrined in the conventions and recommendations of the ILO and offers guidelines for governments, employer organizations, and trade unions regarding these issues. The fourth edition of the Tripartite Declaration was published in 2006.[91]

Other instruments address specific issues of corporate social responsibility. The International Finance Corporation (IFC) laid down the 'IFC Performance Standards on Environmental and Social Responsibility' which govern private investment projects. The FAO 'Voluntary Guidelines on the Responsible Governance of Tenure of Land, Fisheries and Forests in the Context of National Food Security'[92] react to the large-scale sale of farmland to foreign investors ('land grabbing'), sometimes coupled with the subsequent transformation of the land for biofuel or other non-food purposes"', and to other threats to the supply of the local population with adequate and affordable food.[93] The FAO Guidelines, though primarily addressing governments, also refer to the responsibility of non-State businesses.[94]

iii. *The OECD Guidelines for Multinational Enterprises*

The OECD Guidelines for Multinational Enterprises, which were issued in the first version in 2000 and which have been updated in 2011,[95] are designed as non-binding recommendations:

> *Guidelines* are recommendations jointly addressed by governments to multinational enterprises. They provide principles and standards of good practice consistent with applicable laws and internationally recognised standards. Observance of the *Guidelines* by enterprises is voluntary and not legally enforceable. Nevertheless, some matters covered by the *Guidelines* may also be regulated by national law or international commitments.

The Guidelines list general policies and standards to be applied by multinational enterprises while operating in foreign States (Part I). The Guidelines were adopted by the governments of 45 States (the 35 OECD countries plus Argentina, Brazil, Colombia, Costa Rica, Egypt, Lithuania, Morocco, Peru, Romania, and Tunisia).

---

[90] (1978) 17 ILM 422.

[91] (1978) 17 ILM 422; for the current fourth edition see <http://www.ilo.org/empent/Publications/WCMS_094386/lang--en/index.htm> (accessed 23 June 2016).

[92] For the Food and Agriculture Organization of the United Nations, Voluntary Guidelines on the Responsible Governance of Tenure of Land, Fisheries and Forests in the Context of National Food Security (2012) see <http://www.fao.org/docrep/016/i2801e/i2801e.pdf> (accessed 23 June 2016).

[93] BS Gentry, T Sikor, G Auld, AJ Bebbington, et al. 'Changes in Land-Use Governance in an Urban Era' in KC Seto and A Reenberg (eds), *Rethinking Global Land Use in an Urban Era* (MIT Press 2014) 261.

[94] Para 3.2.

[95] The 2000 edition of the Guidelines was published in (2000) 40 ILM 237. On 25 May 2011, the current version of the Guidelines was adopted; see OECD, *OECD Guidelines for Multinational Enterprises* (OECD Publishing 2011).

On the OECD level, the Investment Committee is the forum for the interpretation, implementation, and monitoring of the OECD Guidelines.

Part I of the Guidelines lays down standards for good corporate practice in the areas of disclosure (ch III), human rights (ch IV), employment and industrial relations (ch V), environmental protection (ch VI), combating bribery, bribe solicitation, and extortion (ch VII), protection of consumer interests (ch VIII), science and technology (ch IX), competition (ch X), and taxation (ch XI). The Guidelines (Part I, ch II A) call for 'due diligence' not only within the enterprise, but also in its business relationships and accordingly require enterprises to

10. [c]arry out risk-based due diligence, for example by incorporating it into their enterprise risk management systems, to identify, prevent and mitigate actual and potential adverse impacts as described in paragraphs 11 and 12, and account for how these impacts are addressed. The nature and extent of due diligence depend on the circumstances of a particular situation.
11. [a]void causing or contributing to adverse impacts on matters covered by the Guidelines, through their own activities, and address such impacts when they occur.
12. [s]eek to prevent or mitigate an adverse impact where they have not contributed to that impact, when the impact is nevertheless directly linked to their operations, products or services by a business relationship. This is not intended to shift responsibility from the entity causing an adverse impact to the enterprise with which it has a business relationship.

Additionally, the Guidelines (Part I ch II B) encourage enterprises to

1. [s]upport, as appropriate to their circumstances, cooperative efforts in the appropriate fora to promote Internet Freedom through respect of freedom of expression, assembly and association online.
2. [e]ngage in or support, where appropriate, private or multi-Stakeholder initiatives and social dialogue on responsible supply chain management while ensuring that these initiatives take due account of their social and economic effects on developing countries and of existing internationally recognized standards.

The OECD Guidelines provide for supervisory mechanisms in Part II based on a decision of the OECD Council (which is binding upon OECD members); other adhering countries have followed the implementation procedures on the grounds of a unilateral commitment. Under the Guidelines,[96] National Contact Points (NCP) established by governments monitor compliance with the OECD Guidelines for Multinational Enterprises in 'a manner that is impartial, predictable, equitable and compatible with the standards and principles of the Guidelines'.[97] Some countries have opted for a mono- or inter-ministerial structure of their NCP, whilst other NCPs have a more open design with representatives of the government, trade unions, and enterprises. Any person or organization as well as governments of non-adhering countries and other NCPs may seize an NCP with issues of compliance

---

[96] Part I of the Council Decision and Part I of the attached Procedural Guidance.
[97] Part II Procedural Guidance. ch I C. For a detailed analysis, see J Motte-Baumvol, 'Le règlement des différends à l'intention des entreprises multinationales – Quelques réflexions à partir des principes directeurs de l'OECD' (2014) 118 RGDIP 303.

with the guidelines and thus trigger the 'specific instance procedure'.[98] This procedure includes an initial assessment by the NCP and—if the issue merits further examination—a mediation process between the parties. Concluding the investigation, the NCP submits a 'final statement' on whether or not the multinational enterprise has complied with the Guidelines, if necessary, with recommendations for future conduct. NCPs also monitor subsequent compliance in a follow-up to the final statement. Just like the Guidelines themselves, the recommendations of the NCPs are not legally binding.[99] Still, the statements of NCPs may have considerable impact by 'naming and shaming'. As a rule, complaints (mostly presented by NGOs) will be brought before the NCP of the home State of an enterprise or the NCP of the State where a business or project is located.

Often, the good offices or mediation offered by NCPs facilitate agreements between notifiers and enterprises.[100] Thus, in the *Specific Instance notified by CEDHA, INCASUR Foundation, SOMO and Oxfam Novib concerning Nidera Holding BV*, the Netherlands' NCP mediated an agreement on the enterprises' human rights policy, their procedure as to human rights due diligence and monitoring, their supply chain approach, and grievance mechanism.[101] In other cases, the enterprises refused direct contact with complainants, but issued a voluntary commitment.[102]

If two or more NCPs are involved in a case which relates to several countries (as in the case of a company operated through a foreign subsidiary or of a bi-national joint venture), they shall enter consultations.

The *POSCO* case illustrates the potential of multilateral responsibility as well as the need for coherence and consistency when several NCPs assess the same facts. The *POSCO* case was concerned with the planned construction of an integrated steel plant and power plant in India by the South Korean company POSCO and an Indian subsidiary. The administrator of the funds of a large Dutch pension fund and the Norwegian Bank Investment Management held minority shares in POSCO. Indian, Norwegian, South Korean, and Dutch NGOs claimed that POSCO had

---

[98] See <http://www.state.gov/e/eb/oecd/usncp/specificinstance/> (accessed 23 June 2016).

[99] See *Global Witness v Afrimex Ltd* Final Statement by the UK National Contact Point for the OECD Guidelines for Multinational Enterprises (2008) <www.oecdwatch.org/cases/Case_114/561/at_download/file> (accessed 23 June 2016).

[100] Final Statement by the UK National Contact Point for the OECD Guidelines for Multinational Enterprises *Complaint from the International Union of Food, Agricultural, Hotel, Restaurant, Catering, Tobacco and Allied Workers' Associations against Unilever plc (Doom Dooma factory – Assam – India)* (2010), Annex; Final report of the Netherlands National Contact Point for the OECD Guidelines for Multinational Enterprises on the *Specific Instance notified by Lok Shakti Abhiyan, KTNC Watch, Fair Green and Global Alliance and Forum for Environment and Development concerning an alleged breach of the OECD Guidelines for Multinational Enterprises by the Dutch Pension Fund ABP and its Pension Administrator APG*, para. 4.2 (2013).

[101] Final report of the National Contact Point for the OECD Guidelines in the Netherlands on the *Specific Instance notified by CEDHA, INCASUR Foundation, SOMO and Oxfam Novib concerning Nidera Holding B.V.* (2012); Agreement between Nidera Holdings B.V. and CEDHA, SOMO, Oxfam-Novib and INCASUR, 25 November 2011 <http://oecdwatch.org/cases/Case_220/1000/at_download/file> (accessed 23 June 2016).

[102] Statement by the German National Contact Point for the 'OECD Guidelines for Multinational Enterprises' on the *Complaint Filed against Bayer CropScience by German Watch, Global March, and Coordination gegen Bayer-Gefahren* (2007).

violated the OECD standards with respect to human rights and environmental impacts. They furthermore complained that the investors had not taken appropriate steps to mitigate adverse human rights and environmental impacts in connection with their investment in POSCO. The NGOs submitted notifications to the NCPs of the Netherlands, Norway, and South Korea.[103] Although the Netherlands' NCP and its Norwegian counterpart agreed to cooperate throughout the specific instance and tried to coordinate their operations with the South Korean NCP, the tripartite consultation seems to have been far from perfect.[104] The case documents the risk of inconsistent findings by one or more NCPs: Whilst the NCPs of the Netherlands and Norway found that the notifications raised serious issues of human rights and environmental due diligence, the South Korean NCP's initial assessment concluded that the case did not merit further examination.[105] This incoherence is all the more salient as the corporate social responsibility of minority investors is in a way 'secondary' in terms of being linked to the 'primary responsibility' of the enterprise in which they hold a relatively small capital share.

The OECD Guidelines have the merit of being to date the most comprehensive and most effective multilateral document dealing with corporate social responsibility of multinational enterprises. The inherent weakness of being a non-binding instrument is to some extent compensated by the supervisory function of NCPs which blurs the distinction between 'soft' standards and 'hard' obligations buttressed by palpable sanctions. By now, hundreds of specific instance procedures have turned supervision of compliance by NCPs into a quite effective instrument.

Particularly in context with supply chains, the requirement of 'due diligence' has become a most important standard of corporate social responsibility in connection with human rights violations by business partners.[106] In the case

[103] Final report of the Netherlands National Contact Point for the OECD Guidelines for Multinational Enterprises on the *Specific Instance notified by Lok Shakti Abhiyan, KTNC Watch, Fair Green and Global Alliance and Forum for Environment and Development concerning an alleged breach of the OECD Guidelines for Multinational Enterprises by the Dutch Pension Fund ABP and its Pension Administrator APG*, section 2 with further references (2013); Final Statement of the Norwegian National Contact Point, *Complaint from Lok Shakti Abhiyan, KTNC Watch, Fair Green and Global Alliance and Forum for Environment and Development vs. POSCO (South Korea), ABP/APG and NBIM* (Norway) (2013).
[104] Final report of the Netherlands National Contact Point for the OECD Guidelines for Multinational Enterprises on the *Specific Instance notified by Lok Shakti Abhiyan, KTNC Watch, Fair Green and Global Alliance and Forum for Environment and Development concerning an alleged breach of the OECD Guidelines for Multinational Enterprises by the Dutch Pension Fund ABP and its Pension Administrator APG*, para.2.3 (2013).
[105] Final report of the Netherlands National Contact Point for the OECD Guidelines for Multinational Enterprises on the *Specific Instance notified by Lok Shakti Abhiyan, KTNC Watch, Fair Green and Global Alliance and Forum for Environment and Development concerning an alleged breach of the OECD Guidelines for Multinational Enterprises by the Dutch Pension Fund ABP and its Pension Administrator APG*, section 2 with further references (2013); Final Statement of the Norwegian National Contact Point, *Complaint from Lok Shakti Abhiyan, KTNC Watch, Fair Green and Global Alliance and Forum for Environment and Development vs. POSCO (South Korea), ABP/APG and NBIM (Norway)* (2013), with reference to the South Korean NCP's initial assessment at section 5.
[106] See Ch. VII.3.

DAS Air[107] the British NCP found that an airfreight services company based in the United Kingdom had transported great quantities of cobalt stemming from a conflict zone in the Democratic Republic of the Congo. Although it was notorious that the conflict in the Democratic Republic of the Congo was essentially fuelled by trade in cobalt and other minerals, the company had not questioned the source of its freight, which was transported in violation of a UN Security Council resolution.[108] The NCP found lack of due diligence in the supply chain with respect to the requirements to contribute to economic, social, and environmental progress, respect of human rights and encouragement of business partners to apply principles of corporate conduct compatible with the Guidelines.[109]

Prevailing interpretation tends to extend the UN Guiding Principles on Business and Human Rights as well as OECD Guidelines to the financial sector and, in this context, to minority shareholdings of institutional investors.[110] Thus, in the *Specific Instance notified by Lok Shakti Abhiyan, KTNC Watch, Fair Green and Global Alliance and Forum for Environment and Development concerning an alleged breach of the OECD Guidelines for Multinational Enterprises by the Dutch Pension Fund ABP and its Pension Administrator APG*, the Netherlands' NCP applied the OECD Guidelines to the largest Dutch fund ABP and the corporation APG which administers ABP's pension capital with respect to the South Korean company POSCO, in which APG held a capital share of less than 0.1 per cent. According to the notifiers, the South Korean company and an Indian subsidiary which planned to construct an integrated steel plant and a captive power plant, had failed to carry out both a comprehensive human rights and environmental due diligence and a meaningful consultation with the neighbouring population threatened by displacement. The parties reached an agreement on monitoring the project by an independent review and assessment, and to work for a meaningful multi-stakeholder consultation.[111] This case highlights the leverage of investors in context with corporate social responsibility.

---

[107] Statement by the United Kingdom National Contact Point (NCP) for OECD Guidelines for Multinational Enterprises (NCP): *DAS Air* (2008) <http://www.oecd.org/investment/mne/44479531.pdf> (23 June 2016).

[108] UN SC Res. 1592 (30 March 2005).

[109] Statement by the United Kingdom National Contact Point (NCP) for OECD Guidelines for Multinational Enterprises (NCP): *DAS Air* (2008) <http://www.oecd.org/investment/mne/44479531.pdf> (accessed 21 January 2016), paras 49, 50.

[110] Final report of the Netherlands National Contact Point for the OECD Guidelines for Multinational Enterprises on the *Specific Instance notified by Lok Shakti Abhiyan, KTNC Watch, Fair Green and Global Alliance and Forum for Environment and Development concerning an alleged breach of the OECD Guidelines for Multinational Enterprises by the Dutch Pension Fund ABP and its Pension Administrator APG* (2013), paras 3.3 and 3.4 with further references; Final Statement of the Norwegian National Contact Point, *Complaint from Lok Shakti Abhiyan, KTNC Watch, Fair Green and Global Alliance and Forum for Environment and Development vs. POSCO (South Korea), ABP/APG and NBIM (Norway)* (2013), para. 1.3.2.

[111] Final report of the Netherlands National Contact Point for the OECD Guidelines for Multinational Enterprises on the *Specific Instance notified by Lok Shakti Abhiyan, KTNC Watch, Fair Green and Global Alliance and Forum for Environment and Development concerning an alleged breach of the OECD Guidelines for Multinational Enterprises by the Dutch Pension Fund ABP and its Pension Administrator APG* (2013), para. 4.2.

Meanwhile, the OECD in conjunction with the countries of the International Conference on the Great Lakes Region, representatives of the industrial sector and of the civil society as well as the United Nations, has adopted the 'OECD Due Diligence Guidance for Responsible Supply Chains of Minerals from Conflict-Affected and High-Risk Areas' (2010).

iv. *Other international standards*

With respect to the exploitation of natural resources, a network of companies, governments, and NGOs have launched the 'Extractive Industries Transparency Initiative' (EITI). The EITI has adopted principles and criteria which focus on enhanced participation, transparency, and accountability in the interest of sustainable development.[112]

Individual self-commitments of TNCs to respect human rights and environmental standards reflect an increased sensitivity of TNCs for their social responsibility. Examples for such a self-commitment are the 'Joint Statement on the Baku-Tbilisi-Ceyhan Pipeline Project' (BTC) of 16 March 2003 and the 'BTC Human Rights Undertaking' of 22 September 2003, in which the pipeline company renounces claims inconsistent with international human rights and environmental standards.[113]

The IFC 'Performance Standards on Environmental and Social Responsibility' have inspired private banks to adopt the 'Equator Principles' (2003) for the assessment and management of social and ecological risks to be considered in context with financing large private projects.[114] The International Organization for Standardization (ISO) adopted ISO Standard 26000 on 'Social Responsibility' (2010).[115]

Guidelines for ethical investment strategies such as established by governments for Public Pension Funds or for Sovereign Wealth Funds[116] are another mechanism to indirectly influence the behaviour of TNCs.

---

[112] See EITI Principles and Criteria (2003) <http://eiti.org/eiti/principles> (accessed 23 June 2016).

[113] On complaints about alleged non-compliance against the BTC pipeline company and its largest shareholder BP, UK National Contact Point, revised final statement in the specific instance BTC pipeline (2011).

[114] See Equator Principles, 'Leading Banks Announce Adoption of Equator Principles' (Press Release 4 June 2003) <http://www.equator-principles.com/index.php/all-adoption/adoption-news-by-year/65-2003/167-leading-banks-announce-adoption-of-equator-principles> (accessed 23 June 2016).

[115] See ISO Standard 26000 (2010) <http://www.iso.org/iso/home/standards/iso26000.htm> (accessed 23 June 2016).

[116] The Norwegian Government has adopted such guidelines for its State pension funds, see Guidelines for observation and exclusion from the Government Pension Fund Global's investment universe, available at <http://www.regjeringen.no/en/dep/fin/Selected-topics/the-government-pension-fund/responsible-investments/guidelines-for-observation-and-exclusion.html?id=594254> (accessed 23 June 2016); S Chestermann, 'The Turn to Ethics: Disinvestment from Multinational Corporations for Human Rights Violations— The Case of Norway's Sovereign Wealth Fund' (2008) 23 Am U Int'l L Rev 577.

*v.   The normative impact of international instruments
on corporate social responsibility*

The number and quality of the evolving soft law instruments aiming to control the impact of TNCs on human rights and the environment substantiate
the influence of TNCs—that is 'non-subjects' of public international law—
in today's international economic law on the one hand as well as the growing
importance of legally non-binding mechanisms for international economic relations on the other hand.

Unlike the 1997 OECD Convention on Combating Bribery of Foreign
Public Officials in International Business Transactions,[117] the existing 'codes
of conduct' and other instruments on the social and environmental responsibility of TNCs are not legally binding in international law. However, these
'soft law' standards may, in the long run, catalyse the formation of customary
international law, which directly addresses corporations and gives rise to corporate responsibility.

With respect to the normative impact, there is certain inherent ambiguity in
some 'soft law' standards. The OECD Guidelines for Multinational Enterprises do
not pretend to be legally binding.[118] However, the establishment of NCPs is mandatory for OECD Members (under the OECD Agreement) and other adhering
States (via unilateral commitment). The findings of NCPs are the exercise of public
authority and can have massive impact on an enterprise's standing in the public
eye. Likewise, the UN Principles on Business and Human Rights apparently do not
purport to modify existing rules of international law;[119] still they foster an international consensus on TNCs' obligations under international law and a concurrent
practice of home and host States.

(c) Corporate Social Responsibility and Investment Protection

An emerging issue is the relationship between the standards of corporate social
responsibility and investment protection. Especially human rights protection and
sustainable development are areas with a potential of conflict with investors' rights
under international and domestic law. Agreements between TNCs and host States
may freeze the domestic law applicable to foreign investors or limit their regulatory
liability in so-called 'stabilization clauses'.[120] International treaties on investment
protection limit the regulatory freedom of host States to require foreign investors
to adopt stricter standards, for example with respect to human rights, labour standards, or environmental protection.

---

[117] See S Hobe, 'Non-Governmental Organizations' in R Wolfrum (ed), *The Max Planck
Encyclopedia of Public International Law* (OUP 2012) vol VII, 716 para 16.
[118] OECD, *OECD Guidelines for Multinational Enterprises* (OECD Publishing 2011) 3, 37, 88.
[119] A Flohr, *Self-Regulation and Legalization: Making Global Rules for Banks and Corporations* (2014
Palgrave Macmillan) 12.
[120] See Ch XXXIII.1.

There is a tendency under the OECD Guidelines that investment protection shall not limit corporate social responsibility with respect to the effective protection of human rights obligations of host States under new domestic legislation, but may allow to freeze regulatory liability under existing domestic law.[121] New human rights obligations of host States under international treaties are the benchmark for corporate social responsibility and require specific undertakings to trump accorded stabilization of an investor's liability.[122] The Agreement on the TPP emphasizes the corporate social responsibility of investors:

Article 9.16: Corporate Social Responsibility
The Parties reaffirm the importance of each Party encouraging enterprises operating within its territory or subject to its jurisdiction to voluntarily incorporate into their internal policies those internationally recognised standards, guidelines and principles of corporate social responsibility that have been endorsed or are supported by that Party.

Though this provision defers to the discretion of the parties, it corroborates the tendency to vest the international standards on corporate social responsibility with legal effect.

Select Bibliography

AS Alexandroff and AF Cooper (eds), *Rising States, Rising Institutions: Challenges for Global Governance* (Brookings Institution Press 2010).

S Cassese, 'Administrative Law Without the State? The challenge of Global Regulation' (2005) 37 NYU J Int'l L & Pol 663.

B Craig, *Cyberlaw: The Law of the Internet and Information Technology* (Prentice Hall 2012).

R Hofmann (ed), *Non-State Actors as New Subjects of International Law—From the Traditional State Order Towards the Law of Global Community* (Duncker & Humblot 2000).

T Hale and D Held (eds), *The Handbook of Transnational Governance: Institutions and Innovations* (Polity 2011).

M Karavias, *Corporate Obligations under International Law* (OUP 2013).

R Mares, 'Corporate and State Responsibilities in Conflict-Affected Areas' (2014) 83 Nordic J Int'l L 293.

J Motte-Baumvol, 'Le règlement des différends à l'intention des entreprises multinationales – Quelques réflexions à partir des principes directeurs de l'OECD' (2014) 118 RGDIP 303.

P Muchlinski, 'Corporations in International Law' in R Wolfrum (ed), *The Max Planck Encyclopedia of Public International Law* (OUP 2012) vol II, 797.

P Muchlinski, 'Human Rights and Transnational Corporations: Establishing Meaningful Obligations' in J Faundez and C Tan (eds), *International Economic Law, Globalization and Developing Countries* (Edward Elgar Publishing 2010).

---

[121] UK National Contact Point, revised final statement in the specific instance BTC pipeline, paras 26ff. (2011).

[122] International Finance Corporation and J Ruggie, 'Stabilization Clauses and Human Rights' (2009), <http://www.ifc.org/wps/wcm/connect/9feb5b00488555eab8c4fa6a6515bb18/Stabilization%2BPaper.pdf?MOD=AJPERES> (accessed 23 June 2016).

K Raustiala, 'The Architecture of International Cooperation: Transgovernmental Networks and the Future of International Law' (2002) 43 Va J Int'l L 1.

A-M Slaughter, 'Governing Through Government Networks' in M Byers (ed), *The Role of Law in International Politics* (OUP 2000) 177.

C Walter, 'Subjects of International Law' in R Wolfrum (ed), *The Max Planck Encyclopedia of Public International Law* (OUP 2012) vol IX, 634.

IV

The Legal Sources of International Economic Law

1. International Law as an Order of Transboundary Economic Relations

(a) International economic law and its sources

Public international law is still an order predominantly constituted by States and other traditional subjects of international law such as international organizations. Nevertheless, since the end of the Second World War, the growing protection of human rights and investors has also strengthened the position of private actors (individuals and corporate entities).

Article 38(1) of the Statute of the International Court of Justice enumerates the widely recognized sources of public international law:

(a) international conventions, whether general or particular, establishing rules expressly recognized by the contesting States;
(b) international custom, as evidence of a general practice accepted as law;
(c) the general principles of law recognized by civilized nations;
(d) judicial decisions and the teachings of the most highly qualified publicists of the various nations, as subsidiary means for the determination of rules of law.

Rights established under international law (eg for foreign private investors) are independent of national law and its possible changes. International law and the municipal legal systems must each be seen as legal orders in their own right, however, with manifold contact points and interconnections. The infringement of international obligations, for example by import restrictions or measures directed against a foreign company, whether in conformity with municipal law or not, entail the international responsibility of the State. The mechanisms of enforcement in international law may be less effective or comprehensive than the enforcement of national laws. Still, sanctions establish a strong pull to compliance with international obligations. Breaches of customary law or treaty obligations may trigger a wide range of reactions, ranging from 'political' forms of retaliation (such as discontinuing with economic assistance) to legally relevant countermeasures in law, like non-compliance with treaty concessions or reprisals (such as blocking bank accounts or other assets owned by the violating State).[1] The disruption of financial support, withdrawal of foreign investments, or a trade embargo may raise the political or economic costs which the responsible State has to pay for a breach of international obligations. After the end of the Cold War, the willingness of many States to react forcefully to violations has increased. During the last decades, dispute settlement mechanisms have increased in number and efficiency. Some of these mechanisms have been vested with severe sanctions, such as the dispute settlement mechanism of the World Trade Organization (WTO) with the potentially far-reaching suspension of concessions. These tendencies have resulted in the strengthening of the authority of international law in State practice and enhancing the pull to compliance. International economic relations may also be affected by binding resolutions of the UN Security Council under Chapter VII of the UN Charter, in furtherance of world peace and international security. In the fight against terrorism, the recent practice of the Security Council provides for economic sanctions against individuals and non-State entities ('smart sanctions').[2]

(b) Customary international law

Customary international law is constituted by the practice of States and international organizations and a corresponding legal opinion (sense of obligation or right).[3] Customary international law, in principle, gives way to particular rules or treaties. Exceptions to this 'primacy' of treaties are certain norms which reflect fundamental interests of the international community and which therefore classify as 'peremptory norms' (*jus cogens*).[4] Examples of that kind of norms are the prohibition on the use of force, the right to self-determination of peoples, and elementary human rights.

Despite the rising number of international treaties, general public international law still has a considerable impact on international economic relations. Many treaty clauses stand in close context with customary rules, for example with reference to

[1] For an outline of potential sanctions and sanction mechanisms in international economic law, in particular those with political implications, see AF Lowenfeld, *International Economic Law* (2nd edn, OUP 2008) 847.

[2] Those measures have revealed significant flaws when colliding with fundamental rights on the national level or human rights guarantees of regional organizations; cf ECJ Case C-84/95 *Bosphorus Hava Yollari Turizm ve Ticaret As* [1996] ECR I-3953 paras 19ff; ECJ Joined Cases C-402/05 P and C-415/05 P *Yassin Abdullah Kadi and Al Barakaat International Foundation v Council of the EU and Commission of the EC* (ECJ Judgment) [2008] ECR I-6351 paras 280ff.

[3] Standard cases on the constitution of customary international law are: PCIJ *The Lotus Case (France v Turkey)* [1927] PCIJ Rep Series A No 10; ICJ *Asylum Case (Colombia v Peru)* [1950] ICJ Rep 266; ICJ *Anglo-Norwegian Fisheries Case (UK v Norway)* [1951] ICJ Rep 116; ICJ *North Sea Continental Shelf Cases (Federal Republic of Germany v Denmark and The Netherlands)* [1969] ICJ Rep 3; ICJ *Nicaragua (Nicaragua v United States)* (Merits) [1986] ICJ Rep 14; ICJ *Legality of the Threat or Use of Nuclear Weapons* (Advisory Opinion) [1996] ICJ Rep 226.

[4] See Article 53 of the Vienna Convention on the Law of Treaties; P Czaplinski, 'Ius Cogens and the Law of Treaties' in C Tomuschat and JM Thouvenin (eds), *The Fundamental Rules of the International Legal Order* (Brill Academic Publishers 2006) 83.

'fair and equitable treatment' of foreign investors. Customary principles also guide the interpretation of treaties. In the case *US-Gasoline*, the WTO Appellate Body emphasized that the WTO agreements must not be read in 'clinical isolation from public international law', referring to the general rules of interpretation of treaties.[5]

Rules of customary international law with a strong impact on international economic relations[6] refer to

- State immunity,
- the so-called 'minimum standard' for the treatment of foreign nationals (with rules on expropriation), and
- diplomatic protection.

Customary rules also govern the conditions for the exercise of 'extraterritorial' jurisdiction with respect to situations (certain activities, the status of persons or things) closely connected to other States.

The formation of new customary law is a protracted process. It may take decades until a new rule of customary law is clearly accepted as an existing part of the international legal order. Resolutions of the UN General Assembly cannot substitute State practice and, thereby, create new customary law. However, resolutions of the General Assembly, if truly reflecting (quasi-) universal consensus among UN members, may catalyse the formation of an emerging rule of customary law, even if they are not supported by long and extensive State practice. Some UN resolutions can be considered 'soft law' if they express a quasi-universal legal opinion and turn into customary law in the making with the backing of State practice.

The unanimously adopted Friendly Relations Declaration of 1970[7] contains principles nowadays widely recognized as customary law. This resolution proclaims a duty of all States to cooperate. By contrast, the Charter of Economic Rights and Duties of States of 1974[8] adopted by the UN General Assembly with an overwhelming majority never came near recognition as customary law, because almost all western industrial States rejected the resolution or abstained.

(c) Treaties on international economic transactions

Customary law neither provides for free trade nor for non-discrimination in international economic relations (most-favoured-nation treatment, national treatment) nor for particular forms of dispute settlement. The world trading system, regional or bilateral trade liberalization, the protection of investors beyond the customary minimum standard, and the international monetary system rest on international agreements, often supplemented by informal arrangements (like the establishment of the G20).

---

[5] WTO, *United States: Standards for Reformulated and Conventional Gasoline—Report of the Appellate Body* (1996) WT/DS 2/AB/R [17].
[6] S Zamora, 'Is There Customary International Economic Law?' (1989) 32 GYIL 9.
[7] UNGA Res 2625 (XXV) (1970) UNYB 788.
[8] UNGA Res 3281 (XXIX) (1974) UNYB 402.

Among the early bilateral treaties, the so-called Treaties of Friendship, Commerce and Navigation (FCN Treaties)[9] stand out as predecessors to modern agreements on trade and investment protection law. FCN Treaties typically provide for the freedom of establishment (often including the recognition of corporate status) to the nationals of the contracting States and grant other advantages like most-favoured-nation treatment.[10] During the last decades, many FCN Treaties have been replaced by Bilateral Investment Treaties (BIT).

The most important treaties in economic relations include

- the WTO agreements;
- regional or bilateral free trade agreements and other treaties on economic integration (inter alia, the EU Treaties, the NAFTA Agreement, the MERCOSUR Agreement);
- treaties on investment protection, including the ICSID Convention;
- the Bretton Woods Agreement on the International Monetary Fund (IMF Statute) and the International Bank for Reconstruction and Development (IBRD).

(d) General principles of law

The 'general principles of law recognized by civilized nations'[11] listed in Article 38(1)(c) of the ICJ Statute as one of the sources of public international law play a supplementary role in filling certain 'gaps' in the international legal order left by treaties and customary law. In order to qualify as a general principle of international law, a principle must be recognized in the majority of the legal systems. Practice usually contents itself with looking at the historically significant codifications of the European continent like the French or the German Civil Code (which have often inspired many legal systems on other Continents) and the common law, often also Roman law. As public international law is still essentially a system of coordination among equal States, almost all of the general principles are extracted from the field of private law. Issues like jurisdiction or the scope of human rights are governed by customary law or treaties.

Examples of general principles of international law are:

- the prohibition of the abuse of rights;[12]
- the forfeiture of rights by conduct;
- the restitution of unjust enrichment;[13]

---

[9] For a current analysis of FCN treaties and their importance see AL Paulus, 'Treaties of Friendship, Commerce and Navigation' in R Wolfrum (ed), *The Max Planck Encyclopedia of Public International Law* (OUP 2012) vol IX, 1140.

[10] See ICJ *Case Concerning Elettronica Sicula SpA (ELSI) (United States v Italy)* [1989] ICJ Rep 15.

[11] A classic in this field is B Cheng, *General Principles of Law as Applied by International Courts and Tribunals* (Stevens 1953).

[12] Already established by the PCIJ in the *Chorzow Factory Case* (1927) PCIJ Series A No 9 at 31.

[13] See C Binder and C Schreuer, 'Unjust Enrichment' in R Wolfrum (ed), *The Max Planck Encyclopedia of Public International Law* (OUP 2012) vol X, 588.

- the principle of good faith and the related principle of estoppel;[14]
- the obligation to make reparations for an injury;
- *res iudicata;*[15]
- *negotiorum gestio* (agency without mandate); and
- certain rules of evidence (such as prima facie proof).

In the absence of treaty rules, general principles govern the liability of members of international organizations for the debts of the organization. In this context, the discussion on liability of members refers to the rules for 'piercing the corporate veil' established in the company law of most States.

A practical example for this issue was the financial breakdown of the International Tin Council, which brought members' liability in the focus of interest.[16]

State succession with respect to property and debts, for example in cases of the dissolution of States, is another important field where general principles of law apply.[17] As to succession, liabilities should follow the regime of assets (*res transit cum onere suo*). The prevailing doctrine pleads for allocating State debts, in principle, according the respective share of successor States in the GDP of the predecessor State as the most equitable solution.

2. The Law of the European Union

The system of the European Union[18] has reached a unique degree of legal, economic, and political integration. Even though the European Union is anchored in international treaties (the Treaty on the European Union (TEU) and the Treaty on

---

[14] See T Cottier and JP Müller, 'Estoppel' in R Wolfrum (ed), *The Max Planck Encyclopedia of Public International Law* (OUP 2012) vol III, 671.

[15] See ICJ *UN Administrative Tribunal Case* (Advisory opinion) [1954] ICJ Rep 47, 53; ICJ, *Question of Delimitation of the Continental Shelf between Nicaragua and Colombia* (Jurisdiction) [2016], paras 55ff.

[16] See M Herdegen, 'The Insolvency of International Organizations and the Legal Position of Creditors: Some Observations in the Light of the International Tin Council Crisis' (1988) 35 NILR 135; M Herdegen, 'Bemerkungen zur Zwangsliquidation und zum Haftungsdurchgriff bei internationalen Organisationen' (1987) 47 ZaöRV 537; EJ McFadden, 'The Collapse of Tin: Restructuring a Failed Commodity Agreement' (1986) 80 AJIL 811; M Hartwig, *Die Haftung der Mitgliedstaaten für Internationale Organisationen* (Responsibility of Member States for International Organizations) (Springer 1993); I Seidl-Hohenveldern, 'Piercing the Corporate Veil of International Organizations: The International Tin Council Case in the English Court of Appeals' (1989) 32 GYIL 43.

[17] MT Kamminga, 'State Succession in Respect of Human Rights Treaties' (1996) 7 EJIL 469; PR Williams, 'State Succession and the International Financial Institutions: Political Criteria v. Protection of Outstanding Financial Obligations' (1994) 43 ICLQ 776; P Williams and J Harris, 'State Succession to Debts and Assets: The Modern Law and Policy' (2001) 42 Harv Int'l LJ 355.

[18] P Birkinshaw and M Varney, *The European Union Legal Order after Lisbon* (Kluwer Law International 2010); D Chalmers, G Davies, and G Monti, *European Union Law* (3rd edn, CUP

the Functioning of the European Union (TFEU)), the European legal system can no longer be conceptualized in the established categories of international law. As the European Court of Justice already emphasized many years ago, the European Union forms an autonomous body of law in its own right, based on a transfer of powers, directly conferring rights on individuals.[19] Its founding treaties operate as a kind of constitutional framework.[20]

The system of the European Union is often described as a 'supranational order'. This term tries to indicate that the European Union is not a State on its own but that it is more than just an accumulation of States with common treaty-based obligations.

The law of the European Union claims absolute primacy over the law of its Member States.[21] In case of conflict, EU law ought to prevail. This point of view is often disputed by the municipal courts on the constitutional level. At least as a rule, the constitutional and other courts of Member States recognize the supremacy of EU law and try to avoid conflicts by harmonious interpretation of national law.[22]

3. International Agreements on Private Economic Transactions

A number of international agreements aim to facilitate private economic transactions by harmonizing rules. This technique of regulation is based on the idea of a uniform law (*'loi uniforme'*). It establishes the obligation of the contracting States to adjust their laws and conflict of laws rules according to common standards. Classic examples are agreements on international commercial law, such as the Geneva Convention Providing a Uniform Law for Bills of Exchange and Promissory Notes of 1930 and the two Hague Conventions relating to a Uniform Law on the International Sale of Goods of 1964. The United Nations Convention on Contracts for the International Sale of Goods (CISG) of 1980 contains rules for the sale of goods in a transboundary context. The rules of the Rome Convention on the Law Applicable to Contractual Obligations of 1980 have been transposed into an EU regulation (Rome I). Several agreements have been concluded to unify the rules on international transports by road, rail, sea, or air.

2014); P Craig and G de Búrca, *European Union Law* (6th edn, OUP 2015); J Fairhurst, *Law of the European Union* (11th edn, Longman 2016); R Wallis, *A Guide to European Union Law and Institutions* (2nd edn, Emerald Publishing 2010).

[19] See ECJ Case C-26/62 *van Gend & Loos* [1963] ECR I-25; ECJ Case C-6/64 *Costa/E.N.E.L.* [1964] ECR 1251 (1269).

[20] See ECJ Opinion of the Court 1/91 *European Economic Area* [1993] ECR I-6079: 'The context in which the objective of the agreement is situated also differs from that in which the Community aims are pursued. The European Economic Area is to be established on the basis of an international treaty which merely creates rights and obligations as between the Contracting Parties and provides for no transfer of sovereign rights to the inter-governmental institutions which it sets up. In contrast, the EEC Treaty, albeit concluded in the form of an international agreement, none the less constitutes the constitutional charter of a Community based on the rule of law.'

[21] See ECJ Case C-106/77 *Simmenthal II* [1978] ECR 629 (644ff).

[22] For a good insight into the case law of the courts of different Member States, see P Craig and G de Búrca, *European Union Law* (6th edn, OUP 2015) 268.

A number of agreements refer to issues of jurisdiction and judicial proceedings such as the Convention on the Taking of Evidence Abroad in Civil or Commercial Matters of 1970 (Hague Evidence Convention). Others govern arbitration, for example the Convention on the Recognition and Enforcement of Foreign Arbitral Awards of 1958 (New York Convention).

4. 'Transnational Law' and '*lex mercatoria*'

Over time, international commercial practice has established a broad variety of rules and common concepts for specific transactions. The notion of *lex mercatoria* captures internationally established customary rules or terms with a specific and internationally recognized meaning.[23] In 1987, an arbitral award of the International Chamber of Commerce listed several principles or rules as part of the *lex mercatoria*:

The arbitral tribunal decides that the applicable rules of the *lex mercatoria* should comprise principles such as the one that contracts must prima facie be executed in conformity with the stipulations contained therein (*pacta sunt servanda*), the one that contracts must be executed in good faith, the one that in case that unforeseen difficulties arise after the conclusion of the contract the parties must negotiate in good faith to overcome them, [...] the one that contracts must be interpreted according to the principle of *ut res magis valeat quam pereat (favor validitatis)* and the one that a party's omission to respond to a letter which has been addressed to it by the other party may be considered as an indication for the acceptance of the terms contained therein.[24]

Within the last decades, a number of 'codifications' with a broad range of transnational rules came into existence. In particular, UNIDROIT, the International Institute for the Unification of Private Law, has been very actively involved in the elaboration of such rules. Some of them, like the UNIDROIT Principles of International Commercial Contracts of 2004,[25] identify internationally recognized principles of contract law.

Of particular importance are the rules on the interpretation of certain clauses in international commercial contracts developed and rotationally updated by the International Chamber of Commerce in Paris (the so-called, 'International Commercial Terms', INCOTERMS).[26] Examples for these clauses are 'CIF' ('Cost Insurance Freight') or 'FOB' ('Free on Board').

---

[23] See CB Picker, ID Bunn, and DW Arner, *International Economic Law* (Hart Publishing 2008) 99.

[24] ICC Award 8365 (1997) J Droit Int'l 1078 (1079ff).

[25] S Vogenauer, *Commentary on the UNIDROIT Principles of International Commercial Contracts* (2nd edn, OUP 2015); D Oser, *The Unidroit Principles of International Commercial Contracts* (Brill Academic Publishers 2008); MJ Bonell, *A New Approach to International Commercial Contracts: The Unidroit Principles of International Contracts* (Kluwer Law International 1999); M Heidemann, *Methodology of Uniform Contract Law: The UNIDROIT Principles in International Legal Doctrine and Practice* (Springer 2006).

[26] International Chamber of Commerce, *INCOTERMS 2010* (International Chamber of Commerce 2010); E Jolivet and D Ferrier, *Les Incoterms: etude d'une norme du commerce international* (LexisNexis 2003); J Ramberg, P Rapatout, F Reynolds, and C Debattista, *Incoterms 2000: A Forum of Experts* (International Chamber of Commerce 2008); J Guédon, *Les Incoterms 2000 et leur usage professionnel* (InfoMer 2003).

Building on the expanding range of broadly recognized rules for commercial transactions and international contracts as well as principles common to the laws of many countries, some authors propagate the existence of a 'transnational law', separate both from public international law and national law. However, 'transnational' principles are still far from forming a coherent legal system comparable to a national legal order.

Even the recognition of 'transnational legal principles' cannot be interpreted as the acceptance of a separate and autonomous legal order. In order to be enforceable or otherwise applied by domestic courts or international tribunals, any 'transnational' rule still requires recognition within the framework of municipal law or international law respectively. Nevertheless, quite a number of national legal orders are receptive to the choice of 'transnational' or 'international' principles as the applicable law within the limits of private autonomy. The number of jurisdictions which broadly allow such choices is growing. By choosing such non-national principles, the parties may avoid the undesired application of national law. Sometimes 'transnational' rules may have a more determinate meaning than certain national laws and thus ensure greater legal certainty.

Arbitral practice is particularly inclined to apply generally recognized 'transnational' principles in context with private commercial transactions if the parties have explicitly excluded otherwise applicable national law in favour of such unwritten principles. In those cases, general principles of international contract or commercial law may fill gaps left by the rules expressly negotiated between the parties.

In the *Compañía Valenciana* case,[27] the Cour d'Appel de Paris refused to declare an arbitral award void merely because the arbitral tribunal referred to general principles instead of applying municipal law. Rather, the Cour d'Appel de Paris applying ICC Arbitration Rules allowed the reference to 'the entirety of rules of international commerce, elaborated by practice and endorsed by national jurisprudence'.[28]

In a number of disputes between US nationals and the State of Iran, the Iran–US Claims Tribunal in The Hague referred to generally accepted legal principles.[29] The founding agreement between the United States and Iran allows the Tribunal to apply 'principles of commercial law' as far as the tribunal considers them relevant to the case.[30]

In *Deutsche Schachtbau- und Tiefbohrgesellschaft mbH v R'As al-Khaimah National Oil Co*, English courts recognized an international arbitral award in which the

---

[27] Cour d'Appel de Paris *Compañía Valenciana de Cementos Portland c. Primary Coal* (1990) Rev Arb 701.

[28] Cour d'Appel de Paris (1992) Rev Arb 457: 'L'ensemble des règles du commerce international dégagées par la pratique et ayant reçu la sanction des jurisprudences nationales'.

[29] *Reynolds Tobacco Co v Iran* (1984 III) 7 Iran-USCTR 181 (192); *McCollough & Co v Ministry of Post* (1986 II) 11 Iran-USCTR 3 (29f); *Mobil Oil Iran Inc v Iran 16 Iran*-USCTR 3 (27f); *Iran v United States Case B-1* (1988 II) 19 Iran-USCTR 273 (295); see JR Crook, 'Applicable Law in International Arbitration: The Iran-U.S. Claims Tribunal Experience' (1989) 83 AJIL 278 (280).

[30] Article 33 of the rules of procedure of the Iran-United States Claims Tribunal says: 'The arbitral tribunal shall decide all cases on the basis of respect for law, applying such choice of law rules and principles of commercial and international law as the arbitral tribunal determines to be applicable, taking into account relevant usages of the trade, contract provisions and changed circumstances.'.

arbitral tribunal settled a dispute about crude oil between a German company and an Arab State company on the basis of 'internationally accepted principles of law governing contractual relations'.[31] The tribunal especially referred to international commercial customs on drilling permits.

This case law shows the growing willingness of arbitral tribunals and national courts to recognize international principles on commercial transactions if the parties explicitly agreed so.[32] However, under most national laws, it is at least highly doubtful whether the parties to a contract may completely opt out from municipal law.

Select Bibliography

P Birkinshaw and M Varney, *The European Union Legal Order after Lisbon* (Kluwer Law International 2010).

P Craig and G de Búrca, *European Union Law* (6th edn, OUP 2015).

P Czaplinski, 'Ius Cogens and the Law of Treaties' in C Tomuschat and JM Thouvenin (eds), *The Fundamental Rules of the International Legal Order* (Brill Academic Publishers 2006) 83.

J Fairhurst, *Law of the European Union* (11th edn, Longman 2016).

SE Rolland, *Development at the WTO* (OUP 2012).

T Treves, 'Customary International Law' in R Wolfrum (ed), *The Max Planck Encyclopedia of Public International Law* (OUP 2012) vol II, 937.

R Wallis, *A Guide to European Union Law and Institutions* (2nd edn, Emerald Publishing 2010).

R Wolfrum, 'Sources of International Law' in R Wolfrum (ed), *The Max Planck Encyclopedia of Public International Law* (OUP 2012) vol IX, 299.

S Zamora, 'Is There Customary International Economic Law?' (1989) 32 GYIL 9.

---

[31] English Court of Appeal *Deutsche Schachtbau- und Tiefbohrgesellschaft mbH v R'As al-Khaimah National Oil Co* (1987) 3 WLR 1023.

[32] See SC Boyd, 'The Role of National Law and the National Courts in England' in JDM Lew (ed), *Contemporary Problems in International Arbitration* (Springer 1987) 149.

PART II

INTERNATIONAL ECONOMIC LAW AS AN ORDER OF RULES AND PRINCIPLES

V

Basic Principles of the International Economic Order

1. States' Autonomy in Economic Choices

As a matter of principle, States are free to choose their economic and social system:

Every State possesses a fundamental right to choose and implement its own political, economic and social systems.[1]

Similarly, States are at liberty to maintain or not relations with other economies.[2] This freedom flows from the 'sovereign equality' of States (Article 2(1) UN Charter) and may be exercised by entering treaty commitments. On the one hand, it is certainly true that few treaties and other international instruments provide for a specific economic system like a market economy. On the other hand, international agreements nowadays govern structural economic choices for a very large part of the international community. They do so in particular with provisions on

- the guarantee of private property, the freedom of profession and the freedoms of communication;
- the elimination of non-tariff barriers to trade, including State monopolies;
- the liberalization of the trade in services;
- the freedom of establishment and capital movement;
- the protection of foreign investment; and
- restraints on subsidies.

No country with a pure centrally planned economy is among the members of the World Trade Organization. The CSCE Charter of Paris for a New Europe (1990) proclaims the standard of market economy. The system of a market economy, without being explicitly entrenched in national constitutions, is the

---

[1] ICJ *Military and Paramilitary Activities in and against Nicaragua (Nicaragua v USA)* (Merits) [1986] ICJ Rep 14 para 258.
[2] Ibid.

only economic model compatible with the European Union. The Treaty of the European Union now emphasizes in its Article 3 adherence to the principles of a social market economy:

[…] 3. The Union shall establish an internal market. It shall work for the sustainable development of Europe based on balanced economic growth and price stability, a highly competitive social market economy, aiming at full employment and social progress, and a high level of protection and improvement of the quality of the environment. It shall promote scientific and technological advance […].

The UN Charter adheres to international cooperation including the economic and social sector (Article 1(3), Article 55 *lit* a and b, Article 56) and the principle of 'good-neighborliness' (Article 74). The principle of non-intervention into the internal affairs of other States (Article 2(7) UN Charter) restrains regulatory freedom as to economic activities pursued abroad or things located outside a State's territory ('extraterritorial legislation').

2. Trade Liberalization: Reduction of Tariffs and Elimination of Non-Tariff Barriers

The modern international economic order aims at the liberalization of transboundary economic transactions through the reduction of tariffs and the elimination of other barriers to trade. Trade liberalization reflects the insight that international trade and the division of labour in the international community are advantageous for all the national economies involved. This approach builds on the arguments for free trade stemming from Adam Smith's work on 'The Wealth of Nations' (1776) and the theory of 'comparative advantage' developed by David Ricardo and John Stuart Mill.[3]

In this vein, the Preamble of the WTO Agreement relates trade liberalization to 'the optimal use of the world's resources' and qualifies the agreements on the removal of trade barriers and on the elimination of discriminatory treatment as 'mutually advantageous'.

The principal instruments of trade liberalization are the reduction of tariffs[4] and the elimination of non-tariff barriers (such as quantitative restrictions, sanitary measures, technical norms, obstructive custom procedures, and other specific restrictions of imports).[5] Whilst the principles of 'national treatment' and the 'most-favoured-nation treatment' serve equal competitive conditions in the market, the reduction of tariffs and the elimination of non-tariff barriers directly remove impediments to international trade. On the basis of the GATT, a substantial reduction of tariffs has been reached on a global level.

---

[3] See Ch II.1.　　　　[4] See Article II GATT.　　　　[5] See Article XI GATT.

3. Fair Treatment of Foreign Investors

Over the last decades, foreign investment has come to be recognized as a pivotal factor of development and economic stability. In the so-called 'Monterrey Consensus',[6] the International Conference on Financing for Development (2002) underlined that 'private international capital flows, particularly foreign direct investment, along with international financial stability, are vital complements to national and international development efforts.'

Fair treatment (in a broad sense) of foreign investment is nowadays a cornerstone of international economic law, in terms of customary law (minimum standard) as well as treaty provisions (eg 'fair and equitable treatment' and 'full protection and security').[7]

Investment protection fosters the rule of law. On the other hand, the protection of foreign investment may conflict with legitimate public interests of the host State (like environmental protection) and thus call for a delicate balancing process.

4. Non-discrimination

The elimination of discrimination plays a fundamental role in international trade and investment relations. Non-discrimination of foreign nationals, goods, services, and investments operates on two different levels:

- equal treatment on the international level by extending benefits granted to one State (or nationals, goods, services, and investments of this State) to trade or investment relations with another State (most-favoured-nation treatment); and

- equal treatment in a domestic context by granting national treatment to nationals, goods, services, and investments of other States.

On both levels, non-discrimination ensures a level playing field and equal conditions in competition on national markets. Both most-favoured-nation treatment and national treatment form a cornerstone of the GATT and other WTO agreements as well as of modern investment treaties.

(a) Most-favoured-nation treatment

A most-favoured-nation clause in a treaty allows the parties to that treaty (and their nationals) to benefit from the advantages granted to another (third) State (or its

---

[6] See United Nations *Report of the International Conference of the Financing for Development* (2002) No 20.

[7] See M Paparinskis, *The International Minimum Standard and Fair and Equitable Treatment* (OUP 2013).

nationals) in another treaty concluded between one of the parties to the first treaty and the third State.

Article I(1) of the GATT 1994, for example, states:

With respect to customs duties and charges of any kind imposed on or in connection with importation or exportation or imposed on the international transfer of payments for imports or exports, and with respect to the method of levying such duties and charges, and with respect to all rules and formalities in connection with importation and exportation, and with respect to all matters referred to in paragraphs 2 and 4 of Article III, any advantage, favour, privilege or immunity granted by any contracting party to any product originating in or destined for any other country shall be accorded immediately and unconditionally to the like product originating in or destined for the territories of all other contracting parties.

The application of a most-favoured-nation clause depends on its scope and context. Benefits to be claimed must come within the subject matter of the most-favoured-nation clause and be of the same kind (*ejusdem generis* rule)[8]. The ILC Draft Articles on Most-Favoured-Nation Clauses of 1978[9] provide in Article 9:

1. Under a most-favoured-nation clause the beneficiary State acquires, for itself or for the benefit of persons or things in a determined relationship with it, only those rights which fall within the limits of the subject matter of the clause.
2. The beneficiary State acquires the rights under paragraph 1 only in respect of persons or things which are specified in the clause or implied from its subject matter.

Article 10 of the ILC Articles reads:

1. Under a most-favoured-nation clause the beneficiary State acquires the right to most-favoured-nation treatment only if the granting State extends to a third State treatment within the limits of the subject matter of the clause.
2. The beneficiary State acquires rights under paragraph 1 in respect of persons or things in a determined relationship with it only if they:
   (a) belong to the same category of persons or things as those in a determined relationship with a third State which benefit from the treatment extended to them by the granting State and
   (b) have the same relationship with the beneficiary State as the persons and things referred to in subparagraph (a) have with that third State.

(b) National treatment

National treatment as a treaty obligation may stimulate the elimination of non-tariff barriers to trade, because under this principle such measures must be equally applied to domestic industries.

In rather broad terms, Article III(4) of the GATT provides national treatment for foreign products:

---

[8] See M Hilf and R Geiß, 'Most-Favoured-Nation Clause' in R Wolfrum (ed), *The Max Planck Encyclopedia of Public International Law* (OUP 2012) vol VII, 384.
[9] International Law Commission, *Yearbook of the International Law Commission* (International Law Commission Publications 1978) vol II, Part Two.

The products of the territory of any contracting party imported into the territory of any other contracting party shall be accorded treatment no less favourable than that accorded to like products of national origin in respect of all laws, regulations and requirements affecting their internal sale, offering for sale, purchase, transportation, distribution or use [...].

Most-favoured-nation treatment and national treatment are also standard in modern investment treaties. The US Model Bilateral Investment Treaty 2012, for example, provides:

Article 3: National Treatment

1. Each Party shall accord to investors of the other Party treatment no less favourable than that it accords, in like circumstances, to its own investors with respect to the establishment, acquisition, expansion, management, conduct, operation, and sale or other disposition of investments in its territory.
2. Each Party shall accord to covered investments treatment no less favourable than that it accords, in like circumstances, to investments in its territory of its own investors with respect to the establishment, acquisition, expansion, management, conduct, operation, and sale or other disposition of investments.
3. The treatment to be accorded by a Party under paragraphs 1 and 2 means, with respect to a regional level of government, treatment no less favourable than the treatment accorded, in like circumstances, by that regional level of government to natural persons resident in and enterprises constituted under the laws of other regional levels of government of the Party of which it forms a part, and to their respective investments.

Article 4: Most-Favoured-Nation Treatment

1. Each Party shall accord to investors of the other Party treatment no less favourable than that it accords, in like circumstances, to investors of any non-Party with respect to the establishment, acquisition, expansion, management, conduct, operation, and sale or other disposition of investments in its territory.
2. Each Party shall accord to covered investments treatment no less favourable than that it accords, in like circumstances, to investments in its territory of investors of any non-Party with respect to the establishment, acquisition, expansion, management, conduct, operation, and sale or other disposition of investments.

5. Favourable Conditions for Developing Countries

(a) Preferential treatment

Besides the interest in raising the standard of living and stimulating economic growth, solidarity towards developing countries and regard for their specific needs is a guiding principle of modern international economic law. The WTO Agreement stresses in its preamble that the economic needs of developing countries deserve due consideration:

[...] *Recognizing* further that there is need for positive efforts designed to ensure that developing countries, and especially the least developed among them, secure a share in the growth in international trade commensurate with the needs of their economic development [...].

The demand of less developed countries for greater consideration of their interest, for more 'fairness' in international trade and investment, and for more regulatory freedom in the administration of their resources (including expropriation) is the driving force behind the call for a 'New International Economic Order'.[10]

Apart from direct transfer-payments, there are also other ways to address the specific concerns of developing countries:

- preferential treatment in tariffs;
- ensuring adequate prices for natural resources;
- exemption from certain treaty obligations (temporary or lasting);
- technology transfer; or
- debt-relief, in particular for the least developed countries.

(b) Preferential tariffs

Preferential tariffs are an important vehicle for fostering the economic development of poorer and less industrialized countries. In November 1979, Members of the GATT adopted the decision on Differential and More Favourable Treatment, Reciprocity and Fuller Participation of Developing Countries.[11] As an exemption ('waiver') from most-favoured-nation treatment, this decision gives goods from developing countries a competitive advantage. It provides:

1. Notwithstanding the provisions of Article I of the General Agreement, contracting parties may accord differential and more favourable treatment to developing countries, without according such treatment to other contracting parties.
2. The provisions of paragraph 1 apply to the following:
   a. Preferential tariff treatment accorded by developed contracting parties to products originating in developing countries in accordance with the Generalized System of Preferences;
   b. Differential and more favourable treatment with respect to the provisions of the General Agreement concerning non-tariff measures governed by the provisions of instruments multilaterally negotiated under the auspices of the GATT;
   c. Regional or global arrangements entered into amongst less-developed contracting parties for the mutual reduction or elimination of tariffs and, in accordance with criteria or conditions which may be prescribed by the Contracting Parties, for the mutual reduction or elimination of non-tariff measures, on products imported from one another;
   d. Special treatment on the least developed among the developing countries in the context of any general or specific measures in favour of developing countries.

---

[10] See Ch II.2.
[11] GATT (1979) 26th Supp BISD 203; see A Yusuf, '"Differential and More Favourable Treatment": The GATT Enabling Clause' (1980) 14 JWT 488.

This waiver covers more favourable treatment granted to all developing countries. Preferential treatment confined to certain developing countries requires an additional waiver, unless it is related to a customs union or a free trade area (Article XXIV(5) of the GATT).

(c) Technology transfer

An important concern of developing countries relates to access to the technical know-how and the acquisition of new methods of production and environmental protection.[12] Technology can be directly transferred by industrial countries themselves, by international organizations, and by transnational corporations. Access to technology may be indirectly facilitated through financial support, for example through funds financed by industrialized countries. Within the framework of the United Nations, the United Nations Conference on Trade and Development (UNCTAD) has elaborated an International Code of Conduct for the Transfer of Technology.[13] The UN General Assembly officially took notice of the document and endorsed further efforts in this field without recognizing the content of the document as binding international law.[14]

A kind of technology transfer can already be seen in access to inventions and other innovations by temporal restriction of intellectual property.

A question at issue is the transfer of technology in the context of the extraction of mineral and other resources from the seabed. The depletion of manganese nodules and other forms of seabed mining requires access to high technologies. The United Nations Convention on the Law of the Sea of 1982 (UNCLOS) describes the seabed and its resources as a 'common heritage of mankind' and confers all regulatory powers as to its use to the International Seabed Authority in Jamaica (Part XI of the Convention). The International Seabed Authority does not only regulate the access to the economic use of the seabed (by granting exploration and depletion licences), but also engages in deep-sea-mining through its own 'enterprise'. Particularly controversial is the regime of technology transfer under the auspices of the International Seabed Authority.[15] The International Seabed Authority is supposed to support the transfer of technology in favour of the developing countries (Article 144 UNCLOS). According to the Convention, the parties shall cooperate under fair conditions in the interest of a transfer of marine technology (Part XIV, Article 266 UNCLOS). A major point of contention was the obligation on mining companies to grant access to their technology to the 'enterprise' of the International Seabed Authority

---

[12] See eg H Ballreich, 'Technologietransfer als Völkerrechtsproblem' (1981) 24 GYIL 329; M Waibel and W Alford, 'Technology Transfer' in R Wolfrum (ed), *The Max Planck Encyclopedia of Public International Law* (OUP 2012) vol IX, 801.

[13] See (1980) 19 ILM 773; W Fikentscher, *The Draft International Code of Conduct on the Transfer of Technology* (Wiley-VCH 1980); P Roffe, 'UNCTAD: Code of Conduct on Transfer of Technology' (1985) 19 JWT 669.

[14] See UNGA Res 40/184 (17 December 1985) UN Doc A/RES/40/184.

[15] See SD Yarn, 'The Transfer of Technology and UNCLOS III' (1984) 14 Ga J Int'l & Comp L 121.

'on fair and reasonable commercial terms and conditions', if the 'enterprise' from its point of view is unable to acquire this or a similar technology under adequate conditions on the free market (Annex III, Article 5(3) *lit* a UNCLOS). This regime of a compulsory transfer of technology was a reason for the United States and other industrial countries not to become a party to UNCLOS. In addition, some Western countries were afraid to be outvoted in the International Seabed Authority by the developing countries. Without the technologically advanced Western countries joining, the seabed mining regime of UNCLOS would have been condemned to failure. Under customary law, States can directly proceed with mining on the basis of the priority principle, without requiring any concession. To overcome the concerns of the United States and other countries, the UN General Assembly adopted the Agreement on the Implementation of Part XI of UNCLOS in 1994.[16] By modifying the seabed mining regime of UNCLOS, this agreement essentially accommodates the interests of the industrial countries. It strengthens the position of States like the United States or Russia and other (Western) industrialized countries in the Council of the International Seabed Authority. By balancing competing interests with a realistic regard for major stakeholders in order to reach universal acceptance, this departure from the principle of strict formal equality constitutes an interesting approach for the development of the law of international organizations as well as international economic law.[17] Restructuring the concession regime, the conditions for mining licences were significantly improved for private investors in a way complying with market rules (Annex, Section 5 of the Implementation Agreement).

The preamble of the 1994 Implementation Agreement refers to the changes of the economic and political climate 'including in particular a growing reliance on market principles', which have taken place since the adoption of the Convention in 1982.

The 1994 Implementation Agreement documents a new tendency towards an economic realism. Some even qualify the Agreement as a 'requiem on the new international economic order'.[18] The first application for an exploration undertaking (commenced by Germany) was accepted by the International Seabed Authority in 2005.

The idea of a transfer of technology also plays a significant role in treaties on the protection of the environment. The Montreal Protocol on Substances that Deplete

---

[16] Agreement Relating to the Implementation of Part XI of the UN Convention on the Law of the Sea of 1982 (Annex, Section 3); see DH Anderson, 'Resolution and Agreement Relating to the Implementation of Part XI of the UN Convention on the Law of the Sea: A General Assessment' (1995) 55 ZaöRV 277; G Jaenicke, 'The United Nations Convention on the Law of the Sea and the Agreement Relating to the Implementation of Part XI of the Convention' in U Beyerlin, M Bothe, R Hofmann, and EU Petersmann (eds), *Festschrift für Rudolf Bernhardt* (Springer 1995) 121; BH Oxman et al, 'Law of the Sea Forum: The 1994 Agreement on Implementation of Seabed Provisions of the Convention of the Law of the Sea' (1994) 88 AJIL 687.

[17] See R Wolfrum, 'The Decision-Making Process According to Sec. 3 of the Annex to the Implementation Agreement: A Model to be Followed for other International Economic Organisations?' (1995) 55 ZaöRV 310.

[18] TW Wälde, 'A Requiem for the "New International Economic Order"' in E Hafner et al (eds), *Liber Amicorum Professor Seidl-Hohenveldern* (Brill Academic Publishers 1998) 771.

the Ozone Layer (a protocol to the Vienna Convention for the Protection of the Ozone Layer) requires the parties, with a remarkably extensive wording, to 'take every practical step' to ensure a quick transfer of technology (Article 10A). An amendment to this protocol provides financial support in form of contributions to the Multilateral Fund (Article 10), thus marking a shift from direct technology transfer to financial assistance for acquiring technology on the market. The transfer of technology in terms of Article 4(5) of the United Nations Framework Convention on Climate Change (UNFCCC) also rests on a finance mechanism, which has been institutionalized within the framework of the Global Environmental Facility of the World Bank. In context with environmental standards, developing countries often have a relatively strong bargaining position, as the industrial countries have a significant interest in poorer countries realizing efficient measures of environmental protection.

Technology transfer is also a relevant topic in the still growing sector of 'biotechnology'. The United Nations Convention on Biological Diversity (CBD)[19] stipulates a technology transfer for all forms of exploration of genetic resources and includes an adequate distribution of revenues between the respective countries of origin and their contractual partners (Article 15(7) CBD).[20] The general obligation of the industrial States as to a transfer of technology (Article 16(1) CBD) is embedded in a complex framework of rules (Article 16(2)–(5) CBD), providing mutually agreed conditions. A very controversial issue relates to the transfer of technologies, which are protected by patents and other intellectual property rights. Article 16(2) second sentence of the CBD tries to reconcile the competing interests at stake:

In the case of technology subject to patents and other intellectual property rights, such access and transfer shall be provided on terms which recognize and are consistent with the adequate and effective protection of intellectual property rights.

Concerns about a possible erosion of intellectual property rights, though hardly sustainable, stand behind the United States' non-ratification of the CBD.

(d) Exceptions from general treaty obligations for developing countries

Many agreements address the special interests of developing countries by granting exceptions from general obligations. The TRIPS Agreement, for example, provides a differential treatment for developing countries. Thus, the least developed countries for a transitional period could opt for a far-reaching relief from the obligations under the TRIPS Agreement, extended by the TRIPS Council until 2021, and for patents on pharmaceutical products even until 2033 (Article 66(1) TRIPS).

---

[19] United Nations Convention on Biological Diversity (1992) 31 ILM 818.
[20] For a general analysis see V Normand, 'Access to Genetic Resources and the Fair and Equitable Sharing of Benefits Arising out of their Utilization' (2004) 1 JIB Law 133.

Also, the protection of patents in the pharmaceutical sector may amount to an insuperable barrier of costs for the population of developing countries and frustrate the fight against epidemic diseases.[21] In response to these concerns, Article 8(1) TRIPS provides that

[m]embers may, in formulating or amending their laws and regulations, adopt measures necessary to protect public health and nutrition, and to promote the public interest in sectors of vital importance to their socio-economic and technological development, provided that such measures are consistent with the provisions of this Agreement.

The declaration of the Ministerial Conference in Doha concerning the TRIPS Agreement and public health of November 2001 acknowledges a respectable margin for the members regarding the area of conflict between intellectual or industrial property rights and public health:[22]

[...]
4. We agree that the TRIPS Agreement does not and should not prevent Members from taking measures to protect public health. Accordingly, while reiterating our commitment to the TRIPS Agreement, we affirm that the Agreement can and should be interpreted and implemented in a manner supportive of WTO Members' right to protect public health and, in particular, to promote access to medicines for all.
   In this connection, we reaffirm the right of WTO Members to use, to the full, the provisions in the TRIPS Agreement, which provide flexibility for this purpose.
5. Accordingly and in the light of paragraph 4 above, while maintaining our commitments in the TRIPS Agreement, we recognize that these flexibilities include:
   [...]
   (b) Each Member has the right to grant compulsory licences and the freedom to determine the grounds upon which such licences are granted.
   (c) Each Member has the right to determine what constitutes a national emergency or other circumstances of extreme urgency, it being understood that public health crises, including those relating to HIV/AIDS, tuberculosis, malaria and other epidemics, can represent a national emergency or other circumstances of extreme urgency [...].
6. We recognize that WTO members with insufficient or no manufacturing capacities in the pharmaceutical sector could face difficulties in making effective use of compulsory licensing under the TRIPS Agreement [...].

The so-called 'Medical Decision' of 2003 implements this declaration, waiving certain conditions for compulsory licences under Article 31 of the TRIPS Agreement.[23] An amendment of the TRIPS Agreement facilitating the grant of compulsory licences (Art. 31*bis*) has not yet entered into force.[24]

---

[21] See H Hestermeyer, *Human Rights and the WTO* (OUP 2007); S Joseph, 'Pharmaceutical Cooperations and Access to Drugs: the "Fourth Wave" of Corporate Human Rights Scrutiny' (2003) 25 Hum Rts Q 425.

[22] Declaration on the TRIPS Agreement and Public Health (adopted on 20 November 2001) WT/MIN(01)/DEC/2.

[23] WT/L/540 (1 September 2003); see FM Abbott, 'The WTO Medicines Decision: World Pharmaceutical Trade and the Protection of Public Health' (2005) 99 AJIL 317.

[24] See Ch XVIII.2(b).

6. Sustainable Development

The concept of 'sustainable development' is one of the most salient examples of a soft law standard which has not yet achieved the status of a strict principle of international law, but which has significant consequences for international economic relations. The concept has emerged in international environmental law.

Aiming at a responsible use of natural resources, the concept of sustainable development has a considerable impact. It has found expression in a number of treaties which transform the relatively abstract concept into binding legal rules.[25]

7. Respect for Human Rights

In many ways, the modern international order is interrelated with human rights under customary law and treaties.[26] Human rights like the guarantee of property have a strong impact on the structure of an economic and social system. The protection of human rights may even establish rather finely tuned standards of protection like the precautionary principle in case of possible risks to health or undisturbed family life.[27] Action directed at maximizing economic gains or mere indifference towards elementary rights of the human person may conflict with human rights such as the protection of human health or the prohibition of child labour. On the other hand, the international economic order has become more and more receptive to human rights standards. Collective rights of indigenous groups established under treaty law, possibly even under customary law, affect the depletion of natural resources located within the territories of these groups. Self-commitments, codes of conduct, and other forms of 'soft law', but also possible liability for human rights violations (eg under the US Alien Tort Claims Act) address the responsibility of transnational corporations for compliance with human rights standards and foster the formation of 'hard' international law. Beyond compliance with human rights treaties in a strict sense, certain developments in international economic law may be understood as paying tribute to human rights standards.

---

[25] For further information, see Ch VIII.2.

[26] T Cottier, J Pauwelyn, and E Bürgi (eds), *Human Rights and International Trade* (OUP 2006); C Downes, 'Must the Losers of Free Trade Go Hungry? Reconciling WTO Obligations and the Right to Food' (2007) 47 Va J Int'l L 619; PM Dupuy, E-U Petersmann, and F Francioni (eds), *Human Rights in International Investment Law and Arbitration* (OUP 2009); H Hestermeyer, *Human Rights and the WTO* (OUP 2007); K Mechlem, 'Harmonizing Trade in Agriculture and Human Rights: Options for the Integration of the Right to Food into the Agreement on Agriculture' (2006) 10 Max Planck YB UN L 127; M Ruffert, 'The Protection of Foreign Direct Investment by the European Convention on Human Rights' (2000) 43 GYIL 1166; JG Ruggie, 'Business and Human Rights: The Evolving International Agenda' (2007) 101 AJIL 819; O De Schutter (ed), *Transnational Corporations and Human Rights* (Hart Publishing 2006); I Seidl-Hohenveldern, *International Economic Law* (3rd edn, Kluwer Law International 1999) 130; C Tomuschat, *Human Rights: Between Idealism and Realism* (3rd edn, OUP 2014).

[27] ECtHR *Tatar v Romania* App no 67021/01 (27 January 2009).

Recent discussion in international trade law addresses the implications of the right to 'adequate food' and 'the fundamental right of everyone to be free from hunger' (Article 11(1) and (2) of the UN Covenant on Social, Economic and Cultural Rights). In the context of the protection of intellectual property rights in pharmaceuticals and the production of generic medicinal products for the poor, many refer to 'the right of everyone to the enjoyment of the highest attainable standard of physical and mental health' as enshrined in Article 12(1) of the UN Covenant on Social, Economic and Cultural Rights. The WTO General Council's waiver of conditions for compulsory licences for patents on drugs and the production of generic pharmaceuticals in the fight against endemic diseases in developing countries (the 'Medical Decision' of the WTO)[28] may be understood as responding to concerns on the human right to health.

The globalization of international economic relations assists the protection of human rights in so far as it turns trade sanctions and other economic sanctions into relatively effective tools. Many States or groups of States with a highly developed sensitivity for human rights issues, dispose of a considerable potential for economic sanctions. Thus, globalization of economic relations may, in the long run, contribute to the global protection of a universal standard of human rights.

Select Bibliography

H Fox, *International Economic Law and Developing States* (BICCL 1992).

R Wolfrum and C Kojima (eds), *Solidarity: A Structural Principle of International Law* (Springer 2010).

---

[28] See Section 5(d) in this chapter.

VI

Sovereignty and International Economic Relations

1. A Modern Concept of Sovereignty: Response to Globalization and Deference to Democratic Choices

States are masters of and over their own territory. They have personal jurisdiction over their nationals, individuals, and corporations alike. Thus, States enjoy broad powers to pursue and enforce regulatory interests in an economic context. Each State enjoys freedom from any unilateral constraints and undue interference imposed upon them by other States. This conglomerate of powers and self-determination is commonly called sovereignty.[1] In an economic context, the Charter of Economic Rights and Duties of States of 1974[2] reflects the classic concept of State sovereignty in Article 2(1):

> Every State has and shall freely exercise full permanent sovereignty, including possession, use and disposal, over all its wealth, natural resources and economic activities.

States co-exist in terms of a 'sovereign equality'.[3] The elements of sovereign equality of States are listed in the Friendly Relations Declaration[4] of the UN:

---

[1] For a classic account of sovereignty, see R Jennings and A Watts, *Oppenheim's International Law* (9th edn, OUP 1992) vol II, 122; see also J Bartelson, *A Genealogy of Sovereignty* (CUP 1993); S Besson, 'Sovereignty' in R Wolfrum (ed), *The Max Planck Encyclopedia of Public International Law* (OUP 2012) vol IX, 366; A Chayes and A Handler Chayes, *The New Sovereignty—Compliance with International Regulatory Agreements* (Harvard University Press 1995); FH Hinsley, *Sovereignty* (2nd edn, CUP 1986); A James, *Sovereign Statehood* (Unwin Hyman 1986); H Kelsen, *Das Problem der Souveränität und die Theorie des Völkerrechts* (Mohr 1928). On new concepts of sovereignty, see M Herdegen, 'Souveränität heute' in M Herdegen et al (eds), *Staatsrecht und Politik—Festschrift für Roman Herzog* (CH Beck 2009) 117; G Kreijen (ed), *State, Sovereignty, and International Governance* (OUP 2002); C Schreuer, 'The Waning of the Sovereign State: Towards a New Paradigm for International Law?' (1993) 4 EJIL 447; K Raustiala, 'Rethinking the Sovereignty Debate in International Economic Law' (2003) 6 J Int'l Econ L 841; V Lowe, 'Sovereignty and International Economic Law' in W Shan, P Simons, and D Singh (eds), *Redefining Sovereignty in International Economic Law* (Hart Publishing 2008) 77; JH Jackson, 'Sovereignty: Outdated Concept or New Approaches' in W Shan, P Simons, and D Singh (eds), *Redefining Sovereignty in International Economic Law* (Hart Publishing 2008) 3.

[2] (1974) UNYB 402.

[3] See P Kooijmans, *The Doctrine of the Legal Equality of States* (Sythoff 1964); MN Shaw, International Law (7th edn, CUP 2014) 155; for a classic historical account, see E Witt de Dickinson, *The Equality of States in International Law* (1920).

[4] UNGA Res 2625 (XXV) (24 October 1970) Declaration on Principles of International Law Concerning Friendly Relations and Cooperation Among States in Accordance With the Charter of the United Nations.

All States enjoy sovereign equality. They have equal rights and duties and are equal members of the international community, notwithstanding differences of an economic, social, political or other nature.

In particular, sovereign equality includes the following elements:

a) States are judicially equal;
b) Each State enjoys the rights inherent in full sovereignty;
c) Each State has the duty to respect the personality of other States;
d) The territorial integrity and political independence of the State are inviolable;
e) Each State has the right freely to choose and develop its political, social, economic and cultural systems;
f) Each State has the duty to comply fully and in good faith with its international obligations and to live in peace with other States.

The sovereignty of States has never been understood as absolute. It is embedded in an international legal order governing interests of sovereign entities or interests of the international community as a whole, imposing obligations that extend to the internal sphere of States. The consensual elements of customary rules and treaties link the establishment of international obligations to State sovereignty. In its judgment in the *SS 'Wimbledon'* case, the PCIJ recognized this link:

> The Court declines to see in the conclusion of any treaty by which a State undertakes to perform or refrain from performing a particular act, an abandonment of its sovereignty. [...] [T]he right of entering into international engagements is an attribute of State sovereignty.[5]

Even the limited transfer of elementary sovereign powers to international organizations does not necessarily destroy sovereign statehood. A far-reaching example of such a transfer is the establishment of the European Union. The unparalleled competences of the European Union cover vital economic sectors and include harmonisation of rules for the internal market, competition, monetary and commercial policy.[6] Member States have traded sovereign powers against a share in the administration of the competences transferred and a quota of representation in the European Parliament.

From a traditional and more defensive perspective, sovereignty has come under pressure from manifold sides:

- the dynamic understanding of 'peace' in terms of Chapter VII of the UN Charter and the corresponding powers of intervention of the UN Security Council;
- the development of human rights; and
- the network of agreements on economic relations, especially on free trade and investment protection.

---

[5] PCIJ *SS 'Wimbledon'* (*France, Italy, Japan, and the UK v Germany*) PCIJ Rep Series A No 1, 15 (25).
[6] See P Craig and G de Búrca, *European Union Law* (6th edn, OUP 2015) 73; P Craig and G de Búrca, *The Evolution of EU Law* (2nd edn, OUP 2011).

Under Article 39 of the UN Charter, 'peace' has come to mean more than the mere absence of an armed confrontation between States ('negative' understanding of peace) and now includes respect for fundamental human rights and humanitarian law as well as shelter from prosecution in internal conflicts and human catastrophes ('positive' understanding of peace).[7] Genocide, wilful executions, international terrorism, or widespread hunger may nowadays trigger the vast Chapter VII powers of the UN Security Council for preserving or restoring peace and international security. Mandatory resolutions of the Security Council (such as imposing a trade embargo) will justify restrictive measures under WTO law (Article XXI(c) of the GATT, Article XIV *bis*, section 1(c) of the GATS) and override any other treaty obligation (see Article 103 of the UN Charter).

A modern view of sovereignty sees restraints on sovereign choices through treaties and other consensual arrangements as a rational response to the limited potential and options of individual States. From this perspective, submission to international regulatory regimes enhances a country's status in an interdependent world: sovereignty becomes the status as a recognized member in the international community.[8] The international economic order corroborates this new understanding of sovereignty as status.

In times of economic globalization, two principles co-exist alongside each other under the conceptual roof of modern sovereignty, sometimes in mutual support, sometimes in conflict: reciprocal obligations in the interest of free trade, investment protection, and financial stability on the one hand and national self-determination, and respect to socio-economic choices on the other hand.

In economic as well as in legal terms, globalization with the integration of markets will again and again conflict with national political and societal choices of sovereign States, often enough legitimized by democratic processes. It is a lasting challenge for international economic law to strike an adequate balance between national preferences and the overarching interest in a stable and reliable framework of international economic relations. Even economists who emphasize the benefits of globalization clearly recognize that the elimination of barriers to trade and the free flow of capital cannot trump States' interests and democratic choices.

Democracies have the right to protect their social arrangements, and when this right clashes with the requirements of the global economy, it is the latter that should give way.[9]

From a constitutional and political perspective, an open international economic order draws its legitimacy essentially from treaty arrangements which rest on democratic approval (assent of Congress, Parliament, or even a referendum). The legitimizing force of such assent grows with the degree of textual density and determinacy of international agreements and the predictability of their application in

---

[7] A good insight into the complexity of modern conflicts is given in Report of the UN High-level Panel on Threats, Challenges and Change, *A More Secure World: Our Shared Responsibility* (2004).

[8] See A Chayes and A Handler Chayes, *The New Sovereignty—Compliance with International Regulatory Agreements* (Harvard University Press 1995).

[9] D Rodrik, *The Globalization Paradox* (WW Norton & Co 2011) xix.

the long run. It diminishes as treaty bodies follow a dynamic application of the texts with results not anticipated by States and their constituencies. Informal arrangements and standards hammered out by governments and executive agencies without parliamentary approval are vested with a rather precarious legitimacy in the eyes of national constituencies. Thus, modern sovereignty has to face challenges, which are entirely different from the concept of sovereignty rooted in ideas stemming from the 19th century.

2. The Principle of Non-Intervention

Sovereignty and sovereign equality require that each State can freely determine its internal affairs without intervention from the outside.[10] The principle of non-intervention[11] is universally recognized as one of the cornerstones of international law. The ICJ refers to non-intervention as freedom of choices in the absence of external coercion:

[T]he principle forbids all States or groups of States to intervene directly or indirectly in internal or external affairs of other States. A prohibited intervention must accordingly be one bearing on matters in which each State is permitted, by the principle of State sovereignty, to decide freely. One of these is the choice of a political, economic, social and cultural system, and the formulation of foreign policy. Intervention is wrongful when it uses methods of coercion in regard to such choices, which must remain free ones. The element of coercion, which defines, and indeed forms the very essence of, prohibited intervention, is particularly obvious in the case of an intervention which uses force, either in the direct form of military action, or in the indirect form of support for subversive or terrorist armed activities within another State.[12]

Economic pressure as such will, in principle, not be classified as intervention. An intervention usually requires a noticeable physical element. It is, however, controversial, whether economic pressure can be so compelling as physical coercion as to come within reach of intervention. The Charter of Economic Rights and Duties of States of 1974[13] prohibits the use of such economic measures which aim at the subjection of one State to another in exercising sovereign rights (Article 32).

The principle of non-intervention was often mobilized against the conditions for credits and other financial benefits by the World Bank and other lenders ('conditionality').[14] However, whenever there is no legal claim to unconditional

---

[10] See Article 2(7) of the UN Charter; ICJ *Military and Paramilitary Activities in and against Nicaragua* (*Nicaragua v United States*) (Merits) [1986] ICJ Rep 14; see UNGA Res 2625 (XXV) of 24 October 1970 Declaration on Principles of International Law Concerning Friendly Relations and Co-operation Among States in Accordance with the Charter of the United Nations.

[11] P Kunig, 'Intervention, Prohibition of' in R Wolfrum (ed), *The Max Planck Encyclopedia of Public International Law* (OUP 2012) vol VI, 289.

[12] ICJ *Military and Paramilitary Activities in and against Nicaragua* (*Nicaragua v United States*) (Merits) [1986] ICJ Rep 14 para 205.

[13] (1974) UNYB 402.

[14] W Meng, 'Conditionality of IMF and World Bank Loans: Tutelage over Sovereign States?' (1998) 21 VRÜ 263.

financial assistance, payments may be tied to certain structural reforms and other conditions, at least as long as they do not affect the core of self-determination.

3. State Immunity

The sovereign equality of States is also the root of State immunity from jurisdiction and enforcement measures of other States:[15] *par in parem non habet imperium*. The rules on State immunity govern judicial and administrative proceedings as well as the enforcement of judgments or arbitral awards in other States.

Under international law and the legislation of many States, State immunity does not cover commercial activities (*acta iure gestionis*) as opposed to the exercise of sovereign or public powers (*acta iure imperii*).

States may renounce their claim to immunity either before a dispute arises or after the start of judicial proceedings. Waivers of immunity in favour of creditors are often attached to the emission of State bonds.

(a) From absolute to relative immunity

In classic customary law, it was the doctrine of absolute immunity which prevailed. States could claim immunity for all their activities with a few exceptions (eg actions related to real estate property or counterclaims). Modern international law follows a more functional paradigm and merely recognizes the restricted model of a relative immunity. Immunity only covers sovereign acts (*acta iure imperii*) and does not extend to non-commercial activities (*acta iure gestionis*). Thus, when engaged in business transactions like a private person, States are subject to the jurisdiction of foreign courts like other actors. The restrictive concept of immunity has been adopted by a number of international agreements and municipal laws. It underlies the European Convention on State Immunity of 1972 and the United Nations Convention on Jurisdictional Immunities of States and their Property of 2004[16] as well as the US Foreign Sovereign Immunities Act of 1976 and the British State Immunity Act of 1978.

Immunity clearly applies to the typical exercise of sovereign powers such as the use of the armed forces.[17]

---

[15] H Fox, *The Law of State Immunity* (3rd edn, OUP 2013); A Dickinson, R Lindsay, and JP Loonam, *State Immunity, Selected Materials and Commentary* (OUP 2004); EK Bankas, *The State Immunity Controversy in International Law* (Springer 2005); G Hafner, MG Kohen, and S Breau, *State Practice Regarding State Immunities* (Brill Academic Publishers 2006); P-T Stoll, 'State Immunity' in R Wolfrum (ed), *The Max Planck Encyclopedia of Public International Law* (OUP 2012) vol IX, 498; G Hafner and U Köhler, 'The United Nations Convention on Jurisdictional Immunities of States and their Property' (2004) 35 NYIL 3.

[16] UNGA Res 59/38 (Annex) UN Doc A/Res/59/38 (16 December 2004).

[17] An illustrative example is the bombing of a ship by the Argentine Air Force on the high seas in the Falkland conflict, see US Supreme Court *Argentine Republic v Amerada Hess Shipping Corpn* 488 US 428 (1989); the International Court of Justice held that immunity for sovereign acts applies even in cases where the defendant State had violated fundamental rules of international law (*ius cogens*),

Qualification for purposes of immunity can often prove to be difficult, when States operate on markets like a private business actor while following a public purpose. In those cases, the perspective matters. A subjective perspective would defer to the intentions of the acting State. The objective approach looks at the object (the subject matter) of the transaction or activity in question. The subjective perspective often results in an undue expansion of State immunity. Nowadays, the objective test prevails.[18] However, in certain cases, the focus on the objective 'nature' of the State's transaction or act may be complemented by considering the functional context. The United Nations Convention on State Immunity of 2004 states in Article 2(2):

In determining whether a contract or transaction is a 'commercial transaction' […], reference should be made primarily to the nature of the contract or the transaction, but its purpose should also be taken into account if the parties to the contract or transaction have so agreed, or if, in the practice of the State of the forum, that purpose is relevant to determining the non-commercial character of the contract or transaction.

Even when the functional context matters, remote links to public purposes should be filtered out. Nowadays, the purchase of cigarettes for the armed forces, unlike the purchase of weaponry, would no longer qualify as a sovereign act.[19]

States' engagement on financial markets may give rise to difficult issues. When States act on the capital markets in a way similar to private actors, a strong tendency in international law classifies the recourse to financial instruments like bonds as a commercial transaction despite the underlying public purpose of ensuring State functions.

The US Supreme Court held that the issuance of Argentinean bonds in US-Dollars by the Central Bank of Argentina was a 'commercial activity' subject to the jurisdiction of the United States.[20] According to the terms of the bonds, any payments made with regard to the bonds should be paid in US-Dollars into bank accounts in the United States, Germany, or Switzerland. The US Supreme Court argued that Argentina, by issuing bonds (called 'Bonods'), had acted like a private actor without exercising any sovereign powers:

The Bonods are in almost all respects garden variety debt instruments, and, even when they are considered in full context, there is nothing about their issuance that is not analogous to a private commercial transaction. The fact that they were created to help stabilize Argentina's currency is not a valid basis for distinguishing them from ordinary debt instruments […].[21]

---

eg elementary human rights, ICJ *Jurisdictional Immunities of the State (Germany v Italy: Greece Intervening)* [2012] ICJ Rep 99.

[18] See section 1603(d) of the US Foreign Sovereign Immunities Act of 1976 and section 3(2) of the UK State Immunity Act of 1978.

[19] For a more generous approach, see the French Cour de Cassation in the *Guggenheim case* (1962) 89 J Droit Int'l 432.

[20] US Supreme Court *Republic of Argentina v Weltover Inc* 504 US 607 (1992).

[21] US Supreme Court *Republic of Argentina v Weltover Inc* 504 US 607 at 607 et seq (1992).

The immunity legislation of many States[22] and the European Convention on State Immunity[23] provide a negative list of activities which are not considered sovereign acts. The UN Convention on State Immunity defines 'commercial transactions' in Article 2(1)(c):

(i) any commercial contract or transaction for the sale of goods or supply of services;
(ii) any contract for a loan or other transaction of a financial nature, including any obligation of guarantee or of indemnity in respect of any such loan or transaction;
(iii) any other contract or transaction of a commercial, industrial, trading or professional nature, but not including a contract of employment of persons.

The principle of limited immunity also applies to enforcement measures affecting a foreign State's assets.[24] Such enforcement measures are only allowed if the assets are not designated to be used for sovereign purposes.[25] Unlike the more restrictive legislation of some States,[26] current customary international law does not require that the asset in question stands in a connection with the enforceable claim.[27]

There is a strong, albeit controversial tendency to extend immunity from enforcement to all assets of central banks.[28]

In the *ARA Libertad* case, the International Tribunal for the Law of the Sea held that international law and State immunity from execution cover any warships, as part of the armed forces, even when they are in foreign internal waters.[29] As a provisional measure, the Tribunal ordered Ghana to release the Argentinian warship 'ARA Libertad' which Ghana had impounded in order to enforce a judgment against Argentina in favour of a corporate bond holder (which was a party in *Republic of Argentina v NML Capital, Ltd*[30]).

In *Republic of Argentina v NML Capital, Ltd*, the US Supreme Court held that immunity of foreign State property from execution under the Foreign Sovereign Immunities Act does not preclude a judgment creditor from seeking discovery of property of the debtor State at least as far as such property is located outside the United States. In this case, one of Argentina's bond holders tried to execute judgments against Argentina and had served subpoenas on two banks for records relating to Argentina's international financial transactions. The Supreme Court's

[22] Eg section 3(3) of the UK State Immunity Act of 1978.
[23] Articles 4ff of the European Convention on State Immunity.
[24] See BVerfGE 46, 342; BVerfGE 64, 1 with reference to the jurisprudence of other courts.
[25] See Article 19 of the UN Convention on State Immunity.
[26] See § 1610(a)(2) of the Foreign Sovereign Immunities Act of 1976.
[27] In this respect see BVerfGE 64, 1 (40ff); cf Article 19(1)(c) of the UN Convention on State Immunity.
[28] See Article 21(1)(c) of the UN Convention on State Immunity; see also § 1611(b)(1) of the US Foreign Sovereign Immunities Act.
[29] The 'ARA Libertad' Case (Argentina v Ghana), ITLOS Case No 20 (Order of 15 December 2012).
[30] US Supreme Court *Republic of Argentina v NML Capital, Ltd* 573 US ___ (2014).

judgment allows creditors of foreign States to rely on US Courts as a 'clearinghouse for information'.[31]

The rules on diplomatic and consular immunity set additional limits to coercive measures. Article 22(3) of the Vienna Convention on Diplomatic Relations protects the premises of diplomatic missions against confiscation, levies of execution, or other enforcement measures.

(b) Immunity of State enterprises

State-owned enterprises and other legally independent entities of foreign States may benefit from immunity, as far as they exercise sovereign functions. They can claim immunity from execution for assets which directly serve specific sovereign purposes. As the German Federal Constitutional Court held in the case of the *National Iranian Oil Co*, it is irrelevant whether the assets and the revenue of a State-owned company may be considered a significant part of the State's property or the national budget.[32]

If there are doubts about the classification of acts or assets, the burden of proof calls for a distinction between the State itself and State enterprises. If the acts or assets directly involve a foreign State, State immunity applies as the rule and submission to jurisdiction or execution as the exception (*in dubio pro immunitate*).[33] The opposite principle applies if a State enterprise or another State-owned entity organized in the form of a private corporation claims immunity.

(c) Immunity of international organizations

International organizations may also invoke immunity under certain circumstances. As a rule, the agreement between the organization and the host State (where the organization has its seat) or the founding treaty will define the extent of the immunity. The scope of immunity in customary law, which is relevant *vis-à-vis* non-Member States, is highly controversial. A generous view will grant immunity to all acts which are covered by the purposes of the organization as set out in the founding treaty. As a rather questionable consequence, the distinction between sovereign and commercial acts would become irrelevant. It is, however, hard to understand why an international organization should enjoy broader immunities than their founding States. Therefore, the immunity of international organizations under customary law should follow similar criteria as the immunity of States and hence should exclude commercial activities.[34]

---

[31] See Ginsburg, J., dissenting, US Supreme Court *Republic of Argentina v NML Capital, Ltd* 573 US ___ (2014).

[32] BVerfGE 64, 1 (44).

[33] See Articles 5ff of the Convention on Jurisdictional Immunities of States and their Property.

[34] See § 288(a) of the US International Organizations' Immunity Act of 1945; Italian Corte di Cassazione (1983) Rivista di Diritto Internazionale 187.

4. The Treatment of Foreign Persons

(a) The international minimum standard

Well before the evolution of human rights, customary international law developed rules on the treatment of persons with a nationality other than the host State's.[35]

The level of due treatment under customary law is referred to as the 'international minimum standard', which for a long time contrasted with the almost unlimited discretion of States as to the treatment of their own nationals. The growing impact of human rights has made the differences between nationals and foreigners less important than in the past. Still, the rules on the treatment of foreigners provide additional protection, especially with respect to property and investments.

In its classic version, the minimum standard had a rather narrow scope and merely provided protection against 'outrageous' treatment or wilful failure of action. In the *Neer Claim* (1926), the US–Mexican General Claims Commission defined the minimum standard as a core of decent and reasonable treatment:

[T]he treatment of an alien, in order to constitute an international delinquency should amount to an outrage, to bad faith, to wilful neglect of duty, or to an insufficiency of governmental action so far short of international standards that every reasonable and impartial man would readily recognize its insufficiency. Whether the insufficiency proceeds from the deficient execution of a reasonable law or from the fact that the laws of the country do not empower the authorities to measure up to international standards is immaterial.[36]

Under current international law, the minimum standard has developed in two directions. First, the abstract parameters have become more subtle, raising the level of adequate treatment. 'Outrage', 'bad faith', or the 'wilful neglect of duty' are no longer the predominant criteria. Secondly, the application of the abstract formulas to the concrete case reflects more sensitivity for fairness and legitimate expectations today than in the early 20th century.

Under modern treaties on investment protection, clauses granting 'fair and equitable treatment' and 'full protection and security' very often (but not always) refer to the customary minimum standard. In this context, modern arbitral practice follows a broader, less elementary understanding of the minimum standard. Recognizing the dynamics inherent in the minimum standard, an ICSID tribunal stated in the case *Mondev International v United States of America*:

Neer and like arbitral awards were decided in the 1920s, when the status of the individual in international law, and the international protection of foreign investments, were far less developed than they have since come to be. In particular, both the substantive and procedural rights of the individual in international law have undergone considerable development. In light of these developments it is unconvincing to confine the meaning of 'fair and

---

[35] See K Hailbronner and J Gogolin, 'Aliens' in R Wolfrum (ed), *The Max Planck Encyclopedia of Public International Law* (OUP 2012) vol I, 285 with extensive references.
[36] US–Mexican General Claims Commission *United States v Mexico* (1926) 4 RIAA 60.

equitable treatment' and 'full protection and security' of foreign investments to what those terms—had they been current at the time—might have meant in the 1920s when applied to the physical security of an alien.[37]

A number of modern treaties (including NAFTA) grant 'fair and equitable treatment' and 'full protection and security' with reference to the minimum standard of treatment under customary international law.[38] An important field of application of the international minimum standard covers expropriations. Whilst universal human rights law hardly restrains a State's interference with the property of its own nationals, a State may expropriate foreign property only under certain conditions, that is a public purpose, non-discrimination, and the payment of compensation. Any infringement of those parameters establishes the international responsibility of the host State. The home State of the expropriated owner may exercise diplomatic protection and claim redress.

In addition to the minimum standard with its sometimes soft contours, a vast number of bi- and multilateral treaties protect nationals of one State in another contracting State and grant treatment to more specific or favourable terms. The Treaties of Friendship, Commerce and Navigation[39] were predecessors of many bilateral investment treaties (BITs) and trade agreements with investment protection clauses. Still, customary law continues to play a significant role. Under many modern treaties, certain clauses on the treatment of foreign investors are interpreted in the light of the minimum standard.

(b) The Calvo Doctrine

The minimum standard, which critics often associated with interventionist and presumptuous attitudes of the great powers, has not always met with universal acclaim. For a long time, a strong tendency in Latin American countries followed the standard of national treatment. Foreigners should be entitled to the same treatment as nationals, but not to any better treatment. This concept was developed by the Argentine lawyer Carlos Calvo and is therefore known as the Calvo Doctrine.[40] A conflict between the two standards arises if the treatment of nationals falls below what the minimum standard would require.

Competing for foreign investment and realizing the dissuasive impact of national treatment especially in times of political and economic instability, most Latin American States abandoned the Calvo Doctrine and concluded treaties with modern standards of investment protection. Nevertheless, the Calvo Doctrine

---

[37] *Mondev International Ltd v United States of America*, ICSID Case No ARB(AF)/99/2 (Award) (2003) 42 ILM 85 para 116.

[38] See Ch XXXIV.4.(d) and (e).

[39] A Paulus, 'Treaties of Friendship, Commerce and Navigation' in R Wolfrum (ed), *The Max Planck Encyclopedia of Public International Law* (OUP 2012) vol IX, 498.

[40] P Juillard, 'Calvo Doctrine/Calvo Clause' in R Wolfrum (ed), *The Max Planck Encyclopedia of Public International Law* (OUP 2012) vol I, 1086; DR Shea, *The Calvo Clause* (University of Minnesota Press 1955).

has recently experienced a kind of 'renaissance'. The 'Bolivarian' constitution of Venezuela (1999) and the constitution of Bolivia (2009) espouse the standard of national treatment, denying foreign persons any rights or prerogatives which nationals cannot invoke either. The constitution of Bolivia (2009) bans any privileges for foreign nationals in its Article 320 in very clear terms:

I. Bolivian investment takes priority over foreign investment.

II. All foreign investment is subject to Bolivian jurisdiction, laws and authorities and no-one can claim any exceptional status or appeal to diplomatic protection to obtain a more favourable treatment.

III. Economic relations with foreign states and companies will take place under conditions of independence, mutual respect and fairness. More favorable terms than those established for the Bolivian nationals shall not be granted to foreign States or companies.

IV. The State is independent in all decisions of domestic economic policy and will not accept impositions or conditions of this policy by States, banks or financial institutions, Bolivian or foreign, corporations or transnational enterprises.

V. Public policies will promote the domestic consumption of products made in Bolivia.

It remains to be seen how this revival of the Calvo Doctrine affects foreign investment in Latin America.

5. Diplomatic Protection

(a) General principles

Whenever an act or an omission of a State organ violates the rules on the treatment of foreign nationals, the home State may exercise diplomatic protection.[41] As a precondition for the exercise of diplomatic protection, the injured foreign person must have exhausted all (reasonably available) remedies in the host State (so-called 'local remedies rule').[42]

A State may exercise diplomatic protection in favour of its own nationals (and under certain conditions of stateless persons domiciled on its territory). Although each State determines the conditions for its citizenship, other States need not to unconditionally recognize the conferment of nationality. As the ICJ held in the well-known *Nottebohm* case, nationality, for purposes of diplomatic protection, must rest on a 'genuine link' between the individual and the naturalizing State.[43]

Under the influence of the Calvo Doctrine, some States provided for a waiver of diplomatic protection in contracts with foreign investors. It was and still is, however, questionable, whether a foreigner can waive his right to diplomatic protection

---

[41] CF Amerasinghe, *Diplomatic Protection* (OUP 2008); J Dugard, 'Diplomatic Protection' in R Wolfrum (ed), *The Max Planck Encyclopedia of Public International Law* (OUP 2012) vol III, 114; a classic in this field: EM Borchard, *The Diplomatic Protection of Citizens Abroad* (1915).

[42] AA Cançado Trindade, *The Application of the Rule of Exhaustion of Local Remedies in International Law: Its Rationale in the International Protection of Individual Rights* (CUP 1983).

[43] ICJ *Nottebohm Case (second phase) (Liechtenstein v Guatemala)* [1955] ICJ Rep 4.

with effects for his home State. In the *North American Dredging Co of Texas* case, a Mixed Claims Commission decided that the contractual submission of a US contractor to the exclusive jurisdiction of Mexican courts and the exclusion of diplomatic protection was limited to claims arising directly out of the contract. Other claims arising directly out of breaches of international law, like a denial of justice, still triggered the right to diplomatic protection, irrespective of any such submission agreements.[44] Despite that ruling, a foreign investor cannot be generally denied any chance to make that kind of determination in relation to the host State. This view is supported by the modern perspective on the exercise of diplomatic protection. Modern doctrine shows clear tendencies to consider the exercise of diplomatic protection as a form of 'representative action' of the home State against the host State. In this light, the 'rights' of the home State cannot go any further than the rights of the foreigner himself. Modern investment treaties usually provide dispute settlement by an arbitral institution like the International Centre for the Settlement of Investment Disputes (ICSID). In this context, the contractual submission of an investor to the exclusive jurisdiction of the host State's courts is interpreted narrowly. In the end, the still marginal prominence of the Calvo Doctrine diminishes the relevance of these problems and puts the question for the exact content of the international minimum standard into focus.

The variety of means for diplomatic protection is very broad. The protecting State may enter into negotiations with the host State or take resort to more punitive measures. Those measures include the formal protest, the retorsion (an unfriendly act which is itself in conformity with international law) or the reprisal (a proportionate act which is itself not in conformity with international law but becomes lawful as a reaction to an unlawful act of the other State).

(b) Diplomatic protection of corporations and shareholders

For corporations, either the State where the corporation was founded or the State where the corporation has its seat of management can exercise diplomatic protection. Which of the two links prevails is a matter of controversy. The Draft Articles on Diplomatic Protection of 2006[45] of the International Law Commission, as a rule, favour the State under whose laws the corporation was incorporated. Only under exceptional circumstances, the ILC's Draft Articles allow the State where the corporation has its seat but where it was not incorporated to exercise diplomatic protection (Article 9):

For the purposes of the diplomatic protection of a corporation, the State of nationality means the State under whose law the corporation was incorporated. However, when the corporation is controlled by nationals of another State or States and has no substantial business

---

[44] US–Mexican Claims Commission *North American Dredging Co of Texas v United Mexican States* (1926) 4 RIAA 26 (27ff).
[45] Report on the work of its fifty-eighth session (1 May to 9 June and 3 July to 11 August 2006), UN Doc A/61/10 (16).

activities in the State of incorporation, and the seat of management and the financial control of the corporation are both located in another State, that State shall be regarded as the State of nationality.

In case of measures directed against a company, the home State of the shareholders may not exercise diplomatic protection. As the ICJ stated in the *Barcelona Traction* case:

[A]n act directed against and infringing only the company's rights does not involve responsibility towards the shareholders, even if their interests are affected.[46]

However, certain circumstances allow diplomatic protection of the shareholders by their home State. There is sufficient reason for a 'lifting of the corporate veil', if the corporation is in a state of dissolution or has otherwise lost its capacity to act.[47]

Under Article 11 of the ILC's Draft Articles on Diplomatic Protection of 2006, an injury to the corporation entitles the State of the shareholder's nationality to exercise diplomatic protection if

(a) the corporation has ceased to exist according to the law of the State of incorporation for a reason unrelated to the injury; or
(b) the corporation had, at the date of injury, the nationality of the State alleged to be responsible for causing the injury, and incorporation in that State was required by it as a precondition for doing business there.

Practically important is diplomatic protection if a treaty specifically protects the property rights of shareholders. In this case, measures taken by the host State against the company which affect the value of shares allow diplomatic protection of shareholders.

In the *ELSI* case, the Italian authorities had taken measures against the insolvent Italian subsidiary of a US holding company. The ICJ recognized that the United States could rely on the protection of the parent company under a treaty with Italy.[48]

Most modern treaties protecting shares as an investment provide for arbitration between the investor and the host State. The issue of diplomatic protection only arises if the host State does not comply with an arbitral award (see Article 27(1) of the ICSID Convention).

A direct injury to the rights of shareholders (such as expropriation or other interference with corporate rights) gives rise to diplomatic protection (Article 12 of the ILC's Draft Articles).

The ICJ stated in the *Ahmadou Sadio Diallo* case:

The exercise by a State of diplomatic protection on behalf of a natural or legal person, who is *associé* or shareholder, having its nationality, seeks to engage the responsibility of another State for an injury caused to that person by an internationally wrongful act committed by

[46] ICJ *Barcelona Traction, Light and Power Company (Belgium v Spain)* [1970] ICJ Rep 3 para 46.
[47] ICJ *Barcelona Traction, Light and Power Company (Belgium v Spain)* [1970] ICJ Rep 3 paras 64ff.
[48] ICJ *Elettronica Sicula SpA (ELSI) (United States of America v Italy)* [1989] ICJ Rep 15.

that State. Ultimately, this is no more than the diplomatic protection of a natural or legal person as defined by Article 1 of the ILC draft Articles; what amounts to the internationally wrongful act, in the case of *associés* or shareholders, is the violation by the respondent State of their direct rights in relation to a legal person, direct rights that are defined by the domestic law of that State, as accepted by both Parties, moreover. On this basis, diplomatic protection of the direct rights of *associés* of a SPRL [*sociéte privée à resonsabilité limitée*] or shareholders of a public limited company is not to be regarded as an exception to the general legal régime of diplomatic protection for natural or legal persons, as derived from customary international law.[49]

This distinction between direct and indirect injuries to foreign shareholders has lost much of its relevance, as far as investment treaties also protect corporations controlled directly or indirectly by foreign investors.

6. National Economic Law and the Jurisdiction of States

The national regulation of economic activities presents a broad range of issues. The concept of jurisdiction and its basis from an international perspective must be defined. The territorial scope of application of national laws is in need for clarification. A recurring theme is the exercise of national jurisdiction with extraterritorial effect.

(a) Jurisdiction

The notion of 'jurisdiction' is colourful and vague. The exercise of jurisdiction may take the form of legislation, executive regulation, or administrative orders which allow, enjoin, or prohibit certain behaviour or govern the status of persons (jurisdiction to prescribe). It may also refer to the judicial settlement of disputes (jurisdiction to adjudicate). Finally, the exercise of jurisdiction may contain the enforcement of legal standards (jurisdiction to enforce). The following discussion refers to prescriptive rules which govern or otherwise affect economic activities.

(b) Regulatory competition among States

In the modern world of business, most transboundary business transactions affect the regulatory interests of more than one State. An extensive understanding of territorial jurisdiction (as to the domestic effects of foreign activities) and the regulation of activities abroad on the basis of personal jurisdiction (as to the conduct of a State's own nationals abroad) catalyse 'regulatory competition' among States. Economic activities being subject to more than one municipal law may bring about a 'legal fragmentation' of economic relations which become subject to more than

---

[49] ICJ *Diallo Case* (*Republic of Guinea v Democratic Republic of the Congo*) (Preliminary objections) [2007] ICJ Rep 582 para 64.

one municipal legal order. The merger of major corporations with a global presence is often subject to the scrutiny of two or even more antitrust laws.

Due to the often high transaction costs, competing regulatory claims of two or more States are significant obstacles to world trade. This fosters the interest in harmonizing the rules for the conflict of laws (which determine the relevant national law to be applied in the case) as well as in harmonizing substantive law. In an ideal scenario, a claimant would always end up with the same law applied to his case no matter which State's court decides.

As regards the way jurisdiction is exercised, municipal law should at least consider the legitimate interests of other States instead of insisting on the one-sided enforcement of its own legal standards. However, States and their courts tend to impose their regulatory standards whenever a significant national interest is served by doing so. Especially in the case of applying or not national economic law, the will to fully implement national standards all too often trumps the willingness to make concessions to international comity.

(c) The territorial scope of legislation

As a rule, the laws of a State only apply to its own territory. However, the national regulation of economic activities often has effects which reach beyond a State's boundaries. The 'extraterritorial' application of domestic laws is a central and controversial topic of the international economic order. This extraterritorial reach of national law refers to its application to activities partly or entirely carried out abroad or to the status of persons or things domiciled or located in foreign territory.[50] Extraterritorial application of laws is a common feature of all legal systems, albeit in varying degrees.

How far the implications of extraterritorial legislation may reach can be seen in the case of the US company Paypal, an internet-based service provider offering a payment mechanism for internet shopping. Paypal offers a popular payment method, guaranteeing the confidential treatment of payment information and refund in case of a failed transaction. In 2011, Paypal contacted its partners in Germany and elsewhere in Europe and called upon them to stop selling Cuban

---

[50] American Law Institute, *Restatement of the Law Third, The Foreign Relations Law of the United States* (1987) vol 1, 230ff; J Basedow, 'Private Law Effects of Foreign Export Controls, An International Case Report' (1984) 27 GYIL 109; HG Maier, 'Extraterritorial Jurisdiction at a Crossroads—An Intersection between Public and Private International Law' (1982) 76 AJIL 280; FA Mann, 'The Doctrine of Jurisdiction in International Law' (1964 I) 111 RdC 1; FA Mann, 'The Doctrine of International Jurisdiction Revisited after Twenty Years' (1984) 186 RdC 9; KM Meessen, 'Antitrust Jurisdiction Under Customary International Law' (1984) 78 AJIL 783; KM Meessen (ed), *Extraterritorial Jurisdiction in Theory and Practice* (Martinus Nijhoff Publishers 1996); F Rigaux, 'Droit économique et conflits de souveraineté' (1988) 52 RabelsZ 104; C Ryngaert, *Jurisdiction in International Law* (2nd edn, OUP 2015); T Schultz, 'Carving up the Internet: Jurisdiction, Legal Orders, and the Private/Public International Law Interface' (2004) 1 EJIL 799; PM Roth, 'Reasonable Extraterritoriality: Correcting the "Balance of Interests"' (1992) 41 ICLQ 245.

products such as cigars, if they wished to stay in business with Paypal. With this action, Paypal tried to implement a US trade embargo against Cuba.

For many years, the Congress and the courts of the United States have acted as the main protagonists in extending domestic legislation to transactions or other activities carried out in foreign countries, but affecting regulatory or other jurisdictional interests of the United States. Some of this legislation caused great controversy and conflicts with other affected States.

A very controversial case of an extraterritorial application of national law is the attempt of the US-American legislator to sanction investments of foreign nationals in Cuba. The Cuban Liberty and Democratic Solidarity (Libertad) Act (mostly referred to as Helms–Burton Act) of 1996[51] was meant to protect the interests of US-American nationals (including Cubans in US exile) who were expropriated by the Castro regime by providing sanctions against foreign investors building on these expropriations. The Act should also destabilize the Cuban communist system by countervailing the stimulating effects of foreign investments. Under international law such a sanction regime may not target nationals of other States merely for investing in confiscated land.

In the aforementioned Paypal case, the US company's demand that its European business partners disrupt the sale of Cuban products is nothing but the attempt of a private actor to enforce US legislation banning trade with Cuba. This demand pressed business partners to disregard the European 'Blocking Regulation',[52] which prohibits compliance with the Helms–Burton Act in Europe. Paypal, therefore, may be sanctioned under EU law.[53] This conflict highlights the problems associated with a 'globalization' of laws once more.

Another example of the extraterritorial application of national law is the so-called Iran and Libya Sanctions Act of 1996[54] (since 2006 the Iran Sanctions Act). This Act is directed against commercial dealings with Iran (and previously with Libya) and also restricts activities of foreign nationals who have neither personal nor territorial connections with the United States. The original Act extended until 31 December 2011. The Iran sanctions regime was, however, continued and expanded by the Comprehensive Iran Sanctions, Accountability, and Divestment Act of 2010 (CISADA). The CISADA broadened the extraterritorial scope of application of economic sanctions against Iran to an unparalleled extent. The US executive has taken steps to mitigate conflicts with the European Union and other States. Therefore, the US Congress has allowed the US President to waive sanctions on a case-by-case basis. Since 2008, no sanctions under the US sanctions regime have been applied to any non-US company. After the 2015 agreement on Iran's

---

[51] AF Lowenfeld, 'Agora: The Cuban Liberty and Democratic Solidarity (Libertad) Act' (1996) 90 AJIL 419; JL Snyder and S Agostini, 'New U.S. Legislation to Deter Investment in Cuba' (1996) 30 JWT 37; B Stern, 'Can the United States Set Rules for the World?' (1997) 31 JWT 5.
[52] Council Regulation (EC) No 2271/96 of 22 November 1996 protecting against the effects of the extra-territorial application of legislation adopted by a third country, and actions based thereon or resulting therefrom [1996] OJ L309/1.
[53] See B Fuest, 'Die Bank gewinnt' *Die Welt* (Berlin, 30 July 2011) 15.
[54] (1996) 35 ILM 1273.

nuclear programme (Joint Comprehensive Plan of Action), the United States lifted nuclear-related sanctions on Iran. This measure also affects certain sanctions under the CISADA. The extraterritorial application of laws can conflict with the regulatory interests of other States. These conflicts are rooted in the colliding spheres of sovereignty between States, that is in competing claims to jurisdiction as to the same set of facts.

These conflicts may, in extreme cases, culminate in the enactment of 'blocking statutes' (which order non-compliance with the extraterritorial legislation or non-recognition of judgments) or 'claw-back statutes' (ordering restitution of benefits conferred by extraterritorial legislation) by other States.

As already mentioned, the European Union responded to the Helms–Burton Act with 'blocking' and 'claw-back legislation'.[55] Such legislation has become a common instrument to protect national interests since the 1980s. In 1980, the United Kingdom enacted section 6 of the Protection of Trading Interests Act which was meant to protect defendants having paid multiple damages due to an overseas judgment and provided for recovery of these damages (it was therefore often referred to as the 'British Clawback Statute').[56] The 'blocking regulation' of the European Union responding to US legislation intended to block the recognition and enforcement of American sanctions inside the European Union. The Regulation also applies to the Iran and Libya Sanctions Act of 1996. The Regulation serves as an illustrative example for the clash of diverting economic and political interests. Core passages of the Regulation provide:

THE COUNCIL OF THE EUROPEAN UNION,
[…]
Whereas a third country has enacted certain laws, regulations, and other legislative instruments which purport to regulate activities of natural and legal persons under the jurisdiction of the Member State;

Whereas by their extra-territorial application such laws, regulations and other legislative instruments violate international law and impede the attainment of the aforementioned objectives;

Whereas such laws, including regulations and other legislative instruments, and actions based thereon or resulting therefrom affect or are likely to affect the established legal order and have adverse effects on the interests of the Community and the interests of natural and legal persons exercising rights under the Treaty establishing the European Community;

Whereas, under these exceptional circumstances, it is necessary to take action at Community level to protect the established legal order, the interests of the Community and the interests of the said natural and legal persons, in particular by removing, neutralising, blocking or otherwise countering the effects of the foreign legislation concerned; […] HAS ADOPTED THIS REGULATION:

---

[55] Council Regulation (EC) No 2271/96 of 22 November 1996 protecting against the effects of the extra-territorial application of legislation adopted by a third country, and actions based thereon or resulting therefrom [1996] OJ L 309/1.

[56] See JE Neuhaus, 'Power to Reverse Foreign Judgements: The British Clawback Statute Under International Law' (1981) 81 Colum L Rev 1097.

Article 1

This Regulation provides protection against and counteracts the effects of the extraterritorial application of the laws specified in the Annex of this Regulation, including regulations and other legislative instruments, and of actions based thereon or resulting therefrom, where such application affects the interests of persons, referred to in Article 11, engaging in international trade and/or the movement of capital and related commercial activities between the Community and third countries.

Acting in accordance with the relevant provisions of the Treaty and notwithstanding the provisions of Article 7 (c), the Council may add or delete laws to or from the Annex to this Regulation. [...]

ANNEX: LAWS, REGULATIONS AND OTHER LEGISLATIVE INSTRUMENTS

(1)referred to in Article 1

COUNTRY: UNITED STATES OF AMERICA ACTS

1. 'National Defense Authorization Act for Fiscal Year 1993', Title XVII "Cuban Democracy Act 1992", sections 1704 and 1706' [...].
2. 'Cuban Liberty and Democratic Solidarity Act of 1996' [...].
3. 'Iran and Libya Sanctions Act of 1996' [...].

Extraterritorial application of laws is an important issue when transactions affect the economy of two or more States and no international regulatory regime is in place. It plays a very relevant role in competition (antitrust) law.[57] The United States and the European Union have frequently applied their competition rules to mergers between foreign companies or restrictive practices carried out abroad in cases where these have repercussions on their own markets.

In 2001, the European Commission went as far as entirely prohibiting the merger between two large US corporations, General Electric and Honeywell (as being incompatible with the common market by strengthening an already dominant position in the market for certain jet engines), after the US antitrust authorities had approved the merger.[58]

Extraterritoriality may (egoistically) be driven by national interests or (altruistically) by the concern for global commons or other interests of the international community (such as human rights or biodiversity).

Relying on the protection of the climate as an international concern, the European Union subjected national flights to and from European airports to its scheme of greenhouse gas emission allowances (which can be traded) which imposes considerable costs on non-European as well as European airlines. The calculation of the necessary emission certificates also includes the air-route over the high seas and third countries. In the case *Air Transport Association of America* the European Court of Justice rejected the argument that the EU regime amounts to an excessive extension of its jurisdiction to the high seas and foreign territory and based its extraterritorial application on the territorial link.[59] It is at least arguable

---

[57] DJ Gerber, *Global Competition: Law, Markets, and Globalization* (OUP 2010).

[58] Decision 2004/13/EC of 3 July 2001 [2004] OJ L148/57, confirmed by the Court of First Instance ECJ Case T-210/01 *General Electric Co v Commission of the European Communities* [2005] ECR II-5575; see DJ Gerber, *Global Competition: Law, Markets, and Globalization* (OUP 2010) 95.

[59] ECJ Case C-366/10 *Air Transport Association of America* [2011] ECR I-13755; see B Mayer, 'Case Note' (2012) 49 CML Rev 1113.

that the jurisdiction based on this territorial link must be exercised in terms of proportionality (or reasonableness) and, therefore, cannot extend to the air space outside the European Union without considering clean air as a resource to be shared with other countries. In particular, the governments of the United States, China, and Russia severely criticized the extraterritoriality of the EU emission trade legislation.

The domestic rules on economic activities have mainly a territorial dimension. Their application usually presupposes a nexus of a business transaction to the territory of a certain State. With certain limitations it can also be sufficient that the business transaction merely shows certain effects in that State without directly taking place in its territory.

The most recent blocking order directed against the effects doctrine applied by the EU was ordered by the Russian President in conjunction with the investigations into Gazprom's business activities by the European Commission. In 2011 the European Commission began antitrust investigations in the natural gas sector with unannounced inspections at Gazprom and several other companies. Following the decision of the European Commission to open antitrust proceedings against Gazprom in September 2012,[60] the Russian President signed an executive order on Measures to Protect Russian Federation Interests in Russian Legal Entities' Foreign Economic Activities.[61] Under this order, open joint stock companies, which are on the list of strategic enterprises and strategic joint stock companies,[62] are not allowed to give information to agencies of foreign governments or international organizations and other unions of foreign governments without consent by the Russian Federal Government. The disposal of shares in foreign companies, the right to carry out business in foreign countries, and immovable property located abroad and the amendment of contracts with a foreign counterparts also require prior consent by the Russian Government.[63] The blocking order determines that no consent shall be given if the action in question might harm the economic interests of the Russian Federation.[64] The hastiness the blocking order has been drafted suggests that it aims specifically at the antitrust proceedings of the European Commission against Gazprom.[65] The aim of the blocking order might be to move the solution of

[60] Antitrust: Commission opens proceedings against Gazprom, European Commission Press Release IP/12/937 (4 September 2012) available at <http://europa.eu/rapid/press-release_IP-12-937_en.htm> (accessed 23 June 2016).

[61] Executive Order of the President of the Russian Federation No 1285 of 11 September 2012 on Measures to Protect Russian Federation Interests in Russian Legal Entities' Foreign Economic Activities, see for an unofficial translation M Martyniszyn, 'Legislation Blocking Antitrust Investigations and the September 2012 Russian Executive Order' (2014) 37 World Competition 103, Annex I.

[62] Executive Order of the President of the Russian Federation No 1009 of 4 August 2004 approving the List of Strategic Enterprises and Strategic Joint Stock Companies.

[63] Executive Order of the President of the Russian Federation No 1285 of 11 September 2012 on Measures to Protect Russian Federation Interests in Russian Legal Entities' Foreign Economic Activities 1. a) – c).

[64] Executive Order of the President of the Russian Federation No 1285 of 11 September 2012 on Measures to Protect Russian Federation Interests in Russian Legal Entities' Foreign Economic Activities 2.

[65] S Bennet, 'The European Commission v. Gazprom' (2014) 31 Wisconsin International Law Journal, 887 (890).

the conflict from a judicial to a political level.[66] The wide provisions of the blocking order could have the effect of subjecting decisions of the European Commission concerning the antitrust proceedings to consent of the Russian Federation.

On 22 April 2015 the European Commission sent a Statement of Objections to Gazprom concerning the alleged abuse of its dominant market position which is in breach of Article 102 TFEU and the Antitrust Regulation.[67] In the following, Gazprom has proposed talks and a settlement between the European Commission and Gazprom despite the blocking order.[68] The Russian Federation holds the majority of Gazprom. The antitrust penalty, which can be up to 10 per cent of the company's global revenue, would thus mostly hit the Russian State itself.[69]

(d) Restrictive trends

The recent case-law of the US Supreme Court has shown a clear tendency to restrict the territorial scope of US statutes. The US Supreme Court will not apply statutes with extraterritorial effects, unless the US Congress clearly expressed the intent of extraterritorial application. In *Morrison v National Australia Bank Ltd*,[70] the US Supreme Court established a general presumption against the extraterritorial application of US statutes.

Morrison is a clear 'f³ case': foreign plaintiff, foreign defendant, transaction in foreign territory. In this case, an Australian who had bought shares in an Australian bank in the Australian stock-market had sued the bank for having violated the US Securities and Exchange Act of 1934, because the management of an affiliate company incorporated in Florida supposedly had manipulated the valuation of various assets in the United States (Florida) and, in doing so, indirectly the valuation of the Australian mother bank and its shares (which were also traded in the United States).

The US Supreme Court formulated the presumption that the US Congress only intended to give application to its statutes within the United States: 'When a statute gives no clear indication of an extraterritorial application, it has none.'[71]

---

[66] Ibid.

[67] Antitrust: Commission sends Statement of Objections to Gazprom for alleged abuse of dominance on Central and Eastern European gas supply markets, European Commission Press Release IP/15/4828 (22 April 2015) available at <http://europa.eu/rapid/press-release_IP-15-4828_en.htm> (accessed 23 June 2016); see also Antitrust: Commission sends Statement of Objections to Gazprom—Factsheet, European Commission—Factsheet MEMO/15/4829 (22 April 2015) available at <http://europa.eu/rapid/press-release_MEMO-15-4829_en.htm> (accessed 23 June 2016).

[68] G Steinhauser, 'Gazprom "Still Pushing for EU Antitrust Settlement"' Wall Street Journal (23 July 2015).

[69] S Bennet, 'The European Commission v. Gazprom' (2014) 31 Wisconsin International Law Journal, 887.

[70] US Supreme Court *Robert Morrison et al, Petitioners v National Australia Bank Ltd et al* (2010) 49 ILM 1220; see for further information, PB Stephan, 'Introductory Note to U.S. Supreme Court: Morrison v Australia Nat'l Bank Ltd' (2010) 49 ILM 1217.

[71] US Supreme Court *Robert Morrison et al, Petitioners v National Australia Bank Ltd et al* (2010) 49 ILM 1220 at III.A.; if the statute is not found extraterritorial, a court needs to examine the statute's 'focus' to determine whether the case involves a domestic application of the statute, US Supreme Court *RJR Nabisco Inc, et al v European Community, et al* 579 US___(2016).

As a consequence, the US Securities and Exchange Act of 1934 only applies to manipulations affecting the value of shares which were actually bought in the United States:

The Exchange Act's focus is not on the place where the deception originated, but on purchases and sales of securities in the United States. Section 10(b) applies only to transactions in securities listed on domestic exchanges and domestic transactions in other securities.[72]

In this case, the US Supreme Court also considered *amicus curiae* briefs of foreign industrial associations in favour of non-extraterritoriality.[73]

The *Morrison* ruling severely limits the chances of foreign claims brought before US courts in cases with aggregated foreign elements ('f³ cases').[74] The relevance of the *Morrison* judgment lies more in limiting the scope of statutorily protected interests (in this case the transparency of the US stock market and its protection against deceptive practices) than in restraining extraterritorial application in general.[75] Thus, the ruling does not affect the extraterritorial application of US statutes to protected domestic interests, particularly in antitrust law, where the Congressional intent is clear.

(e) The law of foreign trade and foreign economic relations

Municipal foreign trade law regulates the cross-border movement of goods and services from the inter-State perspective. It does not address the commercial relations between private actors.[76] The broader foreign economic relations law includes the regulation of investments and other capital flows, such as restrictions of foreign investments in strategic sectors like ports or arms and aircraft production.

The 'Commercial Policy' of the European Union (Articles 206f, 215 TFEU) covers trade in goods and services with third countries as well as intellectual property and investment protection, but not the regulation of capital flows (EU monetary policy) or restriction of investments in specific areas (domain of the EU Member States).

The most important instruments of foreign trade law are custom duties, import and export restrictions (prohibitions, prior approval, and quantitative restrictions on imports and exports), and export subsidies. Whether the use of those instruments is desirable or economically reasonable, to a large extent depends on the perspective. Import tariffs, for example, have the advantage of greater transparency over subsidies from an external point of view. On the other hand, such tariffs

---

[72] US Supreme Court *Robert Morrison et al, Petitioners v National Australia Bank Ltd et al* (2010) 49 ILM 1220 Syllabus.

[73] US Supreme Court *Robert Morrison et al, Petitioners v National Australia Bank Ltd et al* (2010) 49 ILM 1220 opinion by Justice Scalia at IV.B.

[74] For an analysis of the legal status quo up to *Morrison*, see JH Knox, 'A Presumption Against Extrajurisdictionality' (2010) 104 AJIL 351.

[75] Similarly, JH Knox 'A Presumption Against Extrajurisdictionality' (2010) 104 AJIL 351.

[76] For a current overview, see RH Folsom, MW Gordon, JA Spanogle, PL Fitzgerald, and MP Van Alstine, *International Business Transactions* (11th edn, West Academic Publishing 2012) 417.

affect pricing and consumption and thus may distort competition just as much as subsidies.

The foreign trade law of the United States follows a flexible structure.[77] The US constitution vests the Congress with the power to 'regulate Commerce with foreign Nations' (Article I, section 8, clause 3). The US Congress passed a number of Acts regulating US foreign trade, often with far-reaching control mechanisms.[78]

European foreign trade law is based on the principle of freedom of transbound-ary economic transactions on goods, capital, and other economic transactions with third parties.[79] In the European Union, EU measures taken under the commercial policy have shaped trade relations with other countries. EU Member States may regulate foreign trade only insofar as the TFEU provides exceptions (eg Articles 346 (1)(b), 347 TFEU) or as secondary EU law authorizes national regulation.

An important feature of foreign trade law is the restriction of export of arms and other strategic materials such as goods, which usually serve civilian (commercial) purposes, but can also have military applications (dual-use goods).

In the United States, the regulation of export controls (eg the Export Administration Regulations administered by the Department of Commerce's Bureau of Industry and Security) is based on specific legislation like the Arms Export Control Act and on emergency powers of the President. In the European Union, a regulation governs the export of dual-use items.[80] The Wassenaar Arrangement on Export Controls for Conventional Arms and Dual-Use Goods and Technologies (1996) replaced the COCOM Regime of the NATO States. It now has about 40 participating States including the Russian Federation and South Africa.

Foreign trade law rests mostly, but not exclusively, on territoriality. On the basis of personal jurisdiction, many States regulate the actions of their nationals abroad, especially in the context of the development and production of nuclear, biological, or chemical weapons in other countries.

Occasionally, States follow a very extensive understanding of territorial or personal jurisdiction and submit even foreign subsidiaries of national corporations to export controls.

The so-called 'pipeline embargo of the United States against the Soviet Union'[81] is illustrative of such an extensive control regime. Targeting the dealings between Western European States and the Soviet Union on the supply of Russian Gas and the delivery of Western pipeline equipment in times of the Cold War, the

---

[77] See ibid 781ff.

[78] Export Administration Act of 1979 (EAA) 50 USCA App § 2401ff; Arms Export Control Act (AECA) 22 USCA § 2778; International Emergency Economic Powers Act (IEEPA) 50 USCA § 1701ff; Trading with the Enemy Act (TWEA) 50 USCA App § 1.

[79] The Regulation (EEC) No 2603/69 of the Council of 20 December 1969 establishing common rules for exports [1969] OJ L324/25 recognizes the freedom of export from the EU (Article 1). Similarly, Council Regulation (EC) No 3285/94 of 22 December 1994 on the common rules for imports [1994] OJ L349/53 establishes the general freedom of import into the EU (Article 1(2)).

[80] Council Regulation (EC) No 428/2009 of 5 May 2009 setting up a Community regime for the control of exports, transfer, brokering, and transit of dual-use items [2009] OJ L 134/1.

[81] AV Lowe, 'International Law Issues Arising in the "Pipeline Dispute": The British Position' (1984) 27 GYIL 54; DF Vagts, 'The Pipeline Controversy: An American Viewpoint' (1984) 27 GYIL 38.

US Government prohibited (subject to prior authorization) the export of technical equipment for the transport of oil and gas which was based on US technology. With reference to the export of goods not originating in the United States, the US control regime did not only extend to US nationals (individuals and companies), but also to foreign subsidiaries of US corporations. Thus, the hard sanctions for an infringement of the US regulations affected even companies incorporated under foreign laws, if only controlled by a US firm. In the so-called *Sensor* case, the Dutch affiliate of a US company had previously agreed to deliver pipeline equipment to a French contractor. The equipment was supposed to be destined for use in a Soviet pipeline project. The Dutch company refused delivery and invoked the US control and sanctions regime. However, a Dutch court rejected this argument and decided in favour of the French contractor.[82] The Dutch court qualified the expansive US regulation and the sanctions for non-compliance as a violation of international law. The Dutch court did not even consider treating the US sanctions as a de facto impediment to contract performance. This case demonstrates that the expansive exercise of jurisdiction depends on the recognition of the other affected States to be effective.

In a scenario like the *Sensor* case, international law (the prohibition of intervention into internal affairs of other States) would not allow an export prohibition addressed to a foreign company, if the only connection of this company to the regulating State is the control by a national corporation. Another possible link might be seen in the 'nationality' of targeted goods stemming from the regulating State. Such a link would be particularly substantial if the export of sensitive high technology were at stake. Finally, it has been discussed in context of the 'pipeline embargo' whether the legitimate application of a foreign export control law can be based on the explicit submission of the foreign company to that law, for example in the form of a voluntary declaration. If a State can entirely prohibit the export of certain goods, it may certainly submit the export of these goods to certain conditions and extend such a submission to future export controls. Submission to the foreign trade law of the State of origin must be seen as a sufficient link for the application of export regulation rules under international law. The recognition of such a submission to foreign laws by other States would depend on whether their laws allow such an autonomous choice.

The foreign trade law of most countries vests the executive with extensive regulatory powers as to the restrictions of import and export. Judicial review of such executive regulation, if available at all, is usually exercised with great restraint.[83] This attitude is due to the highly discretionary character of import and export restrictions which involve sensitive political choices. On the other hand, the excessive

---

[82] President of the District Court of The Hague (1983) 22 ILM 66.

[83] DA Pinkert and TO Blanford, 'Judicial Review of Export Control Determination' (2001) 26 Brooklyn J Int'l L 843; see also the series of decisions in *Bernstein v US Department of Commerce* analysed in JJ Browder, 'Encryption Source Code and the First Amendment' (2000) 40 Jurimetrics 431–44.

judicial restraint may well end up in allowing the exercise of vast discretionary powers for partisan objectives and protectionist policies.

(f) General principles of conflict of laws

Cross-border economic transactions and activities touch the regulatory interests of more than one State. Territoriality and personal links may trigger the exercise of jurisdiction of two or even more States. For competent national courts (or administrative authorities) the question arises, whether their own municipal law or a foreign law has to be applied. The answer follows from the conflict of laws rules of the State of the forum (ie the State of the court that hears a case). Conflict of laws rules usually determine the applicable law in relations between private actors (therefore, in some jurisdictions, the conflict of laws rules are called 'private international law', whilst in other systems this term has a much broader meaning, including substantive rules for cross-border transactions and situations).[84]

A classic example for a conflict of laws situation is the case of *Maharanee of Baroda v Wildenstein*.[85] In this case, the plaintiff, a French resident, had bought a painting from an international art dealer, who was also resident in France. After the painting turned out to likely be a fake, the plaintiff sued for the rescission of the contract, choosing English courts (to secure certain procedural advantages). The plaintiff served proceedings while the defendant was on a visit to England. After assuming jurisdiction, the English Court of Appeal had to decide which law was applicable to the dispute. The latter question is governed by the conflict of laws rules of the State of the forum. Under the English conflict of laws rules, contracts then were subject to the law with the closest connection to the contract, in this case the law of France.

Conflict of laws rules, however, do not only exist in respect of private transactions, but also for administrative law and also criminal law.

The conflict of laws rules determine whether a contract concluded by one of the State's own nationals in a foreign country with a foreign national is 'governed' by the own municipal law of the forum State or whether the dispute has to be settled by the rules of one of the other legal systems involved. Conflict of laws rules merely determine the law to be applied without affecting the preliminary issue of jurisdiction (which relates to the power of the courts of one particular State to decide on the merits of a given case).

Sometimes, conflict of laws rules do not refer to contractual or other relations between private parties, but rather to the regulation of public interests, for example in connection with expropriations or export prohibitions.

---

[84] E Gottschalk, R Michaels, G Ruhl, and J von Hein (eds), *Conflict of Laws in a Globalized World* (CUP 2011); CMV Clarkson and J Hill, *The Conflict of Laws* (4th edn, OUP 2011); D McClean and VR Abou-Nigm, *Morris—The Conflict of Laws* (8th edn, Sweet & Maxwell 2012); A Briggs, *The Conflict of Laws* (3rd edn, OUP 2013).
[85] The English Court of Appeal *Maharanee of Baroda v Wildenstein* [1972] 2 QB 283.

In the *Sensor* case before a Dutch Court,[86] the Dutch conflict of laws rules determined whether or not the US embargo regulation, from the Dutch perspective, affected the performance of a contract on targeted goods between the Dutch subsidiary of a US corporation and a French company so as to relieve the Dutch company of its contractual obligation to deliver.

Foreign public law usually does not lend itself to be 'applied' in the same way as foreign private law (with its rules of contract, tort, or company law). Whilst private laws reconcile the different interests of private parties involved, public law directly relates to the exercise of powers conferred on the State. The 'application' of foreign public law results in the forum State's own sovereignty deferring to sovereign choices of another State. When giving effect to the public laws of another State, courts usually do not enforce foreign rules, but merely recognize certain legal effects of the foreign act in question.

When applying or otherwise deferring to foreign laws, each State insists on respecting fundamental principles and rules of its own legal order. This core of rules and normative values constitutes the 'public order' or *ordre public* as the ensemble of sovereign choices that must not be undermined by the application of foreign private law or the recognition of foreign acts of State.

7. Criteria for Exercising Jurisdiction: Legitimating Links

The exercise of jurisdiction must rest on a sufficient link with the State (unless the State legitimately pursues a concern of the entire international community under the principle of universality). In this respect, the reasoning of the Permanent Court of International Justice in the famous *Lotus* case (1927),[87] which allowed extraterritorial jurisdiction unless it violates a specific prohibition, is not valid any more. In the absence of a legitimizing link, the exercise of jurisdiction with respect to actions taking place in the territory of other States or with respect to activities of foreign nationals would violate the principle of non-intervention in the internal affairs of other States.[88]

---

[86] See Section 6(e) in this Chapter.

[87] PCIJ *France v Turkey* PCIJ Rep Series A No 10, 18–19: '[...] [J]urisdiction [...] cannot be exercised by a State outside its territory except by virtue of a permissive rule derived from international custom or from a convention. It does not, however, follow that international law prohibits a State from exercising jurisdiction in its own territory, in respect of any case which relates to acts which have taken place abroad, and in which it cannot rely on some permissive rule of international law. Such a view would only be tenable if international law contained a general prohibition to States to extend the application of their laws and the jurisdiction of their courts to persons, property, and acts outside their territory, and if, as exception to this general prohibition, it allowed States to do so in certain specific cases. But this is certainly not the case under international law as it stands at present. Far from laying down a general prohibition to the effect that States may not extend the application of their laws and the jurisdiction of their courts to persons, property, and acts outside their territory, it leaves them in this respect a wide measure of discretion which is only limited in certain cases by prohibitive rules.' The circumstances of this case, the collision of a French ship with a Turkish vessel causing loss of life onboard of the latter clearly provided sufficient links with Turkey legitimating the exercise of criminal jurisdiction.

[88] For a general analysis of the problems of jurisdiction, see BH Oxman, 'Jurisdiction of States' in R Wolfrum (ed), *The Max Planck Encyclopedia of Public International Law* (OUP 2012) vol VI, 546; for

In practice, the most important links with a State which legitimize the exercise of its jurisdiction rest on the principle of territoriality and the principle of personality.

The influential Restatement (Third) of the Law (Foreign Relations Law of the United States), elaborated by the American Law Institute,[89] provides an authoritative list of criteria relevant for the exercise of jurisdiction. The Restatement reflects internationally recognized standards when it defines the basis of jurisdiction in § 402:

Subject to § 403, a state has jurisdiction to prescribe law with respect to
(1) (a) conduct that, wholly or in substantial part, takes place within its territory;
    (b) the status of persons, or interests in things, present within its territory;
    (c) conduct outside its territory that has or is intended to have substantial effect within its territory
(2) the activities, interests, status, or relations of its nationals outside as well as within its territory; and
(3) certain conduct outside its territory by persons not its nationals that is directed against the security of the state or against a limited class of other state interests.

(a) Principle of territoriality and the 'effects doctrine'

According to the territoriality principle, the legitimizing link is the location of a person or an object or, alternatively, the performance of an action or the occurrence of effects in the territory of the State which exercising jurisdiction. Jurisdiction based merely on the effects of actions on a State's territory carried out abroad ('effects doctrine') is the most important factor in the extraterritorial application of laws.

The so-called 'effects doctrine' is the most important among the driving forces behind the exercise of jurisdiction over business transactions and other activities in foreign countries. The effects doctrine establishes no jurisdictional category of its own, but is an expansive version of the territoriality principle. According to the effects doctrine, a State has jurisdiction over activities, which are not carried out within the State, but have significant effects in the State's own territory. In the modern world of globalized economic transactions, an unrestrained understanding of the effects doctrine would result in a too broad concept of the legitimate exercise of jurisdiction, with a very high potential for conflicts.

The effects doctrine was applied by the Permanent Court of International Justice in the famous *Lotus* case (1927), concerning Turkey's exercise of criminal jurisdiction over the navigation of a French ship, which had collided with a Turkish ship:

[I]t is certain that the courts of many countries, even of countries which have given their criminal legislation a strictly territorial character, interpret criminal law in the sense

---

the problem of intervention in the context of jurisdiction, see P Kunig, 'Intervention, Prohibition of' in R Wolfrum (ed), *The Max Planck Encyclopedia of Public International Law* (OUP 2012) vol VI, 289.

[89] American Law Institute, 'Restatement (Third) of the Law, The Foreign Relations Law of the United States' (1987) vol 1 § 402.

that offences, the authors of which at the moment of commission are in the territory of another State, are nevertheless to be regarded as having been committed in the national territory, if one of the constituent elements of the offence, and more especially its effects, have taken place there. French courts have, in regard to a variety of situations, given decisions sanctioning this way of interpreting the territorial principle. Again, the Court does not know of any cases in which governments have protested against the fact that the criminal law of some country contained a rule to this effect or that the courts of a country construed their criminal law in this sense. Consequently, once it is admitted that the effects of the offence were produced on the Turkish vessel, it becomes impossible to hold that there is a rule of international law which prohibits Turkey from prosecuting Lieutenant Demons because of the fact that the author of the offence was on board the French ship.[90]

The influence of the effects doctrine is particularly marked in the competition (antitrust) law of many States and its extraterritorial application. US courts have applied US antitrust law to cases with strong links to foreign States.[91]

Similarly, the European Commission and the European Court of Justice are not reluctant to apply and enforce EU competition law whenever restrictive practices or mergers may distort competition in the internal market, whether the source lies inside or outside the European Union.

In the *Wood Pulp* case, the European Commission fined non-EU producers of wood pulp for concluding restrictive price agreements. These price agreements should also extend to the European market. The European Court of Justice considered the application of EU competition law to be justified by the territoriality principle, because the price agreements were intended to take effect within the EU territory as well or at least they factually had such an effect.[92]

In the case *Boeing/McDonnell*, the European Commission, after a vehement controversy with the US Government, submitted the merger of two American airlines to EU competition law as far as it affected the European market. In the end, the Commission allowed the merger, albeit only subject to rigorous conditions.[93] The European Commission completely forbade the acquisition of the US company Honeywell by the US company General Electric because of restraining effects on the competition on the European market.[94] In both cases, the US antitrust authorities had already allowed the mergers to go ahead.

It can be said that under current customary international law, the effects doctrine is limited to cases of a 'substantial, direct and foreseeable effect'[95] on the territory of the regulating State. An example of this restrictive approach is the American Foreign Trade Antitrust Improvements Act (FTAIA) which, as a rule, excludes

---

[90] PCIJ *France v Turkey* PCIJ Rep Series A No 10, 23.
[91] See *United States v Aluminium Co of America (ALCOA)* 148 F.2d 416 (2d Cir 1945).
[92] ECJ Joined Cases 89/85, 104/85, 114/85, 116/85, 117/85, 125/85, 126/85, 127/85, 128/85, 129/85 *Wood-Pulp* [1988] ECR 5193.
[93] [1997] OJ L336/16.   [94] See Section 6(c) in this Chapter and Ch XXIX.2.
[95] American Law Institute, 'Restatement (Third) of the Foreign Relations Law of the United States' (1987) vol 1, § 402(1)(c); Institut de Droit International, 'resolution on multinational companies' [1977-II] Annuaire 343, Article VI(1).

transactions with foreign countries from the application of US competition law. The Sherman Act (§ 6a)[96] provides:

Sections 1 to 7 of this title shall not apply to conduct involving trade or commerce (other than import trade or import commerce) with foreign nations unless—
(1) such conduct has a direct, substantial, and reasonably foreseeable effect—
   (A) on trade or commerce which is not trade or commerce with foreign nations, or on import trade or import commerce with foreign nations; or
   (B) on export trade or export commerce with foreign nations, of a person engaged in such trade or commerce in the United States; and
(2) such effect gives rise to a claim under the provisions of sections 1 to 7 of this title, other than this section.

(b) Principle of personality

Under the personality principle, nationality or the domicile (residence) of an individual or the management seat of a corporation serve as a legitimizing link.

The personality principle, as a rule, does not support the exercise of jurisdiction over foreign subsidiaries of national corporations. The establishment of a subsidiary entity with a legal personality of its own under foreign law cuts off the connection to the home State of the holding company in terms of personal jurisdiction. Hence, in the *Sensor* case,[97] the extension of the US export embargo to foreign subsidiaries of US enterprises met with well-founded criticism in Europe.

(c) Principle of control

In exceptional cases, the exercise of jurisdiction can be justified merely by reference to the (monetary) control of a company over an affiliate company. Even though this form of jurisdiction is always problematic and often leads to regulatory conflicts, there are certain criteria which have a legitimizing effect. Those criteria are mirrored in § 414 of the Restatement (Third) of the Foreign Relations Law of the United States:

(1) Subject to §§ 403 and 441, a state may exercise jurisdiction to prescribe for limited purposes with respect to activities of foreign branches of corporations organized under its laws.
(2) A state may not ordinarily regulate activities of corporations organized under the laws of a foreign state on the basis that they are owned or controlled by nationals of the regulating state. However, under § 403 and subject to § 441, it may not be unreasonable for a state to exercise jurisdiction for limited purposes with respect to activities of affiliated foreign entities
   (a) by direction to the parent corporation in respect of such matters as uniform accounting, disclosure to investors, or preparation of consolidated tax returns of multinational enterprises; or

---

[96] 15 USCA § 6a.   [97] See Section 6(e) in this Chapter.

(b) by direction to either the parent or the subsidiary in exceptional cases, depending on all relevant factors, including the extent to which
  (i) the regulation is essential to implementation of a program to further a major national interest of the state exercising jurisdiction;
  (ii) the national program of which the regulation is a part can be carried out effectively only if it is applied also to foreign subsidiaries;
  (iii) the regulation conflicts or is likely to conflict with the law or policy of the state where the subsidiary is established.
(c) In the exceptional cases referred to in paragraph (b), the burden of establishing reasonableness is heavier when the direction is issued to the foreign subsidiary than when it is issued to the parent corporation.

This provision exhausts the very restrictive scope of the principle of control. As the *Sensor* case[98] illustrates, the attempt of a State to impose an embargo on foreign corporations, which are controlled by domestic companies, overstretches jurisdiction based on control.

(d) Principle of protection of national interests

Besides the territoriality and the personality principle, the principle of protection provides a connection to jurisdiction. The principle of protection allows the exercise of jurisdiction in defence of national security or other important national concerns.

(e) Principle of universality

Finally, in a very limited number of cases without any special territorial or personal link, for purposes of jurisdiction States may rely on the universality principle.[99] The universality principle grants jurisdiction in any case of genocide, piracy, slavery, and possibly certain acts of terrorism.

8. Conflicts of Jurisdiction and Possible Solutions

The extraterritorial application of national laws is one of the salient issues in international economic law. More often than not, regulatory conflicts in economic law are triggered by rules which do not directly aim at business transactions and other activities on foreign territory, but are tailored to govern domestic situations. A meanwhile classical instance is the regulation of internet contents which may come under the jurisdiction of virtually every State on the planet.[100]

---

[98] See Section 6(e) in this Chapter.
[99] L Reydams, *Universal Jurisdiction* (OUP 2004); see also BH Oxman, 'Jurisdiction of States' in R Wolfrum (ed), *The Max Planck Encyclopedia of Public International Law* (OUP 2012) vol VI, 546 paras 37ff.
[100] See Section 10 in this Chapter.

(a) Conflicts of jurisdiction

Problems of jurisdiction do not exclusively relate to the presence of relevant criteria in a given case, but also to the lack of a clear hierarchy among the legitimating links. In the face of parallel jurisdiction of two or more States, undertakings often have to adjust their behaviour and their strategies to more than one legal system. The individual actor will primarily look at the law of the State where he is performing the relevant act. Whenever another State intervenes in this relationship between territory and jurisdiction, the result will be a loss of legal certainty. The 'regulative competition' among States does not only lead to legal uncertainty, but also to problematic choices. In disputes, plaintiffs will look for the most convenient forum for the enforcement of their interests, that is the courts of the State with the law most favourable for their case ('forum shopping').

An expansive exercise of personal jurisdiction might result in a situation where one legal system commands a specific behaviour on the basis of personal jurisdiction while the State where the events occur, prohibits this behaviour on the basis of territorial jurisdiction. In consequence, the actors could be faced with an unsurmountable conflict between competing legal systems. Even where the jurisdictional competition does not culminate in conflicting sanctions, it may force actors to adjust their strategic options to two potentially very different systems of law, for example in competition (antitrust) law.

Conflicts of jurisdiction have frequently occurred between the United States and the European Union or individual European States. As examples of 'exorbitant' extraterritoriality, the anti-Cuban, anti-Libyan, and anti-Iran sanctions statutes did not only meet with strong criticism from other States but Australia, France, Canada, the United Kingdom, and Germany considered this US legislation as an encroachment upon their jurisdiction. Some of these countries reacted with so-called blocking or claw-back statutes.[101]

Conflicting regulations of internet contents have led to discordant standards. Messages covered by free speech in the United States may classify as illegal or even as criminal acts in other countries.[102] In this form of jurisdictional conflict, prescriptive and permissive rules govern the same activity. Members of the internet community (senders, service providers) have to consider the most severe (or most punitive) national standard which could be applied to them.

Apart from outspoken extraterritorial legislation, most controversies relate to the regulation of competition on the transatlantic level.[103] US antitrust law provides significantly higher fines for prohibited practices than EU competition law. In addition, certain features of the US legal system encourage claimants to go to court. Thus, plaintiffs may be granted punitive damages (in antitrust law, treble damages) far exceeding the damage actually suffered.

---

[101] See the French law No 80–538 of 11 July 1980 or the British Protection of Trading Interests Act of 1980; Ch VI 6 (b).

[102] For a comparative analysis, see E Barendt, *Freedom of Speech* (2nd edn, OUP 2007) 39–73.

[103] For a detailed analysis, see D Gerber, *Global Competition: Law, Markets and Globalization* (OUP 2010).

An exceptionally harsh form of conflict appears whenever a court of one State gives an order to the party of a dispute which it cannot comply without violating the laws or the order of a court of another State. An illustrative example of such a predicament is the *Laker* case. The British airline Laker had sued competitors (British Airways and others) in the United States alleging a crowding out in the transatlantic business in violation of US antitrust law. On the basis of a blocking statute, the British Government prohibited the submission of certain documents in the US proceedings. Some of the defendants in the case considered the US proceedings as an abuse of rights and obtained an injunction by the English Court of Appeal ordering Laker to stop the proceedings in the United States. Thereupon, US courts ordered that the defendants should not try to block the US proceedings by seeking relief before English courts. US courts assumed that both the United States and the United Kingdom had jurisdiction in the case.[104] The spiral of contradictory court orders is a very instructive example for the dilemma caused by jurisdictional conflicts. The conflict was finally mitigated by a decision of the House of Lords acknowledging the legality of initiating proceedings in the United States (from a British perspective) and overruling the blocking injunctions by the lower courts.[105] In the end, the case was resolved out of court by amicable settlement.

(b) Balancing regulatory interests

Possible solutions for the problem of jurisdictional conflicts are international agreements on the harmonization of the applicable substantive law (in the sense of a 'uniform law') or the harmonization of the conflict of laws rules. Another approach is the development of criteria restraining the exercise of jurisdiction in cases occurring on or related to foreign territory and affecting the regulatory interest of other States.

In order to avoid regulatory conflicts in cases with links to more than one State, national and international doctrine as well as courts have tried to find operable criteria for limiting the excessive exercise of jurisdiction. The objective is to balance the different interests involved in a fair and adequate manner. This approach to reconcile competing and possibly conflicting regulatory interests is similar to the duty of mutual consideration known in the international law on the relations between neighbouring States.[106] It is unclear to what extent a 'balancing test' is already required by the current state of customary international law and its rules on non-intervention. In any case, the case-law of many States and a strong tendency in the doctrine of international law suggest that the connections to the regulating State, compared with the links to other States, are sufficiently strong to qualify the exercise of jurisdiction as reasonable and plausible.

A more sophisticated model for balancing competing regulatory interests focuses on the 'reasonableness' of the exercise of jurisdiction on the basis of certain criteria.

---

[104] US Court of Appeals *Laker Airways v Sabena* 731 F.2d 909 (DC Cir 1984).
[105] House of Lords *British Airways Board v Laker Airways Ltd* [1985] AC 58.
[106] See Ch VIII.1.

The model of such a 'reasonableness test' is contained in the influential Restatement (Third) of the Law (Foreign Relations Law of the United States) of the American Law Institute. In its famous § 403, the Restatement of the Foreign Relations Law subjects the application of laws with extraterritorial effects to the standard of 'reasonableness'[107] and structures this test by a number of relevant balancing criteria. These criteria determine whether the exercise of jurisdiction is 'unreasonable' or not:

Whether exercise of jurisdiction over a person or activity is unreasonable is determined by evaluating all relevant factors, including, where appropriate:

(a) the link of the activity to the territory of the regulating state, ie, the extent to which the activity takes place within the territory, or has substantial, direct, and foreseeable effect upon or in the territory;

(b) the connections, such as nationality, residence, or economic activity, between the regulating state and the person principally responsible for the activity to be regulated, or between that state and those whom the regulation is designed to protect;

(c) the character of the activity to be regulated, the importance of regulation to the regulating state, the extent to which other states regulate such activities, and the degree to which the desirability of such regulation is generally accepted;

(d) the existence of justified expectations that might be protected or hurt by the regulation;

(e) the importance of the regulation to the international political, legal, or economic system;

(f) the extent to which the regulation is consistent with the traditions of the international system;

(g) the extent to which another state may have an interest in regulating the activity; and

(h) the likelihood of conflict with regulation by another state.

The 'reasonableness test' is a structured balance of interests underlying competing claims to jurisdiction. Unlike the principle of mutual consideration, this rather finely tuned model of balancing has not yet reached the status of customary international law. As a standard of comity among nations, it serves as a guideline for fairness with respect to other States as well as to private actors affected. Despite its welcome restraining effects, the reasonableness test suffers from the indeterminacy of its criteria and the lack of a ranking among the different criteria. In addition, it is questionable whether the judiciary is the proper branch to balance the competing interests. Under the auspices of democracy, it would be desirable that the legislative branch at least addresses the fundamental aspects. Still, if the legislative branch remains silent, it is up to the judiciary to make the necessary determinations. US courts have constantly applied the reasonableness test, regularly resulting in the application of US law.[108]

---

[107] PM Roth, 'Reasonable Extraterritoriality: Correcting the "Balance of Interests"' (1992) 41 ICLQ 245.

[108] See eg the 'classic' cases *Timberlane Lumber Co v Bank of America* 574 F. Supp 1453 (1466) (ND Cal 1983); *Mannington Mills Inc v Congoleum Corpn* 595 F.2d 1287 (3rd Cir 1979); *In Re Insurance Antitrust Litigation* 938 F.2d 919 (9th Cir 1991); for a recent analysis of the reasonableness test with extensive reference, see C Ryngaert, *Jurisdiction in International Law* (2nd edn, OUP 2015) 134–84.

Some time ago, in *Hartford Fire Insurance Co v California*, the US Supreme Court held that a balancing approach in terms of the reasonableness test should be limited to cases in which there is a direct conflict of domestic law and foreign law.[109]

This limitation ignores the fact that not only mandatory rules but also permissive rules are an expression of regulatory choices of other States which deserve respect.

9. The Application of Foreign Laws

Whenever a State wants to exercise sovereign powers to further its own economic interests or other political choices, this State's powers are confined to its own territory. The recognition of regulatory choices made by a foreign State for other countries is a matter of sovereign discretion. States are usually not willing to serve other States' interests or to enforce other States' regulatory choices. Thus, States, as a rule, refuse to enforce a foreign State's tax claims unless a treaty provides otherwise.[110]

In this context, it is important to distinguish the enforcement of a foreign rule or command from the mere recognition of its legal effects for relations among private parties. Whilst States usually do not accept any interference with their regulatory powers in their own territory, they are more receptive to the recognition of foreign sovereign acts such as expropriations already implemented on the foreign territory. This attitude responds to the respect of other States' sovereignty and the idea of reciprocity. Still, States limit the recognition of foreign sovereign acts by a core of mandatory rules protecting fundamental legislative choices and elementary societal values ('public order' or *ordre public*).

In certain situations, States deviate from the practice of non-enforceability of foreign public law. This readiness to give effects to foreign public laws relates to relations among private parties as opposed to claims of the regulating State. In private disputes, the recognition or even enforcement of foreign public law does not directly further the foreign State's own economic interests but preserves an equitable balance between the private interests involved. States will be most willing to give effect to foreign public laws if these pursue interests shared by them. If one State prohibits the export of precious and rare cultural goods, other States will be ready to recognize and even 'enforce' this prohibition, if they share the protected interest or the political choice underlying a foreign rule ('concordance of value judgments', *Wertungsgleichklang*).[111] This concordance of interests and values also have a strong ingredient of reciprocity. A country anxious to protect its cultural heritage against exports will be receptive to similar restraints of other States.

---

[109] See *Hartford Fire Insurance Co v California*, 509 US 764 (1993); for a discussion of that case see AF Lowenfeld, 'Conflict, Balancing of Interests and the Exercise of Jurisdiction to Prescribe: Reflections on the Insurance Antitrust Case' (1995) 89 AJIL 42.
[110] See eg *Peter Buchanan Ltd v McVey* [1955] AC 516.
[111] In German law Gerhard Kegel coined the term *Wertungsgleichklang*, see G Kegel and K Schurig, *Internationales Privatrecht* (9th edn, CH Beck 2004) 1098.

(a) Direct application of foreign public laws ('overriding mandatory rules')

The most deferential form to respect the interests of other States is the direct application of foreign public law.[112] Due to the exceptional character of the application of foreign public law, it requires the existence of a specific rule permitting the application. The Statute of the International Monetary Fund provides a rare instance of a treaty obligation to recognize foreign public laws in its famous Article VIII(2) *lit* b:[113]

Exchange contracts which involve the currency of any member and which are contrary to the exchange control regulations of that member maintained or imposed consistently with this Agreement shall be unenforceable in the territories of any member. In addition, members may, by mutual accord, cooperate in measures for the purpose of making the exchange control regulations of either member more effective, provided that such measures and regulations are consistent with this Agreement.

The application of foreign public laws will usually only be considered if the case has a close connection to the State the law of which is supposed to be applied. Such a rule can be found in Article 9 of Regulation (EC) No 593/2008 of the European Parliament and of the Council of 17 June 2008 on the law applicable to contractual obligations (Rome I):[114]

1. Overriding mandatory provisions are provisions the respect for which is regarded as crucial by a country for safeguarding its public interests, such as its political, social or economic organization, to such an extent that they are applicable to any situation falling within their scope, irrespective of the law otherwise applicable to the contract under this Regulation.
2. Nothing in this Regulation shall restrict the application of the overriding mandatory provisions of the law of the forum.
3. Effect may be given to the overriding mandatory provisions of the law of the country where the obligations arising out of the contract have to be or have been performed, in so far as those overriding mandatory provisions render the performance of the contract unlawful. In considering whether to give effect to those provisions, regard shall be had to their nature and purpose and to the consequences of their application or non-application.

The wording of Article 9 sets a high threshold for qualifying foreign law as such an 'overriding mandatory provision'. Only provisions which are 'regarded as crucial by a country for safeguarding its public interests [...] to such an extent that they are applicable to any situation falling within their scope, irrespective of the law otherwise applicable to the contract under this Regulation' are covered. An additional threshold can be found in section 3 which requires that a mandatory provision of

---

[112] See Pierre Lalive (rapporteur), 'L'application du droit public étranger', partie A, session de Wiesbaden 1975 (resolution on 'The Application of Foreign Public Law', Part A, session of Wiesbaden 1975) (1975) 56 AIDI 550.
[113] See Ch XXXVIII.5.
[114] Regulation (EC) No 593/2008 on the law applicable to contractual obligations (Rome I) [2008] OJ L177/6.

a foreign State may only be given effect 'in so far as those overriding mandatory provisions render the performance of the contract unlawful'.

It is a matter of controversy whether mandatory rules of a State on the verge of bankruptcy which purport to suspend or restructure financial payment obligations of this State (sovereign bonds) may qualify as overriding mandatory provisions in terms of the Rome I Regulation.

A special feature is the so-called act of State doctrine which plays a significant role in US law and to some extent also in British law.[115] According to that doctrine, US courts, in principle, refrain from judicial review over sovereign acts of foreign States.[116] Thus, recognition of foreign sovereign acts does not depend on their conformity with international law (or foreign constitutional law). It is, however, a minimum requirement of the doctrine that the rules of territorial jurisdiction have been obeyed.

In *Allied Bank International v Banco Credito Agricola de Cartago*, the territorial limits for the recognition of foreign sovereign acts determined a legal dispute between US creditors and some banks of Costa Rica.[117] The banks had the obligation to pay off the granted credits in US-Dollars with New York as the place of performance. The Costa Rican banks refused to pay. They invoked the foreign exchange law of Costa Rica which faced a financial crisis and therefore prohibited the performance of such credit obligations. In the light of a statement of the executive, the New York Court of Appeals considered the provisions of the exchange law of Costa Rica as an attempt to respond to the State's foreign indebtedness. In the opinion of the executive, followed by the Court, this objective could not override the contractual obligation. The Court also rejected the defendant's argument because Costa Rica's payment prohibition could, as a rule, not affect a contractual obligation localized in New York and not in Costa Rica.[118]

The act of State doctrine allows certain exceptions. The doctrine does not purport to protect foreign States but to defer to the government's responsibility in conducting foreign affairs. Therefore, the doctrine does not apply before US courts if the executive explicitly waives its application. The US Congress created another exception in the context of allegedly illegal expropriations in Cuba. The Hickenlooper Amendment[119] denies recognition to foreign expropriations which contravene international law unless the US Government intervenes in favour of recognition.

---

[115] See US Supreme Court *Underhill v Hernandez* 168 US 250, 252, 254 (1897); *Banco Nacional de Cuba v Sabbatino* 376 US 398 (1964); Restatement (Third) of US Foreign Relations Law §§ 443ff; CT Ebenroth, *Banking on the Act of State* (Universitätsverlag Konstanz 1985); M Halberstam 'Sabbatino Resurrected: The Act of State Doctrine in the Revised Restatement of U.S. Foreign Relations Law' (1985) 79 AJIL 68; FA Mann, *Foreign Affairs in English Courts* (OUP 1986) 164.
[116] MN Shaw, *International Law* (7th edn, CUP 2014) 129ff; H Fox and P Webb, *The Law of State Immunity* (3rd edn, OUP 2013) 53ff.
[117] New York Court of Appeals *Allied Bank International v Banco Credito Agricola de Cartago* 757 F.2d 516 (2d Cir, 1985).
[118] On the application of foreign exchange law provisions under Article VIII(2)(b) of the Articles of Agreement of the IMF, see *Libra Bank Ltd v Banco Nacional de Costa Rica* 570 F. Supp 870 (SDNY 1983).
[119] 'Second Hickenlooper Amendment' 22 USC § 2370.

(b) Application of domestic law in deference to foreign public law

A common technique of recognition and 'enforcement' is to apply domestic rules in the light of the foreign provisions. Private law terms like 'good faith' or the prohibition of agreements which violate 'public order' or 'public morals' serve as the gateway for such deferential interpretation.

The German *Borax* case illustrates deference to foreign rules triggered by a concordance of political choices. The German Federal Court of Justice qualified a purchase of Borax to be supplied to a country of the Eastern Bloc, which was governed by German law, as a violation of 'good morals' (§ 138 of the German Civil Code), because it went against a strategic US embargo. The Court held that the export embargo not only served US interests but also 'the interests of the entire free Western world and, thereby, also the interests of the Federal Republic of Germany'.[120]

Deferential consideration of foreign laws on the grounds of concordance of legally protected interests or values may result from interests broadly recognized by the international community (even if not strictly mandated by international treaties), such as the protection of the cultural heritage.

In the *Tribal Masks* case, the German Federal Court of Justice held that the export of tribal masks, which was prohibited under the laws of Nigeria, violated the 'good morals' standard under the German Civil Code (§ 138) and that an export contract was therefore void, because an internationally recognized concern like the protection of cultural heritage would also guide the interpretation of national law.[121]

(c) Consideration of foreign public law as fact ('datum')

If foreign laws fail to qualify for recognition as legal rules (eg because they blatantly deviate from domestic standards), they might still be acknowledged as facts (datum). Thus, foreign prohibitions coupled with severe sanctions for non-compliance may operate as a factual barrier to performance and justify non-compliance or even affect the existence of contractual obligations because of a fundamental change of circumstances.

10. Specifics of 'Cyberspace Regulation'

The regulation of what is called 'cyberspace' gives rise to some particular issues. Whilst the extraterritorial application of municipal law in its classic form is historically linked to globalization, the jurisdictional issues in cyberspace relate to its structure[122] and

---

[120] BGHZ 34, 169.   [121] BGHZ 59, 82.

[122] V Boehme-Neßler, *Cyberlaw* (CH Beck 2001); KW Grewlich, *Governance in Cyberspace* (CH Beck 1999); V Röben, 'International Internet Governance' (1999) 42 GYIL 400; S Shipchandler, 'The Wild Web: Non-Regulation as the Answer to the Regulatory Question' (2000) 33 Cornell Int'l LJ 435; J von Bernstorff, 'The Structural Limitations of Network Governance ICANN as a Case in Point' in C Joerges, I-J Sand, and G Teubner (eds), *Transnational Governance and Constitutionalism* (Hart Publishing 2004) 257.

technological developments. The connection of the internet and mobile phones has opened a new dimension in this field. There are many aspects of worldwide communication which require regulation at the international and the national level. Among those issues prominently rank

- the control of certain contents;
- data protection; and
- competition.

One of the salient problems in the regulation of cyberspace is the divergence of regulatory philosophies. The United States, to a large degree, relies on a self-regulation of the private content providers, whilst many EU Member States follow a stricter approach. Under the US constitution, a relatively 'liberal' attitude towards the freedom of speech as one of the privileged fundamental rights prevails.[123] Even though the freedoms of communication rank highly in European constitutions and in the European Convention on Human Rights, certain contents (racist web-pages denying the Holocaust, xenophobic messages, massive infringements of personal rights, child pornography) cannot claim protection against prohibitive standards. In the area of data protection, EU law (Directive 95/46/EC) provides that the transmission of personal data to a third country is only permitted if an appropriate level of protection is ensured.[124] According to a decision of the European Commission, an appropriate level of protection is guaranteed in the United States, if the providers of the data transmission comply with certain standards of protection negotiated with by the US Government (so-called 'EU-US Privacy Shield').[125]

The internet also raises new issues of national jurisdiction. Internet contents addressed to the public at large may be held to be published wherever they can be received. Some national courts are, however, restrictive about assuming jurisdiction merely on grounds of possible access. The German Federal Court of Justice held that internet communications containing defamatory statements about a German plaintiff establish the jurisdiction of the German courts only if they are specifically directed to the German public or are of specific interest to the German public.[126]

A remarkable form of cooperation between public and private actors is the Internet Corporation for Assigned Names and Numbers (ICANN).[127] This corporation is responsible for the distribution and the technical administration of internet addresses (Domain Name System, DNS). ICANN was founded under the laws

---

[123] See US Supreme Court *Reno v American Civil Liberties Union* 521 US 844 (1997).

[124] Directive 95/46/EC of 24 October 1995 on the protection of individuals with regard to the processing of personal data and on the free movement of such data [1995] OJ L281/31.

[125] Commission Implementing Decision of 12 July 2016 pursuant to Directive 95/46/EC of the European Parliament and of the Council on the adequacy of the protection provided by the EU-U.S. Privacy Shield, C(2016) 4176.

[126] BGHZ 184, 313; confirmed in a recent decision of 29 March 2011 (file reference VI ZR 111/10).

[127] J von Bernstorff, 'The Structural Limitations of Network Governance ICANN as a Case in Point' in C Joeges, I-J Sand, and G Teubner (eds), *Transnational Governance and Constitutionalism* (*Hart Publishing* 2004) 257.

of California in accordance with an initiative of the US Department of Commerce and is based on the principle of 'autonomous self-regulation'. The (private) founders and the Department of Commerce fixed the guidelines for the allocation of internet addresses in a Memorandum of Understanding. The directors of ICANN are partly appointed by the holding organizations and partly by international elections. Despite the close interaction with the US Government, ICANN is a non-governmental non-profit organization for internet management. Incorporation in the United States and the still existing links with the US Government have provided the United States with a significant regulatory influence as opposed to other States and the European Union. That could change in the future in light of the US Government's plans to completely withdraw from the administration of domain names and IP addresses and leave this task to ICANN's full responsibility.[128] While proponents of these plans particularly welcome the internet's growing independence, critics urge to promote ICANN's accountability and warn about other governments trying to make use of the power gap and direct the ICANN to an orientation which limits freedom of expression.[129]

Article 4 of the Statute of ICANN requires the institution to act in accordance with the common welfare of the internet community and also refers to international law as far as applicable:

The Corporation shall operate for the benefit of the Internet community as a whole, carrying out its activities in conformity with relevant principles of international law and applicable international conventions and local law and, to the extent appropriate and consistent with these Articles and its Bylaws, through open and transparent processes that enable competition and open entry in Internet-related markets. To this effect, the Corporation shall cooperate as appropriate with relevant international organizations.

An independent review panel has interpreted that clause as a comprehensive reference to international law including general principles of international law such as the good faith principle. The panel based that submission to international standards on ICANN's mission to exercise 'governance of an intrinsically international resource of immense importance to global communications and economies'.[130]

A very important function of ICANN is the protection of trade mark rights and other rights against the abusive obtainment of internet addresses (cyber-squatting). For this purpose, ICANN has developed a dispute resolution mechanism (Uniform

---

[128] US Commerce Department's National Telecommunications and Information Administration, Press Release (14 March 2014) available at <http://www.ntia.doc.gov/press-release/2014/ntia-announces-intent-transition-key-internet-domain-name-functions> (accessed 23 June 2016).

[129] P Rosenzweig, BD Schaefer, JL Gattuso, and D Inserra, 'Protecting Internet Freedom and American Interests: Required Reforms and Standards for ICANN Transition' (16 June 2014) available at <http://www.heritage.org/research/reports/2014/06/protecting-internet-freedom-and-american-interests-required-reforms-and-standards-for-icann-transition> (accessed 23 June 2016).

[130] *ICM Registry, LLC v Internet Corporation for Assigned Names and Numbers ('ICANN')*, International Centre for Dispute Resolution Case No 50 117 T 00224 08 (Declaration of the Independent Review Panel 2010) (2010) 49 ILM 956 paras 140f.

Domain Name Dispute Resolution Policy) in coordination with the World Intellectual Property Organization.[131]

Select Bibliography

CF Amerasinghe, *Diplomatic Protection* (OUP 2008).

J Bartelson, *A Genealogy of Sovereignty* (CUP 1993).

A Chayes and A Handler Chayes, *The New Sovereignty—Compliance with International Regulatory Agreements* (Harvard University Press 1995).

B Craig, *Cyberlaw: The Law of the Internet and Information Technology* (Pearson 2013).

A Dickinson, R Lindsay, and JP Loonam, *State Immunity, Selected Materials and Commentary* (OUP 2004).

H Fox, *The Law of State Immunity* (3rd edn, OUP 2013).

FH Hinsley, *Sovereignty* (2nd edn, CUP 1986).

A James, *Sovereign Statehood* (Unwin Hyman 1986).

G Kreijen (ed), *State, Sovereignty, and International Governance* (OUP 2002).

MK Lewis and S Frankel (eds), *International Economic Law and National Autonomy* (CUP 2010).

V Lowe, 'Sovereignty and International Economic Law' in W Shan, P Simons, and D Singh (eds), *Redefining Sovereignty in International Economic Law* (Hart Publishing 2008) 77.

K Raustiala, 'Rethinking the Sovereignty Debate in International Economic Law' (2003) 6 J Int'l Econ L 841.

C Reed, *Making Laws for Cyberspace* (OUP 2012).

L Reydams, *Universal Jurisdiction* (OUP 2004).

C Ryngaert, *Jurisdiction in International Law* (2nd edn, OUP 2015).

C Schreuer, 'The Waning of the Sovereign State: Towards a New Paradigm for International Law?' (1993) 4 EJIL 447.

---

[131] D Lindsay, *International Domain Name Law, ICANN and the UDRP* (Hart Publishing 2007).

VII

Human Rights and International Economic Relations

International human rights based on custom as well as universal and regional treaties constitute important elements of the international legal order and have a significant impact on international economic relations as well as on national economic laws. Just like fundamental rights on the national level, international human rights do not only protect the private sphere of life but also entrepreneurial activities and property. Social guarantees and collective rights, such as the freedom of association, significantly shape the economic order and employment conditions. Despite their growing importance, the significance of human rights standards for economic life is still being underestimated.

A lively debate addresses the implications of the right to adequate food—as laid down in Article 11 of the International Covenant on Ecnomic, Social and Cultural Rights (ICESCR)—under international trade law, for example.[1] Limitations of the protection of intellectual property rights in favour of the production of generic drugs as part of the drug supply in developing countries are related to the right to health under Article 12 of the ICESCR. Nevertheless, human rights do not directly establish claims against industrialized countries or multinational companies.

The strong interrelation between human rights and the economic order is most visible within human rights regimes which serve as a common roof for politically and economically homogeneous States. The European Convention on Human Rights reflects the dynamic understanding of fundamental rights in context with economic activities in many Contracting States.

An interesting example for the impact of human rights guarantees under the European Convention on the interpretation of the economic order was established by the European Court of Human Rights. In the case *Affaire Groppera Radio AG*, the Court deduced an individual freedom of broadcasting from the freedom of expression as laid down in Article 10 of the European Convention on Human Rights.[2] For the Court, a governmental broadcasting monopoly, under modern

---

[1] K Mechlem, 'Harmonizing Trade in Agriculture and Human Rights: Options for the Integration of the Right to Food into the Agreement on Agriculture' (2006) 10 Max Planck YB UN L 127.

[2] ECtHR *Case of Groppera Radio AG and others v Switzerland* App no 10890/84 (28 March 1990).

technical conditions, is incompatible with the European Convention. The Court has confirmed this interpretation in other cases.[3]

Furthermore, the importance of human rights law is underscored by the fact that many individual freedoms cannot be addressed in isolation from certain material conditions including the right to property. Nevertheless, customary international law still does not recognize a general right to property. Only in the case of foreign nationals, the so-called minimum standard of international law provides some protection of property.[4] For a long time, the ideological heterogeneity of the international community—essentially caused by the influence of the Marxist-Leninist doctrine in many States—hampered the universal acceptance of the right to property as an international human right.[5] The fall of the Iron Curtain and the collapse of socialist systems in Eastern Europe have rekindled the debate on a universal right to property. The German Federal Constitutional Court, for example, still rightly shows some reluctance to recognize the right to property as a right under international customary law.[6]

A number of human rights treaties enshrine the right to property as a human right. Article 1 of Protocol No 1 to the European Convention on Human Rights protects the right to property in the following terms:

Every natural or legal person is entitled to the peaceful enjoyment of his possessions. No one shall be deprived of his possessions except in the public interest and subject to the conditions provided for by law and by the general principles of international law. The preceding provisions shall not, however, in any way impair the right of a State to enforce such laws as it deems necessary to control the use of property in accordance with the general interest or to secure the payment of taxes or other contributions or penalties.

Although this clause, by referring to international law, explicitly guarantees compensation only for the expropriation of foreigners, the European Court of Human Rights requires an adequate compensation also for the expropriation of nationals in terms of a fair balance between the individual interests of the claimant on the one hand and the general interests of the community on the other hand.[7] Under the European Convention, the principle of proportionality requires a compensation, which amounts to the equal value (full compensation) in the case of individual acts of expropriation. In the case of widespread, sectoral expropriations (nationalizations), the compensation may be inferior to the market value but still must be adequate in the light of proportionality.[8] The compensation requirement counteracts

---

[3] ECtHR *Case of Informationsverein Lentia and others v Austria* App nos 13914/88, 15041/89, 15717/89, 15779/89, 17207/90 (1994); see also ECtHR *Case of Centro Europa 7 S.r.l. and Di Stefano v Italy* App no 38433/09 (7 June 2012).

[4] See Ch VI.4(a).

[5] See JG Sprankling, *International Property Law* (OUP 2014), R Dolzer, 'New Foundations of the Law of Expropriation of Alien Property' (1981) 75 AJIL 553.

[6] BVerfGE 112, 1 (32ff).

[7] ECtHR *Case of Sporrong and Lönroth v Sweden* App no 7151/75, 7152/75 (23 September 1982) paras 69ff; *Case of Lithgow and others v United Kingdom* (1986) Series A no 102 paras 120ff.

[8] See ECtHR *Case of Lithgow and others v United Kingdom* Series A no 102 para 121.

tendencies of States towards the nationalization of entire business branches in order to restructure their economies radically.

The Case of *OAO Neftyanaya Kompaniya Yukos v Russia*[9] highlights the relevance of the guarantee of property in regional human rights treaties as a check on the massive abuse of executive powers. In this case, the Russian company Yukos (which owned and controlled a number of corporate entities specialized in the production, refining, and marketing of oil) had lodged an individual complaint against the drastic enforcement measures of the Russian tax authorities in context with Yukos' alleged tax evasion. The Russian Tax Ministry had ordered Yukos to pay about EUR 2.8 billion (in tax arrears, default interest, and penalty). Within a few weeks, before the termination of judicial proceedings, the tax authorities rapidly initiated the enforcement of the tax claim including a substantial enforcement fee and had the shares of several of Yukos' production companies seized and auctioned. In the end, Yukos was liquidated in bankruptcy proceedings. It seems not unfair to assume that the destruction of Yukos and the liquidation of its assets rather than tax collection was the objective of the entire operation. Apart from finding the right to a fair trial violated, the European Court of Human Rights held that the rigid measures of the Russian tax authorities amounted to a disproportionate interference with Yukos' property and therefore violated Article 1 of Protocol 1 of the European Convention on Human Rights:

650. In view of the above considerations, the Court finds that the crux of the applicant company's case did not lay in the attachment of its assets and cash as such, but rather and essentially in the speed with which the authorities demanded the company to pay, in the decision which had chosen the company's main production unit, OAO Yuganskneftegaz, as the item to be compulsorily auctioned in the first instance, and in the speed with which the auction had been carried out.

651. Given the paramount importance of the measures taken by the authorities to the applicant company's future, and notwithstanding the Government's wide margin of appreciation in this field, the Court is of the view that the authorities were obliged to take careful and explicit account of all relevant factors in the enforcement process. Such factors were to include, among other things, the character and the amount of the existing debt as well as of the pending and probable claims against the applicant company, the nature of the company's business and the relative weight of the company in the domestic economy, the company's current and probable economic situation and the assessment of its capacity to survive the enforcement proceedings. Furthermore, the economic and social implications of various enforcement options on the company and the various categories of stakeholders, the attitude of the company's management and owners and the actual conduct of the applicant company during the enforcement proceedings, including the merits of the offers that the applicant company may have made in connection with the enforcement were to be properly considered.

[...]

655. The Court further notes one other factor which seriously affected the company's situation in the enforcement proceedings. The applicant company was subjected to a 7%

---

[9] ECtHR *OAO Neftyanaya Kompaniya Yukos v Russia* App no 14902/04 (20 September 2011).

enforcement fee in connection with the entire amount of its tax-related liability, which constituted an additional hefty sum of over RUB 43 billion (EUR 1.16 billion), the payment of which could not be suspended or rescheduled (...). This was a flat-rate fee which the authorities apparently refused to reduce, and these sums had to be paid even before the company could begin repaying the main body of the debt (...). The fee was by its nature unrelated to the actual amount of the enforcement expenses borne by the bailiffs. Whilst the Court may accept that there is nothing wrong as a matter of principle with requiring a debtor to pay for the expenses relating to the enforcement of a debt or to threaten a debtor with a sanction to incite his or her voluntary compliance with enforcement writs, in the circumstances of the case the resulting sum was completely out of proportion to the amount of the enforcement expenses which could have possibly been expected to be borne or had actually been borne by the bailiffs. Because of its rigid application, instead of inciting voluntary compliance, it contributed very seriously to the applicant company's demise.

[...]

657. On the whole, given the pace of the enforcement proceedings, the obligation to pay the full enforcement fee and the authorities' failure to take proper account of the consequences of their actions, the Court finds that the domestic authorities failed to strike a fair balance between the legitimate aims sought and the measures employed.

In its final judgment on just satisfaction owed to the applicant, the European Court of Human Rights found that an enforcement fee of 4 per cent would have been proportionate and ordered Russia to pay about EUR 1.9 billion in compensation.[10]

The *Yukos* cases also illustrate how human rights protection and investment protection may be intertwined: The controlling shareholders of Yukos initiated arbitrations against Russia (under the Energy Charter Treaty) and were awarded a total of USD50 billion in compensation.[11] The ruling of the European Court of Human Rights and the arbitral awards in the *Yukos* cases are complementary contributions to review and to redress manifest abuses of public power under international standards.

1. The Exploitation of Natural Resources

Some economic activities, in particular the exploitation of natural resources, conflict with the rights and interests of the local population. In this respect, the right to property regarding the traditional living environment of indigenous peoples plays a particularly important role.

In context with the exploitation of natural resources like oil and related foreign investments, the neglect of health and environmental protection or even intimidation mechanisms and the use of outright force by security forces often lead to the disregard of basic human rights standards. The African Commission on Human

---

[10] ECtHR *OAO Neftyanaya Kompaniya Yukos v Russia* App no 14902/04 (Judgment on just satisfaction, 31 July 2014).

[11] Below Ch XXXIV.1(c) iii, 4(f).

and Peoples' Rights had to deal with these problems at a rather early stage of the discussion on indigenous rights in the *Ogoni* case (2001).[12]

In this case, a Nigerian-European consortium was engaged in oil production in the territory of the Ogoni people. The former military government of Nigeria had not carried out a prior environmental and social impact assessment. According to the African Commission, the oil production led to the pollution of air, water, and soil, causing serious harm to the health of the Ogoni people. The population was not involved in the governmental decision-making processes. Additionally, the Nigerian police force destroyed houses and even entire villages of the Ogoni. Some inhabitants, who tried to return to their settlements, were mistreated and in some cases even killed. The Commission stated that these events constituted violations of the human rights guarantees laid down in the African Charter on Human and Peoples' Rights, in particular the right to health (Article 16), the collective right to a generally satisfactory environment (Article 24), the right of sovereignty over natural resources (Article 21), the right to property (Article 14), and the protection of the family (Article 18). However, the Commission did not have to decide on the responsibility of the private oil company.[13] This aspect of corporate responsibility for human rights violations was central to the claims which Ogoni human rights activists and their families brought against companies belonging to the Shell conglomerate before US courts. In a settlement agreement, Shell agreed to pay a considerable amount of compensation.[14]

On the universal level, ILO Convention No 169 of 1989[15] and the UN Declaration on the Rights of Indigenous Peoples of 2007[16] address the issue of indigenous land rights. Both documents recognize the particular relevance of indigenous land for the indigenous identity and call upon States to take the necessary steps to identify and recognize indigenous land rights, to establish procedures of information and participation to recognize and adjudicate those land rights, and to provide compensation for damages.[17] However, the ILO Convention and the UN Declaration do not formulate specific conditions for the establishment of indigenous land rights in domestic law.[18]

The Inter-American Court of Human Rights has rendered several landmark decisions on the right to property of indigenous and similar tribal communities

[12] African Commission on Human and Peoples' Rights, *The Social and Economic Rights Action Center and the Center for Economic and Social Rights v Nigeria*, Comm No 155/96 (2001); F Coomans, 'The Ogoni Case before the African Commission on Human and People's Rights' (2003) 52 ICLQ 749.
[13] See on the responsibility of transnational corporations for human rights violations at section 3 in this Chapter.
[14] <http://wiwavshell.org/documents/Wiwa_v_Shell_agreements_and_orders.pdf> (accessed 23 June 2016); see Section 3(b) in this Chapter.
[15] ILO Convention No 169 concerning Indigenous and Tribal Peoples in Independent Countries (adopted 27 June 1989, entered into force 5 September 1991) 1650 UNTS 383.
[16] United Nations Declaration on the Rights of Indigenous Peoples of 13 September 2007 UN Doc A/61295.
[17] See for a detailed analysis of both documents, G Pentassuglia, 'Towards a Jurisprudential Articulation of Indigenous Land Rights' (2011) 22 EJIL 165 (167ff).
[18] See for a detailed analysis of both documents, G Pentassuglia, 'Towards a Jurisprudential Articulation of Indigenous Land Rights' (2011) 22 EJIL 165 (167ff).

in context with the exploitation of natural resources.[19] In the case of the *Mayagna (Sumo) Awas Tingni Community v Nicaragua*, the Court stressed the role of property for indigenous and like communities as the basis not only of their economic existence but also of their cultural life:

Given the characteristics of the instant case, some specifications are required on the concept of property in indigenous communities. Among indigenous peoples there is a communitarian tradition regarding a communal form of collective property of the land, in the sense that ownership of the land is not concentrated on an individual but rather on the group and its community. Indigenous groups, by the fact of their very existence, have the right to live freely in their own territory; the close ties of indigenous people with the land must be recognized and understood as the fundamental basis of their cultures, their spiritual life, their integrity, and their economic survival. For indigenous communities, relations to the land are not merely a matter of possession and production but a material and spiritual element which they must fully enjoy, even to preserve their cultural legacy and transmit it to future generations.[20]

In this particular case, the Inter-American Court of Human Rights held that deforestation concessions affecting the land of an indigenous community infringed the group's right to property according to Article 21 of the American Convention on Human Rights. In this judgment, the Inter-American Court of Human Rights took a comprehensive approach to define the right to property which also considers the cultural and spiritual relation of an indigenous group with the land.

In the case of the *Saramaka People v Suriname*, the Inter-American Court of Human Rights expanded its perception of the right to property to the traditional use of the natural resources which 'lie on and within the land' and acknowledged the importance of the use of land for the cultural and economic survival of the tribes:

[D]ue to the inextricable connection members of indigenous and tribal peoples have with their territory, the protection of their right to property over such territory, in accordance with Article 21 of the Convention, is necessary to guarantee their very survival. Accordingly, the right to use and enjoy their territory would be meaningless in the context of indigenous and tribal communities if said right were not connected to the natural resources that lie on and within the land. That is, the demand for collective land ownership by members of indigenous and tribal peoples derives from the need to ensure the security and permanence of their control and use of the natural resources, which in turn maintains their very way of life. This connectedness between the territory and the natural resources necessary for their physical and cultural survival is precisely what needs to be protected under Article 21 of the Convention in order to guarantee the members of indigenous and tribal communities' right to the use and enjoyment of their property. From this analysis, it follows that the natural resources found on and within indigenous and tribal people's territories that are protected under Article 21 are those natural resources

---

[19] See generally on the role of indigenous people in the case–law of the IACtHR, L Burgorgue-Larsen and A Úbeda de Torres, *Las decisiones básicas de la Corte Interamericana de Derechos Humanos* (Civitas 2009) 69.

[20] IACtHR *Case of the Mayagna (Sumo) Awas Tingni Community v Nicaragua* (Judgment of 31 August 2001) Series C No 79 (2001) para 149.

traditionally used and necessary for the very survival, development and continuation of such people's way of life.[21]

The right to property of indigenous communities regarding their traditional land under the American Convention on Human Rights does not prevent States from granting concessions for deforestation or mining and other forms of exploiting natural resources. But interference with indigenous land for the exploitation of natural resources must meet three conditions developed by the Inter-American Court of Human Rights:

- an effective participation of the indigenous community in the decision-making process, in conformity with their customs and traditions;
- reasonable benefit for the indigenous community from the economic development in the territory; and
- prior environmental and social impact assessment carried out by independent and capable entities.[22]

More recently, in the case of the *Kichwa Indigenous People of Sarayaku v Ecuador*,[23] the Inter-American Court of Human Rights underlined the right to consultation and its relevance for the preservation of cultural identity:

219. Given the importance that these sites of symbolic value have for the cultural identity of the Sarayaku People, as a collective entity, and their worldview, several of the statements and expert testimonies produced during the proceedings indicate the strong bond that exists between the elements of nature and culture, on the one hand, and each member of the Community's sense of being, on the other. This also highlights the profound impact on the social and spiritual relationships that Community members may have with the different elements of nature that surround them, when these are destroyed or weakened.
220. The Court considers that the failure to consult the Sarayaku People affected their cultural identity, since there is no doubt that the intervention and destruction of their cultural heritage implied a grave lack of respect for their social and cultural identity, their customs, traditions, worldview and way of life, which naturally caused great anguish, sadness and suffering among them.

If the depletion of natural resources on the basis of concessions for deforestation and mining conflicts with property rights of indigenous communities or other guarantees under human rights treaties, a State may not invoke an international agreement on investment protection. In the *Case of the Sawhoyamaxa Indigenous Community v Paraguay*,[24] the Inter-American Court of Human Rights stated:

---

[21] IACtHR *Case of the Saramaka People v Suriname* (Judgment of 28 November 2007) Series C No 172 (2007) para 122; see also on the right to land, JL Zweig, 'A Globally Sustainable Right to Land: Utilizing Real Property to Protect the Traditional Knowledge of Indigenous Peoples and Communities' (2010) 38 Ga J Int'l & Comp L 769.

[22] IACtHR *Case of the Saramaka People v Suriname* (Judgment of 28 November 2007) Series C No 172 (2007) para 129.

[23] IACtHR *Case of the Kichwa Indigenous People of Sarayaku v Ecuador* (Judgment of 27 June 2012) Series C No 245 (2012).

[24] IACtHR *Case of the Sawhoyamaxa Indigenous Community v Paraguay* (Judgment of 29 March 2006) Series C No 146 (2006) para 140.

[T]he enforcement of bilateral commercial treaties negates vindication of non-compliance with state obligations under the American Convention; on the contrary, their enforcement should always be compatible with the American Convention, which is a multilateral treaty on human rights that stands in a class of its own and that generates rights for individual human beings and does not depend entirely on reciprocity among States.

The UN Human Rights Committee has also developed the rights of indigenous peoples to effective participation under Article 27 of the International Covenant on Civil and Political Rights (ICCPR) (minority rights). In the case *Ángela Poma v Peru*, a member of the indigenous community of the Aymara complained that Peru had caused the progressive drainage and degradation of Aymara pasture land by constructing several wells in the area.[25] The Human Rights Committee took the view that

> [...] the admissibility of measures which substantially compromise or interfere with the culturally significant economic activities of a minority or indigenous community depends on whether the members of the community in question have had the opportunity to participate in the decision-making process in relation to these measures and whether they will continue to benefit from their traditional economy. The Committee considers that participation in the decision-making process must be effective, which requires not mere consultation but the free, prior and informed consent of the members of the community. In addition, the measures must respect the principle of proportionality so as not to endanger the very survival of the community and its members.[26]

By insisting on effective participation of minorities, the Human Rights Committee strengthens indigenous land rights.

The decisions of the Inter-American Court of Human Rights have strongly influenced the interpretation of the African Charter on Human and Peoples' Rights. In the case *Endorois v Kenya*,[27] the African Court on Human and Peoples' Rights drew heavily on the case-law of the Inter-American Court of Human Rights and recognized that the deprivation of indigenous land in context with the exploitation of natural resources falls within the scope of Article 14 of the African Charter on Human and Peoples' Rights (right to property).[28] At the same time, the African Court on Human and Peoples' Rights also established standards for the lawful interference with indigenous land, visibly inspired by the Inter-American Court:

- strict proportionality;
- prior consultation; and
- adequate compensation.[29]

---

[25] See UNHRC *Ángela Poma Poma v Peru* UN Doc CCPR/C/95/D/1457/2006.

[26] UNHRC *Ángela Poma Poma v Peru* UN Doc CCPR/C/95/D/1457/2006 para 7.6.

[27] AfCHPR *Centre for Minority Rights Development (Kenya) and Minority Group International on behalf of Endorois Welfare Council v Kenya* (2010) 49 ILM 861.

[28] AfCHPR *Centre for Minority Rights Development (Kenya) and Minority Group International on behalf of Endorois Welfare Council v Kenya* (2010) 49 ILM 861, para 207.

[29] AfCHPR *Centre for Minority Rights Development (Kenya) and Minority Group International on behalf of Endorois Welfare Council v Kenya* (2010) 49 ILM 861, paras 211ff.

For the African Court on Human and Peoples' Rights, even non-traditional forms of land use and disposal fall within the scope of indigenous rights. Thus, the indigenous communities are granted a general right to compensation in the case of third party exploitation of their traditional land. However, for the African Court on Human and Peoples' Rights the right to compensation flows from the specific right to sovereignty over natural resources under the African Convention (Article 21).[30]

In 2010, the Conference of the Member States of the Rio Convention on Biodiversity (CBD) adopted the Nagoya Protocol on Access to Genetic Resources and the Fair and Equitable Sharing of Benefits Arising from Their Utilization. The Protocol explicitly requires an adequate consideration of the interests of local and indigenous communities (Article 4 (2) and (5) *bis*).

The impact of human rights standards brings about a complex regime of property and related rights. This raises the problem of adequately balancing national interests and the majority rule with indigenous and other local rights and interests. In quite a few countries, the national wealth of resources is concentrated in the territory of relatively small indigenous and other tribal or similar communities. This creates tensions between majority concerns and the rights of smaller groups within a society.

The exploitation of some resources stands in close interaction with human rights as well as internal conflicts. Thus, the extraction of so-called 'conflict diamonds' (also known as 'blood diamonds') in Central Africa is associated with human rights violations and organized crime. According to a definition commonly found in UN documents 'conflict diamonds are diamonds that originate from areas controlled by forces or factions opposed to legitimate and internationally recognized governments, and are used to fund military action in opposition to those governments, or in contravention of the decisions of the Security Council'. These diamonds are often extracted under inhuman conditions, for example forced labour, and fuel internal armed conflicts. The 'Kimberley Process', endorsed by the United Nations, established a scheme of certification which shall drain the channels of diamond traffic by rebel groups and local warlords. On 26 February 2003, the WTO Council for Trade in Goods recommended to the General Council to grant requesting members of the WTO a waiver under Article IX:3 and 4 of the WTO Agreement, which covers the Kimberley scheme as far as it may possibly conflict with world trade law, especially Article XIII:1 (non-discriminatory administration of quantitative restrictions), Article I:1 (most favored nation treatment), and Article XI:1 (elimination of quantitative restrictions) of the GATT 1994.[31]

---

[30] AfCHPR *Centre for Minority Rights Development (Kenya) and Minority Group International on behalf of Endorois Welfare Council v Kenya* (2010) 49 ILM 861, paras 252ff.

[31] See <https://www.wto.org/english/news_e/news03_e/goods_council_26fev03_e.htm> (accessed 23 June 2016).

2. Treaties on Economic Cooperation and Economic Integration

There is a marked tendency to include human rights issues in treaties on economic cooperation and economic integration. The Cotonou Agreement between the European Union and the ACP States (ie States of Africa, the Caribbean, and the Pacific region) declares the respect for human rights an essential element of the agreement.[32] The Declaration and Treaty of the Southern African Development Community (SADC Treaty) commits the SADC and its Member States to human rights, democracy, and the rule of law.[33] SADC Member States shall refrain from taking any measure likely to jeopardize the maintenance of its principles, the achievement of its objectives, and the implementation of the provisions of the SADC Treaty.[34]

In the case *Campbell et al v Republic of Zimbabwe*, the SADC Tribunal ruled that the commitment to human rights and rule of law under Article 4(c) of the SADC Treaty establishes a duty on Member States to provide effective judicial protection and to ensure a fair trial in the case of infringements of these standards.[35] According to the Tribunal's judgment, the respect for human rights does not allow any form of racial discrimination including de facto discrimination. Thus, the Tribunal qualified Zimbabwe's constitutional amendment which aimed at the expropriation of white farmers as a violation of the SADC Treaty. The aftermath of the judgment is disillusioning and, in some way, sadly revealing. As in the case of other judgments against Zimbabwe, the Zimbabwean Government flatly refused to recognize the SADC Tribunal's ruling, whilst a South African court ordered its enforcement. In the end, the Member States of SADC de facto suspended the Tribunal and decided to negotiate a new tribunal without jurisdiction over claims of individuals.[36] A new protocol on the SADC Tribunal limits its jurisdiction to advisory opinions and disputes between Member States.

The Treaty on the Economic Community of West African States (ECOWAS) proclaims the 'recognition, promotion and protection of human and peoples' rights in accordance with the provisions of the African Charter on Human and Peoples' Rights'.[37] Individuals may bring complaints about human rights violations before the Community's Court of Justice.[38]

---

[32] Article 9(2) of the Partnership Agreement between the Members of the African, Caribbean, and Pacific Group of States of the one part and the European Community and its Member States of the other part.

[33] Article 4(c) SADC.   [34] Article 6(1) SADC.

[35] SADC Tribunal *Mike Campbell (Pvt) Ltd and Others v Republic of Zimbabwe* Case No 2/2007 (Decision of 28 November 2008) (2009) 48 ILM 530. However, Zimbabwe refused to accept the tribunal's decision.

[36] E de Wet, 'The Rise and Fall of the Tribunal of the Southern African Development Community: Implications for Dispute Settlement in Southern Africa' (2013) 28 ICSID Rev 45.

[37] Article 4(g) ECOWAS Treaty.

[38] Article 10(d) of the Protocol on the Community Court of Justice (A/P.I/7/91) as amended in 2005 by Supplementary Protocol A/SP.1/01/05; see ST Ebobrah, 'Critical Issues in Human Rights

In the case *Koraou v The Republic of Niger*, the Community's Court of Justice decided on traditional forms of slavery of women in Niger.[39]

The trend towards including human rights clauses in economic agreements continued within the Southeast Asian region. The ASEAN Charter of 2007 declares the promotion and protection of human rights both a purpose and principle of the ASEAN Charter.[40] The ASEAN Charter also provides for the establishment of a human rights body, the ASEAN Intergovernmental Commission on Human Rights.[41]

3. Transnational Corporations and Human Rights: Standards and Liability for Violations

Human rights are not only put in jeopardy by direct actions of States, but also by private actors like corporations. A salient issue in modern international economic law is the commitment of multinational companies, in particular transnational corporations (TNCs), to human rights and their responsibility for human rights violations. In a number of cases, TNCs were accused of having violated human rights, indirectly or even by direct action. Indirect entanglements with human rights violations may flow from complicity with the host government or dealings with other companies in a supply chain (lack of 'due diligence', eg as to child labour employed by business partners). Most of these complaints relate to the role of TNCs as investors in countries with a poor human rights record, with a weak government, or torn by civil strife. The exploitation of natural resources in such countries seems to be particularly susceptible to human rights violations.

International law still does not directly extend human rights obligations to private companies as these are not subjects of international law.[42] On the other hand, TNCs may have a considerable impact on the human rights situation in the countries in which they carry out their activities.

On the international level there has always been great reluctance to recognize human rights standards binding upon private corporations. On the UN level, a draft code on *Norms on the Responsibility of Transnational Corporations and Other Business Enterprises with Regard to Human Rights*, which was adopted by the former UN Sub-Commission on the Promotion and Protection of Human Rights, formulated a wide range of human rights obligations directly binding on TNCs.[43]

Mandate of the ECOWAS Court of Justice' (2010) 54 JAL 1; KJ Alter, LR Helfer, and JR McAllister, 'A New International Human Rights Court for West Africa: The ECOWAS Community Court of Justice' (2013) 107 AJIL 737.

[39] ECOWAS Community Court of Justice *Hadijatou Mani Koraou v The Republic of Niger* App no ECW/CCJ/APP/08/08 (Judgment no ECW/CCJ/JUD/06/08 of 27 October 2008) available at <http://www.unhcr.org/refworld/docid/496b41fa2.html> (accessed 23 June 2016).

[40] Articles 1(7), 2(2) ASEAN Charter.   [41] Article 14 ASEAN Charter.

[42] See Ch III.8.

[43] The obligations encompass the right to equal opportunity and non-discriminatory treatment, the right to security of persons, rights of workers, respect for national sovereignty and human rights,

In the end, the draft code did not find enough support and the UN Economic and Social Council (affirming a decision of the Human Rights Commission) declared that the draft had 'no legal standing'.[44] The UN Human Rights Committee, in its General Comment No. 31 on the Nature of the General Legal Obligation on States Parties to the Covenant (2004),[45] expressed the prevailing view when it stated that the obligations of States under Article 2(1) of the UN Covenant on Civil and Political Rights 'do not, as such, have direct horizontal effect as a matter of international law'.

In *Kiobel v Royal Dutch Petroleum*,[46] the United States Court of Appeals for the Second Circuit categorically rejected corporate liability for human rights violations in a lawsuit against Royal Dutch Shell, which was accused of having violated international customary law by aiding and abetting the Nigerian Government in suppressing protests against oil explorations and production activities in the 1990s. In context with an action under the Alien Tort Claims Act (ATCA) or Alien Tort Statute (ATS), the Court of Appeals argued that in international law

[n]o corporation has ever been subject to any form of liability (whether civil, criminal, or otherwise) under the customary international law of human rights. Rather, sources of customary international law have, on several occasions, explicitly rejected the idea of corporate liability. Thus, corporate liability has not attained a discernible, much less universal, acceptance among nations of the world in their relations inter se, and it cannot, as a result, form the basis of a suit under the ATS.[47]

This ruling suffers from not clearly distinguishing between two separate issues: the (controversial) human rights obligations of corporations under international law on the one hand and the corporate liability for the violation of human rights under domestic law on the other.[48] In the end, the US Supreme Court rejected the applicability of the ATCA on grounds of extraterritoriality.[49]

International organizations, such as the United Nations, the International Labour Organization, and the OECD, have taken up the issue of establishing human rights standards for TNCs in the broader context of corporate social responsibility.[50] The UN Guiding Principles on Business and Human Rights are an important step

and obligations with regard to consumer and environmental protection, see (2003) UN Doc E/ CN.4/ Sub.2/2003/12/Rev.2; CF Hillemanns, 'UN Norms on the Responsibilities of Transnational Corporations and Other Business Enterprises with regard to Human Rights' (2003) 4 German LJ 1065 (1067); K Lucke, 'States' and Private Actors' Obligations under International Human Rights Law and the Draft UN Norms' in T Cottier, J Pauwelyn, and E Bürgi (eds), *Human Rights and International Trade* (OUP 2005) 148 (157ff); D Weissbrodt and M Kruger, 'Norms on the Responsibilities of Transnational Corporations and Other Business Enterprises with Regard to Human Rights' (2003) 97 AJIL 901.

[44] UN ECOSOC Decision 2004/279, under (c).
[45] UN Human Rights Committee, General Comment 31, Nature of the General Legal Obligation on States Parties to the Covenant, UN Doc. CCPR/C/21/Rev.1/Add.13 (2004).
[46] *Kiobel v Royal Dutch Petroleum* 621 F.3d 111 (2d Cir 2010).
[47] *Kiobel v Royal Dutch Petroleum* 621, 121, 148 (2d Cir 2010).
[48] See separate opinion of Judge Leval (concurring) in *Kiobel v Royal Dutch Petroleum* (2010) 49 ILM 1510 (1537, 1553f).
[49] See Section 3(b) in this Chapter.   [50] See in more detail Ch III.8.(b).

towards consolidating corporate responsibility with respect to human rights. In the United States, numerous claims for human rights violations by TNCs were based on the ATCA until the restrictive ruling of the US Supreme Court in the *Kiobel* case.[51]

(a) UN Guiding Principles on Business and Human Rights

In 2005, the UN Secretary-General appointed a Special Representative on Human Rights and Transnational Corporations and other Business Enterprises. The Special Representative, John Ruggie, who submitted several reports on 'business and human rights',[52] followed a rather cautious approach on corporate responsibility for human rights violations under existing international law by refusing to accept direct human rights obligations of corporations or other non-State actors.[53] In March 2011, Ruggie presented his final report with the Guiding Principles on Business and Human Rights[54] to the Human Rights Council which endorsed the report by consensus.[55] The UN Guiding Principles on Business and Human Rights ('Ruggie principles') establish three levels of responsibility: the supervisory responsibility of the home States of corporations (essentially based on personal jurisdiction), the responsibility of host States (within territorial jurisdiction) and the corporate responsibility to respect human rights. The UN Guiding Principles call for remedies against business-related human rights abuses:

III. Access to Remedy

A. Foundational Principle
25. As part of their duty to protect against business-related human rights abuse, States must take appropriate steps to ensure, through judicial, administrative, legislative or other

[51] See Section 3(b) in this Chapter.
[52] See eg J Ruggie, 'Business and Human Rights: Further Steps Towards the Operationalization of the "Protect, Respect and Remedy" Framework', Report of the Special Representative of the Secretary-General on the issue of human rights and transnational corporations and other business entities (2010) UN Doc A/HC/14/27.
[53] J Ruggie 'Business and Human Rights: Mapping International Standards of Responsibility and Accountability for Corporate Acts', Report of the Special Representative of the Secretary-General on the Issue of Human Rights and Transnational Corporations (2007) UN Doc A/HRC/4/35, 44; J Ruggie, 'Business and Human Rights: The Evolving International Agenda' (2007) 101 AJIL 819; see also UNHRC Res 8/7 (2008) 'Mandate of the Special Representative of the Secretary-General on the issue of human rights and transnational corporations and other business enterprises' UN Doc A/HRC/Res/8/7: '*Emphasizing* that transnational corporations and other business enterprises have a responsibility to respect human rights'; see R Mares (ed), *The UN Guiding Principles on Business and Human Rights* (Brill 2012).
[54] UNHRC 'Guiding Principles on Business and Human Rights: Implementing the United Nations 'Protect, Respect and Remedy' Framework, Report of the Special Representative of the Secretary-General on the issue of human rights and transnational corporations and other business enterprises' (2011) UN Doc A/HRC/17/31.
[55] UNHRC 'Human rights and transnational corporations and other business enterprises' (2011) UN Doc A/HRC/RES/17/4.

appropriate means, that when such abuses occur within their territory and/or jurisdiction those affected have access to effective remedy.

When defining the scope of human rights responsibility in the foundational principles of corporate responsibility to respect human rights (II.A.), the UN Principles refer to the international bill of rights (constituted by the Universal Declaration on Human Rights and the two UN Covenants on Human Rights of 1966) and the fundamental principles and rights at work as defined by the International Labour Organization:

II. The corporate responsibility to respect human rights

A. Foundational principles

11. Business enterprises should respect human rights. This means that they should avoid infringing on the human rights of others and should address adverse human rights impacts with which they are involved.

12. The responsibility of business enterprises to respect human rights refers to internationally recognized human rights—understood, at a minimum, as those expressed in the International Bill of Human Rights and the principles concerning fundamental rights set out in the International Labour Organization's Declaration on Fundamental Principles and Rights at Work.

The operational principles (II.B of the UN Guiding Principles) emphasize 'human rights due diligence' in investment and other business activities:

B. Operational Principles

[...]

Human rights due diligence

17. In order to identify, prevent, mitigate and account for how they address their adverse human rights impacts, business enterprises should carry out human rights due diligence. The process should include assessing actual and potential human rights impacts, integrating and acting upon the findings, tracking responses, and communicating how impacts are addressed. Human rights due diligence:

(a) Should cover adverse human rights impacts that the business enterprise may cause or contribute to through its own activities, or which may be directly linked to its operations, products or services by its business relationships;

(b) Will vary in complexity with the size of the business enterprise, the risk of severe human rights impacts, and the nature and context of its operations;

(c) Should be ongoing, recognizing that the human rights risks may change over time as the business enterprise's operations and operating context evolve. [...]

(b) OECD Guidelines for Multinational Enterprises

The OECD Guidelines for Multinational Enterprises (2011 edition),[56] as well as the practice of National Contact Points (NCPs) established to monitor compliance with

---

[56] See in more detail Ch III.8(b).

the OECD Guidelines, emphasize the respect of human rights within their own sphere of responsibility and reflect the growing importance of 'human rights due diligence' in the supply chain and other business relations in accordance with the reports of UN Special Rapporteur Ruggie and the Ruggie Principles. The OECD Guidelines state that

[...] Enterprises should, within the framework of internationally recognised human rights, the international human rights obligations of the countries in which they operate as well as relevant domestic laws and regulations:
1. Respect human rights, which means they should avoid infringing on the human rights of others and should address adverse human rights impacts with which they are involved.
2. Within the context of their own activities, avoid causing or contributing to adverse human rights impacts and address such impacts when they occur.
3. Seek ways to prevent or mitigate adverse human rights impacts that are directly linked to their business operations, products or services by a business relationship, even if they do not contribute to those impacts.
4. Have a policy commitment to respect human rights.
5. Carry out human rights due diligence as appropriate to their size, the nature and context of operations and the severity of the risks of adverse human rights impacts.[57]
6. Provide for or co-operate through legitimate processes in the remediation of adverse human rights impacts where they identify that they have caused or contributed to these impacts.

It is not so much the direct responsibility on the grounds of disrespect for human rights, but rather the indirect responsibility of multinational corporations in the context of 'due diligence' in business relations which has become a crucial issue in the practice of NCPs. In the landmark case *Global Witness v Afrimex Ltd*, the British NCP found that the British corporation Afrimex, during its operations in the Democratic Republic of the Congo (DRC), had (besides having paid bribes to a rebel group) violated the OECD Guidelines through neglecting 'due diligence in the supply chain' by purchasing minerals from mines in the DRC that employ child and forced labour.[58]

Occasionally, NCPs turn a tangible and plausible concern about a host State's human rights violations in a particular setting into a thinly substantiated finding that an enterprise having business connections with the host government failed to comply with human rights standards under the OECD Guidelines. Thus in the case *Forum for Environment and Development v Aker Kvaerner ASA*,[59] the NCP of

[57] Part I, Ch IV. Human Rights.
[58] See *Global Witness v Afrimex Ltd* Final Statement by the UK National Contact Point for the OECD-Guidelines for Multinational Enterprises (2008) <http://oecdwatch.org/cases/Case_114/561/at_download/file> (accessed 23 June 2016) para 76: 'The NCP urges UK companies to use their influence over contracting parties and business partners, when trading in natural resources from this region, to ensure that due diligence is applied to the supply chain'. J Letnar Cernic, 'Global Witness v. Afrimex Ltd: Decision Applying OECD Guidelines on Corporate Responsibility for Human Rights' (2009) 13 ASIL Insight No 1.
[59] See *Enquiry from the Forum for Environment and Development on Aker Kvaerner's activities at Guantanamo Bay*, Statement by the Norwegian National Contact Point (2005) <http://www.oecd.org/investment/mne/38038283.pdf> (accessed 23 June 2016).

Norway analysed the maintenance services, for example for the supply of water and electricity, of the subsidiaries of a Norwegian company for the naval bases and the prison on Guantánamo Bay in light of reports on possible human rights violations by the operation of the US detention facilities. The Norwegian NCP concluded that the enterprise should have undertaken a 'thorough and documented assessment of the ethical issues' connected with its operations. However, the Norwegian NCP did not clearly assume a violation of human rights by the US Government or a concurrent complicity of the enterprise. Nor did the Norwegian NCP clarify why maintenance services at a detention facility jeopardize the human rights of prisoners.

A number of cases demonstrate that human rights issues are often closely interwoven with environmental protection, especially in context with the exploitation of natural resources. In the case *Survival International v Vedanta Resources*, the British NCP found that a British mining corporation, operating in India through local subsidiaries, had failed to consult with the tribal peoples which were affected by a projected bauxite mine in their neighbourhood and revered the mining area as sacred. The mining company had failed to use other mechanisms to assess the human rights impact, thus violating the respect for human rights of those affected by its activities,[60] and the requirement of effective mechanisms which foster a relationship of confidence and mutual trust between enterprises and the societies in which they operate.[61] In the follow-up stage of the case, the complainant NGO put forward that the enterprise had not complied with recommendations of the British NCP, whilst the mining company persisted on the unmodified realization of the project as being in conformity with Indian legislation.[62] Some months later, the local Government suspended the mining project with reference to the proceedings before the British NCP since it violated environmental law and indigenous rights.[63] This illustrates that findings of NCPs may have decisive impact on controversial projects.

(c) The US Alien Tort Claims Act (ATCA/ATS)

There are tendencies at the national level to hold individuals as well as corporations accountable for violations of elementary human rights committed abroad. In the United States, a considerable number of claims have been brought before the federal courts on the basis of the Alien Tort Statute of 1789 (ATS),[64] also known as Alien Tort Claims Act (ATCA).[65] The ATCA provides that '[t]he district courts

---

[60] Part I. Ch II. A no. 2.   [61] Part I. Ch II. A no. 7.

[62] *Survival International v Vedanta Resources*, Follow up Final Statement by the UK National Contact Point (2010), paras 11–21.

[63] For a detailed analysis see J Motte-Baumvol, 'Le règlement des différends à l'intention des entreprises multinationales—Quelques réflexions à partir des principes directeurs de l'OECD' (2014) 118 RGDIP 303 (324).

[64] 28 USC § 1350.

[65] See eg *Doe v Unocal* 963 F. Supp 880 (US District CD California 1997); P Muchlinski 'Corporations in International Law' in R Wolfrum (ed), *The Max Planck Encyclopedia of Public International Law* (OUP 2012) vol II, 797 paras 16 and 37; A Clapham, 'Extending International

shall have original jurisdiction of any civil action by an alien for a tort only committed in violation of the law of nations or a treaty of the United States.'

US federal courts have rendered a number of judgments discussing whether and
when human rights violations trigger claims for damages. After its enactment as
part of the Judiciary Act in 1789, the ATCA remained dormant for a long time.
Not until 200 years later, the ATCA was activated in practice as the basis for a civil
law suit against individuals accused of having violated international law. In the case
Filártiga v Peña-Irala in 1980,[66] the United States Court of Appeals for the Second
Circuit held that violations of customary international law including also violations
of contemporary international human rights are actionable under the ATCA. In the
last decades a growing number of claims brought against TNCs under the ATCA
were related to direct human rights violations as well as to 'aiding and abetting'
human rights violations committed by States.

The Supreme Court's ruling in *Sosa v Alvarez-Machain* clarified that the ATCA
was purely a jurisdictional statute.[67] Furthermore, the Court stated that, in order
to bring a legal action in front of the US courts, the right invoked should 'rest on
a norm of international character accepted by the civilized world and defined with
a specificity comparable to the features of the 18th century paradigms we have
recognized'.[68]

However, a number of issues still remain unsettled. It is controversial whether
US law recognizes corporate liability for human rights violations under the ATCA
and, if so, which behaviour qualifies as 'aiding and abetting' in relation to to human
rights violations committed by foreign governments.

In *Khulumani v Barclays National Bank Ltd* (2007), the US Court of Appeals
for the Second Circuit accepted 'aiding and abetting' as a concept of corporate
liability under the ATCA.[69] In this case, plaintiffs argued that TNCs (eg British
Petroleum, Shell Oil, JP Morgan, Citigroup) had aided and abetted the South

---

Criminal Law beyond the Individual to Corporations and Armed Opposition Groups' (2008)
6 JICJ 899 (904ff); D McBarnet and P Schmidt, 'Corporate Accountability Through Creative
Enforcement: Human Rights, the Alien Tort Claims Act and the Limits of Legal Impunity' in D
McBarnet, A Voiculescu, and T Campbell (eds), *The New Corporate Accountability: Corporate Social
Responsibility and the Law* (CUP 2009) 148; A-M Slaughter and DL Bosco, 'Plaintiff 's Diplomacy'
(2000) 79 Foreign Affairs 102; S Joseph, *Corporations and Transnational Human Rights Litigation* (Hart
Publishing 2004) 21; AJ Wilson, 'Beyond Unocal: Conceptual Problems in Using International Norms
to Hold Transnational Corporations Liable Under the Alien Tort Claims Act' in O De Shutter (ed),
Transnational Corporations and Human Rights (Hart Publishing 2006) 43; JA Zerk, *Multinationals
and Corporate Social Responsibility* (CUP 2011) 207; D Scheffer and C Kaeb, 'The Five Levels of CSR
Compliance: The Resiliency of Corporate Liability under the Alien Tort Statute and the Case for a
Counterattack Strategy in Compliance Theory' (2011) 29 Berk J Int'l L 334; B Stephens, J Chomsky,
J Green, P Hoffmann, and M Ratner, *International Human Rights Litigation in US Courts* (2nd edn,
Martinus Nijhoff 2008).

[66] *Filártiga v Peña-Irala* 630 F.2d 876 (2d Cir 1980).
[67] *Sosa v Alvarez-Machain* 542 US 692 (714) (2004); see CM Vázquez, 'Sosa v Alvarez-Machain and
Human Rights Claims against Corporations under the Alien Tort Statute' in T Cottier, J Pauwelyn, and
E Bürgi (eds), *Human Rights and International Trade* (OUP 2005) 137.
[68] *Sosa v Alvarez-Machain* 542 US 692 (725) (2004).
[69] *Khulumani v Barclays National Bank Ltd* 504 F.3d 254 (2d Cir 2007).

African Government's systemic violation of human rights during the Apartheid era by doing business with the regime. The panel issued a fractured decision featuring three different opinions by the three-judge panel. The panel first disagreed about which proper source determines the standard for aiding and abetting liability: domestic US law or customary international law. Secondly, there was a conflict as to the standard, which defined the liability of TNCs for aiding and abetting liability: the pure knowledge or purpose.

The Court held that aiding and abetting does not require purpose but mere knowledge:

[...] [C]ustomary international law requires that an aider and abettor knows that its actions will substantially assist the perpetrator in the commission of a crime or tort in violation of the law of nations.[70]

In *The Presbyterian Church of Sudan v Talisman Energy, Inc*[71] (2009), the US Court of Appeals for the Second Circuit raised the standard for 'aiding and abetting':

[A]pplying international law, we hold the mens rea standard for aiding and abetting liability in ATS actions is purpose rather than knowledge alone. Even if there is a sufficient international consensus for imposing liability on individuals who purposefully aid and abet a violation of international law [...] no such consensus exists for imposing liability on individuals who knowingly (but not purposefully) aid and abet a violation of international law.[72]

In the light of this standard, contributions to the infrastructure of the country facilitating military operations or the contributions to the government's spending (eg by levies on the exploration of crude oil) do not establish liability. The Court was also influenced by the consequences of an all too expansive application of the ATCA:

[...] There is evidence that Southern Sudanese were subjected to attacks by the Government, that those attacks facilitated the oil enterprise, and that the Government's stream of oil revenue enhanced the military capabilities used to persecute its enemies. But if ATS liability could be established by knowledge of those abuses coupled only with such commercial activities as resource development, the statute would act as a vehicle for private parties to impose embargos or international sanctions through civil actions in the USA. Such measures are not the province of private parties but are, instead, properly reserved to governments and multinational organizations.[73]

In the high-profile case *Wiwa v Shell*,[74] plaintiffs invoked the responsibility of Shell under the ATCA for environmental devastation, killings, and other human rights abuses committed by Nigerian police against members and representatives of the Ogoni People. They claimed that a Shell subsidiary engaged in oil production in the territory of the Ogoni People acted in a kind of complicity with Nigerian forces.

---

[70] *Khulumani v Barclays National Bank Ltd et al* (US District Court Southern District of New York 2009) 54.

[71] *The Presbyterian Church of Sudan v Talisman Energy Inc* (2010) 49 ILM 4.

[72] *The Presbyterian Church of Sudan v Talisman Energy Inc* (2010) 49 ILM 4, 15.

[73] *The Presbyterian Church of Sudan v Talisman Energy Inc* (2010) 49 ILM 4, 18.

[74] See Section 1 in this Chapter.

Though Shell denied all responsibility, in 2009, the company entered into a settlement with the plaintiffs agreeing to pay USD 15.5 million.[75] Human rights activists interpret this settlement as a precedent for corporate responsibility for human rights violations.

The United States Court of Appeals for the Second Circuit ruling in the case *Kiobel*, which denied the existence of a corporate liability in customary international law, was criticized in two following decisions by the United States Court of Appeals for the District of Columbia Circuit and the United States Court of Appeals for the Seventh Circuit, which were both rendered before the seminal ruling of the US Supreme Court in *Kiobel*. In *John Doe VIII v EXXON Mobil*,[76] the United States Court of Appeals for the District of Columbia Circuit held:

In sum, the court concludes, guided by *Sosa*, that under the ATS, domestic law, ie, federal common law, supplies the source of law on the question of corporate liability. The law of the United States has been uniform since its founding that corporations can be held liable for the torts committed by their agents. This is confirmed in international practice, both in treaties and in legal systems throughout the world. Given that the law of every jurisdiction in the United States and of every civilized nation, and the law of numerous international treaties, provide that corporations are responsible for their torts, it would create a bizarre anomaly to immunize corporations from liability for the conduct of their agents in lawsuits brought for 'shockingly egregious violations of universally recognized principles of international law.' [...] The analysis of the majority in *Kiobel*, [...] by overlooking the distinction between norms and technical accoutrements in searching for an international law norm of corporate liability in customary international law, misinterpreting *Sosa* in several ways, and selectively ignoring relevant customary international law, is unpersuasive. The issue of corporate liability has remained in the background during the thirty years since the Second Circuit decided *Filartiga* [...] while numerous courts have considered cases against corporations or other juridical entities under the ATS without any indication that the issue was in controversy, whether in ruling that ATS cases could proceed or that they could not on other grounds. Exxon fails to show that a different approach is warranted now.

In the same vein, the United States Court of Appeals for the Seventh Circuit in *Flomo v Firestone Natural Rubber Co LLC*[77] stated:

[S]uppose no corporation had ever been punished for violating customary international law. There is always a first time for litigation to enforce a norm; there has to be. [...] The Alien Tort Statute, moreover, is civil, and corporate tort liability is common around the world. [...] If a plaintiff had to show that civil liability for such violations was itself a norm of international law, no claims under the Alien Tort Statute could ever be successful, even claims against individuals; only the United States, as far as we know, has a statute that provides a civil remedy for violations of customary international law [...].

[75] *Wiwa v Shell* (Settlement Agreement and Mutual Release) <http://wiwavshell.org/documents/Wiwa_v_Shell_agreements_and_orders.pdf> (accessed 23 June 2016).
[76] *John Doe VIII, et al v EXXON Mobil Corp, et al* (decided on 8 July 2011) 84f, footnotes omitted.
[77] United States Court of Appeals of the Seventh Circuit *Flomo v Firestone Natural Rubber Co LLC* (decided on 11 July 2011).

In the *Kiobel* case, the US Supreme Court granted *certoriari* and radically restricted the ambit of the ATCA by applying the presumption confirmed in *Morrison v National Australia Bank Ltd* that the Congress does not generally intend to legislate with extraterritorial effect ('presumption against extraterritoriality'):[78] 'When a statute gives no clear indication of an extraterritorial application, it has none.'[79] The Supreme Court's restrictive approach was also stimulated by the risk of international conflicts raised by a broad extra-territorial application of the ATCA and 'the danger of unwarranted judicial interference in the conduct of foreign policy'.[80]

From an international perspective, the implications of the ATCA gave rise to an ambivalent assessment. Whilst some criticized in the pre-*Kiobel* case law what they perceived as 'human rights imperialism' and a unilateral definition of international standards, others welcomed the existence of a forum for redressing human rights violations within a strong and fair judicial system, granting quality in the administration of justice, as the US federal courts provide. After the US Supreme Court's decision in *Kiobel* the ATCA has lost a lot of its appeal as a means to enforce claims stemming from human rights violations.

Select Bibliography

T Cottier, J Pauwelyn, and E Bürgi (eds), *Human Rights and International Trade* (OUP 2005).

P-M Dupuy, E-U Petersmann, and F Francioni (eds), *Human Rights in International Investment Law and Arbitration* (OUP 2009).

H Hestermeyer, *Human Rights and the WTO* (OUP 2007).

S Joseph, *Blame it on the WTO? A Human Rights Critique* (OUP 2013).

A McBeth, *International Economic Actors and Human Rights* (Routledge 2011).

R Mares (ed), *The UN Guiding Principles on Business and Human Rights: Foundations and Implementation* (Brill 2012).

EP Mendes, *Global Governance, Human Rights and International Law* (Taylor & Francis Ltd 2014).

JC Ochoa Sanchez, 'The Roles and Powers of the OECD National Contact Points Regarding Complaints on an Alleged Breach of the OECD Guidelines for Multinational Enterprises by a Transnational Corporation' (2015) 84 Nordic Journal of International Law 89.

JG Ruggie, 'Business and Human Rights: The Evolving International Agenda' (2007) 101 AJIL 819.

O De Schutter (ed), *Transnational Corporations and Human Rights* (Hart Publishing 2006).

JG Sprankling, *The International Law of Property* (OUP 2014).

K Weidmann, *Der Beitrag der OECD-Leitsätze für multinationale Unternehmen zum Schutz der Menschenrechte* (Duncker & Humblot 2014).

---

[78] US Supreme Court *Kiobel v Royal Dutch Petroleum Co* 133 S.Ct. 1659 (2013) 13.
[79] US Supreme Court *Morrison v National Australia Bank Ltd* 561 U.S. 247 (2010).
[80] US Supreme Court *Kiobel v Royal Dutch Petroleum Co* 133 S.Ct. 1659 (2013) 5.

VIII

Environmental Protection
and Sustainable Development

The framework of international economic law increasingly responds to environmental concerns. Thus, international environmental law[1] is closely interwoven with international trade and investment law. In the modern world, environmental protection has become of paramount importance. The optimal allocation of resources and a maximum of productivity are no longer the dominant and overarching objectives, even of economic policy. The construction of large industrial facilities, the exploitation of natural resources, or the production of energy almost always raise environmental issues. The regulatory framework for environmental protection does not only reflect sensitivity for environmental concerns, but also the degree of risk aversion prevailing in a country. This regulatory framework may determine entrepreneurial choices of where to invest and to do business.

The so-called 'Earth Summit' in Rio de Janeiro in 1992 led to the adoption of several important treaties and other instruments for the protection of the environment. Products of the 'Rio process' are the Framework Convention on Climate Change,[2] the Convention on Biological Diversity (CBD),[3] the Rio Declaration on Environment and Development,[4] the Agenda 21[5] and the Forest Principles.

A constant issue in the context of import restrictions for environmental purposes is their compatibility with the GATT or other rules of WTO law.[6] WTO law in

---

[1] For a general overview of the topic, see U Beyerlin and T Marauhn, *International Environmental Law* (Hart Publishing 2011); D Bodansky, J Brunnee, and E Hey, *The Oxford Handbook of International Environmental Law* (OUP 2007); M Bowman and C Redgwell (eds), *International Law and the Conservation of Biological Diversity* (Kluwer Law International 1996); L Campiglio, L Pineschi, D Siniscalco, and T Treves (eds), *The Environment after Rio: International Law and Economics* (Springer Netherlands 1996); R Dolzer and J Thesing (eds), *Protecting Our Environment* (Konrad Adenauer Stiftung 2000); M Faure and G Skogh, *The Economic Analysis of Environmental Policy and Law* (Edward Elgar Publishing 2003); JC Carlson, GWR Palmer, and BH Weston, *International Environmental Law and World Order* (3rd edn, West Publishers 2012); AC Kiss and D Shelton, *International Environmental Law* (3rd edn, Hotei Publisher 2004); E Louka, *International Environmental Law: Fairness, Effectiveness and World Order* (CUP 2006); P Sands and J Peel, *Principles of International Environmental Law* (3rd edn, CUP 2012); R Wolfrum (ed), *Enforcing Environmental Standards: Economic Mechanisms as Viable Means?* (Springer 1996).

[2] See Section 5 in this Chapter. See Section 6(a) in this Chapter. (1992) 31 ILM 876.

[5] See NA Robinson (ed), *Agenda 21: Earth's Action Plan* (Oceana Publications 1993).

[6] For general remarks on the conflict of trade and environment, see C Robb (ed), *International Environmental Law Reports 2: Trade and Environment* (CUP 2001); P Sands and J Peel, *Principles of*

general and the GATT in particular aim at the liberalization of world trade and the reduction of barriers to trade. WTO law subjects restrictive trade measures to scrutiny, though making allowance for environmental protection (see Article XX(g) of the GATT). Not all measures taken in the name of environmental protection are actually meant to protect the environment but are thinly disguised protectionist measures. More often, authentic environmental protection operates as a trade barrier for products from developing countries or from industrial countries with a different perception of risk. Particular problems are raised by trade restrictions directed against 'production and process methods' (PPMs), which are detrimental to the environment, for example the import prohibition on fish caught by certain catching methods.

1. Transboundary Impacts and Transboundary Harm

A State's sovereignty is limited by the sovereignty of the adjoining States. The law regulating activities with a transboundary impact emphasizes the principle of mutual consideration of interests.[7] A State may not exercise its territorial sovereignty in a way that seriously damages the environment or substantially impairs the ecological balance of neighbour States. This duty of every State to duly consider the environmental integrity of neighbours is not limited to acts and omissions by the State, but also extends to harmful acts of private actors.[8] The duty to respect the environment of other States has been recognized by several arbitral awards and nowadays must be considered customary international law.[9] Due consideration of neighbouring concerns calls for a detailed analysis of the various interests involved and aims at a fair balance.

In the *Pulp Mills* case (*Argentina v Uruguay*), the International Court of Justice (ICJ) held that the operation of industrial facilities in the proximity of border rivers requires an environmental impact assessment. The ICJ derived this duty not only

---

International Environmental Law (3rd edn, CUP 2012) 940; TJ Schoenbaum, 'International Trade and Protection of the Environment: The Continuing Search for Reconciliation' (1997) 91 AJIL 268.

[7] For the historical perspective, see SC McCaffrey, 'The Harmon Doctrine One Hundred Years Later: Buried, Not Praised' (1996) 36 Nat Resources J 965; see generally R Bratspies and R Miller (eds), *Transboundary Harm in International Law* (CUP 2006); G Handl, 'Transboundary Impacts' in D Bodansky, J Brunnee, and E Hey (eds), *The Oxford Handbook of International Environmental Law* (OUP 2007) 531; H Xue, *Transboundary Damage in International Law* (CUP 2003).

[8] See G Handl, 'Transboundary Impacts' in D Bodansky, J Brunnee, and E Hey, *The Oxford Handbook of International Environmental Law* (OUP 2007) 531, 533 with reference to ICJ *Legality of the Threat or Use of Nuclear Weapons* (Advisory Opinion) [1996] ICJ Rep 226 para 29 and ICJ *Case Concerning the Gabčíkovo-Nagymaros Project (Hungary v Slovakia)* [1997] ICJ Rep 7 para 53.

[9] See the arbitral award in the case *Lac Lanoux* (diversion of water in the Pyrenees) (1963) XII RIAA 281; see also A Epiney, 'Lac Lanoux Arbitration' in R Wolfrum (ed), *The Max Planck Encyclopedia of Public International Law* (OUP 2012) vol VI, 626; another 'classic case' *Trail Smelter* (air pollution by a Canadian smelter close to the US border) (1949) III RIAA 1905; see RA Miller, 'Trail Smelter Arbitration' in R Wolfrum (ed), *The Max Planck Encyclopedia of Public International Law* (OUP 2012) vol IX, 1010.

from a treaty which had been concluded between Argentina and Uruguay, but also from customary international law:

[T]he obligation to protect and preserve [...] has to be interpreted in accordance with a practice, which in recent years has gained so much acceptance among States that it may now be considered a requirement under general international law to undertake an environmental impact assessment where there is a risk that the proposed industrial activity may have a significant adverse impact in a transboundary context, in particular, on a shared resource.[10]

This understanding does not only place the duty to assess the cross-border impact on a broad legal basis, but also implies that States must refrain from allowing industrial activities which substantially impair the environment in a neighbour State.[11]

In treaty law, the Convention on Environmental Impact Assessment in a Transboundary Context of 1991, the so-called Espoo-Convention,[12] catalysed the standard of carefully evaluating the cross-border implications of projects for the environment. The Convention, inter alia, covers the construction of crude oil refineries or the construction of large oil and gas pipelines (Annex I, No 1 and 8). The Protocol on Strategic Environmental Assessment to the Convention on Environmental Impact Assessment in a Transboundary Context of 2003 (SEA-Protocol) to the Espoo-Convention contains detailed criteria for the strategic impact assessment of specific plans and programmes.

There is a tendency in international law to subject 'ultra hazardous activities' to strict liability.[13] Such liability does not rest upon the responsible State's negligence or otherwise wrongful conduct, but flows from the high risk of the ultra-hazardous activity.[14] Candidates for this form of strict liability are space operations and nuclear disasters causing vast cross-border contamination (as in Chernobyl 1986), possibly also certain high risk forms of genetic engineering.

A debated issue in international environmental law is the effect of administrative permits for installations with transboundary effects. In many States, neighbours must tolerate activities covered by authorization. In a transboundary context, the authorizing State cannot impose a duty to tolerate on the inhabitants of foreign territory. The authorization shares the territorial limits of national jurisdiction.

In a lawsuit filed before Dutch courts by Dutch tulip-producers against French extractors of potash for the pollution of the water of the Rhine, the French enterprises could not rely on the French authorization to discharge polluted water into the Rhine.[15]

---

[10] ICJ *Case Concerning Pulp Mills on the River of Uruguay (Argentina v Uruguay)* [2010] ICJ Rep 14 para 204.

[11] See N Craik, *The International Law of Environmental Impact Assessment* (CUP 2010). For a rather critical view of this concept, see J Knox, 'The Myth and Reality of Transboundary Environmental Impact Assessment' (2002) 96 AJIL 291.

[12] (1993) 32 ILM 80.

[13] See LFE Goldie, 'Concepts of Strict and Absolute Liability and Ranking of Liability in Terms of Relative Exposure to Risk' (1985) 16 NYIL 174.

[14] For a general outline of the treatment of hazardous substances and activities in international law, see DA Wirth, 'Hazardous Substances and Activities' in D Bodansky, J Brunnee, and E Hey (eds), *The Oxford Handbook of International Environmental Law* (OUP 2007) 394.

[15] See S Nassr-Esfahani and M Wemckstern, 'Der Rheinversalzungsprozess' (1985) 49 RabelsZ 740.

A satisfactory solution normally will have to be sought on the level of an international treaty. Such a treaty exists, for example, between Germany and Austria with respect to the airport in Salzburg.[16]

It is for national law to determine whether the interests of neighbours on the other side of the frontier should be considered before authorization and whether these neighbours should have standing to challenge an authorization.

The German Federal Administrative Court has recognized that Dutch nationals living close to the German border could challenge the permit for a nuclear power plant and invoke certain individual rights (health, life, property) protected under the relevant legislation before the German courts.[17]

2. Sustainable Development

The concept of 'sustainable development'[18] attempts to bring economic development on the one hand and due regard for environmental concerns (including a responsible use of natural resources) on the other hand into balance. Rather than operating as an operable rule of customary law or as a general principle of international law, the concept of sustainable development guides the interpretation of treaties as well as national economic and environmental policies. The United Nations Conference on Environment and Development (UNCED) in Rio (1992) catalysed the recognition of sustainable development as an overarching legal standard. The Rio Declaration on Environment and Development[19] follows an anthropocentric understanding of sustainable development and states as Principle 1:

Human beings are at the centre of concerns for sustainable development. They are entitled to a healthy and productive life in harmony with nature.

The WTO Treaty proclaims 'the optimal use of the world's resources in accordance with the objective of sustainable development' in the preamble. WTO dispute settlement bodies have referred to this principle when balancing free trade and environmental protection.[20]

---

[16] BGBl. 1974 II 13.   [17] BVerwGE 75, 285 (288).

[18] A Boyle and D Freestone, *International Law and Sustainable Development* (OUP 2001); MC Cordonier Segger and A Khalfan, *Sustainable Development Law: Principles, Practices, and Prospects* (OUP 2004); K Ginther, E Denters, and P de Waart, *Sustainable Development and Good Governance* (Springer 1995); D Magraw and LD Hawke, 'Sustainable Development' in D Bodansky, J Brunnee, and E Hey (eds), *The Oxford Handbook of International Environmental Law* (OUP 2007) 613; C Voigt, *Sustainable Development as a Principle of International Law* (Martinus Nijhoff Publishers 2009).

[19] (1992) 31 ILM 876.

[20] See D Magraw and LD Hawke, 'Sustainable Development' in D Bodansky, J Brunnee, and E Hey (eds), *The Oxford Handbook of International Environmental Law* (OUP 2007) 613, 616, and 622; WTO, *United States: Import Prohibition of Certain Shrimp and Shrimp Products—Report of the Appellate Body* (1998) WT/DS58/AB/R.

With the objective to support an environmentally sound development, the Global Environmental Facility was created in the institutional context of the World Bank.[21] The Facility finances measures for environmental protection in developing countries.

3. The Precautionary Principle

One of the prominent standards of international environmental law, as well as of the law of health protection is the 'precautionary principle'.[22] According to that principle, it is not always necessary for States to ascertain a scientifically proven risk before taking measures of protection and prevention. States can take preventive or pre-emptive measures of protection, even if a lack of scientific certainty does not permit a reliable risk assessment, in particular if the chain of causation possibly leading to environmental damages is not fully corroborated or the probability of harm remains to be clarified.

Principle 15 of the Rio Declaration on Environment and Development recognizes the principle of precaution in the field of environmental protection:

In order to protect the environment, the precautionary approach shall be widely applied by States according to their capabilities. Where there are threats of serious or irreversible damage, lack of full scientific certainty shall not be used as a reason for postponing cost-effective measures to prevent environmental degradation.

The precautionary principle does not justify every State action in the prevention of risks. Rather, it presupposes that the available scientific evidence is given full consideration. The precautionary principle can only be invoked if there is a substantial possibility for considerable damage to human health or the environment. The greater the possible damage, the lower is the threshold for possible measures.

In the European Union, the principle of precaution is the overarching standard for environmental policy. EU law also establishes the 'polluter pays' principle, which might extend to precautionary measures. The TFEU states in Article 191(2):

---

[21] For the Statute of the Global Environmental Facility, see (1994) 33 ILM 1273; see also R Dolzer, 'The Global Environment Facility—towards a new concept of the common heritage of mankind?' in G Alfredsson and P Macalister-Smith (eds), *The Living Law of Nations—In Memory of Atle Grahl-Madsen* (Engel 1996) 331.

[22] D Bodansky, 'Scientific Uncertainty and the Precautionary Principle' (1991) 33 Env't 4; CE Foster, *Science and the Precautionary Principle in International Courts and Tribunals* (CUP 2011); D Freestone and E Hey (eds), *The Precautionary Principle and International Law* (Kluwer Law International 1996); H Hohmann, *The Precautionary Legal Duties and Principles of Modern International Environmental Law* (Springer Netherlands 1994); DA Motaal, 'Is the World Trade Organization Anti-Precaution?' (2005) 39 JWT 483; PH Sand, 'The Precautionary Principle: A European Perspective' (2000) 6 Human and Ecological Risk Assessment 445; A Trouwborst, *Evolution and Status of the Precautionary Principle in International Law* (Kluwer Law International 2002); JB Wiener, 'Precaution' in D Bodansky, J Brunnee, and E Hey (eds), *The Oxford Handbook of International Environmental Law* (OUP 2007) 597; S Boutillon, 'The Precautionary Principle: Development of an International Standard' (2001–02) 23 Mich J Int'l L 429; J Peel, 'Precaution—A Matter of Principle, Approach or Process?' (2004) 5 Melb J Int'l L 483.

Union policy on the environment shall aim at a high level of protection taking into account the diversity of situations in the various regions of the Union. It shall be based on the precautionary principle and on the principles that preventive action should be taken, that environmental damage should as a priority be rectified at source and that the polluter should pay.

Under customary law, the precautionary principle does not directly establish rights and obligations. Rather, it helps to define pre-established rules and may guide the interpretation of statutes and treaties.

The European Court of Human Rights reads the precautionary principle into the guarantee of rights which may be affected by measures possibly harming the environment such as the right to private and family life (Article 8 of the European Convention on Human Rights).[23] This approach provides the prevention of environmental damage with anthropocentric underpinnings.

At least to some extent, WTO law is also receptive to the precautionary principle.[24] Members of the WTO may justify restraints on trade with fighting risks even if there is no consensus among scientists about the existence and relevance of risks:

We do not believe that a risk assessment has to come to a monolithic conclusion that coincides with the scientific conclusion or view implicit in the SPS measure. The risk assessment could set out both the prevailing view representing the 'mainstream' of scientific opinion, as well as the opinions of scientists taking a divergent view. Article 5.1 does not require that the risk assessment must necessarily embody only the view of a majority of the relevant scientific community. In some cases, the very existence of divergent views presented by qualified scientists who have investigated the particular issue at hand may indicate a state of scientific uncertainty. Sometimes the divergence may indicate a roughly equal balance of scientific opinion, which may itself be a form of scientific uncertainty. In most cases, responsible and representative governments tend to base their legislative and administrative measures on 'mainstream' scientific opinion. In other cases, equally responsible and representative governments may act in good faith on the basis of what, at a given time, may be a divergent opinion coming from qualified and respected sources. By itself, this does not necessarily signal the absence of a reasonable relationship between the SPS measure and the risk assessment, especially where the risk involved is life-threatening in character and is perceived to constitute a clear and imminent threat to public health and safety. Determination of the presence or absence of that relationship can only be done on a case-to-case basis, after account is taken of all considerations rationally bearing upon the issue of potential adverse health effects.[25]

Despite the broad recognition of precaution, the legitimacy of specific measures is often a matter of controversy. Different degrees of risk perception and risk aversion account for different regulatory philosophies. Residual risks are considered unacceptable in some countries but tolerated in others. In particular, in several fields of

---

[23] On damages to family and private life caused by use of cyanide for the exploration of gold, see ECtHR *Tatar v Romania* App no 67021/01 (27 January 2009).

[24] See HJ Priess and C Pitschas, 'Protection of Public Health and the Role of the Precautionary Principle under WTO Law' (2000–01) 24 Fordham Int'l LJ 519.

[25] On Article 5.7 SPS see WTO, *European Communities: Measures Concerning Meat and Meat Products (Hormones)—Report of the Appellate Body* (1998) WT/DS 26/AB/R, WT/DS 48/AB/R para 194.

high-technology (eg biotechnology) this divergence accounts for significant legal and economic conflicts.

4. Treaties on Pollution Control and on the Liability for Environmental Contaminations

Numerous treaties in the field of international environmental law have established quite a complex architecture of rules. Some fields, such as pollution control or the liability for environmental damage, may have a particular impact on the international economic order. Pollution control often stands behind trade and transport restrictions as a mechanism to prevent environmental damages. Liability for environmental contamination addresses an important corporate risk.

Among the treaties on pollution control[26] affecting international transport and trade is the Basel Convention on the Control of Transboundary Movements of Hazardous Wastes and Their Disposal of 1989.[27] The Basel Convention establishes a regime with the aim of a uniform regulation of the transboundary movement of hazardous wastes. Parties to the Convention may prohibit the import of hazardous wastes or other wastes for disposal (Article 4(1)(a) of the Basel Convention). Other State parties must conform to this decision by prohibiting or not permitting the export of the wastes concerned (Article 4(1)(b) of the Convention). Article 4(1)(c) of the Convention establishes the so-called 'Prior-Informed-Consent Procedure' (PIC), which is often found in the context of international environmental law:

Article 4 section 1
(a) Parties exercising their right to prohibit the import of hazardous wastes or other wastes for disposal shall inform the other Parties of their decision pursuant to Article 13.
(b) Parties shall prohibit or shall not permit the export of hazardous wastes and other wastes to the Parties which have prohibited the import of such wastes, when notified pursuant to subparagraph (a) above.
(c) Parties shall prohibit or shall not permit the export of hazardous wastes and other wastes if the State of import does not consent in writing to the specific import, in the case where that State of import has not prohibited the import of such wastes.

In Article 4, sections 2 to 4, the Basel Convention provides measures to control the traffic with hazardous and other wastes:

Article 4 section 2
Each Party shall take the appropriate measures to: [...]
(e) Not allow the export of hazardous wastes or other wastes to a State or group of States belonging to an economic and/or political integration organization that are Parties,

---

[26] For an outline with a focus on the regulation of toxic substances, see M Pallemaerts, *Toxics and Transnational Law: International and European Regulation of Toxic Substances as Legal Symbolism* (Hart Publishing 2003).

[27] (1989) 28 ILM 657; see K Kummer, *International Management of Hazardous Wastes: The Basel Convention and Related Legal Rules* (OUP 1995).

particularly developing countries, which have prohibited by their legislation all imports, or if it has reason to believe that the wastes in question will not be managed in an environmentally sound manner, according to criteria to be decided on by the Parties at their first meeting;

[...]

(g) Prevent the import of hazardous wastes and other wastes if it has reason to believe that the wastes in question will not be managed in an environmentally sound manner;

[...].

Article 4 section 3

The Parties consider that illegal traffic in hazardous wastes or other wastes is criminal.

Article 4 section 4

Each Party shall take appropriate legal, administrative and other measures to implement and enforce the provisions of this Convention, including measures to prevent and punish conduct in contravention of the Convention.

The Basel Convention bans the import or export of wastes from or to States which are not a party to the Convention in Article 4 section 5:

A Party shall not permit hazardous wastes or other wastes to be exported to a non-Party or to be imported from a non-Party.

This provision aims to protect the integrity of the regulatory framework established by the Basel Convention with respect to non-parties. This is an important feature of modern environmental treaty 'regimes'. They do not only lay down certain objectives for the State Parties but also try to achieve a spill-over effect and to 'motivate' other States to join the regime by direct or indirect economic incentives. The Basel Convention illustrates the importance of international environmental law also in an economic context.

Despite the Basel Convention, controlling the export of toxic wastes from industrial countries to poor countries has remained a matter of concern.[28] As a response, a number of African States adopted the Bamako Convention on the Ban on the Import into Africa and the Control of Transboundary Movement and Management of Hazardous Wastes within Africa (1991).[29]

Another treaty affecting international trade is the Rotterdam Convention on the Prior Informed Consent Procedure for Certain Hazardous Chemicals and Pesticides in International Trade, which entered into force in 2004. According to Article 1, the objective of the Rotterdam Convention

[...] is to promote shared responsibility and cooperative efforts among Parties in the international trade of certain hazardous chemicals in order to protect human health and the environment from potential harm and to contribute to their environmentally sound use, by facilitating information exchange about their characteristics, by providing for a national decision-making process on their import and export and by disseminating these decisions to Parties.

---

[28] For a general outline of the problem, see J Clapp, *Toxic Exports: The Transfer of Hazardous Wastes from Rich to Poor Countries* (Cornell University Press 2001).

[29] (1991) 30 ILM 775.

The very name of the Rotterdam Convention already indicates that it follows the PIC principle.[30] The text of the Convention is an example of the 'soft' character of most environmental treaties. In sensitive areas like international environmental law, 'soft mechanisms' based on consent can be much more efficient than 'hard rules' which merely few States are willing to ratify. The same rationale applies to the Stockholm Convention on Persistent Organic Pollutants ('POPs Convention') which entered into force in 2004.[31] The POPs Convention aims to prevent the bioaccumulation of certain pollutants through the food chain.[32]

Treaties on the liability for environmental contaminations have a significant impact on international business.[33] The Paris Convention on Third Party Liability in the Field of Nuclear Energy of 1960 and the International Convention on Civil Liability for Oil Pollution Damage of 1969 both harmonize the standards of civil liability for particularly severe forms of environmental contamination. The Nagoya–Kuala Lumpur Supplementary Protocol on Liability and Redress to the Cartagena Protocol on Biosafety (2010) addresses the liability of operators for environmental damage caused by the transboundary movement of living genetically modified organisms.

5. Treaties on the Protection of the Atmosphere and for Climate Protection

Two of the fundamental legal instruments for climate protection in general and the protection of the atmosphere in particular[34] are the Vienna Convention for the Protection of the Ozone Layer of 1985 and the Montreal Protocol on Substances that Deplete the Ozone Layer of 1987.[35] The Montreal Protocol obligates its parties to reduce the production and the use of certain ozone-depleting substances continuously (Articles 2Aff; Article 5 contains special provisions for developing countries). The Montreal Protocol lays down extensive import and export restrictions

---

[30] The Rotterdam Convention is therefore often referred to as the 'PIC-Convention'.

[31] (2001) 40 ILM 532.

[32] See MA Olsen, *Analysis of the Stockholm Convention on Persistent Organic Pollutants* (OUP 2003).

[33] See B Baker Röben, 'Civil Liability as a Control Mechanism for Environmental Protection at the International Level' in F Morrison and R Wolfrum (eds), *International, Regional and National Law* (Springer 2000) 821; A Boyle, 'Globalising Environmental Liability: The Interplay of National and International Law' (2005) 17 JEL 3; M Fitzmaurice, 'International Responsibility and Liability' in D Bodansky, J Brunnee, and E Hey (eds), *The Oxford Handbook of International Environmental Law* (OUP 2007) 1010; T Scovazzi, 'State Responsibility for Environmental Harm' (2001) 12 YIEL 43; WR Moomaw, 'Can the International Treaty System Address Climate Change?' (2013) 37 The Fletcher Forum of World Affairs 105.

[34] For a general outline on atmosphere and climate protection, see SO Andersen and K Madhava Sarma, *Protecting the Ozone Layer: the United Nations History* (Routledge 2002); EA Parson, *Protecting the Ozone Layer: Science and Strategy* (OUP 2003); IH Rowlands, 'Atmosphere and Outer Space' in D Bodansky, J Brunnee, and E Hey (eds), *The Oxford Handbook of International Environmental Law* (OUP 2007) 315.

[35] See EA Parson, 'The Montreal Protocol' in PG Le Prestre, JD Reid, and ET Morehouse Jr (eds), *Protecting the Ozone Layer: Lessons, Models and Prospects* (Springer 1998) 127.

from or to States which are not parties to the Protocol in Article 4. These provisions shall restrain ozone-depleting production processes in non-party countries and eliminate competitive advantages of States not bound by its rules on climate protection. This method operates as a 'pull to compliance' or a 'pull to ratification' for States not yet parties to the Protocol.

Another seminal legal instrument for climate protection is the United Nations Framework Convention on Climate Change of 1992 (Rio). Rather than setting precise and immediately operable standards, the Convention provides a gradual specification in subsequent protocols. The ultimate objective of the Convention is to reduce the emission of greenhouse gases in order to protect the ozone layer and to avoid detrimental effects on the environment in general. Despite its character as a framework convention, the Convention itself already contains certain duties to reduce the anthropogenic emission of greenhouse gases like carbon dioxide for industrial countries. However, the Convention did not bring about a significant progress in climate protection.

A first step towards a more efficient regime of climate protection was the Kyoto Protocol of 1997.[36] The Protocol is based on the concept of a common, but differentiated responsibility of States. This approach assumes the common responsibility of all States for the prevention of a further climate change, while taking into account the very different positions of individual States in terms of causation and economic or technical capacity to take measures of reduction. Industrial countries account for two-thirds of the total emission of greenhouse gases. Developing countries and their industries often are not in a position to reduce their emissions effectively. The unequal distribution of the burden often does not follow the rules of logic but rather of political compromise. As a result, even States with high polluting rates are exempt from reduction obligations.

The Protocol requires most industrial States (States with an emission commitment, so-called 'Annex B States') to keep within an assigned emission target, which usually means bringing emissions of carbon dioxide and other greenhouse gases below the levels at a reference date (as a rule 1990) within a certain period. This reference level privileges States such as Russia which had relatively high emissions in past decades, but have long since brought them down through a change of industrial structure or by technological overhaul of entirely outdated installations. Certain adjustments, as for carbon sinks (eg large forested areas), privilege countries like Canada or Russia. Thus, some industrialized States even end up with a commitment of a zero per cent reduction (Russia) or a positive balance allowing them to increase their emission to the reference level.

The Protocol provides some flexible regulatory mechanisms which support international cooperation and technology transfer. It also creates economic incentives.

---

[36] For the text of the Protocol see (1998) 37 ILM 32; see also W Durner, 'The Implementation of the Climate Change' (1999) 37 AVR 357; M Faure, J Gupta, and A Nentjes, *Climate Change and the Kyoto Protocol* (Edward Elgar Publishing 2003); M Grubb, C Vrolijk, and D Brack, *The Kyoto Protocol* (Royal Institute of International Affairs 1999); S Oberthür and H Ott, *The Kyoto Protocol: International Climate Policy for the Twenty-First Century* (Springer 1999).

The 'joint implementation' mechanism (Article 6) allows forms of cooperation between different parties to the Protocol in keeping within the available quota. If keeping within their aggregated quotas, cooperating States may shift parts of their quota among themselves. The 'clean development mechanism' (Article 12) shall stimulate cooperation between industrial and developing countries including technology transfer. By supporting emission-reduction projects in developing countries, parties with an emission reduction or emission limitation commitment ('Annex B States') may benefit from 'certified emission reduction' (CER) credits, which can be set off against their own reduction debit. The system of 'emission trading' (Articles 6 and 17)[37] allows trading with emission certificates which stand for a certain quota of emission reductions. This mechanism establishes some market-oriented incentives for reduction, but in itself does not change the overall emission balance. Emission trading is particularly profitable for States like Russia, which have a very high reference level well above the actual emission levels and a low (or zero) reduction target. These States have a relatively high quota that can be traded.

The Kyoto regime increasingly stands in contrast to reality. The growing economic strength and increase of industries in countries like China and India has resulted in a rising of emissions on a large scale. At the same time, the emissions of industrial countries have increased in absolute terms, even though they got much lower in relation to other countries. Even the technological progress of the last decades and the growing consensus on curbing emissions were insufficient to stop these developments. In all, global emissions have risen to alarming levels since 1990. Still, the entry into force of the Kyoto Protocol in 2005 with its binding commitments marks an important step towards an efficient climate protection strategy.

Under the Kyoto Protocol, the initial period of commitments only extended until 2012. The protracted post-Kyoto negotiations were marked by a most difficult quest for consensus. The UN Climate Conference in Doha (December 2012) adopted an amendment of the Kyoto Protocol which established a new period for the Protocol's operation from 2013 until 2020 with new reduction targets. Only States undertaking new reduction commitments shall participate in emission trading. The few parties accepting these enhanced obligations include the European Union, Australia, Norway, and Switzerland. Whilst the United States by now recognizes the need to dramatically reduce greenhouse emissions, other important players like China and India still show only limited willingness to condition industrial development by clear and operable reduction commitments.

In December 2015, the parties to the Framework Convention on Climate Change adopted a new treaty on climate change, the so-called 'Paris Agreement'.[38] The Paris Agreement commits the parties to the overarching goal of keeping global warming well below the threshold of 2 per cent and establishes the related objectives such as low greenhouse gas emissions and climate-resilient development (Article 2(1)):

[37] D Freestone and C Streck, *Legal Aspects of Carbon Trading: Kyoto, Copenhagen and Beyond* (OUP 2009).
[38] FCCC 'Paris Agreement' (12 December 2015) FCCC/CP/2015/L.9 Annex.

This Agreement, in enhancing the implementation of the Convention, including its objective, aims to strengthen the global response to the threat of climate change, in the context of sustainable development and efforts to eradicate poverty, including by:

(a) Holding the increase in the global average temperature to well below 2 °C above pre-industrial levels and to pursue efforts to limit the temperature increase to 1.5 °C above pre-industrial levels, recognizing that this would significantly reduce the risks and impacts of climate change;

(b) Increasing the ability to adapt to the adverse impacts of climate change and foster climate resilience and low greenhouse gas emissions development, in a manner that does not threaten food production;

(c) Making finance flows consistent with a pathway towards low greenhouse gas emissions and climate-resilient development.

For the implementation of the Agreement, the concept of 'common but differentiated responsibility' serves as a guideline (Article 2(2)):

This Agreement will be implemented to reflect equity and the principle of common but differentiated responsibilities and respective capabilities, in the light of different national circumstances.

The Paris Agreement aims at reaching global peaking of greenhouse gas emissions as soon as possible, 'in the context of sustainable development and efforts to reduce poverty' (Art. 4(1)). Unlike the Kyoto Protocol, the Paris Agreement establishes no 'hard obligations' to reduce carbon emissions. Instead, the Agreement defers to 'nationally determined contributions' to the global response to climate change. The developed country parties shall provide financial resources to assist developing country parties (Article 9). The Paris Conference envisaged a floor of USD 100 billion per year. The Agreement shall enter into force after ratification by at least 55 parties to the Convention accounting for at least 55 per cent of the total greenhouse gas emissions (Article 21).

6. Treaties on Biodiversity, Access to Genetic Resources, and Biosafety

One of the most urgent challenges of environmental protection is the growing reduction of biodiversity. Most areas of 'mega-biodiversity' are situated Latin-American, African, and Asian countries. The density of biodiversity is particularly high in States like Costa Rica, Panama, Colombia, Ecuador, Peru, Bolivia, Brazil, China, Malaysia, and Papua New Guinea.

Recognizing the threat of extinction to many species, a number of treaties and soft-law instruments have been drafted to stop or at least slow down this development. These mechanisms also affect international trade.

(a) The Convention on Biological Diversity as a framework for the protection and sustainable use of biological resources

Modern treaties on the protection of biodiversity do not only lay down mandatory rules, but also provide economic or technological incentives and fair benefit sharing.

The basic international agreement on the protection of biodiversity and access to genetic plant or animal resources was negotiated and adopted at the 'Earth Summit' in Rio de Janeiro in 1992: the Convention on Biological Diversity (CBD).[39] Almost all States are parties to the CBD. The United States has signed, but not ratified the CBD. The CBD can be legitimately called a 'role model convention', as it strikes a balance between the preservation of biodiversity and the economic use of natural (genetic) resources. It also tries to reconcile the interests of (mostly developing) bio-diverse countries and the extractive interests of other (mostly industrial) countries. The CBD aims both at the protection and preservation of biodiversity on the one hand and its sustainable use on the other. At the same time, the CBD's objectives extend to

[...] the fair and equitable sharing of the benefits arising out of the utilization of genetic resources, including by appropriate access to genetic resources and by appropriate transfer of relevant technologies, taking into account all rights over those resources and to technologies, and by appropriate funding (Article 1 CBD).

This goal is particularly important for those developing countries which are providers of genetic materials to the pharmaceutical and chemical industry.

Biological diversity in terms of the CBD, as defined in Article 2(1),

[...] means the variability among living organisms from all sources including, inter alia, terrestrial, marine and other aquatic ecosystems and the ecological complexes of which they are part; this includes diversity within species, between species and of ecosystems.

The central idea, which reconciles preservation of biodiversity and economic utilization, is the 'sustainable use' of natural resources accounting for diversity in terms of an equilibrium of environmental and economic interests. In Article 2(16), the CBD defines sustainable use as

[...] the use of components of biological diversity in a way and at a rate that does not lead to the long-term decline of biological diversity, thereby maintaining its potential to meet the needs and aspirations of present and future generations.

The approach of the CBD to biodiversity is somewhat ambivalent. On the one hand, the preamble considers the preservation of biodiversity as a 'common concern of humankind'. On the other hand, the CBD stresses the sovereignty of States over their own biological resources, and the correlated responsibility for biodiversity and the environment of other States. Article 3 of the CBD provides:

States have, in accordance with the Charter of the United Nations and the principles of international law, the sovereign right to exploit their own resources pursuant to their own environmental policies, and the responsibility to ensure that activities within their

---

[39] See C Bail, R Falkner, and H Marquard (eds), *Reconciling Trade in Biotechnology with Environment and Development? The Cartagena Protocol on Biosafety* (Royal Institute of International Affairs 2002); A Sontot, 'The Convention on Biological Diversity' (2004/05) 7 Bio-Science Law Review 45; F McConnell, *The Biodiversity Convention: A Negotiating History* (Kluwer Law International 1996).

jurisdiction or control do not cause damage to the environment of other States or of areas beyond the limits of national jurisdiction.

States are responsible for the preservation of the biodiversity within their territory and for the sustainable use of their resources in terms of Articles 6 to 14 of the CBD. Article 14 requires an environmental impact assessment and measures to minimize adverse impacts on the environment.

(b) Access to genetic resources

Access to genetic resources[40] is one of the salient issues of biodiversity. The use of genetic resources, often in conjunction with traditional knowledge of indigenous and other local communities, has opened a field of research with most promising prospects for the development of pharmaceuticals and breeding of animals and plants. Many drugs originate in countries of mega-biodiversity and were developed on the basis of the (synthesized or modified) genetic structure of plants and micro-organisms.

The CBD lays down general principles for the access to genetic resources (as defined in Article 2(10) CBD) in its Article 15:

1. Recognizing the sovereign rights of States over their natural resources, the authority to determine access to genetic resources rests with the national governments and is subject to national legislation.
2. Each Contracting Party shall endeavour to create conditions to facilitate access to genetic resources for environmentally sound uses by other Contracting Parties and not to impose restrictions that run counter to the objectives of this Convention.
3. For the purpose of this Convention, the genetic resources being provided by a Contracting Party, as referred to in this Article and Articles 16 and 19, are only those that are provided by Contracting Parties that are countries of origin of such resources or by the Parties that have acquired the genetic resources in accordance with this Convention.
4. Access, where granted, shall be on mutually agreed terms and subject to the provisions of this Article.
5. Access to genetic resources shall be subject to prior informed consent of the Contracting Party providing such resources, unless otherwise determined by that Party.
6. Each Contracting Party shall endeavour to develop and carry out scientific research based on genetic resources provided by other Contracting Parties with the full participation of, and where possible in, such Contracting Parties.

---

[40] See CM Correa, 'Access to Genetic Resources' (1997) 20 W Comp 57; TR Young, 'An Implementation Perspective on International Law of Genetic Resources: Incentive, Consistency, and Effective Operation' (2004) 15 YIEL 3; KT Kate and SA Laird, *The Commercial Use of Biodiversity* (Earthscan Publications 1999); EC Kamau and G Winter, *Genetic Resources, Traditional Knowledge and the Law* (Routledge 2009); MT Mahop, *Intellectual Property, Community Rights and Human Rights* (Routledge 2010); KJ Ni, 'Legal Aspects of Prior Informed Consent on Access to Genetic Resources: An Analysis of Global Lawmaking and Local Implementation Toward an Optimal Normative Construction' (2009) 42 V and J Transnat'l L 227; YG Shim, 'Intellectual Property Protection of Biotechnology and Sustainable Development in International Law' (2003–04) 29 NCJ Int'l L & Com Reg 157.

7. Each Contracting Party shall take legislative, administrative or policy measures, as appro-priate, and in accordance with Articles 16 and 19 and, where necessary, through the financial mechanism established by Articles 20 and 21 with the aim of sharing in a fair and equitable way the results of research and development and the benefits arising from the commercial and other utilization of genetic resources with the Contracting Party providing such resources. Such sharing shall be upon mutually agreed terms.

Central elements of this regime are the sovereign right of States to determine access to their resources and facilitated access for environmentally sound uses on the basis of prior consent as well as a fair and equitable sharing of benefits in mutually agreed terms (Article 19 CBD).

The Bonn Guidelines on Access to Genetic Resources and Equitable Sharing of the Benefits Arising out of their Utilization (2002) specify the standards for a fair and equitable access to genetic resources and the sharing of benefits.[41] At the Nagoya Conference (2010), the Parties to the CBD adopted the Protocol on Access to Genetic Resources and the Fair and Equitable Sharing of Benefits Arising from their Utilization ('Nagoya Protocol'). The Nagoya Protocol also addresses the participation of local and indigenous communities (Article 12) as well as the protection of traditional knowledge.

The CBD does not govern the status and the use of genetic resources without the required consent of the originating State. The Nagoya Protocol partly tries to compensate the deficits of the CBD in Articles 15 and 16:

Article 15. Compliance with Domestic Legislation or Regulatory Requirements on Access and Benefit-sharing
1. Each Party shall take appropriate, effective and proportionate legislative, administrative or policy measures to provide that genetic resources utilized within its jurisdiction have been accessed in accordance with prior informed consent and that mutually agreed terms have been established, as required by the domestic access and benefit-sharing legislation or regulatory requirements of the other Party.
2. Parties shall take appropriate, effective and proportionate measures to address situations of non-compliance with measures adopted in accordance with paragraph 1 above.
3. Parties shall, as far as possible and as appropriate, cooperate in cases of alleged violation of domestic access and benefit-sharing legislation or regulatory requirements referred to in paragraph 1 above.

Article 16. Compliance with Domestic Legislation or Regulatory Requirements on Access and Benefit-sharing for Traditional Knowledge Associated with Genetic Resources
1. Each Party shall take appropriate, effective and proportionate legislative, administrative or policy measures, as appropriate, to provide that traditional knowledge associated with genetic resources utilized within their jurisdiction has been accessed in accordance with prior informed consent or approval and involvement of indigenous and local communi-ties and that mutually agreed terms have been established, as required by domestic access and benefit-sharing legislation or regulatory requirements of the other Party where such indigenous and local communities are located.

---

[41] For a general overview, see V Normand, 'Access to Genetic Resources and the Fair and Equitable Sharing of Benefits Arising Out of Their Utilization' (2004) 1 JIB Law 133.

2. Each Party shall take appropriate, effective and proportionate measures to address situations of non-compliance with measures adopted in accordance with paragraph 1 above.
3. Parties shall, as far as possible and as appropriate, cooperate in cases of alleged violation of domestic access and benefit-sharing legislation or regulatory requirements referred to in paragraph 1 above.

The Andean Community addressed the issue in its Decision No 391 (1996).[42] The Decision declares the genetic resources themselves as well as the resources gained from their utilisation (which contain the genetic information) as part of the 'heritage' of the States of origin (Article 6(1)). It even qualifies both kinds of resources as inalienable (Article 6(2)). In case of an illegal harvesting of genetic resources used for research, the Decision denies recognition of intellectual property rights or other claims associated with these resources (Second Complementary Provision to the Decision). This provision conflicts with the obligations regarding patent protection under the TRIPS Agreement. A number of WTO members, including the European Union support an amendment to the TRIPS Agreement with respect to certified origins of genetic resources in context with patent claims.

(c) Technology transfer

Many countries with regions of abundant mega-biodiversity lack the necessary technological level to use those natural resources effectively and in a sustainable manner. Therefore, a particular concern of the CBD refers to access and transfer of technology. The CBD strives to establish a balance between access to genetic resources and technical or scientific cooperation (Articles 16 to 18). Article 16 CBD provides:

Article 16. Access to and Transfer of Technology
1. Each Contracting Party, recognizing that technology includes biotechnology, and that both access to and transfer of technology among Contracting Parties are essential elements for the attainment of the objectives of this Convention, undertakes subject to the provisions of this Article to provide and/or facilitate access for and transfer to other Contracting Parties of technologies that are relevant to the conservation and sustainable use of biological diversity or make use of genetic resources and do not cause significant damage to the environment.
2. Access to and transfer of technology referred to in paragraph 1 above to developing countries shall be provided and/or facilitated under fair and most favourable terms, including on concessional and preferential terms where mutually agreed, and, where necessary, in accordance with the financial mechanism established by Articles 20 and 21. In the case of technology subject to patents and other intellectual property rights, such access and transfer shall be provided on terms which recognize and are consistent with the adequate and effective protection of intellectual property rights. The application of this paragraph shall be consistent with paragraphs 3, 4 and 5 below.

---

[42] Gaceta Oficial del Acuerdo de Cartagena, Año XII—Número 213, 17 de julio de 1996, 1.

3. Each Contracting Party shall take legislative, administrative or policy measures, as appropriate, with the aim that Contracting Parties, in particular those that are developing countries, which provide genetic resources are provided access to and transfer of technology which makes use of those resources, on mutually agreed terms, including technology protected by patents and other intellectual property rights, where necessary, through the provisions of Articles 20 and 21 and in accordance with international law and consistent with paragraphs 4 and 5 below.

4. Each Contracting Party shall take legislative, administrative or policy measures, as appropriate, with the aim that the private sector facilitates access to, joint development and transfer of technology referred to in paragraph 1 above for the benefit of both governmental institutions and the private sector of developing countries and in this regard shall abide by the obligations included in paragraphs 1, 2 and 3 above.

5. The Contracting Parties, recognizing that patents and other intellectual property rights may have an influence on the implementation of this Convention, shall cooperate in this regard subject to national legislation and international law in order to ensure that such rights are supportive of and do not run counter to its objectives.

The provisions on technology transfer in the CBD are somewhat controversial. The United States in particular is concerned about a possible erosion of intellectual property rights, for example through compulsory licensing. A close reading of Article 16 CBD (especially section 2) does not corroborate these concerns. Still, the United States has refrained from ratifying the CBD and therefore cannot be a party to the subsequent protocols either.

(d) Agreements on access and benefit sharing

In recent years, some agreements on access to genetic resources, benefit sharing, and technology transfer have been concluded between pharmaceutical companies and governmental institutions in charge of biodiversity. In 1991, the US pharmaceutical company MERCK and a governmental agency of Costa Rica concluded a sort of 'pioneer agreement'.[43]

According to that agreement, the governmental agency for biodiversity of Costa Rica (INBio) should provide plants, animals, and soil samples for the exclusive use by MERCK. The company would retain the industrial property rights for the pharmaceuticals developed on the basis of these samples. In return, the company agreed to pay an amount of money to the governmental institute and to share benefits from the marketing of the products developed in context with the cooperation as well as to transfer technological equipment to the governmental agency.

(e) Biosafety

Complying with the mandate under Article 19(3), the Parties to the CBD adopted the Cartagena Protocol on Biosafety to the Convention on Biological Diversity

---

[43] The so-called MERCK-INBio Agreement.

(also known as the 'Biosafety Protocol') in 2000.[44] The Biosafety Protocol governs the movement (especially the import) of living modified organisms (LMOs), that is, genetically modified living organisms.

The Biosafety Protocol establishes the principle of prior information and consent ('advanced informed agreement', AIA). It addresses the conditions for legitimate import and export restrictions and thus regulates trade measures covered by WTO law (GATT and the SPS Agreement). The Biosafety Protocol shows a clear tendency to accord considerably more freedom from trade restrictions to its parties than WTO law (Article XX of the GATT and the SPS Agreement). The relation of the Biosafety Protocol to the WTO agreements is rather unclear. Under the preamble of the Biosafety Protocol, this relation is one of chosen ambiguity. On the one hand, the preamble emphasizes '[…] that this Protocol shall not be interpreted as implying a change in the rights and obligations of a Party under any existing international agreements'. On the other hand, the preamble of the Biosafety Protocol continues with the understanding '[…] that the above recital is not intended to subordinate this Protocol to other international agreements'.

It is a matter of doubt whether the standard for import restrictions under the Biosafety Protocol conforms with or deviates from WTO rules, which are rather strict in terms of the required scientific justification with respect to the health of human beings, plants, and animals. In the same vein as WTO rules, the Protocol calls for a scientific risk assessment as the basis for any import restriction (see Article 10(1)) in terms of Article 15(1) with Annex III and Article 10(6). The risk assessment 'shall be carried out in a scientifically sound manner […] taking into account recognized risk assessment techniques'.

Annex III section 8 of the Biosafety Protocol further specifies the criteria for risk assessment:

To fulfil its objective, risk assessment entails, as appropriate, the following steps:
(a) An identification of any novel genotypic and phenotypic characteristics associated with the living modified organism that may have adverse effects on biological diversity in the likely potential receiving environment, taking also into account risks to human health;
(b) An evaluation of the likelihood of these adverse effects being realized, taking into account the level and kind of exposure of the likely potential receiving environment to the living modified organism;
(c) An evaluation of the consequences should these adverse effects be realized;
(d) An estimation of the overall risk posed by the living modified organism based on the evaluation of the likelihood and consequences of the identified adverse effects being realized;
(e) A recommendation as to whether or not the risks are acceptable or manageable, including, where necessary, identification of strategies to manage these risks; and

---

[44] See C Bail, R Falkner, and H Marquard (eds), *The Cartagena Protocol on Biosafety* (Earthscan Publications 2002); B Eggers and R Mackenzie, 'The Cartagena Protocol on Biosafety' (2000) 3 J Int'l Econ L 525; AL Hobbs, JE Hobbs, and W Kerr, 'The Biosafety Protocol: Multilateral Agreement on Protecting the Environment or Protectionist Club' (2005) 39 JWT 281.

(f) Where there is uncertainty regarding the level of risk, it may be addressed by requesting further information on the specific issues of concern or by implementing appropriate risk management strategies and/or monitoring the living modified organism in the receiving environment.

In its Article 10(6), the Protocol emphasizes the precautionary principle:[45]

Lack of scientific certainty due to insufficient relevant scientific information and knowledge regarding the extent of the potential adverse effects of a living modified organism on the conservation and sustainable use of biological diversity in the Party of import, taking also into account risks to human health, shall not prevent that Party from taking a decision [...].

However, the Biosafety Protocol also allows parties to consider other matters than scientific criteria, thus vesting them apparently with rather broad discretion. Article 26 of the Protocol permits import restrictions for living genetically modified organisms (LMOs) also to be based on 'socio-economic considerations', as long as these are compatible with the international obligations of the respective State. The term 'socio-economic considerations' is the source of a significant degree of uncertainty and results in substantial freedom of the parties. The EU has relied on the precautionary principle as defined by the Protocol and on 'socio-economic considerations' in its controversial policy of suspending authorizations for the marketing of genetically modified organisms (GMOs):

4.339 In light of these risks, governments around the world, since the first commercialisation of GMOs in the early nineties, have started to address the question of how to regulate GMOs. Regulatory approaches range from complete bans to 'laissez faire.' Most, however, consist in setting up an approval system specific to GMOs, based on a case-by-case detailed risk assessment. Often such systems are based on a precautionary approach, and decisions are sometimes made dependent on considerations other than scientific factors, such as, for instance, socio-economic considerations. Furthermore, approval may be subject to post-market surveillance requirements. Given the constant evolution of the science on GMOs, regulatory approaches are under constant review in many countries. [...]
4.342 Against this background the European Communities submits that it is not plausible to argue that GM products are—or should be treated as—equivalent to non-GM products.[46]

This approach has fostered controversies with States following a strictly scientific approach of justifying trade restrictions like the United States (which is not a party to the CBD and, therefore, also not party to the Biosafety Protocol). These different 'regulatory philosophies' have caused trade conflicts within the framework of the WTO.[47]

In 2010, some Parties to the CBD adopted the Nagoya–Kuala Lumpur Supplementary Protocol on Liability and Redress to the Cartagena Protocol on

[45] See JH Adler, 'More sorry than safe: "Assessing the Precautionary Principle and the Proposed International Biosafety Protocol"' (2000) 35 Texas Int'l LJ 173.
[46] WTO, *European Communities: Measures Affecting the Approval and Marketing of Biotech Products—Report of the Panel* (2006) WT/DS291/R, WT/DS292/R, WT/DS293/R [67] paras 4.339 and 4.342.
[47] See PWB Phillips and WA Kerr, 'Alternative Paradigms: The WTO Versus the Biosafety Protocol for Trade in Genetically Modified Organisms' (2000) 34 JWT 63.

Biosafety. The Protocol applies to damages resulting from LMO originating from transboundary movement (Article 3(1)).

7. The Law of Biotechnology

The dynamic development of biotechnology and its utilization in agriculture, in the pharmaceutical industry, and in medical science turned the regulation of this high-technology into one of the central topics of international law.[48] Food, feed, seed, and drugs consisting of or produced from GMO advance on the markets. Genetic engineering also plays a role in medical therapy. In several countries (eg the United States, Argentina, Brazil, and China), genetically modified crops cover vast areas. On the other hand, regulation on the international as well as on the domestic level has to respond to proven or potential risks for human health, and to the environment. The regulation of biotechnology cuts through many areas of law. Restrictive trade measures affect obligations under WTO law. Interferences with the human genome and human life in the early stages affect human rights and human dignity. Despite all inherent risks, biotechnology may contribute to solving some of the problems of a growing world population and to the consequences of climate change in this respect (such as droughts and famines). The Food and Agricultural Organization of the United Nations (FAO) has constantly stressed these positive effects of biotechnology:

Biotechnology can overcome production constraints that are more difficult or intractable with conventional breeding. It can speed up conventional breeding programmes and provide farmers with disease-free planting materials. It can create crops that resist pests and diseases, replacing toxic chemicals that harm the environment and human health, and it can provide diagnostic tools and vaccines that help control devastating animal diseases. It can improve the nutritional quality of the staple foods such as rice and cassava and create new products for health and industrial uses.[49]

Within the framework of the United Nations, the UNESCO issued a declaration on the human genome in 1997. The UNIDO (United Nations Industrial Development Organization) elaborated a Voluntary Code of Conduct for the Release of Organisms into the Environment. The Codex Alimentarius Commission, instituted by the WHO and the FAO, presented guidelines for risk assessment of GMO and genetically modified plants and microorganisms foods derived from biotechnology

Different degrees of risk and risk perception underlie different regulatory 'philosophies' as to controlling genetic engineering and other forms of modern biotechnology. EU law (Directive 2009/41/EC on the contained use of genetically

---

[48] See F Francioni and T Scovazzi (eds), *Biotechnology and International Law* (Irish Academic Press 2006); M Herdegen, 'Biotechnology and Regulatory Risk Assessment' in GA Bermann, M Herdegen, and PL Lindseth (eds), *Transatlantic Regulatory Cooperation* (OUP 2000) 301; M Herdegen, 'The Coexistence of Genetically Modified Crops with other Forms of Farming' (2005) 2 JIB Law 89; M Herdegen and H-G Dederer, *Adventitious Presence of GMOs in Seed* (CH Beck 2001); H Somsen (ed), *The Regulatory Challenge of Biotechnology: Human Genetics, Food and Patents* (Edward Elgar Publishing 2007); D Wüger and T Cottier, *Genetic Engineering and the World Trade System* (CUP 2008).
[49] FAO, 'The State of Food and Agriculture 2003–2004: Agricultural Biotechnology—Meeting the Needs of the Poor?' (2004) 3 Agricultural Series No 35.

modified micro-organisms,[50] Directive 2001/18/EC on the deliberate release into the environment of genetically modified organisms)[51] still tends to classify the mere process of genetic engineering as causing relevant risks warranting specific legislation (process approach). Recent EU legislation on the marketing and labelling of food and feed containing GMO or consisting of GMO[52] is widely based on an understanding of consumer protection, which is somewhat dissociated from scientifically relevant product properties. Thus, food and feed containing only minimum traces of genetically modified material (even if it has no longer an active function) are subject to relatively strict regulation. This tendency may perpetuate prejudices among consumers without a sufficient scientific basis. Even the adventitious and small-scale presence of GMO already authorized in another product raises complex issues of authorization for marketing and labelling.[53] On the other hand, the democratic process will always strive to reflect prevailing societal concerns and expectations. Still, the freedom of States to restrict trade for merely 'socio-economic' reasons may result in curtailing customers' choices.

The laws of other countries, such as the United States or Japan, focus on the properties of the organism to be modified or on the characteristics of the final product (product approach).[54] WTO rules also aim at the strictly scientific justification for restrictive measures.

The tensions between an empirically substantiated risk management on the one hand and strong reservations to genetic engineering on the other hand are exacerbated by the receptivity of many of the EU States to recognize 'socio-economic' concerns as justification of barriers to trade. EU legislation allows Member States to ban the cultivation of genetically modified crops partly or entirely from their territory ('opt out'), thus restraining the marketing of the products concerned.[55] This 'opt out' legislation signifies a fundamentally new approach to free trade which raises sensitive problems. For it allows restrictions of the use of GMO which have been authorized not only for being placed on the market, but also for the very use at issue (ie cultivation) on the basis of a complex process of risk evaluation. Such restrictions of the use of products qualified as 'safe' can only be justified empirically

[50] [2009] OJ L 125/75.

[51] [2001] OJ L 106/1, amended by Directive 2008/27/EC of the European Parliament and of the Council of 11 March 2008, amending Directive 2001/18/EC on the deliberate release into the environment of genetically modified organisms, as regards the implementing powers conferred on the Commission [2008] OJ L 81/45.

[52] Regulation (EC) No 1830/2003 of the European Parliament and of the Council of 22 September 2003 concerning the traceability and labelling of genetically modified organisms and the traceability of food and feed products produced from genetically modified organisms and amending Directive 2001/18/EC [2003] OJ L 268/24.

[53] On the 'contamination' of honey with pollen from authorised GM crops, see ECJ Case C-442/09 *Bablok et al v Freistaat Bayern* [2010] ECR I-7419.

[54] M Herdegen, 'Biotechnology and Regulatory Risk Assessment' in GA Bermann, M Herdegen, and PL Lindseth (eds), *Transatlantic Regulatory Cooperation* (OUP 2000) 301.

[55] Article 26b of Directive (EU) 2015/412 of 11 March 2015 amending Directive 2001/18/EC as regards the possibility for the Member States to restrict or prohibit the cultivation of genetically modified organisms (GMOs) in their territory [2015] OJ L68/1.

(and 'rationally') if the restriction refers to a specific local or regional environment which is particularly sensitive.

Select Bibliography

U Beyerlin and T Marauhn, *International Environmental Law* (Hart Publishing 2011).

D Bodansky, J Brunnee, and E Hey, *The Oxford Handbook of International Environmental Law* (OUP 2007).

S Boutillon, 'The Precautionary Principle: Development of an International Standard' (2001–02) 23 Mich J Int'l L 429.

M Bowman and C Redgwell (eds), *International Law and the Conservation of Biological Diversity* (Kluwer Law International 1996).

AC Kiss and D Shelton, *International Environmental Law* (3rd edn, Hotei Publisher 2004).

D Lanzerath and M Friele (eds), *Concepts and Values in Biodiversity* (Routledge 2014).

E Louka, *International Environmental Law: Fairness, Effectiveness and World Order* (CUP 2006).

P Sands and J Peel, *Principles of International Environmental Law* (3rd edn, CUP 2012).

IX

Good Governance—The Internal Structure of States and Global Economic Integration

The interrelation with and the contribution to 'good governance' is a salient issue of the modern international economic order. In the long run, any market economy system needs reliable rules and effective protection of fundamental civil rights including property to function properly. At the same time, any legal order based on individual freedom cannot ignore some basic economic principles. As history shows, a certain level of political pluralism as well as the protection of civil liberties goes hand in hand with a free market order. The interaction between the rule of law, democracy, and the economic order largely depends on the prevailing political, social, and economic conditions in a State. Experience suggests that both a minimum of economic development (eg as expressed by average per capita income figures) and of social symmetry are essential preconditions for continuing institutional stability and governmental capacity.[1] Conversely, only stable and efficient institutions can guarantee a reliable legal framework and the protection of subjective rights which in turn both form the basis for sustainable economic development, a stable investment climate, and, finally, poverty reduction.

For a well-ordered community, David Hume deduced three basic principles from human nature: first, the right to property; secondly, the right to consensually transfer property; and thirdly, the normative backing of obligations to be fulfilled.[2] These principles also describe basic prerequisites for any social order aiming at functioning markets and prosperity. For mere functionality of markets and competition as well as the successful integration into the world economy, legal certainty and a transparent public administration with a sense of ethics may at an initial stage be as important as the full implementation of democratic principles. States without an institutionally supported pluralism—even though being formally organized as democracies—cannot protect economic and other individual freedoms from the dictates of the majority. A functioning economic order requires the rule of law at least at a minimum level. In the long run, it is essential for States to build up trust

---

[1] See F Zakaria, *The Future of Freedom* (WW Norton & Co 2003) 69.
[2] See D Hume, *A Treatise on Human Nature* (1739–40) Book III, Part II, section IV: Of the transference of property by consent.

of citizens and investors alike in legislation and the administration of justice. These findings stress the impact of legal parameters on economic development.

Economic analysis, especially the New Institutional Economics (NIE), for some time has emphasized the importance of a stable institutional framework for the making and administration of legal rules and the protection of property rights as a condition for economic development.[3] Together with accountability and transparency of public administration under binding legal norms, the standards formulated by NIE are closely related to modern concepts of the rule of law.

With a view to foster the development of market economies in Eastern Europe after the fall of the Iron Curtain, the Charter of Paris for a New Europe of 21 November 1990[4] very clearly stresses the interrelation between economic freedom and political pluralism:

Freedom and political pluralism are necessary elements in our common objective of developing market economies towards sustainable economic growth, prosperity, social justice, expanding employment and efficient use of economic resources. The success of the transition to market economy by countries making efforts to this effect is important and in the interest of us all. It will enable us to share a higher level of prosperity which is our common objective [...].[5]

1. Standards of Good Governance

(a) Historical development

The standards of 'good governance', initially a domain of development policy and international development law, have emerged as a salient aspect of international economic law. Democracy, the rule of law, and a functional economic system stand in close interdependence, and each of them contributes to good governance. The concept governs development cooperation between industrialized and developing countries as well as financial support by the World Bank Group and other international organisations.

Empiric analysis shows that good governance with the rule of law and a solid institutional framework of political control and judicial protection of property rights are crucial for the political, economic, and social development of States.[6] Many States failed because bad governance stifled economic welfare, civic culture, and the effective exercise of State functions. All too often, reliance on revenue from extractive industries and other forms of exploiting natural resources counteract transparent administration, truly representative participation and effective political participation, an open market of ideas, and innovation.

---

[3] DC North, *Institutional Change and Economic Performance* (CUP 1990).
[4] Conference on Security and Co-operation in Europe (CSCE) 'Charter of Paris for a New Europe and Supplementary Document to Give Effect to Certain Provisions of the Charter' (done and entered into force 21 November 1990) (1991) 30 ILM 190.
[5] Ibid.   [6] D Acemoglu and J Robinson, *Why Nations Fail* (Crown Business 2012).

Good governance reaches beyond mere transparency of public administration and democratic mechanisms in the distribution of power in a State. It also encompasses substantive criteria for 'good' government performance. In its Resolution on human rights, democracy, and development of 28 November 1991,[7] the Council of the then European Community, together with the Member States, summed up its components:

[...] 5. The Council stresses the importance of good governance. While sovereign States have the right to institute their own administrative structures and establish their own constitutional arrangements, equitable development can only effectively and sustainably be achieved if a number of general principles of government are adhered to: sensible economic and social policies, democratic decision-making, adequate governmental transparency and financial accountability, creation of a market-friendly environment for development, measures to combat corruption, as well as respect for the rule of law, human rights, and freedom of the press and expression. The Community and Member States will support the efforts of developing countries to advance good governance and these principles will be central in their existing or new development cooperation relationships.[8]

Good governance is a basic principle of the Cotonou Agreement between the European Union and the ACP-States (Articles 8, 9):[9]

[...]
3. In the context of a political and institutional environment that upholds human rights, democratic principles and the rule of law, good governance is the transparent and accountable management of human, natural, economic and financial resources for the purposes of equitable and sustainable development. It entails clear decision-making procedures at the level of public authorities, transparent and accountable institutions, the primacy of law in the management and distribution of resources and capacity building for elaborating and implementing measures aiming in particular at preventing and combating corruption.
Good governance shall underpin the domestic and international policies of the Parties and constitute a fundamental element of this Agreement. The Parties agree that serious cases of corruption, including acts of bribery leading to such corruption, as referred to in Article 97 constitute a violation of that element.[10]

This concept of good governance is rather narrowly formulated and, in consequence, compatible with a broad range of economic and political systems. However, the Cotonou Agreement places good governance in close context with human rights, democracy, and the rule of law.

---

[7] Resolution of the Council and of the Member States Meeting in the Council on Human Rights, Democracy, and Development (1991) 11 Bulletin EC 122.

[8] Ibid.

[9] Partnership Agreement between the Members of the African, Caribbean, and Pacific Group of States on the one part and the European Community and its Members on the other part as of 11 March 2010 (2nd revision), see Agreement amending for the second time the Partnership Agreement between the members of the African, Caribbean, and Pacific Group of States, of the one part, and the European Community and its Member States, of the other part, signed in Cotonou on 23 June 2000, as first amended in Luxembourg on 25 June 2005 [2010] OJ L287/3.

[10] Partnership agreement between the members of the African, Caribbean and Pacific Group of States of the one part, and the European Community and its Member States, of the other part, signed in Cotonou on 23 June 2000 Article 9 (3).

(b) Transparency and the fight against corruption

The elimination of all forms of corruption is a crucial element of legal transparency and legal certainty as well as of an administration truly committed to the public interest and compliance with the law. Bribery is a major obstacle to sustainable economic development and a good investment climate. Often widespread poverty, weak institutions, and indebtedness of a country go hand in hand with a high level of corruption.[11] The lack of legal clarity and all too broad discretion fosters abuse of public authority for personal gain. The United Nations Convention against Corruption (UNCAC) of 2003[12] covers a whole arsenal of preventive and repressive measures against bribery and other forms of corruption. The primary concern of UNCAC is to ensure a certain sense of ethics in public administration. UNCAC also calls on States to take measures against corruption in the private sector (Article 12). The Convention provides an interesting mechanism for recovering assets obtained through corruption and also relies on international cooperation in this context (Articles 51ff).

On the regional level, the Inter-American Convention against Corruption[13] of 1996 has been ground-breaking with regard to the fight against corruption, as it was the first legal instrument addressing the problem of corruption which tried to promote and facilitate cooperation between States by preventive measures. The OECD adopted an Anti-Bribery Convention in 1997,[14] which is also open for accession to non-OECD countries. Within the framework of the Council of Europe, the Criminal Law Convention on Corruption of 27 January 1999[15] and the Civil Law Convention on Corruption of 4 November 1999[16] were elaborated. In the European Union, a number of instruments combat bribery and corruption, for example the Council Framework Decision 2003/568/JHA on combating corruption in the private sector.[17] In Africa, the African Union set a regulatory framework for Africa: the Convention on Preventing and Combating Corruption of 2003.[18]

The Trans-Pacific Partnership Agreement dedicates a whole chapter to anti-corruption and anti-bribery rules. The Agreement provides that each party shall ratify the United Nations Convention against Corruption (Article 26.6.4) and shall fight corruption with criminal sanctions (Article 26.7.1).

Today, bribery of public officials must be considered as a violation of a universally accepted international *ordre public* (the international public order). Therefore, claims based on bribery or other forms of corruption are not recognized by

[11] See the annual Transparency International Corruption Perception Index published by Transparency International (TI), available at <http://www.transparency.org/research/cpi/overview> (accessed 23 June 2016).

[12] UNGA Res 58/4 (31 October 2003) UN Doc A/RES/58/4; see on UNCAC, P Webb, 'The United Nations Convention Against Corruption: Global Achievement or Missed Opportunity?' (2005) 8 J Int'l Econ L 191.

[13] Inter-American Convention against Corruption (29 March 1996) (1996) 35 ILM 724.

[14] OECD Convention on Combating Bribery of Foreign Public Officials in International Business Transactions (1998) 37 ILM 1.

[15] (1999) ETS No 173; (1999) 38 ILM 505.   [16] (2000) ETS No 174.

[17] [2003] OJ L 192/54.   [18] (2004) 43 ILM 5.

international courts and tribunals. In the case *World Duty Free Co Ltd v Kenya* an ICSID tribunal held:

In light of domestic laws and international conventions relating to corruption, and in light of the decisions taken in this matter by courts and arbitral tribunals, this Tribunal is convinced that bribery is contrary to the international public policy of most, if not all, States or, to use another formula, to transnational public policy. Thus, claims based on contracts of corruption or on contracts obtained by corruption cannot be upheld by this Arbitral Tribunal.[19]

By now, this conclusion may be considered a general principle of international law.

The arbitral tribunal stated that it does not matter whether the corrupt action was solicited or otherwise initiated by a public official. The award stresses the interests of the poor which are the real victims of corruption:

The answer, as regards public policy, is that the law protects not the litigating parties but the public; or in this case, the mass of tax-payers and other citizens making up one of the poorest countries in the world.[20]

Recent investment arbitration has corroborated that the provision of bribery is a principle of international public policy which limits party autonomy.[21] In *Niko Resources v Bangladesh* the arbitral tribunal distinguished between contracts which have the object of bribing a civil servant on one hand and contracts obtained by corruption on the other.[22] The arbitral tribunal held that only the first type of contracts is automatically void whilst in the second case an agreement may only be treated as void or invalid if the state party makes a declaration to this effect.

Codes of conduct and other standards for transnational corporations emphasize the need of transparency and ban corruptive practices. Thus, the OECD Guidelines for Multinational Enterprises state in Chapter VII:

Enterprises should not, directly or indirectly, offer, promise, give, or demand a bribe or other undue advantage to obtain or retain business or other improper advantage. Enterprises should also resist the solicitation of bribes and extortion. In particular, enterprises should:
1. Not offer, promise or give undue pecuniary or other advantage to public officials or the employees of business partners. Likewise, enterprises should not request, agree to or accept undue pecuniary or other advantage from public officials or the employees of business partners. Enterprises should not use third parties such as agents and other intermediaries, consultants, representatives, distributors, consortia, contractors and suppliers

---

[19] *World Duty Free Co Ltd v Kenya*, ICSID Case No ARB/00/7 (Award) (2007) 46 ILM 339 para 157.
[20] *World Duty Free Co Ltd v Kenya*, ICSID Case No ARB/00/7 (Award) (2007) 46 ILM 339 para 181.
[21] *Niko Resources (Bangladesh) v People's Republic of Bangladesh et al*, ICSID Case No ARB/10/11 and ARB10/18 (Decision on Jurisdiction 2013) paras 430ff; see AP Llamzon, *Corruption in International Investment Arbitration* (OUP 2014).
[22] *Niko Resources (Bangladesh) v People's Republic of Bangladesh et al*, ICSID Case No ARB/10/11 and ARB10/18 (*Decision on Jurisdiction* 2013) paras 440ff.

and joint venture partners for channelling undue pecuniary or other advantages to public officials, or to employees of their business partners or to their relatives or business associates. [...]

Borderline cases refer to the financial support by corporations for legitimate local projects in context with the application for mining concessions or other authorization of environmentally sensitive projects.[23]

On national level, some States have established rather rigorous standards. The US Foreign Corrupt Practices Act (FCPA)[24] has been known for its sweeping extraterritorial application. The FCPA was enacted in 1977 in response to the Watergate scandal and the growing sensitivity to the distortion of competition and other international implications of corruption. The anti-bribery provisions prohibit not only US persons and businesses, but also foreign companies listed on US stock exchanges (and certain other persons or businesses under territorial jurisdiction of the United States) from making corrupt payment to foreign officials to gain business advantages. In addition, the FCPA also aims at transparency in accounting standards. Under the FCPA a number of important foreign companies were investigated and submitted to serious fines.[25] Other legislation, for example the Dodd–Frank Act, requires oil, gas, and other natural resource companies to publicly disclose detailed information about payments made to government officials. The United States is a founding member of the Open Government Partnership which is committed to transparency and anti-corruption efforts in participating countries.

(c) Due process and fair trial

Within the standards of good governance, the right to due process and fair trial has gained particular importance in international investment law, especially in relation to the treaty standard of 'fair and equitable treatment'. In the case *Mondev International v United States of America*, an ICSID tribunal defined this standard as protecting investors from 'improper and discreditable' judicial decisions:

[...] In the end the question is whether, at an international level and having regard to generally accepted standards of the administration of justice, a tribunal can conclude in the light of all the available facts that the impugned decision was clearly improper and discreditable, with the result that the investment has been subjected to unfair and inequitable treatment.[26]

---

[23] See Norwegian Contact Point *Complaint from the Future In Our Hands (FIOH) against Intex Resources ASA and the Mindoro Nickel Project* Final Statement (2011) 30.

[24] 15 U.S.C. §§ 78dd-1, et seq., amended by the Omnibus Trade and Competitiveness Act of 1988, Pub. L. No. 100-418, § 5003, 102 Stat. 1107, 1415-25 (1988), and the International Anti-Bribery and Fair Competition Act of 1988, Pub. L. 105-366, 112 Stat. 3302 (1998); for an official comprehensive introduction see *The Resource Guide to the U.S. Foreign Corrupt Practices Act*, <http://www.justice.gov/sites/default/files/criminal-fraud/legacy/2015/01/16/guide.pdf> (accessed 23 June 2016).

[25] In a recent case Hewlett-Packard was charged with violating the FCPA by making improper payments to government officials to obtain remunerative public contracts. Eventually the company agreed to pay USD108 million.

[26] *Mondev International Ltd v United States of America*, ICSID Case No ARB(AF)/99/2 (Award) (2003) 42 ILM 85 para 127.

Principles of International Economic Law

Similarly, an ICSID tribunal held in *Loewen v United States of America*:

[W]e take it to be the responsibility of the State under international law and, consequently, of the courts of a State, to provide a fair trial of a case to which a foreign investor is a party. It is the responsibility of the courts of a State to ensure that litigation is free from discrimination against a foreign litigant and that the foreign litigant should not become the victim of sectional or local prejudice.[27]

A number of treaties in investment protection explicitly include due process and non-denial of justice as relevant standards to be observed by the States.

(d) Fundamental rights

The freedom of the press and the freedom of expression as well as the right of the citizens to participate in decision-making are also important elements of good governance. This illustrates the close interdependence between good governance and human rights.[28] However, good governance is not equivalent to human rights.[29] Rather, human rights constitute the legal framework for good governance policies.

(e) Political participation

The early formulation of good governance by development organizations, anxious to avoid the criticism of political interference, referred to political participation of the citizens in rather cautious terms. In the meantime, the World Bank and other international institutions quite openly recognized the interrelation between democratic participation and sound economic development:

In most nondemocratic settings, however, lack of institutionalized accountability has resulted in poor performance in growth and poverty reduction. Even successful developmental states point to an important lesson: undemocratic regimes face serious abuses of state power, and they are prone to rapid policy reversals that can make their development gains fragile. These states are moving to resolve some of these problems by changing their political institutions to increase official accountability.[30]

The checks and balances of participatory democratic regimes—and the procedures for consensus building—limit the scope for rent seeking and drastic policy reversals, offering a much more reliable and sustainable path to development. Participatory political regimes are associated with more stable growth, which is crucial for poverty reduction.[31]

---

[27] *The Loewen Group Inc & Raymond Loewen v United States of America*, ICSID Case No ARB(AF)/98/3 (Award 2003) para 123.

[28] See M Scheinin, 'State Responsibility, Good Governance and Indivisible Human Rights' in H-O Sano and G Alfredsson, *Human Rights and Good Governance: Building Bridges* (Springer 2002) 29, 39ff.

[29] T van Boven, 'Is there an Emerging Right to Good Governance?' in F Coomans et al (eds), *Human Rights from Exclusion to Inclusion: Principles and Practice* (Springer 2000) 329, 337.

[30] World Bank, *World Development Report 2000/2001: Attacking Poverty* (OUP 2001) 113.

[31] World Bank, *World Development Report 2000/2001: Attacking Poverty* (OUP 2001) 113; see on the relation between solid democratic institutions and economic growth, D Acemoglu and J Robinson, *Why Nations Fail* (Crown Business 2012).

2. Global Economic Integration: The Relevance of the Constitutional and Economic Order

The capacity of a State to integrate successfully into the global economy and its openness for global competition considerably depends on its national constitutional order. The normative framework for an effective market economy requires essential elements, such as the guarantee of private property, the freedom of contract, and an effective legal protection of fundamental and other subjective rights. In addition, institutional mechanisms which secure economic stability and which restrain self-serving influences of particular societal groups are also vital for a functioning market economy. These mechanisms include, inter alia, independent central banks and constitutional 'debt brakes', that is rules limiting public borrowing. In these terms, the successful economic development of the Federal Republic of Germany after the Second World War owes much to the normative setting established by the German Basic Law and its emphasis on individual liberty as well as on social responsibility of the State.

Practising excessive caution, the German Federal Constitutional Court assumes a supposedly 'economic neutrality' of the German Basic Law. This assumption does not do justice to the relevance of constitutional principles for the economic order.[32]

As Hernando de Soto highlighted in his famous book *El otro sendero (The Other Path)*,[33] legal uncertainty and an impenetrable jungle of rules coupled with overflowing enactments, inefficiency of public administration, and the lack of an ethical commitment in the public administration generate legal uncertainties and lack of transparency, which force economic actors to do business in the shadow of legality ('underground' or 'shadow economy', black markets). In a number of States in Latin America as in other regions, constitutional reforms reflect and enhance sensitivity for securing property and other fundamental rights and legal certainty as essential preconditions for foreign and domestic investment. The Papal encyclical 'Centesimus Annus' of 1991, in a rather cautious way, also contributed to a more comprehensive understanding of the relation between a social market economy and the right to private property.

The importance of the constitutional order for a functioning economic order and a country's ability to integrate into the world economy is clearly visible in the Eastern European countries. The transition from centrally planned economies to a functioning market economy order could only be realized with a new constitutional basis.[34]

It is not only the global economic development or the international division of labour and international competition which suggest certain standards for the international order of States. Modern international economic law also sets guidelines

---

[32] BVerfGE 4, 7 (17f).   [33] H de Soto, *El otro sendero* (Orell Füssli 1986).
[34] See CG Meyer, 'The Constitutional Development of Eastern Europe: Integration through Reformation' (1992) 32 Va J Int'l L 431.

for the legal order, especially for the constitutional and administrative system.[35] In this context, the principles guiding the WTO, the IMF, and the World Bank[36] are of particular interest.

The so-called 'Washington Consensus', a formula coined by the economist John Williamson, refers to the agenda of political and economic reform in developing countries.[37] It has been summarized as follows: 'Cut back the state, reduce fiscal deficits, get the prices right, liberalize trade and foreign investment, privatize public enterprises and deregulate markets'.[38] Originally, the 'Washington Consensus' referred to the need for a common approach of the institutions based in Washington DC (including the World Bank and the IMF) with regard to their development and financial policy strategies in Latin America.[39] Key elements of the 'Washington Consensus' are: Fiscal Discipline, Public Expenditure Priorities, Tax Reform, Financial Liberalization, Exchange Rates, Trade Liberalization, Foreign Direct Investment, Privatization, Deregulation, and Property Rights.[40] In recent discussions, the 'Washington Consensus' has been subject to criticism for focusing too much on economic development as an end in itself instead of adequately addressing sustainable improvement of the social conditions in a State. However, the opposite approach with protectionist trade policies and restrictions on foreign direct investment that have been implemented in some Latin American countries in recent years have neither substantially raised income levels nor improved the living conditions of the population.

At the United Nations International Conference on Financing for Development in 2002, the heads of State and government adopted the so-called 'Monterrey Consensus'[41] which recommends economic and judicial policies for a favourable investment climate:

To attract and enhance inflows of productive capital, countries need to continue their efforts to achieve a transparent, stable and predictable investment climate, with proper contract enforcement and respect for property rights, embedded in sound macroeconomic policies and institutions that allow businesses, both domestic and international, to operate efficiently

---

[35] See E-U Petersmann, *Constitutional Functions and Constitutional Problems of International Economic Law* (Westview Press 1991).

[36] See S Schlemmer-Schulte, 'The World Bank's Role in the Promotion of the Rule of Law in Developing Countries' in S Schlemmer-Schulte and K-Y Tung (eds), *Liber Amicorum Ibrahim F.I. Shihata: International Finance and Development Law* (Brill Academic Publishers 2001) 677.

[37] J Williamson, 'What Washington Means by Policy Reform' in J Williamson (ed), *Latin American Adjustment: How much has happened?* (Institute for International Economics 1990) 5; J Williamson, 'From Reform Agenda to Damaged Brand Name—A short history of the "Washington Consensus" and suggestions for what to do next' (2003) Finance and Development (September Issue) 10–13.

[38] S Killinger, *The World Bank's Non-Political Mandate* (Heymanns 2003) 12; see on the 'Washington Consensus', M Naim, 'Washington Consensus or Washington Confusion?' (2000) Foreign Pol'y 86.

[39] J Williamson, 'What Should the World Bank Think about the Washington Consensus?' (2000) 15 The World Bank Research Observer 251.

[40] J Williamson, 'What Washington Means by Policy Reform' in J Williamson (ed), *Latin American Adjustment: How much has happened?* (Institute for International Economics 1990) 5.

[41] Monterrey Consensus of the International Conference on Financing for Development of 22 March 2002 as recommended for endorsement by the General Assembly of the UN (A/CONF/198/11, chapter 1, resolution 1, annex).

and profitably and with maximum development impact. Special efforts are required in such priority areas as economic policy and regulatory frameworks for promoting and protecting investments, including the areas of human resource development, avoidance of double taxation, corporate governance, accounting standards, and the promotion of a competitive environment. Other mechanisms, such as public/private partnerships and investment agreements, can be important. We emphasize the need for strengthened, adequately resourced technical assistance and productive capacity-building programmes, as requested by recipients.[42]

In addition, the 'Monterrey Consensus' expresses a commitment to good governance[43] and highlights the relation between good governance and sustainable development:

Good governance is essential for sustainable development. Sound economic policies, solid democratic institutions responsive to the needs of the people and improved infrastructure are the basis for sustained economic growth, poverty eradication and employment creation. Freedom, peace and security, domestic stability, respect for human rights, including the right to development, and the rule of law, gender equality, market-oriented policies, and an overall commitment to just and democratic societies are also essential and mutually reinforcing.[44]

Select Bibliography

A Bianchi and A Peters (eds), *Transparency in International Law* (CUP 2013).

T van Boven, 'Is there an Emerging Right to Good Governance?' in F Coomans et al (eds), *Human Rights from Exclusion to Inclusion: Principles and Practice* (Springer 2000) 329.

DC Esty, 'Good Governance and the World Trade Organization: Building Foundation of Administrative Law' (2007) 10 J Int'l Econ L 509.

AP Llamzon, *Corruption in International Investment Arbitration* (OUP 2014).

D Levi-Faur, *The Oxford Handbook of Governance* (OUP 2012).

H-O Sano and G Alfredsson, *Human Rights and Good Governance. Building Bridges* (Springer 2002).

---

[42] Monterrey Consensus of the International Conference on Financing for Development of 22 March 2002 para 21.

[43] Monterrey Consensus of the International Conference on Financing for Development of 22 March 2002 para 4: 'We commit ourselves to sound policies, good governance at all levels and the rule of law'.

[44] Monterrey Consensus of the International Conference on Financing for Development of 22 March 2002 para 11.

X

Dispute Settlement

1. Mechanisms of International Dispute Settlement

The spectrum of dispute settlement mechanisms in international economic law is as broad as the variety of potential disputes.[1] Each dispute mechanism tries to respond to the different interests involved.

A classical perspective, reflecting Montesquieu's vision of the judge as the 'mouth that pronounces the words of the law', assumes that an international court or tribunal 'states the existing law and does not legislate'.[2] However, it is widely recognized that the process of interpretation and application of rules clarifies and to some extent develops international law.[3]

Judicial and arbitral decisions have shaped the current understanding of customary law, for example as to State immunity and the minimum standard of the treatment of aliens. Still, the principle of consent sets limits to the progressive development of customary law, especially as to balancing conflicting principles and 'discovering' rules which are supposedly inherent in existing law.[4]

Often the text of international agreements gives room for different interpretations. The main parameters governing treaty interpretation are 'the ordinary meaning to be given to the terms of the treaty in their context and in the light of its object and purpose'.[5] In addition, other factors may be considered, for

---

[1] Y Aksar, *Implementing International Economic Law Through Dispute Settlement Mechanisms* (Martinus Nijhoff Publishers 2011); J Collier and V Lowe, *The Settlement of Disputes in International Law* (OUP 1999); J Fawcett, *International Economic Conflicts* (Europa Publications 1977); AF Lowenfeld, *International Litigation and Arbitration* (3rd edn, Thomson West 2006); JG Merrills, *International Dispute Settlement* (5th edn, CUP 2011); H Mosler and R Bernhardt (eds), *Judicial Settlement of International Disputes* (Springer 1974); K Oellers-Frahm and A Zimmermann, *Dispute Settlement in Public International Law* (2nd edn, Springer 2001); E-U Petersmann and G Jaenicke (eds), *Adjudication of International Trade Disputes in International and National Economic Law* (UP 1992).

[2] ICJ, *Legality of the Threat or Use of Nuclear Weapons* (Advisory Opinion) [1996] ICJ Rep 226 para 18. See especially Art 38(1)(c) of the Statute of the ICJ.

[3] See R Higgins, *Problems and Process: International Law and How We Use It* (Clarendon Press, OUP 1994) 202; I Venzke, *How Interpretation Makes International Law: On Semantic Change and Normative Twists* (OUP 2012); AE Boyle and CM Chinkin, *The Making of International Law* (OUP 2007) 268; I Venzke, 'The Role of International Courts as Interpreters and Developers of the Law: Working out the Jurisgenerative Practice of Interpretation' (2012) 34 Loy LA Int'l & Comp L Rev 99.

[4] See on Ronald Dworkin's approach towards understanding and construing law Lord Hoffmann in House of Lords, *Jones v The Kingdom of Saudi Arabia* (2006) 45 ILM 1108.

[5] Art. 31(1) of the Vienna Convention on the Law of Treaties.

example 'subsequent practice in the application of the treaty'.[6] Interpretation must also consider 'any relevant rules of international law applicable in the relation between the parties';[7] this criterion allows for a systemic or integrative interpretation which harmonizes different legal regimes. Thus, agreements on trade and investment can be interpreted in the light of environmental standards or human rights. Dynamic or 'evolutionary' interpretation plays a crucial role in the interpretation of treaties.[8] However, in the area of international trade and investment law most international courts, arbitration tribunals, or other dispute settlement bodies do not push (quasi-)judicial activism as far as the European Court of Justice does in interpreting and developing European Union law in the interest of effectiveness ('*effet utile*').[9]

The dynamic interpretation of treaties in the light of present-day conditions in particular applies to generic clauses such as 'commerce'. In *Dispute regarding Navigational and Related Rights* (*Costa Rica v Nicaragua*) the International Court of Justice held:

[T]here are situations in which the parties' intent upon conclusion of the treaty was, or may be presumed to have been, to give the terms used—or some of them—a meaning or content capable of evolving, not one fixed once and for all, so as to make allowance for, among other things, developments in international law. In such instances it is indeed in order to respect the parties' common intention at the time the treaty was concluded, not to depart from it, that account should be taken of the meaning acquired by the terms in question upon each occasion on which the treaty is to be applied.[10]

Jurisdiction and the legitimacy of judgments, awards, and other decisions on disputes depend on consent. There is some discussion on the legitimacy of rulings which affect not only interests of the parties, but also international common goods and other concerns of the international community as a whole.[11] Internationalized interests such as the protection of climate or biodiversity may be considered in context of systemic interpretation which defers to any international rule binding upon the parties. Moreover, States are still the principal guardians of international concerns within their jurisdiction. In addition, the tendency for enhanced transparency of dispute settlement supports the possibility for non-parties to submit views, inter alia, on aspects of international concern.[12] This tendency is reflected in the

[6] Art 31(3)(b) of the Vienna Convention on the Law of Treaties.
[7] Art 31(3)(c) of the Vienna Convention on the Law of Treaties.
[8] E Bjorge, *The Evolutionary Interpretation of Treaties* (OUP 2014).
[9] See G Conway, *The Limits of Legal Reasoning and the European Court of Justice* (CUP 2012).
[10] ICJ, *Dispute regarding Navigational and Related Rights* (*Costa Rica v Nicaragua*) [2009] ICJ Rep 213 para 64.
[11] See A von Bogdandy and I Venzke, *In Whose Name? A Public Law Theory of International Adjudication* (OUP 2014).
[12] Whilst the independence of a tribunal is commonly seen as a core element favouring democratic legitimacy, EA Posner and J Yoo claim the ineffectiveness of independent tribunals ('Judicial Independence in International Tribunals' (2005) 93 California Law Review 1); see also the response of LR Helfer and A-M Slaughter, 'Why States Create International Tribunals: A Response to Professors Posner and Yoo' (2005) 93 California Law Review 899.

UNCITRAL Rules on Transparency in Treaty-based Investor-State Arbitration and the UN Convention on Transparency in Treaty-based Investor-State Arbitration.[13]

A rough distinction can be made between the settlement of disputes between States and those between private actors. Disputes between States rarely arise from commercial transactions carried out directly between the States as contractual parties. Rather, most interstate disputes are related to measures of economic policy, such as restraints of trade, subsidies, interference with foreign investments, or supply of energy.

The classic forum for the settlement of disputes between States is the International Court of Justice (ICJ) in The Hague. The relevance of the ICJ is limited by its narrow jurisdiction. As to the basis of its jurisdiction, the ICJ is far from being a truly compulsory judicial forum but shows significant similarities with arbitral tribunals. The ICJ only has jurisdiction if the two or more States involved submit to the Court's jurisdiction. Without a submission of both parties, there is no case.

Hence, most interstate disputes of enormous political and economic impact never find their way to the 'World Court'. The jurisdiction of the court can be established in three ways. The Statute of the ICJ provides:

Article 36
1. The jurisdiction of the Court comprises all cases which the parties refer to it and all matters specially provided for in the Charter of the United Nations or in treaties and conventions in force.
2. The states parties to the present Statute may at any time declare that they recognize as compulsory ipso facto and without special agreement, in relation to any other state accepting the same obligation, the jurisdiction of the Court in all legal disputes concerning:
   a. the interpretation of a treaty;
   b. any question of international law;
   c. the existence of any fact which, if established, would constitute a breach of an international obligation;
   d. the nature or extent of the reparation to be made for the breach of an international obligation.
3. The declarations referred to above may be made unconditionally or on condition of reciprocity on the part of several or certain states, or for a certain time [...].

Thus, States may either generally submit certain disputes to the court on the basis of reciprocity ('compulsory jurisdiction' under section 2), they may agree on the jurisdiction of the court within the framework of a treaty (section 1 second alternative) or they may refer an occurring dispute to the court on an ad hoc basis (section 1 first alternative).[14] Section 3 allows certain modifications of the declaration.

For economic disputes, the ICJ has never been the most prominent forum. In international economic law, most cases are referred either to ad hoc arbitral tribunals,

---

[13] See Ch XXXIV.5(e).
[14] For extensive reference in respect of the jurisdiction of the ICJ, see A Zimmermann, Ch Tomuschat, and K Oellers-Frahm (eds), *The Statute of the International Court of Justice: A Commentary* (2nd edn, OUP 2012) Commentary to Article 36.

institutionalized arbitral organizations, or dispute settlement mechanisms within the framework of a treaty (eg the Dispute Settlement Body of the WTO).

Dispute settlement under the Jay Treaty between the United Kingdom and the United States (1794) served as a kind of role model for modern interstate arbitration. The Jay Treaty provided for three joint arbitral commissions (for the settlement of boundaries, for claims of British creditors established before the American revolution, and for claims relating to the British treatment of American shipping in the war with revolutionary France).

An example of an arbitral body established for the settlement of all claims flowing from a specific history context is the Iran–US Claims Tribunal in The Hague.[15] The Tribunal was established to settle claims arising out of the severe conflict between the United States and Iran after the Islamic Revolution (which culminated in the occupation of the US embassy in Tehran) judged by the ICJ in the *Tehran Hostages* case[16] and followed by the retaliatory confiscation of Iranian bank accounts in the United States.[17] Many US citizens and US corporations were affected by measures of the new revolutionary regime. The jurisdiction of the Tribunal is not limited to claims of the two State Parties against one another, but also covers claims of nationals of the two States against the other State (mostly claims of US nationals against Iran).[18] The Tribunal is one of the most influential arbitral tribunals and has rendered a number of significant rulings on questions of international economic law, especially on the expropriation of foreigners and the due amount of compensation.[19] The Tribunal consists of arbitrators nominated by the parties and arbitrators nominated by an independent authority.

In economic disputes, States often prefer flexible dispute settlement mechanisms to the traditional judicial or quasi-judicial mechanisms of classic international law. Many disputes are solved amicably, having regard to the different national interests involved and the economic consequences that follow.

An exceptionally high degree of 'juridification' of dispute settlement has been reached in the World Trade Organization (WTO).[20] The Understanding on Dispute

---

[15] See CR Drahozal and CS Gibson, *The Iran-U.S. Claims Tribunal at 25* (OUP 2007); GH Aldrich, *The Jurisprudence of the Iran-United States Claims Tribunal* (Clarendon Press 1996).

[16] ICJ, *United States Diplomatic and Consular Staff in Tehran (USA v Iran)* [1980] ICJ Rep 3.

[17] D Caron, 'The Nature of the Iran-United States Claims Tribunal and the Evolving Structure of International Dispute Resolution' (1990) 84 AJIL 104.

[18] See (1981) 20 ILM 230.

[19] See A Avanessian, *Iran-United States Claims Tribunal in Action* (Graham & Trotman 1993); JR Crook, 'Applicable Law in International Arbitration: The Iran-U.S. Claims Tribunal Experience' (1989) 83 AJIL 278; JH Crook, DD Caron, and JR Crook, *The Iran-United States Claims Tribunal and the Process of International Claims Resolution* (Transnational Publishers 2000); JJ Van Hof, *Commentary on the UNCITRAL Arbitration Rules: The Application by the Iran-U.S. Claims Tribunal* (Kluwer Law and Taxation Publishers 1991); R Khan, *The Iran-United States Claims Tribunal— Controversies, Cases and Contributions* (Martinus Nijhoff Publishers 1990); RB Lillich and DB Magraw (eds), *The Iran-United States Claims Tribunal: Its Contribution to the Law of State Responsibility* (Transnational Publishers 1998).

[20] See MT Grando, *Evidence, Proof and Fact-Finding in WTO Dispute Settlement* (OUP 2010); Y Guohua, B Mercurio, and L Yongjie, *WTO Dispute Settlement Understanding: A Detailed Interpretation* (Kluwer Law International 2005); WTO (ed), *A Handbook on the WTO Dispute Settlements System*

Settlement within the WTO is characterized by strong quasi-judicial elements and a complex enforcement mechanism. Despite sometimes protracted controversies after rulings on violations of WTO law (on measures of respondents purporting to establish compliance and on retaliation by claimants) the WTO dispute settlement system operates quite effectively.[21]

The European Union has a highly differentiated system of judicial control and dispute settlement as to EU and national acts.[22] The jurisdiction of the Court of Justice extends to disputes between the Member States, disputes between the Union and the Member States, the review of legal acts of the Union, and the interpretation of the law of the European Union.[23] The scope, the efficiency, and the intensity of legal protection available under the EU system are only paralleled by national legal systems.

In classic international law, the access to dispute settlement mechanisms was limited to States. Nowadays, many international treaties do not only recognize rights of individuals,[24] but also provide mechanisms to enforce individual claims and to safeguard individual rights.[25] In the field of human rights, judicial and quasi-judicial mechanisms like the individual complaint under the European Convention on Human Rights (Article 34) extend to disputes which affect the economic order, in particular with respect to property rights.

International investment law is another area where private parties (individuals and corporations) can defend rights vis-à-vis States. The ICSID Convention forms the basis for the settlement of investment disputes between nationals of one Contracting State against another Contracting State, if both parties submit to the jurisdiction of ICSID.[26] Many investment treaties provide for arbitration under the arbitration rules of the United Nations Commission on International Trade Law (UNCITRAL) or the arbitration rules of the International Chamber of Commerce (ICC) in Paris. By referring to the ICSID or another form of arbitration, these

---

(CUP 2004); R Yerxa and B Wilson (eds), *Key Issues in WTO Dispute Settlement: The First Ten Years* (CUP 2005).

[21] See JF Colares, 'The Limits of WTO Adjudication: Is Compliance the Problem?' (2011) 14 J Int'l Econ L 403.

[22] See A Arnull, *The European Union and its Court of Justice* (2nd edn, OUP 2006); G de Búrca and JHH Weiler, *The European Court of Justice* (OUP 2001); MP Maduro, *We, the Court: The European Court of Justice and the European Economic Constitution* (Hart Publishing 1998).

[23] For the structure of competences between the 'General Court' (formerly the 'Court of First Instance') and the 'Court of Justice' (the 'ECJ') see Articles 251ff TFEU.

[24] See K Parlett, *The Individual in the International Legal System* (CUP 2011) 47.

[25] For the field of contractual relations, especially with respect to arbitration, see G Aksen and RB von Mehren (eds), *International Arbitration between Private Parties and Governments* (Practising Law Institute 1982); I Alvik, *Contracting with Sovereignty: State Contracts and International Arbitration* (Hart Publishing 2011); CF Dugan, DJ Wallace, ND Rubins, and B Sahabi, *Investor-State Arbitration* (OUP 2008); SJ Toope, *Mixed International Arbitration: Studies in Arbitration between States and Private Persons* (CUP 1990); N Wühler, 'Mixed Arbitral Tribunals' in R Bernhardt (ed), *Encyclopedia of Public International Law* (1997) vol III, 433.

[26] See Chapter II (Articles 25–27) of the ICSID Convention; see also A Reinisch and L Malintoppi, 'Methods of Dispute Resolution' in P Muchlinski, F Ortino, and C Schreuer (eds), *The Oxford Handbook of International Investment Law* (OUP 2008) 698.

treaties submit the Contracting States to the jurisdiction of the chosen forum of dispute settlement and imply an offer of an arbitration agreement to the private investor (a national of one of the Contracting States).[27] The private investor accepts this offer by initiating arbitral proceedings.

Arbitral proceedings between States and nationals of another State within the framework of an international treaty have a hybrid nature. On the one hand, the structure of the dispute settlement is very similar to private international commercial arbitration. On the other hand, the jurisdiction of the tribunals, the binding structure of the arbitral awards for the State Parties, and the arbitral procedure are clearly based on international law.

The proliferation of dispute settlement mechanisms may be hailed as an important step towards 'legalization' of controversies and towards enhanced compliance with existing obligations. Nevertheless, the growing number of specialized judicial and arbitral institutions may foster an incoherent or 'fragmentized' development of the particular areas of international law (human rights law, trade law, investment, or environmental protection). In some cases, competing jurisdictions of different courts and tribunals create the risk of contradictory rulings.[28]

A paradigmatic example of competing jurisdictions is the dispute between the EU and Chile in the *Swordfish* case.[29] In this case, Chile had denied access to its ports to foreign boats engaged in swordfish-fishing. The EU challenged the measure before the Dispute Settlement Body of the WTO (invoking the transit provisions of the GATT). Chile went to the International Tribunal for the Law of the Sea, relying on the provisions of the UN Convention on the Law of the Sea protecting migratory species.

Similar conflicts of jurisdiction may arise between dispute settlement mechanisms of the WTO and those of regional arrangements (free trade agreements or customs unions).[30] Regarding disputes between Member States of the EU about EU law or the law of the European Atomic Energy Community (EAEC), the European Court of Justice (ECJ) has exclusive jurisdiction (Article 4, section 3 TEU; Article 344 TFEU; Articles 192ff EAEC Treaty). In the *MOX Plant* case, Ireland complained about the discharge of radioactive material from the British nuclear power and research facility at Sellafield into the Irish Sea. Invoking severe harm to the maritime environment, Ireland initiated proceedings under the UN Convention on the Law of the Sea. The ECJ held that, in doing so, Ireland had disregarded the Court's exclusive jurisdiction in disputes covered by EAEC law.[31]

---

[27] See DAR Williams, 'Jurisdiction and Admissibility' in P Muchlinski, F Ortino, and C Schreuer (eds), *The Oxford Handbook of International Investment Law* (OUP 2008) 883.

[28] For a general insight into the problems of jurisdictional conflicts, see N Lavranos, 'Regulating Competing Jurisdictions Among International Courts and Tribunals' (2008) 68 ZaöRV 575; Y Shany, *The Competing Jurisdictions of International Courts and Tribunals* (OUP 2003); Y Shany, *Regulating Jurisdictional Relations Between National and International Courts* (OUP 2007).

[29] See PT Stoll and S Vöneky, 'The *Swordfish* Case, Law of the Sea v. Trade' (2002) 62 ZaöRV 21.

[30] See WTO, *Brazil: Measures Affecting the Import of Retreaded Tyres—Report of the Appellate Body* (2007) WT/DS332/AB/R; WTO, *Mexico: Tax Measures on Soft Drinks and other Beverages—Report of the Appellate Body* (2006) WT/DS308/AB/R.

[31] ECJ, Case C-459/03 *Commission v Ireland* [2006] ECR I-4635, see also MB Volbeda, 'The MOX Plant Case' (2006) 42 Texas Int'l LJ 211.

2. International Commercial Arbitration

For private parties to transboundary economic transactions, international commercial arbitration is very often the first choice as a dispute settlement mechanism.[32]

Most disputes concerning international economic transactions are in the end controversies between private actors. Despite the prominence of cases before the ICJ or the WTO Dispute Settlement Body, international commercial arbitration does not only settle a great number of disputes, but also clarifies or even develops public international law without the same feedback in the media.

There are manifold reasons why the parties to a dispute favour private arbitral proceedings over going to the courts of one particular State.[33] An arbitration agreement allows the parties to determine the procedural rules and the composition of the arbitral tribunal. Time, confidentiality, and costs might also be relevant considerations, even though arbitral proceedings are not always shorter and cheaper than proceedings before public courts. The degree of confidentiality may vary according to the wishes of the parties. An important aspect is the high degree of proficiency of arbitral tribunals and the expertise of arbitrators. Even though many national court rulings on commercial disputes, as a rule, reveal a very high degree of proficiency, a number of arbitrators dispose of exceptional specialized knowledge. Nevertheless, private arbitration also has its own weaknesses. Whenever a party tries to undermine the arbitral process or is unwilling to accept an arbitral award, the lack of authoritative structures of enforcement becomes obvious and leaves the other party with only the recourse to the mechanism of public courts. It may be said that the 'relationship between national courts and arbitral tribunals swings between forced cohabitation and true partnership'.[34] However, in practice there are strong

---

[32] IF Baxter, 'International Business Disputes' (1990) 39 ICLQ 288; KP Berger, *International Economic Arbitration* (Kluwer Law and Taxation Publishers 1993); KP Berger, *Private Dispute Resolution in International Business* (3rd edn, Harcourt Professional Publishing 2015); KP Berger, 'Party Autonomy in the International Economic Arbitration: A Reprisal' (1993) 4 Am Rev Int'l Arb 1; GB Born, *International Commercial Arbitration* (2nd edn, Kluwer Law International 2014) vols I and II; WL Craig, WW Park, and J Paulsson, *International Chamber of Commerce Arbitration* (3rd edn, OUP 2000); GR Delaume, 'State Contracts and Transnational Arbitration' (1981) 75 AJIL 785; H Fox, 'States and the Undertaking to Arbitrate' (1988) 37 ICLQ 1; P Fouchard, E Gaillard, and B Goldman, *Traité de l'arbitrage commercial international* (Litec 1996); H Grigera Naón, *Choice of Law Problems in International Commercial Arbitration* (JCB Mohr 1992); AF Lowenfeld, *International Litigation and Arbitration* (3rd edn, Thomson West 2006); FA Mann, 'State Contracts and International Arbitration' (1967) 42 BYIL 1; ML Moses, *The Principles and Practice of International Commercial Arbitration* (2nd edn, CUP 2012); N Blackaby, C Partasides, A Redfern, and M Hunter, *Redfern and Hunter on International Arbitration* (6th edn, OUP 2015); SM Schwebel, *International Arbitration: Three Salient Problems* (CUP 1987); SI Strong, *Research and Practice in International Commercial Arbitration* (OUP 2009); SJ Toope, *Mixed International Arbitration: Studies in Arbitration between States and Private Persons* (CUP 1990); FB Weigand (ed), *Practitioner's Handbook on International Commercial Arbitration* (2nd edn, OUP 2010); J Paulsson, 'Arbitration in three Dimensions' (2011) 60 ICLQ 291–323.

[33] For a concise presentation of the advantages of arbitration see N Blackaby, C Partasides, A Redfern, and M Hunter, *Redfern and Hunter on International Arbitration* (6th edn, OUP 2015) 31.

[34] N Blackaby, C Partasides, A Redfern, and M Hunter, *Redfern and Hunter on International Arbitration* (6th edn, OUP 2015) 439.

incentives faithfully to comply with an arbitration agreement. The negative social and economic consequences (loss of reputation) in most cases may weigh so much more than the short-term advantages of non-compliance.

Even if the parties to arbitration are willing to comply and cooperate, there are still obstacles inherent to arbitration that have to be overcome. A recurrent problem is the structure of the arbitral process. There is no 'one size fits all' framework which would adequately respond to all potential constellations. For example, the number of arbitrators is usually three. In this case, each party determines one arbitrator and the third arbitrator (chairman) is either determined by the other two arbitrators or by another procedure. This well-proven model fails when more than two parties are taking part in the proceedings. This constellation occurs rather frequently, in particular in cases of large construction projects with several companies involved.[35] In order to solve problems of that kind, some institutions have formulated arbitration rules which try to cover all problematic issues in the form of a 'procedural code'. Even though these sets of arbitration rules do not necessarily solve all problems that may arise in arbitral proceedings, they still provide a very helpful framework and are therefore often referred to in arbitration agreements. Examples are the arbitration rules of the International Chamber of Commerce (ICC),[36] the arbitration rules of the United Nations Commission on International Trade Law (UNCITRAL),[37] and others.[38] Investment arbitration between a private Investor and a host State may follow commercial arbitration rules or a special regime for investment disputes, such as the arbitration rules of the International Centre for the Settlement of Investment Disputes (ICSID).[39]

Although the normative force of international commercial arbitration essentially stems from the autonomy of the parties,[40] recourse to the national legal systems cannot fully be avoided in some cases.[41] National courts play a particularly important role whenever one party no longer stands loyally by the arbitration agreement

[35] See eg the problems in the *Dutco* case before the French *Cour de Cassation* (1992) Rev Arb 470.

[36] See MW Buhler and TH Webster, *Handbook of ICC Arbitration: Commentary, Precedents, Materials* (3rd edn, ICC Publishing 2011); Y Derains and E Schwartz, *A Guide to the ICC Rules of Arbitration* (2nd edn, Kluwer Law International 2005); E Schafer, H Verbist, and C Imhoos, *ICC Arbitration in Practice* (Kluwer Law International 2004).

[37] DD Caron and LM Caplan, *UNCITRAL Arbitration Rules: A Commentary* (2nd edn, OUP 2013); G Sacerdoti, 'The New Arbitration Rules of ICC and UNCITRAL' (1977) 11 JWT 248; TH Webster, *Handbook of UNCITRAL Arbitration: Commentary, Precedents and Models for UNCITRAL-Based Arbitration Rules* (2nd edn, Sweet & Maxwell 2014).

[38] For example MF Gusy, JM Hosking, and FT Schwarz, *A Guide to the ICDR International Arbitration Rules* (OUP 2011); P Turner and R Mohtashami, *A Guide to LCIA Arbitration Rules* (OUP 2009).

[39] See (1976) 15 ILM 701; for an overview of ICSID Arbitration, see R Happ and N Rubins, *Digest of ICSID Awards and Decisions: 1974–2002* (OUP 2013); R Happ and N Rubins, *Digest of ICSID Awards and Decisions: 2003–2007* (OUP 2009); L Reed, J Paulsson, and N Rawding, *Guide to ICSID Arbitration* (2nd edn, Kluwer Law International 2010); C Schreuer, L Malintoppi, A Reinisch, and A Sinclair (eds), *The ICSID Convention: A Commentary* (2nd edn, CUP 2009).

[40] See KP Berger, 'Party Autonomy in the International Economic Arbitration: A Repraisal' (1993) 4 Am Rev Int'l Arb 1.

[41] See N Blackaby, C Partasides, A Redfern, and M Hunter, *Redfern and Hunter on International Arbitration* (6th edn, OUP 2015) 439.

or challenges the arbitrators' ruling. Thus, one party may refuse to take part in the proceedings or may not acknowledge the binding force of an arbitral award against it. Another difficult constellation is the need for provisional measures in cases of the urgent protection of one party's rights. If the arbitration rules do not provide any provisional measures, it may be necessary to go to national courts in order to secure interim protection. Another important function of national courts is the review of arbitral awards. Such a judicial review, however, only becomes relevant if one of the parties does not accept the award and does not comply with its terms. If one party seeks enforcement of the award, it requires the assistance of the national courts. The other party then may challenge the validity of the award (action for nullity) in the State where the arbitration proceedings were held. Today, most States are willing to recognize private arbitral awards. The extent to which national law recognizes private arbitral awards as binding and enforceable essentially depends on its deference to private autonomy and its insistence on compliance with certain domestic standards. For national courts, the extent of judicial scrutiny depends on whether the arbitration proceedings are governed by domestic laws or by the laws of another country. Usually, countries apply their laws of civil procedure to arbitration if the arbitration proceedings and the arbitral tribunal are localized in their own territory.

Recognition is usually denied if certain peremptory rules of the domestic law are disregarded.[42] Such arbitral awards may become unenforceable or may even be nullified by a national court. Some legal orders are more generous than others. The United States tends to be generous in respect of awards in international antitrust disputes,[43] while British courts have admitted the reference to general principles of contract law in an arbitral agreement.[44]

The willingness of States to recognize and enforce (domestic and foreign) arbitral awards flows from the insight that arbitration can be an effective means of dispute settlement without undermining the authority of sovereign States. In order to formulate a uniform standard for arbitral proceedings, UNCITRAL developed a Model Law for national laws of procedure governing arbitration. The UNCITRAL Model Law has been accepted by many States and implemented by their national legislation.[45] The positive attitude of most States towards dispute settlement by arbitration is reflected in the New York Convention on the Recognition and Enforcement of Foreign Arbitral Awards of 1958.[46] The New York Convention covers all foreign arbitral awards, including those which qualify as 'foreign' due to

---

[42] See eg Article V, s 1 of the New York Convention.

[43] See eg US Supreme Court, *Mitsubishi Motors Corp v Soler Chrysler-Plymouth Inc* 473 US 614 (1985).

[44] English Court of Appeal, *Deutsche Schachtbau- und Tiefbohrgesellschaft mbH v R'As al-Khaimah National Oil Co* (1987) 3 WLR 1023; see s 46(1)(a) of the UK Arbitration Act of 1996; (1997) 36 ILM 155.

[45] P Binder, *International Commercial Arbitration and Conciliation in UNCITRAL Model Law Jurisdiction* (3rd edn, Sweet & Maxwell 2008); HC Alvarez, N Kaplan, and DW Rivkin, *Model Law Decisions: Cases Applying the UNCITRAL Model Law on International Commercial Arbitration (1985–2001)* (Kluwer Law International 2003); M Kerr, 'Arbitration and the Courts: The UNCITRAL Model Law' (1985) 34 ICLQ 1.

[46] See H Kronke, P Nacimiento, and D Otto, *Recognition and Enforcement of Foreign Arbitral Awards: A Global Commentary on the New York Convention* (Kluwer Law International 2010); see also

their strong links to another jurisdiction, despite the location of the arbitral tribunal inside the own territory (Article I(1)). Under the Convention, the recognition and enforcement of foreign arbitral awards are the rule and their refusal the exception. Only in particular cases may a Contracting State refuse the recognition or the enforcement. Thus, an award needs not be recognized if the arbitral agreement is invalid under the applicable national law (Article V(1)(a) of the Convention). Recognition may also be refused if the award has been annulled by the competent organs of the State in which the award was rendered (Article V(1)(e)), if the dispute at hand could not have been subject to arbitration in that State (Article V(2)(a)), or if the recognition or the enforcement contravenes the fundamental principles of the State's public order (*ordre public*, Article V(2)(b)). The latter criterion may generate significant uncertainty.

In contractual relations between private corporations and a foreign State, arbitration is the preferred dispute settlement mechanism. For the private party, subjection to the jurisdiction of the contracting State always implies a certain imbalance, given the State's dominion over its own legal order. This lack of parity becomes a critical issue in States with a tendency to mobilize their own legislation or even their own courts for governmental interests in controversies with contractual partners. At the same time, it is usually unacceptable for a State to submit itself to the laws and to the courts of another State. This dilemma is the background of arbitration agreements which purport to isolate the arbitral process from any national law. The arbitral awards based on such an agreement are called 'anational' or 'delocalized'.[47] Sometimes they are referred to as 'floating award' ('*sentence flottante*'). The phenomenon of 'anational' arbitral proceedings is not limited to proceedings between States and private corporations, but also occurs in arbitration between private parties.

The New York Convention of 1958, in principle, does not exclude 'anational' awards from recognition and enforcement.[48] Still, if the parties fail to cooperate loyally, such awards may become the source of considerable legal problems when it comes to recognition and enforcement. All the problems of arbitration, in comparison to 'normal' proceedings before national courts, may accumulate and aggravate in these constellations.

An illustrative example for the problems related to such awards is the saga of the *SEEE* case. The dispute arose in context of a railroad construction project between

L Daradkeh, *Recognition and Enforcement of Foreign Commercial Arbitral Awards* (Lambert Academic Publishing 2010).

[47] See T Rensmann, *Anationale Schiedssprüche* (Duncker & Humblot 1997); P Read, 'Delocalization of International Commercial Arbitration: Its Relevance in the New Millennium' (1999) 10 Am Rev Int'l Arb 177.

[48] See M Herdegen, 'Wirkungen von Schiedssprüchen in Streitigkeiten zwischen Privatpersonen und fremden Staaten' (1989) RIW 329 (336); S Ward Atterbury, 'Enforcement of A-National Arbitral Awards under the New York Convention of 1958' (1992) 32 Va J Int'l L 471; T Rensmann, *Anationale Schiedssprüche* (Duncker & Humblot 1997) 206; US Court of Appeals for the Ninth Circuit *Ministry of Defense of the Islamic Republic of Iran v Gould Inc* 887 F.2d 1357, 1364 (9th Cir 1989).

a French company and Yugoslavia.[49] The dispute was initially decided by an arbitral tribunal consisting of two arbitrators and seated in Lausanne which rendered its award in 1956. The Swiss courts refused recognition of the award, because the local law of the Canton Vaud required an uneven number of arbitrators. However, the Swiss courts did not annul the award either, arguing that the parties to the contract did not want to subject the dispute to Swiss law of procedure. The struggle for the enforcement of the award against Yugoslavia took decades and was taken to the supreme courts of France and the Netherlands. Finally, a decision of a French court of appeal, confirmed by the Cour de Cassation, cleared the way for enforcement of the award. The case impressively illustrates the inherent risks of arbitral proceedings which are detached from any national legal order.

The most adequate solution to the risks of arbitration between States and foreign private parties can be realized within the framework of an international treaty between the State party to the dispute and the home State of the private party. Examples for this solution are the ICSID Convention and the mechanisms of dispute settlement on the basis of bilateral investment treaties. The latter often provide the jurisdiction of the ICSID or an arbitral tribunal constituted under the UNCITRAL rules. In these cases, the rules on commercial arbitration may govern the settlement of non-commercial disputes between a private party and a State.

A problem of international arbitration is the risk of competing proceedings and conflicting awards in the same case. Even though arbitral agreements usually try to avoid that situation, occasionally it happens that two arbitral tribunals may claim jurisdiction over the same case.

A striking example is the case *Czech Republic v CME/Lauder*.[50] The Dutch company CME had made significant investments in the Czech media industry, which were affected by actions of the Czech Government. Lauder, a US national controlling the company, filed a complaint against the Czech Republic on the basis of a bilateral investment treaty (BIT) between the Czech Republic and the United States. The arbitral tribunal was constituted in London, following the UNCITRAL rules. Shortly after the constitution of the tribunal in London, CME instituted proceedings in Stockholm, pursuant to the BIT between the Netherlands and the Czech Republic. Again, UNCITRAL rules were applied. Whilst the London arbitral tribunal rejected Lauder's claims because no actionable interference with the investments could be established, the Stockholm arbitral tribunal decided in favour of CME and assumed that CME de facto had been expropriated. The Czech Republic then went to court in Sweden in order to have this award annulled. The

---

[49] *Société Européenne d'Etudes et d'Entreprises v Republique de Yougoslavie* (1959) 86 J Droit Int'l 1074; see also the judgments of national courts in this case: Canton's Court of Vaud (1958) 47 Rev Crit Dr Intern Priv 359; Swiss Supreme Court (1958) 47 Rev Crit Dr Intern Priv 366 with an annotation by J-F Aubert; Dutch Hoge Raad (1974) Rev Arb 311 (321); Cour d'appel de Rouen (1985) 112 J Droit Int'l 473 with an annotation by B Oppetit, confirmed by the French Cour de Cassation (1987) Rev Arb 149 with an annotation by J-L Delvolvé.

[50] See Svea Court of Appeals, *Czech Republic v CME Czech Republic BV* (2003) 42 ILM 919; G Sacerdoti, 'Investment Arbitration under ICSID and UNCITRAL Rules: Prerequisites, Applicable Law, Review of Awards' (2004) 19 ICSID Rev 1.

Swedish court rejected the Czech argument that the Swedish law on arbitration does not allow parallel proceedings as held in the given case. The court emphasized that it was the Czech Government which had refused to join the cases which would have favoured a uniform final award.

As the *CME* case illustrates, there are good reasons why the claims of a company and the claims of the controlling shareholder should not be separated on a procedural level. It seems reasonable to extend the effects of a binding award against the company to individual shareholders, no matter whether they control the company or not.

3. Jurisdiction of National Courts

Unless there is an agreement on dispute settlement, it is still the national courts which decide any legal dispute. From the perspective of the parties to a dispute, it matters which law of procedure and which substantive law is applied to a case. From the national judge's point of view, the first question is whether his court has jurisdiction to decide the dispute.[51] In the context of cases relating to two or more countries, that is with a view to defining the scope of jurisdiction vis-à-vis other States, this judicial power of adjudication is called international jurisdiction. Without international jurisdiction there will be no case before the courts of a State. Each State determines the ambit of its international jurisdiction for its own courts. In doing so, each State must respect the rules of international law. In case the international jurisdiction of the court is given, the next question is which substantive law applies to the dispute. Despite the theoretical simplicity of this division, there are often constellations which blur the boundaries of the two spheres. In particular, US courts often connect the question of international jurisdiction to the exact content of a particular statute. Whether the court has international jurisdiction or not depends on the interpretation of the statute's wording and is not a question to be decided beforehand. In European law and in particular in the civil law tradition the division is much stronger. Whether a court has 'subject matter jurisdiction' does not depend on the interpretation of the substantive law applicable to the dispute but is determined in the abstract and beforehand by procedural rules.[52]

Under public international law, a State's jurisdiction to adjudicate, like the jurisdiction to prescribe, requires a sufficient (personal, territorial, or other) link to the

---

[51] For a general overview of the topic, see FA Mann, 'The Doctrine of Jurisdiction in International Law (1964-I) 111 RdC 1; FA Mann, 'The Doctrine of International Jurisdiction Revisited after Twenty Years' (1984-III) 186 RdC 9; C Ryngaert, *Jurisdiction in International Law* (2nd edn OUP 2015); P Schlosser, 'Jurisdiction and International Judicial and Administrative Co-operation' (2001) 284 RdC 13; DF Vagts, 'Dispute-Resolution Mechanisms in International Business' (1987-III) 203 RdC 9 (40); H Ward, 'Securing Transnational Corporate Accountability through National Courts' (2001) 24 Hastings Int'l & Comp L Rev 451.

[52] For a detailed analysis of different approaches to jurisdiction, see P Capps, M Evans, and S Konstadinidis (eds), *Asserting Jurisdiction: International and European Legal Approaches* (Hart Publishing 2003).

State concerned. Without such a link, the legitimacy of a decision is questionable and the enforcement of a judgment in other countries may be easily denied. In principle, jurisdiction to adjudicate follows the same principles as the jurisdiction to prescribe.[53] Examples for those links are the nationality of the parties, the place of performance of a contract, or the place where a tort is committed. Also, an agreement by the parties can establish jurisdiction.[54] The presence of a foreign national within the territory of the State may establish jurisdiction to adjudicate, if it creates a substantial personal link such as residence or a branch office. The mere transit of a passenger travelling by plane or other ephemeral presence cannot provide a sufficient basis for the exercise of jurisdiction to adjudicate. Merely 'doing business' within a State's territory does not justify the exercise of jurisdiction over disputes wholly unrelated to the domestic business presence. In such a case, only the principle of universal jurisdiction (for example over particularly grave human rights violations) may justify adjudication by national courts.

National courts and international tribunals have developed various strategies to cope with the problem of competing jurisdictions. A number of treaties address this issue. Still, there remains a considerable potential of jurisdictional conflicts.[55]

(a) European law

In Europe, a relatively high conformity of the rules on international jurisdiction has been reached by the so-called 'Brussels Regime'. This term refers to a set of three legal instruments on international jurisdiction within the European States. The Convention on Jurisdiction and the Enforcement of Judgments in Civil and Commercial Matters of 1968 (Brussels Convention) was concluded between the Member States of the then European Economic Community. The so-called Lugano Convention of 1988 (revised in 2007) is modelled after the Brussels Convention and extends its principles to most Member States of the European Free Trade Association.[56] The Council Regulation (EC) No 44/2001 on Jurisdiction and the Recognition and Enforcement of Judgments in Civil and Commercial Matters (called Brussels I Regulation) incorporated the principles of the Brussels Convention into EU law. The Brussels I Regulation was recast by Regulation (EU) No 1215/2012.[57] The Lugano Convention is still applicable, if the defendant has his domicile in Norway, Iceland, or Switzerland. The Brussels Regime serves as a good example for the successful harmonization of jurisdictional rules on the

---

[53] See Ch VI.7.

[54] A Briggs, *Agreements on Jurisdiction and Choice of Law* (OUP 2008).

[55] For a general insight into the problems of jurisdictional conflicts, see N Lavranos, 'Regulating Competing Jurisdictions Among International Courts and Tribunals' (2008) 68 ZaöRV 575; Y Shany, *The Competing Jurisdictions of International Courts and Tribunals* (OUP 2003); Y Shany, *Regulating Jurisdictional Relations Between National and International Courts* (OUP 2007).

[56] JJ Newton, *Uniform Interpretation of the Brussels and Lugano Conventions* (Hart Publishing 2002).

[57] A Dickinson and E Lein, *The Brussels I Regulation Recast* (OUP 2015); Denmark had initially opted out of the Brussels I regime but later signed an agreement with the European Community to opt-in at will. In 2013 Denmark announced its intention to implement the revised contents of the Brussels I Regulation; see Agreement between the European Community and the Kingdom of Denmark on

regional level. The basic principle of Regulation (EU) No 1215/2012 is the jurisdiction of the courts of the Member State where the defendant has his domicile (Article 5). Special titles of jurisdiction allow actions to be brought in other Member States (Articles 7–9). Of particular relevance is the establishment of jurisdiction based on the place of performance of the contractual obligation in question (Article 7(1)(a)). Under Article 7(2) of the regulation, a person domiciled in the European Union may be sued 'in matters relating to tort, delict or quasi-delict, in the courts for the place where the harmful event occurred or may occur'. As the European Court of Justice held in *Kolassa v Barclays Bank plc*, this jurisdiction applies to actions against the issuer of certificates or other financial instruments for breach of non-contractual information obligations on the basis of the place where the loss occurred, 'particularly when the damage alleged occurred directly in the applicant's bank account held with a bank established within the area of jurisdiction of those courts'.[58] Accordingly, the purchaser of a financial instrument domiciled in Austria may bring an action for damages against a British bank before Austrian courts provided that the damage materialized in an account with a bank established within their local jurisdiction. In a number of cases the courts of a Member State have exclusive jurisdiction (Article 24), for example in proceedings which have as their object immovable property or tenancies of immovable property or which have as their object the validity of the constitution, the nullity or the dissolution of companies or other legal persons or associations of natural or legal persons.

The revised Brussels I Regulation aims at accelerating proceedings in the case of a prorogation of jurisdiction. When the parties have designated a court in an exclusive choice of court agreement, another court seized by a party must suspend its proceedings, if the other party initiates proceedings before the designated court. The revised Regulation also protects arbitration agreements and allows a party to invoke such an agreement before the court of a Member State, even if the other party has initiated proceedings before the courts of another Member State in disregard of the arbitration agreement (recital No 12; Article 1(2)(d)). Moreover, the revised Regulation provides jurisdiction with respect to non-EU defendants in a number of cases. Finally, the revised Regulation facilitates cross-border enforcement of judgments. It eliminates the requisite of the declaration of enforceability which had enabled debtors to raise manifold defences in order to procrastinate the process of enforcement (Article 39).

(b) The Convention on Choice of Court Agreements of 2005

Most legal frameworks on international jurisdiction recognize that the parties to a contract may agree on the court of their choice. In order to provide a stable framework

---

jurisdiction and the recognition and enforcement of judgments in civil and commercial matters [2013] OJ L 79.

[58] ECJ, Case C-375/13 *Kolassa v Barclays Bank plc* [2015] ECLI:EU:C:2015:37 paras 44ff (57). This judgment refers to Council Regulation (EC) No 44/2001.

for choice of court agreements, the Hague Conference on Private International Law in 2005 adopted the Convention on Choice of Court Agreements.[59] This Convention reflects a general standard for choice of court agreements and can therefore be used as a guideline.

According to Article 5(1) of the Convention, 'the court or courts of a Contracting State designated in an exclusive choice of court agreement shall have jurisdiction to decide a dispute to which the agreement applies, unless the agreement is null and void under the law of that State'. Under a valid agreement between the parties, the chosen courts have exclusive jurisdiction, unless otherwise provided in the agreement (Article 3(b)). No jurisdiction chosen by the parties shall be rejected on the grounds that the dispute should be settled before the courts of another State (Article 5(2)). Any judge of a Member State to the Convention is supposed to cease or interrupt proceedings in cases in which the parties agreed on the jurisdiction of another court (Article 6). The Convention also tries to facilitate the recognition and the enforcement of judgments based on a choice of court agreement. Chapter III of the Convention deals with the recognition and the enforcement of judgments. In principle, Contracting States must recognize and enforce judgments based on a choice of court agreement within the terms of the Convention. Only in a limited number of cases, the recognition and enforcement may be refused (Article 9).

(c) Jurisdiction based on domestic business contacts

In the absence of international agreements, the extent of jurisdiction is still determined by the national laws of procedure. While many States massively limit the jurisdiction of their courts in the disputes with an extraterritorial dimension, others open their courts for disputes with strong, even predominant links to foreign States.[60]

Among the States with rather extensive claims to jurisdiction, the United States plays a prominent role.[61] On the one hand, the US practice has often been criticized for being too expansive. On the other hand, the US system is praised as an attractive forum for meritorious claims to which countries with closer links are not very receptive. Within the last years, several decisions of US federal courts including the Supreme Court have substantially restrained the exercise of jurisdiction in various fields. Still, the United States is far from being restrictive as regards the exercise of prescriptive and adjudicative jurisdiction.

---

[59] RA Brand and P Herrup, *The 2005 Hague Convention on Choice of Court Agreements* (CUP 2008); C Thiele, 'The Hague Convention on Choice of Court Agreements: Was It Worth the Effort?' in E Gottschalk, R Michaels, G Rühl, and J van Hein (eds), *Conflict of Laws in a Globalized World* (CUP 2011) 63.

[60] See C Campbell, *International Civil Procedure* (Yorkhill Law Publishing 2007) vols I, II; SR Grubbs, *International Civil Procedure* (Kluwer Law International 2003).

[61] See the respective chapters on US law in C Campbell, *International Civil Procedure* (Yorkhill Law Publishing 2007) vols I, II; SR Grubbs, *International Civil Procedure* (Kluwer Law International 2003).

A very contentious basis for US jurisdiction is the criterion of 'doing business in the United States'. According to that criterion, any business presence in the United States triggers the jurisdiction of US courts.

A prominent example of this approach is the case *TACA International Airlines SA v Rolls-Royce of England Ltd.*[62] In this case, a foreign airline brought an action against the British firm Rolls-Royce for having manufactured an aircraft engine with an alleged defect responsible for an accident in Central America. Although the production and sale of Rolls-Royce aircraft engines was confined to locations outside the United States, the New York courts assumed jurisdiction for the claim, merely because Rolls-Royce had an affiliate company in New York which was exclusively dealing with cars. This very thin connection was considered sufficient in terms of the 'doing business' criterion.

In recent times, US courts have adopted a more restrictive position.[63] The mere business presence in the United States alone no longer establishes the jurisdiction of US courts. The idea of due process[64] requires a 'minimum contact' with the domestic market.[65] The exercise of jurisdiction must also be 'reasonable' in terms of fair play and material justice.[66]

The 'doing business' formula has been reformulated and now requires 'continuous and systematic general business contacts' in the United States. Hence, it is no longer sufficient for jurisdiction in cases of product liability that the product somehow entered the US market. The seller must have intentionally placed the product on the US market for creating a jurisdictional link.[67] A particularly far-reaching case of the establishment of jurisdiction can be found in the form of the Alien Tort Claims Act (ATCA/ATS) of 1789.[68] The ATCA grants jurisdiction to US Federal Courts over 'any civil action by an alien for a tort only, committed in violation of the law of nations or a treaty of the United States'. This unusual provision has experienced a remarkable revival within the last years and has been used very often as a mechanism to counter the structural shortfall of individuals against multinational companies, until the US Supreme Court severely restricted the ATCA's ambit.[69]

(d) The attractions of the US jurisdiction for foreign claimants: some salient features of US law

In cases in which the claimant can opt for several jurisdictions, choosing the most advantageous forum can be decisive for success. The attractiveness of the forum

---

[62] *TACA International Airlines SA v Rolls Royce of England Ltd* 204 NE 2 d 329 (1965).
[63] See US Supreme Court *Helicopteros Nacionales de Colombia v Hall* 466 US 408, 416 (1984).
[64] See Federal Rule of Civil Procedure 4 lit k (2).
[65] *Metropolitan Life Ins Co v Robertson-Ceco Corp* 84 F.3d 560 (567) (2nd Cir, 1996).
[66] US Supreme Court *Asahi Metal Industry Co v Superior Court of California* 480 US 102, 113 (1987).
[67] US Supreme Court *Asahi Metal Industry Co v Superior Court of California* 480 US 102 (1987).
[68] 28 USC § 1350.   [69] For a detailed analysis see Ch VII.3(b).

for the claimant depends on the individual circumstances of the case. It might be the procedural rules or the substantive law which favour the plaintiff. On the other hand, a sober cost–benefit analysis will also consider the implications of a forum choice with respect to other countries with an adjudicatory interest, for example the willingness to cooperate with respect to obtaining evidence abroad or to enforcement.

All the possible problems associated with the choice of a forum that has only limited or questionable links to a particular case have not hindered claimants from all countries to choose the United States as a forum even if other jurisdictions might have appeared to be more adequate. Manifold aspects of procedural and substantive principles traditionally have rendered the US legal system particularly interesting to foreign claimants. In particular, the law of product liability, antitrust law, and the assessment of damages as well as the rules on evidence and the regime of costs have attracted plaintiffs.

The famous English judge Lord Denning used a sarcastic metaphor to illustrate the magnetism of the US legal system:

As a moth is drawn to the light, so is a litigant drawn to the United States. If he can only get his case into their courts, he stands to win a fortune. At no cost to himself and at no risk of having to pay anything to the other side. The lawyers there will conduct the case 'on spec' as we say or on a 'contingency fee' as they say. The lawyers will charge the litigant nothing for their services, but instead they will take 40 per cent of the damages, if they win the case in court, or out of court on a settlement. If they lose, the litigant will have nothing to pay to the other side. The courts in the United States have no such costs deterrent as we have. There is also in the United States a right to trial by jury. These are prone to award fabulous damages. They are notoriously sympathetic and know that the lawyers will take their 40 per cent before the plaintiff gets anything. All this means that the defendant can be readily forced into a settlement. The plaintiff holds all the cards.[70]

In the last decades, case-law has attenuated some of these features, and flocks of US attorneys hovering above the site of man-made disasters in distant corners of the globe have become a much less familiar sight than in the past. Still, the United States remains an enormously popular forum for the truly aggrieved and other claimants from all over the world.

i. Punitive damages

From a claimant's point of view, there are a number of reasons to recommend the United States as the best place for a law suit. One special feature of US law is the 'punitive' (or 'exemplary') damages which not only compensate the actual damage suffered but are also meant to punish and deter. This function of damages is unknown to the tort law of many other countries in which it

---

[70] Lord Denning in *Smith Kline and French Laboratories v Bloch* [1983] 1 WLR 730 (733).

would usually be covered by sanctions under criminal law. Juries all too often tend to side with plaintiffs and have awarded tremendous sums in damages. In the last years, some judgments have interfered with the excessive generosity of juries. The US Supreme Court held that, in particular, the standard of due process, in the interest of fairness, sets limits to the sums of damages that may be awarded.

In *BMW of North America Inc v Gore*, the Supreme Court laid down clear limitations for punitive and exemplary damages.[71] According to the Supreme Court, these damages must stand in an appropriate proportion to

- the degree of reprehensibility of the respondent's conduct;
- the concrete damages suffered by the claimant; and
- other sanctions for comparable misconduct (for example statutory fines).

In this case, the claimant had bought a new car. The car had a defect in the paint which was known to the respondent company (seller and producer) which concealed the damage from the buyer. The reduction of the car's value amounted to USD 4,000. The generous jury, however, awarded USD 2 million as punitive damages. In the light of the three above-mentioned criteria, the Supreme Court considered this sum as 'grossly excessive'.

Recent decisions stress that any damage to third persons not affected by the actual harmful conduct may only be taken into account in context with reprehensibility, but not in terms of enhancing the damage suffered by the claimant.

This case-law significantly reduces the liability risks for the tobacco industry. Thus, the US Supreme Court held that the sum of USD 79.5 million as punitive damages for the death of an addicted smoker could not be justified by the number of other victims of tobacco smoking.[72]

In *Exxon Shipping Co v Baker*, the US Supreme Court took a critical view on the extensive award of punitive damages in the absence of statutory provisions (as they exist in competition law).[73] The case relates to the *Exxon Valdez* incident off the coast of Alaska and the ensuing oil pollution. The concern of the Court extended both to the amount of damages itself as well as to its unpredictability. As to the possible amount of punitive damages, the Court differentiated between liability in antitrust law, competition law, and liability in cases of environmental damage. In antitrust law, punitive damages serve as an important regulatory instrument, creating an incentive for private parties to enforce competition rules. In cases of environmental liability, the primary function of damages is restitution, given the statutory sanctions and the vigilance of environmental NGOs. At least in cases of damages to the marine environment, the Supreme Court held that punitive damages should

---

[71] US Supreme Court *BMW of North America Inc v Gore* 517 US 559, 574 (1996).
[72] US Supreme Court *Philip Morris USA v Williams* 549 US 346 (2007).
[73] US Supreme Court *Exxon Shipping Co v Baker* 554 US 471 (2008).

not exceed the amount for restitution, that is to say a ratio of not more than 1:1 would be appropriate.

ii. Class actions

Another salient feature of the US law of procedure is its receptivity to a multitude of parallel claims. Instead of requiring claims to be filed individually and separately, US law allows the pursuit of concurrent claims in the form of a class action,[74] thus avoiding a host of parallel proceedings. In terms of procedural economy, the judgment of the court extends to all stakeholders in the class action. The concept of class actions is not limited to the US jurisdiction alone. It has also been adopted in Canada, Australia, and Israel. Meanwhile, some kinds of class action made their way to Europe (eg to the United Kingdom and Germany), especially in securities litigation.

iii. Pre-trial discovery of documents

From the plaintiff's point of view, US law of procedure commends itself by the rules on 'pre-trial discovery of documents'. In case of a pre-trial discovery of documents, the respondent must grant the claimant access to certain documents which are potentially relevant to a forthcoming case. The claimant does not have to specify which information is contained in the documents he is interested in. It suffices that the documents might contain relevant information. Such gathering of evidence often amounts to a 'fishing expedition' without concrete points of reference. In most countries, such discovery of documents is considered as an undue intrusion and violation of the respondent's rights. Often, the mere threat of a cumbersome pre-trial discovery of documents with all its possible implications induces respondents to enter into negotiations about an 'amicable' settlement, even though the claim stands little chance of success. Despite all legitimate criticism, the idea underlying the pre-trial discovery of documents has some merit. Under certain conditions, the imbalance of power between large corporations and less financially strong claimants might justify such a mechanism to redress equality of conditions in civil litigation. In any case, pre-trial discovery must not operate as pure chicanery and an abuse of rights.

(e) Forum shopping

The concurrence of jurisdictions and the natural tendency of claimants to select the forum most advantageous for them, is one of the side-effects of globalized litigation in modern business and leads to what is called 'forum shopping'.[75] The claimants'

---

[74] See R Mulheron, *The Class Action in Common Law Legal Systems—A Comparative Perspective* (Hart Publishing 2004).
[75] A Bell, *Forum Shopping and Venue in Transnational Litigation* (OUP 2003); J Pauwelyn and LE Salles, 'Forum Shopping Before International Tribunals' (2009) 42 Cornell Int'l LJ 77.

interest in securing the most favourable conditions for their case is perfectly legitimate. However, forum shopping becomes problematic if the country of choice has only a relatively weak connection with the dispute.

In order to cope with excesses of forum shopping, Anglo-American case-law developed the doctrine of *forum non conveniens*.[76] According to that doctrine, a court may dismiss any case in which it has international jurisdiction on the grounds that the case can practically be dealt with more adequately by the courts of another country which also has jurisdiction in the case.[77]

In the *Gas Plant Disaster at Bhopal* case, US courts applied that doctrine and dismissed an action against the US chemical company Union Carbide.[78] Claimants held the US company responsible for a devastating explosion in one of its gas plants (run by Union Carbide India Ltd (UCIL)) in India with numerous victims. US federal courts considered the courts of India the appropriate forum, given the territorial link to the accident and the ability of Indian courts to handle the case despite its complexity.

The doctrine of *forum non conveniens* is often applied in a flexible manner. In the *Asbestos* case,[79] the House of Lords did not dismiss a case of tort liability even though the dispute had a much closer connection to the country it originated from than to the United Kingdom. South African workers had sued the South African affiliate of a British company in London for having them exposed to carcinogenic dusts in a South African plant and thereby having caused serious health damage. The House of Lords did not admit the respondent's plea of *forum non conveniens*. The House of Lords argued that the financially weak claimants could not rely on any legal aid under the law of South Africa. This approach opens the concept of *forum non conveniens* for elements of social justice and due process.

4. Obtaining Evidence Abroad

Access to evidence abroad is one of the most controversial issues in international procedural law.[80] The access to documents located in other countries and the hearing of witnesses domiciled abroad may often conflict with the sovereignty of other States and with foreign laws. All this might result in noticeable delays or even plain non-cooperation defeating the access to evidence. The practice of US courts

---

[76] See RA Brand and SR Jablonski, *Forum Non Conveniens* (OUP 2007).

[77] See House of Lords *Spiliada Maritime Corp v Cansulex Ltd* [1987] 1 AC 460 (474) per Lord Goff of Chieveley.

[78] *In re Union Carbide Corp Gas Plant Disaster at Bhopal, India* 634 F.Supp 842 (SDNY 1986); 809 F.2d 195 (2nd Cir 1987).

[79] *Lubbe v Cape Plc* [2001] 1 AC 1545; for an exception from the *forum non conveniens* principle in civil law suits based on human rights violations, see US Court of Appeals (2nd Cir) *Wiwa v Royal Dutch Petroleum Co* (2001) 40 ILM 481.

[80] For a compendium of special features of different laws of procedure, see SR Grubbs, *International Civil Procedure* (Kluwer Law International 2003); D Campbell, *Serving Process and Obtaining Evidence Abroad* (Kluwer Law International 1998).

to sidestep the channels of international judicial assistance and to seek evidence through orders to the parties more than once caused resentments in European States.[81]

In the *Volkswagen* case,[82] a US court ordered the respondent, a German car manufacturer, to grant to the claimant free access to its factories in Germany, to allow direct contact with the workers, and to submit construction plans located abroad.

Behind this expansive practice, often considered as unduly intrusive and invasive to foreign sovereignty, stands the idea that jurisdiction to adjudicate does not only extend to the claimant as a legal subject, but also to assets under his control for the purpose of obtaining evidence, no matter whether situated in the United States or abroad. From this somehow parochial perspective, claiming jurisdiction over evidence located in foreign assets does not violate the sovereignty of any other country but it is simply the effective exercise of domestic jurisdiction in the interest of the administration of justice. Many, if not most, other States are not willing to share this perspective.

The formal gathering of evidence (like the hearing of witnesses) abroad is always subject to the territorial sovereignty of the State concerned. A number of treaties facilitate the access to evidence. One of the most important treaties in this field is the Convention on the Taking of Evidence Abroad in Civil or Commercial Matters (1970) adopted by the Hague Conference on Private International Law. Many industrial countries are parties to this Convention (eg the United States, France, Germany, and the United Kingdom). Under this Convention, 'a judicial authority of a Contracting State'[83] may request assistance in gathering evidence from the competent organs of any other party to the Convention. The requested assistance can only be denied under certain circumstances (Articles 11 and 12 of the Convention).

Special problems are associated with orders of extraterritorial pre-trial discovery of documents. The relation of pre-trial discovery of documents located abroad to the mechanism of judicial assistance under this Convention remains very controversial, as pre-trial discovery goes against the legal tradition of many countries. Article 23 of the Convention addresses this conflict:

A Contracting State may at the time of signature, ratification or accession, declare that it will not execute Letters of Request issued for the purpose of obtaining pre-trial discovery of documents as known in Common Law countries.

France, Germany, and the United Kingdom made such a declaration. In the case *Aérospatiale* the US Supreme Court held that the 1970 Convention presented no obstacle to pre-trial discovery of documents located abroad.[84]

---

[81] See American Law Institute, *Restatement (Third) of the Foreign Relations Law of the United States* (1987) vol 1, Comments to § 474 (551).

[82] *Volkswagenwerk AG v Superior Court, Alameda County,* 123 Cal App 3 d 503 (1981).

[83] Article 1, s 1 of the Convention.

[84] *Société Nationale Industrielle Aérospatiale v United States District Court for the District of Iowa,* 482 US 522 (1987); cf GB Born and S Hoing, 'Comity and the Lower Courts: Post-Aérospatiale

In this case, a claim based on product liability was brought before the US courts against two French companies owned by the French State. The French companies were ordered to submit certain documents located in France. They argued that for obtaining evidence abroad, the 1970 Convention on the Taking of Evidence Abroad in Civil or Commercial Matters excluded any mechanism other than a request for judicial assistance. The Supreme Court rejected that objection and ruled that the Convention does not supersede US procedural law on evidence. However, the Court stressed that international comity required US courts to consider the interests of other States. From an international perspective, this ruling is rather unsatisfactory and clashes with the possible rejection of pre-trial discovery under Article 23 of the 1970 Convention.

Under certain circumstances, US law provides that parties to a dispute before a 'foreign or international tribunal' may ask for the assistance of US courts to obtain evidence.[85] In *Intel Corp v Advanced Micro Devices Inc*,[86] the US Supreme Court decided that this provision also applies to proceedings before institutions not to be classified as courts in the strict sense, such as antitrust proceedings before the European Commission.

In the *Intel* case, the company AMD had filed a complaint against Intel before the Directorate-General for Competition of the European Commission. After AMD had failed with its attempt to have the European Commission request certain documents from the US courts, which Intel had submitted in another antitrust case in Alabama, AMD sought the assistance of the US courts for ordering Intel to hand over the documents to the Directorate-General for Competition. The Supreme Court held that the mechanism of judicial assistance is not confined to court proceedings and it established criteria for cooperation. US courts should consider the nature of the dispute, the willingness of foreign dispute settlement bodies to cooperate reciprocally, and the reasonableness of the requested cooperation in terms of proportionality.

Recent decisions of the US courts have even extended the principles of pre-trial discovery to commercial arbitration outside the United States.[87] Under this new case law, a party to arbitral proceedings may request pre-trial discovery of certain documents before US courts. Parties to an arbitral agreement should therefore consider the exclusion of intrusive measures like pre-trial discovery.

Applications of the Hague Evidence Convention' (1990) Int'l Law 393; DJ Gerber, 'International Discovery after Aérospatiale: The Quest for an Analytical Framework' (1988) 82 AJIL 521.

[85] 28 USC § 1782[a].   [86] 542 US 241 (2004).

[87] United States District Court (ND Ga, Atlanta Division) *In re Roz Trading Ltd* 469 F.Supp 2d 1221 (2006).

5. Service of Process, Recognition,
and Enforcement of Foreign Judgments

In principle, States are free to allow or refuse the serving of foreign juridical documents. For international cooperation in this field,[88] the Convention on the Service Abroad of Judicial and Extrajudicial Documents in Civil or Commercial Matters of 1965 (the so called 'Hague Service Convention') plays an important role. The Hague Service Convention limits the grounds on which contracting States may refuse the service of documents. The Convention provides in Article 13(1):

Where a request for service complies with the terms of the present Convention, the State addressed may refuse to comply therewith only if it deems that compliance would infringe its sovereignty or security.

That provision significantly limits States' discretion in refusing a request for service. In many cases which affect its *ordre public*, the requested State may opt for refusing the service of documents rather than wait for the refusal of recognition and enforcement of the judgment.

In the *Napster* case, the German Constitutional Court blocked the service of process against a German publishing company to be sued in the United States in an interim decision. The Constitutional Court indicated that, given the circumstances of the case (a class action in the United States with a monstrous damages claim of USD 17 billion), the fundamental rights of the defendant may be violated if the service aims at intimidating the defendant. The German Constitutional Court stated that the duty to cooperate in legal matters reaches its limits,

[...] where the foreign claim asserted by the law suit—at least as far as the amount of the claim is concerned—is devoid of any substance. If law suits before the courts are used in an obviously abusive manner by public pressure and the risk of a negative judgement in order to influence a market participant, this may violate German constitutional law.[89]

Judgments of national courts are not automatically valid and enforceable in any other foreign State. They require the recognition and an enforcement order in the State concerned. Most States are receptive to the recognition and enforcement of foreign judgments, if they fulfil certain requirements. Common criteria found in the legislation of many countries are that the foreign judgment is based on recognized international jurisdiction, that the judgment does not conflict with the fundamental principles of the recognizing State's own legal order (*ordre public*) and that reciprocity is granted. A typical example for an infringement of the *ordre public* of many European States is excessive punitive damages.[90]

Some international treaties govern the conditions for recognition and enforcement of judgments. The 'Brussels regime', building first on the Brussels Convention

---

[88] See D Campbell, *Serving Process and Obtaining Evidence Abroad* (Kluwer Law International 1998).
[89] BVerfGE 108, 238 (248); see also BVerfGE 114, 396 (Provisional Measures).
[90] See BGHZ 118, 312.

of 1968 and the Lugano Convention of 1998, now incorporated into EU law by the Council Regulation (EC) No 44/2001 on jurisdiction and the recognition and enforcement of judgments in civil and commercial matters, also contains detailed provisions on recognition and enforcement of foreign judgments.

Select Bibliography

Y Aksar, *Implementing International Economic Law Through Dispute Settlement Mechanisms* (Martinus Nijhoff Publishers 2011).

N Blackaby, C Partasides, A Redfern, and M Hunter, *Redfern and Hunter on International Arbitration* (6th edn, OUP 2015).

J Collier and V Lowe, *The Settlement of Disputes in International Law* (OUP 1999).

A Dickinson and E Lein, *The Brussels I Regulation Recast* (OUP 2015).

MT Grando, *Evidence, Proof and Fact-Finding in WTO Dispute Settlement* (OUP 2010).

JH Jackson, *The Jurisprudence of the GATT and the WTO: Insights on Treaty Law and Economic Relations* (CUP 2007).

AF Lowenfeld, *International Litigation and Arbitration* (3rd edn, Thomson West 2006).

JG Merrills, *International Dispute Settlement* (5th edn, CUP 2011).

H Mosler and R Bernhardt (eds), *Judicial Settlement of International Disputes* (Springer 1974).

K Oellers-Frahm and A Zimmermann, *Dispute Settlement in Public International Law* (2nd edn, Springer 2001).

WTO (ed), *A Handbook on the WTO Dispute Settlements System* (CUP 2004).

PART III

WORLD TRADE LAW AND REGIONAL TRADE AGREEMENTS

XI

History and Development of World Trade Law

1. Development up to the Uruguay Round

As early as in 1941, the Atlantic Charter[1] emphasized non-discriminatory access to markets and raw materials as a principle of the post-war order and expressed the commitment to intensive international cooperation in the interest of improved labour standards, social security, and economic progress in the post-war order:

The President of the United States of America and the Prime Minister, Mr. Churchill, representing His Majesty's Government in the United Kingdom, being met together, deem it right to make known certain common principles in the national policies of their respective countries on which they base their hopes for a better future for the world. [...]

Fourth, they will endeavour, with due respect for their existing obligations, to further the enjoyment by all States, great or small, victor or vanquished, of access, on equal terms, to the trade and to the raw materials of the world which are needed for their economic prosperity;

Fifth, they desire to bring about the fullest collaboration between all nations in the economic field with the object of securing, for all, improved labour standards, economic advancement and social security; [...].

After the end of the Second World War, the Economic and Social Council of the United Nations convened a number of conferences on trade and employment, responding to an initiative of the United States (the conferences of London in October 1946, Geneva in August 1947, and Havana from November 1947 until March 1948).[2] After the organization of the international monetary and finance system with the International Monetary Fund and the International Bank for Reconstruction and Development (World Bank), this process aimed at new structures for international trade with an International Trade Organization (ITO) as an institutional platform. The Havana Charter of 1948[3] encapsulated these structures in a comprehensive framework. The Havana Charter contained rules not only for all areas of trade, but also for competition, development, and the labour market. In the end, the Charter proved to be an over-ambitious instrument at its time and never

---

[1] See M Bennouna, 'Atlantic Charter' in R Wolfrum (ed), *The Max Planck Encyclopedia of Public International Law* (OUP 2012) vol I, 734.

[2] See M Matsushita, TJ Schoenbaum, PC Mavroidis, and M Hahn (eds), *The World Trade Organization* (3rd edn, OUP 2015) 1f.

[3] See G Sacerdoti, 'Havana Charter' in R Wolfrum (ed), *The Max Planck Encyclopedia of Public International Law* (OUP 2012) vol IV, 718.

entered into force. The main reason was growing opposition in the US Congress which was afraid that the Charter might establish too far-reaching restraints on the foreign trade policy of the United States.

Shortly before the Havana Conference, negotiations on the reduction of tariffs and other aspects of free trade led to the General Agreement on Tariffs and Trade (GATT). The GATT was signed on 31 October 1947 and entered into force on 1 January 1948, according to a protocol on its preliminary application. The GATT was meant to be an integral element of the Havana framework. The protocol on the preliminary application of the GATT was meant to bridge the often lengthy process of parliamentary ratification. Up to now, the GATT has been the cornerstone of the world trade system.

The 'grandfather clause' of the protocol allowed the Contracting States to maintain 'existing legislation', that is municipal law already in force on 30 October 1947, even if it conflicted with Part II of the GATT. After the failure of the Havana Charter, the 'provisional' GATT became the new framework for world traders. The GATT assumed some of the functions assigned originally to the ITO and became a sort of de facto international organization with a somehow unclear legal status.[4] The basis was Article XXV which provided for joint action of the contracting parties:

1. Representatives of the contracting parties shall meet from time to time for the purpose of giving effect to those provisions of this Agreement which involve joint action and, generally, with a view to facilitating the operation and furthering the objectives of this Agreement. Wherever reference is made in this Agreement to the contracting parties acting jointly they are designated as the CONTRACTING PARTIES.
2. The Secretary-General of the United Nations is requested to convene the first meeting of the CONTRACTING PARTIES, which shall take place not later than March 1, 1948.
3. Each contracting party shall be entitled to have one vote at all meetings of the CONTRACTING PARTIES.
4. Except as otherwise provided for in this Agreement, decisions of the CONTRACTING PARTIES shall be taken by a majority of the votes cast.
5. In exceptional circumstances not elsewhere provided for in this Agreement, the CONTRACTING PARTIES may waive an obligation imposed upon a contracting party by this Agreement; Provided that any such decision shall be approved by a two-thirds majority of the votes cast and that such majority shall comprise more than half of the contracting parties. The CONTRACTING PARTIES may also by such a vote
   (i) define certain categories of exceptional circumstances to which other voting requirements shall apply for the waiver of obligations, and
   (ii) prescribe such criteria as may be necessary for the application of this paragraph.

In order to eliminate trade barriers, Member States have periodically conducted negotiation rounds. The earlier rounds (in Geneva in 1947, in Annecy in 1949,

[4] See M Matsushita, TJ Schoenbaum, PC Mavroidis, and M Hahn (eds), *The World Trade Organization* (3rd edn, OUP 2015) 2 f.

in Torquay in 1950/51, again in Geneva in 1956, 1960–62 (so-called 'Dillon Round'), and 1964–67 (so-called 'Kennedy Round')) focused on the reduction of tariffs. Since the so-called Tokyo Round (1973–79) the focus of negotiations shifted on the elimination of non-tariffs barriers to trade. The so-called Uruguay Round (1986–94), which began in Punta del Este, led to far-reaching changes of the world trade system with the newly founded World Trade Organization. Under the auspices of the World Trade Organization, the current Doha Round started in 2001.

In the light of their power, transferred by the Member States, to regulate trade the European Communities have been treated like a member to the GATT. In 1994, the European Community (now replaced by the European Union) acceded formally to the GATT and the other WTO agreements.

2. The Uruguay Round

The 'Uruguay Round'[5] brought about comprehensive reform of the world trading system with

- a new institutional framework based on the World Trade Organization (WTO);
- a dispute settlement mechanism with strong quasi-judicial elements; and
- a number of new agreements extending the scope of world trade law.

The final Act of the 'Uruguay Round' with the bundle of new agreements and other documents[6] was signed in Marrakesh in April 1994 and entered into force on 1 January 1995.

The revised GATT ('GATT 1994')[7] consists of the pre-existing GATT as amended in the past ('GATT 1947'), of new understandings on various GATT provisions, and the Marrakesh Protocol to the GATT 1994. Article 1 of the GATT 1994 states:

1. The General Agreement on Tariffs and Trade 1994 ('GATT 1994') shall consist of:
   (a) the provisions in the General Agreement on Tariffs and Trade, dated 30 October 1947, annexed to the Final Act Adopted at the Conclusion of the Second Session of the Preparatory Committee of the United Nations Conference on Trade and

---

[5] See GR Winham, 'An Interpretative History of the Uruguay Round Negotiation' in PFJ Macrory, AE Appleton, and MG Plummer (eds), *The World Trade Organization: Legal, Economic and Political Analysis* (Springer 2005) vol I, 3.
[6] The final Act of the Uruguay Round of April 1994 with its Protocols (in particular the Agreement Establishing the World Trade Organization, the Agreement on Trade and Goods, the General Agreement on Tariffs and Trade 1994, the Uruguay Round Protocol GATT 1994, the Agreement on Trade in Services, the Agreement on Trade-Related Aspects of International Property Rights, including Trade in Counterfeit Goods, the Understanding on Rules and Procedures Governing the Settlement of Disputes) is published in (1994) 33 ILM 1125.
[7] (1994) 33 ILM 28. In the following text, the term 'GATT' will be used as reference to the GATT 1994, which includes the GATT 1947.

Employment (excluding the Protocol of Provisional Application), as rectified, amended or modified by the terms of legal instruments which have entered into force before the date of entry into force of the WTO Agreement;
(b) the provisions of the legal instruments set forth below that have entered into force under the GATT 1947 before the date of entry into force of the WTO Agreement:
    (i)   protocols and certifications relating to tariff concessions;
    (ii) protocols of accession (excluding the provisions *(a)* concerning provisional application and withdrawal of provisional application and *(b)* providing that Part II of GATT 1947 shall be applied provisionally to the fullest extent not inconsistent with legislation existing on the date of the Protocol);
    (iii) decisions on waivers granted under Article XXV of GATT 1947 and still in force on the date of entry into force of the WTO Agreement;
    (iv) other decisions of the CONTRACTING PARTIES to GATT 1947;
(c) the Understandings set forth below:
    (i)   Understanding on the Interpretation of Article II:1(b) of the General Agreement on Tariffs and Trade 1994;
    (ii) Understanding on the Interpretation of Article XVII of the General Agreement on Tariffs and Trade 1994;
    (iii) Understanding on Balance-of-Payments Provisions of the General Agreement on Tariffs and Trade 1994;
    (iv) Understanding on the Interpretation of Article XXIV of the General Agreement on Tariffs and Trade 1994;
    (v) Understanding in Respect of Waivers of Obligations under the General Agreement on Tariffs and Trade 1994;
    (vi) Understanding on the Interpretation of Article XXVIII of the General Agreement on Tariffs and Trade 1994; and
(d) the Marrakesh Protocol to GATT 1994.

The substantive principles of the GATT 1947 are continued by the GATT 1994. In institutional terms, the crucial achievement of the 'Uruguay Round' is the establishment of the World Trade Organization (WTO). The WTO law considerably extends the reach of world trade law. The General Agreement on Trade in Services (GATS)[8] now covers the service sector. The Agreement on Trade-Related Aspects of Intellectual Property Rights (TRIPS)[9] and the Agreement on Trade-Related Investment Measures (TRIMS)[10] bring new areas within the ambit of the WTO regime. Specific agreements address sanitary and phytosanitary measures, technical barriers to trade, safeguards, trade in the agricultural sector, anti-dumping measures, as well as subsidies and countervailing measures. The new Dispute Settlement Understanding (DSU) vests the WTO regime with mechanisms which are more judicial than political in character and with palpable sanctions. The dispute settlement system has strongly enhanced the pull to compliance.

   [8] (1994) 33 ILM 44.
   [9] (1994) 33 ILM 81.
   [10] See ML de Sterlini, 'The Agreement on Trade-Related Investment Measures' in PFJ Macrory, AE Appleton, and MG Plummer (eds), *The World Trade Organization: Legal, Economic and Political Analysis* (Springer 2005) vol I, 437.

The new Agreement on Government Procurement (GPA),[11] replacing a previous GPA, opens the access to public procurement also on the regional and local level and applies to the procurement of goods and services for water and energy supply as well as transportation, whilst no agreement could be achieved on public procurement in the area of telecommunication systems.

It must be conceded that the main beneficiaries from the trade liberalization agreed upon in the 'Uruguay Round' are the industrialized States of North America, Europe, and Asia with highly competitive producers of goods and services. Still, significant welfare gains have accrued or will, in the long run, accrue to many developing countries. In any case, due consideration of developing countries, especially those with an economy essentially based on agriculture, remains a lasting challenge for the WTO regime,[12] especially as about three-quarters of the WTO members are developing countries.[13]

3. Post-Uruguay Perspectives and Challenges for the WTO System

In November 2001, a new world trade round was opened at the WTO meeting in Doha (Qatar). The Doha Ministerial Conference adopted the 'Doha Declaration'[14] which outlines the agenda for negotiations on further development of the WTO system. A separate declaration lists a number of 'implementation-related issues and concerns'.[15] Among the issues of negotiation are more support for the least developed countries, the progressive liberalization of markets for services, the resolution of intellectual property controversies (eg with respect to patents for biotechnological inventions), measures of environmental protection, and the further elimination or reduction of measures distorting international competition, especially export subsidies for agricultural products and electronic commerce.

The Sixth Ministerial Conference of December 2005 in Hong Kong[16] has brought about a package of measures to support the least developed countries. The industrialized countries and the willing emerging market countries shall grant duty- and quota-free access to these countries' markets for at least 97 per cent of

---

[11] BM Hoekman and PC Mavroidis (eds), *Law and Policy in Public Purchasing: The WTO Agreement on Government Procurement* (University of Michigan Press 1997); P Trepte, 'The Agreement on Government Procurement' in PFJ Macrory, AE Appleton, and MG Plummer (eds), *The World Trade Organization: Legal, Economic and Political Analysis* (Springer 2005) vol I, 1123; S Arrowsmith and RD Anderson, *The WTO Regime on Government Procurement: Challenge and Reform* (CUP 2011).

[12] See Ministerial Declaration (14 November 2001) WT/MIN(01)/DEC/1; see M Matsushita, TJ Schoenbaum, PC Mavroidis, and M Hahn (eds), *The World Trade Organization* (3rd edn, OUP 2015) 19–26.

[13] P van den Bossche and W Zdouc, *The Law and Policy of the World Trade Organization* (3rd edn, CUP 2013) 105.

[14] Ministerial Declaration (14 November 2001) WT/MIN(01)/DEC/1.

[15] Decision on 'implementation-related issues and concerns' (14 November 2001) WT/MIN (01)/17.

[16] See Ministerial Declaration (18 December 2005) WT/MIN(05)/DEC.

their products. In addition, export subsidies and other measures to support agricultural exports shall be further reduced until 2013. Despite this progress, further negotiations failed. The informal Ministerial Conference of July 2008 was hampered by insurmountable frictions between industrialized countries on one side, and developing and emerging countries on the other. Especially the issue of fair market access for agricultural goods remains controversial. In recent negotiations, the so-called Group of 21 (G-21), led by China, India, and Brazil, has gained increasing influence vis-à-vis the traditionally dominant powers, that is the United States, the European Union, and Japan.

The Ministerial Conference in Bali (December 2013) succeeded in negotiating the Agreement on Trade Facilitation. The Agreement's objective is to facilitate importation, exportation, and transit, inter alia, by enhancing the transparency and non-discrimination of custom procedures, reducing the complexity of custom formalities, promoting customs cooperation, and establishing a Committee on Trade Facilitation. For implementation purposes, the Agreement grants special and differential treatment to developing and least developed countries. According to some estimate, the Agreement has the potential of adding USD 1 trillion to the world economy. Together with a number of Ministerial decisions, the Agreement forms part of the so-called 'Bali Package' and was hailed as an important breakthrough in the Doha Development Agenda after years of stand-still. However, in July 2014, India blocked the necessary approval of the Bali Agreement. India insisted in linking the adoption of the Agreement on Trade Facilitation with an agreement on food security which would change rules on agricultural subsidies and give developing countries more freedom to buy food at administered prices from domestic farmers in order to build public food stocks or provide food aid.

At its Nairobi session of December 2015, the Ministerial Conference adopted a declaration on the gradual elimination of export subsidies in the agricultural sector.[17] Furthermore, the Ministerial Conference established rules regarding International Food Aid. Such aid must take account of the local markets of the aid-receiving countries, food aid shall only be given in a needs-driven manner and shall not serve market interests of the donor.[18] Preference shall be given to cash-based food aid[19] or food aid stemming from local or regional sources.

Apart from specific trade issues, the inclusion of common environmental standards ('Greening the GATT') ranks highly in the agenda of the world trading system.[20] The World Trade Organization has established a Committee on Trade and Environment (CTE) in order to examine the interrelation between trade liberalization, economic development, and environmental protection. Another important

---

[17] Ministerial Declaration (19 December 2015) WT/MIN(15)/45.
[18] Ministerial Declaration (19 December 2015) WT/MIN(15)/45 para. 23.
[19] Ministerial Declaration (19 December 2015) WT/MIN(15)/45 para. 25.
[20] See E Brown Weiss and JH Jackson (eds), *Reconciling Environment and Trade* (2nd edn, Brill Academic Publishers 2008); P Sands, *Principles of International Environmental Law* (1st edn, CUP 1995) vol I, 687; TJ Schoenbaum, 'International Trade and Protection of the Environment, the Continuing Search for Reconciliation' (1997) 91 AJIL 268; S Shaw and R Schwartz, 'Trade and Environment in the WTO. State of Play' (2002) 36 JWT 129.

issue is the inclusion of core labour standards on the basis of cooperation between the World Trade Organization and the International Labour Organization.[21]

Select Bibliography

C Bjørnskov and KM Lind, 'Where Do Developing Countries Go After Doha? An Analysis of WTO Positions and Potential Alliances' (2002) 36 JWT 543.

E Bohne, *The World Trade Organization: Institutional Development and Reform* (Palgrave Macmillan 2010) 165ff.

DZ Cass, *The Constitutionalization of the World Trade Organization: Legitimacy, Democracy, and Community in the International Trading System* (OUP 2005).

T Cottier and M Elsig (eds), *Governing the World Trade Organization: Past, Present and Beyond Doha* (CUP 2011).

J Davidow and H Shapiro, 'The Feasibility and Worth of a WTO Competition Agreement' (2003) 37 JWT 49.

A Dunkel, 'The Uruguay Round and the World Economy' (1987) 42 Außenwirtschaft 7.

BM Hoekman and MM Kostecki, *The Political Economy of the World Trading System* (3rd edn, OUP 2009).

S Lester, B Mercurio, and A Davies, *World Trade Law: Text, Materials and Commentary* (2nd edn, Hart Publishing 2012).

R Senti and P Conlan, *WTO: Regulation of World Trade after the Uruguay Round* (Schulthess 1998).

T Stewart, *The GATT Uruguay Round: A Negotiating History* (Kluwer Law International 1999).

P Sutherland, 'The Politics of Trade Policy Development—the New Complexity' in PFJ Macrory, AE Appleton, and MG Plummer (eds), *The World Trade Organization: Legal, Economic and Political Analysis* (Springer 2005) vol 1, 27.

M Trebilcock, R Howse, and A Eliason, *The Regulation of International Trade* (4th edn, Routledge 2012).

E Vranes, *Trade and Environment. Fundamental Issues in International Law, WTO Law and Legal Theory* (OUP 2009).

GR Winham, 'An Interpretative History of the Uruguay Round Negotiation' in PFJ Macrory, AE Appleton, and MG Plummer (eds), *The World Trade Organization: Legal, Economic and Political Analysis* (Springer 2005) vol 1, 3.

[21] For the relationship of WTO law and labour law standards, see K Addo, 'The Correlation between Labour Standards and International Trade. Which Way Forward?' (2002) 36 JWT 285; C MacCrudden and A Davies, 'A Perspective on Trade and Labour Rights' (2000) 3 J Int'l Econ L 43; VA Leary, 'The WTO and the Social Clause: Post-Singapore' (1997) 1 EJIL 118.

XII

The World Trade Organization

1. The WTO as an Institutional Platform for Trade Relations

The World Trade Organization (WTO) is the centre of the new world trade system and operates as the institutional basis for the relations among its members, as governed by all trade agreements and instruments included in the annexes to the WTO Agreement.[1] Article II:1 of the WTO Agreement provides:

The WTO shall provide the common institutional framework for the conduct of trade relations among its Members in matters related to the agreements and associated legal instruments included in the Annexes to this Agreement.

2. Members of the WTO

The contracting parties to the General Agreement on Tariffs and Trade 1947 (GATT 1947) as well as the European Community were founding members of the WTO. Article XI:1 of the WTO Agreement states:

The contracting parties to GATT 1947 as of the date of entry into force of this Agreement, and the European Communities, which accept this Agreement and the Multilateral Trade Agreements and for which Schedules of Concessions and Commitments are annexed to GATT 1994 and for which Schedules of Specific Commitments are annexed to GATS shall become original Members of the WTO.

The WTO members (as of July 2016 164) do not only include States, but also other separate customs territories possessing full autonomy in trade relations covered by WTO law, for example Hong Kong or Macao (Article XII:1 first sentence of the WTO Agreement). The inclusion of autonomous customs areas allows entities with disputed status under international law, as for example Chinese Taipei, to join the WTO. China acceded in December 2001,[2] Chinese Taipei in 2002. Russia became

---

[1] See WJ Davey, 'Institutional Framework' in PFJ Macrory, AE Appleton, and MG Plummer (eds), *The World Trade Organization: Legal, Economic and Political Analysis* (Springer 2005) vol 1, 51.

[2] For the status of China within the WTO, see D Bhattasali, S Li, and W Martin (eds), *China and the WTO: Accession, Policy Reform, and Poverty Reduction Strategies* (World Bank Publications 2004); for China's role with regard to regional trade agreements, see F Snyder, 'China, Regional Trade Agreements and WTO Law' (2009) 43 JWT 1.

a member of the WTO in 2012.[3] Most (about three-quarters) of the WTO members are developing countries. The current 'Doha Round' documents the rising influence of countries like Brazil, China, and India.

The European Community (not, however, the European Atomic Energy Community and the then still existing European Coal and Steel Community) ratified the WTO agreements in 1994.[4] Under the Treaty on European Union (TEU) as modified by the Lisbon Treaty (Article 1 paragraph 3 third sentence), the European Union replaced and succeeded the European Community. Despite the membership of the European Union, the Member States of the European Union still remain members of the WTO as well. The underlying reason is that, despite the broad regulatory powers of the European Union to regulate internal and external trade, some residual competences affecting the WTO agreements still lie with the Member States of the European Union.[5] These residual powers have been permanently shrinking (see Article 207 of the Treaty on the Functioning of the European Union (TFEU)). If one of the Member States of the European Union violates WTO law, this non-compliance establishes responsibility of the European Union as a whole, whether the infringement was triggered by a measure of the European Union or not. Under international law, the internal distribution of competencies within the European Union does not matter for the purpose of joint responsibility. If a measure of the European Union violates WTO law, possible sanctions may affect even Member States of the European Union which have voted against the measure in the Council of the European Union.

According to Article IX:1 third sentence of the WTO Agreement, the European Union has as many votes as it has Member States:

Where the European Communities exercise their right to vote, they shall have a number of votes equal to the number of their member States which are Members of the WTO.

The concurrent membership may prove to be difficult in cases of divergent political positions of the European Union and its Member States. In order to ensure a coherent position within the WTO, the European Union and its Member States exercise their powers jointly and do not act as separate entities.[6] The European Commission usually represents the European Union as well as its Member States in the decision-making process of the WTO. The Commission consults the Member States in order to reach a consensus and thus operates as unifying actor in issues of trade policy.[7]

---

[3] On the accession process of new WTO Members, see World Trade Organization (ed), *A Handbook on Accession to the WTO* (CUP 2008); II Kavass, 'WTO Accession: Procedure, Requirements and Costs' (2007) 41 JWT 453.

[4] Council Decision 94/800/EC (22 December 1994) concerning the conclusion on behalf of the European Community, as regards matters within its competence, of the agreements reached in the Uruguay Round multilateral negotiations [1994] OJ L 336/1–2.

[5] This point was already raised by the ECJ *WTO-Agreement Opinion 1/94* [1994] ECR I-5267.

[6] See Article 207(1) first sentence TFEU.

[7] See eg the Report of the Appellate Body regarding trade restricting measures by France in WTO, *European Communities: Measures Affecting Asbestos and Asbestos-Containing Products—Report of the Appellate Body* (2001) WT/ DS135/AB/R.

3. Organs of the WTO

The supreme organ of the WTO is the Ministerial Conference with representatives of all the members, which shall meet at least once every two years (Article IV:1 first sentence WTO Agreement).

Article IV:1 second and third sentence of the WTO Agreement defines the functions of the Ministerial Conference:

The Ministerial Conference shall carry out the functions of the WTO and take actions necessary to this effect. The Ministerial Conference shall have the authority to take decisions on all matters under any of the Multilateral Trade Agreements, if so requested by a Member, in accordance with the specific requirements for decision-making in this Agreement and in the relevant Multilateral Trade Agreement.

As representative organ which meets on a more regular basis, the General Council plays a central role under Article IV:2–4 of the WTO Agreement:

2. There shall be a General Council composed of representatives of all the Members, which shall meet as appropriate. In the intervals between meetings of the Ministerial Conference, its functions shall be conducted by the General Council. The General Council shall also carry out the functions assigned to it by this Agreement. The General Council shall establish its rules of procedure and approve the rules of procedure for the Committees provided for in paragraph 7.
3. The General Council shall convene as appropriate to discharge the responsibilities of the Dispute Settlement Body provided for in the Dispute Settlement Understanding. The Dispute Settlement Body may have its own chairman and shall establish such rules of procedure as it deems necessary for the fulfilment of those responsibilities.
4. The General Council shall convene as appropriate to discharge the responsibilities of the Trade Policy Review Body provided for in the TPRM. The Trade Policy Review Body may have its own chairman and shall establish such rules of procedure as it deems necessary for the fulfilment of those responsibilities.

As Article IV:5 first sentence of the WTO Agreement provides, three special councils, set up for particular sectors, operate under the guidance of the General Council:

- the Council for Trade in Goods;
- the Council for Trade in Services; and
- the Council for Trade-Related Aspects of Intellectual Property Rights.

Article IV:7 of the WTO Agreement provides for the establishment of committees with specified competences:

The Ministerial Conference shall establish a Committee on Trade and Development, a Committee on Balance-of-Payments Restrictions and a Committee on Budget, Finance and Administration, which shall carry out the functions assigned to them by this Agreement and by the Multilateral Trade Agreements, and any additional functions assigned to them by the General Council, and may establish such additional Committees with such functions as it may deem appropriate. As part of its functions, the Committee on Trade and Development shall periodically review the special provisions in the Multilateral Trade Agreements in favour of the least-developed country Members and report to the General Council for appropriate action. Membership in these Committees shall be open to representatives of all Members.

The Secretariat is headed by the Director-General (Article VI:1 of the WTO Agreement). The international responsibility of the Director-General and the staff of the Secretariat are incompatible with instructions from governments or other forms of influence from outside (Article VI:4 of the WTO Agreement).

Under Article VIII:1 of the WTO Agreement, the WTO has international legal personality and the legal capacity as well as the privileges and immunities warranted by its functions:

1. The WTO shall have legal personality, and shall be accorded by each of its Members such legal capacity as may be necessary for the exercise of its functions.
2. The WTO shall be accorded by each of its Members such privileges and immunities as are necessary for the exercise of its functions.
3. The officials of the WTO and the representatives of the Members shall similarly be accorded by each of its Members such privileges and immunities as are necessary for the independent exercise of their functions in connection with the WTO.
4. The privileges and immunities to be accorded by a Member to the WTO, its officials, and the representatives of its Members shall be similar to the privileges and immunities stipulated in the Convention on the Privileges and Immunities of the Specialized Agencies, approved by the General Assembly of the United Nations on 21 November 1947.
5. The WTO may conclude a headquarters agreement.

One of the salient features of the WTO system is the Dispute Settlement Body (DSB), established under the Dispute Settlement Understanding (DSU).[8] Its functions are carried out by the General Council (Article IV:3 of the WTO Agreement). Within the DSB, the performing units are the panels and the Appellate Body. Panels are set up ad hoc, while the Appellate Body is a standing body. The panel and Appellate Body reports adopted by the DSB play a crucial role in the understanding, interpretation, and development of WTO law. Although there is no doctrine of *stare decisis* in WTO law, the Appellate Body held that '[...] adopted panel reports are an important part of the GATT acquis. [...] They create legitimate expectations among WTO Members and, therefore, should be taken into account.'[9]

---

[8] For more details about the dispute settlement system of the WTO, see later at Ch XX.
[9] WTO, *Japan: Taxes on Alcoholic Beverages—Report of the Appellate Body* (1996) WT/DS8/AB/R para 14.

The Appellate Body assumes that even unadopted panel reports might be considered relevant as it believes 'that a panel could find useful guidance in the reasoning of an unadopted panel report that it considered to be relevant.'[10]

The principle governing the functioning and development of the WTO system is decision-making by consensus:

The WTO shall continue the practice of decision-making by consensus followed under GATT 1947. Except as otherwise provided, where a decision cannot be arrived at by consensus, the matter at issue shall be decided by voting (Article IX of the WTO Agreement).[11]

The principle of consensus often delays decision-making processes. It protects, however, members or group of members against being overruled by majorities. In negotiations, drafts on different issues are submitted to approval in a single package. A most important exception to decision-making by consensus applies in the settlement of trade disputes. Panel reports and Appellate Body reports are adopted by reverse consensus (ie if they are not rejected with unanimity).

Article IX:2 of the WTO Agreement vests the Ministerial Conference and the General Council with the competence to adopt binding interpretations of WTO law and requires a three-quarters majority of the Members:

The Ministerial Conference and the General Council shall have the exclusive authority to adopt interpretations of this Agreement and of the Multilateral Trade Agreements. In the case of an interpretation of a Multilateral Trade Agreement in Annex 1, they shall exercise their authority on the basis of a recommendation by the Council overseeing the functioning of that Agreement. The decision to adopt an interpretation shall be taken by a three-fourths majority of the Members. This paragraph shall not be used in a manner that would undermine the amendment provisions in Article X.

'In exceptional circumstances', the Ministerial Conference may decide to waive an obligation imposed on a Member State by the WTO Agreement or any of the Multilateral Trade Agreements ('waiver', Article IX paragraphs 3 and 4 of the WTO Agreement).[12]

Select Bibliography

P van den Bossche and W Zdouc, *The Law and Policy of the World Trade Organization* (3rd edn, CUP 2013).
DZ Cass, *The Constitutionalization of the World Trade Organization* (OUP 2005).
I van Damme, *Treaty Interpretation by the WTO Appellate Body* (OUP 2009).

[10] WTO, *Argentina: Measures Affecting Imports of Footwear, Textiles, Apparel and other Items— Report of the Appellate Body* (1998) WT/DS56/AB/R para 43.

[11] See note 1 to Article IX of the WTO Agreement: 'The body concerned shall be deemed to have decided by consensus on a matter submitted for its consideration, if no Member, present at the meeting when the decision is taken, formally objects to the proposed decision.'

[12] See I Feichtner, *The Law and Politics of WTO Waivers: Stability and Flexibility in Public International Law* (CUP 2012).

JF Dennin (ed), *Law and Practice of the World Trade Organization* (Oceana Publications).

P van Dijck and G Faber (eds), *Challenges to the New World Trade Organization* (Kluwer Law 1996).

BM Hoekman, A Mattoo, and P English (eds), *Development, Trade, and the WTO: A Handbook* (The World Bank 2002).

JH Jackson, *The World Trading System* (2nd edn, MIT Press 1997).

JH Jackson, *The Jurisprudence of GATT and the WTO: Insights on Treaty Law and Economic Relations* (CUP 2000).

JH Jackson and A Sykes (eds), *Implementing the Uruguay Round* (Clarendon Press 1997).

S Lester, B Mercurio, and A Davies, *World Trade Law: Text, Materials and Commentary* (2nd edn, Hart 2012).

PFJ Macrory, AE Appleton, and MG Plummer (eds), *The World Trade Organization: Legal, Economic and Political Analysis* (Springer 2005) vols 1–3.

M Matsushita, TJ Schoenbaum, PC Mavroidis, and M Hahn (eds), *The World Trade Organization: Law, Practice, and Policy* (3rd edn, OUP 2015).

M Trebilcock, R Howse, and A Eliason, *The Regulation of International Trade* (4th edn, Routledge 2012).

World Trade Organization (ed), *A Handbook on the WTO Dispute Settlement System* (CUP 2004).

World Trade Organization (ed), *Guide to GATT Law and Practice: Analytical Index* (CUP 2012).

XIII

The Multilateral and the Plurilateral Agreements on Trade

1. Multilateral and Plurilateral Trade Agreements: Concentric Circles

The WTO Agreement distinguishes between the Multilateral Trade Agreements and the Plurilateral Trade Agreements. The multilateral agreements are binding on all WTO members and must be ratified, together with the WTO Agreement, as a whole ('single undertaking approach'). Plurilateral agreements are optional in character and only obligate those members which choose to ratify them. Accordingly, Article II:2 and 3 of the WTO Agreement states:

2. The agreements and associated legal instruments included in Annexes 1, 2 and 3 (hereinafter referred to as 'Multilateral Trade Agreements') are integral parts of this Agreement, binding on all Members.

3. The agreements and associated legal instruments included in Annex 4 (hereinafter referred to as 'Plurilateral Trade Agreements') are also part of this Agreement for those Members that have accepted them, and are binding on those Members. The Plurilateral Trade Agreements do not create either obligations or rights for Members that have not accepted them.

The interplay of the various trade agreements adds to the complex texture of WTO law. Moreover, the different meanings of certain terms as well as specific and general exceptions often turn the understanding of the trade agreements into a difficult labour. However, the extensive case-law established by panel and Appellate Body reports by now provides fairly reliable guidance and fosters a consistent application of WTO law.

The Multilateral Trade Agreements include

- the General Agreement on Tariffs and Trade 1994 (GATT 1994) (Annex 1A);
- the Agreement on the Application of Sanitary and Phytosanitary Measures (SPS Agreement) (Annex 1A);
- the Agreement on Technical Barriers to Trade (TBT Agreement) (Annex 1A);
- the Agreement on Trade-Related Investment Measures (TRIMS) (Annex 1A);
- General Agreement on Trade in Services (GATS) (Annex 1B);

- The Agreement on Trade-Related Aspects of Intellectual Property Rights (TRIPS) (Annex 1C);
- the Dispute Settlement Understanding (DSU) (Annex 2); and
- the Trade Policy Review Mechanism (Annex 3).

The Plurilateral Trade Agreements (Annex 4) still in force are

- the Agreement on Trade in Civil Aircraft (Annex 4(a)); and
- the Agreement on Government Procurement (Annex 4(b)).

The plurilateral International Dairy Agreement (Annex 4(c)) and the International Bovine Meat Agreement (Annex 4(d)) were terminated in 1997.

2. The GATT 1994 and Related Trade Agreements

In practical terms, the GATT 1994 is the most significant multilateral trade agreement.[1] Understandings of several Articles of the GATT 1994 and other Multilateral Trade Agreements concretise or supplement provisions of the GATT 1994. Thus, the GATT 1994 must be read in context with the Agreement on Implementation of Article VI of the General Agreement on Tariffs and Trade 1994 (Anti-Dumping) and the Agreement on Implementation of Article VII of the General Agreement on Tariffs and Trade 1994 (Customs Valuation).[2] The SPS Agreement stands in close context with the GATT. It establishes standards for conformity of sanitary and phytosanitary measures with the GATT 1994 (Article 2.4 of the SPS Agreement). Besides, it also has an autonomous scope of application, for example non-discriminatory measures. The TBT Agreement contains specific rules for technical barriers to trade.

The GATT 1994 and the GATS each have their own ambit of application. In some cases, the scope of the GATT 1994 and of the GATS may overlap,[3] when restraints to services affect the trade in goods, as the Appellate Body stated in the 'Banana Dispute' (*EC—Bananas III*):

Certain measures could be found to fall exclusively within the scope of the GATT 1994, when they affect trade in goods as goods. Certain measures could be found to fall exclusively within the scope of the GATS, when they affect the supply of services as services. There is yet a third category of measures that could be found to fall within the scope of both the GATT 1994 and the GATS. These are measures that involve a service relating to a particular good or a service supplied in conjunction with a particular good. In all such cases in this third

---

[1] See K Kennedy, 'GATT 1994' in PFJ Macrory, AE Appleton, and MG Plummer (eds), *The World Trade Organization: Legal, Economic and Political Analysis* (Springer 2005) vol 1, 89.
[2] I Forrester and OE Odarda, 'The Agreement on Customs Valuation' in PFJ Macrory, AE Appleton, and MG Plummer (eds), *The World Trade Organization: Legal, Economic and Political Analysis* (Springer 2005) vol 1, 531.
[3] See E Vranes, 'The Overlap between GATT and GATS: A Methodological Mate' (2009) 36 LIEI 215.

category, the measure in question could be scrutinized under both the GATT 1994 and the GATS.[4]

Thus, the GATT and the GATS may overlap in the case of import licensing procedures[5] or services for the distribution of imported products.[6]

The TRIMS[7] applies 'to investment measures related to trade in goods only'.[8] It provides in Article 2:

1. Without prejudice to other rights and obligations under GATT 1994, no Member shall apply any TRIM that is inconsistent with the provisions of Article III or Article XI of GATT 1994.
2. An illustrative list of TRIMs that are inconsistent with the obligation of national treatment provided for in paragraph 4 of Article III of GATT 1994 and the obligation of general elimination of quantitative restrictions provided for in paragraph 1 of Article XI of GATT 1994 is contained in the Annex to this Agreement.

The 'illustrative list' contained in the Annex reads:

1. TRIMs that are inconsistent with the obligation of national treatment provided for in paragraph 4 of Article III of GATT 1994 include those which are mandatory or enforceable under domestic law or under administrative rulings, or compliance with which is necessary to obtain an advantage, and which require:
   (a) the purchase or use by an enterprise of products of domestic origin or from any domestic source, whether specified in terms of particular products, in terms of volume or value of products, or in terms of a proportion of volume or value of its local production; or
   (b) that an enterprise's purchases or use of imported products be limited to an amount related to the volume or value of local products that it exports.
2. TRIMs that are inconsistent with the obligation of general elimination of quantitative restrictions provided for in paragraph 1 of Article XI of GATT 1994 include those which are mandatory or enforceable under domestic law or under administrative rulings, or compliance with which is necessary to obtain an advantage, and which restrict:
   (a) the importation by an enterprise of products used in or related to its local production, generally or to an amount related to the volume or value of local production that it exports;
   (b) the importation by an enterprise of products used in or related to its local production by restricting its access to foreign exchange to an amount related to the foreign exchange inflows attributable to the enterprise; or

---

[4] WTO, *European Communities: Regime for the Importation, Sale and Distribution of Bananas—Report of the Appellate Body* (1997) WT/DS27/AB/R para 221.

[5] WTO, *European Communities: Regime for the Importation, Sale and Distribution of Bananas—Report of the Appellate Body* (1997) WT/DS27/AB/R para 222.

[6] WTO, *China: Measures Affecting Trading Rights and Distribution Services for Certain Publications and Audiovisual Entertainment Products—Report of the Panel* (2009) WT/DS363/R paras 7.127.

[7] See TL Brewer and S Young, 'Investment Issues at the WTO: The Architecture of Rules and the Settlement of Disputes' (1998) J Int'l Econ L 457; see ML de Sterlini, 'The Agreement on Trade-Related Investment Measures' in PFJ Macrory, AE Appleton, and MG Plummer (eds), *The World Trade Organization: Legal, Economic and Political Analysis* (Springer 2005) vol 1, 437.

[8] Article 1 of the TRIMS Agreement.

(c) the exportation or sale for export by an enterprise of products, whether specified in
  · terms of particular products, in terms of volume or value of products, or in terms of
    a proportion of volume or value of its local production.

The TRIMS Agreement, above all, applies to the compulsory use of domestic raw materials, the compulsory purchase of domestic precursors to certain goods or the requirement to reach a fixed volume of domestic sales (local content/local performance requirements). In the negotiations of the Uruguay Round, the United States pushed in vain for a comprehensive ban of trade related investment measures.

In case of a conflict of the GATT with the other Multilateral Trade Agreements, the General Interpretative Note to Annex 1A of the WTO Agreement provides:

In the event of conflict between a provision of the General Agreement on Tariffs and Trade 1994 and a provision of another agreement in Annex 1A to the Agreement Establishing the World Trade Organization (referred to in the agreements in Annex 1A as the 'WTO Agreement'), the provision of the other agreement shall prevail to the extent of the conflict.

The conflicting term of the GATT will not be applied for the purposes of the other agreement, but only as far as the conflict is concerned.

XIV

The GATT

1. Objectives and Basic Principles

The General Agreement on Tariffs and Trade 1994 (hereinafter simply referred to as GATT) aims at international trade liberalization by progressively eliminating or restricting barriers to trade and other protectionist interferences with competition on the world market as well as the national markets. The underlying model of world trade follows the principles of market economy.

The Preamble of the GATT sets out the objectives and purposes as well as the principles of the GATT:

Recognizing that their relations in the field of trade and economic endeavour should be conducted with a view to raising standards of living, ensuring full employment and a large and steadily growing volume of real income and effective demand, developing the full use of the resources of the world and expanding the production and exchange of goods,

Being desirous of contributing to these objectives by entering into reciprocal and mutually advantageous arrangements directed to the substantial reduction of tariffs and other barriers to trade and to the elimination of discriminatory treatment in international commerce,

Have through their Representatives agreed as follows: [...].

The fundamental principles of the GATT are the principle of non-discrimination, in the form of the most-favoured-nation principle and the national treatment principle, and the principle of liberalization by means of the elimination or restriction of tariffs as well as of non-tariff barriers to trade.[1]

Reciprocity is another important principle of the GATT.[2] The principle refers to a balance of mutual benefits and obligations between the contracting parties. It also governs the system of sanctions for non-compliance (suspension of concessions). From a purely economic point of view, the principle of reciprocity has a problematic side. The overall economic benefit of unilateral compliance with treaty obligations may be higher than full non-compliance in terms of reciprocity. However, in the long run, reciprocity creates a strong incentive to compliance. The principle of reciprocity suffers an exception in favour of developing countries. Article XXXVI:8 of the GATT provides:

---

[1] See para 3 of the Preamble to the GATT.   [2] See eg Articles XXIII and XXVIII GATT.

The developed contracting parties do not expect reciprocity for commitments made by them in trade negotiations to reduce or remove tariffs and other barriers to the trade of less-developed contracting parties.

This provision, along with other exceptions in favour of developing countries, responds to pre-existing inequalities within the community of States which present a major challenge to the world trade system.

2. Most-Favoured-Nation Treatment

One of the elementary instruments of the GATT regime is the most-favoured-nation treatment. Article I:1 of the GATT provides:

With respect to customs duties and charges of any kind imposed on or in connection with importation or exportation or imposed on the international transfer of payments for imports or exports, and with respect to the method of levying such duties and charges, and with respect to all rules and formalities in connection with importation and exportation, and with respect to all matters referred to in paragraphs 2 and 4 of Article III, any advantage, favour, privilege or immunity granted by any contracting party to any product originating in or destined for any other country shall be accorded immediately and unconditionally to the like product originating in or destined for the territories of all other contracting parties.

Many other provisions of the GATT, like Article V (Freedom of Transit), Article IX:1 (Marks of Origin), Article XIII:1 (Non-discriminatory Administration of Quantitative Restrictions), and Article XVII:1 (State Trading Enterprises) refer to most-favoured-nation treatment.

'Most-favoured-nation treatment' essentially means that trade advantages granted to one contracting party must be granted to all other parties.[3] By referring to Article III:2 and 4, Article I:1 of the GATT extends the most-favoured-nation treatment also to internal taxes and other internal charges as well as import regulations. In terms of Article I:1 of the GATT, most-favoured-nation treatment must be accorded 'immediately and unconditionally' and thus does not depend on any service, benefit or other advantage granted in return.

Most-favoured-nation treatment prohibits de jure as well as de facto discriminations.[4] Regulations that openly discriminate against goods originating in a certain country are regarded as de jure discriminations. The most-favoured-nation principle also applies to hidden or indirect privileges, which prove advantageous for goods originating from certain States only.[5] According to the Appellate Body Report in *Canada—Autos*, discrimination not only exists when

[…] the failure to accord an 'advantage' to like products of all other Members appears *on the face* of the measure, or can be demonstrated on the basis of the words of the

---

[3] See Ch V.4(a).

[4] For a general outline, see J Ya Qin, 'Defining Nondiscrimination under the Law of the World Trade Organization' (2005) 23 BU Int'l LJ 215.

[5] See WTO, *Canada: Certain Measures Affecting the Automotive Industry—Report of the Appellate Body* (2000) WT/DS139/AB/R paras 77ff; this case was about privileged tariffs for automobiles and

measure. Neither the words '*de jure*' nor '*de facto*' appear in Article I:1. Nevertheless, we observe that Article I:1 does not cover only 'in law', or *de jure*, discrimination. As several GATT panel reports confirmed, Article I:1 covers also 'in fact', or *de facto*, discrimination.[6]

(a) The condition of 'likeness'

The most-favoured-nation treatment only applies to 'like' products. Thus, the first and foremost issue in context of the most-favoured-nation treatment is whether certain goods and products favoured are 'like'. The term 'like products' is used in different contexts within the GATT 1994 (eg Articles I:1, II:2, III:2, III:4, VI:1, IX:1, XI:2(c), XIII:1, XVI:4, and XIX:1 of the GATT). The meaning of the term 'like products' varies according to the context.[7] The Appellate Body used the image of an accordion to capture the spectrum of possible meanings:

[T]here can be no one precise and absolute definition of what is 'like'. The concept of 'likeness' is a relative one that evokes the image of an accordion. The accordion of 'likeness' stretches and squeezes in different places as different provisions of the *WTO Agreement* are applied.[8]

According to the case-law of the Dispute Settlement Body, the term 'like' in Article I:1 of the GATT reaches at least as far as the term 'like' in Article III:2 first sentence of the GATT.[9] The criteria developed under Article III of the GATT[10] by WTO jurisprudence for determining the 'likeness' of products also apply to Article I:1 GATT.[11]

(b) Exceptions

i. Customs unions and free-trade areas

Several exceptions apply to the most-favoured-nation treatment. An important exception relates to customs unions and free-trade areas (Article XXIV paragraphs 4 to 12 of

---

parts of automobiles of foreign producers with a production site within the importing State (Canada); these privileges related to US products on the basis of a bilateral agreement between Canada and the United States.

[6] WTO, *Canada: Certain Measures Affecting the Automotive Industry—Report of the Appellate Body* (2000) WT/DS139/AB/R para 78.

[7] See WM Choi, '*Like Products' in International Trade Law: Towards a Consistent GATT/WTO Jurisprudence* (OUP 2003).

[8] WTO, *Japan: Taxes on Alcoholic Beverages—Report of the Appellate Body* (1996) WT/DS8/AB/R, WT/DS10/AB/R, WT/DS11/AB/R 21.

[9] WTO, *Indonesia: Certain Measures Affecting the Automobile Industry—Report of the Panel* (1998) WT/DS54/R WT/DS55/R, WT/DS59/R, WT/DS64/R para 14.141.

[10] See Section 3(b)(i) in this Chapter.

[11] See WTO, *Indonesia: Certain Measures affecting the Automobile Industry—Report of the Panel* (1998) WT/DS54/R para 14.141.

the GATT).[12] The application of the most-favoured-nation principle would defeat the objective of such preferential trade agreements between two or more States by extending concessions within the ambit of the GATT to all members of the WTO. The reasoning behind the exception for customs unions and free-trade areas is the assumption that, on balance, the overall benefits of these arrangements for world trade outweigh possible disadvantages. This assumption has been challenged.[13] Still, as experience with regional liberalization shows, preferential trade arrangements (PTAs) foster the willingness to support liberalization on the global level.

In order to avoid the abusive claim of the exception for preferential trade arrangements, the GATT defines the scope of this privilege rather narrowly in Article XXIV:8:

For the purposes of this Agreement:
(a) A customs union shall be understood to mean the substitution of a single customs territory for two or more customs territories, so that
  (i) duties and other restrictive regulations of commerce (except, where necessary, those permitted under Articles XI, XII, XIII, XIV, XV and XX) are eliminated with respect to substantially all the trade between the constituent territories of the union or at least with respect to substantially all the trade in products originating in such territories, and,
  (ii) subject to the provisions of paragraph 9, substantially the same duties and other regulations of commerce are applied by each of the members of the union to the trade of territories not included in the union;
(b) A free-trade area shall be understood to mean a group of two or more customs territories in which the duties and other restrictive regulations of commerce (except, where necessary, those permitted under Articles XI, XII, XIII, XIV, XV and XX) are eliminated on substantially all the trade between the constituent territories in products originating in such territories.

The key condition for preferential trade agreements is that they liberalize 'substantially all the trade between the constituent territories'. Thus, customs unions and free-trade areas must at least cover the bulk of the respective trade volumes. It is a matter of controversy whether they must also cover all or almost all relevant economic sectors. In reaction to the rapid proliferation of regional free-trade areas (especially in Europe, the Americas, and Asia), the Committee on Regional Trade Agreements (CRTA) was established in 1996. This Committee scrutinizes regional trade agreements as to their compatibility with Article XXIV:8 of the GATT.

Currently, there are about 250 regional and bilateral trade agreements. The maze of free-trade areas, customs unions, and regional economic communities has been compared to a 'spaghetti bowl'.[14] The European Union and the United States have

---

[12] See L Bartels and F Ortino, *Regional Trade Agreements and the WTO Legal System* (OUP 2007).

[13] J-A Crawford and RV Fiorentino, 'The Changing Landscape of Regional Trade Agreements' (2005) 8 WTO Discussion Paper 16.

[14] The term was first used by J Bhagwati in 'U.S. Trade Policy: The Infatuation with Free Trade Agreements' in J Bhagwati and AO Krueger, *The Dangerous Drift to Preferential Trade Agreements* (AEI Press 1995). See on the 'spaghetti-bowl'-effect, JHB Pauwelyn, 'Adding Sweeteners to Softwood Lumber: The WTO-NAFTA "Spaghetti Bowl" is Cooking' (2006) 9 J Int'l Econ L 197;

entered into a kind of competition for extended preferential trade relations with other countries, for example in Latin America or in South East Asia. In particular, the preferential trade agreements between economically strong WTO members (like the free-trade agreements between the European Union and South Korea[15] or between the United States and South Korea)[16] foster concern among other members. The increase of preferential trade agreements has eroded the most-favoured-nation treatment and often supplants it in practice by 'least-favoured-nation treatment'.[17] Thus, the general reduction of tariffs has become all the more important to neutralize the competitive advantages of such preferential arrangements.

ii. Preferences for developing countries

In 1965, a Part IV (Trade and Development) was added to the GATT. Part IV provides exceptions to the most-favoured-nation clause to allow preferential treatment for developing countries. It exempts general tariff preferences for finished and semi-finished products originating in those countries from the most-favoured-nation treatment.[18] Article XXXVI:1 GATT sets out the reasons for the preferential treatment of developing countries:

The contracting parties,
(a) recalling that the basic objectives of this Agreement include the raising of standards of living and the progressive development of the economies of all contracting parties, and considering that the attainment of these objectives is particularly urgent for less-developed contracting parties;
(b) considering that export earnings of the less-developed contracting parties can play a vital part in their economic development and that the extent of this contribution depends on the prices paid by the less-developed contracting parties for essential imports, the volume of their exports, and the prices received for these exports;
(c) noting, that there is a wide gap between standards of living in less-developed countries and in other countries;
(d) recognizing that individual and joint action is essential to further the development of the economies of less-developed contracting parties and to bring about a rapid advance in the standards of living in these countries;
(e) recognizing that international trade as a means of achieving economic and social advancement should be governed by such rules and procedures—and measures in conformity with such rules and procedures—as are consistent with the objectives set forth in this Article;

---

see also R Leal-Arcas, 'Proliferation of Regional Trade Agreements: Complementing or Supplanting Multilateralism?' (2011) 11 Chi J Int'l L 597.

[15] [2011] OJ L 127/6 (8ff).

[16] Available at <http://www.ustr.gov/trade-agreements/free-trade-agreements/korus-fta/final-text> (accessed 23 June 2016).

[17] P Lloyd, 'Global Economic Integration' (2010) 15 Pacific Economic Review 71 (81).

[18] For the broader perspective, see JP Trachtman and C Thomas (eds), *Developing Countries in the WTO Legal System* (OUP 2009); SE Rolland, *Development at the WTO* (OUP 2012); GA Bermann and PC Mavroidis (eds), *WTO Law and Developing Countries* (CUP 2011).

(f) noting that the CONTRACTING PARTIES may enable less-developed contracting parties to use special measures to promote their trade and development;
agree as follows [...].

The GATT specifies the term 'developing countries' in Article XVIII:1 as 'those contracting parties the economies of which can only support low standards of living and are in the early stages of development'.

In practice, classification of a State as a developing country is self-judging. When a country claims status as a developing country, this self-assessment is, as a rule, accepted by the other Member States on a regular basis. China claimed in the accession process developing country status, but many commitments assumed by China do not support this claim.

WTO law accords particularly privileged position to those States classified as the 'least developed countries' by the United Nations.[19] For this group of States, the obligations under the multilateral WTO Agreements are not categorically binding. Article XI:2 of the WTO Agreement states:

The least-developed countries recognized as such by the United Nations will only be required to undertake commitments and concessions to the extent consistent with their individual development, financial and trade needs or their administrative and institutional capabilities.

An important exception from the most-favoured-nation principle results from a waiver under Article XXV:5 of the GATT. This 'waiver clause' provides:

In exceptional circumstances not elsewhere provided for in this Agreement, the CONTRACTING PARTIES may waive an obligation imposed upon a contracting party by this Agreement; *Provided* that any such decision shall be approved by a two-thirds majority of the votes cast and that such majority shall comprise more than half of the contracting parties. The CONTRACTING PARTIES may also by such a vote
  (i) define certain categories of exceptional circumstances to which other voting requirements shall apply for the waiver of obligations, and
  (ii) prescribe such criteria as may be necessary for the application of this paragraph.

Such a waiver, approved by a two-thirds majority, has allowed preferential conditions for developing countries in the past and present. On this basis, the members adopted the decision on 'Differential and More Favourable Treatment, Reciprocity and Fuller Participation of Developing Countries' of 28 November 1979.[20] This decision, also called 'enabling clause', provides:

1. Notwithstanding the provisions of Article I of the General Agreement, contracting parties may accord differential and more favourable treatment to developing countries, without according such treatment to other contracting parties.

---

[19] For an analysis of recent developments regarding LDCs in the Doha Round, see C Carrère and J De Melo, 'The Doha Round and Market Access for LDCs: Scenarios for the EU and US Markets' (2010) 44 JWT 251.

[20] Differential and More Favourable Treatment, Reciprocity and Fuller Participation of Developing Countries (1979) GATT 26th Supp BISD (L/4903); see A Yusuf, 'Differential and More Favourable Treatment: The GATT Enabling Clause' (1980) 14 JWT 488.

2. The provisions of paragraph 1 apply to the following:
   (a) Preferential tariff treatment accorded by developed contracting parties to products originating in developing countries in accordance with the Generalized System of Preferences,
   (b) Differential and more favourable treatment with respect to the provisions of the General Agreement concerning non-tariff measures governed by the provisions of instruments multilaterally negotiated under the auspices of the GATT;
   (c) Regional or global arrangements entered into amongst less-developed contracting parties for the mutual reduction or elimination of tariffs and, in accordance with criteria or conditions which may be prescribed by the Contracting Parties, for the mutual reduction or elimination of non-tariff measures, on products imported from one another;
   (d) Special treatment on the least developed among the developing countries in the context of any general or specific measures in favour of developing countries.

In these terms, goods originating from developing countries may be granted a competitive advantage exempted from most-favoured-nation treatment.[21] The 1979 Decision permits developed members to set up 'Generalized System of Preferences' (GSP) schemes.[22] Under GSP programmes, developed countries offer non-reciprocal preferential treatment (such as zero or low duties on imports) to goods originating from developing countries. A number of WTO members, for example Australia, Canada, the European Union, Japan, and the United States, have established such GSP schemes.

The 1979 Decision does not justify discrimination between developing countries by selective preferences (except for least developed countries). Article 2(a) of the 1979 Decision with footnote 3 thereto requires 'non-discriminatory preferences beneficial to the developing countries in order to increase the export earnings, to promote the industrialization, and to accelerate the rates of economic growth of these countries [...]'.[23] As the Appellate Body Report in *EC—Tariff Preferences* stated, identical treatment must be available to all similarly-situated developing countries, in other words to all GSP beneficiaries with 'similar development, financial and trade needs'.[24]

The agreement between the European Union (formerly the European Community) and its Member States with the so-called ACP States (the Agreement of Cotonou of 2000, successor to the Lomé Conventions) raised problems as to preferences for selected developing countries. Under Article XXV:5 of the GATT, a waiver was granted for a limited period of time (until 2007). The Cotonou

---

[21] See K Kennedy, 'Special and Differential Treatment of Developing Countries' in PFJ Macrory, AE Appleton, and MG Plummer (eds), *The World Trade Organization: Legal, Economic and Political Analysis* (Springer 2005) vol 1, 1523.

[22] See NB dos Santos, R Farias, and R Cunha, 'Generalized System of Preferences in General Agreement on Tariffs and Trade/World Trade Organization: History and Current Issues' (2005) 39 JWT 637.

[23] Generalized System of Preferences (1971) GATT BISD 18S/24.

[24] WTO, *European Communities: Conditions for the Granting of Tariff Preferences to Developing Countries—Report of the Appellate Body* (2004) WT/DS246/AB/R para 165.

Agreement was altered and now operates as an umbrella for individual Economic Partnership Agreements with ACP States or groups of States.[25] These Partnership Agreements must now meet the standard of Article XXIV:8(b) of the GATT ('substantially all trade').

The 1979 Decision is also the legal basis for preferential trade agreements between developing countries and the Global System of Trade Preferences (GSTP) under which concessions are granted among developing countries.

3. National Treatment

(a) Article III:1 of the GATT: equality of competitive conditions

A fundamental principle of the GATT aims at national treatment, that is non-discrimination between imported and domestic products. Article III of the GATT requires that imported products are subject to the same treatment as domestic goods with respect to internal charges and other internal regulations relating to the marketing of products. The standard of national treatment ensures fair competition between domestic and imported goods as to market access. At the same time, national treatment contributes to the overall reduction of barriers to trade for equal treatment and requires States to extend all barriers to market access of imported products to domestic products. Thus, the principle of national treatment curbs the appetite of States to restrain the marketing of imported goods.

In terms of Article III:1 of the GATT, the contracting parties

[...] recognize that internal taxes and other internal charges, and laws, regulations and requirements affecting the internal sale, offering for sale, purchase, transportation, distribution or use of products, and internal quantitative regulations requiring the mixture, processing or use of products in specified amounts or proportions, should not be applied to imported or domestic products so as to afford protection to domestic production.

The thrust of Article III:1 of the GATT is to eliminate protectionist discrimination. As the Appellate Body emphasized in *Japan — Alcoholic Beverages II*, the central objective of Article III is to ensure the equality of competitive conditions for imported and domestic goods:

The broad and fundamental purpose of Article III is to avoid protectionism in the application of internal tax and regulatory measures. More specifically, the purpose of Article III 'is to ensure that internal measures "not be applied to imported or domestic products so as to afford protection to domestic production"'. Toward this end, Article III obliges Members of the WTO to provide equality of competitive conditions for imported products in relation

---

[25] For a critical recent analysis of the Economic Partnership Agreements, see JJ Hallaert, 'Economic Partnership Agreements: Tariff Cuts, Revenue Losses and Trade Diversion in Sub-Saharan Africa' (2010) 44 JWT 223.

to domestic products. '[T]he intention of the drafters of the Agreement was clearly to treat the imported products in the same way as the like domestic products once they had been cleared through customs. Otherwise indirect protection could be given'. Moreover, it is irrelevant that 'the trade effects' of the tax differential between imported and domestic products, as reflected in the volumes of imports, are insignificant or even non-existent; Article III protects expectations not of any particular trade volume but rather of the equal competitive relationship between imported and domestic products. Members of the WTO are free to pursue their own domestic goals through internal taxation or regulation so long as they do not do so in a way that violates Article III or any of the other commitments they have made in the WTO Agreement.[26]

Article III:1 of the GATT guides the interpretation of the following operative paragraphs of Article III which implement the overarching objective of equal competitive conditions. This understanding of Article III:1 of the GATT as a guideline was also stressed by the Appellate Body in *Japan—Alcoholic Beverages II*:

The terms of Article III must be given their ordinary meaning—in their context and in the light of the overall object and purpose of the WTO Agreement. Thus, the words actually used in the Article provide the basis for an interpretation that must give meaning and effect to all its terms. The proper interpretation of the Article is, first of all, a textual interpretation. Consequently, the Panel is correct in seeing a distinction between Article III:1, which 'contains general principles', and Article III:2, which 'provides for specific obligations regarding internal taxes and internal charges' [...] Article III:1 articulates a general principle that internal measures should not be applied so as to afford protection to domestic production. This general principle informs the rest of Article III. The purpose of Article III:1 is to establish this general principle as a guide to understanding and interpreting the specific obligations contained in Article III:2 and in the other paragraphs of Article III, while respecting, and not diminishing in any way, the meaning of the words actually used in the texts of those other paragraphs. In short, Article III:1 constitutes part of the context of Article III:2, in the same way that it constitutes part of the context of each of the other paragraphs in Article III. Any other reading of Article III would have the effect of rendering the words of Article III:1 meaningless, thereby violating the fundamental principle of effectiveness in treaty interpretation. Consistent with this principle of effectiveness, and with the textual differences in the two sentences, we believe that Article III:1 informs the first sentence and the second sentence of Article III:2 in different ways.[27]

The scope of Article III is not restricted to products covered by tariff concessions under Article II, as the Appellate Body clarified in *Japan—Alcoholic Beverages II*:

The broad purpose of Article III of avoiding protectionism must be remembered when considering the relationship between Article III and other provisions of the WTO Agreement. Although the protection of negotiated tariff concessions is certainly one purpose of Article III, [...] the statement in Paragraph 6.13 of the Panel Report that 'one of the main purposes of

[26] WTO, *Japan: Taxes on Alcoholic Beverages—Report of the Appellate Body* (1996) WT/DS8/AB/R, WT/DS10/AB/R and WT/DS11/AB/R -16.

[27] WTO, *Japan: Taxes on Alcoholic Beverages—Report of the Appellate Body* (1996) WT/DS8/AB/R, WT/DS10/AB/R and WT/DS11/AB/R 17ff.

Article III is to guarantee that WTO Members will not undermine through internal measures their commitments under Article II' should not be overemphasized. The sheltering scope of Article III is not limited to products that are the subject of tariff concessions under Article II. The Article III national treatment obligation is a general prohibition on the use of internal taxes and other internal regulatory measures so as to afford protection to domestic production. This obligation clearly extends also to products not bound under Article II. [...] This is confirmed by the negotiating history of Article III [...].[28]

The broad scope of Article III of the GATT is further determined and specified by Annex I to the GATT. The first paragraph of the annotation to Article III in Annex I clarifies that Article III of the GATT also applies to internal measures imposed at the moment or place of importation:

Any internal tax or other internal charge, or any law, regulation or requirement of the kind referred to in paragraph 1 which applies to an imported product and to the like domestic product and is collected or enforced in the case of the imported product at the time or point of importation, is nevertheless to be regarded as an internal tax or other internal charge, or a law, regulation or requirement of the kind referred to in paragraph 1, and is accordingly subject to the provisions of Article III.

By referring only to 'products' (and not to production methods), the annotation to Article III of the GATT limits the scope of application of this article in an important respect. Article III does not extend to measures relating to methods of production (like environmentally friendly ways of production). In the Panel Report *US—Tuna II* (which was finally not adopted, but is still relevant as guidance to interpretation), the Panel

[...] noted that Article III calls for a comparison between the treatment accorded to domestic and imported like products, not for a comparison of the policies or practices of the country of origin with those of the country of importation. The Panel found therefore that the Note ad Article III could only permit the enforcement, at the time or point of importation, of those laws, regulations and requirements that affected or were applied to the imported and domestic products considered *as products*. The Note therefore could not apply to the enforcement at the time or point of importation of laws, regulations or requirements that related to policies or practices that could not affect the product as such, and that accorded less favourable treatment to like products not produced in conformity with the domestic policies of the importing country.[29]

Thus, so-called 'process and production methods' (PPMs) restricting the import of goods are not covered by Article III, but by Article XI of the GATT. This, however, only applies to PPMs which have no influence on the product as such (non-product related PPMs).[30]

---

[28] WTO, *Japan: Taxes on Alcoholic Beverages—Report of the Appellate Body* (1996) WT/DS8/AB/R, WT/DS10/AB/R, and WT/DS11/AB/R.

[29] GATT, *United States: Restrictions on Import of Tuna—Report of the Panel* (1994) DS29/R para 5.8.

[30] See GATT, *United States: Restrictions on Imports of Tuna—Report of the Panel* (1991) DS21/R–39S/155 paras 5.11–5.14; GATT, *United States: Restrictions on Import of Tuna—Report of the Panel* (1994) DS29/R para 5.8.

(b) Article III:2 of the GATT: internal charges

Article III:2 of the GATT requires national treatment for taxes and other charges on imported products:

> The products of the territory of any contracting party imported into the territory of any other contracting party shall not be subject, directly or indirectly, to internal taxes or other internal charges of any kind in excess of those applied, directly or indirectly, to like domestic products. Moreover, no contracting party shall otherwise apply internal taxes or other internal charges to imported or domestic products in a manner contrary to the principles set forth in paragraph 1.

The structure of Article III:2 of the GATT is rather complex. The first sentence covers all cases in which imported products can be qualified as 'like products' in comparison to domestic goods. The second sentence prohibits protectionist discrimination directed against foreign goods which are 'directly competitive or substitutable'. This meaning follows from the annotation (Ad Article III Paragraph 2) in Annex I to the GATT:

> A tax conforming to the requirements of the first sentence of paragraph 2 would be considered to be inconsistent with the provisions of the second sentence only in cases where competition was involved between, on the one hand, the taxed product and, on the other hand, a directly competitive or substitutable product which was not similarly taxed.

The concurrence of two regulatory standards in Article III:2 of the GATT illustrates that 'likeness' in terms of the first sentence has to be understood narrowly, as likeness of a product must be distinguished from being directly competitive or substitutable in terms of the annotation to the second sentence.[31] Once the 'likeness' in terms of Article III:2 first sentence of the GATT is established, the competitive relationship does not need to be considered.

i. *'Like products' (Article III:2 first sentence of the GATT)*

As results from established case-law, four criteria determine whether imported and domestic products are 'like' in terms of Article III:2 first sentence of the GATT:

- the products' properties, nature, and quality;
- their end uses in a given market;
- consumers' tastes and habits; and
- the tariff classification of the products based on the Harmonized System.[32]

---

[31] WTO, *Japan: Taxes on Alcoholic Beverages—Report of the Appellate Body* (1996) WT/DS8/AB/R, WT/DS10/AB/R, and WT/DS11/AB/R 19ff.

[32] Working Party Report *Border Tax Adjustments* (1970) BISD 185/97 para 18; WTO, *Canada: Certain Measures Concerning Periodicals—Report of the Appellate Body* (1997) WT/DS31/AB/R para 20. The tariff classification as a criterion of the WTO jurisprudence was recognized later than the other criteria, see WTO, *Japan: Taxes on Alcoholic Beverages—Report of the Appellate Body* (1996) WT/DS8/ AB/R, WT/DS10/AB/R, and WT/DS11/AB/R 20ff; WTO, *Mexico: Tax Measures on Soft Drinks and other Beverages—Report of the Panel* (2005) WT/DS308/R para 8.29 mentions 'the

In the Report *Philippines — Taxes on Distilled Spirits*,[33] the Appellate Body had to analyse a tax regime for distilled spirits of the Philippines which drew a distinction based on the raw materials used.

This regime privileged (sugar-based) spirits produced from 'designated raw materials' (including sugar of the cane, used exclusively in domestic production) over spirits stemming from other raw materials. The Philippines contended that (domestic) sugar-based spirits and (imported) spirits produced from other raw material, despite similarities of the final product, were not 'like' in the light of Article III:2 of the GATT.

The Appellate Body held that 'likeness' does not depend on the use of particular raw materials, but on the competitive relationship between the compared products. The decisive criterion is the degree in which products are substitutable on the relevant market:

125. We consider that, in spite of differences in the raw materials used to make the products, if these differences do not affect the final products, these products can still be found to be 'like' within the meaning of Article III:2 of the GATT 1994. Article III:2, first sentence, refers to 'like products', not to their raw material base. If differences in raw materials leave fundamentally unchanged the competitive relationship among the final products, the existence of these differences would not necessarily negate a finding of 'likeness' under Article III:2. As we have explained above, the determination of what are 'like products' under Article III:2 is not focused exclusively on the physical characteristics of the products, but is concerned with the nature and the extent of the competitive relationship between and among the products. We consider, therefore, that as long as the differences among the products, including a difference in the raw material base, leave fundamentally unchanged the competitive relationship among the final products, the existence of these differences does not prevent a finding of 'likeness' if, by considering all factors, the panel is able to come to the conclusion that the competitive relationship among the products is such as to justify a finding of 'likeness' under Article III:2. [...]

148. We observe that both the analysis of 'likeness' under Article III:2, first sentence, of the GATT 1994, and the analysis of direct competitiveness and substitutability under Article III:2, second sentence, require consideration of the competitive relationship between imported and domestic products. However, 'likeness' is a narrower category than 'directly competitive and substitutable'. Thus, the degree of competition and substitutability that is required under Article III:2, first sentence, must be higher than that under Article III:2, second sentence. On this point, we recall that, in *Canada—Periodicals*, the Appellate Body considered that a relationship of 'imperfect substitutability' would still be consistent with the notion of 'directly competitive or substitutable products', under the second sentence of Article III:2 of the GATT 1994, and that '[a] case of perfect substitutability would fall within Article III:2, first sentence'. In *Korea—Alcoholic Beverages*, the Appellate Body observed that ' "like products" are a subset of directly competitive or substitutable products', so that 'perfectly substitutable products fall within Article III:2, first sentence', while 'imperfectly substitutable products can be assessed under Article III:2, second sentence'.

---

products properties, nature and quality; their end uses in a given market; consumers' tastes and habits; and the tariff classification of the products based on the Harmonized System'.

[33] WTO, *Philippines: Taxes on Distilled Spirits—Report of the Appellate Body* (2011) WT/DS403/AB/R.

149. We do not understand the statements by the Appellate Body in *Canada—Periodicals* and in *Korea—Alcoholic Beverages* to mean that only products that are perfectly substitutable can fall within the scope of Article III:2, first sentence. This would be too narrow an interpretation and would reduce the scope of the first sentence essentially to identical products. Rather, we consider that, under the first sentence, products that are close to being perfectly substitutable can be 'like products', whereas products that compete to a lesser degree would fall within the scope of the second sentence.[34]

According to this understanding, products that are perfectly substitutable or at least close to being perfectly substitutable qualify for 'likeness' under the first sentence of Article III:2 of the GATT. If there is a lesser degree of competition between the products, the second sentence of Article III:2 becomes relevant.

It has long been a matter of controversy whether the 'aims and effects' of a measure may co-determine 'likeness'.[35] Regulatory aims and effects may affect consumer attitudes and habits, for example with respect to enhanced environmental standards. If regulatory standards have over time transformed consumer perceptions and habits through internalization (like sensitivity to low emissions), they shape market conditions and can hardly be ignored. Nevertheless, consumer preferences which essentially depend on a challenged measure cannot automatically eliminate the 'likeness' of imported and domestic products.[36] Otherwise, regulatory measures with a chilling effect on the sale of imported products would be self-justifying. As a rule, measures which typically result in significant competitive advantages for domestic products should be faded out in the analysis of a product's properties and of consumer attitudes.

In the case *US—Taxes on Automobiles*,[37] the Panel considered the taxation of particularly energy-inefficient cars ('gas guzzler tax') in the United States which aimed at preserving fossil fuels. In its Report (which was finally not adopted), the Panel could not find a protectionist intention of the US measure and therefore concluded that 'gas guzzlers' and more energy-efficient cars were not 'like products' in terms of Article III:2 first sentence of the GATT. Later, panel and Appellate Body reports tended to be rather reluctant to determine 'likeness' in Article III:2 first sentence of the GATT in the light of the 'aims and effects' of a challenged measure. In the Report *Japan — Taxes on Alcoholic Beverages*, the Panel rejected the 'aims and effects' of a measure as a distinguishing parameter for the properties of products. As the Panel rightly indicated, the consideration of 'aims and effects' of a measure might circumvent the application of General Exceptions in Article XX of the GATT.[38]

---

[34] WTO, *Philippines: Taxes on Distilled Spirits—Report of the Appellate Body* (2011) WT/DS403/AB/R paras 125, 148, 149.

[35] See J Ya Qin, 'Defining Nondiscrimination Under the Law of the World Trade Organization' (2005) 23 BU Int'l LJ 215, 242ff.

[36] See WTO, *European Communities: Measures Affecting Asbestos and Asbestos-Containing Products—Report of the Appellate Body* (2001) WT/DS135/AB/R para 123.

[37] GATT, *United States: Taxes on Automobiles—Report of the Panel* (1994) DS31/R paras 5.24–5.26.

[38] WTO, *Japan: Taxes on Alcoholic Beverages—Report of the Panel* (1996) WT/DS8/R, WT/DS10/R, and WT/DS11/R para 6.16; approved by WTO, *Japan: Taxes on Alcoholic Beverages—Report of the Appellate Body* (1996) WT/DS8/AB/R, WT/DS10/AB/R, and WT/DS11/AB/R 18.

In this context, the competitive relationship between domestic and imported goods is not just determined by current consumer habits. Otherwise, discriminatory taxes or other charges might defeat substitutability from the very beginning. This corroborates that criteria for 'likeness' which are dependent on regulatory measures must be viewed with great caution. Therefore, it is important whether there is a latent demand in case the challenged measure is eliminated. In this context, the Appellate Body Report in the case *Philippines—Distilled Spirits* rightly called for a hypothetical consideration of consumer attitudes:

We do not agree with the Philippines that Article III:2, second sentence, of the GATT 1994 requires *identity* in the 'nature and frequency' of the consumers' purchasing behaviour. If that were the case, the competitive relationship between the imported and domestic products in a given market would only be assessed with reference to *current* consumer preferences. However, as the Appellate Body expressly held in *Korea—Alcoholic Beverages*, 'the requisite relationship *may* exist between products that are not, at a given moment, considered by consumers to be substitutes but which are, nonetheless, *capable* of being substituted for one another'. Therefore, requiring identity in frequency and nature of consumers' purchase decisions, as suggested by the Philippines, would not sufficiently account for *latent* demand for imported distilled spirits in the Philippine market.[39]

The relevant competitive relationship between domestic and imported goods depends on the market conditions of the State where the product is being sold. Consumers in one country may subtly differentiate between all kinds of distilled spirits, whilst in others price and alcohol content, regardless of raw materials and production methods, determine market shares. As the Appellate Body indicated in *Philippines—Distilled Spirits*, certain differentiations may be relevant in one State, but may be negligible from the perspective of consumers in other States:

The determination of 'likeness' under Article III:2, first sentence, of the GATT 1994 should be made on a case-by-case basis. If two spirits are considered to be 'like products' in a given market, this does not necessarily mean that they would be considered 'like products' in another market. It is thus conceivable that brandy and whisky made from designated raw materials and those made from non-designated raw materials may be considered as 'like products' by consumers in the Philippine market, but that they may not be considered as 'like products' by consumers in another market. As we have explained above, we consider that, in order to establish whether two products are 'like' within the meaning of Article III:2 of the GATT 1994, a panel needs to examine the nature and the extent of the competitive relationship between and among products, which will depend on the market where these products compete.[40]

Looking at markets, not from a global view, but from country to country, implies considerable deference to cultural diversity and social realities in world trade law.

---

[39] WTO, *Philippines: Taxes on Distilled Spirits—Report of the Appellate Body* (2011) WT/DS403/AB/R para 218.
[40] WTO, *Philippines: Taxes on Distilled Spirits—Report of the Appellate Body* (2011) WT/DS403/AB/R para 168.

ii. 'Directly Competitive or Substitutable Products' (Article III:2 second sentence of the GATT)

Article III:2 second sentence of the GATT calls for a three-step-analysis. The Panel Report *Mexico—Taxes on Soft Drinks* summarizes the approach as follows:

> There are three elements to be considered to determine whether a measure is inconsistent with Article III:2, second sentence: first, whether the imported products and the domestic products are 'directly competitive or substitutable products' which are in competition with each other; second, whether the directly competitive or substitutable imported and domestic products are 'not similarly taxed'; and third, whether the dissimilar taxation of the directly competitive or substitutable imported and domestic products is 'applied [...] so as to afford protection to domestic production'.[41]

An important, albeit not exclusive criterion for determining whether imported and domestic products are 'directly competitive or substitutable' is cross-price elasticity. The relevance of this criterion was stressed by the Appellate Body in the Report *Japan—Alcoholic Beverages II*:

> If imported and domestic products are not 'like products' for the narrow purposes of Article III:2, first sentence, then they are not subject to the strictures of that sentence and there is no inconsistency with the requirements of that sentence. However, depending on their nature, and depending on the competitive conditions in the relevant market, those same products may well be among the broader category of 'directly competitive or substitutable products' that fall within the domain of Article III:2, second sentence. How much broader that category of 'directly competitive or substitutable products' may be in any given case is a matter for the panel to determine based on all the relevant facts in that case. As with 'like products' under the first sentence, the determination of the appropriate range of 'directly competitive or substitutable products' under the second sentence must be made on a case-by-case basis.
>
> In this case, the Panel emphasized the need to look not only at such matters as physical characteristics, common end-uses, and tariff classifications, but also at the 'market place'. This seems appropriate. The GATT 1994 is a commercial agreement, and the WTO is concerned, after all, with markets. It does not seem inappropriate to look at competition in the relevant markets as one among a number of means of identifying the broader category of products that might be described as 'directly competitive or substitutable'.
>
> Nor does it seem inappropriate to examine elasticity of substitution as one means of examining those relevant markets. The Panel did not say that cross-price elasticity of demand is '*the* decisive criterion' for determining whether products are 'directly competitive or substitutable'. The Panel stated the following:
>
> In the Panel's view, the decisive criterion in order to determine whether two products are directly competitive or substitutable is whether they have common end-uses, *inter alia*, as shown by elasticity of substitution [...].
>
> We agree. And, we find the Panel's legal analysis of whether the products are 'directly competitive or substitutable products' in paragraphs 6.28–6.32 of the Panel Report to be correct.[42]

[41] WTO, *Mexico: Tax Measures on Soft Drinks and Other Beverages—Report of the Panel* (2005) WT/DS308/R para 8.66; the term 'so as to afford protection' can be found in Article III:1 of the GATT at the very end.

[42] WTO, *Japan: Taxes on Alcoholic Beverages—Report of the Appellate Body* (1996) WT/DS8/AB/R, WT/DS10/AB/R, and WT/DS11/AB/R 25.

The demarcation of the scope of the first and the second sentence of Article III:2 of the GATT can be quite a subtle undertaking. In *Japan—Alcoholic Beverages II*, the Appellate Body found that, compared with the Japanese liquor shochu, vodka is a 'like product' in terms of the first sentence, whilst whisky, Brandy, and other distilled liquors are competitive products under the second sentence of Article III:2 of the GATT.[43] The dispute was triggered by Japan's taxation of distilled spirits which privileged shochu over other alcoholic beverages.

(c) Article III:4 of the GATT: the general principle of national treatment

In general terms, Article III:4 of the GATT enshrines the principle of national treatment for imported goods which are 'like' those goods of domestic origin:

> The products of the territory of any contracting party imported into the territory of any other contracting party shall be accorded treatment no less favourable than that accorded to like products of national origin in respect of all laws, regulations and requirements affecting their internal sale, offering for sale, purchase, transportation, distribution or use. The provisions of this paragraph shall not prevent the application of differential internal transportation charges which are based exclusively on the economic operation of the means of transport and not on the nationality of the product.

Article III:4 of the GATT must be seen in the light of the anti-protectionist objective of Article III:1 of the GATT, which aims at achieving equal competitive conditions. The competitive relationship is an essential criterion for 'likeness' in Article III:4. However, the wording of Article III:4 does not allow a precise definition of 'likeness' with reference to the two sentences of Article III:2 of the GATT. In this respect, the Appellate Body interprets Article III:4 of the GATT in broader terms than Article III:2 first sentence of the GATT. In *EC—Asbestos*, the Appellate Body held that 'likeness' in terms of Article III:4 of the GATT includes all cases of 'likeness' in terms of the first sentence of Article III:2 and reaches into the product scope of the second sentence:

> [...] [W]e conclude that the scope of 'like' in Article III:4 is broader than the scope of 'like' in Article III: 2, first sentence. Nonetheless, we note [...] that Article III: 2 extends not only to 'like products', but also to products which are 'directly competitive or substitutable', and that Article III: 4 extends only to 'like products'. In view of this different language, and although we need not rule, and do not rule, on the precise product scope of Article III: 4, we do conclude that the product scope of Article III: 4, although broader than the *first* sentence of Article III: 2, is certainly *not* broader than the *combined* product scope of the *two* sentences of Article III: 2 of the GATT 1994.[44]

With some uncertainty on the conceptual periphery of 'likeness', the product scope of Article III:2 first sentence of the GATT forms the core of the broader concept

[43] WTO, *Japan: Taxes on Alcoholic Beverages—Report of the Appellate Body* (1996) WT/DS8/AB/R, WT/DS10/AB/R, and WT/DS11/AB/R para 31.

[44] WTO, *European Communities: Measures Affecting Asbestos and Asbestos-Containing Products—Report of the Appellate Body* (2001) WT/DS135/AB/R para 99.

of 'likeness' in terms of Article III:4. Thus, the four criteria which determine the product scope under Article III:2 first sentence of the GATT are sufficient (though not necessary) to establish 'likeness' in terms of Article III:4 of the GATT:

We note that these four criteria comprise four categories of 'characteristics' that the products involved might share: (i) the physical properties of the products; (ii) the extent to which the products are capable of serving the same or similar end-uses; (iii) the extent to which consumers perceive and treat the products as alternative means of performing particular functions in order to satisfy a particular want or demand; and (iv) the international classification of the products for tariff purposes.[45]

The four criteria may overlap. The physical properties, end-uses, and consumer perceptions are interrelated. In *EC—Asbestos*,[46] the Appellate Body took the view that risks to health stemming from the physical properties of a product can be considered a relevant criterion for the exclusion of 'likeness' also in the light of consumer perceptions.

In this case, Canada complained about a French marketing and import prohibition on asbestos fibres and products containing asbestos. Canada argued that asbestos fibres and other industrial fibres free of asbestos (PCG fibres) were 'like products' for construction purposes. The European Community relied on the carcinogenic properties of asbestos products and held that the inherent risks made these products different from asbestos-free fibres.

The Appellate Body rejected the Canadian argument and emphasized the close connection between carcinogenic product properties and consumer habits:

[...] [E]vidence relating to consumers' tastes and habits would establish that the health risks associated with chrysotile asbestos fibres influence consumers' behaviour with respect to the different fibres at issue. We observe that, as regards *chrysotile asbestos and PCG fibres*, the consumer of the fibres is a *manufacturer* who incorporates the fibres into another product, such as cement-based products or brake linings. We do not wish to speculate on what the evidence regarding these consumers would have indicated; rather, we wish to highlight that consumers' tastes and habits regarding *fibres*, even in the case of commercial parties, such as manufacturers, are very likely to be shaped by the health risks associated with a product which is known to be highly carcinogenic. A manufacturer cannot, for instance, ignore the preferences of the ultimate consumer of its products. If the risks posed by a particular product are sufficiently great, the ultimate consumer may simply cease to buy that product. This would, undoubtedly, affect a manufacturer's decisions in the marketplace. Moreover, in the case of products posing risks to human health, we think it likely that manufacturers' decisions will be influenced by other factors, such as the potential civil liability that might flow from marketing products posing a health risk to the ultimate consumer, or the additional costs associated with safety procedures required to use such products in the manufacturing process.[47]

[45] WTO, *European Communities: Measures Affecting Asbestos and Asbestos-Containing Products— Report of the Appellate Body* (2001) WT/DS135/AB/R para 101.
[46] WTO, *European Communities: Measures Affecting Asbestos and Asbestos-Containing Products— Report of the Appellate Body* (2001) WT/DS135/AB/R.
[47] WTO, *European Communities: Measures Affecting Asbestos and Asbestos-Containing Products— Report of the Appellate Body* (2001) WT/DS135/AB/R para 122.

The consideration of health issues also touches on the scope of the general exception of Article XX(b) of the GATT. In the context of 'likeness', health-related consumer perceptions and preferences merely refer to the competitive relationship between products without pre-empting the justification of trade measures under Article XX of the GATT.[48]

Reference to consumer habits and expectations in domestic markets as a criterion for 'likeness' under Article III:4 might in the end favour domestic goods which respond to consumer sensitivities. As long as these preferences are not triggered by regulation, but by prevailing societal sensitivities (in particular to health risks), they are a legitimate factor of competition.

Reliance on consumer perceptions relates to cultural diversity. The same holds true for the criterion of end uses, which are equally shaped by the cultural and socio-economic context. Thus, in poorer countries 'likeness' of food products will often cover more varieties of food than in more affluent countries where large sectors of the population can afford subtle differentiation as to end uses and product characteristics. In a society which sharply differentiates between single malt and blended whisky, 'likeness' of spirits has another connotation than in societies where alcoholic beverages more or less indiscriminately serve the purpose of exhilaration and where the price, rather than nuances of taste, dictates consumer choices. On the other hand, even in poor countries religion and other socio-cultural habits may foster differentiation between comparable products.

Whether treatment is 'less favourable' than for domestic goods depends on competitive disadvantages.[49] In the case *Korea—Measures Affecting Imports of Fresh, Chilled and Frozen Beef*, the Appellate Body analysed a sales system with a dual structure for imported products and domestic products as to its impact on the equality of competitive conditions:

[...] [T]he Korean measure formally separates the selling of imported beef and domestic beef. However, that formal separation, *in and of itself*, does not necessarily compel the conclusion that the treatment thus accorded to imported beef is less favourable than the treatment accorded to domestic beef. To determine whether the treatment given to imported beef is less favourable than that given to domestic beef, we must [...] inquire into whether or not the Korean dual retail system for beef modifies the *conditions of competition* in the Korean beef market to the disadvantage of the imported product.[50]

The prohibition of discriminatory treatment applies to disadvantages directly targeting imported goods as well as to 'hidden' (indirect) discrimination.

An illustrative example of indirect discrimination is provided by the case *Dominican Republic—Cigarettes*.[51] The law of the Dominican Republic established

---

[48] WTO, *European Communities: Measures Affecting Asbestos and Asbestos-Containing Products—Report of the Appellate Body* (2001) WT/DS135/AB/R para 115.

[49] WTO, *European Communities: Measures Affecting Asbestos and Asbestos-Containing Products—Report of the Appellate Body* (2001) WT/DS135/AB/R para 100.

[50] WTO, *Korea: Measures Affecting Imports of Fresh, Chilled and Frozen Beef—Report of the Appellate Body* (2000) WT/DS61/AB/R para 144.

[51] WTO, *Dominican Republic: Measures Affecting the Importation and Internal Sale of Cigarettes—Report of the Panel* (2004) WT/DS302/R.

a requirement to affix a tax stamp on imported cigarettes in the territory of the Dominican Republic, under the supervision of the local tax authorities. Despite the formally equal application of the measure to domestic and foreign products, the Panel qualified this measure as a particular impediment for the import of cigarettes because of the additional burden placed on imports:

In this respect, the Panel finds that, although the tax stamp requirement is applied in a formally equal manner to domestic and imported cigarettes, it does modify the conditions of competition in the marketplace to the detriment of imports. The tax stamp requirement imposes additional processes and costs on imported products. It also leads to imported cigarettes being presented to final consumers in a less appealing manner.[52]

(d) Article III:8 of the GATT: derogations from national treatment obligations

Article III:8 of the GATT contains two derogations from the principle of national treatment under Article III:

(a) The provisions of this Article shall not apply to laws, regulations or requirements governing the procurement by governmental agencies of products purchased for governmental purposes and not with a view to commercial resale or with a view to use in the production of goods for commercial sale.
(b) The provisions of this Article shall not prevent the payment of subsidies exclusively to domestic producers, including payments to domestic producers derived from the proceeds of internal taxes or charges applied consistently with the provisions of this Article and subsidies effected through governmental purchases of domestic products.

Article III:8(a) became relevant in the context of domestic (local) content requirements under the TRIMS Agreement which prohibits trade-related investment measures inconsistent with Article III of the GATT (Article 2.2).[53]

The exceptions under Article III:8(a) apply only in the context of a competitive relationship between a domestic and an imported product. In *Canada—Renewable Energy*, the Appellate Body held that the government purpose must relate directly to the purchase of the goods which are subject to a discriminatory regime:

[...] Article III:8(a) stipulates conditions under which derogation from the obligations in Article III takes place. The derogation in Article III:8(a) becomes relevant only if there is discriminatory treatment of foreign products that are covered by the obligations in Article III, and this discriminatory treatment results from laws, regulations, or requirements governing procurement by governmental agencies of products purchased. Both the obligations in Article III and the derogation in Article III:8(a) refer to discriminatory treatment of products. Because Article III:8(a) is a derogation from the obligations contained in other paragraphs of Article III, we consider that the same discriminatory

---

[52] WTO, *Dominican Republic: Measures Affecting the Importation and Internal Sale of Cigarettes—Report of the Panel* (2004) WT/DS302/R paras 7.196.
[53] See Ch XIII.2.

treatment must be considered both with respect to the obligations of Article III and with respect to the derogation of Article III:8(a). Accordingly, the scope of the terms 'products purchased' in Article III:8(a) is informed by the scope of 'products' referred to in the obligations set out in other paragraphs of Article III. Article III:8(a) thus concerns, in the first instance, the product that is subject to the discrimination. The coverage of Article III:8 extends not only to products that are identical to the product that is purchased, but also to 'like' products. In accordance with the Ad Note to Article III:2, it also extends to products that are directly competitive to or substitutable with the product purchased under the challenged measure. For convenience, this range of products can be described as products that are in a competitive relationship. What constitutes a competitive relationship between products may require consideration of inputs and processes of production used to produce the product. In its rebuttal of Canada's claim under Article III:8(a), the European Union acknowledges that the cover of Article III:8(a) may also extend to discrimination relating to inputs and processes of production used in respect of products purchased by way of procurement. Whether the derogation in Article III:8(a) can extend also to discrimination of the kind referred to by the European Union is a matter we do not decide in this case.[54]

Accordingly, the Appellate Body concluded that the purchase of green energy for governmental purposes did not exempt the discriminatory domestic content regulations for electricity generators operated by private energy producers from the rules on national treatment, because there is no direct competition between green energy suppliers and producers of electricity generators.[55]

4. The Reduction of Tariffs and Non-Tariff Barriers to Trade

The most-favoured-nation principle and the national treatment principle address barriers to trade only in the context of equality of competitive conditions and do not address trade restrictions as such. By contrast, other GATT principles and rules directly eliminate or reduce barriers to trade. In a two-tiered approach, the GATT aims at tariff reduction and establishes the 'tariffs-only principle' which severely limits the arsenal of protectionist measures.

(a) The reduction of tariffs

In the history of the GATT, the first negotiation rounds essentially focused on the reduction of tariffs. The resulting commitments of each member are listed in the so-called 'Schedules of Concessions' annexed to the GATT. According to Article II:7

---

[54] WTO, *Canada: Certain Measures Affecting the Renewable Energy Generation Sector—Report of the Appellate Body* (2013) WT/DS412/AB/R, WT/DS426/AB/R para 5.63.

[55] WTO, *Canada: Certain Measures Affecting the Renewable Energy Generation Sector— Report of the Appellate Body* (2013) WT/DS412/AB/R, WT/DS426/AB/R paras 5.54ff; see also WTO, *India: Certain Measures Relating to Solar Cells and Solar Modules* (2016), WT/DS456/R, paras 55ff.

of the GATT, these schedules are an integral aspect of Part I of the Agreement. The concessions of each Member State regarding tariffs and other import-related charges listed in individual schedules are a cornerstone of trade liberalization. Article II:1(b) of the GATT provides:

The products described in Part I of the Schedule relating to any contracting party, which are the products of territories of other contracting parties, shall, on their importation into the territory to which the Schedule relates, and subject to the terms, conditions or qualifications set forth in that Schedule, be exempt from ordinary customs duties in excess of those set forth and provided therein. Such products shall also be exempt from all other duties or charges of any kind imposed on or in connection with the importation in excess of those imposed on the date of this Agreement or those directly and mandatorily required to be imposed thereafter by legislation in force in the importing territory on that date.

The specific tariffs must be seen as a ceiling ('bound tariffs'). The tariffs actually levied are often significantly lower than the tariff concessions would allow. The so-called nomenclature consists of a complex system of classifications and covers all kinds of products for tariff purposes. This classification is based on the 'Harmonized System' (HS) of the World Customs Organization (WCO), which is seated in Brussels.

The Ministerial Declaration on Trade in Information Technology Products (Information Technology Agreement) of 1996[56] establishes a far-reaching exemption from tariffs on certain products of information technology. Sections 1 and 2 of the Declaration provide:

1. Each party's trade regime should evolve in a manner that enhances market access opportunities for information technology products.
2. Pursuant to the modalities set forth in the Annex to this Declaration, each party shall bind and eliminate customs duties and other duties and charges of any kind, within the meaning of Article II:1(b) of the General Agreement on Tariffs and Trade 1994, with respect to the following:
   (a) all products classified (or classifiable) with Harmonized System (1996) ('HS') headings listed in Attachment A to the Annex to this Declaration; and
   (b) all products specified in Attachment B to the Annex to this Declaration, whether or not they are included in Attachment A;
   through equal rate reductions of customs duties beginning in 1997 and concluding in 2000, recognizing that extended staging of reductions and, before implementation, expansion of product coverage may be necessary in limited circumstances.

(b) The prohibition of import- and export-related barriers to trade (Article XI of the GATT)

Even though non-tariff barriers to trade are undesirable from the perspective of global liberalization, the GATT does not ban these impediments altogether. Article

---

XI:1 of the GATT establishes a general prohibition on quantitative and other restrictions to trade which are directly linked to the import or export of goods:

No prohibitions or restrictions other than duties, taxes or other charges, whether made effective through quotas, import or export licences or other measures, shall be instituted or maintained by any contracting party on the importation of any product of the territory of any other contracting party or on the exportation or sale for export of any product destined for the territory of any other contracting party.

Import-related measures can be considered 'restrictions' in terms of Article XI:1 of the GATT whenever their structure and practical application obstructs market access, significantly increases transaction costs, or causes a degree of legal uncertainty which has a deterrent effect on the import of goods. As to the inhibitory effect of uncertainties, the Panel Report in the case *Colombia—Ports of Entry* stated:

[...] [A] number of GATT and WTO panels have recognized the applicability of Article XI:1 to measures which create uncertainties and affect investment plans, restrict market access for imports or make importation prohibitively costly, all of which have implications on the competitive situation of an importer. Moreover, it appears that findings in each of these cases were based on the design of the measure and its potential to adversely affect importation, as opposed to a standalone analysis of the actual impact of the measure on trade flows.[57]

Import-related barriers to trade are subject to a strict standard of control under the GATT. WTO members may only adopt measures specifically targeting or affecting the import (or export) of goods within the rather narrow corridor of exceptions, in particular under Article XX of the GATT. By contrast, WTO members may, as a rule, apply so-called 'internal' restrictions, in other words measures generally restricting market access at will, even if the regulation extends to imported goods, as long as they comply with national treatment under Article III of the GATT. Due to the different standards in Article III and Article XI of the GATT, the distinction between barriers to trade in terms of Article III of the GATT and import restrictions in terms of Article XI of the GATT is crucial.[58] The comment on Article III in Annex I to the GATT clarifies that the application of internal restrictions to imported products is covered by Article III and not Article XI of the GATT:

Any internal tax or other internal charge, or any law, regulation or requirement of the kind referred to in paragraph 1 which applies to an imported product and to the like domestic product and is collected or enforced in the case of the imported product at the time or point of importation, is nevertheless to be regarded as an internal tax or other internal charge, or a law, regulation or requirement of the kind referred to in paragraph 1, and is accordingly subject to the provisions of Article III.

---

[57] WTO, *Colombia: Indicative Prices and Restrictions on Ports of Entry—Report of the Panel* (2009) WT/DS366/R para 7.240.

[58] See E Vranes, 'The WTO and Regulatory Freedom: WTO Disciplines on Market Access, Non-Discrimination and Domestic Regulation Relating to Trade in Goods and Services' (2009) 12 JIEL 953.

As previously mentioned, this comment is interpreted as being applicable only to barriers to trade which directly relate to product properties and not to PPMs. The latter fall exclusively within the scope of application of Article XI:1 of the GATT. Measures related to the production process mostly serve the goal of environmental protection.

In sum, general market restrictions for certain products are not categorically prohibited by the GATT. However, they cannot be used as protectionist instruments because any distortion of competitive conditions in favour of domestic products would conflict with Article III of the GATT.

In contrast to the free movement of goods under EU law (Article 34 TFEU), which even targets non-discriminatory measures, the GATT does not contain a general prohibition on barriers to the cross-border movement of goods. Thus, the GATT does not call for general and unqualified market access for imported goods but rather aims at market access free from discrimination. However, the SPS and the TBT Agreements subject even non-discriminatory (non-protectionist) measures to scrutiny.

Article XI:2 of the GATT exempts certain measures from the general prohibition under paragraph 1:

The provisions of paragraph 1 of this Article shall not extend to the following:
(a) Export prohibitions or restrictions temporarily applied to prevent or relieve critical shortages of foodstuffs or other products essential to the exporting contracting party;
(b) Import and export prohibitions or restrictions necessary to the application of standards or regulations for the classification, grading or marketing of commodities in international trade;
(c) Import restrictions on any agricultural or fisheries product, imported in any form, necessary to the enforcement of governmental measures which operate:
    (i)   to restrict the quantities of the like domestic product permitted to be marketed or produced, or, if there is no substantial domestic production of the like product, of a domestic product for which the imported product can be directly substituted; or
    (ii) to remove a temporary surplus of the like domestic product, or, if there is no substantial domestic production of the like product, of a domestic product for which the imported product can be directly substituted, by making the surplus available to certain groups of domestic consumers free of charge or at prices below the current market level; or
    (iii) to restrict the quantities permitted to be produced of any animal product the production of which is directly dependent, wholly or mainly, on the imported commodity, if the domestic production of that commodity is relatively negligible.
    [...]

The exception of Article XI:2(a) of the GATT has only recently turned into an issue of major interest in the context of China's restriction on the export of raw materials important for various industrial sectors.[59] In the case *China—Measures Related to*

---

[59] See WTO, *China: Measures Related to the Exportation of Various Raw Materials—Report of the Appellate Body* (2012) WT/DS394/AB/R, WT/DS395/AB/R, and WT/DS398/AB/R; WTO, *China: Measures Related to the Exportation of Rare Earths, Tungsten, and Molybdenum—Report of the Panel* (2014) WT/DS431/R, WT/DS432/R, and WT/DS433/R. On this issue B Karapinar, 'Export Restrictions and the WTO Law: How to Reform the "Regulatory Deficiency"' (2011) 45 JWT 1139.

the Exportation of Various Raw Materials,[60] China invoked this exception to justify export restrictions on certain raw materials (eg bauxite, silicon carbide, and yellow phosphorus). The wording of Article XI:2(a) indicates that this exception merely applies to 'temporary' measures and thus only covers shortages of goods which are not permanent in nature. The permanent preservation of exhaustible resources is the domain of Article XX(g) of the GATT. For this reason, the Panel Report in *China—Measures Related to the Exportation of Various Raw Materials* rightly interpreted the exception narrowly:

Article XI:2 (a) permits the application of restrictions or prohibitions 'temporarily' to address 'critical shortages' of 'essential products'. The Panel concluded that a product may be 'essential' within the meaning of Article XI:2 (a) when it is 'important' or 'necessary' or 'indispensable' to a particular Member. This may include a product that is an input to an important product or industry. The determination of whether a particular product is 'essential' to a Member must take into consideration the particular circumstances faced by that Member at the time in which a Member seeks to justify a restriction or prohibition under Article XI:2 (a). The Panel concluded that the term 'critical shortage' in Article XI:2 (a) refers to situations or events that are grave or provoking crises and which can be relieved or prevented through the application of measures on a 'temporary', and not an indefinite or permanent, basis. [61]

The Appellate Body agreed on the essence of the argument:

We note that the Panel found that the word 'temporarily' suggests 'a fixed time-limit for the application of a measure', and also expressed the view that a 'restriction or ban applied under Article XI:2(a) must be of a limited duration and not indefinite'. We have set out above our interpretation of the term 'temporarily' as employed in Article XI:2(a). In our view, a measure applied 'temporarily' in the sense of Article XI:2(a) is a measure applied in the interim, to provide relief in extraordinary conditions in order to bridge a passing need. It must be finite, that is, applied for a limited time. Accordingly, we agree with the Panel that a restriction or prohibition in the sense of Article XI:2(a) must be of a limited duration and not indefinite.[62]

Unlike the Panel, the Appellate Body found that measures under Article IX.2(a) must not be subject to a time-limit fixed in advance:

The Panel further interpreted the term 'limited time' to refer to a 'fixed time-limit' for the application of the measure. To the extent that the Panel was referring to a time-limit fixed in advance, we disagree that 'temporary' must always connote a time-limit fixed in advance. Instead, we consider that Article XI:2(a) describes measures applied for a limited duration, adopted in order to bridge a passing need, irrespective of whether or not the temporal scope of the measure is fixed in advance.[63]

---

[60] WTO, *China: Measures Related to the Exportation of Various Raw Materials—Report of the Panel* (2011) WT/DS394/R, WT/DS395/R, and WT/DS398/R.

[61] WTO, *China: Measures Related to the Exportation of Various Raw Materials—Report of the Panel* (2011) WT/DS394/R, WT/DS395/R, and WT/DS398/R para 7.354.

[62] WTO, *China: Measures Related to the Exportation of Various Raw Materials—Report of the Appellate Body* (2012) WT/DS394/AB/R, WT/DS395/AB/R, and WT/DS398/AB/R para 330.

[63] WTO, *China: Measures Related to the Exportation of Various Raw Materials—Report of the Appellate Body* (2012) WT/DS394/AB/R, WT/DS395/AB/R, and WT/DS398/AB/R para 331.

Another exception is established by Article XII:1 of the GATT:

Notwithstanding the provisions of paragraph 1 of Article XI, any contracting party, in order to safeguard its external financial position and its balance of payments, may restrict the quantity or value of merchandise permitted to be imported, subject to the provisions of the following paragraphs of this Article.

5. General Exceptions (Article XX of the GATT)

(a) General aspects

Besides the particular exceptions to specific provisions, Article XX of the GATT contains General Exceptions applicable to all GATT obligations:

Article XX: General Exceptions
Subject to the requirement that such measures are not applied in a manner which would constitute a means of arbitrary or unjustifiable discrimination between countries where the same conditions prevail, or a disguised restriction on international trade, nothing in this Agreement shall be construed to prevent the adoption or enforcement by any contracting party of measures:
(a) necessary to protect public morals;
(b) necessary to protect human, animal or plant life or health;
(c) relating to the importations or exportations of gold or silver;
(d) necessary to secure compliance with laws or regulations which are not inconsistent with the provisions of this Agreement, including those relating to customs enforcement, the enforcement of monopolies operated under paragraph 4 of Article II and Article XVII, the protection of patents, trade marks and copyrights, and the prevention of deceptive practices;
(e) relating to the products of prison labour;
(f) imposed for the protection of national treasures of artistic, historic or archaeological value;
(g) relating to the conservation of exhaustible natural resources if such measures are made effective in conjunction with restrictions on domestic production or consumption;
(h) undertaken in pursuance of obligations under any intergovernmental commodity agreement which conforms to criteria submitted to the CONTRACTING PARTIES and not disapproved by them or which is itself so submitted and not so disapproved;
(i) involving restrictions on exports of domestic materials necessary to ensure essential quantities of such materials to a domestic processing industry during periods when the domestic price of such materials is held below the world price as part of a governmental stabilization plan; *Provided* that such restrictions shall not operate to increase the exports of or the protection afforded to such domestic industry, and shall not depart from the provisions of this Agreement relating to non-discrimination;
(j) essential to the acquisition or distribution of products in general or local short supply; *Provided* that any such measures shall be consistent with the principle that all contracting parties are entitled to an equitable share of the international supply of such products, and that any such measures, which are inconsistent with the other provisions of

the Agreement shall be discontinued as soon as the conditions giving rise to them have ceased to exist. The CONTRACTING PARTIES shall review the need for this sub-paragraph not later than 30 June 1960.

(b) The 'chapeau' of Article XX of the GATT

All measures within the General Exceptions must conform to the so-called 'chapeau' of Article XX of the GATT[64] which requires

that such measures are not applied in a manner which would constitute a means of arbitrary or unjustifiable discrimination between countries where the same conditions prevail, or a disguised restriction on international trade [...].

According to the Appellate Body Report *US—Shrimp* (often simply referred to as the 'shrimp/turtle case'), the 'chapeau' of Article XX GATT is an expression of the principle of good faith[65] and aims at a proper balance of obligations and their exceptions. The enumerated exceptions cannot justify a measure which is discriminatory or is applied abusively or arbitrarily. This also excludes clearly disproportionate measures:

158. The chapeau of Article XX is, in fact, but one expression of the principle of good faith. This principle, at once a general principle of law and a general principle of international law, controls the exercise of rights by states. One application of this general principle, the application widely known as the doctrine of *abus de droit*, prohibits the abusive exercise of a state's rights and enjoins that whenever the assertion of a right, impinges on the field covered by [a] treaty obligation, it must be exercised bona fide, that is to say, 'reasonably.' An abusive exercise by a Member of its own treaty right thus results in a breach of the treaty rights of the other Members and, as well, a violation of the treaty obligation of the Member so acting. Having said this, our task here is to interpret the language of the chapeau, seeking additional interpretative guidance, as appropriate, from the general principles of international law.

159. The task of interpreting and applying the chapeau is, hence, essentially the delicate one of locating and marking out a line of equilibrium between the right of a Member to invoke an exception under Article XX and the rights of the other Members under varying substantive provisions (e.g., Article XI) of the GATT 1994, so that neither of the competing rights will cancel out the other and thereby distort and nullify or impair the balance of rights and obligations constructed by the Members themselves in that Agreement. The location of the line of equilibrium, as expressed in the chapeau, is not fixed and unchanging; the line moves as the kind and the shape of the measures at stake vary and as the facts making up specific cases differ.[66]

---

[64] See L Bartels, 'The Chapeau of the General Exceptions in the WTO GATT and GATS Agreements: A Reconstruction' (2015) 109 AJIL 95.

[65] For a general analysis of the good faith principle in WTO law, see M Panizzon, *Good Faith in the Jurisprudence of the WTO: The Protection of Legitimate Expectations, Good Faith Interpretation and Fair Dispute Settlement* (Hart Publishing 2006).

[66] WTO, *United States: Import Prohibition of Certain Shrimp and Shrimp Products—Report of the Appellate Body* (1998) WT/DS58/AB/R paras 158ff.

Forms of abuse as targeted by the 'chapeau' may be seen in the entirely uncompromising enforcement of national legislation with extraterritorial effects or in the complete denial of negotiations aiming at a fair balance of interests.[67] Some measures do not apply equally to foreign and domestic products, but are, nevertheless, recognized as reasonable and necessary, such as charges justified by the objectively higher administrative burden triggered by imported goods. In any case, critical scrutiny under the 'chapeau' aims at proportionality, requiring that no less invasive means are available.[68]

(c) Production-related measures

An issue cutting across some exceptions under Article XX (especially *lits* a and g) is raised by regulatory measures which do not refer to the imported products as such, but to certain PPMs.[69] Such measures mostly serve environmental protection. PPMs may also relate to human rights, labour conditions (child labour), or the protection of animals, as in the *EC—Seal Products* case.[70] Such measures target production methods in other countries. Measures aiming at the preservation of 'global commons', for example the atmosphere or biodiversity, compliance with human rights, or certain labour standards at the international level tend indirectly to regulate behaviour in foreign territory or on the high seas. This extraterritorial effect invites challenges to production-related restrictions of imports. In particular, measures serving environmental protection are controversial, because they may increase production costs and thus deteriorate the terms of trade for developing countries.

In *US—Shrimp*, the Appellate Body presented a landmark report which is receptive to the justification of PPM-related measures under Article XX.

The dispute was triggered by a US import prohibition on shrimps and shrimp products which were caught with certain fishing methods affecting turtle populations. Several Asian States as the main producers of shrimps filed a complaint.

Initially, GATT panels were reluctant to admit environmental measures with an extraterritorial effect under Article XX.[71] Following the unadopted Panel Report in *US—Tuna II*,[72] the Appellate Body in *US—Shrimp*[73] took the view that

---

[67] For measures relating to the preservation of endangered species, see WTO, *United States: Import Prohibition of Certain Shrimp and Shrimp Products—Report of the Appellate Body* (1998) WT/DS58/AB/R paras 166ff.

[68] WTO, *United States: Standards for Reformulated and Conventional Gasoline—Report of the Appellate Body* (1996) WT/DS2/AB/R.

[69] S Lester and B Mercurio with A Davies and K Leitner, *World Trade Law* (Hart Publishing 2008) 388ff; T Cottier and M Oesch, 'Direct and Indirect Discrimination in WTO and EU Law', in SE Gaines, BE Olsen, and KE Sorensen (eds), *Liberalising Trade in the EU and WTO* (CUP 2012) 166ff.

[70] WTO, *European Communities—Measures Prohibiting the Importation and Marketing of Seal Products*, WT/DS400/AB/R and WT/DS401/AB/R.

[71] See eg GATT, *United States: Restrictions on Imports of Tuna—Report of the Panel* (1991) DS21/R–39S/155 paras 5.24ff.

[72] GATT, *United States: Restrictions on Imports of Tuna—Report of the Panel* (1994) DS29/R para 5.20.

[73] WTO, *United States: Import Prohibition of Certain Shrimp and Shrimp Products—Report of the Appellate Body* (1998) WT/DS58/AB/R paras 121ff.

production-related import restrictions can, in principle, be justified by the protection of exhaustible natural resources under Article XX(g) of the GATT.

(d) Measures necessary to protect public morals (Article XX(a) of the GATT)

For a long time the public morals exception had little practical significance. The underlying reason seems twofold: first, relatively pluralist liberal attitudes among most WTO members in respect of products with 'moral implications', such as printed materials and, second, non-discriminating application of the few restrictions to imported and domestic products. With the accession of China, a different attitude appeared among major players, namely, a legally entrenched concern to fencing-off prevailing political societal perceptions against destabilizing influences from outside. This vests the public morals exception with new interest.

The term 'public morals' refers to a wide range of cultural, social, and ethical perceptions and values which are rooted or prevailing in a national or regional context. Article XX(a) of the GATT therefore suggests a very broad margin of appreciation, albeit falling short of a self-judging clause. In the leading case *US—Gambling*, the Panel Report analysed a public morals exception in WTO law, for the first time, under Article XIV(a) of the GATS, which essentially corresponds to Article XX(a) of the GATT.[74] The Panel came down with an approach widely deferring to the societal standards invoked by a member. The Panel in *China—Publications and Audiovisual Products* followed the same line of argument:

We note that the panel and Appellate Body in *US—Gambling* examined the meaning of the term 'public morals' as it is used in Article XIV(a) of the GATS, which is the GATS provision corresponding to Article XX(a). The panel in *US—Gambling*, in an interpretation not questioned by the Appellate Body, found that 'the term "public morals" denotes standards of right and wrong conduct maintained by or on behalf of a community or nation'. The panel went on to note that 'the content of these concepts for Members can vary in time and space, depending upon a range of factors, including prevailing social, cultural, ethical and religious values.' The panel went on to note that Members, in applying this and other similar societal concepts, 'should be given some scope to define and apply for themselves the concepts of "public morals" … in their respective territories, according to their own systems and scales of values.' Since Article XX(a) uses the same concept as Article XIV(a), and since we see no reason to depart from the interpretation of 'public morals' developed by the panel in *US—Gambling*, we adopt the same interpretation for purposes of our Article XX(a) analysis.[75]

In the dispute *China—Publications and Audiovisual Products*, the United States challenged restrictive measures established by China to control the content and

[74] WTO, *United States: Measures Affecting the Cross-Border Supply of Gambling and Betting Services—Report of the Appellate Body* (2005) WT/DS285/AB/R paras 6.461, 6.465.
[75] WTO, *China: Measures Affecting Trading Rights and Distribution Services for Certain Publications and Audiovisual Entertainment Products—Report of the Panel* (2009) WT/DS363/R para 7.759.

distribution of foreign print materials and audiovisual products. A point of contention was that China had reserved the control of contents as well as the entire import for State-owned enterprises. Whilst China invoked the protection of public morals (Article XX(a) of the GATT), the United States complained about the disproportionality of the Chinese control regime. The Appellate Body qualified the State's import monopoly as disproportionate because less invasive alternatives would have been available (eg import by private companies and control of contents by the government).[76]

The scope of the 'public morals exception' is broad enough to cover measures to protect animal welfare, as illustrates the case *EC—Seal Products*. This dispute referred to a ban of the European Union on the marketing of seal products (subject to narrow exceptions, such as hunting by indigenous communities). The ban was inspired by moral disapproval of cruel killing methods. In this case, the Appellate Body held that members have a wide discretion as to the level of protection of moral concerns. Therefore, the European Union was not required to extend the protection of animal welfare to slaughterhouses and terrestrial wildlife hunts in terms of a strictly consistent approach to animal welfare.[77] 'Public morals' are very much shaped by the history of ways of life, religious traditions, and socio-economic parameters. This explains why measures based on 'public morals' often escape scrutiny as to consistency.

It is open to discussion how far the scope of 'public morals' may reach. In context with PPMs, human rights and labour standards (especially if broadly recognized in customary law or in widely ratified universal treaties) are plausible candidates. If such standards, for example on child labour or forced labour, justify import restrictions, Article XX(a) of the GATT would have considerable implications for human rights activism under WTO law.

(e) Measures necessary to protect human, animal, or plant life or health (Article XX(b) of the GATT)

The exception of Article XX(b) of the GATT for 'measures necessary to protect human, animal, or plant life or health' allows import restrictions and other barriers to trade which avert dangers or risks to health resulting from product properties. The scope of this exception covers standards for gasoline directed at the protection of clean air[78] as well as restrictions on carcinogenic substances like asbestos.[79] It is

---

[76] WTO, *China: Measures Affecting Trading Rights and Distribution Services for Certain Publications and Audiovisual Entertainment Products—Report of the Appellate Body* (2009) WT/ DS363/ AB/R.

[77] WTO, *European Communities: Measures Prohibiting the Importation and Marketing of Seal Products—Report of the Appellate Body* (2014) WT/DS400/AB/R and WT/DS401/AB/R paras 5.131ff, 5.200ff.

[78] See WTO, *United States: Standards for Reformulated and Conventional Gasoline—Report of the Appellate Body* (1996) WT/DS2/AB/R paras 155ff.

[79] WTO, *European Communities: Measures Affecting Asbestos and Asbestos-Containing Products—Report of the Appellate Body* (2001) WT/DS135/AB/R paras 157ff.

an unsettled issue whether Article XX(b) also applies to measures protecting human life or health in the State of origin of a product.[80] The wording 'necessary to protect' suggests a more restrictive interpretation. Still, it is at least arguable that Article XX(b) covers production-related measures which target child labour and inhuman labour conditions.

The application of Article XX(b) of the GATT raises particular difficulties when different regulatory philosophies (expressing different societal perceptions) with respect to risks and precaution collide. The hard cases are triggered by risk scenarios in which available scientific knowledge has not (yet) reliably established or dismissed a causal link between certain product properties and potential damages to health. The SPS Agreement[81] lays down rather detailed standards for the evaluation and management of health risks. Compliance of measures with the SPS standards means conformity with Article XX(b) of the GATT (Article 2(4) of the SPS Agreement).

Members may rely on Article XX(b) once a scientifically identified risk is established. It is then not necessary to quantify the risk as to the period of time the risk takes to materialize.[82] If the causal link is substantiated, the appropriate level of protection falls within the discretion of WTO members.[83]

(f) Measures necessary to secure compliance with certain laws or regulations (Article XX(d) of the GATT)

Article XX(d) of the GATT covers measures necessary to secure the compliance with certain laws or regulations which are in conformity with the GATT, for example tax and customs laws or rules on patent protection.

In *India—Certain Measures Relating to Solar Cells and Solar Modules*, India tried to defend local content requirements for solar cells and solar modules under Article XX(d) and, inter alia, invoked international instruments on climate change and a national action plan. The Panel found that the terms 'laws or regulations' must be construed narrowly and concluded that these terms 'refer to legally enforceable rules of conduct under the domestic legal system of the WTO Member concerned, and do not include general objectives'.[84]

---

[80] In WTO, *European Communities: Conditions for the Granting of Tariff Preferences for Developing Countries—Report of the Panel* (2003) WT/DS246/R para 7.210 the Panel found 'that the policy reflected in the Drug Arrangements' did not purport 'human life or health *in the European Communities* and, therefore [...] are not a measure [...] under Article XX(b) of GATT 1994'.

[81] See Ch XV.

[82] WTO, *European Communities: Measures Affecting Asbestos and Asbestos-Containing Products—Report of the Appellate Body* (2001) WT/DS135/AB/R para 167.

[83] WTO, *European Communities: Measures Affecting Asbestos and Asbestos-Containing Products—Report of the Appellate Body* (2001) WT/DS135/AB/R para 168: '[...] WTO members have the right to determine the level of protection of health that they consider appropriate in a given situation'.

[84] WTO, *India: Certain Measures Relating to Solar Cells and Solar Modules—Report of the Panel* (2016) WT/DS456/R para 7.311.

These measures are subject to a two-tiered test:[85]

1. the measure must serve the compliance with laws or regulations which are in conformity with the GATT; and

2. the measure must be proportionate.

As the Appellate Body held in *Korea—Measures Affecting Imports of Fresh, Chilled and Frozen Beef*, the test of proportionality

[...] involves in every case a process of weighing and balancing a series of factors which prominently include the contribution made by the compliance measure to the enforcement of the law or regulation at issue, the importance of the common interests or values protected by that law or regulation, and the accompanying impact of the law or regulation on imports or exports.[86]

A crucial aspect of proportionality is that the measure must be necessary. A measure fails this test if the same result could have been achieved by a measure with a less trade-restricting effect. In *Dominican Republic—Import and Sale of Cigarettes* the Appellate Body upheld the Panel Report's finding that the requirement that the tag on imported cigarettes certifying the payment of taxes was attached within the Dominican Republic prior to final packaging was unnecessary. For it was possible to reach the objective by attaching these tags during the production process.[87]

The higher the relative importance of the protected interest is, the easier it is to justify a measure of enforcement:

It seems to us that a treaty interpreter assessing a measure claimed to be necessary to secure compliance of a WTO-consistent law or regulation may, in appropriate cases, take into account the relative importance of the common interests or values that the law or regulation to be enforced is intended to protect. The more vital or important those common interests or values are, the easier it would be to accept as 'necessary' a measure designed as an enforcement instrument.[88]

(g) Measures relating to the conservation of exhaustible natural resources (Article XX(g) of the GATT)

Over time, the exception for measures relating to the conservation of exhaustible resources (Article XX(g) of the GATT) has become relevant in a number of different contexts. The exception covers two types of measures:

(1) the preservation of mineral, fossil, and other resources used for energy generation or the production of industrial goods; and

(2) environmental protection.

---

[85] See WTO, *Korea: Measures Affecting Imports of Fresh, Chilled and Frozen Beef—Report of the Appellate Body* (2000) WT/DS161/AB/R para 157.

[86] WTO, *Korea: Measures Affecting Imports of Fresh, Chilled and Frozen Beef—Report of the Appellate Body* (2000) WT/DS161/AB/R para 164.

[87] WTO, *Dominican Republic: Measures Affecting the Importation and Internal Sale of Cigarettes—Report of the Appellate Body* (2005) WT/DS302/AB/R para 72.

[88] See WTO, *Korea: Measures Affecting Imports of Fresh, Chilled and Frozen Beef—Report of the Appellate Body* (2000) WT/DS161/AB/R para 162.

The term 'exhaustible natural resources' also includes clean air, as the Panel Report in *US—Gasoline* recognized:

In the view of the Panel, clean air was a resource (it had value) and it was natural. It could be depleted. The fact that the depleted resource was defined with respect to its qualities was not, for the Panel, decisive. Likewise, the fact that a resource was renewable could not be an objection. A past panel had accepted the renewable stocks of salmon could constitute an exhaustible natural resource. Accordingly, the Panel found that a policy to reduce the depletion of clean air was a policy to conserve a natural resource within the meaning of Article XX(g).[89]

By contrast, 'climate' as such hardly qualifies as a 'exhaustible natural resource', but is rather a state of conditions resulting from the interplay of physical components. The depletable ozone layer is a doubtful candidate because it cannot be exploited like other natural substances. Therefore, it is difficult to bring sustainability criteria for bio-fuel production (such as those established under EU law) within the ambit of Article XX(g) of the GATT.[90]

Article XX(g) covers measures relating to the conservation of exhaustible natural resources only, 'if such measures are made effective in conjunction with restrictions on domestic production or consumption'.

This wording requires a fair and balanced treatment of domestic and foreign production or of domestic and foreign consumption which genuinely aims at conservation and avoids unfair distribution of the burden associated with this objective as to the access to natural resources ('even-handedness'). The Panel Report in *China—Rare Earths*,[91] which was later confirmed by the Appellate Body,[92] makes abundantly clear that the preservation of exhaustible natural resources under Article XX(g) cannot justify restrictions on export combined with unrestricted access of domestic industries to raw materials:

In the Panel's view, the assessment of compliance with subparagraph (g) should focus on the architecture and the design of the challenged measure to determine whether it has a substantial link with conservation, e.g. whether it supports, assists, or contributes to conservation of the resources at issue since the object of the analysis under subparagraph (g) is for the Panel to determine whether China's export quotas on rare earths, tungsten, and molybdenum

---

[89] WTO, *United States: Standards for Reformulated and Conventional Gasoline—Report of the Panel* (1996) WT/DS2/R para 6.37. The Panel Report was essentially confirmed by the Appellate Body, WTO, *United States: Standards for Reformulated and Conventional Gasoline—Report of the Appellate Body* (1996) WT/DS2/AB/R paras 14ff.

[90] See WT Douma, 'Legal Aspects of the European Union's Biofuels Policy: Protection or Protectionism?' (2010) 53 GYIL 371; S Switzer and JA McMahon, 'EU Biofuels Policy—Raising the Question of WTO Compatibility' (2011) 60 ICLQ 713.

[91] WTO, *China: Measures Related to the Exportation of Rare Earths, Tungsten, and Molybdenum— Report of the Panel* (2014) WT/DS431/R, WT/DS432/R, and WT/DS433/R, para 7.328; see also WTO, *China: Measures Related to the Exportation of Various Raw Materials—Reports of the Appellate Body* (2012) WT/DS394/AB/R, WT/DS395/AB/R, and WT/DS398/AB/R.

[92] WTO, *China: Measures Related to the Exportation of Rare Earths, Tungsten, and Molybdenum— Reports of the Appellate Body* (2014) WT/DS431/AB/R, WT/DS432/AB/R, and WT/DS433/AB/R; see also the case note by E Trujillo in (2015) 109 AJIL 616.

are about conservation. As the Panel discussed above, subparagraph (g) includes several elements that together impose requirements that aim at ensuring that measures invoked as exceptions for conservation are really about conservation. In the Panel's view, the even-handedness requirement of subparagraph (g) mentioned by the Appellate Body serves as an analytical tool to help in assessing whether the challenged measure assists, supports, or contributes to conservation of the concerned natural resources. As the Panel sees it, measures allegedly adopted for the conservation of natural resources situated within a Member's territory cannot be said to 'relate to' conservation if such measures exempt or otherwise do not control domestic actions that deplete or deteriorate the natural resource in question. In other words, if domestic users of a resource are exempted from the domestic restriction, it will be difficult to conclude that a GATT-inconsistent measure supposedly justified under Article XX(g) properly 'relates to' conservation, since unregulated domestic exploitation could undermine such conservation—and this would be especially the case when the majority of what is to be conserved is consumed only domestically. In the present case, the Panel recalls that China's consumers represent an important share of world consumption of rare earths that China says it wants to conserve; China, accordingly, must be able to demonstrate that it is taking action to regulate the domestic consumption that constitutes a significant share of the global usage of rare earths and that is a serious threat to conservation.[93]

In sum, the Panel concluded:

[…] [T]he 'even-handedness' criterion is satisfied where the regulating Member can show that, in addition to its GATT-inconsistent measures, it has also imposed real conservation restrictions on the domestic production or consumption of the resource subject to its GATT-inconsistent measures. These domestic measures must distribute the burden of conservation between foreign and domestic consumers in an even-handed or balanced manner. However, 'even-handedness' under subparagraph (g) does not require the Panel to assess the effects of the concerned restrictions. Instead, the relevant 'balance' or 'even-handedness' under subparagraph (g) is structural or regulatory. The balanced or even-handed nature of the domestic and foreign restrictions should be evident from the design, structure, and architecture of the challenged measure. Therefore, the Panel believes that issues relating to the effects of China's challenged export quotas on prices, as well as the question why the challenged export quotas were not filled and what effect if any an unfilled export quota has on foreign consumers, are concerned with the application and effects of the challenged export quotas, which are properly assessed under the chapeau of Article XX.[94]

The exception of Article XX(g) of the GATT does not only apply to measures protecting mineral or other inanimate resources, but also covers import restrictions for the protection of endangered species which live partly inside, partly outside the territory, the territorial sea, or the exclusive economic zone of a WTO Member State (eg migratory marine species).

In the case *US—Shrimp*, the Appellate Body stated that migration established a sufficient nexus for the protection of endangered sea turtles and that the preservation of endangered species is now recognized as an interest of the whole international

---

[93] WTO, *China: Measures Related to the Exportation of Rare Earths, Tungsten, and Molybdenum—Report of the Panel* (2014) WT/DS431/R, WT/DS432/R, and WT/DS433/R, para 7.328.
[94] WTO, *China: Measures Related to the Exportation of Rare Earths, Tungsten, and Molybdenum—Report of the Panel* (2014) WT/DS431/R, WT/DS432/R, and WT/DS433/R, para 7.337.

community.[95] In this context, universal treaties for the protection of endangered species as well as the commitment to 'sustainable development' in the preamble of the WTO Agreement support a broad interpretation of Article XX(g) in favour of measures with an extraterritorial reach. The Appellate Body stated:

130. From the perspective embodied in the preamble of the WTO Agreement, we note that the generic term 'natural resources' in Article XX(g) is not 'static' in its content or reference but is rather 'by definition, evolutionary'. [...] It is, therefore, pertinent to note that modern international conventions and declarations make frequent references to natural resources as embracing both living and non-living resources [...].

131. Given the recent acknowledgement by the international community of the importance of concerted bilateral or multilateral action to protect living natural resources, and recalling the explicit recognition by WTO Members of the objective of sustainable development in the preamble of the WTO Agreement, we believe it is too late in the day to suppose that Article XX(g) of the GATT 1994 may be read as referring only to the conservation of exhaustible mineral or other non-living natural resources. Moreover, two adopted GATT 1947 panel reports previously found fish to be an 'exhaustible natural resource' within the meaning of Article XX(g). We hold that, in line with the principle of effectiveness in treaty interpretation measures to conserve exhaustible natural resources, whether *living* or *non-living*, may fall within Article XX(g).[96]

(h) Measures essential to the acquisition or distribution of products in general or local short supply (Article XX(j) of the GATT)

Under Article XX(j), members may take measures

essential to the acquisition or distribution of products in general or local short supply; Provided that any such measures shall be consistent with the principle that all contracting parties are entitled to an equitable share of the international supply of such products, and that any such measures, which are inconsistent with the other provisions of the Agreement shall be discontinued as soon as the conditions giving rise to them have ceased to exist. [...].

In *India—Certain Measures Relating to Solar Cells and Solar Modules*[97], India relied on this exception to justify local content requirements for solar cells and solar modules. It advanced an 'evolutionary interpretation' and argued that Article XX(j) covers measures which address the lack of domestic manufacturing capacity and the dependence of solar product developers on imported products. The Panel rejected this approach and concluded that

[...] the terms 'products in general or local short supply' refer to a situation in which the quantity of available supply of a product, from all sources, does not meet demand in

---

[95] WTO, *United States: Import Prohibition of Certain Shrimp and Shrimp Products—Report of the Appellate Body* (1998) WT/DS58/AB/R para 131.

[96] WTO, *United States: Import Prohibition of Certain Shrimp and Shrimp Products—Report of the Appellate Body* (1998) WT/DS58/AB/R para 131f.

[97] WTO, *India: Certain Measures Relating to Solar Cells and Solar Modules—Report of the Panel* (2016) WT/ DS456/ R.

a relevant geographical area or market. We do not consider that India's manufacturing capacity for solar cells and modules is irrelevant to the question of whether those are 'products in general or local short supply' in India. Rather, our view is that a product is 'in general or local short supply' when the quantity of available supply of that product, from all sources, does not meet demand in the relevant geographical area or market in question. This includes all available sources of supply, including both foreign and domestic sources. Domestic manufacturing capacity is therefore one variable that must be taken into account to assess whether solar cells and modules are products in short supply in India. In other words, our view is that a lack of domestic production in the products at issue is a necessary, but not sufficient, condition for finding that supply of that product, from all sources, does not meet demand in the relevant geographical area or market in question.[98]

This interpretation rightly takes account of the global supply of goods. As a consequence, it severely restricts the practical ambit of this exception in a world with integrated markets.

6. Security Exceptions (Article XXI of the GATT)

Article XXI of the GATT allows WTO members to take measures for the protection of their security interests.[99] Paragraph b has a particularly broad scope:

Nothing in this Agreement shall be construed [...]
(b) to prevent any contracting party from taking any action which it considers necessary for the protection of its essential security interests
  (i) relating to fissionable materials or the materials from which they are derived;
  (ii) relating to the traffic in arms, ammunition and implements of war and to such traffic in other goods and materials as is carried on directly or indirectly for the purpose of supplying a military establishment;
  (iii) taken in time of war or other emergency in international relations; [...].

The wording of the provision ('which it considers necessary') vests the contracting parties with a very wide margin of appreciation, making the exception more or less 'self-judging'. Article XXI(b)(iii) covers trade restrictions in time of military confrontation and severe tensions. It is arguable that this exception applies to restrictions of trade in response to serious breaches of international law like the violation of fundamental human rights. Under current international law, massive violations of elementary human rights or other fundamental rules (self-determination, protection of diplomatic missions) qualified as a breach of obligations *erga omnes* violate the interests of each member of the international

---

[98] WTO, *India: Certain Measures Relating to Solar Cells and Solar Modules—Report of the Panel* (2016) WT/DS456/R para 7.234.

[99] See AS Alexandroff and R Sharma, 'The National Security Provision—GATT Article XXI' in PFJ Macrory, AE Appleton, and MG Plummer (eds), *The World Trade Organization: Legal, Economic and Political Analysis* (Springer 2005) vol 1, 1571.

community.[100] Otherwise, for such violations of international law only unilateral sanctions in the form of trade restrictions based on the general rules of state responsibility are justified (as a form of reprisal or retaliation). Furthermore, the exception of Article XXI(c) of the GATT allows the Member States to obey binding obligations under Chapter VII of the UN Charter serving the maintenance of international peace and security.

7. Safeguard Measures (Article XIX of the GATT)

The exception of Article XIX:1(a) of the GATT allows contracting parties to take emergency measures for the protection of domestic industries, if

> [...] as a result of unforeseen developments and of the effect of the obligations incurred by a contracting party under this Agreement, including tariff concessions, any product is being imported into the territory of that contracting party in such increased quantities and under such conditions as to cause or threaten serious injury to domestic producers in that territory of like or directly competitive products, the contracting party shall be free, in respect of such product, and to the extent and for such time as may be necessary to prevent or remedy such injury, to suspend the obligation in whole or in part or to withdraw or modify the concession.

A similar exception applies to the import of goods which are subject to a preference (Article XIX:1(b) of the GATT).

The Agreement on Safeguards[101] lays down special procedural requirements which govern the exceptions under Article XIX of the GATT. In practice, the application of the safeguard clause of Article XIX was circumvented for a long time by the agreements which established a special regime for certain goods outside the GATT framework. One of those regimes resulted from the former World Textile Agreement with its import quotas. A number of voluntary export restraints,[102] in the form of intergovernmental agreements or unilateral measures, in many areas eroded GATT principles (eg the most-favoured-nation treatment and the prohibition of non-tariff barriers to trade). In the long run, the protectionist cover resulting from such voluntary export restraints isolates certain markets, disadvantages consumers, and curbs innovation. Over the years, all these special regimes in many areas led to a 'GATT à la carte'. Under Article 11(1)(b) of the Agreement on Safeguards there is no more room for self-restraining agreements.

---

[100] JA Frowein, 'Obligations erga omnes' in R Wolfrum (ed), *The Max Planck Encyclopedia of Public International Law* (OUP 2012) vol VII, 916.

[101] See AO Sykes, *The WTO Agreement on Safeguards: A Commentary* (OUP 2006); YS Lee, 'The Agreement of Safeguards' in PFJ Macrory, AE Appleton, and MG Plummer (eds), *The World Trade Organization: Legal, Economic and Political Analysis* (Springer 2005) vol I, 749.

[102] See K Jones, 'Voluntary Export Restraints: Political Economy, History and the Role of the GATT' (1989) 23 JWT 125.

8. Waivers

The 'waiver clause' of Article XXV:5 of the GATT was of great practical importance, especially for the preferential treatment of developing countries[103] in terms
of the Enabling Clause.[104] Since the establishment of the WTO, Article IX:3 of
the WTO Agreement serves as a general basis for waivers. Under this provision,
the contracting parties may, by a three-quarters majority, decide that certain obligations under the WTO Agreement or any other of the multilateral agreements
do not apply to one of the parties or a group of parties. Such a waiver calls for
'exceptional circumstances'. The 'Understanding in respect of Obligations under
the General Agreement on Tariffs and Trade 1994', which is part of the GATT,[105]
lays down the procedure for the granting of waivers in more detail and applies to
waivers which were granted under the GATT 1947 and are still in force.

9. Burden of Proof

According to the case-law of the Dispute Settlement Body, a WTO member which
complains about a measure merely has to provide *prima facie* evidence that the
measure is inconsistent with the GATT. By contrast, the member relying on an
exception (eg under Article XX of the GATT) has to provide full evidence.[106]

Select Bibliography

GENERAL LITERATURE

PC Mavroidis, *The General Agreement on Tariffs and Trade: A Commentary* (OUP 2005).
PC Mavroidis, *Trade in Goods* (2nd edn, OUP 2012).
R Wolfrum, PT Stoll, and HR Hestermeyer (eds), *WTO: Trade in Goods* (Brill Academic
  Publishers 2010).

GENERAL EXCEPTIONS (ARTICLE XX OF THE GATT)

L Bartels, 'The Chapeau of the General Exceptions in the WTO GATT and GATS
  Agreements: A Reconstruction' (2015) 109 AJIL 95.

---

[103] See Section 2(b)(ii) in this Chapter.
[104] Differential and More Favourable Treatment, Reciprocity and Fuller Participation of Developing
Countries (1979) GATT 26th Supp BISD (L/4903).
[105] See Introductory Note to GATT 1994 1(c)(v); see I Feichtner, *The Law and Politics of WTO
Waivers: Stability and Flexibility in Public International Law* (CUP 2012).
[106] WTO, *Japan: Measures Affecting the Importation of Apples—Report of the Appellate Body* (2003)
WT/DS245/AB/R para 160; see generally MT Grando, *Evidence, Proof, and Fact-Finding in WTO
Dispute Settlement* (OUP 2009).

L Bartels, 'Article XX of GATT and the Problem of Extraterritorial Jurisdiction. The Case of Trade Measures for the Protection of Human Rights' (2002) 36 JWT 353.

SECURITY EXCEPTIONS (ARTICLE XXI OF THE GATT)

D Eisenhut, 'Sovereignty. National Security and International Treaty Law' (2010) 48 AVR 437.
MJ Hahn, 'Vital Interests and the Law of GATT: An Analysis of GATT's Security Exception' (1991) 12 Mich J Int'l L 558.

SAFEGUARD MEASURES (ARTICLE XIX OF THE GATT)

MJ Hahn, 'Balancing or Bending? Unilateral Reactions to Safeguard Measures' (2005) 39 JWT 301.
YS Lee, Safeguard Measures in World Trade: The Legal Analysis (3rd edn, Edward Elgar Publishing 2014).

XV

The Agreement on the Application of Sanitary and Phytosanitary Measures (SPS)

The Agreement on Sanitary and Phytosanitary Measures (SPS Agreement)[1] establishes standards for trade restrictions which shall protect the life and health of humans, animals, and plants. The SPS standards are far more specific than the exception of Article XX(b) of the GATT. The SPS Agreement 'applies to all sanitary and phytosanitary measures which may, directly or indirectly, affect international trade' (Article 1.1 first sentence) and requires that '[s]uch measures shall be developed and applied in accordance with the provisions of this Agreement'. In legal terms, the SPS Agreement has a double function: it subjects even non-discriminatory and otherwise GATT-consistent measures to rather detailed requirements. At the same time, conformity of measures with the SPS Agreement always signifies conformity with the GATT.

Sanitary and phytosanitary measures are defined in Annex A(1) to the SPS Agreement:

Sanitary or phytosanitary measure—Any measure applied:
(a) to protect animal or plant life or health within the territory of the Member from risks arising from the entry, establishment or spread of pests, diseases, disease-carrying organisms or disease-causing organisms;
(b) to protect human or animal life or health within the territory of the Member from risks arising from additives, contaminants, toxins or disease-causing organisms in foods, beverages or feedstuffs;
(c) to protect human life or health within the territory of the Member from risks arising from diseases carried by animals, plants or products thereof, or from the entry, establishment or spread of pests; or
(d) to prevent or limit other damage within the territory of the Member from the entry, establishment or spread of pests.

Sanitary or phytosanitary measures include all relevant laws, decrees, regulations, requirements and procedures including, *inter alia*, end product criteria; processes and production methods; testing, inspection, certification and approval procedures; quarantine treatments including relevant requirements associated with the transport of animals or plants, or with

---

[1] D Prévost and P van den Bossche, 'The Agreement on the Application of Sanitary and Phytosanitary Measures' in PFJ Macrory, AE Appleton, and MG Plummer (eds), *The World Trade Organization: Legal, Economic and Political Analysis* (Springer 2005) vol 1, 231.

the materials necessary for their survival during transport; provisions on relevant statistical methods, sampling procedures and methods of risk assessment; and packaging and labelling requirements directly related to food safety.

Measures coming within this definition are subject to the SPS Agreement, even if they pursue broader goals of environmental protection.[2] The Panel Report in *EC—Biotech Products* extends the 'spread of pests' as defined in Annex A(1)(a), (b), (c), and (d) to measures against the unwanted spread of genetically modified organisms.[3]

As a comprehensive legal framework for sanitary and phytosanitary measures, the SPS Agreement has its own scope of application which is autonomous from the GATT. In addition, measures which comply with the SPS Agreement are regarded as being in conformity with the GATT, as Article 2.4 of the SPS Agreement states:

Sanitary or phytosanitary measures which conform to the relevant provisions of this Agreement shall be presumed to be in accordance with the obligations of the Members under the provisions of GATT 1994 which relate to the use of sanitary or phytosanitary measures, in particular the provisions of Article XX(b).

The three overarching parameters for sanitary and phytosanitary measures are

* their limitation to the necessary extent (Articles 2.1 and 2.2);
* support by scientific evidence (Articles 2.2, 5.2); and
* guidance of risk assessment by international standards (Articles 3, 5.1).

According to Article 2.2,

Members shall ensure that any sanitary or phytosanitary measure is applied only to the extent necessary to protect human, animal or plant life or health, is based on scientific principles and is not maintained without sufficient scientific evidence, except as provided for in paragraph 7 of Article 5.

In principle, WTO members must be guided by available 'international standards, guidelines or recommendations' (Article 3.1). Measures that conform to such international standards shall be deemed necessary (Article 3.2). A member's risk assessment may go beyond internationally recognized standards, if this choice of a higher level of protection is scientifically justified or meets the requirements of Article 5 paragraphs 1 to 8 (Article 3.3 first sentence). Article 3.4 refers, in particular, to

the relevant international organizations and their subsidiary bodies, in particular the Codex Alimentarius Commission, the International Office of Epizootics, and the international and regional organizations operating within the framework of the International Plant Protection Convention […].

    [2] WTO, *European Communities: Measures Affecting the Approval and Marketing of Biotech Products—Report of the Panel* (2006) WT/DS291/R para 7.203.
    [3] WTO, *European Communities: Measures Affecting the Approval and Marketing of Biotech Products—Report of the Panel* (2006) WT/DS291/R paras 7.231ff.

The Codex Alimentarius, elaborated by a common commission of the Food and Agricultural Organization and the World Health Organization, lays down particularly important health standards for food, which have become a point of reference for risk assessment all over the world.

Risk assessment and the determination of the appropriate level of protection must take into account methods developed by the relevant international organizations (Article 5.1) as well as available scientific evidence (Article 5.2).

In the 'hormones dispute' (*EC—Hormones US*),[4] the Appellate Body made some important clarifications on the necessary scientific substantiation as the basis of sanitary and phytosanitary measures. In this dispute, the United States challenged a regulation of the European Community which prohibited the marketing and import of beef stemming from hormone-treated cattle. By prescribing a zero level of hormones in meat, the European Community opted for a stricter level of health protection than the tolerance standard of the Codex Alimentarius Commission. The European Community tried to justify its measures invoking potential health risks caused by even low hormone level residues. The United States considered the European policy as an expression of overstrained risk-aversion, inspired by 'phantom risks'.

The Appellate Body held that mere theoretical uncertainty about the harmful effects of a substance on human health does not meet the standard of adequate scientific evidence. Only a 'scientifically identified risk' may trigger legitimate measures. The theoretical possibility of harmful effects alone lacks a minimum of an empirical support.[5] There must be a 'rational relationship' between the risk assessment on the one hand and the trade-restrictive measure on the other.[6] This 'rational relationship' does not necessarily need to rest on prevailing scientific opinion. It may also be established on the basis of minority views within the scientific community:

We do not believe that a risk assessment has to come to a monolithic conclusion that coincides with the scientific conclusion or view implicit in the SPS measure. The risk assessment could set out both the prevailing view representing the 'mainstream' of scientific opinion, as well as the opinions of scientists taking a divergent view. Article 5.1 does not require that the risk assessment must necessarily embody only the view of a majority of the relevant scientific community. In some cases, the very existence of divergent views presented by

[4] WTO, *European Communities: Measures Concerning Meat and Meat Products (Hormones)—Report of the Appellate Body* (1998) WT/DS26/AB/R and WT/DS48/AB/R; see MM Slotboom, 'The Hormones Case: An Increased Risk of Illegality of Phytosanitary Measures' (1999) 36 CML Rev 401; VR Walker, 'Keeping the WTO from Becoming the "World Trans-Science Organization": Scientific Uncertainty, Science Policy and Factfinding in the Growth Hormones Dispute' (1998) 31 Cornell Int'l LJ 251.
[5] WTO, *European Communities: Measures Concerning Meat and Meat Products (Hormones)—Report of the Appellate Body* (1998) WT/DS26/AB/R and WT/DS48/AB/R para 186.
[6] WTO, *European Communities: Measures Concerning Meat and Meat Products (Hormones)—Report of the Appellate Body* (1998) WT/DS26/AB/R and WT/DS48/AB/R paras 193f.

qualified scientists who have investigated the particular issue at hand may indicate a state of scientific uncertainty. Sometimes the divergence may indicate a roughly equal balance of scientific opinion, which may itself be a form of scientific uncertainty. In most cases, responsible and representative governments tend to base their legislative and administrative measures on 'mainstream' scientific opinion. In other cases, equally responsible and representative governments may act in good faith on the basis of what, at a given time, may be a divergent opinion coming from qualified and respected sources. By itself, this does not necessarily signal the absence of a reasonable relationship between the SPS measure and the risk assessment, especially where the risk involved is life-threatening in character and is perceived to constitute a clear and imminent threat to public health and safety. Determination of the presence or absence of that relationship can only be done on a case-by-case basis, after account is taken of all considerations rationally bearing upon the issue of potential adverse health effects.[7]

A source must be recognized as 'qualified and respectable' whenever its views are based on methods which the scientific community recognizes as sustainable (even if controversial).

The Panel in *Japan—Apples*, which was confirmed by the Appellate Body,[8] held that only recognized scientific methods can provide 'sufficient scientific evidence' in terms of Article 2.2 of the SPS Agreement and that unproved hypotheses are inadequate.[9]

The Appellate Body does not insist on evidence only under laboratory conditions, but allows a risk assessment guided by practical reason with regard to the conditions of real life:

It is essential to bear in mind that the risk that is to be evaluated in a risk assessment under Article 5.1 is not only risk ascertainable in a science laboratory operating under strictly controlled conditions, but also risk in human societies as they actually exist, in other words, the actual potential for adverse effects on human health in the real world where people live and work and die.[10]

In *EC—Hormones*, the European Community's prohibition, based on adequately substantiated presumptions, fell short of the standards of science-based rationality.

A crucial issue is the relation between the standards of the SPS Agreement and the principle of precaution. If scientific evidence does not (yet) provide reliable guidance, members still may take sanitary and phytosanitary measures. The SPS Agreement allows members to opt for a particularly high level of protection (paragraph 6 of the Preamble, Article 3.3). In the light of insufficient scientific evidence, members may take provisional measures unsupported by international

[7] WTO, *European Communities: Measures Concerning Meat and Meat Products (Hormones)—Report of the Appellate Body* (1998) WT/DS26/AB/R and WT/DS48/AB/R para 194.
[8] WTO, *Japan: Measures Affecting the Importation of Apples—Report of the Appellate Body* (2003) WT/DS245/AB/R.
[9] WTO, *Japan: Measures Affecting the Importation of Apples—Report of the Panel* (2003) WT/DS245/R para 8.92f.
[10] WTO, *European Communities: Measures Concerning Meat and Meat Products (Hormones)—Report of the Appellate Body* (1998) WT/DS26/AB/R and WT/DS48/AB/R para 187.

standards under Article 5.7. The standard of 'sufficient scientific evidence' (Article 2.2), by including minority views in the scientific community, allows measures to counter possible harmful effects even if they do not result from a reliable chain of causation. Within these parameters, the SPS Agreement embodies the widely recognized precautionary principle.[11] In *EC—Hormones*, the Appellate Body emphasized that the precautionary principle, whilst reflected in the SPS Agreement, does not justify a departure from the standards of justification laid down in Articles 5.1 and 5.2 of the SPS Agreement:[12]

It appears to us important, nevertheless, to note some aspects of the relationship of the precautionary principle to the SPS Agreement. First, the principle has not been written into the SPS Agreement as a ground for justifying SPS measures that are otherwise inconsistent with the obligations of Members set out in particular provisions of that Agreement. Secondly, the precautionary principle indeed finds reflection in Article 5.7 of the SPS Agreement. We agree, at the same time, with the European Communities, that there is no need to assume that Article 5.7 exhausts the relevance of a precautionary principle. It is reflected also in the sixth paragraph of the preamble and in Article 3.3. These explicitly recognize the right of Members to establish their own appropriate level of sanitary protection, which level may be higher (i.e., more cautious) than that implied in existing international standards, guidelines and recommendations. Thirdly, a panel charged with determining, for instance, whether 'sufficient scientific evidence' exists to warrant the maintenance by a Member of a particular SPS measure may, of course, and should, bear in mind that responsible, representative governments commonly act from perspectives of prudence and precaution where risks of irreversible, e.g. life-terminating, damage to human health are concerned. Lastly, however, the precautionary principle does not, by itself, and without a clear textual directive to that effect, relieve a panel from the duty of applying the normal (i.e. customary international law) principles of treaty interpretation in reading the provisions of the SPS Agreement.[13]

The required risk assessment does not demand that a scientifically substantiated risk is quantified in terms of a tolerance level.[14] A member may also opt for excluding residual risks altogether ('zero-risk level').[15] Thus, the SPS Agreement leaves room for the different degrees of risk aversion among members. Within sustainable scientific parameters, the SPS Agreement thus defers to cultural diversity expressed in sanitary and phytosanitary measures.

---

[11] See I Cheyne, 'Risk and Precaution in World Trade Organization Law' (2006) 40 JWT 837; L Gruszczynski, *Regulating Health and Environmental Risks Under WTO Law: A Critical Analysis of the SPS Agreement* (OUP 2010) 177ff.

[12] For a critical appraisal of the regulation of health and environmental risks in general, see L Gruszczynski, *Regulating Health and Environmental Risks Under WTO Law: A Critical Analysis of the SPS Agreement* (OUP 2010) chs 4, 5, and 6, with an emphasis on the hormones dispute at 219ff.

[13] WTO, *European Communities: Measures Concerning Meat and Meat Products (Hormones)— Report of the Appellate Body* (1998) WT/DS26/AB/R and WT/DS48/AB/R para 124.

[14] WTO, *European Communities: Measures Concerning Meat and Meat Products (Hormones)— Report of the Appellate Body* (1998) WT/DS26/AB/R and WT/DS48/AB/R para 186.

[15] WTO, *Australia: Measures Affecting Importation of Salmon—Report of the Appellate Body* (1998) WT/DS18/AB/R para 125.

In *Australia—Salmon*, the Appellate Body further specified the required elements of a risk assessment under Article 5.1 of the SPS Agreement.[16] When assessing risks, members must take three steps:

[W]e consider that, in this case, a risk assessment within the meaning of Article 5.1 must:
(1) *identify* the diseases whose entry, establishment or spread a Member wants to prevent within its territory, as well as the potential biological and economic consequences associated with the entry, establishment or spread of these diseases;
(2) *evaluate the likelihood* of entry, establishment or spread of the diseases, as well as the associated potential biological and economic consequences; and
(3) evaluate the likelihood of entry, establishment or spread of these diseases *according to the SPS measures which might be applied.*[17]

In *Japan—Apples*, the Panel and the Appellate Body[18] provided some fine-tuning of the standards for risk management.[19]

This dispute referred to far-reaching restrictions on the import of apples from the United States, with the objective to prevent the spread of fire blight in Japan. These measures ranged from intensive examinations over quarantines to a total import ban. The Panel and the Appellate Body subjected the Japanese risk management to a scrutiny of proportionality. A 'rational or objective relationship' between a sanitary or phytosanitary measure and the given scientific evidence cannot be assumed, if the measure stands in 'clear disproportion'[20] to the detectable risk. The Panel qualified the measure at issue as excessive in the light of the established risk and concluded

[...] that the phytosanitary measure at issue is clearly disproportionate to the risk identified on the basis of the scientific evidence available. In particular, some of the requirements applied by Japan as integral parts of the measure at issue are, either individually or when applied cumulatively with the other requirements of that measure, not supported by sufficient scientific evidence within the meaning of Article 2.2 of the SPS Agreement.[21]

The Appellate Body confirmed this conclusion.[22]

If relevant scientific evidence is insufficient, Article 5.7 allows provisional measures. As the Appellate Body indicated in *Japan—Apples*, the available scientific

---

[16] WTO, *Australia: Measures Affecting Importation of Salmon—Report of the Appellate Body* (1998) WT/DS18/AB/R.
[17] WTO, *Australia: Measures Affecting Importation of Salmon—Report of the Appellate Body* (1998) WT/DS18/AB/R para 121.
[18] WTO, *Japan: Measures Affecting the Importation of Apples—Report of the Appellate Body* (2003) WT/DS245/AB/R.
[19] See G Goh, 'Tipping the Apple Cart: The Limits of Science and Law in the SPS Agreement After Japan—Apples' (2006) 40 JWT 655.
[20] WTO, *Japan: Measures Affecting the Importation of Apples—Report of the Panel* (2003) WT/DS245/R paras 8.198f; WTO, *Japan: Measures Affecting the Importation of Apples—Report of the Appellate Body* (2003) WT/DS245/AB/R para 163.
[21] WTO, *Japan: Measures Affecting the Importation of Apples—Report of the Panel* (2003) WT/DS245/R para 8.198.
[22] WTO, *Japan: Measures Affecting the Importation of Apples—Report of the Appellate Body* (2003) WT/DS245/AB/R para 163.

evidence must be considered 'insufficient' in terms of Article 5.7, if it does not permit an adequate assessment of risks under Article 5.1 of the SPS Agreement:

'Relevant scientific' evidence will be 'insufficient' within the meaning of Article 5.7 if the body of available scientific evidence does not allow, in quantitative or qualitative terms, the performance of an adequate assessment of risks as required under Article 5.1 and as defined in Annex A to the SPS Agreement.[23]

According to the Appellate Body Report in *Japan—Agricultural Products*, a member which resorts to provisional measures must subsequently try to gather further information and review the measures within reasonable time.[24]

The SPS Agreement has become the crucial frame of reference for divergent regulatory philosophies in regard to risks associated with new technologies.[25] The standards of the SPS Agreement, as interpreted in panel and Appellate Body reports, ensure a rather high degree of rationality of risk assessment and risk management in the light of available scientific evidence. They seriously curtail the members' discretion to give leeway to a marked risk aversion. This scrutiny of rationality particularly affects WTO members with strong sensitivity to all kinds of possible risks prevailing in societal perceptions and, consequently, in regulatory attitudes. Thus, 'socio-economic' resentments, for example in relation to genetically modified products (food, feed, seed, or pharmaceuticals), fall short of a rational justification under the SPS Agreement.[26]

The dispute *EC—Biotech Products*[27] is the first leading case over conflicting regulatory philosophies in the sector of biotechnology. In this case, the United States and other States complained against a moratorium of the European Community on the approval of the marketing of genetically modified products in the period of 1998–2004. The EC moratorium signified a *de facto* import ban on GMO products.

According to the Panel Report, the EC moratorium on the approval of biotech products fell within the scope of the SPS Agreement pursuant to Annex A(1).[28] As the moratorium had no regulatory content, it did not qualify as a 'measure' in terms of Article 5.1 and Annex A(1).[29] The Panel, however, considered the moratorium as a violation of the duty to timely process under Article 8 of the SPS Agreement

---

[23] WTO, *Japan: Measures Affecting the Importation of Apples—Report of the Appellate Body* (2003) WT/DS245/AB/R para 179.

[24] WTO, *Japan: Measures Affecting Agricultural Products—Report of the Appellate Body* (1999), WT/DS76/AB/R paras 92ff.

[25] N Covelli and V Hohots, 'The Health Regulation of Biotech Foods under The WTO Agreements' (2003) 6 J Intl Econ L 773.

[26] See M Herdegen, 'Biotechnology and Regulatory Risk Assessment' in G Bermann, M Herdegen, and P Lindseth (eds), *Transatlantic Regulatory Co-operation: Legal Problems and Political Prospects* (OUP 2001) 301.

[27] WTO, *European Communities: Measures Affecting the Approval and Marketing of Biotech Products—Report of the Panel* (2006) WT/DS291/R, WT/DS292/R, and WT/DS293/R.

[28] WTO, *European Communities: Measures Affecting the Approval and Marketing of Biotech Products—Report of the Panel* (2006) WT/DS291/R, WT/DS292/R, and WT/DS293/R paras 7.231ff.

[29] WTO, *European Communities: Measures Affecting the Approval and Marketing of Biotech Products—Report of the Panel* (2006) WT/DS291/R, WT/DS292/R, and WT/DS293/R paras 7.1343ff (7.1383).

in connection with Annex C(1)(a).[30] As the Panel underlined, a member may not invoke a moratorium to escape the risk assessment required by the SPS Agreement. Nor does the precautionary principle dispense with the duty to reach a decision without undue delay:

The other consideration to be noted relates to the use of procedural delay as an instrument to manage or control risks. It is useful to illustrate this using an example. For instance, if the European Communities delayed the completion of a particular approval procedure because existing legislation precluded it from imposing a traceability requirement for a GMO which would facilitate the withdrawal of the product in the event of unforeseen adverse effects on human health or the environment, the European Communities would effectively use procedural delay as a substitute for a substantive risk management measure (the traceability requirement) that would not be imposable under existing approval legislation. In our view, however, the pursuit of a risk management objective would not justify a delay in the completion of an approval procedure and hence would be inconsistent with Annex C(1)(a), first clause. If procedural delay could be used, directly or indirectly, as an instrument to manage or control risks, then Members could evade the obligations to be observed in respect of substantive SPS measures, such as Article 5.1, which requires that SPS measures be based on a risk assessment. Clearly, we cannot interpret Annex C(1)(a), first clause, in a manner which would nullify or impair the usefulness and intended effect of other provisions of the SPS Agreement. Indeed, as we see it, a central purpose of Annex C(1)(a), first clause, is precisely to prevent a situation where Members avoid the substantive disciplines which Articles 2 and 5 of the SPS Agreement impose with respect to substantive SPS decisions by not reaching final substantive decisions on applications for marketing approval.[31]

Select Bibliography

L Gruszczynski, *Regulating Health and Environmental Risks Under WTO Law: A Critical Analysis of the SPS Agreement* (OUP 2010).

D Prévost and P van den Bossche, 'The Agreement on the Application of Sanitary and Phytosanitary Measures' in PFJ Macrory, AE Appleton, and MG Plummer (eds), *The World Trade Organization: Legal, Economic and Political Analysis* (Springer 2005) vol 1, 231.

R Wolfrum, PT Stoll, and A Seibert-Fohr (eds), *WTO—Technical Barriers and SPS Measures* (Brill Academic Publishers 2007).

---

[30] WTO, *European Communities: Measures Affecting the Approval and Marketing of Biotech Products—Report of the Panel* (2006) WT/DS291/R, WT/DS292/R, and WT/DS293/R para 7.1569.

[31] WTO, *European Communities: Measures Affecting the Approval and Marketing of Biotech Products—Report of the Panel* (2006) WT/DS291/R, WT/DS292/R, and WT/DS293/R para 7.1517.

XVI

The Agreement on Technical Barriers to Trade

1. Relevance and Scope

The Agreement on Technical Barriers to Trade (TBT Agreement)[1] applies to technical regulations and other technical standards related to product characteristics or production processes such as labelling requirements. Technical requirements (regulations and standards) in terms of the TBT Agreement are, as a rule, less of a threat to international trade than the restrictive measures covered by the SPS Agreement which impede the market access to the product as such (eg because of its contents or composition). This difference justifies and explains a far more lenient standard of scrutiny for technical barriers to trade. Still, many technical provisions, such as requirements for labelling, may have a strong effect on market shares in light of consumer attitudes. A number of technical regulations are inspired by protectionist motives or have at least a protectionist effect by distorting competitive conditions in favour of domestic products, especially in context with the protection of public health.

'Technical regulations' refer to requirements for product characteristics and production processes which are mandatory. Annex 1.1 defines a 'technical regulation' as follows:

Document which lays down product characteristics or their related processes and production methods, including the applicable administrative provisions, with which compliance is mandatory. It may also include or deal exclusively with terminology, symbols, packaging, marking or labelling requirements as they apply to a product, process or production method.

By contrast, 'standards' are non-binding (Annex 1.2). The distinction raises problems, when legislation or other forms of regulation condition the voluntary use of labels and other characteristics by mandatory requirements. In *US—Tuna II—'Dolphin-Safe'*, the Appellate Body qualified regulatory requirements for the voluntary use of the label 'dolphin safe' as a technical regulation:

[...] [A] determination of whether a particular measure constitutes a technical regulation must be made in the light of the characteristics of the measure at issue and the circumstances of the case. In this case, we note that the US measure is composed of legislative and

---

[1] AE Appleton, 'The Agreement on Technical Barriers to Trade' in PFJ Macrory, AE Appleton, and MG Plummer (eds), *The World Trade Organization: Legal, Economic and Political Analysis* (Springer 2005) vol 1, 371.

regulatory acts of the US federal authorities and includes administrative provisions. In addition, the measure at issue sets out a single and legally mandated definition of a 'dolphin-safe' tuna product and disallows the use of other labels on tuna products that do not satisfy this definition. In doing so, the US measure prescribes in a broad and exhaustive manner the conditions that apply for making any assertion on a tuna product as to its 'dolphin-safety', regardless of the manner in which that statement is made. As a consequence, the US measure covers the entire field of what 'dolphin-safe' means in relation to tuna products. For these reasons, we find that the Panel did not err in characterizing the measure at issue as a 'technical regulation' within the meaning of Annex 1.1 to the TBT Agreement.[2]

2. National Treatment

Technical rules are subject to the national treatment principle and the most-favoured-nation principle (Article 2.1). National treatment requires 'even-handedness' of technical requirements. This standard is violated when a measure is designed or applied in a manner that amounts to arbitrary or unjustifiable, de jure or de facto discrimination.[3]

The principle of national treatment prohibits all forms of discrimination against imported products, but allows WTO members to pursue legitimate public interests such as the protection of health (as a kind of inherent limitation of the principle), as long as they act in an 'even-handed' manner and do not distort competitive conditions to the detriment of imported products.[4]

Thus, in *US—Clove Cigarettes*, the Appellate Body recognized the legitimate interest to reduce youth smoking, when it examined the ban on cigarettes with characterizing flavours other than tobacco and menthol:

[…] [T]he object and purpose of the *TBT Agreement* is to strike a balance between, on the one hand, the objective of trade liberalization and, on the other hand, Members' right to

---

[2] WTO, *United States: Measures Concerning the Importation, Marketing and Sale of Tuna and Tuna Products—Report of the Appellate Body* (2012) WT/DS381/AB/R para 199.

[3] See WTO, *United States: Certain Country of Origin Labelling (COOL) Requirements—Report of the Appellate Body* (2012) WT/DS384/AB/R and WT/DS386/AB/R para 293 on Country of Origin Labelling ('COOL') for imported livestock which creates incentives for meat producers to rely exclusively on US livestock; WTO, *United States: Measures Concerning the Importation, Marketing and Sale of Tuna and Tuna Products—Report of the Appellate Body* (2012) WT/DS381/AB/R paras 284, 297 on 'dolphin-safe' tuna labels establishing a *de facto* discrimination against Mexican tuna products; WTO, *United States: Measures Affecting the Production and Sale of Clove Cigarettes—Report of the Appellate Body* (2012) WT/DS406/AB/R paras 95, 175ff. (182), 215 on the prohibition of cigarettes containing a flavour, herb, or spice, except for menthol and tobacco, which primarily affects clove cigarettes imported from Indonesia.

[4] WTO, *United States: Measures Affecting the Production and Sale of Clove Cigarettes—Report of the Appellate Body* (2012) WT/DS406/AB/R para 182: '[…] in making a determination of whether a measure is *de facto* inconsistent with Article 2.1, "a panel must carefully scrutinize the particular circumstances of the case, that is, the design, architecture, revealing structure, operation, and application of the technical regulation at issue, and, in particular, whether that technical regulation is even-handed." '; WTO, *United States: Measures Concerning the Importation, Marketing and Sale of Tuna and Tuna Products—Report of the Appellate Body* (2012) WT/DS381/AB/R para 225.

regulate. This object and purpose therefore suggests that Article 2.1 should not be interpreted as prohibiting any detrimental impact on competitive opportunities for imports in cases where such detrimental impact on imports stems exclusively from legitimate regulatory distinctions. [5]

On the other hand, the Appellate Body underlined the equality of competitive conditions which calls for a consistent regulatory design:

[…] [T]he context and object and purpose of the *TBT Agreement* weigh in favour of reading the 'treatment no less favourable' requirement of Article 2.1 as prohibiting both *de jure* and *de facto* discrimination against imported products, while at the same time permitting detrimental impact on competitive opportunities for imports that stems exclusively from legitimate regulatory distinctions.[6]

As the US ban essentially targeted clove cigarettes imported from Indonesia, whilst exempting menthol cigarettes which essentially stemmed from domestic production, the Appellate Body considered the ban to be discriminatory:

[…] Given the above, the design, architecture, revealing structure, operation, and application of Section 907(a)(1)(A) strongly suggest that the detrimental impact on competitive opportunities for clove cigarettes reflects discrimination against the group of like products imported from Indonesia. The products that are prohibited under Section 907(a)(1)(A) consist primarily of clove cigarettes imported from Indonesia, while the like products that are actually permitted under this measure consist primarily of domestically produced menthol cigarettes.[7]

---

[5] WTO, *United States: Measures Affecting the Production and Sale of Clove Cigarettes—Report of the Appellate Body* (2012) WT/DS406/AB/R para 175. See also para 180: […] 'Similarly to Article III:4 of the GATT 1994, Article 2.1 of the *TBT Agreement* requires WTO Members to accord to the group of imported products treatment no less favourable than that accorded to the group of like domestic products. Article 2.1 prescribes such treatment specifically in respect of technical regulations. For this reason, a panel examining a claim of violation under Article 2.1 should seek to ascertain whether the technical regulation at issue modifies the conditions of competition in the market of the regulating Member to the detriment of the group of imported products vis-à-vis the group of like domestic products'.

[6] WTO, *United States: Measures Affecting the Production and Sale of Clove Cigarettes—Report of the Appellate Body* (2012) WT/DS406/AB/R para 175.

[7] WTO, *United States: Measures Affecting the Production and Sale of Clove Cigarettes—Report of the Appellate Body* (2012) WT/DS406/AB/R para 224. See also the concluding comments:

235. In reaching this conclusion, we wish to clarify the implications of our decision. We do not consider that the *TBT Agreement* or any of the covered agreements is to be interpreted as preventing Members from devising and implementing public health policies generally, and tobacco-control policies in particular, through the regulation of the content of tobacco products, including the prohibition or restriction on the use of ingredients that increase the attractiveness and palatability of cigarettes for young and potential smokers. Moreover, we recognize the importance of Members' efforts in the World Health Organization on tobacco control.

236. While we have upheld the Panel's finding that the specific measure at issue in this dispute is inconsistent with Article 2.1 of the *TBT Agreement*, we are not saying that a Member cannot adopt measures to pursue legitimate health objectives such as curbing and preventing youth smoking. In particular, we are not saying that the United States cannot ban clove cigarettes: however, if it chooses to do so, this has to be done consistently with the *TBT Agreement*. Although Section 907(a)(1)(A) pursues the legitimate

In *US—Tuna II*, the Appellate Body held that requirements for 'tuna safe' labelling were not adequately calibrated to the risks for dolphins by certain fishing methods, because they comprehensively responded to these risks in the Eastern Tropical Zone (the fishing zone of the Mexican fleet) whilst allowing certain fishing methods other than setting on dolphins (the method used by the Mexican fleet) which have also detrimental effects on dolphin populations in zones preferred by US vessels.[8]

National treatment under Article 2.1 of the TBT Agreement calls for a fair balance between free trade and the pursuit of legitimate interest. It aims at minimizing adverse effects on producers or users of imported products in the same way as the 'chapeau' of Article XX of the GATT calls for restraint in applying the general exceptions, as the Appellate Body held in *US—Clove Cigarettes*:

As we have observed above, the balance that the preamble of the *TBT Agreement* strikes between, on the one hand, the pursuit of trade liberalization and, on the other hand, Members' right to regulate, is not, in principle, different from the balance that exists between the national treatment obligation of Article III and the general exceptions provided under Article XX of the GATT 1994. The second recital of the preamble links the two Agreements by expressing the 'desire' 'to further the objectives of the GATT 1994', while the 'recognition' of a Member's right to regulate in the sixth recital is balanced by the 'desire' expressed in the fifth recital to ensure that technical regulations, standards, and conformity assessment procedures do not create unnecessary obstacles to international trade. We note, however, that in the GATT 1994 this balance is expressed by the national treatment rule in Article III:4 as qualified by the exceptions in Article XX, while, in the *TBT Agreement*, this balance is to be found in Article 2.1 itself, read in the light of its context and of its object and purpose.[9]

3. Proportionality

Under Article 2.2, technical regulations may not restrict international trade beyond the extent necessary to protect a legitimate interest:

Members shall ensure that technical regulations are not prepared, adopted or applied with a view to or with the effect of creating unnecessary obstacles to international trade. For this purpose, technical regulations shall not be more trade-restrictive than necessary to fulfil a

---

objective of reducing youth smoking by banning cigarettes containing flavours and ingredients that increase the attractiveness of tobacco to youth, it does so in a manner that is inconsistent with the national treatment obligation in Article 2.1 of the *TBT Agreement* as a result of the exemption of menthol cigarettes, which similarly contain flavours and ingredients that increase the attractiveness of tobacco to youth, from the ban on flavoured cigarettes.

[8] WTO, *United States: Measures Concerning the Importation, Marketing and Sale of Tuna and Tuna Products—Report of the Appellate Body* (2012) WT/DS381/AB/R paras 284ff.

[9] WTO, *United States: Measures Affecting the Production and Sale of Clove Cigarettes—Report of the Appellate Body* (2012) WT/DS406/AB/R para 109.

legitimate objective, taking account of the risks non-fulfilment would create. Such legitimate objectives are, *inter alia*: national security requirements; the prevention of deceptive practices; protection of human health or safety, animal or plant life or health, or the environment. In assessing such risks, relevant elements of consideration are, *inter alia*: available scientific and technical information, related processing technology or intended end-uses of products.

Legitimate objectives of technical regulations are also mentioned in Article 5.4:

In cases where a positive assurance is required that products conform with technical regulations or standards, and relevant guides or recommendations issued by international standardizing bodies exist or their completion is imminent, Members shall ensure that central government bodies use them, or the relevant parts of them, as a basis for their conformity assessment procedures, except where, as duly explained upon request, such guides or recommendations or relevant parts are inappropriate for the Members concerned, for, *inter alia*, such reasons as: national security requirements; the prevention of deceptive practices; protection of human health or safety, animal or plant life or health, or the environment; fundamental climatic or other geographical factors; fundamental technological or infrastructural problems.

Article 2.2 of the TBT Agreement calls for a test of proportionality, as the Appellate Body stated in *US—Tuna II*:

[…] Both the first and second sentence of Article 2.2 refer to the notion of 'necessity'. These sentences are linked by the terms '[f]or this purpose', which suggests that the second sentence qualifies the terms of the first sentence and elaborates on the scope and meaning of the obligation contained in that sentence. The Appellate Body has previously noted that the word 'necessary' refers to a range of degrees of necessity, depending on the connection in which it is used. In the context of Article 2.2, the assessment of 'necessity' involves a relational analysis of the trade-restrictiveness of the technical regulation, the degree of contribution that it makes to the achievement of a legitimate objective, and the risks non-fulfilment would create. We consider, therefore, that all these factors provide the basis for the determination of what is to be considered 'necessary' in the sense of Article 2.2 in a particular case.[10]

In this case, the Appellate Body listed a number of criteria which govern the balancing of the regulatory objective with the effects on trade:

[…] In sum, we consider that an assessment of whether a technical regulation is 'more trade-restrictive than necessary' within the meaning of Article 2.2 of the *TBT Agreement* involves an evaluation of a number of factors. A panel should begin by considering factors that include: (i) the degree of contribution made by the measure to the legitimate objective at issue; (ii) the trade-restrictiveness of the measure; and (iii) the nature of the risks at issue and the gravity of consequences that would arise from non-fulfilment of the objective(s) pursued by the Member through the measure. In most cases, a comparison of the challenged measure and possible alternative measures should be undertaken. In particular, it may be relevant for the purpose of this comparison to consider whether the proposed alternative is less trade restrictive, whether it would make an equivalent contribution to the relevant

---

[10] WTO, *United States: Measures Concerning the Importation, Marketing and Sale of Tuna and Tuna Products—Report of the Appellate Body* (2012) WT/DS381/AB/R para 318.

legitimate objective, taking account of the risks non-fulfilment would create, and whether it is reasonably available.[11]

In *US—Country of Origin Labeling (COOL)* the Appellate Body considered the informational requirements in regulations for the labelling of meat as a disproportionate burden on importers of meat and meat processors:

[…] [T]he informational requirements imposed on upstream producers under the COOL measure are disproportionate as compared to the level of information communicated to consumers through the mandatory retail labels. That is, a large amount of information is tracked and transmitted by upstream producers for purposes of providing consumers with information on origin, but only a small amount of this information is actually communicated to consumers in an understandable manner, if it is communicated at all. Yet, nothing in the Panel's findings or on the Panel record explains or supplies a rational basis for this disconnect. Therefore, we consider the manner in which the COOL measure seeks to provide information to consumers on origin, through the regulatory distinctions described above, to be arbitrary, and the disproportionate burden imposed on upstream producers and processors to be unjustifiable.[12]

Just as the SPS Agreement, the TBT Agreement defers to international standards according to its Article 2.4:

Where technical regulations are required and relevant international standards exist or their completion is imminent, Members shall use them, or the relevant parts of them, as a basis for their technical regulations except when such international standards or relevant parts would be an ineffective or inappropriate means for the fulfilment of the legitimate objectives pursued, for instance because of fundamental climatic or geographical factors or fundamental technological problems.

International standards are only relevant under Article 2.4 of the TBT if they are set by bodies whose standardization activity is widely recognized and which are open to all WTO members, such as the Codex Alimentarius Commission.[13]

Recognized international standards must be considered as guidelines and as standards of review for national regulations, even if they were established after a technical regulation. In *EC—Sardines*, the Appellate Body (affirming the Panel Report) recognized this dynamic impact of international standards.[14] WTO members must, therefore, review and, if necessary, modify their regulations in the light of new international standards.

---

[11] WTO, *United States: Measures Concerning the Importation, Marketing and Sale of Tuna and Tuna Products—Report of the Appellate Body* (2012) WT/DS381/AB/R para 322.
[12] WTO, *United States: Certain Countries of Origin Labelling Requirements—Report of the Appellate Body* (2012) WT/DS384/AB/R, WT/DS/386/AB/R para 347.
[13] WTO, *United States: Measures Concerning the Importation, Marketing and Sale of Tuna and Tuna Products—Report of the Appellate Body* (2012) WT/DS381/AB/R paras 355 (with reference to a TBT Committee Decision), 378. On the Codex Alimentarius as a relevant international standard, see WTO, *European Communities: Trade Descriptions of Sardines—Report of the Appellate Body* (2002) WT/DS231/AB/R paras 217ff.
[14] WTO, *European Communities: Trade Descriptions of Sardines—Report of the Appellate Body* (2002) WT/DS231/AB/R para 205.

Select Bibliography

AE Appleton, 'The Agreement on Technical Barriers to Trade' in PFJ Macrory, AE Appleton, and MG Plummer (eds), *The World Trade Organization: Legal, Economic and Political Analysis* (Springer 2005) vol 1, 371.

R Wolfrum, PT Stoll, and A Seibert-Fohr (eds), *WTO—Technical Barriers and SPS Measures* (Brill Academic Publishers 2007).

XVII

The General Agreement on Trade in Services (GATS)

1. Scope and Relevance

Besides the GATT, which has served as the legal core of the world trading system, the General Agreement on Trade in Services (GATS)[1] has become more and more important, sometimes applying concurrently with the GATT.[2] The GATS defines its scope of application in Article I:

1. This Agreement applies to measures by Members affecting trade in services.
2. For the purposes of this Agreement, trade in services is defined as the supply of a service:
   (a) from the territory of one Member into the territory of any other Member;
   (b) in the territory of one Member to the service consumer of any other Member;
   (c) by a service supplier of one Member, through commercial presence in the territory of any other Member;
   (d) by a service supplier of one Member, through presence of natural persons of a Member in the territory of any other Member.
3. For the purposes of this Agreement:
   (a) 'measures by Members' means measures taken by:
      (i) central, regional or local governments and authorities; and
      (ii) non-governmental bodies in the exercise of powers delegated by central, regional or local governments or authorities;
   In fulfilling its obligations and commitments under the Agreement, each Member shall take such reasonable measures as may be available to it to ensure their observance by regional and local governments and authorities and non-governmental bodies within its territory;
   (b) 'services' includes any service in any sector except services supplied in the exercise of governmental authority;
   (c) 'a service supplied in the exercise of governmental authority' means any service which is supplied neither on a commercial basis, nor in competition with one or more service suppliers.

---

[1] See ME Footer and C George, 'The General Agreement on Trade in Services' in PFJ Macrory, AE Appleton, and MG Plummer (eds), *The World Trade Organization: Legal, Economic and Political Analysis* (Springer 2005) vol 1, 799.

[2] On the relationship between GATT and GATS, see E Vranes, 'The Overlap between GATT and GATS: A Methodological Mate' (2009) 36 LIEI 215.

Thus, the GATS extends to all measures which affect trade in services and covers all services in any sector, except those 'supplied in the exercise of governmental authority' (Article I:3(b)).

The GATS, like the GATT, enshrines the most-favoured-nation principle (Article II:1 of the GATS). Exemptions from Article II of the GATS are listed in the Annex on Article II to the GATS. In parallel to the GATT exception for free trade agreements and customs unions, the GATS exempts agreements aimed at the liberalization of trade in services from the most-favoured-nation principle (Article V).

A number of important GATS provisions do not apply generally, but are only binding for States having entered 'specific commitments' for certain service sectors (eg telecommunication services).[3] This includes 'all measures of general application' (Article VI:1, 3, 5, and 6), the obligation to grant free market access (Article XVI) and national treatment (Article XVII). In addition, the GATS establishes a special regime for several sectors (such as the film industry, financial services or shipping).

Some commitments under the GATS generally prohibit restrictive measures, even if these are applied in a non-discriminatory manner (see for standards of qualification, technical standards and licensing requirements, Article VI:4 and 5 of the GATS).

A most relevant obligation in context with free market access under specific commitments refers to the prohibition of quantitative restrictions. Article XVI:2 of the GATS provides:

In sectors where market-access commitments are undertaken, the measures which a Member shall not maintain or adopt either on the basis of a regional subdivision or on the basis of its entire territory, unless otherwise specified in its Schedule, are defined as:
(a) limitations on the number of service suppliers whether in the form of numerical quotas, monopolies, exclusive service suppliers or the requirements of an economic needs test;
(b) limitations on the total value of service transactions or assets in the form of numerical quotas or the requirement of an economic needs test;
(c) limitations on the total number of service operations or on the total quantity of service output expressed in terms of designated numerical units in the form of quotas or the requirement of an economic needs test;
(d) limitations on the total number of natural persons that may be employed in a particular service sector or that a service supplier may employ and who are necessary for, and directly related to, the supply of a specific service in the form of numerical quotas or the requirement of an economic needs test;
(e) measures which restrict or require specific types of legal entity or joint venture through which a service supplier may supply a service; and
(f) limitations on the participation of foreign capital in terms of maximum percentage limit on foreign shareholding or the total value of individual or aggregate foreign investment.

In *US—Gambling*, the Appellate Body has qualified the categorical prohibition of certain services (zero quota) as a 'numerical quota' encompassed by Article XVI:2(a) of the GATS:

[A] 'numerical quota' within Article XVI:2(a) appears to mean a quantitative limit on the number of service suppliers. The fact that the word 'numerical' encompasses things

---

[3] B Mathew, *The WTO Agreements on Telecommunications* (Peter Lang 2003).

which 'have the characteristics of a number' suggests that limitations 'in the form of a numerical quota' would encompass limitations which, even if not in themselves a number, have the characteristics of a number. Because zero is *quantitative* in nature, it can, in our view, be deemed to have the 'characteristics of' a number—that is, to be 'numerical'.[4]

In this case, the State of Antigua and Barbuda had complained about US federal laws establishing a general ban on cross-border gambling and betting services on the US market.

The principle of national treatment (Article XVII of the GATS) prohibits unequal terms of marketing which distort competition in favour of domestic service suppliers under specific commitments. In *China—Publications and Audiovisual Products*, the Panel qualified restrictions on the marketing of imported print and audiovisual products as a violation of the national treatment principle in Article XVII:

Since the measures at issue have the effect of prohibiting foreign service suppliers from wholesaling imported reading materials, while like Chinese suppliers are permitted to do so, these measures clearly modify the conditions of competition to the detriment of the foreign service supplier and thus constitutes 'less favourable treatment' in terms of Article XVII.[5]

Following the model of the GATT (Article XX), the GATS contains a list of 'general exceptions' under a common 'chapeau' in Article XIV:

Subject to the requirement that such measures are not applied in a manner which would constitute a means of arbitrary or unjustifiable discrimination between countries where like conditions prevail, or a disguised restriction on trade in services, nothing in this Agreement shall be construed to prevent the adoption or enforcement by any Member of measures:

(a) necessary to protect public morals or to maintain public order;

(b) necessary to protect human, animal or plant life or health;

(c) necessary to secure compliance with laws or regulations which are not inconsistent with the provisions of this Agreement including those relating to:

(i) the prevention of deceptive and fraudulent practices or to deal with the effects of a default on services contracts;

(ii) the protection of the privacy of individuals in relation to the processing and dissemination of personal data and the protection of confidentiality of individual records and accounts;

(iii) safety;

(d) inconsistent with Article XVII, provided that the difference in treatment is aimed at ensuring the equitable or effective imposition or collection of direct taxes in respect of services or service suppliers of other Members;

---

[4] WTO, *United States: Measures Affecting the Cross-Border Supply of Gambling and Betting Services—Report of the Appellate Body* (2005) WT/DS285/AB/R para 227; see JP Trachtman, 'United States: Measures Affecting the Cross-Border Supply of Betting and Gambling Services. WT/DS285/AB/R' (2005) 99 AJIL 861; see also P Delimatsis, 'Don't Gamble with GATS—The Interaction between Articles VI, XVI, XVII and XVIII GATS in the Light of the US—Gambling Case' (2006) 40 JWT 1059.

[5] WTO, *China: Measures Affecting Trading Rights and Distribution Services for Certain Publications and Audiovisual Entertainment Products—Report of the Panel* (2009) WT/DS363/R para 7.996.

(e) inconsistent with Article II, provided that the difference in treatment is the result of an agreement on the avoidance of double taxation or provisions on the avoidance of double taxation in any other international agreement or arrangement by which the Member is bound.

The terms 'public morals' and 'public order' (Article XIV(a)) are receptive to all kinds of moral standards and societal perceptions which may prevail in a Member State, as the Appellate Body emphasized in its Report *US—Gambling*.[6] However, a member may only invoke the public order exception if 'a genuine and sufficiently serious threat is posed to one of the fundamental interests of society' (see note 5 of Article XIV(a)). Still, the exceptions of Article XIV(a) are broad enough to accommodate a variety of cultural idiosyncrasies. They open the gate widely for societal, and to some extent political, sensibilities.

In order to conform to the general exceptions, restrictive measures must always be a proportionate means to serve the objectives in Article XIV. Proportionality calls for a rational comparison between the measure to be applied and less restrictive alternatives and, in addition, requires a balancing of the respective interests involved.[7]

2. Telecommunications Services

Recognizing particular features of telecommunications services, the GATS establishes a special regime for this sector in the Annex on Telecommunications. Section 1 of this Annex provides:

Recognizing the specificities of the telecommunications services sector and, in particular, its dual role as a distinct sector of economic activity and as the underlying transport means for other economic activities, the Members have agreed to the following Annex with the objective of elaborating upon the provisions of the Agreement with respect to measures affecting access to and use of public telecommunications transport networks and services. Accordingly, this Annex provides notes and supplementary provisions to the Agreement.

Access to public telecommunication networks and services is of crucial relevance to providers from other members.[8] Section 5(a) of the Annex on Telecommunications provides that the obliged members must grant 'access to and use of public telecommunications transport networks and services on reasonable and non-discriminatory terms and conditions'.

---

[6] WTO, *United States: Measures Affecting the Cross-Border Supply of Gambling and Betting Services—Report of the Appellate Body* (2005) WT/DS285/AB/R para 299, upholding the finding of the Panel, WT/DS285/R (2004) paras 6.461ff.

[7] WTO, *United States: Measures Affecting the Cross-Border Supply of Gambling and Betting Services—Report of the Appellate Body* (2005) WT/DS285/AB/R paras 306ff.; WTO, *China: Measures Affecting Trading Rights and Distribution Services for Certain Publications and Audiovisual Entertainment Products—Report of the Appellate Body* (2009) WT/DS363/AB/R paras 244ff.

[8] For a general insight into the field of telecommunications within WTO law, see M Bronckers and P Larouche, 'Telecommunications Services' in PFJ Macrory, AE Appleton, and MG Plummer (eds), *The World Trade Organization: Legal, Economic and Political Analysis* (Springer 2005) vol 1, 989.

These conditions also apply to certain end user services. Section 5(b) of the Annex on Telecommunications states:

(b) Each Member shall ensure that service suppliers of any other Member have access to and use of any public telecommunications transport network or service offered within or across the border of that Member, including private leased circuits, and to this end shall ensure, subject to paragraphs (e) and (f), that such suppliers are permitted:

   (i)   to purchase or lease and attach terminal or other equipment which interfaces with the network and which is necessary to supply a supplier's services;

  (ii) to interconnect private leased or owned circuits with public telecommunications transport networks and services or with circuits leased or owned by another service supplier; and

 (iii) to use operating protocols of the service supplier's choice in the supply of any service, other than as necessary to ensure the availability of telecommunications transport networks and services to the public generally.

Under specific commitments, so-called reference papers substantiate the undertaken obligations. In this context, the elimination of certain practices restricting competition plays an important role. Thus, the reference papers, though only to a limited extent, vest WTO law with an antitrust dimension.

In *Mexico—Telecoms*,[9] the Panel Report established a breach of competition law obligations under the GATS for the first time. The dispute referred to a rather peculiar regulatory interplay between the Mexican authority for telecommunications and the largest telecommunications company in Mexico (Telmex). Mexican regulation entrusted the Mexican carrier with the regulatory fixing of fees for transferring incoming international calls.

Telmex established a schedule of minimum fees for all foreign telecommunications service providers. All other domestic operators were not allowed to charge less than the established fees for interconnecting calls. In addition, shares of the domestic market for international calls were determined by quotas, according to the rate of incoming international calls (regardless of outbound overseas calls). This system resulted in a kind of antitrust charging system and an anti-competitive allocation of market shares.

According to the Panel Report, Mexico had infringed its commitments under the Annex on Telecommunications (section 5 (a) and (b)). In addition, Mexico had committed itself in its reference paper to take reasonable measures to prevent anti-competitive practices by providers with a dominant position and to ensure cost-oriented rates for the interconnection of calls. The Panel found:

Mexico has not met its obligations under Section 5(a) of the GATS Annex on Telecommunications since it fails to ensure access to and use of public telecommunications transport networks and services on reasonable terms to United States service suppliers for the cross-border supply, on a facilities basis in Mexico, of the basic telecommunications

---

[9] WTO, *Mexico: Measures Affecting Telecommunications Services—Report of the Panel* (2004) WT/DS204/R; see E Fox, 'The WTO's First Antitrust Case—Mexican Telecom: A Sleeping Victory for Trade and Competition' (2006) 9 J Intl Econ L 271; CM Chung, 'Interpretation of "Interconnection" by the WTO Mexico—Telecommunications Panel: A Critique' (2007) 41 JWT 783.

services at issue. [...] Mexico has not met its obligations under Section 5(b) of the GATS Annex on Telecommunications, since it fails to ensure that United States commercial agencies, whose commercial presence Mexico has committed to allow, have access to and use of private leased circuits within or across the border of Mexico, and are permitted to interconnect these circuits to public telecommunications transport networks and services or with circuits of other service suppliers.[10]

Regional agreements such as the Comprehensive Economic and Trade Agreement (CETA) and the agreement on the Trans-Pacific Partnership (TPP) contain rather extensive provisions on telecommunications services.

3. WTO Law and Financial Services

The Fifth Protocol to GATS (1998)[11] with its reference to the new schedule of commitments in financial services aims at the liberalization of cross-border trade in financial services.[12] The obligation to grant market access, including possible participation of foreign banks and insurance companies in domestic corporations, varies according to the individual commitments undertaken by WTO members. The United States, the country with the largest financial markets, as well as India and Thailand have committed themselves to the most-favoured-nation principle with only a limited number of exemptions.

In the Annex on Financial Services, the GATS establishes specific rules for the financial sector which have great potential for cross-border services but also create opportunities for tax evasion.

Section 2 of the Annex on Financial Services allows for restrictive measures based on prudential reasons:

Domestic Regulation
(a) Notwithstanding any other provisions of the Agreement, a Member shall not be prevented from taking measures for prudential reasons, including for the protection of investors, depositors, policy holders or persons to whom a fiduciary duty is owed by a financial service supplier, or to ensure the integrity and stability of the financial system. Where such measures do not conform with the provisions of the Agreement, they shall not be used as a means of avoiding the Member's commitments or obligations under the Agreement.
(b) Nothing in the Agreement shall be construed to require a Member to disclose information relating to the affairs and accounts of individual customers or any confidential or proprietary information in the possession of public entities.

In *Argentina—Measures Relating to Trade in Goods and Services* the Panel Report clarified the meaning of 'prudential reasons'. In this case, Argentina had adopted

---

[10] WTO, *Mexico: Measures Affecting Telecommunications Services—Report of the Panel* (2004) WT/DS204/R para 8.1.
[11] Fifth Protocol to the General Agreement on Trade in Services (1997) S/L/45.
[12] M Yokoi-Arai, 'GATS Prudential Carve Out in Financial Services and its Relation with Prudential Regulation' (2008) 57 ICLQ 623.

several measures to close tax loopholes for financial services.[13] The measures covered services with connection to a so-called 'non-cooperative country', that is a country not cooperating with the Argentinian administration in matters of tax transparency.

Countries could qualify for cooperative status, if they had signed agreements on a broad information exchange in tax matters or had initiated negotiations on such an agreement, even if they did not effectively exchange information during the negotiations. To defend non-conformity with the most-favoured nation and national treatment obligations, Argentina relied on paragraph 2(a) of the GATS Annex on Financial Services. The Panel found a violation of the most-favoured-nation clause of Article II:1 GATS. As for the likeness of the services, the Panel concluded, that the 'services and service suppliers of cooperative and non-cooperative countries are like by reason of origin.' The Panel Report defines 'prudential reasons' as 'preventive or precautionary reasons'[14] which 'motivate financial sector regulators to act to prevent a risk, injury or danger that does not necessarily have to be imminent'.[15] The Panel rejected Argentina's defence under Article XIV(c) of the GATS (enforcement of tax laws) and held that the 'chapeau' of Article XIV of the GATS precludes arbitrary and unjustified discrimination between countries where like conditions prevail (as between 'non-cooperative' countries and 'cooperative' countries which do not participate in the information exchange).[16]

4. Trade in Services Agreement (TiSA)

Outside the framework of GATS the Trade in Services Agreement (TiSA) is currently negotiated by a number of WTO members including the European Union and the United States, with the objective of liberalizing trade in services. TiSA shall be based on the principles of the GATS and facilitate trade in services, especially in the sector of finance, telecommunications and e-commerce.[17]

Select Bibliography

SCOPE AND RELEVANCE

C Arup, *The World Trade Organization Knowledge Agreements* (2nd edn, CUP 2008) 165.

---

[13] WTO, *Argentina—Measures Relating to Trade in Goods and Services—Report of the Panel* (2015) WT/DS453/R; WTO, *Argentina—Measures Relating to Trade in Goods and Services—Report of the Appellate Body* (2016) WT/DS453/AB/R.
[14] WTO, *Argentina: Measures Relating to Trade in Goods and Services—Report of the Panel* (2015) WT/DS453/R para 7.868.
[15] WTO, *Argentina: Measures Relating to Trade in Goods and Services—Report of the Panel* (2015) WT/DS453/R para 7.879.
[16] WTO, *Argentina—Measures Relating to Trade in Goods and Services—Report of the Panel* (2015) WT/DS453/R paras 7.153ff; on the scope of Article 2(a) of the Annex on Financial Services see also WTO, *Argentina—Measures Relating to Trade in Goods and Services—Report of the Appellate Body* (2016) WT/DS453/AB/R paras 6.251ff.
[17] European Commission, <http://ec.europa.eu/trade/policy/in-focus/tisa/> accessed 23 June 2016.

P Delimatsis, *International Trade in Services and Domestic Regulations: Necessity, Transparency and Regulatory Diversity* (OUP 2008).

ME Footer and C George, 'The General Agreement on Trade in Services' in PFJ Macrory, AE Appleton, and MG Plummer (eds), *The World Trade Organization: Legal, Economic and Political Analysis* (Springer 2005) vol 1, 799.

M Krajewski, *National Regulation and Trade Liberalization in Services: The Legal Impact of the General Agreement on Trade in Services (GATS) on National Regulatory Autonomy* (Kluwer Law International 2003).

A Matoo, RM Stern, and G Zanini, *A Handbook of International Trade in Services* (OUP 2007).

R Wolfrum, PT Stoll, and C Feinaugle, *WTO—Trade in Services* (Brill Academic Publishers 2008).

TELECOMMUNICATIONS SERVICES

C Blouin, 'The WTO Agreement on Basic Telecommunications: A Reevaluation' (2000) 24 Telecommunications Policy 135.

HJ Broadman and C Balassa, 'Liberalizing International Trade in Telecommunications Services' (1993) 28 The Columbia Journal of World Business 30.

M Bronckers and P Larouche, 'Telecommunications Services' in PFJ Macrory, AE Appleton, and MG Plummer (eds), *The World Trade Organization: Legal, Economic and Political Analysis* (Springer 2005) vol 1, 989.

WTO LAW AND FINANCIAL SERVICES

R Bismuth, 'Financial Sector Regulation and Financial Services Liberalization at the Crossroads: The Relevance of International Financial Standards in WTO Law' (2010) 44 JWT 489.

SJ Key, 'Financial Services' in PFJ Macrory, AE Appleton, and MG Plummer (eds), *The World Trade Organization: Legal, Economic and Political Analysis* (Springer 2005) vol 1, 955.

XVIII

The Agreement on Trade Related Aspects of Intellectual Property Rights (TRIPS)

1. General Aspects

The scope of patents, trademarks, and other intellectual property rights is territorial. In international trade the availability and protection of intellectual property rights in the country of destination becomes a crucial issue. If the country of destination does not effectively protect property rights, this vulnerability of intellectual property rights will affect the willingness to 'export' certain forms of knowledge. Still, intellectual property rights and their protection were long relegated to the margin of the world trading system. The exception of Article XX(d) of the GATT allows measures for the protection of intellectual property rights. During the negotiations of the Uruguay Round, industrialized countries, led by the United States pushed hard for a specific treaty regime on the protection of intellectual property rights: the Agreement on Trade-Related Aspects of Intellectual Property Rights (TRIPS Agreement),[1] one of the multilateral WTO agreements.

The TRIPS Agreement provides for national treatment (Article 3) and most-favoured-nation treatment (Article 4). Article 7 sets out the general objectives.

The protection and enforcement of intellectual property rights should contribute to the promotion of technological innovation and to the transfer and dissemination of technology, to the mutual advantage of producers and users of technological knowledge and in a manner conducive to social and economic welfare and to a balance of rights and obligations.

The TRIPS Agreement applies to copyright and related rights (Articles 9ff), trademarks (Articles 15ff), geographical indications (Articles 22ff), industrial designs (Articles 25ff), patents (Articles 27ff), layout designs (topographies) of integrated circuits (Articles 35ff), the protection of undisclosed information (Articles 39ff), and the control of anti-competitive practices in contractual licences (Articles 40ff).

---

[1] (1994) 33 ILM 81; see T Cottier, 'The Agreement on Trade-Related Aspects of Intellectual Property Rights' in PFJ Macrory, AE Appleton, and MG Plummer (eds), *The World Trade Organization: Legal, Economic and Political Analysis* (Springer 2005) vol 1, 1041.

The TRIPS Agreement also aims at the effective enforcement of intellectual property rights (Articles 41ff), including provisional measures of protection (Article 50).[2]

Special rules apply to developing countries and countries in transition (Article 65(2)–(5); see also Article 67). Among the least developed countries, few opted for the transitional regime under Article 66(1).

2. Patent Rights

(a) Scope of patentability

A particularly important TRIPS Agreement is Article 27 on the mandatory scope of patents available for inventions:

Article 27 Patentable Subject Matter
1. Subject to the provisions of paragraphs 2 and 3, patents shall be available for any inventions, whether products or processes, in all fields of technology, provided that they are new, involve an inventive step and are capable of industrial application.[3] Subject to paragraph 4 of Article 65, paragraph 8 of Article 70 and paragraph 3 of this Article, patents shall be available and patent rights enjoyable without discrimination as to the place of invention, the field of technology and whether products are imported or locally produced.
2. Members may exclude from patentability inventions, the prevention within their territory of the commercial exploitation of which is necessary to protect *ordre public* or morality, including to protect human, animal or plant life or health or to avoid serious prejudice to the environment, provided that such exclusion is not made merely because the exploitation is prohibited by their law.
3. Members may also exclude from patentability:
   (a) diagnostic, therapeutic and surgical methods for the treatment of humans or animals;
   (b) plants and animals other than micro-organisms, and essentially biological processes for the production of plants or animals other than non-biological and microbiological processes. However, Members shall provide for the protection of plant varieties either by patents or by an effective *sui generis* system or by any combination thereof. The provisions of this subparagraph shall be reviewed four years after the date of entry into force of the WTO Agreement.

Under Article 27(1) in principle all inventions are patentable. The public order reservation of Article 27(2) allows exclusion of certain inventions from patentability only if all practically relevant forms of exploitation are prohibited by law and violate the public order or morality.[4]

---

[2] See eg ECJ Case C-53/96 *Hermès International v FHT Marketing Choice BV* [1998] ECR I-3603; ECJ Joined Cases C-300/98 and C-392/98 *Parfums Christian Dior v Tuk Consultancy BV* [2000] ECR I-11307.

[3] Note to Article 27: 'For the purposes of this Article, the terms "inventive step" and "capable of industrial application" may be deemed by a Member to be synonymous with the terms "non-obvious" and "useful" respectively'.

[4] M Herdegen, 'TRIPS Agreement, art. 27 para 4' in T Cottier and P Véron (eds), *Concise International and European IP Law* (3rd edn, Kluwer Law International 2015).

The judgment of the European Court of Justice in the case *Brüstle v Greenpeace*[5] raises serious issues under Article 27(2). The European Court of Justice held that stem cell procedures are categorically excluded from patentability under Article 6(2)(c) of the Biotechnology Directive 98/44/EC, if the cells are produced from human embryos *in vitro*. This categorical exclusion violates the TRIPS Agreement whenever the exploitation of the invention is allowed (as is the case under German law).

The Committee on Economic, Social and Cultural Rights, established under the International Covenant on Social, Economic and Cultural Rights (ICESCR), adopted the General Comment No 17 (2005) on Article 15(1)(c) of the ICESCR[6] which lays down limitations for intellectual property rights:

[...] Ultimately, intellectual property is a social product and has a social function. [...] States parties thus have a duty to prevent unreasonably high costs for access to essential medicines, plant seeds or other means of food production, or for schoolbooks and learning materials, from undermining the rights of large segments of the population to health, food and education. Moreover, States parties should prevent the use of scientific and technical progress for purposes contrary to human rights and dignity, including the rights to life, health and privacy, eg by excluding inventions from patentability whenever their commercialization would jeopardize the full realization of these rights. [...]

These limitations do not easily meet the standards under the TRIPS Agreement.

Many inventions, especially in the pharmaceutical sector, build on exploitation of genetic resources in countries of great biodiversity. There is much support for a possible exclusion of such inventions from patentability, if genetic resources were exploited with due authorization of the host country. Such exclusion, as already established by Decision No 391 of the Andean Commission,[7] would require an amendment to Article 27.

(b) Compulsory licences and access to pharmaceuticals

Article 31 of the TRIPS Agreement governs the possible grant of compulsory licences. Such compulsory licences allow exploiting the patent on a product or a process without the consent of the right holder:

Where the law of a Member allows for other use[8] of the subject matter of a patent without the authorization of the right holder, including use by the government or third parties authorized by the government, the following provisions shall be respected:
(a) authorization of such use shall be considered on its individual merits;
(b) such use may only be permitted if, prior to such use, the proposed user has made efforts to obtain authorization from the right holder on reasonable commercial terms and conditions and that such efforts have not been successful within a reasonable period of time.

---

[5] ECJ Case C-34/10 *Oliver Brüstle v Greenpeace eV* paras 34ff.
[6] E/C.12/GC/17 (2006) para 35.
[7] Decision No 391 of the Andean Commission: Common Regime on Access to Genetic Resources.
[8] Note to Article 31: ' "Other use" refers to use other than that allowed under Article 30.'

This requirement may be waived by a Member in the case of a national emergency or other circumstances of extreme urgency or in cases of public non-commercial use. In situations of national emergency or other circumstances of extreme urgency, the right holder shall, nevertheless, be notified as soon as reasonably practicable. In the case of public non-commercial use, where the government or contractor, without making a patent search, knows or has demonstrable grounds to know that a valid patent is or will be used by or for the government, the right holder shall be informed promptly;

(c) the scope and duration of such use shall be limited to the purpose for which it was authorized, and in the case of semi-conductor technology shall only be for public non-commercial use or to remedy a practice determined after judicial or administrative process to be anti-competitive;

(d) such use shall be non-exclusive;

(e) such use shall be non-assignable, except with that part of the enterprise or goodwill which enjoys such use;

(f) any such use shall be authorized predominantly for the supply of the domestic market of the Member authorizing such use;

(g) authorization for such use shall be liable, subject to adequate protection of the legitimate interests of the persons so authorized, to be terminated if and when the circumstances which led to it cease to exist and are unlikely to recur. The competent authority shall have the authority to review, upon motivated request, the continued existence of these circumstances;

(h) the right holder shall be paid adequate remuneration in the circumstances of each case, taking into account the economic value of the authorization;

(i) the legal validity of any decision relating to the authorization of such use shall be subject to judicial review or other independent review by a distinct higher authority in that Member;

(j) any decision relating to the remuneration provided in respect of such use shall be subject to judicial review or other independent review by a distinct higher authority in that Member;

(k) Members are not obliged to apply the conditions set forth in subparagraphs (b) and (f) where such use is permitted to remedy a practice determined after judicial or administrative process to be anti-competitive. The need to correct anti-competitive practices may be taken into account in determining the amount of remuneration in such cases. Competent authorities shall have the authority to refuse termination of authorization if and when the conditions which led to such authorization are likely to recur;

(l) where such use is authorized to permit the exploitation of a patent ('the second patent') which cannot be exploited without infringing another patent ('the first patent'), the following additional conditions shall apply:

   (i) the invention claimed in the second patent shall involve an important technical advance of considerable economic significance in relation to the invention claimed in the first patent;

   (ii) the owner of the first patent shall be entitled to a cross-licence on reasonable terms to use the invention claimed in the second patent; and

   (iii) the use authorized in respect of the first patent shall be non-assignable except with the assignment of the second patent.

Thus, Article 31 subjects compulsory licences to a number of conditions such as the use of a patent primarily serving as supply of the domestic market (*lit* f) or an adequate compensation paid to the right holder (*lit* h). In the case of a 'national emergency or other circumstances of extreme urgency' (*lit* b second and third sentence) compulsory access to patents is facilitated.

Compulsory licences are a sharp instrument to provide access to a patented invention. When in March 2012 the Indian patent office for the first time granted a compulsory licence on a patented drug, this decision stirred considerable controversy. The Indian Patent Office, finding that the German company Bayer had failed to make a patented cancer drug available in sufficient quantities and at a reasonable price in India, allowed a domestic company to produce a generic version of the drug at a fraction of the price charged by the patent holder.[9] This development caused strong deep among some Members of the US Congress which they articulated in a letter to President Obama in June 2013:

[...] [T]he intellectual property (IP) climate has become increasingly challenging in India. US companies have suffered from a whole host of IP issues in areas including information technology, renewable energy and biopharmaceuticals. For example, last year several biopharmaceutical companies inappropriately had their patents revoked or their appeals denied by the Indian courts to market a variety of life-saving drugs in India. Additionally, the Indian Government issued its first compulsory license (CL) on a stage three liver and kidney cancer drug. It has been reported that additional drugs may be subject to CLs imminently and that the decisions related to these CLs are being improperly driven by an interest in growing the pharmaceutical market in India. These actions by the Indian Government greatly concern us because innovation and the protection of intellectual property are significant driving engines of the U.S. economy.[10]

For some time, the terms for compulsory licensing have been a disputed issue, in particular as to the supply of poor countries with patented pharmaceuticals. Under the conditions laid down in Article 31, many developing countries considered the possible grant of compulsory licences as inadequate as a mechanism to ensure the supply of pharmaceuticals at sustainable prices. Apart from the compensation to the right holder, many developing countries do not have a pharmaceutical sector able to provide their own population with medicines. However, countries like India have considerable production capacities which also allow supplying other countries with pharmaceuticals at relatively low prices. From a broader human rights perspective, critical analysis has emphasized possible tensions between patent protection under the TRIPS Agreement and the right to health under Article 12 of the International Covenant on Social, Economic and Cultural Rights (ICESCR). With respect to food and, in particular, agricultural products covered by intellectual property rights, a similar discussion emerged in the light of the right to adequate food (Article 11 of the ICESCR).

---

[9] *Economic Times, Natco Pharma bags licence to sell Bayer's cancer drug Nexavar* (13 March 2012).
[10] Letter available at <http://paulsen.house.gov/uploads/India%20IP%20Letter%20Signed.pdf> (accessed 23 June 2016).

A conflict of interests between industrialized and developing countries emerged in context with the fight against epidemic diseases and the lack of nutrition. In this field, patent protection may account for a serious cost barrier in less developed countries.[11] The TRIPS Agreement is receptive to this kind of vital concerns. According to Article 8.1

Members may, in formulating or amending their laws and regulations, adopt measures necessary to protect public health and nutrition, and to promote the public interest in sectors of vital importance to their socio-economic and technological development, provided that such measures are consistent with the provisions of this Agreement.

The Doha Ministerial Declaration on the TRIPS Agreement and Public Health of 14 November 2001[12] responds to public health concerns of developing countries, in particular in context with the fight against pandemic diseases (eg in South Africa):[13]

[...]
4. We agree that the TRIPS Agreement does not and should not prevent Members from taking measures to protect public health. Accordingly, while reiterating our commitment to the TRIPS Agreement, we affirm that the Agreement can and should be interpreted and implemented in a manner supportive of WTO Members' right to protect public health and, in particular, to promote access to medicines for all.
   In this connection, we reaffirm the right of WTO Members to use, to the full, the provisions in the TRIPS Agreement, which provide flexibility for this purpose.
5. Accordingly and in the light of paragraph 4 above, while maintaining our commitments in the TRIPS Agreement, we recognize that these flexibilities include:
   [...]
   (b) Each Member has the right to grant compulsory licences and the freedom to determine the grounds upon which such licences are granted.
   (c) Each Member has the right to determine what constitutes a national emergency or other circumstances of extreme urgency, it being understood that public health crises, including those relating to HIV/AIDS, tuberculosis, malaria and other epidemics, can represent a national emergency or other circumstances of extreme urgency. [...]
6. We recognize that WTO members with insufficient or no manufacturing capacities in the pharmaceutical sector could face difficulties in making effective use of compulsory licensing under the TRIPS Agreement. We instruct the Council for TRIPS to find an expeditious solution to this problem and to report to the General Council before the end of 2002.

In 2003, the General Council of the WTO adopted the Decision on Implementation of paragraph 6 of the Doha Declaration on the TRIPS Agreement and Public

[11] H Hestermeyer, *Human Rights and the WTO: The Case of Patents and Access to Medicines* (OUP 2007); S Joseph, 'Pharmaceutical Corporations and Access to Drugs: The "Fourth Wave" of Corporate Human Rights Scrutiny' (2003) 25 Hum Rts Q 425.
[12] Declaration on the TRIPS Agreement and Public Health (2001) WT/MIN(01)/DEC/2.
[13] See RE Mshomba, *Africa and the World Trade Organization* (CUP 2009) 100; see also AD Mitchell and T Voon, 'Patents and Public Health in the WTO, FTAs and Beyond: Tension and Conflict in International Law' (2009) 43 JWT 571.

Health.[14] The Decision facilitates the granting of compulsory licences in cases in which production and export of patented pharmaceuticals serve the healthcare of developing countries. On the basis of Article IX:3 and 4 of the WTO Agreement, the Decision contains a waiver from the requirement of production mainly for the domestic market (Article 31(f) of the TRIPS Agreement) and modifies the required compensation (Article 31(h) of the TRIPS Agreement):

2. The obligations of an exporting Member under Article 31(f) of the TRIPS Agreement shall be waived with respect to the grant by it of a compulsory licence to the extent necessary for the purposes of production of a pharmaceutical product(s) and its export to an eligible importing Member(s) in accordance with the terms set out below in this paragraph:

(a) the eligible importing Member(s) has made a notification to the Council for TRIPS, that:

   (i) specifies the names and expected quantities of the product(s) needed;

   (ii) confirms that the eligible importing Member in question, other than a least developed country Member, has established that it has insufficient or no manufacturing capacities in the pharmaceutical sector for the product(s) in question in one of the ways set out in the Annex to this Decision; and

   (iii) confirms that, where a pharmaceutical product is patented in its territory, it has granted or intends to grant a compulsory licence in accordance with Article 31 of the TRIPS Agreement and the provisions of this Decision;

(b) the compulsory licence issued by the exporting Member under this Decision shall contain the following conditions:

   (i) only the amount necessary to meet the needs of the eligible importing Member(s) may be manufactured under the licence and the entirety of this production shall be exported to the Member(s) which has notified its needs to the Council for TRIPS;

   (ii) products produced under the licence shall be clearly identified as being produced under the system set out in this Decision through specific labelling or marking. Suppliers should distinguish such products through special packaging and/or special colouring/shaping of the products themselves, provided that such distinction is feasible and does not have a significant impact on price; and

   (iii) before shipment begins, the licensee shall post on a website the following information:—the quantities being supplied to each destination as referred to in indent (i) above; and—the distinguishing features of the product(s) referred to in indent (ii) above;

(c) the exporting Member shall notify the Council for TRIPS of the grant of the licence, including the conditions attached to it. The information provided shall include the name and address of the licensee, the product(s) for which the licence has been granted, the quantity(ies) for which it has been granted, the country(ies) to which the product(s) is (are) to be supplied and the duration of the licence. The notification shall also indicate the address of the website referred to in subparagraph (b)(iii) above.

---

[14] Decision of the General Council on the Implementation of paragraph 6 of the Doha Declaration on the TRIPS Agreement and Public Health (2003) WT/L/540 and Corr. 1; see FM Abbott, 'The WTO Medicines Decision: The Political Economy of World Pharmaceutical Trade and the Protection of Public Health' (2005) 99 AJIL 317.

3. Where a compulsory licence is granted by an exporting Member under the system set
   out in this Decision, adequate remuneration pursuant to Article 31(h) of the TRIPS
   Agreement shall be paid in that Member taking into account the economic value to the
   importing Member of the use that has been authorized in the exporting Member. Where
   a compulsory licence is granted for the same products in the eligible importing Member,
   the obligation of that Member under Article 31(h) shall be waived in respect of those
   products for which remuneration in accordance with the first sentence of this paragraph
   is paid in the exporting Member.

The amendment of the TRIPS Agreement (Decision on an amending protocol
adopted by the General Council in 2005)[15] integrates the substance of the 2003
Decision (which will apply until the amendment comes into force) into the TRIPS
Agreement (Article 31*bis*), with a view to facilitating the supply of pharmaceuticals
to developing and, particularly, the least developed countries. The new Article 31*bis*
provides:

1. The obligations of an exporting Member under Article 31(f) shall not apply with
   respect to the grant by it of a compulsory licence to the extent necessary for the
   purposes of production of a pharmaceutical product(s) and its export to an eligible
   importing Member(s) in accordance with the terms set out in paragraph 2 of the
   Annex to this Agreement.
2. Where a compulsory licence is granted by an exporting Member under the system set
   out in this Article and the Annex to this Agreement, adequate remuneration pursuant to
   Article 31(h) shall be paid in that Member taking into account the economic value to the
   importing Member of the use that has been authorized in the exporting Member. Where
   a compulsory licence is granted for the same products in the eligible importing Member,
   the obligation of that Member under Article 31(h) shall not apply in respect of those
   products for which remuneration in accordance with the first sentence of this paragraph
   is paid in the exporting Member.
3. With a view to harnessing economies of scale for the purposes of enhancing purchasing
   power for, and facilitating the local production of, pharmaceutical products: where a
   developing or least developed country WTO Member is a party to a regional trade agreement within the meaning of Article XXIV of the GATT 1994 and the Decision of 28
   November 1979 on Differential and More Favourable Treatment Reciprocity and Fuller
   Participation of Developing Countries (L/4903), at least half of the current membership
   of which is made up of countries presently on the United Nations list of least developed
   countries, the obligation of that Member under Article 31(f) shall not apply to the extent
   necessary to enable a pharmaceutical product produced or imported under a compulsory
   licence in that Member to be exported to the markets of those other developing or least
   developed country parties to the regional trade agreement that share the health problem
   in question. It is understood that this will not prejudice the territorial nature of the patent rights in question.
   [...]

The new regime under the 2003 waiver and the following amendment of the TRIPS
Agreement allows countries with a large pharmaceutical sector like India (which has

---

[15] Decision of the General Council on the Amendment of the TRIPS Agreement (2005) WT/
L/641.

accordingly amended its patent law) to produce patented products and to export them to eligible countries with affordable prices under compulsory licences. It seems that this new regime brought some relief to populations in poor countries which are affected by endemic diseases.

(c) Patents in biotechnology

Patents on biotechnological inventions are an issue of particular relevance and ongoing controversy. The broad scope of Article 27(1) also ensures patentability of inventions in the field of biotechnology, subject to the narrow exceptions in Article 27(3). Still, patents on plants and animals and, even more, patents on human DNA sequences, meet criticism, driven either by ethical convictions or by concerns about the stifling effect of patents on research and industrial development or on medical treatment.

For a number of developing countries (especially those harbouring great bio-diversity and indigenous populations), the protection of traditional knowledge is a matter of concern. Patents on certain ingredients of pharmaceuticals occurring in nature may ultimately result in an 'appropriation' of traditional knowledge by foreign companies.[16] A special problem is patent protection for DNA sequences (genes or gene fragments) of a natural origin for which new methods of synthesizing or isolation have been developed.

US Courts qualify isolated or synthesized DNA sequences which (essentially) correspond to natural substances as capable of being patented. This highly contro-versial position was affirmed by the US Court of Appeals for the Federal Circuit in *Association for Molecular Pathology et al v US Patent and Trademark Office, et al* as to the patenting of genes potentially responsible for breast cancer.[17]

In the European Union, the Biotechnology Directive (Directive 98/44/EC),[18] after a protected and controversial legislative process, meant a breakthrough for patent protection of biotechnological inventions.[19] Article 3 of the Directive estab-lishes the principle of patentability of inventions involving biological material:

1. For the purposes of this Directive, inventions which are new, which involve an inventive step and which are susceptible of industrial application shall be patentable even if they concern a product consisting of or containing biological material or a process by means of which biological material is produced, processed or used.

---

[16] For an outline of the problems in this field, see K Aoki, 'Neocolonialisms, Anticommons Property and Biopiracy in the (Not-So-Brave) New World Order of Intellectual Property Protection' (1998) 6 Global Legal Studies Journal 11; M Blakeney (ed), *Intellectual Property Aspects of Ethnobiology* (Sweet & Maxwell 1999).

[17] US Court of Appeals for the Federal Circuit *Association for Molecular Pathology et al v US Patent and Trademark Office et al* 94 USPQ 2d (SDNY 29 March 2010). See KJ Liddle, 'Gene Patents: The Controversy and the Law in the Wake of the Myriad' (2011) 44 Suffolk U L Rev 683.

[18] Directive 98/44/EC of the European Parliament and of the Council on the legal protection of biotechnological inventions [1998] OJ L 213/13.

[19] See M Herdegen, 'Patenting Human Genes and other Parts of the Human Body under EC Biotechnology Directive' (2000/01) 3 Bio-Science Law Review 102.

2. Biological material which is isolated from its natural environment or produced by means of a technical process may be the subject of an invention.

The criterion of 'industrial application' must be interpreted in the light of the 23rd recital in the preamble to the Directive:

(23) Whereas a mere DNA sequence without indication of a function does not contain any technical information and is therefore not a patentable invention; [...].

In Article 5, the Directive establishes the patentability of elements of the human body including gene sequences if isolated or produced by means of a technical process:

1. The human body, at the various stages of its formation and development, and the simple discovery of one of its elements, including the sequence or partial sequence of a gene, cannot constitute patentable inventions.
2. An element isolated from the human body or otherwise produced by means of a technical process, including the sequence or partial sequence of a gene, may constitute a patentable invention, even if the structure of that element is identical to that of a natural element.
3. The industrial application of a sequence or a partial sequence of a gene must be disclosed in the patent application.

Certain inventions, for example essentially biological processes for the production of plants and animals, are excluded from patentability on grounds of their object or kind of process (Article 4 of the Directive). Certain inventions are considered unpatentable for reasons of public policy or morality (Article 6 of the Directive). Thus, Article 6(2) of the Directive, inter alia, extends non-patentability to processes for cloning human beings (*lit* a) and processes involving the use of human embryos (*lit* c). On the basis of a rather broad interpretation of this provision, the European Court of Justice held that inventions involving human embryonic stem cells may not be patented.[20]

A particularly controversial issue refers to the 'absolute protection' for DNA sequences. Such absolute protection, as it is known in the field of traditional chemical or physical substances, is most problematic, because an isolated or synthesized gene segment may have multiple functions and some of them may be discovered after the patent was granted. This multi-functionality of DNA sequences as information carriers suggests that patent protection should be limited to the functions described in the patent application ('functional limitation').[21] By contrast, the guidelines of the US Patent and Trademark Office (Utility Examination Guidelines)[22] are comparatively generous as to the absolute protection of patents

[20] ECJ Case C-34/10 *Oliver Brüstle v Greenpeace eV* [2011] ECR I-9821.
[21] M Herdegen, 'Patenting Human Genes and Other Parts of the Body Under EC Law' (2002) European Biopharmaceutical Review 43 (44). See § 1a (3) of the German Patent Act.
[22] Federal Register Vol 66/4 (2001) 1092.

on genes or DNA sequences, without limits resulting from the functions disclosed by the inventor.

3. The Protection of Intellectual Property Rights in Broader International Context

The protection of intellectual property rights under the TRIPS Agreement stands in context with a number of other international agreements. The Paris Convention for the Protection of Industrial Property of 1883 covers patents, utility models, industrial designs, trademarks, service marks, trade names, indications of source or appellations of origin and the repression of unfair competition (Article 1(2)). The Convention provides for national treatment (Article 2). A cornerstone of the Paris Convention is the principle of priority established by Article 4 A:

(1) Any person who has duly filed an application for a patent, or for the registration of a utility model, or of an industrial design, or of a trademark, in one of the countries of the Union, or his successor in title, shall enjoy, for the purpose of filing in the other countries, a right of priority during the periods hereinafter fixed.

(2) Any filing that is equivalent to a regular national filing under the domestic legislation of any country of the Union or under bilateral or multilateral treaties concluded between countries of the Union shall be recognized as giving rise to the right of priority.

(3) By a regular national filing is meant any filing that is adequate to establish the date on which the application was filed in the country concerned, whatever may be the subsequent fate of the application.

The most important treaties on copyright agreements are the (Revised) Berne Convention for the Protection of Literary and Artistic Works of 1886 and the (Revised) Universal Copyright Convention of 1952. The International Convention for the Protection of New Varieties of Plants (UPOV) is of relevance for rights of the breeder with respect to the use of propagating material of protected varieties (Articles 14ff). The 1989 Treaty of Washington on Intellectual Property in Respect of Integrated Circuits addresses the protection of intellectual property in the field of micro-electronic technologies, for example with respect to computer topographies. The 2006 Singapore Treaty on the Law of Trademarks is another important agreement. The World Intellectual Property Organization (WIPO), established under the 1967 Stockholm Convention and based in Geneva, provides an inter-governmental forum for promoting intellectual property and cooperates with other international organizations.

Under the Convention on the Grant of European Patents (European Patent Convention) of 1973 (as amended in 2000), the European Patent Office issues European patents. These patents may be described as a bundle of national patents, having the same effect as a national patent in all contracting States (which include all Member States of the European Union). Article 2 of the European Patent Convention provides:

(1) Patents granted under this Convention shall be called European patents.
(2) The European patent shall, in each of the Contracting States for which it is granted, have the effect of and be subject to the same conditions as a national patent granted by that State, unless this Convention provides otherwise.

In the European Union, legislation created a 'unitary patent' issued by the European Patent Office, which shall have uniform effect and enjoy equal protection in all EU Member States.[23] An agreement among EU Member States establishes a Unified Patent Court.[24] The first unified patent can only be issued after the Agreement on a Unified Patent Court has entered into force.

The International Treaty on Plant Genetic Resources for Food and Agriculture (FAO 'Seed Treaty'),[25] addresses so-called farmers' rights and provides for the protection of traditional knowledge about crops by States Parties (Article 9.2(b)). The Treaty serves as a basis for a multilateral system of facilitated access to plant genetic resources for food and agricultural purposes (Articles 10ff). Under this system, recipients may not be able to invoke intellectual property rights that limit facilitated access to plant genetic resources (Article 12.3(d)). A material transfer agreement (MTA) shall govern distribution of benefits and other aspects of the transfer of plant genetic resources (Article 12.4).

Recent developments include agreements with 'TRIPS-plus' standards, for example the free trade agreements of the United States with Australia (Article 17.1.4.) or with Jordan (Article 4.19). The 2011 Anti-Counterfeiting Trade Agreement (ACTA) was negotiated between Australia, Canada, the European Union (and its Member States), Japan, Jordan, Morocco, Mexico, New Zealand, Switzerland, Singapore, South Korea, the United Arab Emirates, and the United States. ACTA does not create new substantive standards of protection, but aims to effectively enforce existing TRIPS obligations. ACTA, inter alia, provides civil liability for damages of infringers (Article 9) and criminal sanctions at least in cases of wilful trademark counterfeiting and of copyright or related rights piracy (Article 23). The ACTA provisions on enforcement in the digital environment (Articles 27ff), for example on disclosure of information by online service providers, have triggered a vivid controversy. Somehow ambiguously, ACTA maintains the contracting parties' freedom to limit liability of online service providers 'while preserving the legitimate interests of rights holders' (note 13 to Article 27). ACTA has drawn criticism for having been negotiated outside the WTO and without the involvement of the

---

[23] See Articles 3 and 5(2) of Regulation (EU) No 1257/2012 of 17 December 2012 implementing enhanced cooperation in the area of the creation of unitary patent protection [2012] OJ L361/1.
[24] See Agreement on a Unified Patent Court, Council of the European Union, Doc 2013/C 175/01.
[25] See C Fowler, 'Plant Genetic Resources for Food and Agriculture—Developments in International Law and Politics' (2004/05) 7 Bio-Science Law Review 53; T Stoll, 'The FAO "Seed Treaty"—New International Rules for the Conservation and Sustainable Use of Plant Genetic Resources for Food and Agriculture' (2004) 1 Journal of International Biotechnology Law 239.

WIPO.[26] The European Parliament rejected the ratification of ACTA in July 2012, fearing undue interferences with the freedom of internet.

Select Bibliography

GENERAL ASPECTS

FM Abbott, 'Toward a New Era of Objective Assessment in the Field of TRIPS and Variable Geometry for the Preservation of Multilateralism' (2005) 8 EJIL 77.

C Arup, *The World Trade Organization Knowledge Agreements* (2nd edn, CUP 2008) 285.

CM Correa, *Trade-Related Aspects of Intellectual Property Rights: A Commentary on the TRIPS Agreement* (OUP 2007).

T Cottier, 'The Agreement on Trade-Related Aspects of Intellectual Property Rights' in PFJ Macrory, AE Appleton, and MG Plummer (eds), *The World Trade Organization: Legal, Economic and Political Analysis* (Springer 2005) vol 1, 1041.

T Cottier and P Véron (eds), *Concise International and European IP Law* (3rd edn, Kluwer Law International 2015).

AM Mitchell and T Voon, 'TRIPS' in D Bethlehem, D McRae, R Neufeld, and I van Damme (eds), *The Oxford Handbook of International Trade Law* (OUP 2009) 186.

PATENT RIGHTS

FM Abbott, 'The WTO Medicines Decision: World Pharmaceutical Trade and the Protection of Public Health' (2005) 99 AJIL 317.

M Adcock and M Llewelyn, 'TRIPS and the Patentability of Micro-Organisms' (2000/01) 3 Bio-Science Law Review 91.

PW Grubb and PR Thomsen, *Patents for Chemicals, Pharmaceuticals and Biotechnology* (5th edn, OUP 2010).

M Herdegen, 'Patents on Parts of the Human Body—Salient Issues under EC and WTO Law' (2002) 5 Journal of World Intellectual Property 145.

GP Hestermeyer, *Human Rights and the WTO* (OUP 2007).

R Kampf, 'Patents versus Patients?' (2002) 40 AVR 90.

N Pires de Carvalho, *The TRIPS Regime of Patents and Test Data* (4th edn, Wolters Kluwer Law & Business 2014).

THE PROTECTION OF INTELLECTUAL PROPERTY RIGHTS IN BROADER INTERNATIONAL CONTEXT

SD Anderman (ed), *International Property and Competition Law: New Frontiers* (OUP 2011).

L Bently and B Sherman, *Intellectual Property Law* (4th edn, OUP 2014).

C Colston and J Galloway, *Modern Intellectual Property Law* (3rd edn, Routledge 2010).

T Cottier and P Véron (eds), *Concise International and European IP Law* (3rd edn, Kluwer Law International 2015).

---

[26] An analysis of the WTO's usual relationship with the WIPO is given in V Hrbatá, 'No International Organization is an Island ... the WTO's Relationship with the WIPO: A Model for the Governance of Trade Linkage Areas?' (2010) 44 JWT 1.

GB Dinwoodie, WO Hennesy, S Perimutter, and GW Austin, *Intellectual Property Law and Policy* (2nd edn, LexisNexis 2008).

G Dutfield and U Suthersanen, *Global Intellectual Property Law* (Edward Elgar Publishing 2008).

JJ Fawcett and P Torremans, *Intellectual Property and Private International Law* (2nd edn, OUP 2011).

P Goldstein, *International Intellectual Property Law, Cases and Materials* (4th edn, Foundation Press 2015).

CA Nard, MJ Madison, and M McKenna, *The Law of Intellectual Property* (4th edn, Wolters Kluwer Law & Business 2013).

XIX

Subsidies and Anti-dumping Measures

State subsidies are a major factor in the distortion of international competition.[1] Industrialized countries account for the great bulk of subsidies (especially in the agricultural sector). Although subsidies are a popular instrument of State intervention in the economy, the GATT only addresses them in a rather rudimentary and cautious way. Under the general provision of Article XVI:1 of the GATT, subsidies which may change competitive conditions in favour of domestic products must be notified. Paragraphs 2 to 4 of Article XVI of the GATT specifically refer to export subsidies. According to paragraph 3, subsidies on the export of primary products shall be avoided. The Subsidies Code of 1979 banned subsidies on the export of finished products. Under Article VI:3 of the GATT, countervailing duties on subsidized products may not go beyond neutralizing the competitive advantage of a subsidy.

1. Subsidies and Countervailing Measures (SCM Agreement)

The Agreement on Subsidies and Countervailing Measures (SCM Agreement),[2] negotiated during the Uruguay Round as one of the multilateral trade agreements, establishes a regime for subsidies which is much tighter than pre-existing rules.[3] The SCM Agreement defines a 'subsidy' in Article 1.1:

For the purpose of this Agreement, a subsidy shall be deemed to exist if:
(a) (1) there is a financial contribution by a government or any public body within the territory of a Member (referred to in this Agreement as 'government'), i.e. where:

---

[1] See eg P Poretti, *The Regulation of Subsidies Within the General Agreement on Trade in Services of the WTO: Problems und Prospects* (Kluwer Law International 2009); for an overview of the importance and the problems of subsidies for the world economy, see WTO, *World Trade Report* (2008) 34 <https://www.wto.org/english/res_e/publications_e/wtr08_e.htm> (accessed 23 June 2016).

[2] See PA Clarke and GN Horlick, 'The Agreement on Subsidies and Countervailing Measures' in PFJ Macrory, AE Appleton, and MG Plummer (eds), *The World Trade Organization: Legal, Economic and Political Analysis* (Springer 2005) vol 1, 679; for a critical analysis, see DP Steger, 'The Subsidies and Countervailing Measures Agreement: Ahead of its Time or Time for Reform?' (2010) 44 JWT 779.

[3] See MS Slotboom, 'Subsidies in WTO Law and in EC Law. Broad and Narrow Definitions' (2002) 36 JWT 517.

    (i)   a government practice involves a direct transfer of funds (e.g. grants, loans, and equity infusion), potential direct transfers of funds or liabilities (e.g. loan guarantees);

    (ii)   government revenue that is otherwise due is foregone or not collected (e.g. fiscal incentives such as tax credits);

    (iii) a government provides goods or services other than general infrastructure, or purchases goods;

    (iv) a government makes payments to a funding mechanism, or entrusts or directs a private body to carry out one or more of the type of functions illustrated in (i) to (iii) above which would normally be vested in the government and the practice, in no real sense, differs from practices normally followed by governments; or

  (2) there is any form of income or price support in the sense of Article XVI of GATT 1994; and

(b) a benefit is thereby conferred.

The determination of a 'benefit' within the meaning of Article 1.1(b) depends on a market oriented perspective. To qualify as a benefit, a financial contribution by a government or any public body must be more favourable than prevailing market conditions under the same circumstances. Article 14 second sentence of the SCM establishes parameters for the determination and the calculation of a benefit:

Article 14

For the purpose of Part V [Countervailing Measures], any method used by the investigating authority to calculate the benefit to the recipient conferred pursuant to paragraph 1 of Article 1 shall be provided for in the national legislation or implementing regulations of the Member concerned and its application to each particular case shall be transparent and adequately explained. Furthermore, any such method shall be consistent with the following guidelines:

(a) government provision of equity capital shall not be considered as conferring a benefit, unless the investment decision can be regarded as inconsistent with the usual investment practice (including for the provision of risk capital) of private investors in the territory of that Member;

(b) a loan by a government shall not be considered as conferring a benefit, unless there is a difference between the amount that the firm receiving the loan pays on the government loan and the amount the firm would pay on a comparable commercial loan which the firm could actually obtain on the market. In this case the benefit shall be the difference between these two amounts;

(c) a loan guarantee by a government shall not be considered as conferring a benefit, unless there is a difference between the amount that the firm receiving the guarantee pays on a loan guaranteed by the government and the amount that the firm would pay on a comparable commercial loan absent the government guarantee. In this case the benefit shall be the difference between these two amounts adjusted for any differences in fees;

(d) the provision of goods or services or purchase of goods by a government shall not be considered as conferring a benefit unless the provision is made for less than adequate remuneration, or the purchase is made for more than adequate remuneration. The adequacy of remuneration shall be determined in relation to prevailing market conditions for the good or service in question in the country of provision or purchase (including price, quality, availability, marketability, transportation and other conditions of purchase or sale).

A benefit is, thus, conferred if the recipient obtained a financial contribution at better terms than the marketplace offers in the same situation. In *Canada— Aircraft*, the Panel compared the market conditions and the government's terms:

[T]he word 'benefit', as used in Article 1.1(b), implies some kind of comparison. This must be so, for there can be no 'benefit' to the recipient unless the 'financial contribution' makes the recipient 'better off' than it would otherwise have been, absent that contribution. In our view, the marketplace provides an appropriate basis for comparison in determining whether a 'benefit' has been 'conferred', because the trade-distorting potential of a 'financial contribution' can be identified by determining whether the recipient has received a 'financial contribution' on terms more favourable than those available to the recipient in the market.[4]

This comparison with market conditions corresponds to the so-called 'private investor test' ('rational investor test') practised under the EU law on State aids.[5]

Indirect economic advantages for the State flowing from subsidised productivity (eg increased tax revenues) cannot be offset against the benefits granted by the government.[6]

Sometimes, the determination of the relevant market (which provides the comparative parameters for the benefit analysis) raises difficult issues. When the government creates a demand for new products or services conforming to particular regulatory standards (eg energy from renewable sources), this new market is governed by other conditions than the broader unregulated market (eg the wholesale market for energy from all possible sources). In such a new market, governmental regulation sets the prevailing standards of the market conditions. If the market for regulated products or services is considered relevant for the benefit analysis, the government may provide financial incentives for the products or services which conform to market conditions (unless the incentives distort competition within the new market).

In this sense, in *Canada—Renewable Energy*, the Appellate Body deferred to the government's choice of an energy-mix with support for regulated wind power and solar production of electricity which creates a new market:

[...] [A] distinction should be drawn between, on the one hand, government interventions that create markets that would otherwise not exist and, on the other hand, other types of government interventions in support of certain players in markets that already exist, or to correct market distortions therein. Where a government creates a market, it cannot be said that the government intervention distorts the market, as there would not be a market if the government had not created it. While the creation of markets by a government does not *in and of itself* give rise to subsidies within the meaning of the SCM Agreement, government interventions in existing markets may amount to subsidies when they take the form of a

---

    [4] WTO, *Canada: Measures Affecting the Export of Civilian Aircraft—Report of the Panel* (1999) WT/DS70/R paras 9.111ff.
    [5] ECJ Case C-234/84 *Kingdom of Belgium v Commission* [1986] ECR 2263 para 14.
    [6] WTO, *European Communities and Certain Member States: Measures Affecting Trade in Large Civil Aircraft—Report of the Panel* (2010) WT/DS316/R para 7.429.

financial contribution, or income or price support, and confer a benefit to specific enterprises or industries.[7]

This approach vests members with broad freedom to promote 'green' energy with financial support, such as guaranteed prices paid by public entities.

The SCM Agreement only targets subsidies which are 'specific', that is which benefit a specific company, specific groups of enterprises, or specific industry sectors (Article 1.2). Article 2 of the SCM Agreement further defines the elements of 'specificity':

Article 2: Specificity

2.1 In order to determine whether a subsidy, as defined in paragraph 1 of Article 1, is specific to an enterprise or industry or group of enterprises or industries (referred to in this Agreement as 'certain enterprises') within the jurisdiction of the granting authority, the following principles shall apply:

  (a) Where the granting authority, or the legislation pursuant to which the granting authority operates, explicitly limits access to a subsidy to certain enterprises, such subsidy shall be specific.

  (b) Where the granting authority, or the legislation pursuant to which the granting authority operates, establishes objective criteria or conditions governing the eligibility for, and the amount of, a subsidy, specificity shall not exist, provided that the eligibility is automatic and that such criteria and conditions are strictly adhered to. The criteria or conditions must be clearly spelled out in law, regulation, or other official document, so as to be capable of verification.

  (c) If, notwithstanding any appearance of non-specificity resulting from the application of the principles laid down in subparagraphs (a) and (b), there are reasons to believe that the subsidy may in fact be specific, other factors may be considered. Such factors are: use of a subsidy programme by a limited number of certain enterprises, predominant use by certain enterprises, the granting of disproportionately large amounts of subsidy to certain enterprises, and the manner in which discretion has been exercised by the granting authority in the decision to grant a subsidy. In applying this subparagraph, account shall be taken of the extent of diversification of economic activities within the jurisdiction of the granting authority, as well as of the length of time during which the subsidy programme has been in operation.

2.2 A subsidy which is limited to certain enterprises located within a designated geographical region within the jurisdiction of the granting authority shall be specific. It is understood that the setting or change of generally applicable tax rates by all levels of government entitled to do so shall not be deemed to be a specific subsidy for the purposes of this Agreement.

2.3 Any subsidy falling under the provisions of Article 3 shall be deemed to be specific.

2.4 Any determination of specificity under the provisions of this Article shall be clearly substantiated on the basis of positive evidence.

A benefit lacks 'specificity' if it is granted according to general criteria which do not privilege particular sectors (such as start-up aid for new businesses or benefits for

---

[7] WTO, *Canada: Certain Measures Affecting the Renewable Energy Generation* Sector—*Report of the Appellate Body* (2013) WT/DS412/AB/R and WT/DS426/AB/R para 5.188.

the hiring of persons after long-term unemployment). The SCM Agreement qualifies certain subsidies, such as incentives for certain businesses within a designated area (Article 2.2) and export subsidies (Article 2.3), automatically as 'specific'.

According to the clearly prevailing view, exchange rate manipulations which keep the value of a State's currency low in the interest of exports do not qualify as a 'specific benefit' nor do they depend on the specific performance of exports and therefore cannot be considered as export subsidies under Article 3.1(a) of the SCM Agreement either.

The SCM Agreement originally followed a three-tiered regime for the admissibility of subsidies, distinguishing between three categories of subsidies according to a 'traffic light' model. These categories were:

- prohibited subsidies ('red box');
- actionable subsidies ('amber box'); and
- non-actionable subsidies ('green box'), which no longer exist as a separate category.

The legitimate (non-actionable) subsidies were listed in the catalogue of Article 8. This provision has expired (Article 31). Thus, the only two remaining categories of subsidies governed by the SCM Agreement are prohibited and actionable subsidies. A special and differentiated regime applies to developing countries (Article 27).

Article 3 addresses the prohibited subsidies:

3.1 Except as provided in the Agreement on Agriculture, the following subsidies, within the meaning of Article 1, shall be prohibited:
    (a) subsidies contingent, in law or in fact, whether solely or as one of several other conditions, upon export performance, including those illustrated in Annex I;
    (b) subsidies contingent, whether solely or as one of several other conditions, upon the use of domestic over imported goods.
3.2 A Member shall neither grant nor maintain subsidies referred to in paragraph 1.

Export subsidies (*lit* a) can be made dependent on the export performance either by law ('de jure export-contingency') or by a factual link ('de facto export-contingency'), as footnote 4 of the SCM Agreement clarifies.[8] To establish factual dependence, it must be shown that the subsidy purports to create export incentives, which would not exist otherwise in the light of the natural interplay of supply and demand.

The disputes over subsidies for the European and the United States aircraft industry provided occasion to clarify the scope of prohibited export subsidies.

In *EC—Large Civil Aircraft*,[9] the United States had complained about subsidies for the Airbus consortium (start-up assistance by the European Investment Bank

---

[8] It reads: 'This standard is met when the facts demonstrate that the granting of a subsidy, without having been made legally contingent upon export performance, is in fact tied to actual or anticipated exportation or export earnings. The mere fact that a subsidy is granted to enterprises which export shall not for that reason alone be considered to be an export subsidy within the meaning of this provision.'

[9] WTO, *European Communities and Certain Member States: Measures Affecting Trade in Large Civil Aircraft—Report of the Panel* (2010) WT/DS316/R; WTO, *European Communities and Certain*

and financial support by EU Member States). In turn, the European Community initiated a dispute settlement procedure (*US—Large Civil Aircraft*[10]) because of subsidies granted to Boeing (through military contracts).

The Appellate Body in *EC—Large Civil Aircraft*[11] focused on incentives which were alien to undistorted market conditions:

> [W]e do *not* suggest that the standard is met merely because the granting of the subsidy is designed to increase a recipient's production, even if the increased production is exported in whole. We also do *not* suggest that the fact that the granting of the subsidy may, in addition to increasing exports, *also* increase the recipient's domestic sales would prevent a finding of *de facto* export contingency. Rather, we consider that the standard for *de facto* export contingency under Article 3.1(a) and footnote 4 of the *SCM Agreement* would be met when the subsidy is granted so as to provide an incentive to the recipient to export in a way that is not simply reflective of the conditions of supply and demand in the domestic and export markets undistorted by the granting of the subsidy.[12]

According to the Appellate Body, a parameter indicative of a de facto export subsidy is the (actual or expected) ratio of export rates and of the domestic sales rate before and after the granting of the subsidy, with hypothetical development based on the performance of a profit-maximizing company:

> [W]here relevant evidence exists, the assessment could be based on a comparison between, on the one hand, the ratio of *anticipated* export and domestic sales of the subsidized product that would come about in consequence of the granting of the subsidy, and, on the other hand, the situation in the absence of the subsidy. The situation in the absence of the subsidy may be understood on the basis of historical sales of the same product by the recipient in the domestic and export markets before the subsidy was granted. In the event that there are no historical data untainted by the subsidy, or the subsidized product is a new product for which no historical data exists, the comparison could be made with the performance that a profit-maximizing firm would hypothetically be expected to achieve in the export and domestic markets in the absence of the subsidy. Where the evidence shows, all other things being equal, that the granting of the subsidy provides an incentive to skew anticipated sales towards exports, in comparison with the historical performance of the recipient or the hypothetical performance of a profit-maximizing firm in the absence of the subsidy, this would be an indication that the granting of the subsidy is in fact tied to anticipated exportation within the meaning of Article 3.1(a) and footnote 4 of the SCM Agreement.[13]

Member States: Measures Affecting Trade in Large Civil Aircraft—Report of the Appellate Body (2011) WT/DS316/AB/R.

[10] WTO, *United States: Measures Affecting Trade in Large Civil Aircraft—Report of the Appellate Body* (2012) WT/DS353/AB/R; for a general insight into the complex field of aircrafts and WTO law, see RO Cunningham and P Lichtenbaum, 'The Agreement on Trade in Civil Aircraft and Other Issues Relating to Civil Aircraft in the GATT/WTO System' in PFJ Macrory, AE Appleton, and MG Plummer (eds), *The World Trade Organization: Legal, Economic and Political Analysis* (Springer 2005) vol 1, 1165.

[11] WTO, *European Communities and Certain Member States: Measures Affecting Trade in Large Civil Aircraft—Report of the Appellate Body* (2011) WT/DS316/AB/R.

[12] WTO, *European Communities and Certain Member States: Measures Affecting Trade in Large Civil Aircraft—Report of the Appellate Body* (2011) WT/DS316/AB/R para 1045.

[13] WTO, *European Communities and Certain Member States: Measures Affecting Trade in Large Civil Aircraft—Report of the Appellate Body* (2011) WT/DS316/AB/R para 1047.

This understanding of Article 3.1(a) of the SCM Agreement essentially follows the respective interpretation of the Appellate Body in *Canada—Aircraft*.[14] It also guides the Panel Report in *US—Aircraft*.[15]

'Actionable subsidies' fall under Part III of the SCM Agreement. 'Actionable subsidies' are not per se prohibited, but members must avoid detrimental effects on the interests of other Member States. Article 5 of the SCM Agreement provides:

No Member should cause, through the use of any subsidy referred to in paragraphs 1 and 2 of Article 1, adverse effects to the interests of other Members, i.e.:
(a) injury to the domestic industry of another Member;
(b) nullification or impairment of benefits accruing directly or indirectly to other Members under GATT 1994 in particular the benefits of concessions bound under Article II of GATT 1994;
(c) serious prejudice to the interests of another Member.

This Article does not apply to subsidies maintained on agricultural products as provided in Article 13 of the Agreement on Agriculture.

A key notion is the 'serious prejudice to the interests of another Member' in terms of Article 5(c). Article 6.1–3 provide guidance on the circumstances which allow assuming a 'serious prejudice':

6.1 Serious prejudice in the sense of paragraph (c) of Article 5 shall be deemed to exist in the case of:
(a) the total ad valorem subsidization of a product exceeding 5 per cent:
(b) subsidies to cover operating losses sustained by an industry;
(c) subsidies to cover operating losses sustained by an enterprise, other than one-time measures which are non-recurrent and cannot be repeated for that enterprise and which are given merely to provide time for the development of long-term solutions and to avoid acute social problems;
(d) direct forgiveness of debt, i.e. forgiveness of government-held debt, and grants to cover debt repayment.
6.2 Notwithstanding the provisions of paragraph 1, serious prejudice shall not be found if the subsidizing Member demonstrates that the subsidy in question has not resulted in any of the effects enumerated in paragraph 3.
6.3 Serious prejudice in the sense of paragraph (c) of Article 5 may arise in any case where one or several of the following apply:
(a) the effect of the subsidy is to displace or impede the imports of a like product of another Member into the market of the subsidizing Member;
(b) the effect of the subsidy is to displace or impede the exports of a like product of another Member from a third country market;
(c) the effect of the subsidy is a significant price undercutting by the subsidized product as compared with the price of a like product of another Member in the same market or significant price suppression, price depression or lost sales in the same market;

---

[14] WTO, *Canada: Measures Affecting the Export of Civilian Aircraft—Report of the Appellate Body* (1999) WT/DS70/AB/R.
[15] WTO, *United States: Measures Affecting Trade in Large Civil Aircraft—Report of the Panel* (2011) WT/DS353/R para 7.1516.

(d) the effect of the subsidy is an increase in the world market share of the subsidizing Member in a particular subsidized primary product or commodity as compared to the average share it had during the previous period of three years and this increase follows a consistent trend over a period when subsidies have been granted.

In *US—Upland Cotton*,[16] the Appellate Body specified the requirements of Article 6.3(c).[17] In this case, Brazil complained about a billion-dollar bundle of support measures for the United States cotton industry. Rejecting the US view that the relevant ('same') market within the meaning of Article 6.3(c) can only be a national market, the Appellate Body considered the world market as relevant, if there is global competition between the subsidized product and the like product of another member, and if competitive conditions (including transport costs) justify the assumption of a global market:

[R]ecalling that one accepted definition of 'market' is 'the area of economic activity in which buyers and sellers come together and the forces of supply and demand affect prices', it seems reasonable to conclude that two products would be in the same market if they were engaged in actual or potential competition in that market. Thus, two products may be 'in the same market' even if they are not necessarily sold at the same time and in the same place or country. As the Panel correctly pointed out, the scope of the 'market', for determining the area of competition between two products, may depend on several factors such as the nature of the product, the homogeneity of the conditions of competition, and transport costs. This market for a particular product could well be a 'world market'.[18]

The SCM Agreement contains its own mechanisms for resolving disputes and provides for specific remedies (Articles 4 and 7). One form of remedy is the recovery of subsidies already disbursed. Countervailing duties must conform to Article VI of the GATT and the SCM Agreement (Article 10 of the SCM Agreement). The determination of countervailing duties is subject to Article 19.

According to Article 32.1, '[n]o specific action against a subsidy of another Member can be taken except in accordance with the provisions of GATT 1994, as interpreted by this Agreement.'

In the 'Byrd Amendment' case (*US—Offset Act*), the Appellate Body qualified a measure as 'specific' in terms of Article 32.1, if it responds to acts for which the subsidy is 'constitutive'.[19] The Appellate Body further clarified that a measure is directed 'against' subsidies if it has a dissuasive effect on the practice of granting subsidies by another State:

We agree with the Panel that our statement in *US—1916 Act*—to the effect that 'the ordinary meaning of the phrase "specific action against dumping" of exports within the meaning

[16] WTO, *United States: Subsidies on Upland Cotton—Report of the Appellate Body* (2005) WT/DS/267/AB/R; see RH Steinberg, 'United States: Subsidies on Upland Cotton, WTO Doc WT/DS267/AB/R' (2005) 99 AJIL 852.

[17] For an analysis of the legal development following *United States: Subsidies on Upland Cotton*, see D Coppens, 'WTO Disciplines on Export Credit Support for Agricultural Products in the Wake of the US—Upland Cotton Case and the Doha Round Negotiations' (2010) 44 JWT 349.

[18] WTO, *United States: Subsidies on Upland Cotton—Report of the Appellate Body* (2005) WT/DS/267/AB/R para 408.

[19] WTO, *United States: Continued Dumping and Subsidy Offset Act of 2000—Report of the Appellate Body* (2003) WT/DS217/AB/R and WT/DS234/AB/R para 242.

of Article 18.1 is action that is taken in response to situations presenting the constituent elements of "dumping" ' [...]—is not conclusive as to the nature of the condition flowing from the term 'against'. The Panel took the position that an action operates 'against' dumping or a subsidy within the meaning of Article 18.1 of the Anti-Dumping Agreement and Article 32.1 of the SCM Agreement if it has an *adverse bearing* on dumping or subsidization.[20]

Countervailing measures must keep within the framework of the SCM Agreement.[21] This constitutes a severe limitation in the possibilities of action that may be taken by individual Member States.

The 'Byrd Amendment' case (*US—Offset Act*) turned on a US law under which revenues from anti-dumping and countervailing duties were distributed among US companies which had complained about the foreign dumping measures and subsidies. The Appellate Body regarded this form of compensation for domestic industries as a response falling out of the enumerative countermeasures permitted under the SCM Agreement.[22]

2. The Agreement on Agriculture

A most contentious issue are subsidies in the agricultural sector.[23] In particular, the European Union and—to a lesser extent—Japan and the United States, with their agricultural subsidies, are responsible for a massive distortion of international competition. Export-oriented emerging and developing countries are primarily affected by subsidies granted by industrialized WTO Members to their agricultural sector.[24] On the other hand, agricultural subsidies of developed countries often lower world market prices for many agricultural products. In particular, least developed countries which are net importers of agricultural products may indirectly benefit from subsidies.

The Agreement on Agriculture (AoA)[25] aims at gradually reducing agricultural subsidies. The AoA modifies the 'traffic light' approach of the SCM Agreement. There is no category of prohibited subsidies ('red box'). Subsidies with distorting effects on international trade are subject to the commitment of gradual reduction

---

[20] WTO, *United States: Continued Dumping and Subsidy Offset Act of 2000—Report of the Appellate Body* (2003) WT/DS217/AB/R and WT/DS234/AB/R para 247, footnote omitted.

[21] WTO, *United States: Continued Dumping and Subsidy Offset Act of 2000—Report of the Appellate Body* (2003) WT/DS217/AB/R and WT/DS234/AB/R para 273.

[22] WTO, *United States: Continued Dumping and Subsidy Offset Act of 2000—Report of the Appellate Body* (2003) WT/DS217/AB/R and WT/DS234/AB/R paras 273f.

[23] See T Beierle, 'Agricultural Trade Liberalization—Uruguay, Doha, and Beyond' (2002) 36 JWT 1089; DK Das, 'The Doha Round of Multilateral Trade Negotiations and Trade in Agriculture' (2006) 40 JWT 259; W Koo and PL Kennedy, 'The Impact of Agriculture Subsidies on Global Welfare' (2006) 88 AJAE 1219.

[24] For an insight of the importance of agriculture for African countries in the Doha round negotiations, see RE Mshomba, *Africa and the World Trade Organization* (CUP 2009) 143.

[25] See JA McMahon, 'The Agreement on Agriculture' in PFJ Macrory, AE Appleton, and MG Plummer (eds), *The World Trade Organization: Legal, Economic and Political Analysis* (Springer 2005) vol 1, 187.

('amber box' measures). 'Green box' measures are non-distortive subsidies which are permanently permitted under the AoA and which could even be expanded. Some distortive subsidies are exempted from reduction commitments under certain conditions ('blue box' measures).

Export subsidies (in terms of Article 1(e)) are subject to reduction commitments (Articles 3.3 and 9). Article 3.3 incorporates the commitments of members under their schedule:

Subject to the provisions of paragraphs 2(b) and 4 of Article 9, a Member shall not provide export subsidies listed in paragraph 1 of Article 9 in respect of the agricultural products or groups of products specified in Section II of Part IV of its Schedule in excess of the budgetary outlay and quantity commitment levels specified therein and shall not provide such subsidies in respect of any agricultural product not specified in that Section of its Schedule.

Under Article 9.1, several categories of export subsidies are subject to reduction commitments. Article 9.2(b)(iv) sets the reduction export subsidies and the quantities benefiting from such subsidies in relation to 1986–90 base period levels, requiring that

[…] the Member's budgetary outlays for export subsidies and the quantities benefiting from such subsidies, at the conclusion of the implementation period, are no greater than 64 per cent and 79 per cent of the 1986–1990 base period levels, respectively. For developing country Members these percentages shall be 76 and 86 per cent, respectively […].

According to Article 10.1 of the AoA, a member must not use export subsidies, which are not subject to the reduction commitment under Article 9.1 of the AoA, in ways leading to a circumvention of the rules on export subsidies:

Export subsidies not listed in paragraph 1 of Article 9 shall not be applied in a manner which results in, or which threatens to lead to, circumvention of export subsidy commitments; nor shall non-commercial transactions be used to circumvent such commitments.

In this light, it is controversial, whether export credits (by which developed countries grant financial aid to other countries importing agricultural products from the donor country) are subject to the contractual reduction commitments as well.

Articles 6 and 7, in conjunction with Annex 2 to the AoA, refer to subsidies which do not relate to export ('domestic support'). A number of internal subsidies which serve regional, social, and environmental interests as well as certain forms of direct payment (eg under certain structural adjustment or disaster relief programmes) qualify as 'green box' measures. Other domestic subsidies are subject to reduction commitments. However, some subsidies are exempted from the reduction commitment ('blue-box' measures), such as direct payments under production-limiting programmes (Article 6.5(a)).

The Tenth Ministerial Conference of December 2015 in Nairobi has agreed on the elimination of all export subsidies.[26] The Ministerial Decision of 19 December 2015 regarding export competition aims at entirely abolishing export subsidies in

---

[26] See Ministerial Decision (19 December 2015) WT/MIN(15)/45.

the long run whilst considering the specific needs and wishes of developing countries. According to this decision, developed countries are required to eliminate all scheduled export subsidies as of the date of adoption[27] whereas developing countries may do so until the end of 2018.[28] Least-developed and net food-importing countries are exempted from the obligation to eliminate scheduled export subsidies. Developing countries shall continue to benefit from Article 9.4 of the Agreement on Agriculture until 2023, least-developed countries and net food-importing countries until 2030.[29] All three groups of countries benefit from special treatment concerning certain forms of export credits.[30]

The SCM Agreement excludes subsidies allowed under the Agreement on Agriculture from the scope of prohibited export subsidies and actionable subsidies (Article 3.1 and Article 5 second sentence). However, the exemption under Article 13 of the AoA expired by the end of 2003.[31]

3. Dumping and Anti-dumping Measures

As the GATT does not categorically prohibit subsidies, it does not categorically ban dumping measures either. 'Dumping' in this context refers to the marketing of exported goods at a price lower than its normal value.

Article VI:1 second sentence of the GATT clarifies the conditions of dumping:

For the purposes of this Article, a product is to be considered as being introduced into the commerce of an importing country at less than its normal value, if the price of the product exported from one country to another
(a) is less than the comparable price, in the ordinary course of trade, for the like product when destined for consumption in the exporting country, or,
(b) in the absence of such domestic price, is less than either
    (i) the highest comparable price for the like product for export to any third country in the ordinary course of trade, or
    (ii) the cost of production of the product in the country of origin plus a reasonable addition for selling cost and profit.

Dumping is a widespread mechanism for expanding market share in countries of import. Occasionally, the export price is even below the manufacturing costs. Article VI:1 of the GATT denounces the distortive effects of dumping:

The contracting parties recognize that dumping, by which products of one country are introduced into the commerce of another country at less than the normal value of the products, is to be condemned if it causes or threatens material injury to an established industry in the territory of a contracting party or materially retards the establishment of a domestic industry.

---

[27] Ministerial Decision (19 December 2015) WT/MIN(15)/45 para 6.
[28] Ministerial Decision (19 December 2015) WT/MIN(15)/45 para 7.
[29] Ministerial Decision (19 December 2015) WT/MIN(15)/45 para 8.
[30] Ministerial Decision (19 December 2015) WT/MIN(15)/45 paras 16, 17.
[31] See Article 1(f) of the Agreement on Agriculture.

In Article VI:2, the GATT allows members to neutralize or prevent dumping by levying anti-dumping duties, which can reach up to the amount of the 'dumping margin':[32]

In order to offset or prevent dumping, a contracting party may levy on any dumped product an anti-dumping duty not greater in amount than the margin of dumping in respect of such product. For the purposes of this Article, the margin of dumping is the price difference determined in accordance with the provisions of paragraph 1.

The Agreement on Implementation of Article VI of the GATT 1994 (Anti-Dumping Agreement)[33] establishes standards for 'specific measures' against dumping.[34] Dumping strategies often take more or less recursive forms in order to avoid countermeasures. In the case of 'assembly-dumping', importers do not introduce the end product but just major components and have them assembled in 'screwdriver factories' in the country of import in order to pass them off as 'domestic' product. In those cases, anti-dumping measures met difficulties in the past.[35]

Article 2.1 of the Anti-Dumping Agreement defines dumping as follows:

For the purpose of this Agreement, a product is to be considered as being dumped, i.e. introduced into the commerce of another country at less than its normal value, if the export price of the product exported from one country to another is less than the comparable price, in the ordinary course of trade, for the like product when destined for consumption in the exporting country.

Article 3.1 provides, that 'a determination of injury for purposes of Article VI of GATT 1994 shall be based on positive evidence and involve an objective examination of both (a) the volume of the dumped imports and the effect of the dumped imports on prices in the domestic market for like products, and (b) the consequent impact of these imports on domestic producers of such products.' In Art. 3.2, the Anti-Dumping Agreement lays down how the authorities shall examine price undercutting or other distortive effects on imports on the price level of like domestic products. As the Appellate Body held in the case China—HP-SSST the verification of 'price undercutting' calls for a dynamic evaluation of price developments:

[...] [T]hat the term 'price undercutting' in Article 3.2 is used in present participle, [suggests] that the inquire under Article 3.2 concerns pricing conduct that continues over time. Hence, Article 3.2 does not ask the question of whether an investigating authority can

---

[32] See R Bierwagen, *GATT Article VI and the Protectionist Bias in Antidumping Laws* (Wolters Kluwer Law & Business 1990); see also PA Clarke and GN Horlick, 'Injury Determinations in Antidumping and Countervailing Duty Investigations' in PFJ Macrory, AE Appleton, and MG Plummer (eds), *The World Trade Organization: Legal, Economic and Political Analysis* (Springer 2005) vol 1, 735.

[33] See E Vermulst, *The WTO Anti-Dumping Agreement: A Commentary* (OUP 2005); PFJ Macrory, 'The Anti-Dumping Agreement' in PFJ Macrory, AE Appleton, and MG Plummer (eds), *The World Trade Organization: Legal, Economic and Political Analysis* (Springer 2005) vol 1, 485.

[34] WTO, *United States: Continued Dumping and Subsidy Offset Act of 2000—Report of the Appellate Body* (2003) WT/DS217/AB/R and WT/DS234/AB/R paras 264f.

[35] See eg GATT, *European Economic Community: Regulation on Imports of Parts and Components—Report of the Panel* (1990) L/6657–37S/132; adopted by the Council on 16 May 1990, GATT C/M/241 para 26.

identify an isolated instance of the dumped imports being sold at lower prices than the domestic like products. Rather, a proper reading of 'price undercutting' under Article 3.2 suggests that the inquire requires a dynamic assessment of price developments and trends in the relationship between the prices of the dumped imports and those of domestic like products over the entire period of investigation (POI).'[36]

This approach to price developments is justified by the evolutionary relation between the price of dumped imports and those of domestic products.

Select Bibliography

I van Bael and J-F Bellis, *EU Anti-Dumping and Other Trade Defence Instruments* (5th edn, Wolters Kluwer Law & Business 2011).

L Brink and DJ Ikenson, 'Reforming the Antidumping Agreement: A Road Map for WTO Negotiations' (2002) Cato Institute Trade Policy Analysis No 21.

TW Huang, *Trade Remedies* (Kluwer Law International 2003).

JA McMahon, *The WTO Agreement on Agriculture: A Commentary* (OUP 2007).

JA McMahon and MG Desta (eds), *Research Handbook on the WTO Agriculture Agreement* (Edward Elgar Publishing 2012).

R Wolfrum, PT Stoll, and M Koebele (eds), *WTO—Trade Remedies* (Brill Academic Publishers 2007).

---

[36] WTO, *China: Measures Imposing Anti-Dumping Duties on High-Performance Stainless Steel Seamless Tubes ('HP-SSST') from Japan/the European Union—Reports of the Appellate Body* (2015) WT/DS454/AB/R and WT/DS460/AB/R para 5.159.

XX

Dispute Settlement in the WTO

Under the GATT 1947, a formalized dispute settlement regime emerged based on Article XXII (consultations)[1] and Article XXIII (complaints about nullification or impairment of benefits). The GATT regime contained elements of objective legal analysis provided by committees (panels) of three independent experts, rendering an advisory opinion (panel report). Still, dispute settlement was characterized by diplomatic negotiation and the pursuit of consensus.[2] A defending party could obstruct panel proceedings and the adoption of a panel report.

The Understanding on Rules and Procedures Governing the Settlement of Disputes (DSU), addressing the weaknesses of the old GATT regime, was one of the key elements of the reform in the Uruguay Round. The DSU depoliticizes the whole dispute settlement and essentially converts it into a quasi-judicial procedure. The DSU establishes a permanent Dispute Settlement Body (DSB). Under Article 2.1 second sentence of the DSU,

[...] the DSB shall have authority to establish panels, adopt panel and Appellate Body reports, maintain surveillance of implementation of rulings and recommendations, and authorize suspension of concessions and other obligations under the covered agreements.

The DSU facilitates the adoption of the findings and recommendations given by expert committees dealing with a dispute[3] and introduces an appeal mechanism. In addition, the DSU has sped up the entire dispute settlement process. Under the reserved principle of consensus, a panel report is now considered as adopted unless either of the parties files a formal appeal or the Dispute Settlement Body unanimously opts for non-adoption (Article 16.4 of the DSU). A standing Appellate Body[4] serves as a second instance for the review of panel reports on points of

---

[1] See C Schuchhardt, 'Consultations' in PFJ Macrory, AE Appleton, and MG Plummer (eds), *The World Trade Organization: Legal, Economic and Political Analysis* (Springer 2005) vol 1, 1197.

[2] RE Hudec, *'Enforcing International Trade Law: The Evolution of the Modern GATT Legal System'* (Lexis Law Publishers 1993).

[3] W Zdouc, 'The Panel Process' in PFJ Macrory, AE Appleton, and MG Plummer (eds), *The World Trade Organization: Legal, Economic and Political Analysis* (Springer 2005) vol 1, 1233.

[4] See V Donaldson, 'The Appellate Body: Institutional and Procedural Aspects' in PFJ Macrory, AE Appleton, and MG Plummer (eds), *The World Trade Organization: Legal, Economic and Political Analysis* (Springer 2005) vol 1, 1277; see also M Matsushita, 'Some Thoughts on the Appellate Body' in PFJ Macrory, AE Appleton, and MG Plummer (eds), *The World Trade Organization: Legal, Economic and Political Analysis* (Springer 2005) vol 1, 1389.

law (Article 17). Appellate Body reports are adopted by the Dispute Settlement Body, unless it decides within 30 days by consensus that the report will not be adopted (Article 17.14). Panel reports or Appellate Body reports adopted by the Dispute Settlement Body are binding on the parties to the dispute. The period of time between the establishment of a panel and the consideration of the report by the Dispute Settlement Body generally ought not to exceed nine months, in case of an appeal 12 months (Article 20 first sentence). The Appellate Body allows written statements (*amicus curiae* briefs) submitted by individuals and by non-governmental organizations (NGOs) which it is free to consider or not. This practice has drawn harsh criticism from WTO members.[5]

When a panel or the Appellate Body concludes that a measure is incompatible with the WTO agreement, it will recommend that the member concerned 'brings the measure into conformity' with the infringed agreement (Article 19.1 first sentence). Moreover, they may suggest specific ways to implement recommendations (Article 19.1 second sentence).

Within 30 days after the adoption of the panel or the Appellate Body report, the member concerned has to notify its intent to implement the recommendations (Article 21.3 first sentence). In case immediate implementation is impossible, the Member State will be granted a fixed period for implementation (Article 21.3 second sentence).

Despite the sometimes ambiguous language of the DSU, which uses misleading terms like 'recommendation', the member found in breach of WTO law clearly has an obligation of full compliance in terms of withdrawing the wrongful measure. According to Article 3.7 fourth sentence, non-consensual settlement of disputes primarily aims at 'withdrawal' of the measure concerned. Under the prevailing, though controversial, view the obligations of the member concerned in terms of a recommendation are purely prospective (conformity *ex nunc*) and do not include redress for the past.[6] This view deviates from general principles of State responsibility for an internationally wrongful act, which require prospective compliance with international obligations as well as retrospective restitution ('wiping out the consequences of the wrongful act').[7] However, Article 22.8 supports the prospective understanding of countermeasures as a lever.

Relying on Article 4.7 of the SCM Agreement ('withdrawal' of a prohibited subsidy) as *lex specialis* to the general rules of the DSU, the compliance Panel in *Australia—Automotive Leather II (Article 21.5—US)* instructed Australia to seek

---

[5] See generally B Stern, 'The Intervention of Private Entities and States as "Friends of the Court" in WTO Dispute Settlement Procedures' in PFJ Macrory, AE Appleton, and MG Plummer (eds), *The World Trade Organization: Legal, Economic and Political Analysis* (Springer 2005) vol 1, 1427.

[6] On this issue, see P Eeckhout, 'Remedies and Compliance' in D Bethlehem, D McRae, R Neufeld, and I Van Damme (eds), *The Oxford Handbook of International Trade Law* (OUP 2009) 448.

[7] *Case Concerning the Factory at Chorzów (Germany v Poland)* (Merits) PCIJ Rep Series A No 17 para 47; A Tanzi, 'Restitution' in R Wolfrum (ed), *The Max Planck Encyclopedia of Public International Law* (OUP 2012) vol VIII, 972.

repayment of prohibited export subsidies, thus giving 'withdrawal' a retrospective dimension.[8]

Disagreements about the due implementation of the recommendations shall be settled on the basis of a panel report (if possible by the original panel). The panel report shall, as a rule, be released within 90 days (Article 21.5).

If the member concerned does not comply with recommendations and decisions of the Dispute Settlement Body, the complaining member may request authorization to take specific countermeasures (Article 22). These countermeasures include compensation and suspension of concessions under WTO law (Article 22.1 first sentence). Payment of compensation is voluntary (Article 22.1 third sentence). If an agreement on compensation is not reached within a specified period of time (20 days after the expiration of the reasonable period of time in terms of Article 21.3), the member affected by the infringement may claim the suspension of treaty obligations towards the defaulting member. Article 22.2 reads:

If the Member concerned fails to bring the measure found to be inconsistent with a covered agreement into compliance therewith or otherwise comply with the recommendations and rulings within the reasonable period of time determined pursuant to paragraph 3 of Article 21, such Member shall, if so requested, and no later than the expiry of the reasonable period of time, enter into negotiations with any party having invoked the dispute settlement procedures, with a view to developing mutually acceptable compensation. If no satisfactory compensation has been agreed within 20 days after the date of expiry of the reasonable period of time, any party having invoked the dispute settlement procedures may request authorization from the Dispute Settlement Body to suspend the application to the Member concerned of concessions or other obligations under the covered agreements.

The Dispute Settlement Body authorizes countermeasures as applied for within 30 days after the expiry of the reasonable period of time in terms of Article 21.3, unless the application is rejected by consensus (Article 22.6 first sentence). In case the member concerned objects to the approved countermeasures, the issue is submitted to arbitral proceedings (either before the original panel or by an arbitrator appointed by the Director-General, Article 22.6 sentences 2 and 3).

The deadlines for the settlement of a dispute about the due implementation in terms of Article 21.5 of the DSU on the one hand and for the approval of countermeasures under Article 22.6 of the DSU on the other hand are difficult to reconcile. As the Appellate Body stated in the 'bananas dispute' between the United States and the EC (*EC—Bananas III*), the affected member may not take unilateral measures without the authorization of the Dispute Settlement Body.[9] In practice, both the dispute settlement procedure (Article 21.5) and the countermeasures procedure (Article 22.2) will be initiated immediately after the expiry of the reasonable period of time in terms of Article 21.3. The countermeasures

---

[8] WTO, *Australia: Subsidies Provided to Producers and Exporters of Automotive Leather—Recourse to Article 21.5 of the DSU by the United States—Report of the Panel* (2000) WT/DS126/R paras 6.18–6.49.

[9] WTO, *United States: Import Measures on Certain Products from the European Communities—Report of the Appellate Body* (2000) WT/DS165/AB/R paras 93ff.

procedure will be suspended until the dispute on implementation is resolved in accordance with Article 21.5.

When considering the suspension of concessions or other obligations, the complaining member shall be guided by the principles of Article 22.3:

In considering what concessions or other obligations to suspend, the complaining party shall apply the following principles and procedures:
(a) the general principle is that the complaining party should first seek to suspend concessions or other obligations with respect to the same sector(s) as that in which the panel or Appellate Body has found a violation or other nullification or impairment;
(b) if that party considers that it is not practicable or effective to suspend concessions or other obligations with respect to the same sector(s), it may seek to suspend concessions or other obligations in other sectors under the same agreement;
(c) if that party considers that it is not practicable or effective to suspend concessions or other obligations with respect to other sectors under the same agreement, and that the circumstances are serious enough, it may seek to suspend concessions or other obligations under another covered agreement;
(d) in applying the above principles, that party shall take into account:
(i) the trade in the sector or under the agreement under which the panel or Appellate Body has found a violation or other nullification or impairment, and the importance of such trade to that party;
(ii) the broader economic elements related to the nullification or impairment and the broader economic consequences of the suspension of concessions or other obligations; [...].

As a rule, the impairment by the violation of WTO law and countermeasures should be symmetrical (Article 22.3 *lit* a). If symmetry is not practicable or effective, countermeasures may also extend to other sectors under the infringed agreement (*lit* b). Thus, in response to measures affecting the automobile sector, countermeasures may target the sector of consumer electronics. In exceptional cases, concessions or other obligations under an agreement other than the infringed WTO agreement may be suspended (*lit* c). Countermeasures relating to other sectors or to other agreements than those affected by violation are referred to as 'cross-retaliation'. This form of countermeasures increases the non-calculable risks of violation and thus enhances the pull of the entire WTO system to compliance. The suspension of obligations of the injured member serves as an incentive for the violating member to revert to compliance. In addition, countermeasures also compensate, at least prospectively, the injury suffered by the complaining member.

The suspension of concessions and other obligations are subject to proportionality. According to Article 22.4, '[t]he level of the suspension of concessions or other obligations authorized by the Dispute Settlement Body shall be equivalent to the level of the nullification or impairment.'

The exclusivity of the mechanisms provided by the DSU with respect to unilateral measures is vital for the WTO system as a multilateral system based on law. Article 23 explicitly underlines this understanding which rules out unilateral options not covered by the rules and procedures of the DSU:

Strengthening of the Multilateral System

1. When Members seek the redress of a violation of obligations or other nullification or impairment of benefits under the covered agreements or an impediment to the attainment of any objective of the covered agreements, they shall have recourse to, and abide by, the rules and procedures of this Understanding.

2. In such cases, Members shall:

    (a) not make a determination to the effect that a violation has occurred, that benefits have been nullified or impaired or that the attainment of any objective of the covered agreements has been impeded, except through recourse to dispute settlement in accordance with the rules and procedures of this Understanding, and shall make any such determination consistent with the findings contained in the panel or Appellate Body report adopted by the Dispute Settlement Body or an arbitration award rendered under this Understanding;

    (b) follow the procedures set forth in Article 21 to determine the reasonable period of time for the Member concerned to implement the recommendations and rulings; and

    (c) follow the procedures set forth in Article 22 to determine the level of suspension of concessions or other obligations and obtain Dispute Settlement Body authorization in accordance with those procedures before suspending concessions or other obligations under the covered agreements in response to the failure of the Member concerned to implement the recommendations and rulings within that reasonable period of time.

The strict priority of the multilateral dispute settlement regime limits the application of existing instruments under domestic law against trade restrictions or distortions of competition by other members. This is particularly true for US law (with sections 301–310 of the Trade Act and similar provisions)[10] and, albeit to a much lesser extent, for the comparable instruments of the European Union.

It would be misleading to consider the sanction regime mechanism a modification of the alteration of the treaty obligations. Compensation and the suspension of obligations are not a kind of equivalent to compliance with the violating member's obligations. A member cannot buy release from its obligations under the WTO agreements by paying compensation or by suffering countermeasures taken by an injured member. The rules on sanctions leave the primary duty to abide by the rules of WTO law unaffected. There is the alternative to the duty of compliance, as the first two sentences of Article 22.1 corroborate:

Compensation and the suspension of concessions or other obligations are temporary measures available in the event that the recommendations and rulings are not implemented within a reasonable period of time. However, neither compensation nor the suspension of concessions or other obligations is preferred to full implementation of a recommendation to bring a measure into conformity with the covered agreements.

The DSU rules on compensation and the suspension of obligations have weaknesses. They do not envisage payment of compensation to the affected industries. In

---

[10] See WTO, *United States: Sections 301–310 of the Trade Act of 1974—Report of the Panel* (1999) WT/DS152/R.

addition, countermeasures may target companies which are by no means involved, as beneficiaries or otherwise, in impairment of obligations under WTO law. So far, compensation rests on an agreement between the parties to the dispute. Developing countries are often entirely unable to make effective use of possible countermeasures in a way that would be economically practicable. Thus, it should be considered amplifying the compensation regime of the DSU and to providing for compensation imposed by the Dispute Settlement Body rather than relying on consensus.

The DSU marks a significant change from the emphasis on political consensus to clearly regulated procedures with strong judicial elements. Most disputes focus on non-tariff barriers. Disputes about anti-dumping tariffs have also begun to play an important role. The overall balance for the dispute settlement system under the DSU in terms of compliance and efficiency is affected by the dilatory practice of members with respect to a timely implementation as well as by difficulties in identifying effective countermeasures.[11]

The United States has tended duly to implement recommendations, if the withdrawal of measures does not involve the US Congress and lies within the powers of the Executive. In the case *US—1916 Act*,[12] the United States failed for years to repeal anti-dumping legislation (15 USC § 72) providing for penalties in cases in which under WTO law only anti-dumping duties could be properly imposed.[13] In the case of the *US—Offset Act (Byrd Amendment)*,[14] the United States refused to implement recommendations for many years and was therefore targeted by countermeasures of the European Union and other members. On the other side of the Atlantic, the saga of the 'banana disputes' over the EC banana regime, with a lengthy sequence of half-hearted steps towards implementation, is equally telling about legislative attitudes towards compliance.[15] In the 'hormones dispute' (*EC—Hormones*)[16] the European Community either had to lift the import ban on hormone-treated beef or to provide a risk assessment according to the requirements of WTO law. After the expiry of the deadline set for implementing the recommendations, the United

---

[11] See generally AW Shoyer, EM Solovy, and AW Koff, 'Implementation and Enforcement of Dispute Settlement Decisions' in PFJ Macrory, AE Appleton, and MG Plummer (eds), *The World Trade Organization: Legal, Economic and Political Analysis* (Springer 2005) vol 1, 1341.

[12] WTO, *United States: Anti-Dumping Act of 1916—Report of the Appellate Body* (2000) WT/DS136/AB/R.

[13] See WTO, *United States: Anti-dumping Act of 1916—Report of the Appellate Body* (2000) WT/DS136/AB/R and WT/DS162/AB/R.

[14] WTO, *United States: Continued Dumping and Subsidy Offset Act of 2000—Report of the Panel* (2002) WT/DS217/R and WT/DS234/R; WTO, *United States: Continued Dumping and Subsidy Offset Act of 2000—Report of the Appellate Body* (2003) WT/DS217/AB/R and WT/DS234/AB/R.

[15] BL Brimeyer, 'Bananas, Beef, and Compliance in the World Trade Organization: The Inability of the WTO Dispute Settlement Process to Achieve Compliance from Superpower Nations' (2001) 10 Minn J Global Trade 133 (147ff); A Imdad Ali, 'Non-Compliance and Ultimate Remedies Under the WTO Dispute Settlement System' (2003) 14 Journal of Public and International Affairs paper 1.

[16] WTO, *European Community: Measures Concerning Meat and Meat Products (Hormones)— Report of the Panel* (1998) WT/DS26/R and WT/DS48/R; WTO, *European Community: Measures Concerning Meat and Meat Products (Hormones)—Report of the Appellate Body* (1998) WT/DS26/AB/R and WT/DS48/AB/R; WTO, *United States: Continued Suspension of Obligations in the EC—Hormones Dispute—Report of the Panel* (2008) WT/DS320/R and respective *Report of the Appellate Body* (2008) WT/DS320/AB/R.

States and Canada were authorized to apply countermeasures. When the European Community notified the revision of the directive at issue, the full implementation of the DSU's ruling still remained controversial. Thus, the United States and Canada maintained their countermeasures for some time.

The WTO dispute settlement system also allows so-called 'non-violation complaints'[17] under Article XXIII(b) of the GATT, Article XXIII:3 of the GATS, Article 64 of the TRIPS Agreement and Article 26 of the DSU. Following this form of complaint, a member can react to measures by other member States which impair a benefit of the complaining Member regardless of the legality of the challenged measure. The conditions under which such a complaint is permissible were specified by the Panel in *Japan—Film*:

The text of Article XXIII:1(b) establishes three elements that a complaining party must demonstrate in order to make out a cognizable claim under Article XXIII:1(b):

(1) application of a measure by a WTO Member;
(2) a benefit accruing under the relevant agreement; and
(3) nullification or impairment of the benefit as the result of the application of the measure.[18]

Select Bibliography

M Bronckers and N van den Broek, 'Financial Compensation in the WTO: Improving the Remedies of WTO Dispute Settlement' (2005) 8 J Int'l Econ L 101.

T Cottier, 'Dispute Settlement in the World Trade Organization: Characteristics and Structural Implications for the European Union' (1998) 35 CML Rev 325.

Y Guohua, B Mercurio, and L Yongjie, *WTO Dispute Settlement Understanding: A Detailed Interpretation* (Kluwer Law International 2005).

R Howse, 'The World Trade Organization 20 Years on: Global Governance by Judiciary' (2016) 27 EJIL 9–77.

L Hsu, 'Non-violation Complaints—World Trade Organization Issues and Recent Free Trade Agreements' (2005) 39 JWT 205.

JH Jackson, 'The International Status of WTO Dispute Settlement Reports: Obligation to Comply or Option to "Buy Out"?' (2004) 98 AJIL 109.

T Jürgensen, 'Crime and Punishment: Retaliation under the World Trade Organization Dispute Settlement System' (2005) 39 JWT 327.

PC Mavroidis, 'No Outsourcing of Law? WTO Law as Practiced by WTO Courts' (2008) 102 AJIL 421.

---

[17] L Hsu, 'Non-violation Complaints—World Trade Organization Issues and Recent Free Trade Agreements' (2005) 39 JWT 205; F Roessler and P Gappah, 'A Re-Appraisal of Non-Violation Complaints Under the WTO Dispute Settlement Procedures' in PFJ Macrory, AE Appleton, and MG Plummer (eds), *The World Trade Organization: Legal, Economic and Political Analysis* (Springer 2005) vol 1, 1371.

[18] WTO, *Japan: Measures Affecting Consumer Photographic Film & Paper—Report of the Panel* (1998) WT/DS44/R para 10.41.

D Palmeter and PC Mavroidis, *Dispute Settlement in the World Trade Organization: Practice and Procedure* (2nd edn, CUP 2004).

EU Petersmann, *The GATT/WTO Dispute Settlement System* (Wolters Kluwer Law & Business 1997).

S Shadikhodjaev, *Retaliation in the WTO Dispute Settlement System* (Kluwer Law International 2009).

TP Stewart (ed), *Handbook of WTO/GATT Dispute Settlement* (2007) 3 vols.

I Van Damme, 'Jurisdiction, Applicable Law and Interpretation' in D Bethlehem, D McRae, R Neufeld, and I Van Damme, *The Oxford Handbook of International Trade Law* (OUP 2009) 298.

CM Vázquez and JH Jackson, 'Some Reflections on compliance with WTO Dispute Settlement Decisions' (2002) 33 Law and Policy in International Business 555.

E Vranes, 'Principles and Emerging Problems of WTO Cross Retaliation' (2001) 1 EuZW 10.

R Wolfrum, PT Stoll, and K Kaiser (eds), *WTO Institutions and Dispute Settlement* (Brill Academic Publishers 2006).

World Trade Organization (ed), *A Handbook on the WTO Dispute Settlement System* (CUP 2004).

XXI

WTO Law in Broader Perspective:

The Interplay with Other Regimes of International Law

WTO law is not categorically separated from other rules and principles of public international law. There are many linkages to other rules of customary law and to international treaties. Sometimes, WTO agreements explicitly refer to obligations or standards established in context with other regimes. Thus, the security exception of Article XXI(c) of the GATT is linked to obligations under Articles 25 and 48 of the UN Charter. Under Articles 2.2, 3.1, and 3.2 of the SPS Agreement, the guidelines of international expert bodies like the Codex Alimentarius Commission operating within other international organisations may serve as the basis for risk assessment.[1]

Problems arise when treaties lay down objectives which collide with free trade. Sometimes these conflicts can be easily reconciled by exceptions in the multilateral WTO agreements. The preamble of the Agreement Establishing the WTO recognizes 'sustainable development' as an interest of the world trading system and thus opens the door for international rules serving this objective. This deference to environmental concerns supports an extensive understanding of 'exhaustible natural resources' in Article XX(g) of the GATT including living endangered species of animals and other living resources.[2] A particularly large potential for conflict flows from multilateral treaties which explicitly allow restrictive measures which are at least prima facie banned under WTO law.

The Biosafety Protocol of Cartagena allows restrictions on the import of living genetically modified organisms in terms which are probably broader than the respective WTO standards.[3] Conflict-prone is also the relationship of the UNESCO Convention of 2005 on Cultural Diversity (Convention on the Protection and Promotion of the Diversity of Cultural Expressions)[4] with WTO law. The

---

[1] WTO, *European Communities: Measures Concerning Meat and Meat Products (Hormones)—Report of the Appellate Body* (1998) WT/DS26/AB/R and WT/DS48/AB/R paras 160ff.

[2] See WTO, *United States: Import Prohibition of Certain Shrimp and Shrimp Products—Report of the Appellate Body* (1998) WT/DS58/AB/R paras 130f.

[3] See AL Hobbs, JE Hobbs, and WE Kerr, 'The Biosafety Protocol: Multilateral Agreement on Protecting the Environment or Protectionist Club?' (2005) 39 JWT 281; see also DA Motaal, 'Is the World Trade Organization Anti-Precaution?' (2005) 39 JWT 483.

[4] See M Hahn, 'A Clash of Cultures? The UNESCO Diversity Convention and International Trade Law' (2006) 9 J Int'l Econ L 515; J Wouters and B De Meester, 'The UNESCO Convention on Cultural Diversity and WTO Law: A Case Study in Fragmentation of International Law' (2008) 42 JWT 205.

UNESCO Convention affirms the 'cultural sovereignty' of States and provides great latitude for protectionist measures (Article 2 principle no 2). The Convention expressly allows far-reaching regulation and other measures for the protection and promotion of culture, including preferential treatment for domestic cultural goods and services as well as subsidies (Article 6.2). The negotiation of the UNESCO Convention was vigorously supported by France and Canada and strongly opposed by the United States and Israel. In the meantime, the European Union and many of its Member States as well as most other States have ratified the Convention.

It is widely recognized that the WTO agreements must be interpreted in light of other international law rules.[5] According to Article 3.2 second sentence of the DSU, the WTO dispute settlement system serves

[...] to preserve the rights and obligations of Members under the covered agreements, and to clarify the existing provisions of those agreements in accordance with customary rules of interpretation of public international law.

In *United States—Gasoline*, the Appellate Body underlined that the WTO rules are not to be read in 'clinical isolation from public international law', making particular reference to the rules of interpretation laid down in Articles 31ff of the Vienna Convention on the Law of Treaties.[6] When WTO law and obligations under other treaties conflict, the latter obligations are merely relevant, if at least all parties to a dispute are also parties to that other treaty. Article 31(3)(c) of the Vienna Convention on the Law of Treaties establishes that the interpretation of a treaty provision must take into account 'together with the context [...] any relevant rules of international law applicable in the relations between the parties'. Thus, WTO law may not hold another treaty against a member not having ratified this treaty.

In consequence, the provisions of the Biosafety Protocol do not affect the trade relations of the United States and of other States, which have not ratified the Protocol. The Panel in *EC—Biotech Products* stated:

Taking account of the fact that Article 31(3)(c) mandates consideration of other applicable rules of international law, and that such consideration may prompt a treaty interpreter to adopt one interpretation rather than another, we think it makes sense to interpret Article 31 (3)(c) as requiring consideration of those rules of international law which are applicable in the relations between all parties to the treaty which is being interpreted. Requiring that a treaty be interpreted in the light of other rules of international law which bind the States parties to the treaty ensures or enhances the consistency of the rules of international law applicable to these States and thus contributes to avoiding conflicts between the relevant rules. [...] Turning to the Biosafety Protocol, we note that it entered into force only on

[5] See J Pauwelyn, 'The Application of Non-WTO Rules of International Law in WTO Dispute Settlement' in PFJ Macrory, AE Appleton, and MG Plummer (eds), *The World Trade Organization: Legal, Economic and Political Analysis* (Springer 2005) vol 1, 1405.
[6] WTO, *United States: Standards for Reformulated and Conventional Gasoline—Report of the Appellate Body* (1996) WT/DS2/AB/R para 17.

11 September 2003, i.e., after this Panel was established by the Dispute Settlement Body. Among the WTO Members parties to the Biosafety Protocol is the European Communities. Argentina and Canada have signed the Biosafety Protocol, but have not ratified it since. Hence, they are not parties to it. The United States has not signed the Biosafety Protocol. While this does not preclude the United States from ratifying the Protocol, the United States has so far not done so. Accordingly, it, too, is not a party to the Biosafety Protocol. We do not consider that the rules of the Biosafety Protocol can be deemed to be applicable to the United States merely because the United States participates in the Protocol's Clearing-House Mechanism. It follows that the Biosafety Protocol is not in force for Argentina, Canada or the United States. We deduce from this that the Biosafety Protocol is not 'applicable' in the relations between these WTO Members and all other WTO Members. As we have said above, in our view, the mere fact that WTO Members like Argentina and Canada have signed the Biosafety Protocol does not mean that the Protocol is applicable to them. In view of the fact that several WTO Members, including the Complaining Parties to this dispute, are not parties to the Biosafety Protocol, we do not agree with the European Communities that we are required to take into account the Biosafety Protocol in interpreting the multilateral WTO agreements at issue in this dispute.[7]

The relevance of other international treaty regimes for the interpretation of WTO law cannot be taken for granted even in cases in which all parties to a dispute, but not all WTO Member States, are bound by the respective treaty. If the other treaty allows measures in conflict with WTO law, why should the Dispute Settlement Body, established in order to ensure compliance with WTO law, selectively recognize and enforce rules which deviate from its own treaty regime? If it did, the WTO rulings would differentiate the applicable standards according to ratification of non-WTO agreements by parties to a dispute.

In this context, it must be clearly distinguished between treaties which may generate genuine conflicts with WTO law (eg the Biosafety Protocol or the UNESCO Convention of Cultural Diversity) and other agreements, which serve objectives recognized in WTO law, even if colliding with free trade. The more the WTO is receptive to the objectives enshrined in another treaty, the lesser is the potential for conflicts. Treaties which are widely recognized and ratified by most States, but not by all WTO members, such as the Washington Convention on the Trade in Endangered Species of Wild Fauna and Flora (CITES) and the UN Convention on the Law of the Sea, may serve as a normative guidance as far as they express the general and uncontroversial recognition of a concern or interest by the international community at large, which are also shared by the WTO regime. This holds particularly true for environmental concerns which can be linked to exceptions under WTO law, for example the exception for the protection of 'exhaustible natural resources' under Article XX(g) of the GATT. Agreements serving such broadly recognized concerns like the protection of endangered species may be taken into account when interpreting WTO law, even if not all parties to the dispute are also parties of those treaties.[8] The

---

[7] WTO, *European Communities: Measures Affecting the Approval and Marketing of Biotech Products—Report of the Panel* (2006) WT/DS291/R para 7.70.
[8] See WTO, *United States: Import Prohibition of Certain Shrimp and Shrimp Products—Report of the Appellate Body* (1998) WT/DS58/AB/R paras 130f.

limits of an harmonious interpretation are reached when, on the instrumental level, a treaty provides for measures in conflict with WTO law.

A controversial issue is the relation of WTO law to regional or bilateral rules on free trade. In *Brazil—Tyres*[9] the Appellate Body had to review import restrictions on retreaded tyres, which Brazil had adopted in the interest of environmental protection and public health. After a MERCOSUR tribunal had qualified these import restrictions as a violation of the provisions of the MERCOSUR Free Trade Agreement,[10] Brazil granted an exemption for tyres imported from other MERCOSUR States. The Appellate Body considered this limited exemption as an 'arbitrary or unjustifiable discrimination' in terms of the 'chapeau' of Article XX of the GATT,[11] even though Brazil had done nothing else but to comply with its obligations under the MERCOSUR arbitral decision. The Appellate Body argued that, in the MERCOSUR proceedings, Brazil had failed to invoke an exception under the MERCOSUR agreements which corresponds to Article XX(b) of the GATT and that, therefore, the exemption granted did not necessarily result from a conflict between WTO law and Brazil's obligation under MERCOSUR law.[12]

Finally, customary law may influence the understanding and interpretation of WTO rules. This holds true particularly for universal human rights and environmental standards. Thus, a member cannot rely on the exception for public morals or public order under Article XX(a) of the GATT or Article XIV(a) of the GATS to enforce domestic standards which violate customary international law.

Possible conflicts of WTO law with other international legal regimes are not confined to substantive law, but may also extend to dispute settlement provisions. An illustrative example is the *Swordfish* case.[13] This dispute was triggered by restrictions imposed by Chile on the entry of foreign swordfish vessels to Chilean ports. The European Community filed a complaint against Chile under the DSU, especially relying on the freedom of transit under Article V of the GATT. Chile and the European Community went to the International Tribunal for the Law of the Sea (ITLOS), with both parties invoking the UN Convention on the Law of the Sea, especially the rules on the conservation of highly migratory species (Article 64 in conjunction with Articles 116 to 119). On the basis of an understanding between the parties, both disputes had been temporarily suspended in order to allow an

---

[9] WTO, *Brazil: Measures Affecting the Import of Retreaded Tyres—Report of the Appellate Body* (2007) WT/DS332/AB/R.

[10] See F Morosini, 'The MERCOSUR Trade and Environment Linkage Debate: the Disputes over Trade in Retreaded Tires' (2010) 44 JWT 1127.

[11] WTO, *Brazil: Measures Affecting the Import of Retreaded Tyres—Report of the Appellate Body* (2007) WT/DS332/AB/R para 228.

[12] WTO, *Brazil: Measures Affecting the Import of Retreaded Tyres—Report of the Appellate Body* (2007) WT/DS332/AB/R para 234; see A Davies, 'Interpreting the Chapeau of GATT Article XX in Light of the "New" Approach in Brazil—Tyres' (2009) 43 JWT 507.

[13] J Hillman, 'Conflicts Between Dispute Settlement Mechanisms in Regional Trade Agreements and the WTO—What Should the WTO Do?' (2009) 42 Cornell Int'l LJ 193; M Rau, 'Comment: The *Swordfish* Case: Law of the Sea v. Trade' (2002) 62 ZaöRV 37.

amicable solution. In the end, the parties to the dispute came to a settlement under certain agreed terms so that the case was removed from ITLOS' list of cases.[14]

The relation between the WTO dispute settlement regime and specific mechanisms of dispute resolution under free trade agreements may sometimes give rise to controversy.[15] In *Mexico—Taxes on Soft Drinks*, the Appellate Body rejected the suggestion that the WTO regime should give way to dispute settlement under NAFTA.[16]

Select Bibliography

WB Chambers, *Inter-Linkages: The Kyoto Protocol and the International Trade and Investment Regimes* (United Nations University Press 2001).

SH Cleveland, 'Human Rights Sanctions and International Trade: A Theory of Compatibility' (2002) 5 J Intl Econ L 133.

T Cottier, J Pauwelyn, and E Bürgi (eds), *Human Rights and International Trade* (OUP 2005).

J Gama Sa Cabral and GG Lucarelli De Salvio, 'Considerations on the Mercosur Dispute Settlement Mechanism and the Impact of its Decisions in the WTO Dispute Resolution System' (2008) 42 JWT 1013.

A Green, 'Climate Change, Regulatory Policy and the WTO' (2005) 8 J Int'l Econ L 143.

D Haan, 'Linkages between International Financial and Trade Institutions' (2000) 34 JWT 1.

G Marceau, 'A Call for Coherence in International Law' (1999) 33 JWT 87.

M Matsushita, 'Governance of International Trade Under WTO Agreements—Relationships between WTO Agreements and Other Trade Agreements' (2004) 38 JWT 185.

B McGrady, 'Fragmentation of International Law or "Systemic Integration" of Treaty Regimes: EC—Biotech Products and the Proper Interpretation of Article 31(3)(c) of the Vienna Convention on the Law of Treaties' (2008) 42 JWT 589.

J Pauwelyn, *Conflict of Norms in Public International Law: How WTO Law Relates to Other Rules of International Law* (CUP 2003).

J Pauwelyn, 'The Role of Public International Law in the WTO: How Far Can We Go?' (2001) 95 AJIL 535.

---

[14] See ITLOS order 2009/1 in List of Cases No. 7 of 16 December 2009.

[15] See eg JG Sá Cabral and GG Lucarelli De Salvio, 'Considerations on the Mercosur Dispute Settlement Mechanism and the Impact of its Decisions in the WTO Dispute Resolution System' (2008) 42 JWT 1013.

[16] WTO, *Mexico: Tax Measures on Soft Drinks and Other Beverages—Report of the Appellate Body* (2006) WT/DS308/AB/R paras 46ff.

XXII

WTO Law in Domestic Law

There is a long-standing controversy on whether the domestic law of WTO members should give direct effect to the WTO agreements. This issue relates to the application of WTO agreements by national authorities and national courts in context with restrictive trade measures. Direct application of WTO law by domestic authorities and courts raises a number of conflicting considerations. On the one hand, deference to the WTO agreements avoids the violation of international obligations, trade conflicts, and possible sanctions which hurt domestic industries. All too often, legislative bodies and executive authorities serenely ignore clear obligations under WTO law, as the practice of many members including the European Union, the United States and, more recently, China amply demonstrates. Therefore, judicial control of conformity (if available) matters. On the other hand, the provisions of the GATT and, after 1994, of other WTO agreements have often been perceived as too indeterminate to be directly applied. National courts are unduly afraid to preempt their own government in addressing trade conflicts and negotiations on the international level. These concerns have lost much of their weight after the reform of the world trading system in 1994. The dispute settlement regime has diminished the political element in settling trade conflicts in favour of quasi-judicial mechanisms. Over the years, panels and Appellate Body have considerably clarified the content of WTO law and settled controversies on interpretation. At least after a binding decision of the Dispute Settlement Body (DSB) asserting a violation of the treaties, administrative authorities and courts should defer to WTO law,[1] unless the national legislation clearly directs to ignore even clearly identified international obligations.

Still, national courts continue to be most reluctant to consider the WTO agreements as 'self-executing' or to be directly applicable. Thus, US courts have shown little inclination to apply the GATT when scrutinizing domestic measures.[2]

When ratifying the WTO agreements, the US Congress took pains to minimize their impact on the application of existing US law. The Uruguay Round Agreements Act (URAA) states in section 102(a)(1):

---

[1] See JM Beneyto, 'The EU and the New WTO: Direct Effect of the New Dispute Settlement System?' (1996) 7 EuZW 295.

[2] See eg *Suramerica de Aleaciones Laminadas, CA v United States*, 966 F 2 d 660 (Fed Cir 1992); for the effects of Dispute Settlement Body decisions in the US legal order, see G Gattinara, 'The Relevance of WTO Dispute Settlement Decisions in the US Legal Order' (2009) 36 LIEI 285.

No provision of any of the Uruguay Round Agreements, nor the application of any such provision to any person or circumstance, that is inconsistent with any law of the United States shall have effect.

According to Section 102(a)(2) of the URAA,

[n]othing in this Act shall be construed—
(A) to amend or modify any law of the United States, including any law relating to—
    (i)   the protection of human, animal, or plant life or health,
    (ii) the protection of the environment, or
    (iii) worker safety, or
(B) to limit any authority conferred under any law of the United States, including section 301 of the Trade Act of 1974,
unless specifically provided for in this Act.

In the European Union, an extensive discussion has focused on the applicability of WTO law by the European Court of Justice, in particular in actions of annulment challenging trade measures under secondary EU law.[3] The European Court of Justice, in other contexts sensitive to international obligations of the European Union, has never been very receptive to the invocation of world trade law. Decades ago, the European Court of Justice found the GATT 1947 too vague to be directly applicable (or self-executing) and held that 'Article XI of the General Agreement is not capable of conferring on citizens of the Community rights which they can invoke before the courts'.[4]

Elaborating this approach, the European Court of Justice based non-application on the 'indeterminate' content of provisions of the GATT, specific mechanisms of dispute settlement, the equally restrictive practice of other members (reciprocity), as well as the necessary 'room for manoeuvre' for the European Community (as it then existed) in negotiations.[5] In context with the 'bananas dispute',[6] the

---

[3] See P Ruttley and M Weisberger, 'The WTO Agreement in European Community Law: Status, Effect and Enforcement' in PFJ Macrory, AE Appleton, and MG Plummer (eds), *The World Trade Organization: Legal, Economic and Political Analysis* (Springer 2005) vol 1, 1459; see also A von Bogdandy, 'Legal Effects of World Trade Organization Decisions Within European Union Law: A Contribution to the Theory of the Legal Acts of International Organizations and the Action for Damages Under Article 288(2) EC' (2005) 39 JWT 45; see also M Bronckers, 'From Direct Effect to "Muted Dialogue"—Recent Developments in the European Courts' Case Law on the WTO and Beyond' (2008) 11 J Int'l Econ L 885.

[4] ECJ Joined Cases C-21 to 24/72 *International Fruit Co v Produktschap voor Groenten en Fruit* [1972] ECR 1219 (1228).

[5] See ECJ Case C-149/96 *Portugal v Council* [1999] ECR I-8425, 8438f.

[6] This dispute referred to massive restrictions by the European Community on the import of bananas from Central and South American countries, discriminating 'dollar bananas' against products from European States and from the so-called ACP States (African, Caribbean, and Pacific States associated with the European Community). The German government argued that these import restrictions were contrary to the GATT 1947. The repeatedly modified European banana regime triggered a number of complaints under the GATT and later under the WTO Dispute Settlement Understanding (DSU). In 1994, a Panel Report concluded that the EC measures violated the GATT: GATT, *European Economic Community: Import Regime for Bananas—Report of the Panel* (1994) DS38/R; see also WTO, *European Communities: Regime for the Importation, Sale and Distribution of Bananas—Report of the Appellate Body* (1997) WT/DS27/AB/R.

European Court rejected scrutiny of legislative measures violating the GATT 1947, even when a Member State challenged their legality:

In the absence of [...] an obligation following from GATT itself, it is only if the Community intended to implement a particular obligation entered into within the framework of GATT, or if the Community act expressly refers to specific provisions of GATT, that the Court can review the lawfulness of the Community act in question from the point of view of the GATT rules [...].[7]

This case illustrates the broader implications of this narrow view. In the EU Council, the claimant, Germany, as a major importing country, had voted against a regulation restricting the import of the popular 'dollar bananas' from Central and South America. Still, Germany may be targeted, just like any EU Member State, by countermeasures responding to the violation of WTO agreements. Denying judicial relief means exposing all EU Member States to sanctions under WTO law.

International agreements ratified by the European Union are binding upon the EU organs (Article 216(2) of the TFEU). Still, the Council of the European Union, in a far-reaching unilateral interpretation, categorically declared in the preamble to its decision on the ratification of the WTO agreements that WTO law shall not be directly applicable in judicial proceedings:

[B]y its nature, the Agreement establishing the World Trade Organization, including the Annexes thereto, is not susceptible to being directly invoked in Community or Member State courts [...].[8]

Like the proviso in favour of existing national legislation formulated by the Congress of the United States, this declaration of the Council of the European Union seriously affects the pull to compliance with obligations under WTO law.

Despite sharp criticism,[9] the European Court of Justice maintained its restrictive jurisprudence even after the new WTO regime with the new dispute settlement mechanism came into force.[10] The European Court of Justice has shown an astonishing lack of sensitivity for the binding effect of international legal obligations for the European Union. It is most irritating that not even EU Member States can claim relief against violations of WTO obligations before the European Court of Justice and thus avert their own co-responsibility.

[7] ECJ Case C-280/93 *Germany v Council* [1994] ECR I-5039, 5073f.
[8] Council Decision (EC) 800/1994 concerning the conclusion on behalf of the European Community, as regards matters within its competence, of the agreements reached in the Uruguay Rounds multilateral negotiations (1986–94) [1994] OJ L 336/1.
[9] See JM Beneyto, 'Direct Effect of the New Dispute Settlement System?' (1996) 7 EuZW 295; U Everling, 'Will Europe Slip on Bananas? The Bananas Judgment of the Court of Justice and National Courts' (1996) 33 CML Rev 401.
[10] Current jurisprudence of the ECJ still sticks to a restrictive approach: ECJ Case C-149/96 *Portugal v Council* [1999] ECR I-8425 paras 25ff; Case C-307/99 *OGT Fruchthandelsgesellschaft v Hauptzollamt Hamburg-St Annen* [2001] ECR I-3159 paras 22ff. The ECJ also refers to the courts of other Member States, which also deny a direct application of WTO law on the municipal level. An exception was accepted for the interpretation of municipal law in conformity with WTO law in ECJ Joined Cases C-300/98 and 392/98 *Parfums Christian Dior SA v Tuk Consultancy BV and Assco Gerüste GmbH and Rob van Dijk v Wilhelm Layher GmbH & Co KG and Layher BV* [2000] ECR I-11307.

In the *van Parys* case, the European Court of Justice refused to review an EC regulation (again on a banana market regime), even though the Dispute Settlement Body had found a violation of WTO law and had set a time limit for the implementation of its recommendations (Article 21 paragraph 3 of the DSU). The European Court relied on the option of negotiations on implementation between the parties of countermeasures.[11] This view ignores that compensation or countermeasures do not discharge the Member States from the primary obligations under the WTO rules (Article 22.1 second sentence of the DSU) and that the suspension of certain concessions also depends on the extent of the infringement (Article 22.4 of the DSU).

In the *FIAMM* case, the European Court of Justice carried its refusal to review EU legislation in the light of WTO law to the next level. In this case, European exporters of products which were targeted by US sanctions against the amended European banana trade regime brought an action against the European Community. The amended banana trade regime purported to implement a finding by the Dispute Settlement Body (DSB) that the previous regime violated WTO law. Under Article 22.6 of the DSU, arbitrators had found that the amended banana regime also did not conform to WTO law after the DSB had authorized the United States to level customs duties on European imports. Up to a certain amount, the United States imposed an import duty, inter alia, on products such as batteries covered by the business activities of the plaintiffs. The European Court of Justice held that, in actions for damages caused by retaliating measures, individuals cannot rely on rulings by the DSB. In the view of the European Court of Justice, decisions of the DSB must be treated as substantive WTO law which, according to established case law, does not provide a justiciable standard for review of European legislation:

127. In holding that the WTO rules which have been found by a decision of the DSB to have been infringed cannot, notwithstanding the expiry of the period of time laid down for implementing that decision, be relied upon before the Community courts for the purpose of having the legality of the conduct of the Community institutions reviewed by the Community courts in the light of those rules, the Court has necessarily excluded such a review in the light of the DSB decision itself.

128. A DSB decision, which has no object other than to rule on whether a WTO member's conduct is consistent with the obligations entered into by it within the context of the WTO, cannot in principle be fundamentally distinguished from the substantive rules which convey such obligations and by reference to which such a review is carried out, at least when it is a question of determining whether or not an infringement of those rules or that decision can be relied upon before the Community courts for the purpose of reviewing the legality of the conduct of the Community institutions.

129. A recommendation or a ruling of the DSB finding that the substantive rules contained in the WTO agreements have not been complied with is, whatever the precise legal effect attaching to such a recommendation or ruling, no more capable than those rules of conferring upon individuals a right to rely thereon before the Community courts for the purpose of having the legality of the conduct of the Community institutions reviewed.[12]

---

[11] ECJ Case C-377/02 *Léon van Parys v Belgisch Interventie- en Restitutiebureau (BIRB)* [2005] ECR I-1465 paras 45ff.

[12] ECJ Joined Cases C-120/06 P and C-121/06 P *FIAMM* [2008] ECR I-6531 paras 127–129.

In addition, the European Court of Justice indicated that enterprises exporting goods to the markets of other WTO members must carry the risk of punitive measures adopted under Article 22 of the DSU:

An economic operator whose business consists in particular in exporting goods to the markets of non-member States must therefore be aware that the commercial position which he has at a given time may be affected and altered by various circumstances and that those circumstances include the possibility, which is moreover expressly envisaged and governed by Article 22 of the DSU, that one of the non-member States will adopt measures suspending concessions in reaction to the stance taken by its trading partners within the framework of the WTO and will for this purpose select in its discretion, as follows from Article 22(3)(a) and (f) of the DSU, the goods to be subject to those measures.[13]

This signifies that, in the end, private businesses in the European Union must bear the retaliatory consequences of measures which the European Union adopts in a specific sector in violation of WTO law without compensation, even if they operate in an entirely different sector.

Nevertheless, the European Court of Justice recognizes effects of procedural issues of the WTO agreements in domestic law. Thus, in the *Dior* case the Court held that the courts of the EU Member States must consider the provision of Article 50 of the TRIPS Agreement as far as possible, when deciding on provisional measures for the protection of intellectual property rights:

In a field to which TRIPs applies and in respect of which the Community has already legislated, as is the case with the field of trade marks, it follows from the judgment in Hermès, in particular paragraph 28 thereof, that the judicial authorities of the Member States are required by virtue of Community law, when called upon to apply national rules with a view to ordering provisional measures for the protection of rights falling within such a field, to do so as far as possible in the light of the wording and purpose of Article 50 of TRIPs.[14]

Courts of WTO members are willing to give effect to WTO law, if provisions of domestic law refer to WTO standards and if these provisions confer a specific right which individuals can invoke in judicial proceedings. Such provisions, which can be found in EU law as well as in the law of the United States, often allow affected domestic industries to seek relief against the violation of WTO rules by other States. A famous example is section 301 of the US Trade Act of 1974 which enables US enterprises to claim governmental action in response to foreign trade measures.[15]

---

[13] Ibid, para 186.

[14] ECJ Joined Cases C-300/98 and 392/98 *Parfums Christian Dior SA v Tuk Consultancy BV and Assco Gerüste GmbH and Rob van Dijk v Wilhelm Layher GmbH & Co KG and Layher BV* [2000] ECR I-11307 para 47; see also ECJ Case C-53/96 *Hermès International v FHT Marketing Choice BV* [1998] ECR I-3603.

[15] For this and other mechanisms in US law, see JN Bhagwati and HC Patrick (eds), *Aggressive Unilateralism: America's 301 Trade Policy and the World Trading System* (University of Michigan Press 1990); BE Clubb, *United States Foreign Trade Law* (Little Brown & Co Law & Business 1991) vol 1, 232; M Nettesheim, 'Section 301 of the Trade Act of 1974: Response to Unfair Foreign Trade' in E Grabitz and A von Bogdandy (eds), U.S. *Trade Barriers: A Legal Analysis* (Oceana Publications 1991) 355.

The European counterpart to the US mechanism is the Regulation [EC] No 3286/94.[16] Under this Regulation, European enterprises or EU Member States may seize the European Commission and apply for an adequate response to trade restrictions taken by third States in violation of international obligations. The relevant provisions of the Regulation state:

Article 2
Definitions
1. For the purposes of this Regulation, 'obstacles to trade' shall be any trade practice adopted or maintained by a third country in respect of which international trade rules establish a right of action. Such a right of action exists when international trade rules either prohibit a practice outright, or give another party affected by the practice a right to seek elimination of the effect of the practice in question [...].

Article 3
Complaint on behalf of the Community industry
1. Any natural or legal person, or any association not having legal personality, acting on behalf of a Community industry which considers that it has suffered injury as a result of obstacles to trade that have an effect in the market of the Community may lodge a written complaint [...].

Article 4
Complaint on behalf of Community enterprises
1. Any Community enterprise, or any association, having or not legal personality, acting on behalf of one or more Community enterprises, which considers that such Community enterprises have suffered adverse trade effects as a result of obstacles to trade that have an effect in the market of a third country may lodge a written complaint [...].

In *Fediol III*, the European Court of Justice upheld the right of individual applicants to challenge the refusal of the Commission to intervene in the light of the GATT.[17] Moreover, the European Court of Justice reviewed an anti-dumping regulation of the Council as to its conformity with the Anti-Dumping Code, on the grounds that the preamble to the Regulation itself referred to the Anti-Dumping Code.[18]

Select Bibliography

A Antoniadis, 'EU and WTO Law: A Nexus of Reactive, Coactive, and Proactive Approaches' (2007) 6 World Trade Review 45.
G de Búrca and J Scott (eds), *The EU and the WTO: Legal and Constitutional Issues* (Hart Publishing 2001).

[16] Council Regulation (EC) 3286/94 laying down Community procedures in the field of the common commercial policy in order to ensure the exercise of the Community's rights under international trade rules, in particular those established under the auspices of the World Trade Organization [1994] OJ L 349/71.
[17] ECJ Case C-70/87 *Fediol v Commission* [1989] ECR 1781 (1830ff).
[18] ECJ Case C-69/89 *Nakajima v Council* [1991] ECR 2069 (2177ff).

XXIII

The Regional Integration of Markets

1. Forms of Regional Market Integration (Free Trade Areas, Customs Unions, and Economic Communities)

The basis of all forms of regional or bilateral economic integration is the elimination or progressive reduction of tariffs and of other trade restrictions between the contracting States. The elimination of such 'internal barriers' to the trade between the Member States characterizes the elementary type of regional economic integration: the free trade area or free trade zone. A more advanced form is the customs union. Whilst the free trade area merely eliminates tariffs in between members, the customs union additionally establishes a single external tariff for imports from third countries. This single external tariff avoids problems with the movement of imported goods associated with individual tariffs. The General Agreement on Tariffs and Trade 1994 (GATT) defines the terms 'free trade area' and 'customs union' in Article XXIV:8:

(a) A customs union shall be understood to mean the substitution of a single customs territory for two or more customs territories, so that
   (i) duties and other restrictive regulations of commerce [...] are eliminated with respect to substantially all the trade between the constituent territories of the union or at least with respect to substantially all the trade in products originating in such territories, and
   (ii) [...], substantially the same duties and other regulations of commerce are applied by each of the Members of the union to the trade of territories not included in the union [...];
(b) A free-trade area shall be understood to mean a group of two or more customs territories in which the duties and other restrictive regulations of commerce [...] are eliminated on substantially all the trade between the constituent territories in products originating in such territories.

In a free trade area, the lack of a common external tariff makes the State with the lowest tariff the first choice for the import of foreign goods. Complicated mechanisms are designed to neutralize possible distortions resulting from different external tariffs. So-called rules of origin determine whether a good shall benefit from the advantages of the free trade agreement or not. An example for such 'rules of origin'[1]

---

[1] See S Inama, *Rules of Origin in International Trade* (CUP 2009); for 'rules of origin' in the WTO context, see H Imagawa and E Vermulst, 'The Agreement on Rules of Origin' in PFJ Macrory,

can be found in the Revised Treaty of Chaguaramas Establishing the Caribbean Community Including the CARICOM Single Market and Economy. Article 84 of the Treaty provides:

Community Rules of Origin

1. Subject to the provisions of this Article, goods that have been consigned from one Member State to a consignee in another Member State shall be treated as being of Community origin, where the goods:

    (a) have been wholly produced within the Community; or

    (b) have been produced within the Community wholly or partly from materials imported from outside the Community or from materials of undetermined origin by a process which effects a substantial transformation characterized:

       (i) by the goods being classified in a tariff heading different from that in which any of those materials is classified; or

       (ii) in the case of the goods set out in the List in Schedule I to this Treaty (hereinafter referred to as 'the List'), only by satisfying the conditions therefor specified.

2. Goods that have been consigned from one Member State to a consignee in another Member State for repair, renovation or improvement shall, on their return to the Member State from which they were exported, be treated for the purpose of re-importation only, in like manner as goods which are of Community origin, provided that the goods are reconsigned directly to that Member State from which they were exported and the value of materials imported from outside the Community or of undetermined origin which have been used in the process of repair, renovation or improvement does not exceed:

    (a) in the case where the goods have undergone the process of repair, renovation or improvement in a More Developed Country, 65 per cent of the cost of repair, renovation or improvement;

    (b) in the case where the goods have undergone the process of repair, renovation or improvement in a Less Developed Country, 80 per cent of the cost of repair, renovation or improvement [...].

The rules of origin shall ensure that only products which originate in the territory of the Member States benefit from the reduction of internal tariffs. Possible criteria are a given ratio of domestic and foreign components of a product, the place where the product is finished, or the place where crucial steps of the production process are undertaken.[2] Rules of origin will not entirely eliminate the distortion of trade between the Member States of a free trade area caused by different tariffs. Therefore, in the long run, there is a strong pull for free trade areas to develop into customs unions. The Common Market for South America (MERCOSUR) and the Caribbean Free Trade Association (CARIFTA), which became the Caribbean Community (CARICOM), have moved in this direction. The Revised Treaty of Chaguaramas Establishing the Caribbean Community Including the CARICOM Single Market and Economy introduced a common external tariff for certain goods:

AE Appleton, and MG Plummer (eds), *The World Trade Organization: Legal, Economic and Political Analysis* (Springer 2005) vol I, 601.

[2] See eg Article 4(1) of the EFTA Treaty; Decision No 293 of the Commission of the Andean Pact (1993) 32 ILM 172.

ARTICLE 82

Establishment of Common External Tariff

The Member States shall establish and maintain a common external tariff in respect of all goods which do not qualify for Community treatment in accordance with plans and schedules set out in relevant determinations of COTED [Council for Trade and Economic Development].

Sometimes, the effective realization of a free trade area is hampered by lasting difficulties. An example is the Commonwealth of Independent States (CIS) which was formed by the now independent republics of the former Soviet Union. The economic relations between the CIS States could only be stabilized by a number of bilateral and multilateral agreements.[3]

The WTO encourages the regional integration of markets.[4] Article XXIV:4 of the GATT provides:

The contracting parties recognize the desirability of increasing freedom of trade by the development, through voluntary agreements, of closer integration between the economies of the countries parties to such agreements. They also recognize that the purpose of a customs union or of a free-trade area should be to facilitate trade between the constituent territories and not to raise barriers to the trade of other contracting parties with such territories.

As an exception to the most-favoured-nation treatment, Article XXIV:5 of the GATT accordingly allows customs unions and free trade areas. Articles V and V *bis* of the General Agreement on Trade in Services (GATS) similarly endorse bilateral or regional economic integration of markets for services. This endorsement of preferential trade agreements reflects the widespread, though controversial, understanding that economic cooperation on the regional level also has a stimulating effect on the global economy. As a precondition, the GATT requires that the preferential arrangements extend to 'substantially all the trade' (Article XXIV:8).[5] The last decades have witnessed a proliferation of free trade areas and customs unions. Both the United States and the European Union have concluded a number of so-called 'Preferential Trade Agreements' (PTAs). The importance of PTAs essentially depends on the volume of the internal trade between the State Parties. Preferential trade relations on a regional or bilateral basis do not only increase the welfare of the respective nations.[6] The creation of large trading blocs might also threaten to fragment the global economy and to disadvantage the countries whose exports do not significantly benefit from preferential arrangements.

The European Union, which emerged from the European Communities, is based upon a customs union (Article 28(1) of the TFEU). As a very advanced system of economic integration, the European Union has established an internal market

---

[3] R Dragneva and J De Kort, 'The Legal Regime for Free Trade in the Commonwealth of Independent States' (2007) 56 ICLQ 233.

[4] For the broader perspective, see L Bartels and F Ortino (eds), *Regional Trade Agreements and the WTO Legal System* (OUP 2006).

[5] See Ch XIV.2(b)(i).

[6] For a more economic analysis, see JJ Hallaert, 'Proliferation of Preferential Trade Agreements: Quantifying its Welfare Impact and Preference Erosion' (2008) 42 JWT 813.

with free movement of goods, persons, services, capital, and payments and with the power to harmonize national laws in the interest of a functioning internal market. Moreover, the European Union has a common agricultural policy, a competition regime, and a common commercial policy which covers trade and investment relations with other States, a close economic coordination with a regime of fiscal discipline, and a common currency (European Economic and Monetary Union). Implementing its 2006 Global Europe[7] vision, the European Union has pursued a rather active strategy by negotiating a number of trade agreements or comprehensive economic agreements (including investments), whilst other negotiations are still ongoing. The European Union became a model for 'economic communities' in other regions of the world. However, the degree of economic and political integration of the European Union, so far, stands unparalleled. Examples of an increased economic integration are the common market of the parties to the Andean Community of Nations (Comunidad Andina, CAN), the Central American Common Market (CACM; Mercado Común Centroamericano, MCCA), and the Economic Community of West African States (ECOWAS). Some of these communities have to date achieved only a rather modest degree of integration. Often, the lack of true political commitment among governments as well as the low volume of trade between the Member States hamper further integration.

2. The Free Movement of Goods and Services in the European Union

(a) Free movement of goods

The European Union has accomplished an internal market (Article 3(3) of the TEU, Article 26(2) of the TFEU) with a number of components beyond free movement of goods and services (including free movement of workers, freedom of establishment, free movement of payments and capital). Still, the free movement of goods is a central element of the European internal market. According to Article 28(1) of the TFEU,

[t]he European Union shall comprise a customs union which shall cover all trade in goods and which shall involve the prohibition between Member States of customs duties on imports and exports and of all charges having equivalent effect, and the adoption of a common customs tariff in their relations with third countries.

The basic rule on the elimination of non-tariff barriers to trade is enshrined in Article 34 of the TFEU which states that '[q]uantitative restrictions on imports and all measures having equivalent effect shall be prohibited between Member States'.

---

[7] European Commission, 'Global Europe: Competing in the World—A Contribution to the EU's Growth and Jobs Strategy' (Staff Working Document) COM(2006) 567 final.

Article 35 of the TFEU contains a similar prohibition for the export of goods. In contrast to the GATT, European Union law does not only prohibit discriminating restrictions on import or export within the common market, but also non-discriminating measures affecting trade between Member States, unless they can be justified as necessary means to satisfy a recognized interest. The famous '*Dassonville* formula' of the European Court of Justice defines the term 'measures having equivalent effect' within the prohibition of Article 34 of the TFEU as broadly as possible:

All Trading rules enacted by Member States which are capable of hindering, directly or indirectly, actually or potentially, intra-community trade are to be considered as measures having an effect equivalent to quantitative restrictions.[8]

Under this broad understanding, Articles 34 and 35 of the TFEU apply to any conceivable, discriminatory and non-discriminatory, direct and indirect hindrances to trade within the internal market. The prohibition of 'measures having equivalent effect' extends to statutory rules on the ingredients of products,[9] on returnable bottles for certain beverages,[10] on medical prescription for certain drugs and exclusive sale of drugs in pharmacies,[11] as well as to governmental support for campaigns in favour of domestic products.[12] Even restrictions on the use of goods (as environmental conditions for the use of private watercraft) qualify as hindrance to trade under Article 34 of the TFEU if they affect consumer decisions.[13]

The European Court of Justice exempts selling arrangements which affect domestic products in the same way as imported products (such as the prohibition on a resale at a loss or closing hours) from the prohibition in Article 34 of the TFEU.[14] The Court states that '[i]t follows that Article 30 of the Treaty is to be interpreted as not applying to legislation of a Member State imposing a general prohibition on resale at a loss'.[15]

---

[8] ECJ Case C-8/74 *SA ÉTS. Fourcroy v Dassonville* [1974] ECR 837 (852).

[9] See on the German 'purity standard' for beer ECJ Case C-178/84 *Commission v Germany* [1987] ECR 1227.

[10] ECJ Case C-302/86 *Commission v Denmark* [1988] ECR 4607.

[11] ECJ Case C-322/01 *Deutscher Apothekerverband eV v DocMorris* ECJ [2003] ECR I-12887.

[12] ECJ Case C-249/81 *Commission v Ireland* [1982] ECR 4005.

[13] ECJ Case C-142/05 *Åklagaren v Mickelsson and Roos* [2009] ECR I-4273.

[14] ECJ Joined Cases C-267/91 and C-268/91 *Criminal Proceedings against Bernard Keck and Daniel Mithouard* [1993] ECR I-6097 para 17: '[T]he application to products from other Member States of national provisions restricting or prohibiting certain selling arrangements is not such as to hinder trade between Member States, within the meaning of that definition, so long as those provisions apply to all relevant traders operating within the national territory and so long as they affect in the same manner, in law and in fact, the marketing of domestic products and of those from other Member States. Provided that those conditions are fulfilled, the application of such rules to the sale of products from another Member State meeting the requirements laid down by that State is not by nature such as to prevent their access to the market or to impede access any more than it impedes the access of domestic products. Such rules therefore fall outside of Article 30 [now Article 34] of the Treaty.'

[15] ECJ Joined Cases C-267/91 and C-268/91 *Criminal Proceedings against Bernard Keck and Daniel Mithouard* [1993] ECR I-6097 Summary.

The effects of this case law, which meant to limit the scope of Article 34 of the TFEU,[16] in some cases can be difficult to ascertain.[17] Very often, selling arrangements are closely connected with the Community-wide distribution of certain goods. Consequently, the European Court of Justice has put some restrictions on the movement of goods, which purported to protect the integrity of competition, under the scrutiny of Articles 34 and 36 of the TFEU.

The prohibition of non-tariff barriers to trade is not absolute. Member States may justify restrictions if they apply indiscriminately and are necessary to satisfy a mandatory requirement like an effective fiscal supervision, the protection of public health, environmental protection, fair trading, and consumer protection. These 'inherent limits' to Article 34 of the TFEU were recognized by the European Court of Justice in the famous *Cassis de Dijon* case.[18] In addition, Article 36 of the TFEU provides explicit exceptions:

The provisions of Articles 34 and 35 shall not preclude prohibitions or restrictions on imports, exports or goods in transit justified on grounds of public morality, public policy or public security; the protection of health and life of humans, animals or plants; the protection of national treasures possessing artistic, historic or archaeological value; or the protection of industrial and commercial property. Such prohibitions or restrictions shall not, however, constitute a means of arbitrary discrimination or a disguised restriction on trade between Member States.

The exceptions under Article 36 of the TFEU and the inherent limits to Article 34 of the TFEU overlap. It is a matter of controversy whether discriminatory measures may also fall under the inherent limits or whether they can only be justified under Article 36 of the TFEU.

Any justifications of restrictions on the free movement of goods, by the inherent limitations to Article 34 of the TFEU or under Article 36 of the TFEU, are subject to a strict scrutiny of proportionality which also calls for a consistent approach to the public interest pursued.[19]

In a case similar to *Dominican Republic—Import and Sale of Cigarettes*,[20] the European Court of Justice had to rule on provisions for the import of ultra-high

---

[16] Article 34 of the TFEU for example does also not apply to sales restrictions on Sundays, ECJ Joined Cases C-69/93 and C-258/93 *Punto Casa* [1994] ECR I-2355; see also ECJ Case C-317/91 *Quattro v Quadra* [1993] ECR I-6227.

[17] See N Reich, 'The "November Revolution" of the European Court of Justice: Keck, Meng and AUDIRevisited' (1994) 31 CML Rev 459.

[18] ECJ Case 120/78 *Rewe-Zentral v Federal Monopoly Administration for Spirits* [1979] ECR 649 (662), usually referred to as the 'Cassis de Dijon' case. 'In the absence of common rules relating to the production and marketing of alcohol [...] it is for the Member States to regulate all matters relating to the production and marketing of alcohol and alcoholic beverages on their own territory. Obstacles to movement within the Community resulting from disparities between the national laws relating to the marketing of the products in question must be accepted in so far as those provisions may be recognized as being necessary in order to satisfy mandatory requirements relating in particular to the effectiveness of fiscal supervision, the protection of public health, the fairness of commercial transactions and the defence of the consumer.'

[19] ECJ Case 120/78 *Rewe-Zentral v Federal Monopoly Administration for Spirits* [1979] ECR 649; ECJ Case C-178/84 *Commission v Germany* [1987] ECR 1227.

[20] WTO, *Dominican Republic: Measures Affecting the Importation and Internal Sale of Cigarettes—Report of the Appellate Body* (2005) WT/DS302/AB/R; see Ch XIV.3(c) and 5(f).

temperature milk into the United Kingdom which required a prior import licence and conditioning distribution in certain parts of the country on a second heating and repacking. This system, practically amounting to an import ban, did not pass the test of proportionality.[21]

Restrictive measures based on potential threats to human health require a risk assessment in the light of available scientific information.[22] This condition is quite similar to the standards for risk assessment under the Agreement on the Application of Sanitary and Phytosanitary Measures (SPS Agreement).[23] In the absence of harmonization by the European Union, the treaty provisions on the free movement of goods establish the principle of mutual recognition, subject to the 'inherent limits' and the exceptions under Article 36 of the TFEU. Extensive secondary legislation of the European Union harmonizes standards for products, labelling, and marketing. To the extent that EU harmonization is exhaustive, it bars unilateral measures protecting specific interests.

(b) Free movement of services

The freedom of services (Articles 56ff of the TFEU) covers the freedom to provide and to receive services all over the European Union as well as cross-border movement of services. Thus, legislation which precludes the sale or use of foreign decoders providing access to satellite broadcasting services from other Member States in context with territorial licensing of transmission rights (eg as to sports events) interferes with the freedom of services, as the European Court of Justice held in the *Football Association Premier League* case.[24] When companies or natural persons (like a doctor or a lawyer) provide services in a Member State different from their home country, the freedom of establishment (Articles 49ff of the TFEU) may apply, if they have organized a basis in the country of destination. If, for example, an insurance company from Member State A provides services in Member State B through a local branch or subsidiary, such activity is covered by the freedom of establishment. If, however, the services are provided without any such basis in B by a subsidiary in B, this activity is subject to the freedom to provide services (Article 57 of the TFEU). The distinction between the freedom of establishment and the freedom to provide services depends on several criteria such as duration, regularity, and continuity of the provided services and the kind of infrastructure in the Member State where the service is provided.[25] Like the free movement of goods and the other 'market freedoms', the freedom to provide services operates both

---

[21] ECJ Case C-124/81 *Commission v United Kingdom* [1983] ECR 203.
[22] ECJ Case C-192/01 *Commission v Denmark* [2003] ECR I-9693 paras 45ff; the case was about vitamin additives in food.
[23] See Ch XV.
[24] ECJ Joined Cases C-403/08 and C-429/08 *Football Association Premier League Ltd and Others v QC Leisure and Others* [2011] ECR I-9083.
[25] ECJ Case C-55/94 *Gebhard v Consiglio dell'Ordine degli Avvocati e Procuratori di Milano* [1995] ECR I-4165 para 27; ECJ Case C-215/01 *Bruno Schnitzer* [2003] ECR I-14 847 para 32.

as a prohibition of discrimination and as a general prohibition of disproportionate restrictions.[26] Apart from 'inherent limits', there are also exceptions for public policy, public security, and public health (Articles 62, 52(1) of the TFEU). A number of directives, including the Directive 2006/123/EC on services in the internal market,[27] harmonize applicable standards or otherwise facilitates the exercise of the freedom of services.

3. EFTA and the European Economic Area

The European Free Trade Association (EFTA), founded in 1960,[28] ranked among the most important free trade areas for a long time. The attraction of the European Communities (now the European Union), as a much more advanced form of integration, accounts for the accession of the former EFTA members Denmark, the United Kingdom, Portugal, Finland, Austria, and Sweden to the European Union. Iceland, Liechtenstein, Norway, and Switzerland are the only remaining members of the EFTA.

The Agreement on the European Economic Area (EEA) of 1992[29] opened the internal market of the European Union for the remaining EFTA members (except Switzerland). The EEA Agreement establishes an association with the European Union in terms of Article 217 of the TFEU. The EEA constitutes a large European free trade zone unfolding an enormous economic potential. The Member States of the EEA, with more than 500 million inhabitants, account for significantly more than 40 per cent of world trade. After the Swiss people rejected the EEA Agreement, Switzerland (which already had concluded a free trade agreement with the European Community) entered into a number of bilateral arrangements with the European Union (eg on free movement of persons, agriculture, civil aviation, elimination of border controls, and the taxation of savings). In certain areas of law, Swiss legislation unilaterally brings its domestic law in line with EU law without international obligation ('autonomous implementation'). Swiss citizens, goods, and services now enjoy full access to the internal market of the European Union.

The EEA Agreement (in force since 1994) reflects the principles which govern the internal market of the European Union and EU competition law. The

[26] ECJ Case C-55/94 *Gebhard v Consiglio dell'Ordine degli Avvocati e Procuratori di Milano* [1995] ECR I-4165 para 37.
[27] Directive of the European Parliament and of the Council (EC) 2006/123 on services in the internal market [2006] OJ L 376/36.
[28] EFTA Convention 370 UNTS 5.
[29] Decision of the Council and the Commission (EC) 1994/1 on the conclusion of the Agreement on the European Economic Area between the European Communities, their Member States, and the Republic of Austria, the Republic of Finland, the Republic of Iceland, the Principality of Liechtenstein, the Kingdom of Norway, the Kingdom of Sweden, and the Swiss Confederation [1994] OJ L1/3; the EEA Agreement was concluded between the European Community, the (meanwhile extinct) European Coal and Steel Community and their Member States on the one side and the EFTA States on the other side.

provisions on the free movement of goods, the free movement of workers, the right of establishment, the free movement of services and capital, as well as the supervision of competition are modelled after the EU system. The provisions of the EEA Agreement shall be construed in accordance with prior rulings of the European Court of Justice if their content is identical with the rules of EU law (Article 6 of the EEA Agreement).

The complexity of the institutional structure of the EEA Agreement reflects conflicting objectives. On the one hand, the European Union is interested in dynamically extending its own rules on the development of the internal market to the entire EEA. On the other hand, EFTA States reject being subject to 'foreign' regulatory powers. Finally, the EEA system must ensure uniform standards applicable to the entire EEA. The Agreement provides for the establishment of an EEA Council as the supreme political body (Articles 89ff). Its functions are set out in Article 89 of the Agreement:

Article 89
1. An EEA Council is hereby established. It shall, in particular, be responsible for giving the political impetus in the implementation of this Agreement and laying down the general guidelines for the EEA Joint Committee.
   To this end, the EEA Council shall assess the overall functioning and the development of the Agreement. It shall take the political decisions leading to amendments of the Agreement.
2. The Contracting Parties, as to the Community and the EC Member States in their respective fields of competence, may, after having discussed it in the EEA Joint Committee, or directly in exceptionally urgent cases, raise in the EEA Council any issue giving rise to a difficulty.
3. [...].

The EEA Council is composed of members of the Council of the European Union and the European Commission and one member from each EFTA State (Article 90.1). Crucial functions lie with the EEA Joint Committee (Articles 92ff). Article 93 of the EEA Agreement provides:

1. The EEA Joint Committee shall consist of representatives of the Contracting Parties.
2. The EEA Joint Committee shall take decisions by agreement between the Community, on the one hand, and the EFTA States speaking with one voice, on the other.

This mechanism pushes the EFTA States to reach consensus among them. Newly created EU law shall be adopted for purposes of the EEA on the basis of decisions of the EEA Joint Committee (Articles 98ff of the EEA Agreement). Details are set out in the Annexes to the EEA Agreement.

For the implementation of the treaty provisions and for monitoring mechanisms, the EEA Agreement establishes a two-pronged model. For the EFTA States, the EFTA Surveillance Authority monitors compliance with the EEA Agreement. Article 108.1 of the EEA Agreement states:

The EFTA States shall establish an independent surveillance authority (EFTA Surveillance Authority) as well as procedures similar to those existing in the Community including procedures for ensuring the fulfilment of obligations under this Agreement and for control of the legality of acts of the EFTA Surveillance Authority regarding competition.

In addition, the EFTA Surveillance Authority exercises control of restrictive practices and mergers of companies with respect to the impact on trade between the EFTA States (Articles 55ff). In cases affecting the trade between EU Member States, the European Commission will decide (Articles 56, 57.2). A submission to the jurisdiction of the European Court of Justice in Luxembourg to rule on the application of the EEA Agreement was not acceptable for the EFTA States. A small exception to this rule is contained in Article 111.3 first sentence of the Agreement:

> If a dispute concerns the interpretation of provisions of this Agreement, which are identical in substance to corresponding rules of the Treaty establishing the European Economic Community and the Treaty establishing the European Coal and Steel Community and to acts adopted in application of these two Treaties and if the dispute has not been settled within three months after it has been brought before the EEA Joint Committee, the Contracting Parties to the dispute may agree to request the Court of Justice of the European Communities to give a ruling on the interpretation of the relevant rules.

After the European Court of Justice had rejected the establishment of an EEA Court (with five judges of the European Court of Justice and three judges appointed by the EFTA States),[30] the EEA Agreement now follows a two-tiered system of judicial protection. Alongside the European Court of Justice, an EFTA Court has been established with jurisdiction defined in Article 108.2 of the EEA Agreement:[31]

> The EFTA States shall establish a Court of Justice (EFTA Court).
> The EFTA Court shall, in accordance with a separate agreement between the EFTA States, with regard to the application of this Agreement be competent, in particular, for:
> (a) actions concerning the surveillance procedure regarding the EFTA States;
> (b) appeals concerning decisions in the field of competition taken by the EFTA Surveillance Authority;
> (c) the settlement of disputes between two or more EFTA States.

Disputes concerning the interpretation or application of the EEA Agreement can be brought before the EEA Joint Committee by the European Union or an EFTA State (Article 111). If the dispute concerns the interpretation of provisions, which are identical in substance to corresponding rules of EU treaties or secondary EU law, the parties may request the European Court of Justice to rule on the interpretation (Article 111.3). A court or tribunal of an EFTA State may request the European Court of Justice to decide on the interpretation of an EEA standard (Article 107 of the EEA Agreement, Protocol 34).

---

[30] ECJ Opinion of the Court 1/91 *Opinion delivered pursuant to the second subparagraph of Article 228 (1) of the Treaty—Draft agreement between the Community, on the one hand, and the countries of the European Free Trade Association, on the other, relating to the creation of the European Economic Area* [1991] I-6079.

[31] See C Baudenbacher, P Tresselt, and T Örlygsson (eds), *The EFTA Court: Ten Years On* (Hart Publishing 2005).

4. The North American Free Trade Agreement (NAFTA)

The North American Free Trade Agreement (NAFTA) of 1992[32] emerged from the free trade agreement concluded between Canada and the United States in 1988.[33] Its parties are the United States, Canada, and Mexico. The NAFTA established a large free trade area with a population of about 475 million, constituting an important counterweight to the European Union, Japan, and China. The objectives of the NAFTA are defined in Article 102:

Objectives
1. The objectives of this Agreement, as elaborated more specifically through its principles and rules, including national treatment, most-favored-nation treatment and transparency, are to:
   a) eliminate barriers to trade in, and facilitate the cross-border movement of, goods and services between the territories of the Parties;
   b) promote conditions of fair competition in the free trade area;
   c) increase substantially investment opportunities in the territories of the Parties;
   d) provide adequate and effective protection and enforcement of intellectual property rights in each Party's territory;
   e) create effective procedures for the implementation and application of this Agreement, for its joint administration and for the resolution of disputes; and
   f) establish a framework for further trilateral, regional and multilateral cooperation to expand and enhance the benefits of this Agreement.
2. The Parties shall interpret and apply the provisions of this Agreement in the light of its objectives set out in paragraph 1 and in accordance with applicable rules of international law.

Principles of NAFTA are national treatment as a basic principle and, in some areas, the most-favoured-nation treatment. For the trade in goods (Part II), the NAFTA provides for national treatment (Article 301), for the elimination or reduction of tariffs (Article 302), as well as for the elimination of restrictions on import and export (Article 309). Certain goods benefit from the most-favoured-nation treatment with respect to tariffs (Article 308). Only goods originating in the territory of one of the Parties to NAFTA qualify for the elimination or reduction of tariffs. Article 401 refers to the materials used as well as to the production process:

Except as otherwise provided in this Chapter, a good shall originate in the territory of a Party where:
a) the good is wholly obtained or produced entirely in the territory of one or more of the Parties, as defined in Article 415;
b) each of the non-originating materials used in the production of the good undergoes an applicable change in tariff classification set out in Annex 401 as a result of production

---

[32] See (1993) 32 ILM 289ff, 605ff.
[33] See (1988) 27 ILM 281; see FM Abbott, 'North American Free Trade Agreement' in R Wolfrum (ed), *The Max Planck Encyclopedia of Public International Law* (OUP 2012) vol VII, 776; FP Cantin and AF Lowenfeld, 'Rules of Origin, The Canada-U.S. FTA, and the Honda Case' (1993) 87 AJIL 375.

occurring entirely in the territory of one or more of the Parties, or the good otherwise satisfies the applicable requirements of that Annex where no change in tariff classification is required, and the good satisfies all other applicable requirements of this Chapter;

c) the good is produced entirely in the territory of one or more of the Parties exclusively from originating materials; or

d) except for a good provided for in Chapters 61 through 63 of the Harmonized System, the good is produced entirely in the territory of one or more of the Parties but one or more of the non-originating materials provided for as parts under the Harmonized System that are used in the production of the good does not undergo a change in tariff classification because

   (i) the good was imported into the territory of a Party in an unassembled or a disassembled form but was classified as an assembled good pursuant to General Rule of Interpretation 2(a) of the Harmonized System, or

   (ii) the heading for the good provides for and specifically describes both the good itself and its parts and is not further subdivided into subheadings, or the subheading for the good provides for and specifically describes both the good itself and its parts, provided that the regional value content of the good, determined in accordance with Article 402, is not less than 60 percent where the transaction value method is used, or is not less than 50 percent where the net cost method is used, and that the good satisfies all other applicable requirements of this Chapter.

Market access of agricultural products is subject to Part II, Chapter 7, Section A. NAFTA restrains technical barriers to trade (Part III). Part IV establishes rules for government procurement. In Part V, Chapter 11 on investment, inter alia, grants a minimum standard of treatment (Article 1105), compensation for expropriation (Article 1110), and provides for the settlement of disputes between private investors and a Party (Article 1122).[34] To trade in services (Part V, Chapter 12), NAFTA grants national treatment (Article 1202) as well as most-favoured-nation treatment (Article 1203). Special rules apply to the telecommunication sector (Chapter 13) and to financial services (Chapter 14). Chapter 15 deals with competition, monopolies, and State-owned enterprises. Part VI, Chapter 17 is dedicated to intellectual property. NAFTA provides for a binational panel review of a final anti-dumping or countervailing duty determination by the competent authority of an importing Party (eg the US Department of Commerce). Upon request by an involved party, a binational panel of five experts shall replace judicial review and rule on the correct application of the laws of the importing country (Chapter 19, Article 1904). NAFTA establishes exceptions with regard to the matters covered by Article XX of the GATT (Article 2101), to national security (Article 2102), and to problems with the balance of payments (Article 2104). The institutional structure of NAFTA is rather lean. The Free Trade Commission (with members of cabinet rank), inter alia, reviews the implementation of the Agreement, oversees its further elaboration, and resolves disputes on interpretation or application of the Agreement (Article 2001.1). The Secretariat (Article 2002) comprises national sections.

---

[34] See GN Horlick and AL Marti, 'NAFTA Chapter 11 B—A Private Right of Action to Enforce Market Access through Investments' (1997) 14 J Int'l Arbit 43.

5. Regional Integration in South America

(a) The Latin American integration association

The States of Central and South America have concluded a number of agreements on economic integration. Under the Treaty of Montevideo of 1960, several South American countries established the Latin American Free Trade Association (ALALC).[35] In 1980, the Agreement on the Latin American Integration Association (Asociación Latinoamericana de Integración, ALADI)[36] replaced the original Montevideo Treaty. Its Member States are Argentina, Bolivia, Brazil, Chile, Colombia, Cuba, Ecuador, Mexico, Panama, Paraguay, Peru, Uruguay, and Venezuela. The organs of the ALADI are the Council of Ministers of Foreign Affairs, the Evaluation and Convergence Conference, the Committee of Representatives, and the General Secretariat (Articles 28, 29 of the Agreement). Under Article 30 of the Agreement,

[t]he Council shall have the following powers:
To issue general rules aimed at a better compliance with the objectives of the Association, as well as at the harmonious development of the integration process;
To examine the results of the tasks carried out by the Association;
To adopt corrective measures of multilateral scope, following the recommendations adopted by the Conference as per terms of article 33, caption a) of the present Treaty;
To establish the guide-lines to be followed by the other bodies of the Association in their tasks;
To set the basic rules to govern the relations of the Association with other regional associations, international organizations or agencies;
To review and update basic rules governing convergence and cooperation agreements with other developing countries and the respective areas of economic integration;
To take cognizance of questions submitted by the other political bodies and decide upon them;
To delegate upon the other political bodies the power to decide on specific matters aimed at a better compliance with the Association objectives;
To accept accession of new Member countries;
To adopt amendments and additions to the Treaty as per precepts of article 61; To appoint the Secretary-General; and
To adopt its own Rules of Procedure.

(b) The Andean Community

Within the ALADI, several Andean countries moved to strengthen sub-regional integration by concluding the Cartagena Agreement on Subregional Integration (Andean Pact) in 1969.[37] Under the Agreement of Trujillo of 1996 modifying the

---

[35] See S Montt, 'Latin American Integration Association' in R Wolfrum (ed), *The Max Planck Encyclopedia of Public International Law* (OUP 2012) vol VI, 699.
[36] (1981) 20 ILM 672.
[37] (1989) 28 ILM 1165; see FV García Amador, *El ordenamiento jurídico andino, Un nuevo derecho Comunitario* (Edicionas De Palma 1977).

Cartagena Agreement, the Andean Community of Nations (Communidad Andina de Naciones, CAN) emerged from the Andean Pact.[38] Current membership comprises Bolivia, Colombia, Ecuador, and Peru. Argentina, Brazil, Chile, Paraguay, and Uruguay are associate members. Inspired by the European model of integration, the Andean Community has a rather complex organizational structure. The main organs are the Andean Presidential Council, the Andean Council of Foreign Affairs, the Commission of the Andean Community, the General Secretariat, the Court of Justice, and the Andean Parliament. There are also several advisory bodies. The broader Andean Integration System (Article 16 of the Cartagena Agreement) also comprises a number of other institutions like the Andean Development Corporation, the Latin American Reserve Fund (FLAR), the Andean Health Organization, and the Consultative Council of the Indigenous People (Article 7 of the Cartagena Agreement). The Andean Presidential Council (Articles 11ff of the Cartagena Agreement) is composed of the leaders of the Member States and formulates guidelines. The Andean Council of Foreign Ministers (Articles 15ff of the Cartagena Agreement) formulates a common foreign policy as to sub-regional integration issues, concludes the international agreements of the Andean Community, and shares law-making functions with the Commission (Article 16 of the Cartagena Agreement). The Commission (Articles 21ff of the Cartagena Agreement), in which each Member is represented, defines the Andean Community policy in the areas of trade and investment and takes the necessary measures to implement the objectives of the Cartagena Agreement (Article 22 of the Cartagena Agreement). Decisions and resolutions of the Council of Foreign Ministers of the Commission and the General Secretariat shall be directly applicable (self-executing) in the Member States (Article 3.1 of the Treaty Creating the Court of Justice of the Cartagena Agreement, Articles 40f of the Cartagena Agreement), unless incorporation into national law is explicitly provided for (Article 3.2 of the Treaty Creating the Court of Justice of the Cartagena Agreement). The General Secretariat (Articles 29ff of the Cartagena Agreement), based in Lima, operates as the executive body of the Andean Community. The Court of Justice of the Andean Community,[39] with its seat in Quito, is modelled on the Court of Justice of the European Communities (now the European Union).

Its jurisdiction covers actions of annulment of secondary Andean law, actions for non-compliance, requests by national courts for binding preliminary interpretations and actions on omission as well as arbitral functions and labour disputes (Articles 17ff of the Treaty Creating the Court of Justice of the Cartagena Agreement). The direct applicability of decisions and resolutions of the Community Organs addressed to Member States as well as the binding effect of preliminary rulings of

---

[38] RA Porrata-Doria Jr, 'Andean Community of Nations (CAN)' in R Wolfrum (ed), *The Max Planck Encyclopedia of Public International Law* (OUP 2012) vol I, 381.

[39] CE Daly Gimón, *Tribunal de Justicia e Institutionalidad en la Comunidad Andina de Naciones* (Editorial Adadémia Espanola 2011); RA Porrata-Doria Jr, 'Andean Community of Nations, Court of Justice' in R Wolfrum (ed), *The Max Planck Encyclopedia of Public International Law* (OUP 2012) vol I, 385.

the Court of Justice support the supremacy of the Andean Community law and the inapplicability of domestic law in case of conflict.[40]

Under the Cartagena Agreement, internal tariffs were eliminated. As the progressive establishment and uniform implementation of a common external tariff (see Article 62.2(f) of the Cartagena Agreement) met with difficulties, the Andean Community is an imperfect customs union. The Andean Community has a common regime for foreign investment (Article 55 of the Cartagena Agreement, Decision 291) and for intellectual property rights (Article 55 of the Cartagena Agreement, Decision 486) as well as for Andean multinational enterprises (Article 56 of the Cartagena Agreement, Decision 292).

(c) MERCOSUR

The Common Market of South America (Mercado Común del Sur, MERCOSUR; in Portuguese: MERCOSUL)[41] was established in 1991 by the Treaty of Asunción,[42] as modified by the Protocol of Ouro Preto of 1994. Members are Argentina, Brazil, Paraguay, Uruguay, and Venezuela. Associate members currently are Chile, Colombia, Ecuador, Guyana, Peru, and Suriname. Subject to approval by all Member States, Bolivia is about to join the MERCOSUR as a full member. With a common external tariff still subject to many exceptions, a yet imperfect customs union has been established. A safeguard clause allows Member States to establish temporary import quotas on certain goods if a dramatic increase of imports threatens the national market and may cause significant damage to the economy.

In contrast to the European Union or the Andean Pact, the founders of MERCOSUR opted for a simple institutional system without complex institutional mechanisms of supranational decision-making. Instead, the Member States have attempted to reduce the economic asymmetries gradually by means of intergovernmental cooperation. The coordination of economic policies between Argentina and Brazil had to overcome significant obstacles especially in the monetary sector. The MERCOSUR has led to a significant revival of trade between its Member States and a significant increase in the gross national product of the four founding States. The growth of the MERCOSUR economies (also driven by the export of commodities) and the volume of trade within in the common market (especially between Argentina and Brazil) turned the MERCOSUR into one of the more successful projects of regional integration worldwide, despite often divergent economic policies of its members and occasional trade conflicts between Argentina and Brazil.

---

[40] See L Sáchica, *Introducción al derecho comunitario andino* (Témis 1990); E Tremolado Alvarez, *El derecho andino en Colombia* (Universidad Externado de Colombia 2007).

[41] PB Cassella, 'Legal Features and Institutional Perspectives for the MERCOSUR' (1998) 31 VRÜ 523; MT Franca Filho, L Lixinski, and MB Olmos Giupponi (eds), *The Law of Mercosur* (Hart Publishing 2010); JP Schmidt, 'MERCOSUR' in R Wolfrum (ed), *The Max Planck Encyclopedia of Public International Law* (OUP 2012) vol VII, 110.

[42] (1991) 30 ILM 1041.

The current organizational structure of MERCOSUR rests on the Protocol of Ouro Preto of 1994.[43] This Protocol also established the legal personality of MERCOSUR in international law and under domestic law (Articles 34 and 35). The main organs of MERCOSUR are the Common Market Council, the Common Market Group, the Trade Commission, the Common Parliament Committee, the Socio-economic Advisory Forum, and the Administrative Office. The Common Market Council is the supreme decision-making body. It is composed of the foreign and economic ministers of the Member States. The Common Market Group is the executive organ of MERCOSUR. In this organ, each Member State is represented with four regular and four substitute members which constitute the National Section of the respective Member State. The Common Market Group is assisted by the MERCOSUR Trade Commission, which supervises the application of common trade policy instruments, monitors the development of the common market, and makes regulatory proposals.

Legal sources of the MERCOSUR under the founding Agreement with its Protocols and Amendments are the international agreements concluded by the MERCOSUR as well as the decisions of the Common Market Council, the resolutions of the Common Market Group, and the guidelines of the Trade Commission. The Member States are bound to incorporate the acts of the MERCOSUR institutions into domestic law (Article 40 of the Protocol of Ouro Preto). The Protocol of Brasilia of 1991[44] deals with the settlement of disputes within MERCOSUR.

The mechanisms of dispute settlement are now governed by the Olivos Protocol of 2002 (as modified in 2007).[45] If a dispute cannot be settled between the parties, they can jointly submit their controversy to the Common Market Group for consideration (Article 6.2). In the absence of a solution of the dispute, any party can initiate arbitral proceedings before an ad hoc tribunal (Articles 9ff of the Protocol). The Permanent Tribunal of Revision (Tribunal Permanente de Revisión, TPR) reviews arbitral awards (Articles 17ff). The parties can also directly submit a dispute to the Permanent Tribunal of Revision (Article 23). In their home State, private parties can lodge a complaint before the National Section of the Common Market Group (Articles 39ff). The Common Market Group may call for the opinion of an expert group after a preliminary examination of the complaint. Where the expert group unanimously concludes the complaint against a Member State well founded, any other Member State may require remedial measures or withdrawal of the disputed measures, and may, after the lapse of a short time, initiate arbitral proceedings (Article 44.1). The advanced level of integration in the MERCOSUR seems to call for an institutionally more developed system of dispute settlement.

The Declaration of Cuzco (2004) proclaimed the project of the South American Community of Nations (Comunidad Suramericana de Naciones, CSN) as a

---

[43] (1995) 34 ILM 1244.   [44] (1997) 36 ILM 691.
[45] See M Klumpp, 'Mercosur, Permanent Appeals Court' in R Wolfrum (ed), *The Max Planck Encyclopedia of Public International Law* (OUP 2012) vol VII, 117.

continental free trade zone which comprises the MERCOSUR and the Andean Community. By bilateral agreements, the Member States of the Andean Community have each agreed on a free trade zone with the Member States of MERCOSUR. Conversely, Argentina, Brazil, Paraguay, Uruguay, and Chile joined the Andean Community as associate members. These free trade agreements cover approximately 80 per cent of the trade between the two blocks. In 2007, the name of the CSN was changed into Union of South American Nations (Unión de Naciones Suramericanas, UNASUR). In May 2008, the constitutive treaty of UNASUR, which also operates as a political organization, was signed in Brasilia. UNASUR, with its 12 Member States, includes all member countries of the MERCOSUR and of the Andean Community.

(d) Pacific Alliance

In 2011 Chile, Colombia, Mexico, and Peru established the Pacific Alliance (Alianza del Pacífico), a promising framework for free trade agreements. The main objective is economic integration with free circulation of goods, services, capital, and persons. The Pacific Alliance also fosters close cooperation with the Asia-Pacific region.[46]

The Alliance is rather simply structured. Apart from meetings of the Presidents of the four countries as the supreme forum for decision-making (body on summits), there are only two other bodies: the Council of Ministers (integrated by the ministers of foreign trade and foreign affairs) and the High-Level Group (with the vice-ministers of foreign trade and foreign affairs).

A considerable number of States supporting the Alliance and its integration agenda have observer status, including Canada, China, France, Japan, Spain, South Korea, and the United States.

In South America, economic integration within the Pacific Alliance competes with MERCOSUR which also has a social dimension.

6. Regional Integration in Central America and the Caribbean

(a) Central American integration system

The Central American Integration System (Sistema de Integración Centroamericano, SICA) emerged from the Central American Common Market (MCCA) in 1993. Members are Belize, Costa Rica, El Salvador, Guatemala, Honduras, Nicaragua, and Panama. The bodies of this organization include the Presidents' Summit, the Council of Ministers of Foreign Affairs, the Central American Parliament, the

---

[46] See <https://alianzapacifico.net/en/what-is-the-pacific-alliance/#strategic-value> (accessed 22 February 2016).

Central American Court of Justice[47] (which also hears claims presented by private persons), the Secretariat, and the Executive and the Consultation Committee.

(b) Caribbean Community

Within the framework of the Caribbean Community (CARICOM),[48] the Revised Treaty of Chaguaramas on the Caribbean Community Including the CARICOM Single Market and Economy provides the basis for a common external tariff and a close coordination of trade policies. Members of CARICOM are Antigua and Barbuda, the Bahamas, Barbados, Belize, Dominica, Grenada, Guyana, Haiti, Jamaica, Montserrat, St Kitts and Nevis, St Lucia, St Vincent and the Grenadines, Suriname, and Trinidad and Tobago. Anguilla, Bermuda, the British Virgin Islands, the Cayman Islands, and the Turks and Caicos Islands are Associates. Aruba, Colombia, Curaçao, the Dominican Republic, Mexico, Puerto Rico, Sint Maarten, and Venezuela have observer status. The international jurisdiction of the Caribbean Court of Justice[49] (which is also the highest court of appeal for those Commonwealth members which have shifted this function from the Privy Council to the Caribbean Court) extends to disputes between the CARICOM States, to preliminary rulings at the request of national courts, and to applications from private persons. In *Trinidad Cement Ltd v Caribbean Community*, the Court admitted a direct challenge by a private party against decisions of the organs of CARICOM, invoking the principle of 'legal accountability'.[50]

7. Regional Integration in Asia and the Pacific

(a) ASEAN

The Association of Southeast Asian Nations (ASEAN) was founded in 1967 and initially intended to contain the Communist expansion. It currently includes Brunei, Cambodia, Indonesia, Laos, Malaysia, Myanmar, the Philippines, Singapore, Thailand, and Vietnam. On the basis of an agreement of 1977, the Member States of ASEAN have granted each other preferential tariffs. The Agreement of the ASEAN Free Trade Area (AFTA) provides for the gradual removal of barriers to trade. An important mechanism for economic integration within ASEAN is the 'Common Effective Preferential Tariff (CEPT) Scheme', adopted on the basis of an agreement of 2002 which aims at a substantial reduction of tariffs for a great

---

[47] See R Virzo, 'Central American Court of Justice' in R Wolfrum (ed), *The Max Planck Encyclopedia of Public International Law* (OUP 2012) vol II, 33.
[48] D Byron and C Malcolm, 'Caribbean Community (CARICOM)' in R Wolfrum (ed), *The Max Planck Encyclopedia of Public International Law* (OUP 2012) vol I, 1125.
[49] D Byron and C Malcolm, 'Caribbean Court of Justice (CCJ)' in R Wolfrum (ed), *The Max Planck Encyclopedia of Public International Law* (OUP 2012) vol I, 1130.
[50] Caribbean Court of Justice, *Trinidad Cement Ltd v The Caribbean Community* CCJ App no AR 3 of 2008 (Judgment of 5 February 2009) CCJ 2 (OJ) para 32.

number of products and the removal of non-tariff barriers to trade. The ASEAN Charter of 2007 vests ASEAN with legal personality.

(b) ACFTA and Other Free Trade Agreements of ASEAN States

On 1 January 2010, the free trade agreement between the ASEAN States and China (ASEAN-China Free Trade Agreement, ACFTA)[51] came into effect. ACFTA brings about the elimination of tariffs on about 90 per cent of the goods, first for only six ASEAN States (Brunei, Indonesia, Malaysia, Philippines, Singapore, and Thailand) and China. After a transitional period, the liberalization of trade now applies to all ASEAN States and China. With a population of almost 2 billion, the ACFTA is the largest free trade zone in the world in terms of population alone. In economic terms, ACFTA ranks third after the European Economic Area and NAFTA. Besides ACFTA, the ASEAN States concluded free trade agreements with Australia and New Zealand, India, Japan, and South Korea. An ASEAN-initiated free trade agreement between these countries as well as China, the Regional Comprehensive Economic Partnership (RCEP),[52] is in the stadium of negotiations.

(c) SAFTA

The Agreement on the South Asian Free Trade Area (SAFTA)[53] between Bangladesh, Bhutan, India, Maldives, Nepal, Pakistan, Afghanistan, and Sri Lanka establishes the gradual elimination of most tariff and non-tariff barriers to trade and services. The SAFTA Agreement, in force since 2006, provides for the phased reduction of tariffs differentiating between the non-least developed Contracting States (India, Pakistan, and Sri Lanka) and the least developed Contracting States (Nepal, Bhutan, Bangladesh, Afghanistan, and the Maldives).

(d) APEC

For the Pacific region, the Asia-Pacific Economic Cooperation (APEC) was founded in 1989 with its headquarters in Singapore. Its Member States include Australia, Brunei, Chile, China, Hong Kong, Indonesia, Japan, Canada, Malaysia, Mexico, New Zealand, Papua New Guinea, Peru, the Philippines, Russia, Singapore, South Korea, Chinese Taipei (Taiwan), Thailand, the United States, and Vietnam. The 21 Member States of APEC have agreed on a comprehensive liberalization programme on their meeting in Vancouver in November 1997. As opposed to other

---

[51] For the development of ACFTA, see S Inama, 'The Association of South East Asian Nations— People's Republic of China Free Trade Area: Negotiating Beyond Eternity With Little Trade Liberalization?' (2005) 39 JWT 559.

[52] Yoshifumi Fukunaga, 'ASEAN's Leadership in the Regional Comprehensive Economic Partnership' (2014) 2 Asia & the Pacific Policy Studies 103–115.

[53] See R Islam, 'An Appraisal of the South Asian Free Trade Agreement and Its Consistency with the WTO Rules on Preferential Trade Agreements' (2010) 44 JWT 1187.

economic areas, APEC is based on non-binding agreements and makes decisions by consensus.

(e) Trans-Pacific Trade Relations

The Agreement on Trans-Pacific Strategic Economic Partnership (TPSEP) provides a framework for the liberalization of trade in goods and services. Since 2006, the TPSEP Agreement has been in force between Brunei, Chile, New Zealand, and Singapore (P4).

The United States entered into negotiations with the P4 and other APEC countries on a new broader trade agreement in the Pacific Rim. In 2015, the United States, Australia, Brunei, Canada, Chile, Japan, Malaysia, Mexico, New Zealand, Peru, Singapore, and Vietnam concluded the negotiations on the Trans-Pacific Partnership (TPP). The TPP agreement provides for trade liberalization and investment protection as well as for the protection of intellectual property and common labour standards.[54]

8. Regional Integration in Africa

The Economic Community of West African States (ECOWAS; Communauté Économique des États de l'Afrique de l'Ouest, CEDEAO),[55] established in 1975, is a customs union. Members are Benin, Burkina Faso, Ivory Coast, Gambia, Ghana, Guinea, Guinea-Bissau, Cape Verde, Liberia, Mali, Niger, Nigeria, Senegal, Sierra Leone, and Togo.

The Common Market for Eastern and Southern Africa (COMESA)[56] was formed in 1994 and comprises 20 Member States (Angola, Egypt, Ethiopia, Burundi, Djibouti, Eritrea, Kenya, Comoros, the Democratic Republic of Congo, Libya, Madagascar, Malawi, Mauritius, Rwanda, Zambia, the Seychelles, Sudan, Swaziland, Uganda, and Zimbabwe). In addition to the commonly agreed programme for the reduction or elimination of tariffs, a number of COMESA countries are negotiating on the elimination of non-tariff barriers to trade as well.

Burundi, Kenya, Rwanda, Tanzania, and Uganda established the Eastern African Community (EAC)[57] as a framework for a customs union. The institutional structure includes organs with representatives of the Member States, a secretariat, and the Court of Justice of the EAC.[58]

The Community of Sahel Saharan States (CEN-SAD) aims at free movement of persons, free establishment, and free trade of goods and services. Many of its 28 Member States are already party to other free trade arrangements.

---

[54] See in Section 10(b) in this Chapter The Agreement on the Trans-Pacific Partnership (TPP).

[55] See JE Okolo, 'ECOWAS Regional Cooperation Regime' (1989) 32 GYIL 111.

[56] R Akombe Kwamboka, *Regional Integration and the Challenge of Economic Development: The Case of the Common Market for Eastern and Southern Africa (COMESA)* (Rutgers University 2005).

[57] A Ajulu, *The Making of a Region: The Revival of the East African Community* (Institute for Global Dialogue 2005).

[58] See AP van der Mei, 'Regional Integration: The Contribution of the Court of Justice of the ECA' (2009) 69 ZaöRV 403.

South Africa and 14 other States form the Southern African Development Community (SADC), which was initially designed as a free trade zone and aims at the creation of a common market. Although not designed as a human rights court in the strict sense, the SADC Tribunal issued landmark rulings on the principles of rule of law and human rights. The Tribunal's ruling in the case of *Campbell et al v Republic of Zimbabwe*[59] met with massive opposition by the Government of Zimbabwe which refused to recognize the judgment. Consequently, the Member States of SADC de facto suspended the operation of the Tribunal.[60]

The ambitious project of the African Economic Community (AEC) under the Abuja Treaty of 1991[61] is inspired by the European Union. The AEC Treaty envisages implementation in several stages within 34 years. The existing regional economic communities in Africa are considered building blocks of the AEC (Article 88(1) of the AEC Treaty). The AEC pursues the ambitious aim of establishing a common currency and an African Central Bank.

The AEC stands in a complex relationship with the African Union.[62] The African Economic Community shall form an integral part of the African Union (Article 98(1) of the AEC Treaty). The African Court of Justice and Human Rights, which belongs to the institutional system of the African Union, has jurisdiction over disputes between the Members of the African Economic Community. The relations between the African Union and the regional economic communities of Africa are governed by a protocol of 2007.

9. Bilateral Trade Agreements of the European Union and of the United States

For the current trade policy of the European Union and of the United States, the establishment of free trade areas by bilateral trade agreements ranks as one of the strategic objectives. The United States concluded bilateral free trade agreements, inter alia, with Australia, Chile, the Central American States and the Dominican Republic (CAFTA-DR), Colombia, and Peru. In economic terms the Korea–United States Free Trade Agreement (KORUS FTA), in force since March 2012, has been the most important free trade agreement of the United States since NAFTA.[63] Central issues covered by US free trade agreements are tariff-exemptions for almost all goods, market access for financial and other services, and investment protection.

---

[59] SADC Tribunal, *Mike Campbell (Pvt) Ltd and Others v Republic of Zimbabwe* Case No 2/2007 (Decision of 28 November 2008) (2009) 48 ILM 530.

[60] E de Wet, 'The Rise and Fall of the Tribunal of the Southern African Development Community: Implications for Dispute Settlement in Southern Africa' (2013) 28 ICSID Rev 45–63.

[61] Treaty Establishing the African Economic Community of 1991 (Abuja Treaty) (1991) 30 ILM 1241.

[62] RF Oppong, 'The African Union, African Economic Community and Africa's Regional Economic Communities: Untangling a Complex Web' (2010) 18 African Journal of International and Comparative Law 92.

[63] See YS Lee, 'The Beginning of Economic Integration Between East Asia and North America?—Forming the Third Largest Free Trade Area Between the United States and the Republic of Korea' (2007) 41 JWT 1091.

The European Union and its Member States concluded free trade agreements, inter alia, with Argentina, Chile, Colombia, Mexico, Peru, and South Africa.

After the extension of the European Union's external powers, especially in the areas of investment and intellectual property rights, by the Lisbon Treaty, the European Union seeks comprehensive economic agreements with its trade partners. The first treaty in force was the free trade agreement between the European Union and the Republic of Korea.[64] The Agreement provides for the progressive elimination of tariffs for industrial products and most agricultural goods as well as for the far-reaching liberalization of trade in services. Specific commitments address non-tariff barriers in the sectors of automobiles, pharmaceuticals, and electronics. The agreement also covers the topics investments, competition, government procurement, intellectual property rights, and transparency as well as sustainable development.

In 2014, the European Union and Canada concluded negotiations on the Comprehensive Economic and Trade Agreement (CETA).[65] A similar agreement with Singapore followed.[66]

Some East-Asian States like Japan, Malaysia, and Vietnam are engaged in more or less advanced negotiations with the European Union on the one hand and the United States on the other. In 2015, Vietnam and the European Union concluded the negotiations on a free trade agreement, which is the most ambitious and comprehensive free trade agreement between the European Union and a developing country so far.[67] Regional trade agreements, agreements between major economic powers, face fundamental as well as more technical criticism. A serious concern is the challenge to a multilateral approach. Certainly, reducing protectionism on a global scale may be more conducive to economic growth and prosperity than an even more massive elimination of barriers to free trade which is confined to a regional context. Still, bilateral or regional liberalization of trade may have an important 'spill over' effect in terms of weaning industries and domestic politics from protectionist measures and thus foster receptivity for equality of competitive conditions which is a paramount objective of the current world trade system.[68] Very often, the benefits of trade liberalization accrue essentially to big transnational corporations, whilst only rather modest 'trickle down effects' reach medium and small enterprises. However, it is difficult to make generalizing forecasts. The benefits for employment and for public budget, which in the end affect every citizen, must also be considered.

---

[64] Free Trade Agreement between the European Union and its Member States, of the one part, and the Republic of Korea, of the other part [2011] OJ L127/6.

[65] See Section 10(a) in this Chapter.

[66] See for the text of the EU-Singapore Free Trade Agreement at <http://trade.ec.europa.eu/doclib/press/index.cfm?id=961> (accessed 23 June 2016).

[67] EU and Vietnam reach agreement on free trade deal European Commission Press release IP/15/5467 (4 August 2015) <http://europa.eu/rapid/press-release_IP-15-5467_en.htm> (accessed 23 June 2016).

[68] See Article III:1 of the GATT: 'The contracting parties recognize that internal taxes and other internal charges, and laws, regulations and requirements affecting the internal sale, offering for sale, purchase, transportation, distribution or use of products, and internal quantitative regulations requiring the mixture, processing or use of products in specified amounts or proportions, should not be applied to imported or domestic products so as to afford protection to domestic production'.

Preferential Trade Agreements of the European Union[69]

Preferential Trade Agreements of the European Union in place

Albania, Algeria, Antigua, Bahamas, Barbados, Barbuda, Belize, Bosnia-Herzegovina, Chile, Colombia, Costa Rica, Dominica, Dominican Republic, Egypt, El Salvador, Former Yugoslav Republic of Macedonia, Grenada, Guatemala, Guyana, Haiti, Honduras, Israel, Jamaica, Jordan, Lebanon, Madagascar, Mauritius, Mexico, Montenegro, Nicaragua, Occupied Palestinian Territory, Panama, Papua New Guinea, Peru, Republic of Korea (South Korea), Serbia, Seychelles, Singapore, South Africa, St Kitts and Nevis, St Lucia, St Vincent and the Grenadines, Suriname, Switzerland, Syria, Trinidad and Tobago, Ukraine, Zimbabwe

Countries with which the United States has a bilateral free trade agreement in place[70]

Australia, Bahrain, Canada, Chile, Colombia, Costa Rica, Dominican Republic, El Salvador, Guatemala, Honduras, Israel, Jordan, Republic of Korea (South Korea), Mexico, Morocco, Nicaragua, Oman, Panama, Peru, Singapore

---

10. Mega-regional Trade Agreements: CETA, TPP, TTIP, and beyond

A recent and salient feature of sub-global trade liberalization are the so-called 'mega-regionals', that is, trade agreements which span regions far apart from each other and often have an intercontinental reach. These agreements tend to pursue a broader agenda of economic integration than traditional free trade agreements. Mega-regionals, beyond trade liberalization, cover important issues such as investment protection. They govern gigantic trade and capital flows. An important aspect of mega-regionals is regulatory cooperation (eg under CETA and TTIP). Regulatory cooperation bodies are an institutional mechanism for the exchange of information, for consultation, and for the consideration of respective regulations of the parties as well as for the development of common standards. TTIP has the potential to bring about a realignment of global economic governance. Together with the Trans-Pacific Partnership (TTP), TTIP would become one of the pillars of a bipolar order, which rests on trans-pacific cooperation and transatlantic cooperation in trade and investment. TTIP and the TTP stand in a synergetic as well as competitive relationship. In the long run, the dynamics of regulatory cooperation between the European Union and the United States may be the crucial factor in global standard setting for products and services and the removal of non-tariff barriers to trade. In addition, cooperation between the European Union and the United States in competition law may give transatlantic cooperation an edge over its transpacific counterpart. CETA, the comprehensive economic agreement between Canada and the European Union, pursues an agenda similar to TTIP. The opening of the negotiations

---

[69] <http://trade.ec.europa.eu/doclib/docs/2012/november/tradoc_150129.pdf> (accessed 23 June 2016).
[70] <http://www.ustr.gov/trade-agreements/free-trade-agreements> (accessed 9 February 2016).

on the settlement of investment disputes under CETA, with the objective to put pressure on the US Government in the TTIP negotiations, bears witness to the strategic interplay between parallel treaty regimes governing transatlantic relations.

(a) The Comprehensive Economic and Trade Agreement (CETA)

In 2014, Canada and the European Union finished negotiations on the Comprehensive Economic and Trade Agreement (CETA).[71] The preamble of CETA emphasizes the parties' commitment to sustainable development, labour and environmental protection, as well as their attachment to international security, human rights, democracy, and the rule of law. These objectives demonstrate that trade liberalization and investment protection are embedded in a broader political context and that the parties of CETA undertook many regulatory approaches.

Apart from covering the core issues of trade liberalization including tariff elimination, CETA, inter alia, contains chapters on trade remedies (anti-dumping and countervailing duties, safeguards), technical barriers to trade, sanitary and phytosanitary measures, investment, cross-border trade in services, financial and telecommunications services, recognition of professional qualifications, electronic commerce, competition policy, state enterprises and monopolies, government procurement, intellectual property, and regulatory cooperation. It also addresses labour standards (with reference to ILO Declaration on Fundamental Principles and Rights at Work and its Follow up as adopted in 1998), and environmental protection. CETA establishes a dispute settlement system with arbitral panels of independent experts.

(b) The Agreement on the Trans-Pacific Partnership (TPP)

In February 2016, twelve countries of the Pacific Rim signed the Agreement on the Trans-Pacific Partnership (TPP).[72] Parties are Australia, Canada, Brunei, Chile, Japan, Malaysia, Mexico, New Zealand, Peru, Singapore, the United States, and Vietnam. It is remarkable that China stays outside the TPP. The United States were the major driving force behind the TPP which reflects the American 'Pivot to Asia' strategy. Like CETA, the TPP Agreement covers the protection of investments (chapter 9). Its impact on the global political and economic order may even overshadow the Transatlantic Trade and Investment Partnership the negotiation of which aroused a most lively interest on both sides of the Atlantic and generated an unprecedented public controversy within the European Union.

In many respects, the TPP Agreement pursues a similar agenda as CETA. But for many of its parties, the TPP standards will have a far more significant impact on national legislation and on regulatory practice. This holds true for financial services (chapter 11), telecommunications services (chapter 13), state-owned enterprises, and designated monopolies (chapter 17), and intellectual property rights (chapter 18, with refined standards as to effective market protection of pharmaceutical products or as to copyright infringements in the online environment). In some sensitive areas, the TPP Agreement defers to regulatory philosophies of parties, for example with respect to products of modern biotechnology (Article 2.29). The Agreement dedicates a special chapter to labour standards (chapter 19). The chapter on the environment (chapter 20) makes particular reference to trade and biodiversity (Article 20.13) and the transition to a low emission economy (Article 20.15). Other chapters cover development (chapter 23) as well as transparency and anti-corruption (chapter 26).

On an inter-governmental level, the Agreement is administered by the TPP Commission (chapter 27). The dispute settlement (chapter 28) is modelled after the WTO system. It includes an arbitral panel consisting of independent experts which shall make an objective assessment (Article 28.11). In compliance with the panel's findings, parties shall eliminate nonconformity of national measures 'whenever possible' (Article 28.18.2). In case of non-implementation, remedies are compensation and suspension of benefits (Article 28.19).

Its complex and detailed texture within often very strict standards for restrictive trade measures or regulatory frameworks as to competition law, intellectual property, or other trade-related areas, the TPP Agreement sets an ambitious model for other mega-regionals with heterogeneous parties.

(c) The Transatlantic Trade and Investment Partnership Agreement (TTIP)

The relevance of liberalization of transatlantic trade can hardly be overestimated. Trade between the European Union and the United States accounts for about a third of the entire world trade. The European Union and the United States concluded several agreements on mutual recognition, for example as to product-related standards. In 2007, the EU–US summit adopted the Framework Agreement on the Advancement of Transatlantic Economic Integration. Since 2013, the European Union and the United States have been engaged in negotiations on the TTIP. TTIP shall considerably reduce existing tariffs, and average custom duties are already relatively low (about 2 per cent).[73] However, it is important to differentiate between the custom duties for individual goods. Whilst more than half of EU–US trade is not subject to any custom duties at all, tariffs for the remaining trade are marked by a notable spread and occasionally reach prohibitive dimensions (1 per cent on many raw materials, 30 per cent for clothes, 53 per cent US custom duties on raw tobacco). Sometimes the European Union and the United States charge different duties for the same product (eg cars). TTIP will also eliminate or reduce non-tariff barriers to trade. Many industrial sectors suffer from different technical requirements (eg components of cars) or standards for the production process (hygienic standards for food production). Regular cooperation under TTIP shall facilitate recognition of equivalent standards or contribute to a harmonized approach. This regulatory cooperation has the potential to establish common standards which may operate as a global benchmark in international trade. The negotiation mandate of

[73] European Commission, *Fact Sheet on Trade in Goods and Customs Duties in TTIP* <http://trade.ec.europa.eu/doclib/html/152998.htm> (accessed 23 June 2016).

the European Commission laid down by the Council of the European Union[74] contains an important reservation in favour of 'cultural and linguistic diversity' and policies in support of the cultural sector. The directive aims at preserving the quality of public utilities and excludes services in the exercise of governmental authority. The European Commission shall aim at the elimination or lowering of non-tariff barriers to trade such as technical standards for automobile components. According to rather optimistic expectations, TTIP will increase the transatlantic trade volume both for the European Union and the United States by about EUR 100 billion within a decade.

Critics fear an erosion of the multilateral approach to progressive trade liberalization under the WTO. Voices warn against lower standards of health and environmental protection under TTIP's trade and investment rules. Many challenges to TTIP ignore already existing commitments, especially under WTO law. The European Commission pursues an ambitious negotiation agenda as to high labour and environmental standards.

(d) Implications for the World Trading System

From a global perspective, mega-regionals have an ambivalent impact on trade liberalization, competitiveness, and balance of negotiation power. On the one hand, critics consider mega-regional agreements as a particular challenge to the WTO as the global forum for trade liberalization and are concerned about the risk for non-parties to be marginalized. Even more than other free trade agreements, mega-regionals erode the principle of most-favoured-nation treatment within the WTO. Dispute settlement may compete with the WTO Dispute Settlement Body in the interpretation of rules which incorporate obligations under the WTO treaties or establish similar standards. This might severely impair the guiding function of the WTO panel and Appellate Body reports.

On the other hand, mega-regionals operate as fore runners in the sense that they put pressure on WTO members to agree to further trade liberalization which may pave the way for bridging differences within the WTO and reaching consensus on a global level. This holds particularly true for agreements which include economically and politically powerful States with different regulatory philosophies or conflicting industrial or agricultural interests such as the TPP. For example, the TPP Agreement commits parties to cooperate within the WTO towards elimination of export subsidies for agricultural products (Article 2.23). Mega-regionals also give a voice to smaller countries in a sub-global framework.

Moreover, mega-regionals bring up important objectives which transcend economic development. Thus, the preamble of CETA affirms the commitment of both sides as parties to the UNESCO Convention on the Protection and Promotion of the Diversity of Cultural Expressions and recognizes that

---

[74] Council of the European Union Directives for the negotiation on the Transatlantic Trade and Investment Partnership between the European Union and the United States of America [17 June 2013] Doc 11103/13 DCL 1 (declassified 9 October 2014).

States have the right to preserve, develop and implement their cultural policies, and to support their cultural industries for the purpose of strengthening the diversity of cultural expressions, and preserving their cultural identity, including through the use of regulatory measures and financial support.[75]

Furthermore, mega-regionals are committed to the standards of proportionality and transparency and, in the context of investment protection, to fairness and access to justice. These standards are important elements of 'good governance' on the domestic and international plane. The dispute settlement mechanism will contribute to consistency and accountability of legislative and executive action, which in terms of a spillover effect will benefit citizens also in a purely domestic context.

Finally, mega-regionals respond to concerns which are voiced also under the WTO system. Both CETA and the TPP Agreement respond to political complaints about excessive limitations of regulatory freedom by trade liberalization. Thus, in the preamble of the TPP Agreement, the parties

[r]ecognize their inherent right to regulate and resolve to preserve the flexibility of the Parties to set legislative and regulatory priorities, safeguard public welfare, and protect legitimate public welfare objectives, such as public health, safety, the environment, the conservation of living or non-living exhaustible natural resources, the integrity and stability of the financial system and public morals.[76]

The TPP Agreement expresses a commitment to 'promote transparency, good governance and rule of law' in its preamble.

Select Bibliography

FORMS OF REGIONAL MARKET INTEGRATION (FREE TRADE AREAS, CUSTOMS UNIONS, AND ECONOMIC COMMUNITIES)

L Bartels and F Ortino, *Regional Trade Agreements and the WTO Legal System* (OUP 2006).
A Dür and M Elsig (eds), *Trade Cooperation: The Purpose, Design and Effects of Preferential Trade Agreements* (CUP 2014).
DA Gantz, 'Regional Trade Agreements' in D Bethlehem, D McRae, R Neufeld, and I Van Damme (eds), *The Oxford Handbook of International Trade Law* (OUP 2009) 237.
B Hoeckman and R Newfarmer, 'Preferential Trade Agreements, Investment Disciplines and Investment Flows' (2005) 39 JWT 949.

---

[75] In a less emphatic manner, the preamble of the TPP Agreement also recognizes the importance of cultural identity and diversity:

the provisions of this Agreement preserve the right to regulate within their territories and resolving to preserve their flexibility to achieve legitimate policy objectives, such as public health, safety, environment, public morals and the promotion and protection of cultural diversity.

[76] In similar terms, the preamble of CETA states the understanding of the parties that

the provisions of this Agreement preserve the right to regulate within their territories and resolving to preserve their flexibility to achieve legitimate policy objectives, such as public health, safety, environment, public morals and the promotion and protection of cultural diversity.

C Kaufmann, 'Customs Unions' in R Wolfrum (ed), *The Max Planck Encyclopedia of Public International Law* (OUP 2012) vol II, 982.

M Köbele, 'Free Trade Areas' in R Wolfrum (ed), *The Max Planck Encyclopedia of Public International Law* (OUP 2012) vol IV, 239.

S Lester and B Mercurio, *Bilateral and Regional Trade Agreements* (CUP 2009).

THE FREE MOVEMENT OF GOODS AND SERVICES IN THE EUROPEAN UNION

M Adenas and W-H Roth (eds), *Services and Free Movement in EU Law* (OUP 2003).

P Oliver (ed), *Oliver on Free Movements of Goods in the European Union* (5th edn, Hart Publishing 2010).

EFTA AND THE EUROPEAN ECONOMIC AREA

O Jacot-Guillarmod (ed), *Accord EEE-Commentaire et Réflexions/EWR-Abkommen* (Schultheiss 1992).

S Norberg, 'The Agreement on a European Economic Area' (1992) 29 CML Rev 1171.

P Oliver (ed), *Oliver on Free Movements of Goods in the European Union* (5th edn, Hart Publishing 2010).

A Toledano Laredo, 'The EEA Agreement: An Overall View' (1992) 29 CML Rev 1199.

THE NORTH AMERICAN FREE TRADE AGREEMENT (NAFTA)

FM Abbott, *Law and Policy of Regional Integration: The NAFTA and Western Hemispheric Integration in the World Trade Organization System* (Aspen Publishers 1995).

SA Baker and SB Battram, 'The Canada—United States Free Trade Agreement' (1989) 23 Int'l Law 37.

JH Bello, AF Holmer, and JJ Norton (eds), *The North American Free Trade Agreement. A New Frontier in International Trade and Investment in the Americas* (American Bar Association 1994).

K Kennedy (ed), *The First Decade of NAFTA: The Future of Free Trade in North America* (Brill Academic Publishers 2004).

JJ Norton (ed), *NAFTA and Beyond. A New Framework for Doing Business in the Americas* (Springer 1995).

SJ Rubin and DC Alexander, *NAFTA and the Environment* (Kluwer Law International 1996).

JL Siqueiros, 'NAFTA Institutional Arrangements and Dispute Settlement Procedures' (1993) 23 California Western International Law Journal 383.

REGIONAL INTEGRATION IN SOUTH AMERICA

C Chatterjee, 'The Treaty of Asunción: An Analysis' (1992) 26 JWT 63.

MT Franca Filho, L Lixinski, and MB Olmos Giupponi (eds), *The Law of Mercosur* (Hart Publishing 2010).

G Mancero-Bucheli, 'Anti-Competitive Practices by Private Undertakings in Ancom and Mercosur: An Analysis from the Perspective of EC Law' (1998) 47 ICLQ 149.

H Moavro, PW Orieta, and RG Parera, *Las Instituciones del Mercosur* (Centro Interdisciplinario de Estudios Sobre el Desarollo Latinoamericano 1997).

TA O'Keefe, 'How the Andean Pact Transformed Itself into a Friend of Foreign Enterprise' (1996) 30 Int'l Law 811.

TA O'Keefe, *Latin American and Caribbean Trade Agreements: Keys to a Prosperous Community of the Americas* (Martinus Nijhoff Publishers/Brill Academic Publishers 2009).

J Vervaele, 'Mercosur and Regional Integration in South America' (2005) 54 ICLQ 387.

REGIONAL INTEGRATION IN CENTRAL AMERICA AND THE CARIBBEAN

TA O'Keefe, *Latin American and Caribbean Trade Agreements: Keys to a Prosperous Community of the Americas* (Martinus Nijhoff Publishers/Brill Academic Publishers 2009).

REGIONAL INTEGRATION IN ASIA AND THE PACIFIC

E Aryeetey, J Court, M Nissanke, and B Weder (eds), *Asia and Africa in the Global Economy* (UNUP 2003).

M Beeson, *Institutions of the Asia Pacific: ASEAN, APEC and Beyond* (Routledge 2009).

HS Kartadjoemena, 'ASEAN and the International Trading System: Regional Trade Arrangement vs. the WTO' in M Than (ed), *ASEAN Beyond the Regional Crisis* (Institute of Southeast Asian Studies 2001).

S Narine, *Explaining ASEA: Regionalism in Southeast Asia* (Lynne Rienner Publishers 2002).

G Thompson (ed), *Economic Dynamism in the Asia-Pacific: Growth of Integration and Competitiveness* (Taylor & Francis 1998).

REGIONAL INTEGRATION IN AFRICA

RK Akombe, *Regional Integration and the Challenge of Economic Development: The Case of the Common Market for Eastern and Southern Africa (COMESA)* (Rutgers University 2005).

A Geda and H Kebret, 'Regional Economic Integration in Africa: A Review of Problems and Prospects with a Case Study of COMESA' (2008) 17 Journal of African Economies 357.

T Hartzenberg, 'Regional Integration in Africa' (2011) WTO Staff Working Paper ERSD-2011–14.

BILATERAL TRADE AGREEMENTS OF THE EUROPEAN UNION AND OF THE UNITED STATES

GA Berman, M Herdegen, and P Lindseth (eds), *Transatlantic Regulatory Co-operation* (OUP 2001).

M Herdegen, 'Legal Challenges for Transatlantic Economic Integration' (2008) CML Rev 1581.

PART IV
INTERNATIONAL BUSINESS LAW

XXIV

International Sales and Contract Law

1. Introduction

(a) International agreements on private international law and uniform law

The harmonization of rules is an elementary concern of international commerce. In international business relations, the parties have a vital interest in reliably knowing their mutual rights and obligations. A contract does not necessarily settle all contentious issues and may give rise to controversies and lead to litigation. It may be a matter of doubt which law applies to the contractual relation and the courts in different countries may reach different conclusions in this context. International agreements on the applicable law respond to this problem. Even then, the disparities among national laws persist, for instance, with respect to the rights of the buyer or seller of goods. Only more ambitious treaties harmonizing substantive law can reliably establish uniform standards (*loi uniforme*) for the countries concerned. These uniform rules dispense the parties from ascertaining the particularities of foreign laws. They restrain the interest of parties to look for a forum with a law particularly favourable to their case.

The United Nations Commission on International Trade Law (UNCITRAL) was established by the United Nations General Assembly by its resolution 2205 (XXI) of 17 December 1966 to promote the 'progressive harmonization and unification of the law of international trade'. It mainly serves to prepare and promote the use and adoption of a variety of legislative and non-legislative instruments in a number of key areas of commercial law such as dispute resolution, international contract practices, insolvency, electronic commerce, international payments, secured transactions, procurement, and sale of goods.[1]

According to II.8 of Resolution 2205 (XXI) the Commission 'shall further the progressive harmonization and unification of the law of international trade' by:

(a) coordinating the work of organizations active in this field and encouraging cooperation among them;

---

[1] See for further detail, UNCITRAL, *The UNCITRAL Guide* (2007) <http://www.uncitral.org/pdf/english/texts/general/06-50941_Ebook.pdf> (accessed 23 June 2016).

(b) promoting wider participation in existing international conventions and wider accept-
     ance of existing model and uniform laws;
(c) preparing or promoting the adoption of new international conventions, model laws,
     and uniform laws and promoting the codification and wider acceptance of international
     trade terms, provisions, customs, and practices, in collaboration, where appropriate,
     with the organizations operating in this field;
(d) promoting ways and means of ensuring a uniform interpretation and application of
     international conventions and uniform laws in the field of the law of international trade;
(e) collecting and disseminating information on national legislation and modern legal
     developments, including case-law, in the field of the law of international trade;
(f) establishing and maintaining a close collaboration with the United Nations Conference
     on Trade and Development;
(g) maintaining liaison with other United Nations organs and specialized agencies con-
     cerned with international trade;
(h) taking any other action it may deem useful to fulfil its functions.

The most prominent uniform framework for international business relations is the
UN Convention on Contracts for the International Sale of Goods (CISG) of 1980.
The Hague Convention on the Law Applicable to Contracts for the International
Sale of Goods of 1986 aims to unify the rules on the conflict of laws. Within
the European Union, the EEC Convention on the Law Applicable to Contractual
Obligations (the 'Rome Convention') of 1980 was replaced by the Regulation (EC)
No 593/2008 ('Rome I Regulation').[2] Among Latin American States, a number of
treaties on the unification of the rules on the conflict of laws are in force. Under
the auspices of the OAS, an Inter-American Private Law framework has emerged.[3]
It comprises the Inter-American Convention on International Commercial
Arbitration, the Inter-American Convention on Personality and Capacity of
Juridical Persons in Private International Law, the Inter-American Convention
on Contracts for the International Carriage of Goods by Road, the Model Inter-
American Law on Secured Transactions, the Negotiable Uniform Bill of Lading for
the International Carriage of Goods by Road, and the Non-negotiable Uniform Bill
of Lading for the International Carriage of Goods by Road.

(b) Incoterms

The established usage of standard terms with an internationally recognized
meaning contributes to uniform rules whenever the parties refer to these terms.
Incoterms (International Commercial Terms), a series of three-letter trade terms,
stand for well-established standard obligations in context with the transportation
and delivery of goods.

The Incoterms are published by the International Chamber of Commerce (ICC).
They date back to the year 1936 and are updated periodically. They cover mainly

---

[2] Regulation (EC) No 593/2008 on the law applicable to contractual obligations (Rome I) [2008]
OJ L177/6.
[3] See (1994) 33 ILM 732.

the tasks, costs, and risks involved in the delivery of goods. The eighth version, the Incoterms 2010, was published in early 2011.

The Incoterms contain rules for modalities of transport in general such as:

- EXW—Ex Works (named place of delivery),
- FCA—Free Carrier (named place of delivery),
- CPT—Carriage Paid To (named place of destination),
- CIP—Carriage and Insurance Paid to (named place of destination),
- DAT—Delivered at Terminal (named terminal at port or place of destination),
- DAP—Delivered at Place (named place of destination),
- DDP—Delivered Duty Paid (named place of destination),

and special rules for Sea and Inland Waterway Transport such as:

- FAS—Free Alongside Ship (named port of shipment),
- FOB—Free on Board (named port of shipment),
- CFR—Cost and Freight (named port of destination),
- CIF—Cost, Insurance and Freight (named port of destination).

The rule 'Ex Works' means that the seller delivers by placing the goods at the disposal of the buyer at the former's premises or at another place. This indicates the minimum obligation for the seller because he neither needs to load the goods on any collecting vehicle nor is he concerned with any applicable export clearance requirement.[4] In contrast, 'Delivery Duty Paid' represents the maximum obligation for the seller. He bears all the costs and risks involved in bringing the goods to the named place of destination (including the responsibility for the export and import clearance).[5] 'Free on Board' is used for waterway transport. It obliges the seller to deliver the goods on board of the vessel chosen by the buyer at the named port of shipment (or procures the goods already so delivered).[6] The moment at which the goods are on board of the vessel is decisive as the risk of loss or damages concerning the goods passes over to the buyer who then bears all the costs from that moment onwards. The seller is obliged to clear the goods for export while import restrictions are the buyer's responsibility. The term 'Cost, Insurance and Freight' also requires the seller to deliver the goods on board of the vessel nominated by the buyer at the destined port of shipment (or procures the goods already so delivered).[7] Furthermore, the seller must contract for and pay the costs and freight necessary to bring the goods to the named port of destination and contract for insurance cover against the buyer's risk of loss or damage to the goods during carriage. Thus, the costs accrued up to delivery to the agreed point of destination are assumed by the

---

[4] See ICC, *Incoterms 2010* (2010) Guidance Note EXW.

[5] See ICC, *Incoterms 2010* (2010) Guidance Note DDP.

[6] See ICC, *Incoterms 2010* (2010) Guidance Note FOB: 'the reference to "procure" caters for multiple sales down a chain'.

[7] See ICC, *Incoterms 2010* (2010) Guidance Note CIF.

seller, while the risk of loss of and damages to the goods passes over (to the buyer) when the goods are on board of the vessel.[8]

An important issue is the incorporation of Incoterms into a contract under the CISG. In *BP Oil International Ltd v Empresa Estatal Petróleos de Ecuador*, a US Court of Appeals ruled on a contracted 'CFR' shipment:

> The CISG incorporates Incoterms through article 9(2), [...] Even if the usage of Incoterms is not global, the fact that they are well known in international trade means that they are incorporated through article 9(2). [...] Shipments designated 'CFR' require the seller to pay the costs and freight to transport the goods to the delivery port, but pass title and risk of loss to the buyer once the goods 'pass the ship's rail' at the port of shipment. The goods should be tested for conformity before the risk of loss passes to the buyer. [...] In the event of subsequent damage or loss, the buyer generally must seek a remedy against the carrier or insurer.[9]

Thus, under trade rules, Incoterms convey a specific meaning to contractual obligations.

2. The Rome Convention, the Rome I Regulation, and the Common European Law on Sales

The Regulation (EC) No 593/2008 ('Rome I Regulation') on the law applicable to contractual obligations modernizes and replaces the Convention on the Law Applicable to Contractual Obligations of 1980 (the 'Rome Convention') except with respect to some overseas territories of the Member States (Article 24).

The 'Rome I Regulation' applies 'in situations involving a conflict of laws, to contractual obligations in civil and commercial matters' (Article 1(1)). Certain matters such as the status or legal capacity of natural persons, obligations arising out of family relationships, arbitration agreements, and agreements on the choice of court or the constitution of trusts remain outside the scope of the regulation. The applicable law does not need to be the law of a Member State of the European Union (Article 2).

The regulation is founded on the principle of party autonomy. Parties may choose the law which shall govern their contract (Article 3(1)(a)). However, if all relevant criteria point to a country other than the country whose law has been chosen, the choice of law of the parties shall not prejudice the application of non-derogable rules of that other country (Article 3(3)). If the parties have not chosen the applicable law, the general rule is that a contract shall be subject to the law of the country with which it is most closely connected (Article 4(4)). Article 4(1) lays down criteria for the specific contracts:

(a) a contract for the sale of goods shall be governed by the law of the country where the seller has his habitual residence;

---

[8] See ICC, *Incoterms 2010* (2010) Guidance Note CIF.
[9] *BP Oil International v Empresa Estatal Petroleos de Ecuador* 332 F.3d 333 (5th Cir 2003).

(b) a contract for the provision of services shall be governed by the law of the country where the service provider has his habitual residence;

(c) a contract relating to a right in rem in immovable property or to a tenancy of immovable property shall be governed by the law of the country where the property is situated;

(d) notwithstanding point (c), a tenancy of immovable property concluded for temporary private use for a period of no more than six consecutive months shall be governed by the law of the country where the landlord has his habitual residence, provided that the tenant is a natural person and has his habitual residence in the same country;

(e) a franchise contract shall be governed by the law of the country where the franchisee has its habitual residence;

(f) a distribution contract shall be governed by the law of the country where the distributor has his habitual residence;

(g) a contract for the sale of goods by auction shall be governed by the law of the country where the auction takes place, if such a place can be determined;

(h) a contract concluded within a multilateral system which brings together or facilitates the bringing together of multiple third-party buying and selling interests in financial instruments, as defined by Article 4(1), point (17) of Directive 2004/39/EC, in accordance with non-discretionary rules and governed by a single law, shall be governed by that law.

If the contract is not covered by Article 4(1) or if more than one of the listed criteria apply to a contract, the habitual residence of the party required to effect the characteristic performance of the contract, in principle, determines the country whose law shall govern the contract (Article 4(2)), unless all circumstances indicate a closer connection of the contract with another country (Article 4(3)).

Mandatory provisions of a country with extraterritorial effect may override the law otherwise applicable. Under Article 9(1), 'mandatory provisions are provisions the respect for which is regarded as crucial by a country for safeguarding its public interests, such as its political, social or economic organization'. Such provisions may relate to import or export bans or to national security. Article 9(3) of the Regulation narrowly conditions deference to mandatory provisions:

Effect may be given to the overriding mandatory provisions of the law of the country where the obligations arising out of the contract have to be or have been performed, in so far as those overriding mandatory provisions render the performance of the contract unlawful. In considering whether to give effect to those provisions, regard shall be had to their nature and purpose and to the consequences of their application or non-application.

In the case of *Paypal* (a US financial services corporation requiring European business partners not to sell Cuban products targeted by a US embargo)[10], Article 9(3) leaves no room for giving effect to the US embargo, as the contract obligations are not to be performed within the United States.

---

[10] See Cuban Democracy Act (1992) <http://www.treasury.gov/resource-center/sanctions/documents/cda.pdf> (accessed 26 January 2016).

In 2011, the European Commission submitted a proposal for a regulation on a Common European Law on Sales.[11] The draft regulation intends to overcome the divergences in the contract laws by establishing a common regime for cross-border sales within the European Union. The Commission draft draws on the Convention on the International Sale of Goods (CISG), the UNIDROIT Principles and the current state of the Common Frame of Reference.[12] The Common European Law on Sales shall apply to contracts on the sale of goods, contracts on the supply of digital contents and related service. The Common European Law on Sales shall only apply on an optional basis, on the basis of the agreement between the parties.[13] In relations between a trader and a consumer, the agreement on the use of the Common European Sales Law shall only be valid if the consumer's consent is given by an explicit statement which is separate from the statement indicating the agreement to conclude a contract.[14] At least one of the contracting parties must be a small or a medium-sized enterprise (SME), that is a trader which employs fewer than 250 persons and whose annual turnover or annual balance does not exceed a certain amount.[15] Under currently prevailing conditions, SMEs, as a rule, find themselves forced to agree to apply the law of larger business partners with all the resulting complications.[16]

3. UN Convention on Contracts for the International Sale of Goods (CISG)

For some time, steps to harmonize the substantive rules for contracts for the sale of goods have met with very modest success. The 'Hague Uniform Laws' of 1964, that is the Convention relating to a Uniform Law on the International Sale of Goods[17] and the Convention relating to the Formation of Contracts for the International Sale of Goods,[18] did not reflect the views of many developing countries and were only ratified by a relatively small number of states. As the Hague Convention failed to qualify as a universal standard,[19] UNCITRAL drafted and adopted the UN Convention on Contracts for the International Sale of Goods of 1980 (CISG).[20]

---

[11] Proposal for a Regulation of the European Parliament and the Council on a Common European Sales Law (11 October 2011) 2011/0284 (COD).

[12] Second Progress Report on The Common Frame of Reference (25 July 2007) COM(2007) 447.

[13] Article 8(1) Reg-2011/0284 (COD).   [14] Article 8(1) Reg-2011/0284 (COD).

[15] Article 7 Reg-2011/0284 (COD).

[16] Reg-2011/0284 (COD) Context of the Proposal.

[17] <http://www.cisg.law.pace.edu/cisg/text/ulis.html> (accessed 23 June 2016).

[18] <http://www.unidroit.org/instruments/international-sales/international-sales-ulfc-1964-en> (accessed 23 June 2016).

[19] M Ndulo, 'The Vienna Sales Convention 1980 and the Hague Uniform Laws on international Sale of Goods 1964: A Comparative Analysis' (1989) 38 ICLQ 1.

[20] (1980) 19 ILM 668.

In its preamble, the CISG puts emphasis on the connection of friendly relations among States and the development of international trade on the basis of equality and mutual benefit. The CISG strives to integrate and balance the principles of different legal systems around the world and to 'take into account the different social, economic and legal systems' (preamble). The CISG purports to provide a universally applicable framework for sales which is appropriate for transactions of an international character.[21] The fundamental principles underlying the CISG are the autonomy of the parties and freedom of contract (see Articles 6, 8, and 9). The Convention recognizes usages which in international trade 'are widely known and regularly observed by parties to contracts of the type involved in the particular trade concerned' (Article 9(2)).

Until June 2016, 85 States had ratified the CISG[22] including the United States, China, Russia, France, Canada, and Germany. Some significant trading countries such as South Africa and the United Kingdom have not yet ratified the CISG.

As a successful endeavour to combine principles of different legal systems, the CISG has inspired other initiatives at the international level and is considered a kind of *lingua franca* in international business.[23]

(a) Scope of application of the CISG

The CISG unifies only a part of the law on international sale of goods, that is the formation of the contract (Part II) and the rights and obligations of the parties under the contract (Part III). The CISG does not address substantive issues of validity such as fraud, duress, and mistake or the legal capacity of a party and leaves them to be settled by the applicable domestic law.[24] In doing so, the Convention remains a fragmentary framework of only imperfect harmonization. In terms of Article 4(1), the Convention covers

[...] only the formation of the contract of sale and the rights and obligations of the seller and the buyer arising from such a contract. In particular, except as otherwise expressly provided therein, this Convention is not concerned with:
(a) the validity of the contract or of any of its provisions or of any usage;
(b) the effect which the contract may have on the property in the goods sold.

---

[21] UNCITRAL *Commentary on the Draft Convention on Contracts for the International Sale of Goods prepared by the Secretariat ('Secretariat Commentary')* (1979) UN Doc A/CONF. 97/5 Article 1 No 4.

[22] <http://www.uncitral.org/uncitral/en/uncitral_texts/sale_goods/1980CISG_status.html> (accessed 23 June 2016).

[23] P Schlechtriem, in H Flechtner, H Brand, and M Walter (eds), *Drafting Contracts under the CISG* (OUP 2007) 167; S Kröll, LA Mistelis, and P Perales Viscasillas, 'Introduction to the CISG' in S Kröll, LA Mistelis, and P Perales Viscasillas, *UN Convention on Contracts for the International Sale of Goods (CISG)* (CH Beck 2011) 19 paras 28ff.

[24] See *Geneva Pharmaceutical Technology Corp v Barr Laboratories, Inc* 201 F. Supp 2d 236 (SDNY 2002) para 25.

To determine applicable domestic law, the court must engage in a traditional conflict of laws analysis to determine the substantive law.[25]

Under Article 1, the CISG is only applicable to contracts on the sale of goods
between parties whose places of business[26] are located in different States (test of
internationality). The CISG applies when the States are Contracting States (Article
1(1)(a)) or when the rules of private international law lead to the application of the
law of a Contracting State (Article 1(1)(b)). Whilst subparagraph (1)(a) introduces
an autonomous criterion for the application of the CISG (location of the place of
business in Contracting States) and supersedes conflict of laws rules, subparagraph
(1)(b) refers to conflict of laws and indicates that the Convention will then be
applied as part of the domestic law of Contracting States.[27] Since many aspects
of the sale of goods are not covered by the Convention and have to be resolved
by domestic law anyhow, national courts and arbitral tribunals tend to apply the
Convention on the basis of subparagraph (1)(b).[28] Under the alternative of subparagraph (1)(b), the CISG may be applied even if a party is not from a Contracting
State. Article 95, however, allows Contracting States to decide not to be bound by
Article 1(1)(b).

The United States ratified the CISG with a reservation opting out of Article 1 (1)
(b). By making this reservation, the US Government was concerned that US law
would more often be displaced than foreign law:

Subparagraph 1(b) would displace our own domestic law more frequently than foreign law.
By its term, subparagraph 1(b) would be relevant only in sales between parties in the United
States (a Contracting State) and a non-Contracting State. Under subparagraph 1(b), when
private international law points to the law of a foreign non-Contracting State the Convention
will not displace that foreign law, since subparagraph 1(b) makes the Convention applicable only when 'the rules of private international law lead to the application of the law of a
Contracting State'. Consequently, when those rules point to United States law, subparagraph 1(b) would normally operate to displace United States law (the Uniform Commercial
Code) and would not displace the law of the foreign Non-Contracting State.[29]

The Uniform Commercial Code (UCC), which has been adopted by all US states,
departs from the CISG in some areas, especially with respect to the law governing the form of the contract. The CISG also does not accept the US Statute of
Frauds and the Parole Evidence Rule providing that extrinsic evidence (oral or written) of prior or contemporaneous agreements or negotiations is not admissible to

---

[25] See *Geneva Pharmaceutical Technology Corp v Barr Laboratories, Inc* 201 F. Supp 2d 236 (SDNY 2002) para 26.
[26] Determined by Article 10 CISG without reference to nationality, place of incorporation or place of head office; see also Article 1(3) of the CISG.
[27] LA Mistelis, 'Article 1' in S Kröll, LA Mistelis, and P Perales Viscasillas (eds), *UN Convention on Contracts for the International Sale of Goods (CISG)* (CH Beck 2011) 21 para 5.
[28] With further references, see LA Mistelis, 'Article 1' in S Kröll, LA Mistelis, and P Perales Viscasillas (eds), *UN Convention on Contracts for the International Sale of Goods (CISG)* (CH Beck 2011) 21 para 5.
[29] US State Department, *Legal Analysis of the UN Convention on Contracts for the International Sale of Goods* (1990) Appendix B.

contradict, vary, or modify an unambiguous written contract if considered by the parties to be the final and complete expression of the agreement.[30]

In *MCC-Marble Ceramic Center, Inc v Ceramica Nuova D'Agostino*,[31] the US Court of Appeals for the Eleventh Circuit held:

[T]he language of Article 8(3) that 'due consideration is to be given to all relevant circumstances of the case' seems adequate to override any domestic rule that would bar a tribunal from considering the relevance of other agreements [...] Article 8(3) relieves tribunals from domestic rules that might bar them from 'considering' any evidence between the parties that is relevant. This added flexibility for interpretation is consistent with a growing body of opinion that the 'parole evidence rule' has been an embarrassment for the administration of modern transactions [...] This is not to say that parties to an international contract for the sale of goods cannot depend on written contracts or that parole evidence regarding subjective contractual intent always prevents a party relying on a written agreement from securing summary judgment. To the contrary, most cases will not present a situation (as exists in this case) in which both parties to the contract acknowledge a subjective intent not to be bound by the terms of a pre-printed writing. In most cases, therefore, article 8(2) of CISG will apply, and objective evidence will provide the basis for the court's decision [...] Consequently, a party to a contract governed by CISG will not be able to avoid the terms of a contract and force a jury trial simply by submitting an affidavit which states that he or she did not have the subjective intent to be bound by the contract's terms.

The fact that the parties have their places of business in different States must be disregarded if this fact does not appear from the contract, other dealings between the parties or information by the parties (Article 1(2)).

The CISG does not explicitly define a contract on the sale of goods. Nevertheless, essential elements can be deduced from Articles 30 and 50 of the CISG: the delivery of goods, documents and transfer of property on the side of the seller, the payment of the purchase price and taking delivery on the side of the buyer.[32] Framework contracts such as distributorship agreements obliging the contracting parties to agree to sales contracts already determining the main rights and obligations (*essentialia negotii*) fall under the CISG.[33] This does not apply if distribution agreements themselves do not cover the sale of specific goods and do not contain the essential terms defining quantity and price. Barter does not fall within the CISG's scope of application.[34]

---

[30] *TeeVee Tunes, Inc et al v Gerhard Schubert GmbH* 2006 WL 2463537 (SDNY 2006).

[31] *MCC-Marble Ceramic Center, Inc v Ceramica Nuova D'Agostino, SpA* 144 F.3d 1384 (11th Cir 1998).

[32] I Schwenzer and P Hachem, 'Article 1' in P Schlechtriem and I Schwenzer (eds), *Commentary on the UN Convention on the International Sale of Goods (CISG)* (4th edn, OUP 2016) para 8.

[33] LA Mistelis, 'Article 1' in S Kröll, LA Mistelis, and P Perales Viscasillas (eds), *UN Convention on Contracts for the International Sale of Goods (CISG)* (CH Beck 2011) 21 para 5.

[34] LA Mistelis, 'Article I' in S Kröll, LA Mistelis, and P Perales Viscasillas (eds), *UN Convention on Contracts for the International Sale of Goods (CISG)* (CH Beck 2011) 21 para 5 and para 30; I Schwenzer and P Hachem, 'Article 1' in P Schlechtriem and I Schwenzer (eds), *Commentary on the UN Convention on the International Sale of Goods (CISG)* (4th edn, OUP 2016) para 11.

'Goods' in terms of the CISG[35] must be moveable and tangible. Intangibles such as intellectual property rights or shares in companies are not covered. According to Article 2, the CISG does not apply to sales

(a) of goods bought for personal, family, or household use, unless the seller, at any time before or at the conclusion of the contract, neither knew nor ought to have known that the goods were bought for any such use;
(b) by auction;
(c) on execution or otherwise by authority of law;
(d) of stocks, shares, investment securities, negotiable instruments, or money;
(e) of ships, vessels, hovercraft, or aircraft;
(f) of electricity.

Article 3(1) of the CISG includes the supply of goods to be manufactured or produced. Whether hybrid contracts with a sales element are covered or not by the CISG depends on a case-by-case analysis. Distribution agreements, franchising agreements, or agreements regarding finance are widely held to fall outside the scope of the Convention.

(b) Opting out

As the provisions of the CISG are of a dispositive character, parties may opt out of the CISG altogether or in part (Article 6). Although the CISG is gaining more and more acceptance, a number of standard form contracts contain a choice of law clause and opt out of the CISG.[36] Exporters in the United States still widely opt out of the CISG in their contracts.[37]

Whether the choice of the law of a country implies a derogation from the CISG depends on the wording and the context. If the parties refer to the law of a non-contracting State (eg the United Kingdom) or specifically choose domestic sales law of a contracting State (eg the Civil and the Commercial Code of Germany), they opt out of the CISG. If, however, the parties simply refer to the law of a contracting State (eg the law of Germany), this reference is to be understood as triggering the application of the CISG as part of the chosen national law.

---

[35] LA Mistelis, 'Article 1' in S Kröll, LA Mistelis, and P Perales Viscasillas (eds), *UN Convention on Contracts for the International Sale of Goods (CISG)* (CH Beck 2011) 21 paras 36ff; I Schwenzer and P Hachem, 'Article 1' in P Schlechtriem and I Schwenzer (eds), *Commentary on the UN Convention on the International Sale of Goods (CISG)* (4th edn, OUP 2016) paras 16ff. It is irrelevant for the application of the CISG whether or not the respective contract is of civil or commercial nature, see I Schwenzer and P Hachem, 'Article 1' in P Schlechtriem and I Schwenzer (eds), *Commentary on the UN Convention on the International Sale of Goods (CISG)* (4th edn, OUP 2016) para 6.

[36] See eg the choice of English law by Grain and Feed Association (GAFTA) or the Federation of Oils, Seeds and Fats Association (FOSFA).

[37] See with further reference LA Mistelis, 'Article 6' in S Kröll, LA Mistelis, and P Perales Viscasillas (eds), *UN Convention on Contracts for the International Sale of Goods (CISG)* (CH Beck 2011) 99 para 13.

The German Federal Court of Justice held:

The Court of Appeals was correct to apply the CISG and also to affirm the Convention's application in case the seller's general terms and conditions had become part of the contract. As the Court of Appeals properly explained, the referral to German law [...] in principle leads to the authority of the CISG. This law of sales, as part of German law and as special law for the international sale of goods, has priority over non-uniform German sales law. The parties do not assert that in this case something else should apply as an exception.[38]

(c) Formation of the contract and pre-contractual liability

Part II of the CISG (Articles 14–24) governs the formation of the contract. Article 92 of the CISG allows a contracting State to 'declare at the time of signature, ratification, acceptance, approval or accession that it will not be bound by Part II of this Convention'. Scandinavian States in particular have made such a declaration.[39]

For the conclusion of a contract, the CISG follows the established pattern of offer and corresponding acceptance 'reaching' the respective addressee.[40] In terms of Article 23 of the CISG, 'a contract is concluded at the moment when an acceptance of an offer becomes effective in accordance with the provisions of this Convention'. '[A]n offer, declaration of acceptance or any other indication of intention "reaches" the addressee when it is made orally to him or delivered by any other means to him personally, to his place of business or mailing address or, if he does not have a place of business or mailing address, to his habitual residence' (Article 24). An offer may be revoked if the revocation reaches the offeree before he has dispatched an acceptance (Article 16(1)). In contrast to Article 2 of the UCC, under the CISG the offeror's right and power to withdraw an offer is limited, and an offer cannot be revoked 'if it was reasonable for the offeree to rely on the offer as being irrevocable and the offeree has acted in reliance of the offer' (Article 16 (2)(b) CISG).

Whether or not a statement or conduct amounts to acceptance is subject to the rules on interpretation in Article 8(1) and (2).[41] In the absence of any further indication of acceptance, mere silence or inactivity itself cannot be regarded as an acceptance (Article 18(1) of the CISG). Specific circumstances indicating acceptance of an offer may be a particular agreement of the parties to that effect that the practices established between the parties, or the usages that are binding upon the parties pursuant to Article 9 of the CISG. Furthermore, reasons of good faith

---

[38] BGH NJW 1999, 1259; English translation <http://www.unilex.info/case.cfm?id=356> (accessed 23 June 2016).

[39] F Ferrari, 'Introduction to Articles 14–24' in S Kröll, LA Mistelis, and P Perales Viscasillas (eds), *UN Convention on Contracts for the International Sale of Goods (CISG)* (CH Beck 2011) 207 para 1.

[40] F Ferrari, 'Introduction to Articles 14–24' in S Kröll, LA Mistelis, and P Perales Viscasillas (eds), *UN Convention on Contracts for the International Sale of Goods (CISG)* (CH Beck 2011) 207 para 4.

[41] OLG Frankfurt 9 U 13/00 (30 August 2000), English translation available at <http://cisgw3.law.pace.edu/cases/000830g1.html> (accessed 23 June 2016).

(equity) may establish acceptance despite the offeree's silence. Thus, in the case *Filanto v Chilewich*, the United States Federal District Court for New York held:

An offeree who, knowing that the offeror has commenced performance, fails to notify the offeror of its objection to the terms of the contract within a reasonable time will, under certain circumstances, be deemed to have assented to those terms.[42]

The receipt of a commercial letter of confirmation does not usually amount to an acceptance of the terms therein.[43] If, however, a reply to an offer, which purports to be an acceptance, contains additional or different terms which do not materially alter the terms of the offer, it may constitute acceptance (Article 19).[44] In consequence, the CISG and the UCC provisions (section 2–207) lead to different results in case the additional or different terms are to be considered material. While under the UCC there would be a contract excluding the differing or additional terms, under the CISG there would be no formation of the contract at all. In *Calzaturificio Claudia Snc v Olivieri Footwear Ltd*, the United States Southern District Court held:

Material modifications, including the delivery terms, often occur in the routine exchange of the buyer's printed purchase order and the seller's printed acknowledgment of sale form [...]. Under the CISG no contract results from such an exchange if the purported acceptance contains additional or different terms that materially alter the offer.[45]

The CISG does not establish any requirement as to form (Article 11), thus dispensing with any formal standard under domestic law such as the US Statute of Frauds.[46]

(d) Obligations of the seller

The seller is obligated to 'deliver the goods, hand over any documents relating to them and transfer the property in the goods, as required by the contract and this Convention' (Article 30). Articles 31–34 address the place and time of delivery and the handing over of documents. The delivered goods must be of the 'quantity, quality and description required by the contract and which are contained or packaged in the manner required by the contract' (Article 35(1)). Subject to the parties agreeing otherwise, the delivered goods must conform to the requirements of Article 35(2). In particular, they must be fit for purposes for which goods of the same description would be ordinarily used (Article 35(2)(a)) and for any particular purpose expressly or impliedly made known to the seller (Article 35(2)(b)). In the *New Zealand Mussels* case, the German Federal Court of Justice held that the seller has no

---

[42] *Filanto v Chilewich* 89 F.Supp 1229 (SDNY 1992).

[43] F Ferrari, 'Introduction to Articles 14–24' in S Kröll, LA Mistelis, and P Perales Viscasillas (eds), *UN Convention on Contracts for the International Sale of Goods (CISG)* (CH Beck 2011) paras 8f.

[44] If the offeror wants to object to the modifications, he must do so without undue delay. Otherwise the terms of the contract will be the terms of the offer with the modifications contained in the acceptance.

[45] *Calzaturificio Claudia snc v Olivieri Footwear Ltd* Westlaw 164824 (SDNY 1998).

[46] See *TeeVee Tunes, Inc et al v Gerhard Schubert GmbH* 2006 WL 2463537 (SDNY 2006).

obligation to ensure that a product conforms to standards applicable in the country of destination (such as the tolerance level established by the German health authority for cadmium in mussels) unless the seller was aware of the particular provisions.[47] The burden of proof for non-conformity is of considerable practical relevance and follows the principle that a party bears the onus of proof for circumstances on which it relies.[48] In *Chicago Prime Packers Inc v Northam Food Trading*, a case concerning the delivery of pork back ribs, the US Court of Appeal (7th Circuit) held that the buyer bears the burden of proof for non-conformity:

The CISG does not state expressly whether the seller or buyer bears the burden of proof as to the product's conformity with the contract. Because there is little case law under the CISG, we interpret its provisions by looking to its language and to the general principles upon which it is based. [...]. The CISG is the international analogue to Article 2 of the Uniform Commercial Code (UCC). Many provisions of the UCC and the CISG are the same or similar, and '[c]aselaw interpreting analogous provisions of Article 2 of the [UCC], may [...] inform a court where the language of the relevant CISG provision tracks that of the UCC. [...] A comparison with the UCC reveals that the buyer bears the burden of proving non-conformity under the CISG. [...] Accordingly, just as a buyer-defendant bears the burden of proving breach of the implied warranty of fitness for ordinary purpose under the UCC, under the CISG, the buyer-defendant bears the burden of proving non-conformity at the time of transfer.[49]

Under the CISG, the buyer must examine the goods within as short a period as is practicable under the given circumstances and must notify the lack of conformity in terms of Articles 38–40. Failure to give proper notice may defeat or limit buyers' rights (Articles 39, 44), unless the seller knew or should have known the facts establishing non-conformity (Article 40). As a rule, the delivered goods must be free from rights of third parties (Articles 41 and 42). Article 39 CISG is comparable to the rules of the UCC (section 2–607).

In the case of a breach by the seller, the buyer has various rights (see Article 45). Remedies depend on the nature of the breach. Some rights such as declaring the contract void (Article 49(1)(a)) or requiring the delivery of substitute goods (Article 46(2)) depend on a 'fundamental breach'. In terms of Article 25, a breach of contract committed by one of the parties is fundamental

if it results in such detriment to the other party as substantially to deprive him of what he is entitled to expect under the contract, unless the party in breach did not foresee and a reasonable person of the same kind in the same circumstances would have not foreseen such a result.[50]

---

[47] BGHZ 129, 75, English translation available at <http://cisgw3.law.pace.edu/cases/950308g3.html> (accessed 23 June 2016).

[48] BGH NJW 2002, 1651 ('CISG powdered-milk case').

[49] *Chicago Prime Packers Inc v Northam Food Trading* 408 F.3d 894 (7th Cir 2005).

[50] See with regard to the concept of 'fundamental breach', F Ferrari, 'Fundamental Breach of Contract Under the UN Sales Convention' (2006) 25 JL & Com 489; L Graffi, 'Case Law on the Concept of "Fundamental Breach" in the Vienna Sales Convention' (2003) 3 IBLJ 338; C Pauly, 'The Concept of Fundamental Breach as an International Principle to Create Uniformity of Commercial Law' (2000) 19 JL & Com 221 (225).

Questions as to when belated performance, the delivery of deficient goods, or the violation of other contractual obligations constitute a fundamental breach depend on the circumstances.[51] A fundamental breach does not only depend on the objective relevance of a deviation from contractual standards, but also on its irremediable nature.

In a case in which three delivered inflatable triumphal arches did not suit the contractual purpose as an advertising medium near motor racing tracks, the Commercial Court of the Swiss Canton Aargau[52] concluded that the buyer was not entitled to declare the contract void because the defect did not amount to a fundamental breach:

The term fundamental breach of contract according to Art. 49(1)(a) CISG is defined in Art. 25 CISG. According to this Article, the condition for a fundamental breach of contract is an especially weighty impairment of the buyer's interest in the performance. Yet, besides the objective weight or importance of a defect, it is decisive of the substantiality of a breach of contract, whether the defect can be removed by subsequent repair or substitute delivery. The UN Sales Law proceeds from the fundamental precedence of preservation of the contract, even in case of an objective fundamental defect. When in doubt, the contract is to be maintained even in case of fundamental defects, and an immediate contract avoidance should stay exceptional. Because, as long as and so far as (even) a fundamental defect can still be removed by remedy or replacement, the fulfillment of the contract by the seller is still possible and the buyer's essential interest in the performance is not yet definitively at risk. According to doctrine as well as jurisdiction of the UN Sales Law, an objective fundamental defect does not mean a fundamental breach of contract when the defect is removable and the seller agrees to remedy this defect without creating unreasonable delay or burden on the buyer. That the buyer is obliged to accept a remedy (subsequent cure of the defect) offered by the seller results from Art. 48(2) CISG. According to this provision, when the seller notifies the buyer of his readiness for performance, the buyer may not within a reasonable period of time 'resort to any remedy which is inconsistent with performance by the seller'. For this reason, the buyer does not have the right to avoid the contract even in case of an objective fundamental defect as long as and as far as the seller comes up with a remedy (subsequent cure of the defect) and such is still possible.[53]

The concept of fundamental breach differs from the 'perfect tender rule' under the UCC (section 2–601) which allows for cancellation even if the non-conformity is not serious and the buyer would substantially receive the performance.

Non-conformity amounting to a fundamental breach can also be triggered in case of impliedly issued purposes in the meaning of Article 35(2) of the CISG. The US District Court of Louisiana stated in *Medical Marketing International, Inc v Internazionale Medico Scientifica*:

The Convention also provides that in an international contract for goods, goods conform to the contract if they are fit for the purpose for which goods of the same description would

---

[51] F Ferrari, 'Fundamental Breach of Contract Under the UN Sales Convention' (2006) 25 JL & Com 489 (499).

[52] Commercial Court of the Canton of Aargau (*Inflatable Triumphal Arch* case) (Judgment of 5 November 2002) <http://cisgw3.law.pace.edu/cases/021105s1.html> (accessed 23 June 2016).

[53] Commercial Court of the Canton of Aargau (*Inflatable triumphal arch* case) (Judgment of 5 November 2002) <http://cisgw3.law.pace.edu/cases/021105s1.html> (accessed 23 June 2016).

ordinarily be used or are fit for any particular purpose expressly or impliedly made known to the seller and relied upon by the buyer. CISG Article 35(2). To avoid a contract based on the non conformity of goods, the buyer must allege and prove that the seller's breach was 'fundamental' in nature, CISG Article 49. A breach is fundamental when it results in such detriment to the party that he or she is substantially deprived of what he or she is entitled to expect under the contract, unless the party in breach did not foresee such result, CISG Article 25.[54]

In the case of non-conformity, 'the buyer may require the seller to remedy the lack of conformity by repair, unless this is unreasonable having regard to all the circumstances' (Article 46(3)).

The buyer may fix an additional period of time of reasonable length for performance by the seller (in reference to German law often called *Nachfrist*) and may also resort to avoidance after this period (Article 49(1)(b)) even though the non-conformity does not amount to a fundamental breach. The requirement of a fundamental breach or of giving the seller a second chance as a condition for avoidance is an expression of the Convention's tendency to uphold the concluded contract as far as possible.

In the case of non-conformity of the goods delivered, the buyer 'may reduce the price in the same proportion as the value that the goods actually delivered had at the time of the delivery bears to the value that conforming goods would have had at that time' (Article 50). Irrespective of exercising his right to other remedies (Article 45(2)), the buyer may claim damages in accordance with Articles 74–77. Article 74 limits the parties' liability to compensate only the losses which were foreseeable at the time the contract was concluded.

The seller may rely on the general exception of Article 79, according to which a party 'is not liable for a failure to perform any of his obligations if he proves that the failure was due to an impediment beyond his control and that he could not reasonably be expected to have taken the impediment into account at the time of the conclusion of the contract or to have avoided or overcome it or its consequences'. It is a matter of controversy whether the seller's duty to deliver goods conforming to the standards under Article 35 of the CISG falls within the obligations covered by Article 79.[55]

In a case concerning a sale of vine wax supposed to protect vines from drying out in order to reduce infection risks, the seller had obtained the vine wax from a third party. The German Federal Court of Justice, without squarely deciding the issue, interpreted the exemption rule in accordance with the contractual risk:

The possibility of exemption under CISG Art. 79 does not change the allocation of the contractual risk. According to the [CISG], the reason for the seller's liability is that he has agreed to provide the purchaser with goods that are in conformity with the contract. If the

---

[54] *Medical Marketing v Internazionale Medico Scientifica* WL 311945 (ED La 1999).
[55] The prevailing view now holds Article 79 applicable also in case of defective delivery, see YM Atamer 'Art. 79' in S Kröll, LA Mistelis, and P Perales Viscasillas (eds), *UN Convention on Contracts for the International Sale of Goods (CISG)* (CH Beck 2011) 1054 para 12.

supplier's breach of the contract is a general impediment within the meaning of CISG Art. 79 at all, it is generally an impediment that the seller must avoid or overcome according to the content of the contract of sale. This follows the typical meaning of such a contract [...]. From the buyer's point of view, it makes no difference whether the seller produces the goods himself—with the consequence that the non-performance is generally in his actual control so that, as a rule, a dispensation pursuant to CISG Art. 79(1) is generally excluded—or whether the seller obtains the goods from suppliers. Just as in the case of unspecified obligations, where the seller is liable for the timely delivery by his supplier [...], he is also responsible to see that his supplier delivers defect-free goods. In this respect, the [CISG] does not distinguish between an untimely delivery and a delivery of goods not in conformity with the contract. For both breaches of contract the same standard of liability applies. [...] Pursuant to CISG Art. 79, the seller's exemption from consequences of goods not in conformity with the contract can only be considered—if at all [...]—when the non- conformity cannot be deemed to be within the seller's control. Because the seller has the risk of acquisition (as shown), he can only be exempted under CISG Art. 79 (1) or (2) (even when the reasons for the defectiveness of the goods are—as here—within the control of his supplier or his sub-supplier) if the defectiveness is due to circumstances out of his own control and out of each of his suppliers' control.[56]

(e) Obligations of the buyer

The buyer's elementary obligations are to pay the price for the goods and take delivery of them (Article 53). The loss of or damage to the goods after the risk has passed to the buyer does not relieve him of his obligation to pay the price, unless the loss or damage is due to an act or omission of the seller (Article 66).

When a contract has been validly concluded without expressly or implicitly fixing or determining the price, 'the parties are considered, in the absence of any indication to the contrary, to have impliedly made reference to the price generally charged at the time of the conclusion of the contract for such goods sold under comparable circumstances in the trade concerned' (Article 55). On the other hand, a sufficiently determined price is a prerequisite for a valid contract under Article 14(1). The interplay between Article 14(1) and Article 55 is one of the most controversial questions raised by the Convention.[57]

As a general rule, the buyer must pay the price at the seller's place of business (Article 57(1)(a)) or, if the payment is to be made against the handing over of the goods or of documents, at the place of the handing over (Article 57(1)(b)). The place of payment may be a criterion triggering the jurisdiction of courts.

EC Regulation No 44/2001[58] ('Brussels Regulation') establishes jurisdiction based on the place of performance in Article 5(1)(b). This provision, however,

---

[56] See BGHZ 141, 129 (*Vine wax* case); English translation <http://cisgw3.law.pace.edu/cases/990324g1.html> (accessed 23 June 2016).
[57] UNCITRAL, *Digest of Case Law on the United Nations Convention on the International Sale of Goods* (2012) Article 14 paras 14–17.
[58] [2001] OJ L12/1.

contains an autonomous definition of the place of performance which does refer to delivery (and not to payment):

For the purpose of this provision and unless otherwise agreed, the place of performance of the obligation in question shall be:
– in the case of the sale of goods, the place in a Member State where, under the contract, the goods were delivered or should have been delivered
[…].

Thus, Article 57 of the CISG does not trigger jurisdiction on the basis of the Brussels Regulation.[59]

Remedies for a breach of contract by the buyer are established in Articles 61 to 65. Non-payment or belated payment may establish claims to damages (Article 74) or to interest (Article 78).

With respect to the reimbursement of legal fees, a US Court of Appeals held in *Zapata Hermanos v Hearthside Baking*:

Although Article 74's principle of full compensation appears to support the view that litigation expenses should be recoverable in order to make the aggrieved party whole, such an interpretation would be contrary to the principle of equality between buyers and sellers as expressed in Articles 45 and 61. If legal expenses were awarded as damages under Article 74, an anomaly would result where only a successful claimant would be able to recover litigation expenses. The ability to recover damages under Article 74 is grounded on a breach of contract; thus, a successful respondent will not be able to recover its legal expenses if the claimant has not committed a breach of contract. Therefore, the purpose of awarding attorneys' fees and costs, to make a prevailing party whole for costs incurred in litigation, will not be realized in those cases where the respondent prevails. Remedies are the core of contract law, and to interpret Article 74 to create unequal recovery of damages between buyers and sellers is contrary to the design of the Convention. However, Article 74 does not preclude a court or arbitral tribunal from awarding a party its attorneys' fees and costs when the contract provides for their payment or when authorized by applicable rules.[60]

(f) Product liability under the CISG

The CISG 'does not apply to the liability of the seller for death or personal injury caused by the goods to any person'. Thus, liability of the seller for personal injury is subject to the applicable domestic law. Damages to property, however, fall within the scope of the CISG. In any case, the CISG only addresses the relationship between buyer and seller and not consumer claims against manufacturers who have not sold the purchased goods to the consumer.

Despite the limited scope of the CISG, product liability under domestic law (general tort law and more specific consumer protection law) may raise issues under the Convention. Thus, a buyer may bring a tort claim for product liability without

---

[59] See recent case-law by the ECJ Case C-381/08 *Car Trim GmbH v KeySafety Systems Srl* [2010] ECR I-1255, 1282.
[60] *Zapata Hermanos v Hearthside Baking* 313 F.3d 385 (7th Cir 2002).

having complied with the notification regime of the CISG. On the one hand, the Convention purports to establish uniform rules for contractual obligations (see Article 7(1)). On the other hand, liability for torts remains a domain of domestic law. Therefore, national courts should distinguish between specific 'contractual interests' and 'extra-contractual duties' in the particular case.[61]

4. Electronic Commerce

Transactions, especially the sale of goods or the supply of services, on the basis of communications through electronic systems such as the Internet ('e-commerce') have become a common feature in international business relations.

Bodies like UNCITRAL strive for a regulation of electronic commerce law on the basis of

- non-discrimination;
- technological neutrality; and
- functional equivalence.[62]

The principle of non-discrimination means that communications via electronic systems are not denied legal effects or enforceability solely on account of their form of transmission. Technological neutrality aims at neutrality of regulation with respect to the technology used thereby allowing technological advancements. The principle of functional equivalence refers to the suitability of electronic communication for the same purposes and functions as communications in the traditional paper-based system (written form, signature).

International commerce with electronic means of communication requires a set of internationally recognized rules which establish legal certainty. UNCITRAL has adopted

- the UNCITRAL Model Law on Electronic Commerce with Guide to Enactment, with additional Article 5 as adopted in 1998;[63]
- the UNCITRAL Model Law on Electronic Signatures with Guide to Enactment in 2001;[64] and
- the United Nations Convention on the Use of Electronic Communications in International Contracts in 2005.[65]

---

[61] See P Schlechtriem, 'The Borderland of Tort and Contract—Opening a New Frontier?' (1988) 21 Cornell Int'l LJ 473.

[62] See with respect hereto and the following <http://www.uncitral.org/uncitral/en/uncitral_texts/electronic_commerce/1996Model.html> (accessed 23 June 2016).

[63] See Guide to Enactment <http://www.uncitral.org/pdf/english/texts/electcom/05-89450_Ebook.pdf> (accessed 23 June 2016).

[64] See Guide to Enactment <http://www.uncitral.org/pdf/english/texts/electcom/ml-elecsig-e.pdf> (accessed 23 June 2016).

[65] See Explanatory note <http://www.uncitral.org/pdf/english/texts/electcom/06-57452_Ebook.pdf> (accessed 23 June 2016).

The UNCITRAL Model Law on Electronic Commerce is the only Model law adopted by a considerable number of States including major North American countries. In the United States, the Model Law was implemented by many States, in Canada by all provinces.

In 2009, UNCITRAL published a guide on the main legal issues arising out of the use of electronic signatures and authentication methods in international transactions.[66]

Select Bibliography

MG Bridge, *The International Sale of Goods* (3rd edn, OUP 2013).

Center for Transnational Law (ed), *Law and Practice of Export Trade* (Quadis 2001).

M Davies and DV Snyder, *International Transactions in Goods* (OUP 2014).

F Ferrari, *International Sale of Goods* (Helbing & Lichtenhahn 1999).

F Ferrari, *Contracts for the International Sale of Goods: Applicability and Applications of the 1980 United Nations Sales Conventions* (Martinus Nijhoff 2011).

RA Hillman and JJ Rachlinski, 'Standard-Form Contracting in the Electronic Age' (2002) 77 NYU L Rev 429.

S Kröll, L Mistelis, and P Perales Viscasillas (eds), *UN Convention on Contracts for the International Sale of Goods (CISG)* (CH Beck 2011).

TA Kumar, 'Common Problems with E-Commerce in the Global Economy' (2000) 28 Int'l Bus Law 387.

C Murray, D Holloway, D Timson-Hunt, and G Dixon, *Schmitthoff: The Law and Practice of International Trade* (12th edn, Sweet & Maxwell 2012).

M Parmentier, 'Uniform Sales Law' in R Wolfrum (ed), *The Max Planck Encyclopedia of Public International Law* (OUP 2013) vol X, 154.

C Reed, *Making Laws for Cyberspace* (OUP 2012).

P Schlechtriem and I Schwenzer (eds), *Commentary on the UN Convention on the International Sale of Goods (CISG)* (3rd edn, OUP 2010).

R Schulze (ed), *Common European Sales Law(CESL)* (CH Beck, Hart Publishing, Nomos 2012).

---

[66] <http://www.uncitral.org/pdf/english/texts/electcom/08-55698_Ebook.pdf> (accessed 23 June 2016).

XXV

Letters of Credit

Letters of credit[1] play an important role in international sales as an instrument for payment in international documentary sales. They establish an undertaking of a bank acting on behalf of the buyer or the seller. The 'documentary credit' guarantees fulfilment of the seller's claim of payment upon presentation of certain documents. The 'standby letter of credit' secures the obligation of the seller to perform the sales contract for the benefit of the buyer.

1. Documentary Credit

On the basis of an agreement between the applicant (buyer) and his bank, the applicant's bank (issuing bank) undertakes to honour the issued letter of credit against the presentation of certain documents. The documents to be presented may be commercial invoices, bills of lading, certificates of quality, or other papers. The letter of credit establishes a contractual claim of the beneficiary (seller) to payment against the issuing bank. As an absolute ('abstract') obligation on the bank, the letter of credit guarantees payment once the formal conditions under the letter are fulfilled. The undertaking under a letter of credit is independent of the validity of the contract of sale and of the buyer's payment obligations thereunder (principle of independence). For the buyer the old maxim applies: 'Pay first and then litigate'. As a rule, letters of credit (though subject to expiration within a given period of time) are irrevocable, because revocable letters usually do not provide the seller with the required assurance of payment.

If the issuing bank honours its commitment under the letter of credit, the applicant must reimburse the bank and pay a fee. If, however, the issuing bank makes undue payment without presentation of the proper documents, it may not claim reimbursement. Many controversies arise from disputes over the underlying sales contract which drives the buyer to prevent the bank from making payment to the seller. In international transactions, the issuing bank will often engage other banks (usually situated at or near the seller's place of business) such as a confirming bank (assuming an additional payment obligation of its own, if so required by the seller),

---

[1] E Adodo, *Letters of Credit: The Law and Practice of Compliance* (OUP 2014); JF Dolan, *The Law of Letters of Credit* (4th edn, AS Pratt & Sons 2007).

a nominated bank (authorized by the issuing bank to make payment under the letter of credit without assuming an obligation towards the seller), or an advising bank (assisting in checking the authenticity of the credit).

Some States apply the law applicable to the seat of the issuing bank,[2] others the law under which the bank was incorporated. International business usually follows the Uniform Customs and Practice for Documentary Credits (UCP) published by the International Chamber of Commerce, currently UCP 600 (2007).[3] The UCP applies to all credits 'where they are incorporated into the text of the Credit' (Article 1 of the UCP). The UCP is a codification of internationally accepted banking customs and practice regarding letters of credit.[4] In the United States, the Uniform Commercial Code (UCC) allows the parties to exclude its application, for example by incorporating the UCP into the letter of credit.[5]

Most international credits refer to the UCP. The UCP is neither a statute nor a code. It is a set of rules established by the world banking community under the aegis of the International Chamber of Commerce.[6]

Some courts apply the UCP, even if the agreement between the parties makes no explicit reference to it.

In the case of Siporex Trade SA v Banque Indosuez, Siporex Trade contracted to sell tallow cotton seed oil to Comdel. Payment was to be made by an irrevocable letter of credit. In accordance with the contract, Comdel instructed Banque Indosuez to issue a performance guarantee in favour of Siporex Trade S.A. by Comdel by 7 December 1984. Siporex stated the letter of credit issued by Comdel was not in conformity with the agreement contracted by both parties. Comdel was unable to cure the defects in the letter of credit prior to the 7 December, 1984 deadline. Three days later, Siporex issued letters of demand to Banque Indosuez for payment under the performance bond. Siporex maintained the performance bond created an absolute guarantee on the part of Bank Indosuez. Siporex contended it could draw on the guarantee if Comdel did not issue a letter of credit or if the issuance did not precisely conform to the full requirements of the underlying contract. Banque Indosuez denied liability contending the bond was a conditional and not absolute obligation. If the performance guarantee was absolute, the contracting parties had to express this clearly in their contract and not merely implied.

The case mainly concerns the demand of a performance guarantee in favour of Siporex Trade SA but there are similarities between letters of credit and performance bonds in general. The English High Court found that Banque Indosuez was liable and that the performance bond was an absolute guarantee: '[A]lthough

---

[2] BGH (1971) WM 158 (159).

[3] International Chamber of Commerce, *Uniform Customs and Practice for Documentary Credits (UCP)* (2007 Revision) Publication No 600.

[4] G Xiang and RP Buckley, 'The Unique Jurisprudence of Letters of Credit: Its Origin and Sources' (2003) 4 SDILJ 91.

[5] G Folsom and F Spanogle, *International Business Transactions* (10th edn, West Group 2009) 300.

[6] M Wayne, 'The Uniform Customs and Practice as a Source of Documentary Credit Law in the United States, Canada and Great Britain: A Comparison of Application and Interpretation' (1989) 7 Ariz J Int'l & Comp L 148.

there was no reference to the UCP [...] the court relied on UCP Article 3 for its conclusion'.[7]

The obligation to pay depends on presentation of the documents that correspond to the letter of credit. Article 13(a) provides:

If a credit that reimbursement is to be obtained by a nominated bank ('claiming bank') claiming on another party ('reimbursing bank'), the credit must state if the reimbursement is subject to the ICC rules for bank-to-bank reimbursements in effect on the date of issuance of the credit.

The issuing bank must honour a presentation that appears, on its face, strictly to comply with the terms and condition of the letter of credit (principle of strict compliance).[8] If this condition is not met, the issuer should dishonour the presentation. If the issuing bank, even in good faith, deviates from the exact stipulations in the letter of credit, by paying on lenient terms not clearly authorized by its customer (the buyer) or insisting on stricter terms, it does so at its own risk.

The independence of the letter of credit from the underlying sales contract severs the issuing bank's obligations from the seller's compliance with the sales contract (principle of severance).

As the Court of Appeals of New York held in *Maurice O'Meara v National Park Bank of New York*,[9] the issuing bank has neither the right nor the obligation to verify whether the description of the goods in the presented documents meets the quality required under the contract of sale, unless the letter of credit expressly provides so.

There is, however, an important exception to the independence principle, namely the case of fraud. If the presented documents are demonstrably forged or fraudulent, the buyer may apply for a court order (injunction) which prohibits payment by the issuing bank. In the famous case *Sztejn v J Henry Schroder Banking Co*,[10] the buyer brought an action against the issuing bank before payment because the documents presented by the seller were fraudulent. A US Federal District Court held:

[W]here the seller's fraud has been called to the bank's attention before the drafts and documents have been presented for payment, the principle of the independence of the bank's obligation under the letter of credit should not be extended to protect the unscrupulous seller. It is true that even though the documents are forged or fraudulent, if the issuing bank has already paid the draft before receiving notice of the seller's fraud, it will be protected if it exercised reasonable diligence before making such payment.

In the absence of an injunction in a case of fraudulent documents, the issuing bank may choose either to honour or to dishonour the demand for payment, as long as it acts in good faith, considering that the bank has the burden of proving fraud. In most cases, the bank will opt for paying rather than defending itself in litigation for wrongful dishonour.

---

[7] *Siporex Trade SA v Banque Indosuez* [1986] 2 Lloyd's Rep 146.
[8] *JH Rayner and Co v Hambro's Bank Ltd* [1943] English Court of Appeal 1 KB 37.
[9] *Maurice O'Meara v National Park Bank of New York* 239 NY 386 (NY 1925) Cardozo J dissenting.
[10] 31 NYD S 2d 631(1941).

The UCP contains no provision for the case of fraud, thus leaving regulation to domestic law. The UCC deals with fraud and forgery in Article 5 (§ 5–109):

(a) If a presentation is made that appears on its face strictly to comply with the terms and conditions of the letter of credit, but a required document is forged or materially fraudulent, or honour of the presentation would facilitate a material fraud by the beneficiary on the issuer or applicant:

    (1) the issuer shall honour the presentation, if honour is demanded by (i) a nominated person who has given value in good faith and without notice of forgery or material fraud, (ii) a confirmer who has honoured its confirmation in good faith, (iii) a holder in due course of a draft drawn under the letter of credit which was taken after acceptance by the issuer or nominated person, or (iv) an assignee of the issuer's or nominated person's deferred obligation that was taken for value and without notice of forgery or material fraud after the obligation was incurred by the issuer or nominated person; and

    (2) the issuer, acting in good faith, may honour or dishonour the presentation in any other case.

(b) If an applicant claims that a required document is forged or materially fraudulent or that honour of the presentation would facilitate a material fraud by the beneficiary on the issuer or applicant, a court of competent jurisdiction may temporarily or permanently enjoin the issuer from honouring a presentation or grant similar relief against the issuer or other persons only if the court finds that:

    (1) the relief is not prohibited under the law applicable to an accepted draft or deferred obligation incurred by the issuer;

    (2) a beneficiary, issuer, or nominated person who may be adversely affected is adequately protected against loss that it may suffer because the relief is granted;

    (3) all of the conditions to entitle a person to the relief under the law of this State have been met; and

    (4) on the basis of the information submitted to the court, the applicant is more likely than not to succeed under its claim of forgery or material fraud and the person demanding honour does not qualify for protection under subsection (a)(1).

This legislation aims at a fair balance between the functionality of required documents on the basis of the independent principle and material justice.

2. Standby Letters of Credit

The standby letter of credit is a mechanism to alleviate the buyer's risk of non-performance by the seller. It constitutes a commitment by the seller's bank that must be honoured upon submission of a *pro forma* declaration by the buyer that the seller has not complied with his contractual obligations. Often, the buyer's bank will additionally assume an obligation of payment upon presentation of documents. After paying, the buyer's bank will transmit the documents to the seller's bank and ask for reimbursement on the basis of the standby letter of credit. After reimbursement, the seller's bank will demand reimbursement by the seller.

Standby letters of credit may be governed by UCC Article 5, the UCP 600,[11] the Uniform Rules for Demand Guarantees (URDG) issued by the International Chamber of Commerce[12] and the International Chamber of Commerce's International Standby Practices (ISP 98).[13] The UN Convention on Independent Guarantees and Standby Letters of Credits (1995) has been ratified by eight States (Belarus, Ecuador, El Salvador, Gabon, Kuwait, Liberia, Panama, and Tunisia). The United States has signed, but not yet ratified the UN Convention.

Select Bibliography

E Adodo, *Letters of Credit: The Law and Practice of Compliance* (OUP 2014).
N Enonchong, *The Independence Principle of Letters of Credit and Demand Guarantees* (OUP 2011).
D Horowitz, *Letters of Credit and Demand Guarantees: Defences to Payment* (OUP 2010).
MS Kurkela, *Letters of Credit and Bank Guarantees under International Trade Law* (2nd edn, OUP 2007).

---

[11] Article 1 of UCP 600 (Application of UCP) provides: 'The Uniform Customs and Practice for Documentary Credits, 2007 Revision, ICC Publication no. 600 ("UCP") are rules that apply to any documentary credit ("credit") (including, to the extent to which they may be applicable, any standby letter of credit) when the text of the credit expressly indicates that it is subject to these rules. They are binding on all Parties thereto unless expressly modified or excluded by the credit'.

[12] International Chamber of Commerce, *Uniform Rules for Demand Guarantees* (1992) Publication No 455.

[13] International Chamber of Commerce, *International Standby Practices* (1998) Publication No (590).

XXVI
International Building and Construction Contracts

An important area of international business refers to international construction contracts.[1] These contracts belong to the category of long-term contracts which are particularly sensitive to unforeseen developments.[2]

1. FIDIC Manuals

The FIDIC (Fédération Internationale des Ingénieurs Conseils), the International Association of Consulting Engineers, has adopted various sets of standard terms (contract-types of manuals) which international usage incorporates into the contracts. The parties in a FIDIC contract are

- the employer/contracting authority;
- the contractor; and
- the engineer administering the contract on behalf of the employer/contracting authority.

FIDIC contract terms govern issues like status and functions of the engineer (including power to vary works) and the possibility of re-measurement. They aim at a calculable and balanced management and allocation of risks adjusted to the different types of contract.

- Conditions of Contract for Construction (New Red Book), for building and engineering works to be constructed in accordance with the employer's design;
- Harmonised Conditions of Contract for Construction (Pink Book);
- Conditions for Electrical and Mechanical Works and for Building and Engineering Works Designed by the Contractor (New Yellow Book);

---

[1] P Joussen, *Der Industrieanlagen-Vertrag* (2nd edn, Verlag Recht und Wirtschaft 1997); F Nicklisch, 'The BOT-Model—The Contractor's Role as Builder—Contract Structure Risk Allocation and Risk Management' (1992) 9 ICLR 425; F Nicklisch (ed), *Betreibermodelle—BOT/PPP-Vorhaben im In- und Ausland* (CH Beck 2007).

[2] F Nicklisch, 'The BOT-Model—The Contractor's Role as Builder—Contract Structure Risk Allocation and Risk Management' (1992) 9 ICLR 425.

- Conditions for Contract for Engineering, Procurement and Construction (EPC)/Turnkey Projects (Silver Book);
- Short Form of Contract (Green Book/Mini-Red Book), for building and engineering works of relatively small scale.

2. Long-term Contracts (BOT, BOO, BOOT, BLOT, BOTT)

A special form of building contract provides that contractors shall also operate the building or installation for a given time. These contracts refer to the operation of infrastructures (such as toll-roads, toll-bridges, airports, and harbours) or power plants. The classical form of this kind of contract refers to BOT (build, operate, transfer) projects, which provides for a transfer at an established time.[3] These projects are characterized by their highly complex nature and coined by the cooperation of several participants from different branches. The loyal cooperation of governmental institutions is essential for the project's progress or success. Administrative interferences may be assumed as a 'creeping expropriation' or as a comparable treaty violation, especially an expropriation of contractual rights.[4] In addition, a treaty violation normally implies a damage claim for the investor.

The most famous BOT project is the Channel Tunnel Project.[5] The project rests on a treaty between France and the United Kingdom from 1986. This agreement is also the basis for the concessions granted to the private investors. In addition, both countries passed domestic legislation on the project (in the United Kingdom, the British Channel Tunnel Act of 1987). The main concessionaire is the Channel Tunnel Group/France—Manche (CTG/F–M), which consists of several banks and construction companies from both countries.

As domestic legislation prohibits any public subsidies for the Channel Tunnel Project (see section 2 of the Channel Tunnel Act), the project depended on private funding. Variations of contracts on building and subsequent operation are BOO contracts (build, own, operate), BOOT contracts (build, own, operate, transfer), BOTT contracts (build, own, train, transfer) and BLOT contracts (build, own, lease, operate, transfer). BOO contracts usually allocate benefits as well as the risks associated with the project to the investor.

Select Bibliography

J Denwar, *International Project Finance—Law and Practice* (2nd edn, OUP 2015).
BC Esty, *Modern Project Finance: A Casebook* (John Wiley & Sons 2007).

---

[3] F Nicklisch, 'The BOT-Model—The Contractor's Role as Builder—Contract Structure Risk Allocation and Risk Management' (1992) 9 ICLR 425.
[4] R Dolzer and C Schreuer, *Principles of International Investment Law* (2nd edn, OUP 2012) 115.
[5] R Goy, 'Le Tunnel sous la Manche' (1986) 32 AFDI 741; M Herdegen, 'Der Konzessionsvertrag aus öffentlich-rechtlicher Sicht: das Beispiel des Kanaltunnelprojekts' in F Nicklisch (ed), *Rechtsfragen privatfinanzierter Projekte* (CF Müller 1994) 41.

SL Hofmann, *The Law and Business of International Project Finance: A Resource for Governments, Sponsors, Lawyers, and Project Participants* (3rd edn, CUP 2007).

A Kramer and P Fusaro, *Energy and Environmental Project Finance Law and Taxation—New Investment Techniques* (OUP 2010).

F Nicklisch, 'The BOT Model—The Contractor's Role as Builder—Contract Structure Risk Allocation and Risk Management' (1992) 9 ICLR 425.

I Siddiky, *Cross-Border Pipeline Arrangements: What would a Single Regulatory Framework Look Like?* (Kluwer Law International 2011).

XXVII

International Company, Competition, and Tax Law

1. Relevance

International company law governs the corporate issues of cross-border activities of companies.[1] Each private corporation is subject to the law of its 'home State' which governs its establishment as a legal person (incorporation), its organization, and the legal position of shareholders and other associates. Other aspects of company law are liabilities towards creditors and the relation with dominant or dependent companies within a group. The proper law of a company is either the law of the State in which the company is incorporated or the law of the State where the real seat of management (or administrative centre) is located.

A key aspect of international company law is the recognition of a corporation as legal person outside its home country. The internationally recognized legal capacity to conclude contracts, to hold property, and to have standing before courts is fundamental to a company's radius of action. It is also important that the law of a single jurisdiction governs core internal issues, thus ensuring a uniform regime at least for corporate organization in accordance with the founders' intent.

2. The Proper Law of a Corporation

The law governing a company ('home law') follows the place of incorporation or the seat of administration (management and control). The nationality of shareholders with a controlling interest (control theory) usually does not establish a jurisdictional link (except in times of war).

(a) The theory of incorporation

The 'place of incorporation theory' (*lex incorporationis*) refers to the law under which the corporation was incorporated as the proper law governing the corporate

---

[1] H Eidenmuller, 'The Transnational Law Market, Regulatory Competition, and Transnational Corporations' (2011) 18 Ind J Global Legal Stud 707; P Muchlinski, 'Corporations in International Law' in R Wolfrum (ed), *The Max Planck Encyclopedia of Public International Law* (OUP 2012) vol II, 797.

structure and internal relations within the corporation. This approach defers to the founders' choice of law. The incorporation doctrine has the advantage that it is easy to establish where the corporation was founded. The place of incorporation remains stable, even if the seat of management changes. As a factor for determining jurisdiction over a company, the place of incorporation allows the founders to choose the governing law. This approach fuels a regulatory competition between countries for the most 'liberal' corporate law. However, contrary to popular perception, this competition does not simply mean a race to the bottom which favours the laxest system. Companies and their shareholders often have a genuine interest in high standards of shareholder protection, as an element of a good investment climate.

The State of Delaware (United States) provides a particularly attractive corporate law that is often chosen by many US companies and even by corporations whose business is focused on the European Union. The advantages of incorporation under the law of Delaware are significant: a clearly structured legal order with a well-developed body of case-law, competitive taxation, and modest regulatory interference.

The possibility of 'jurisdiction shopping' has drawn some criticism in cases where the company's business is conducted wholly or essentially outside the country of incorporation. Sometimes, founders, driven by regulatory arbitrage, choose to do business in a country under the umbrella of a so-called 'pseudo-foreign corporation'. This is a corporation incorporated in a certain jurisdiction only for the purpose of minimizing liability, taxes, or regulatory interference.

Despite all possible criticism, the incorporation doctrine prevails in Anglo-American company laws (for example United States, United Kingdom, Australia, Canada, India, Hong Kong) and several countries of continental Europe (the Netherlands and Spain).

(b) The real seat theory

The 'real seat theory' considers the actual centre of administration (as opposed to the seat as defined in the articles of agreement) as the relevant criterion for jurisdiction. The Federal Court of Justice of Germany defined the seat of administration as 'the operational base of the management and the representative organs, that is the place where the key executive decisions are taken and effectively implemented in the current corporate management.'[2]

The criterion of the seat of management defers to the relationship between jurisdiction and the corporation's business operations and thus bases jurisdiction on a substantial operational link between a corporation and its 'home State'. The seat of management doctrine has to cope with several problems. Transferring the corporation's seat of management into another country always entails the liquidation of

---

[2] BGHZ 97, 269 (272).

the former corporation. Determination of the main seat of management of international corporations may be difficult, if key managerial decisions are not taken at a single headquarter.

The seat of management doctrine has traditionally been adopted in many countries of Continental Europe including Austria, France, Germany, Italy, Luxembourg, and Switzerland. However, in the recent past, some European countries like Germany and Switzerland have become receptive to the incorporation approach and now allow a transfer of the real seat of administration without a necessary change in the company's status. Several rulings of the European Court of Justice catalysed this development.

Germany has considerably softened the long-practised real seat approach.[3] After a change in German company law, the corporate seat is determined by the company's statutes. This allows the company, a joint stock company (Aktiengesellschaft) or a German Private Limited Company (GmbH), to move the seat of management to another country without losing its corporate status under German law.

3. Recognition of Foreign Corporations and Deference to 'Home' Regulation

The recognition of a corporation established in one State as a legal person in other countries is crucial for international business. Similarly, it is important that the law under which a company was incorporated governs the organization and the internal relations between the actors within a corporation (corporate bodies and representatives as well as shareholders) also from the perspective of other jurisdictions. The recognition of this exclusive jurisdiction of a company's 'home State' over its status as a legal person and its internal affairs is an issue of the conflict of laws. Problems of the legal status arise when a country does not recognize the legal personality of a foreign corporation, because the corporation does not conduct substantial business or maintain a genuine link with the State of incorporation.

As the European Court of Justice held, under the freedom of establishment within the European Union (Article 49 of the TFEU) Member States must recognize companies established under the law of another Member State, even if the real seat or the main place of business are not located in the country of incorporation. The European Court of Justice stated in the *Ueberseering* case:

[W]here a company formed in accordance with the law of a Member State ('A') in which it has its registered office is deemed, under the law of another Member State ('B'), to have moved its actual centre of administration to Member State B, Articles 43 EC and 48 EC

---

[3] German Act to Modernize the Law on Private Limited Companies and to Combat Abuses (MoMiG 23 October 2008).

[now Articles 49 and 54 TFEU] preclude Member State B from denying the company legal capacity and, consequently, the capacity to bring legal proceedings before its national courts for the purpose of enforcing rights under a contract with a company established in Member State B.[4]

On the other hand, deference to the law of the country in which a company is established also extends to the conditions for continued existence. If, for example, under Hungarian company law the real seat of administration must be located in Hungary, freedom of establishment under EU law does not allow a Hungarian company to move its headquarters to Italy without its dissolution in Hungary and reestablishment in Italy.[5]

International treaties often provide for the recognition of foreign companies or corporations. The German–US Treaty of Friendship, Commerce, and Navigation[6] states in Article XXV(5) second sentence:

Companies constituted under the applicable laws and regulations within the territories of either Party shall be deemed companies thereof and shall have their juridical status recognized within the territories of the other Party.

Under the German–US Treaty, the German Federal Court of Justice recognizes the legal status of a corporation established in the United States only if there are minimal contacts with the United States.[7]

According to the 'internal affairs doctrine',[8] only a single State as 'home State' should have jurisdiction to regulate the internal affairs of a corporation. As the US Supreme Court held in *Edgar v MITE Corp*:

The internal affairs doctrine is a conflict of laws principle which recognizes that only one State should have the authority to regulate a corporation's internal affairs-matters peculiar to the relationships among or between the corporation and its current officers, directors, and shareholders-because otherwise a corporation could be faced with conflicting demands [...]. The [Illinois] Act thus applies to corporations that are not incorporated in Illinois and have their principal place of business in other States. Illinois has no interest in regulating the internal affairs of foreign corporations.[9]

---

[4] ECJ Case C-208/00 *Überseering* [2002] ECR I-9919 para 22; W-H Roth, 'From Centros to Ueberseering: Free Movement of Companies, Private International Law, and Community Law' (2003) 52 ICLQ 177.

[5] ECJ Case C-210/06 *Cartesio* [2008] ECR I-9641. See also V Petronella, 'The Cross-Border Transfer of the Seat after Cartesio and the Non-Portable Nationality of the Company' (2010) 21 Eur Bus L Rev 245.

[6] AL Paulus, 'Treaties of Friendship Commerce and Navigation' in R Wolfrum (ed), *The Max Planck Encyclopedia of Public International Law* (OUP 2012) vol X, 1140; LB Barnes, 'State Regulation of Foreign Investment' (1975) 9 Cornell Int'l LJ 82; JT Haight, 'Restrictive Business Practices Clause in United States Treaties: An Antitrust Tranquilizer for International Trade' (1960) 70 Yale LJ 240.

[7] BGH GRUR 2005, 55 (56) (*GEDIOS* case).

[8] See 'The Internal Affairs Doctrine: Theoretical Justifications and Tentative Explanations for Its Continued Primacy' (2001–02) 115 HLR 1480.

[9] 457 US 624 (645–646) (1982).

As the founders choose the place and law of incorporation, the internal affairs doctrine defers to their intent and objective.

The scope of 'internal affairs' is not carved in stone and may be defined differently in different jurisdictions.[10] 'Internal affairs' can overlap with jurisdiction over consumer protection or regulation of securities. Moreover, deference to the law of incorporation and to the founders' intent will not always trump legitimate regulatory interests of another country, based on a substantial link of regulatory issue with that country (for example protection of minority shareholders domiciled in the country or business contacts).

Under EU law on freedom of establishment, interferences into the internal affairs of a company established in another Member State may be justified by general interests, such as the protection of minority shareholders, creditor protection, or participation of employees in the management.[11] As the European Court of Justice set out in the *Inspire Art* judgment, these interests allow a Member State to limit the activities of a foreign company within its own territory only in terms of strict proportionality:

[I]t is clear from settled case-law [...] that the fact that a company does not conduct any business in the Member State in which it has its registered office and pursues its activities only or principally in the Member State where its branch is established is not sufficient to prove the existence of abuse or fraudulent conduct which would entitle the latter Member State to deny that company the benefit of the provisions of Community law relating to the right of establishment [...].[12]

4. EU Company Law: the *Societas Europaea*

In the European Union, several directives on the harmonization of European company law, for example on acquisitions, were enacted (on the basis of what is now Article 50(2)(g) of the TFEU).[13] EU law has also developed new corporate forms like the *Societas Europaea* (SE).[14] The SE was established by Council Regulation (EC) No 2157/2001 on the Statute for a European Company.[15] For an SE, EU law is the 'home law' governing corporate issues. An SE can be registered in any Member State of the European Union. Its administration can be moved within the

---

[10] See M Stevens, 'Internal Affairs Doctrine: California versus Delaware in a Fight to Regulate Foreign Corporations' (2007) 48 BLCR 1047.

[11] ECJ Case C-167/01 *Inspire Art* [2003] ECR I-10195 paras 82ff.

[12] ECJ Case C-167/01 *Inspire Art* [2003] ECR 1-10195 paras 82ff, 139.

[13] M Szydlo, 'The Right of Companies to Cross-Border Conversion under the TFEU Rules on Freedom of Establishment' (2010) 7 ECFR 414; J Borg-Barthet, 'A New Approach to the Governing Law of Companies in the EU: A Legislative Proposal' (2010) 6 J Priv Int'l L 589.

[14] AW Grumberg and C Le Gall-Robinson, 'Societas Europaea: Ombres et Lumières—Societas Europaea: Shadows and Lights' (2006) 6 IBLJ 741; N Lenoir, 'The Societas Europaea (SE) in Europe—A Promising Start and an Option with Good Prospects' (2008) 4 ULR 13; WG Ringe, 'The European Company Statute in the Context of Freedom of Establishment' (2007) 7 JCLS 185.

[15] [2001] OJ L294/1.

European Union. The subscribed capital shall be expressed in Euro and shall not be less than EUR 120,000 (Article 4). The Regulation sets out conditions for founding and transformation in its Article 2:

1. Public limited-liability companies such as referred to in Annex I, formed under the law of a Member State, with registered offices and head offices within the Community may form an SE by means of a merger provided that at least two of them are governed by the law of different Member States.
2. Public and private limited-liability companies such as referred to in Annex II, formed under the law of a Member State, with registered offices and head offices within the Community may promote the formation of a holding SE provided that each of at least two of them:
   (a) is governed by the law of a different Member State, or
   (b) has for at least two years had a subsidiary company governed by the law of another Member State or a branch situated in another Member State.
3. Companies and firms within the meaning of the second paragraph of Article 48 of the Treaty and other legal bodies governed by public or private law, formed under the law of a Member State, with registered offices and head offices within the Community may form a subsidiary SE by subscribing for its shares, provided that each of at least two of them:
   (a) is governed by the law of a different Member State, or
   (b) has for at least two years had a subsidiary company governed by the law of another Member State or a branch situated in another Member State.
4. A public limited-liability company, formed under the law of a Member State, which has its registered office and head office within the Community may be transformed into an SE if for at least two years it has had a subsidiary company governed by the law of another Member State.
5. A Member State may provide that a company the head office of which is not in the Community may participate in the formation of an SE provided that company is formed under the law of a Member State has its registered office in that Member State and has a real and continuous link with a Member State's economy.

Beyond enhanced mobility, transforming a company into an SE allows strategic choices often hampered by the corset of national company law. Companies may opt between a two-tier system or a one-tier system of corporate governance. The one-tier system (Article 43) follows the model of British and US company law. The two-tier system (Article 39) is inspired by the German model (with an executive board and a supervisory board). The participation of employees in the corporate governance of an SE is an important issue for companies established in an EU country with strong labour rights in the management (representation in the supervisory board or even the executive board), especially for large companies under the German system of co-determination. According to Article 37(8) of the Directive 2001/86/EC,[16] the management shall negotiate the framework of participation with the employee representatives:

Member States may condition a conversion to a favourable vote of a qualified majority or unanimity in the organ of the company to be converted within which employee participation is organised.

---

[16] [2001] OJ L294/22.

If no agreement can be reached, the pre-existing system of participation continues to apply (Article 7 and Annex of the Directive). In an SE, the multinational base of employee participation significantly reduces the influence of national trade unions and, in the end, fosters a new culture of participation.

In 2016, more than 2,488 SEs were registered in the Member States of the European Union. Examples of important corporations converted into or founded as an SE are Allianz SE, BASF SE, Airbus Group SE and SCOR SE, the first French company converted into an SE.

5. Corporate Governance

For some time, corporate governance has been the conceptual platform for corporate and individual accountability and transparency. In the 1990s and early 2000s, reckless management and fraudulent practices (highlighted in the Enron or World-Com scandals), often culminating in the corporation's financial collapse fuelled the demand for improved standards of governance in the interest of creditors, shareholders, and the public at large. New rules on conflicts of interest as well as mechanisms of internal and external control emerged.

The United States and many European and other countries have responded in several ways to corporate governance issues. Some countries, besides legislative measures, rely on soft law-like codes of conduct for corporate governance. In 2002, the US Congress enacted the Sarbanes–Oxley Act (SOX).[17] The Act establishes tighter standards of corporate responsibility and new criminal sanctions, addresses auditor independence, and enhances financial disclosures. As mandated by the Sarbanes–Oxley Act, the Securities and Exchange Commission (SEC) issued a number of implementing rules, in particular on increased accountability of CEOs and CFOs, on disclosure of financial information and avoidance of conflicts of interests.

Under the Sarbanes–Oxley Act, the Public Company Accounting Oversight Board (PCAOB),[18] a private sector non-profit corporation, oversees the audit of public companies, to protect the interests of investors and of the public at large in informative, accurate, and independent audit reports. The PCAOB operates under the supervision of the SEC.

The SOX standards are binding for every company listed on the New York Stock Exchange (NYSE). Therefore, the US corporate governance rules affect management standards worldwide. On the other hand, for a number of foreign corporations (including several large German companies), the burden of compliance

---

[17] R Romano, 'The Sarbanes-Oxley Act and the Making of Quack Corporate Governance' (2005) 114 Yale LJ 1521; LE Mitchell, 'The Sarbanes-Oxley Act and the Reinvention of Corporate Governance' (2003) 48 Villanova L Rev 1189.
[18] DM Nagy, 'Playing Peekaboo with Constitutional Law: The PCAOB and Its Public/Private Status' (2005) 80 Notre Dame L Rev 975.

with the new US standards outweighed the benefits of access to the NYSE. Thus, administrative costs and complexity of financial disclosures under the SOX fuelled a process of delisting and deregistration from the SEC.

Select Bibliography

U Bernitz and WG Ringe, *Company Law and Economic Protectionism: New Challenges to European Integration* (OUP 2011).

KJ Hopt, E Wymeersch, H Kanda, and H Baum, *Corporate Governance in Context: Corporations, States, and Markets in Europe, Japan, and the US* (OUP 2005).

R Kraakman, J Armour, P Davies, L Enriques, HB Hansmann, G Hertig, KJ Hopt, H Kanda, and EB Rock, *The Anatomy of Corporate Law—A Comparative and Functional Approach* (2nd edn, OUP 2009).

C Padgett, *Corporate Governance: Theory and Practice* (Palgrave Finance, Palgrave Macmillan 2011).

S Rammeloo, *Corporations in Private International Law—A European Perspective* (OUP 2001).

B Tricker, *Corporate Governance: Principles, Policies and Practices* (3rd edn, OUP 2015).

J Vermeylen and IV Velde, *European Cross-Border Mergers and Reorganisations: Law and Practice* (OUP 2012).

XXVIII

International Accounting Standards

International accounting standards play a crucial role for any internationally operating public company. These standards are the basis for international annual accounts and other financial statements. On a global level, the standards of the International Accounting Standards Board (IASB) enjoy broad recognition. However, in the United States specific domestic standards (US-GAAP) prevail. Gradual convergence between these competing standards is an important objective.

The IASB,[1] a private and independent organization, was established in 2001 by organizations representing accounting professions and took over from the International Accounting Standards Committee (IASC). The 14 board members are selected as a group of experts with various kinds of practical or academic experience. The IASB adopted the International Financial Reporting Standards (IFRS) which replace the International Accounting Standards (IAS) established by its predecessor body. The International Financial Reporting Interpretations Committee (IFRIC) adopts clarifying interpretations of the IFRS.

The IASB is currently working on a revision of the Conceptual Framework for Financial Reporting which was elaborated by its predecessor body IASC. After temporarily suspending the project in 2010, the IASB expects it to be completed in 2016. The Framework states consistent concepts and accounting policies underlying IFRS. The Exposure Draft IASB Framework as of October 2015 deals with:[2]

(a) the objective of financial reporting;

(b) the qualitative characteristics of useful financial reporting;

(c) financial statements and the reporting entity;

(d) the elements of financial statements;

(e) recognition and derecognition;

(f) the measurement;

(g) presentation and disclosure; and

(h) concepts of capital and capital maintenance.

---

[1] DS Ruder, CT Canfield, and HT Hollister, 'Creation of World Wide Accounting Standards: Convergence and Independence' (2005) 25 Northwest J Int'l Law Bus 513.

[2] See for the progress of the Conceptual Framework <http://www.ifrs.org/Current-Projects/IASB-Projects/Conceptual-Framework/Pages/Conceptual-Framework-Summary.aspx> (accessed 23 June 2016).

Under EU law, publicly traded companies incorporated under the law of a Member State must prepare their annual accounts in accordance with the IFRS.[3] The referral to the IFRS in EU law is an example of the outsourcing of legislative functions to non-governmental organizations.

In the United States, annual accounts must conform to the United States Generally Accepted Accounting Principles (US-GAAP). The US-GAAP were developed by the Financial Accounting Standards Board (FASB), the American Institute of Certified Public Accountants (AICPA), and the Security and Exchange Commission (SEC). Every foreign company which is listed on a US Stock Exchange is subject to the US-GAAP. Thus, European companies, listed in the European Union and in the United States, must bear the double burden of publishing their annual accounts in accordance with the IFRS and the US-GAAP.

The IASB and the FASB are constantly updating their standards. The SEC is considering annual accounts submitted according to the IFRS. In addition, the ISAB and the FASB agreed on a roadmap for convergence. Until its temporal suspension in 2010, the Conceptual Framework was a joint project of the IASB and the FASB; since the restart in 2012 it is carried on by the IASB only.

Select Bibliography

B Mackenzie, D Coetsee, T Njikizana, R Chamboko, and B Colyvas, *Wiley IFRS 2014: Interpretation and Application of International Financial Reporting Standards* (11th edn, John Wiley & Sons 2014).

PWC, *Manual of Accounting: IFRS 2015* (Tottel Publishing 2014).

---

[3] Article 4 of Regulation (EC) No 1606/2002 on the application of international accounting standards [2002] OJ L243/1.

XXIX

International Competition Law

1. National and International Rules against Anti-Competitive Behaviour

Competition law (in the United States antitrust law) is a framework of rules to promote and maintain undistorted competition. These rules prohibit restrictive practices of undertakings, restrain monopolies, prohibit the abuse of a dominant market position, and control mergers. Some countries have established specific regulatory mechanisms apart from general competition law to establish and foster competition in markets traditionally governed by network oligopolies or in markets opened after the demise of State monopolies (markets for energy, postal services, railway transport). The most developed and most influential systems of competition law are the US antitrust law and the competition law of the European Union,[1] which also includes rules on subsidies. The European Union is the only system of regional economic integration with a common competition law and supranational law enforcement (through the European Commission).

In today's world, enterprises pursuing international marketing strategies and restrictive practices or mergers affect competition in many countries. Consequently, many practices and transactions appear on the screen of several antitrust authorities distributed over different States. The application of competition law, with all its territorial limitations, often has far-reaching cross-border effects. Interference with the configuration of products like computer software on the basis of national competition law may disrupt international marketing strategies and the prohibition of a merger between foreign corporations will affect concentration processes in other countries. These extraterritorial implications suggest some kind of convergence of competition laws or, at least, some mutual consideration of cross-border effects by national authorities.

A truly international framework with binding competition rules is not in sight.[2] There are, however, rudimentary rules for undistorted competition in regulated sectors (telecommunications services) under the GATS.[3] A number of bilateral

---

[1] J Basedow, 'Antitrust or Competition Law, International' in R Wolfrum (ed), *The Max Planck Encyclopedia of Public International Law* (2012) vol I, 450.
[2] See E Fox, 'Toward World Antitrust and Market Access' (1997) 92 AJIL.
[3] See Ch XVII.2.

agreements and memoranda of understanding establish a close cooperation in competition cases. Finally, general international law governs the legitimate reach of national competition laws.

A number of codes of conduct and guidelines on the control of anticompetitive business practices have established international standards over time. The OECD Guidelines for Multinational Enterprises (first issued in 1976, most recently updated in 2011)[4] provide in Part I, chapter X:

Enterprises should:
1. Carry out their activities in a manner consistent with all applicable competition laws and regulations, taking into account the competition laws of all jurisdictions in which the activities may have anticompetitive effects.
2. Refrain from entering into or carrying out anti-competitive agreements among competitors, including agreements to:
   a) fix prices;
   b) make rigged bids (collusive tenders);
   c) establish output restrictions or quotas; or
   d) share or divide markets by allocating customers, suppliers, territories or lines of commerce.
3. Co-operate with investigating competition authorities by, among other things and subject to applicable law and appropriate safeguards, providing responses as promptly and completely as practicable to requests for information, and considering the use of available instruments, such as waivers of confidentiality where appropriate, to promote effective and efficient co-operation among investigating authorities.
4. Regularly promote employee awareness of the importance of compliance with all applicable competition laws and regulations, and, in particular, train senior management of the enterprise in relation to competition issues.

In 1980, the UN General Assembly adopted the Set of Multilaterally Agreed Equitable Principles and Rules for the Control of Restrictive Business Practices elaborated by the United Nations Conference for Trade and Development (UNCTAD Code or RBP Rules).[5] A particular concern of the UNCTAD Code is due consideration for the welfare of developing countries. The Munich Group of competition lawyers has elaborated a catalogue of principles for an international competition law (Draft International Antitrust Code).[6] The Munich Code formulates a core of antitrust principles. National treatment is a key principle of the Draft International Antitrust Code.

The Draft Code is above all inspired by the antitrust law of the United States and the European Union. The Code addresses horizontal and vertical restraints, control of concentration and restructuring as well as abuse of dominant position. It also provides liability of undertakings for any damages caused by the infringements

---

[4] OECD, *OECD Guidelines for Multinational Enterprises* (2011).
[5] UNCTAD/RBP/CONF/10/Rev.2.
[6] See SW Waller, 'The Internationalization of Antitrust Enforcement' (1997) 77 BULR 347; DJ Gifford, 'The Draft International Antitrust Code Proposed at Munich: Good Intentions Gone Awry' (1997) 6 Minn J Global Trade 1.

upon the rights or interest of other persons, including consumers.[7] The Code also provides for the establishment of an International Antitrust Authority and an International Antitrust Panel.[8]

In the European Union and in the United States private rights of action of competitors play an important role in ensuring compliance with competition rules. Reflecting the US American approach, the TPP Agreement recognizes that private rights of action operate as an important mechanism for the enforcement of competition laws (Article 16.3). Directive 2014/104/EU on certain rules governing actions for damages under national law for infringements of the competition law provisions of the Member States and of the European Union[9] strengthens the position of the victims of infringements of EU antitrust law. It provides for a right to full compensation (Article 3). In the case of the passing-on of overcharges, direct and indirect purchasers may claim compensation (Articles 12–16). The Directive establishes rules on the disclosure of evidence in civil proceedings (Articles 5–8) and on the joint and several liability of infringers (Article 11).

2. The Application of Competition Law and Extraterritorial Effects

The application of national competition laws is not confined to practices carried out within the territory of the respective State. The 'effects doctrine' establishes jurisdiction of any State over behaviour that has anticompetitive effects in its own territory.[10] The effects doctrine, serving as a basis for the application of US antitrust law, is meanwhile internationally accepted and is also practised by the European Union.

For some time, in the United States and elsewhere, a widely shared tendency has tried to contain the scope of the effects doctrine. The doctrine shall only apply if conduct in a foreign state has a 'substantial effect' on domestic markets. According to the Foreign States Trade Antitrust Improvement Act (FTAIA) of 1982 the US antitrust law (the Sherman Act) shall not be applied to anticompetitive conduct in context with trade or commerce with foreign nations, unless it has a 'direct, substantial and reasonably foreseeable effect' on the US market:

U.S.C. § 6a. Conduct involving trade or commerce with foreign nations
Sections 1 to 7 of this title shall not apply to conduct involving trade or commerce (other than import trade or import commerce) with foreign nations unless—
(1) such conduct has a direct, substantial, and reasonably foreseeable effect—
  (A) on trade or commerce which is not trade or commerce with foreign nations, or on import trade or import commerce with foreign nations; or

---

[7] Draft Antitrust Code, Article 15(6).   [8] Draft Antitrust Code, Article 19(1)b–c.
[9] Directive 2014/104/EU of 26 November 2014 on certain rules governing actions for damages under national law for infringements of the competition law provisions of the Member States and of the European Union [2014] OJ L349/1.
[10] See Ch VI.7(a) and 8(b).

(B) on export trade or export commerce with foreign nations, of a person engaged in such trade or commerce in the United States; and

(2) such effect gives rise to a claim under the provisions of sections 1 to 7 of this title, other than this section [...].

In *Hartford Fire Insurance Co v California*,[11] the US Supreme Court applied the Sherman Act on the basis of the effects doctrine in its restrained version and assumed US antitrust jurisdiction in a case of foreign companies acting in a foreign market. In *Hartford*, reinsurance companies incorporated and doing business in the United Kingdom had taken concerted action to induce US insurers to abandon certain policy practices that were advantageous to their consumers, but costly to reinsurers. Several US States then filed an action against the British reinsurance companies for violations of US antitrust law. In *Hartford*, the defendant asserted that the United States lacked jurisdiction over their acts and that various statutes exempted them from liability. But the US Supreme Court held that

[...] it is well established by now that the Sherman Act applies to foreign conduct that was meant to produce, and did in fact produce, some substantial effect in the United States. Such is the conduct alleged here: that the London reinsurers engaged in unlawful conspiracies to affect the market for insurance in the United States and that their conduct in fact produced substantial effect.[12]

In *Hoffmann-La Roche Ltd v Empagran SA*, the US Supreme Court adopted a restrictive approach.[13] In this case, vitamin purchasers filed a class action alleging that foreign vitamin manufacturers and distributors were engaged in a price-fixing conspiracy which raised vitamin prices in the United States and several foreign countries. This worldwide price-fixing conspiracy was economically the biggest ever detected. A number of foreign plaintiffs brought a class action in the United States although their damage had occurred outside the United States.

The Supreme Court denied the application of the Sherman Act:

[...] The FTAIA exception does not apply here for two reasons.

First, this Court ordinarily construes ambiguous statutes to avoid unreasonable interference with other nations' sovereign authority. This rule of construction reflects customary international law principles and cautions courts to assume that legislators take account of other nations' legitimate sovereign interests when writing American laws. It thereby helps the potentially conflicting laws if different nations work together in harmony. While applying America's antitrust laws to foreign conduct can interfere with a foreign nation's ability to regulate its own commercial affairs, courts have long held such application nonetheless reasonable, and hence consistent with prescriptive comity principles, insofar as the laws reflect a legislative effort to redress domestic antitrust injury caused by foreign anticompetitive conduct. However, it is not reasonable to apply American laws to foreign conduct insofar as

---

[11] 509 US 764 (1993).   [12] 509 US 764 (1993) para 2909.

[13] *Hoffmann-La Roche Ltd v Empagran SA* 542 US 155 (2004); See M Fitzpatrick, 'Hoffman-La Roche Ltd v. Empagran S.A.: The Supreme Court Trusts that Foreign Nations Can Preserve Competition without American Interference' (2005) 13 TJICL 357; F Harry, 'The Vitamins Case: Cartel Prosecutions and the Coming of International Competition Law' (2001) 68 Antitrust LJ 711.

that conduct causes independent foreign harm that alone gives rise to a plaintiff's claim. The risk of interference is the same, but the justification for the interference seems insubstantial. While some of the anticompetitive conduct alleged here took place in America, the higher foreign prices are not the consequence of any domestic anticompetitive conduct sought to be forbidden by Congress, which rather wanted to release domestic (and foreign) anticompetitive conduct from Sherman Act constraint when that conduct causes foreign harm. Contrary to respondents' claim, the comity concerns remain real as other nations have not in all areas adopted antitrust laws similar to this country's and, in any event, disagree dramatically about appropriate remedies. Respondents' alternative argument that case-by-case comity analysis is preferable to an across the board exclusion of foreign injury cases is too complex to prove workable.

Second, the FTAIA's language and history suggest that Congress designed the Act to clarify, perhaps to limit, but not to expand, the Sherman Act's scope as applied to foreign commerce. There is no significant indication that at the time Congress wrote the FTAIA courts would have thought the Sherman Act applicable in these circumstances, nor do the six cases on which respondents rely warrant a different conclusion [...].[14]

The European Commission applies EU competition law to mergers and other conduct in foreign countries, if the competition in the internal market of the European Union or in the European Economic Area (EEA) is significantly affected.

In 1997, the Commission objected to the merger of the two leading US aircraft companies in the *Boeing/McDonnell* case:[15]

[...] Not only does the operation have a Community dimension within the legal sense of the Merger Regulation, it also has an important economic impact on the large commercial jet aircraft market within the EEA, [...]

The relevant market for the purposes of assessing the operation is the world market for large commercial jet aircraft. The EEA is an integral and important part of this world market, and its competitive structure is very similar. [...]

It is therefore evident that the operation is of great significance in the EEA as it is in the world market of which the EEA is an important part.[16]

The European Commission's position fuelled a political confrontation between the European Union and the US Government and drew some criticism as undue interference with US competition policy. In the end, the Commission authorized the merger, after Boeing had accepted far-reaching conditions.

In 2001, the European Commission entirely blocked the General Electric/Honeywell merger.[17] The Commission stated:

The product markets that are affected by the combination of the GE and Honeywell businesses are part of the aerospace and power systems industries. In these sectors, the transaction brings about significant horizontal, vertical and conglomerate effects [...].[18]

For all those reasons, it should be concluded that the proposed merger would lead to the creation or strengthening of a dominant position on the markets for large commercial jet

---

[14] 542 US 155 (2004) paras 2361f.
[15] WE Kovacic, 'Transatlantic Turbulence: The Boeing-McDonnell Douglas Merger and International Competition Policy' (2001) 68 Antitrust LJ 805.
[16] [1998] OJ L336/16.   [17] [2004] OJ L48/2 (8–84).   [18] [2004] OJ L48/2 (8).

aircraft engines, large regional jet aircraft engines, corporate jet aircraft engines, avionics and non-avionics products, as well as small marine gas turbine, as a result of which effective competition in the common market would be significantly impeded. The proposed merger should therefore be declared incompatible with the common market [...].[19]

These cases illustrate the need for bilateral cooperation between antitrust authorities.

3. Bilateral Cooperation

In the absence of a harmonized antitrust regime, effective cooperation among competition authorities is an important objective. The United States as well as the European Union have entered into a number of bilateral agreements and memoranda of understanding on cooperation with other States. In 1991, the European Union and the United States concluded the 1991 Competition Cooperation Agreement.[20] The EU/US Agreement provides for notification and exchange of information (Article III) as well as for cooperation and coordination between the EU/US competition authorities (Article IV).

The 'positive comity' procedure allows a party to request the other party to take appropriate measures against anti-competitive activities affecting the requesting Party's interests (Article V).[21] The European Union and the United States entered

---

[19] [2004] OJ L48/2 (567).

[20] Agreement between the Government of the United States of America and the Commission of the European Communities regarding the application of their competition laws [1995] OJ L95/47.

[21] Article V provides: 'Cooperation regarding anticompetitive activities in the territory of one Party that adversely affect the interests of the other Party

1. The Parties note that anticompetitive activities may occur within the territory of one Party that, in addition to violating that Party's competition laws, adversely affect important interests of the other Party. The Parties agree that it is in both their interests to address anticompetitive activities of this nature.
2. If a Party believes that anticompetitive activities carried out on the territory of the other Party are adversely affecting its important interests, the first Party may notify the other Party and may request that the other Party's competition authorities initiate appropriate enforcement activities. The notification shall be as specific as possible about the nature of the anticompetitive activities and their effects on the interests of the notifying Party, and shall include an offer of such further information and other cooperation as the notifying Party is able to provide.
3. Upon receipt of a notification under paragraph 2, and after such other discussion between the Parties as may be appropriate and useful in the circumstances, the competition authorities of the notified Party will consider whether or not to initiate enforcement activities, or to expand ongoing enforcement activities, with respect to the anticompetitive activities identified in the notification. The notified Party will advise the notifying Party of its decision. If enforcement activities are initiated, the notified Party will advise the notifying Party of their outcome and, to the extent possible, of significant interim developments.
4. Nothing in this Article limits the discretion of the notified Party under its competition laws and enforcement policies as to whether or not to undertake enforcement activities with respect to the notified anticompetitive activities, or precludes the notifying Party from undertaking enforcement activities with respect to such anticompetitive activities.'

into a separate Agreement on 'positive comity' (1998)[22] which lays down further details of cooperation.

Under Article IV(2) of the 1998 Agreement the parties shall coordinate their enforcement activities:

[...] In considering whether particular enforcement activities should be coordinated, the Parties shall take account of the following factors, among others:
(a) the opportunity to make more efficient use of their resources devoted to the enforcement activities;
(b) the relative abilities of the Parties' competition authorities to obtain information necessary to conduct the enforcement activities;
(c) the effect of such coordination on the ability of both Parties to achieve the objectives of their enforcement activities; and
(d) the possibility of reducing costs incurred by persons subject to the enforcement activities.

The 'traditional comity' procedure ensures that each party duly considers important interests of the other party (Article VI of the 1991 Cooperation Agreement). The Cooperation Agreement lists a number of factors to be considered in an accommodation of competing interests in Article VI(3):

Where it appears that one Party's enforcement activities may adversely affect important interests of the other Party, the Parties will consider the following factors, in addition to any other factors that appear relevant in the circumstances, in seeking an appropriate accommodation of the competing interests:
(a) the relative significance to the anticompetitive activities involved of conduct within the enforcing Party's territory as compared to conduct within the other Party's territory;
(b) the presence or absence of a purpose on the part of those engaged in the anticompetitive activities to affect consumers, suppliers, or competitors within the enforcing Party's territory;
(c) the relative significance of the effects of the anticompetitive activities on the enforcing Party's interests as compared to the effects on the other Party's interests;
(d) the existence or absence of reasonable expectations that would be furthered or defeated by the enforcement activities;
(e) the degree of conflict or consistency between the enforcement activities and the other Party's laws or articulated economic policies; and
(f) the extent to which enforcement activities of the other Party with respect to the same persons, including judgments or undertakings resulting from such activities, may be affected.

Cooperation between the EU/US authorities under the 1991 Agreement finds its limits in the existing laws of both parties (Article IX). Despite this exception, the discretionary powers of competition authorities, often coupled with a margin of appreciation, leave ample space for intensive cooperation. In practice, transatlantic cooperation works well. There are even joint case teams.

---

[22] [1998] OJ L173/28.

4. Convergences and Divergences between EU Competition Law and US Antitrust Law

Since its inception in the late 19th century, US antitrust law played a pioneering role in the world, which builds on its innovative force, its subtly structured development over the years, its effective enforcement, and its impact for most large companies with a presence in the US market. Nowadays, EU competition law and US antitrust law follow similar objectives with similar mechanisms. They both control restrictive agreements (horizontal agreements or cartels and vertical agreements such as exclusive dealings agreements) and other restrictive practices, the abuse of a dominant position, and mergers. US antitrust concepts like the 'essential facilities doctrine' now form the basis for restraining the exercise of dominant positions coupled with a copyright or with technical standards in EU competition law.[23] Under both systems, there is an ongoing discussion as to which extent they should ultimately protect undistorted competition as an end in itself, or rather other consumers' interests and other concerns.

For some time, US antitrust practice has strongly leaned towards consumer welfare. In the European Union, and previously under German competition law, the traditional focus was on freedom to compete and on protection against distorting interferences. In the 2000s, the European Commission adopted the 'more economic approach',[24] which results in considerable convergence with US antitrust policy. The more economic approach reflects current economic thinking about competition, incentives, and efficiency. It enhances the weight of consumers' interests in the overall balance of relevant factors and increases the discretionary element in the application of competition law.

Despite all the convergence, there are marked divergences. Unlike EU competition law, US antitrust law strongly relies on private enforcement (with the incentive of treble damages) and on sanctions under criminal law. EU law tends to be more sensitive about the anti-competitive risks associated with a dominant position and the interests of newcomers in an entirely unhampered market entry than US antitrust law. The European Commission is less shy than US authorities in siphoning off the fruits of innovation.

---

[23] See ECJ Case C-418/01 *IMS Health* [2004] ECR I-5038 para 38: '[I]n order for the refusal by an undertaking which owns a copyright to give access to a product or service indispensable for carrying on a particular business to be treated as abusive, it is sufficient that *three cumulative conditions* be satisfied, namely, that that refusal is preventing the emergence of a new product for which there is a potential consumer demand, that it is unjustified and such as to exclude any competition on a secondary market.'

[24] N Forwood, 'The Commission's More Economic Approach—Implications for the Role of the EU Courts, the Treatment of Economic Evidence and the Scope of Judicial Review' (2009) Eur Competition L Ann 255; J Basedow, 'The Modernization of European Competition Law: A Story of Unfinished Concepts' (2007) 42 Texas Int'l LJ 429.

The famous *Microsoft* case[25] illustrates these transatlantic divergences. In 2004, the European Commission decided that Microsoft had abused its dominant position (Article 102 of the TFEU, Article 54 of the EEA Agreement) by:

- refusing to supply interoperability information and allow its use for the purpose of developing and distributing work group server operating system products,
- making the availability of the Windows Client PC Operating System conditional on the simultaneous acquisition of Windows Media Player (WMP).[26]

The Commission imposed the highest fine so far in EU history (about EUR 500 million, to which about EUR 280 million were added later). The European Court of First Instance upheld the Commission's decision.[27] The European Commission's requirement of server interoperability information cuts deeply into intellectual property rights. Heavy criticism in the United States challenged the Commission's position as inhibiting innovation processes.[28]

The EC Merger Regulation (Regulation (EC) No 139/2004)[29] aims at an ex ante prevention of creating an anti-competitive activity. As the Court of First Instance held in *Gencor Ltd v Commission of the European Communities*,[30]

[...] Community jurisdiction is therefore founded, first and foremost, on the need to avoid the establishment of market structures which may create or strengthen a dominant position, and not on the need to control directly possible abuses of a dominant position.[31]

The US merger control adopts the 'SLC test' which refers to a 'substantial lessening of competition' by the proposed concentration.[32] The EU law which abandoned the previously applied 'dominant position' follows a similar approach as US antitrust law. The EC Merger Control establishes the 'SIEC test' which focuses on a 'significant impediment to effective competition'.[33]

An important issue of undistorted competition relates to State aid.[34] In the European Union, Article 107(1) of the TFEU establishes a general prohibition of aid granted by Member States affecting trade between the Member States:

Save as otherwise provided in the Treaties, any aid granted by a Member State or through State resources in any form whatsoever which distorts or threatens to distort competition by

[25] B Canetti, 'Microsoft Champions Intellectual Property Rights and Loses to European Union Competition Law: Proceeding under Article 82 of the EC Treaty' (2004) 1 JLTP 171.
[26] [2007] OJ L32/33.   [27] ECJ Case T-201/04 *Microsoft* [2004] ECR II-4463.
[28] SA Mota, 'Hide It or Unbundle It: A Comparison of the Antitrust Investigations against Microsoft in the U.S. and the E.U.' (2005) 3 Pierce Law Review 183; A Cohen, 'Surveying the Microsoft Antitrust Universe' (2004) 19 BTLJ 333; N Economides and I Lianos, 'A Critical Appraisal of Remedies in the E.U. Microsoft Cases' (2010) 2 CBLR 346.
[29] [2004] OJ L24/1.   [30] CFI Case T-102/96 *Gencor* ECR II-759.
[31] CFI Case T-102/96 *Gencor* ECR II-759 para. 106.
[32] DS Evans and AJ Padilla, 'Demand-side Efficiencies in Merger Control' (2003) 26 W Comp 167.
[33] Article 2(2), (3) of the EC Merger regulation; N Levy, 'The EU's SIEC Test Five Years On: Has It Made a Difference' (2010) 6 Eur Competition J 211.
[34] L Rubini, 'The Elusive Frontier: Regulation under EC State Aid Law' (2009) 3 Eur St Aid LQ 277.

favouring certain undertakings or the production of certain goods shall, in so far as it affects trade between Member States, be incompatible with the internal market.

There is, however, a number of exceptions for State aid which either are or may be declared compatible with the internal market (Article 107(2), (3) of the TFEU). The control of State aid lies with the European Commission (Article 108 of the TFEU).

In the European internal market, State enterprises (public undertakings) and private undertakings with a special mandate under the law, still play a significant role in the internal market. Article 106(2) of the TFEU tries to establish a balance between the general interest in served and undistorted competition:

Undertakings entrusted with the operation of services of general economic interest or having the character of a revenue-producing monopoly shall be subject to the rules contained in the Treaties, in particular to the rules on competition, in so far as the application of such rules does not obstruct the performance, in law or in fact, of the particular tasks assigned to them. The development of trade must not be affected to such an extent as would be contrary to the interests of the Union.

Select Bibliography

D Broder, *U.S. Antitrust Law and Enforcement—A Practice Introduction* (2nd edn, OUP 2011).

MM Dabbah, *International and Comparative Competition Law (Antitrust and Competition Law)* (CUP 2010).

J Drexl, WS Grimes, CA Jones, RJR Peritz, and ET Swaine, *More Common Ground for International Competition Law?* (Edward Elgar Publishing 2011).

A Ezrachi, *EU Competition Law* (4th edn, Hart Publishing 2014).

AT Guzman, *Cooperation, Comity, and Competition Policy* (OUP 2011).

R Nazzini, *The Foundations of European Union Competition Law—The Objective and Principles of Article 102* (OUP 2011).

CJ Noonan, *The Emerging Principles of International Competition Law* (OUP 2008).

R Whish and D Bailey, *Competition Law* (8th edn, OUP 2015).

F Wijckmans and F Tuytschaever, *Vertical Agreements in EU Competition Law* (2nd edn, OUP 2011).

XXX

International Tax Law

International tax law covers the rules on taxation in cross-border contexts. National tax law reaches out to bases of taxation located abroad, if nationals or persons domiciled within the country earn income or hold assets in foreign territory. A State's tax jurisdiction also extends to foreign persons who earn income or hold property within the State.

Customary international law requires a personal or territorial link for exercising tax jurisdiction. The Restatement (Third) of the US Foreign Relations Law[1] provides in § 412:

(1) A state may exercise jurisdiction to tax the income of
   (a) a person, whether natural or juridical, who is a national, resident, or domiciliary of the state, whether the source of the income is within or without the state;
   (b) a natural or juridical person who is not a national, resident, or domiciliary of the state but who is present or does business in the state, but only with respect to income derived from or associated with presence or doing business within the state; and
   (c) a natural or juridical person who is not a national, resident or domiciliary of the state and is not present or doing business therein, with respect to income derived from property located in the territory of the state.
(2) A state may exercise jurisdiction to tax property located within its territory, without regard to the nationality, domicile, residence, or presence of the owner of the property.
(3) A state may exercise jurisdiction to tax transfer of wealth
   (a) if the wealth consists of property located in its territory, or
   (b) if the transfer is made by or to a national, resident, or domiciliary of the state.
(4) A state may exercise jurisdiction to tax a transaction that occurs, originates, or terminates in its territory or that has a substantial relation to the state, without regard to the nationality, domicile, residence, or presence of the parties to such a transaction.

The 'world income principle' signifies an unrestricted tax liability covering all income or taxable assets, regardless of where the financial basis of taxation is located. The principle of unrestricted tax liability can only be applied on the basis of a personal link (nationality or residence of natural persons, place of incorporation, or real seat of administration of corporations). Common practice of States subjects foreign persons without residence in the country only to limited tax liability, that is to say taxation on sources of income or property located in their territory (source principle).

---

[1] American Law Institute, *Restatement of the Law Third, The Foreign Relations Law of the United States* (1987) 1.

Double taxation is a central issue of international tax law. It arises when two countries impose taxes on the same source of income or on the same basis of taxation like property.

Avoidance of double taxation and fair allocation of taxes is the objective of bilateral treaties on double taxation (far more than 1,000 worldwide).[2] Many bilateral treaties follow the OECD Model Tax Convention on Income and on Capital, which was first presented in 1963 and has been updated since then.[3] The OECD Model Tax Convention applies to persons who are residents of one or more of the Contracting States. The OECD Model Tax Convention covers all taxes on income, on total capital, or on elements of income or of capital, including taxes on gains from the alienation of movable or immovable property, taxes on the total amounts of wages or salaries paid by enterprises, as well as taxes on capital appreciation.[4]

Among the mechanisms to avoid an undue double tax burden, treaty practice provides for allocating certain forms of income for the purpose of taxation, either to the State of residence or to the source State. Thus, double taxation treaties tend to subject revenue of shipping companies or airlines only to taxation by the seat State.

Article 4 Resident

2. Where by reason of the provisions of paragraph 1 an individual is a resident of both Contracting States, then his status shall be determined as follows:

    a) he shall be deemed to be a resident only of the State in which he has a permanent home available to him; if he has a permanent home available to him in both States, he shall be deemed to be a resident only of the State with which his personal and economic relations are closer (centre of vital interests);

    b) if the State in which he has his centre of vital interests cannot be determined, or if he has not a permanent home available to him in either State, he shall be deemed to be a resident only of the State in which he has an habitual abode;

    c) if he has an habitual abode in both States or in neither of them, he shall be deemed to be a resident only of the State of which he is a national;

    d) if he is a national of both States or of neither of them, the competent authorities of the Contracting States shall settle the question by mutual agreement [...].

If the seat State refrains from taxation, these companies enjoy full exemption. Tax benefits provide a strong incentive for shipping companies to take their seat in countries like Costa Rica, Liberia, or Panama.

Article 8 Shipping, Inland Waterways Transport and Air Transport

1. Profits from the operation of ships or aircraft in international traffic shall be taxable only in the Contracting State in which the place of effective management of the enterprise is situated.

---

[2] Y Margalioth, 'International Taxation' in R Wolfrum (ed), *The Max Planck Encyclopedia of Public International Law* (OUP 2012) vol XI, 769.

[3] Articles of the OECD Model Tax Convention on Income and on Capital (July 2014) <http:// www.keepeek.com/Digital-Asset-Management/oecd/taxation/model-tax-convention-on-income-and-on-capital-condensed-version-2014_mtc_cond-2014-en#> (accessed 23 June 2016).

[4] Article 2(2) of the OECD Model Tax Convention on Income and on Capital.

2. Profits from the operation of boats engaged in inland waterways transport shall be taxable only in the Contracting State in which the place of effective management of the enterprise is situated.

3. If the place of effective management of a shipping enterprise or of an inland waterways transport enterprise is aboard a ship or boat, then it shall be deemed to be situated in the Contracting State in which the home harbour of the ship or boat is situated, or, if there is no such home harbour, in the Contracting State of which the operator of the ship or boat is a resident [...].

In addition to the OECD Model, the United Nations adopted a model tax convention between developed and developing countries (1980 United Nations Model Double Taxation Convention between Developed and Developing Countries)[5]. Many countries have drafted a model treaty on taxation as a basis for further negotiations.[6]

Foreign-based companies (off-shore companies) established in tax oases or low-tax countries (for example the Bahamas, Liechtenstein, Panama, the Netherlands Antilles, and the British Virgin Islands) play an important role in taking advantage of different levels of taxation. These companies, often operating as holding companies, are an instrument for shifting profits to low-tax countries. However, States may subject the profits of such foreign-based companies to taxation, if the companies are managed and controlled within their territory or by their own nationals or if the transfer of profits amounts to an abuse of legal options.

A contentious issue of extraterritorial enforcement of tax law relates to measures taken by a government to coerce foreign banks to disclose accounts held by nationals abroad, as practised by US tax authorities against the Swiss bank UBS with a John Doe Summons. It is controversial whether doing business in the United States subjects a bank to US jurisdiction as to accounts established abroad, especially if the coercion of the foreign bank circumvents an inter-governmental request provided in a bilateral treaty on taxation.[7]

In order to combat tax evasion, in October 2014 more than 50 States signed the OECD Multilateral Competent Authority Agreement on Automatic Exchange of Financial Account Information[8] which aims at implementing the OECD Standard for Automatic Exchange of Financial Account Information in Tax Matters.[9] Under the Agreement, States will automatically exchange financial data in conformity

[5] United Nations Model Double Taxation Convention between Developed and Developing Countries UNDoc ST/ESA/PAD/SER.E/21 (updated 2011).

[6] United States Income Model Tax Convention of 15 November 2006 <http://www.irs.gov/pub/irs-trty/model006.pdf> (accessed 23 June 2016).

[7] M Schaub, 'Zur völkerrechtlichen Zulässigkeit des amerikanischen Editionsbefehls an die UBS im Streit um die Kundendaten' (2011) 71 ZaöRV 807.

[8] See at <http://www.oecd.org/ctp/exchange-of-tax-information/multilateral-competent-authority-agreement.pdf> (accessed 23 June 2016).

[9] See at <http://www.keepeek.com/Digital-Asset-Management/oecd/taxation/standard-for-automatic-exchange-of-financial-account-information-for-tax-matters_9789264216525-en> (accessed 23 June 2016).

with the Multilateral Convention on Mutual Administrative Assistance in Tax Matters.[10] The information exchange shall begin in 2017.

Select Bibliography

A Amatucci, E Gonzalez, and C Trzaskalik, *International Tax Law* (Kluwer Law International 2006).

BJ Arnold and MJ McIntyre, *International Tax Primer* (2nd edn, Kluwer Law International 2002).

HJ Ault and BJ Arnold, *Comparative Income Taxation: A Structural Analysis* (3rd edn, Kluwer Law International 2010).

R Avi-Yonah, *International Tax as International Law: An Analysis of the International Tax Regime* (CUP 2007).

R Avi-Yonah, N Sartori, and O Marian, *Global Perspectives on Income Taxation Law* (OUP 2011).

MJ Graetz, *Foundations of International Income Taxation* (Foundation Press 2003).

CH Gustafson, RJ Peroni, and RC Pugh, *Taxation of International Transactions: Materials, Texts and Problems* (4th edn, West St Paul 2011).

Y Margalioth, 'International Taxation' in R Wolfrum (ed), *The Max Planck Encyclopedia of Public International Law* (OUP 2012) vol IX, 769.

[10] See at <http://www.keepeek.com/Digital-Asset-Management/oecd/taxation/the-multilateral-convention-on-mutual-administrative-assistance-in-tax-matters_9789264115606-en> (accessed 23 June 2016).

PART V

THE INTERNATIONAL LAW
OF FOREIGN INVESTMENT

PART V

THE INTERNATIONAL LAW OF FOREIGN INVESTMENT

XXXI

Foreign Investment in Practice

1. Economic and Political Relevance

Foreign investment is a crucial factor for economic and social development, sustained economic growth, poverty reduction, improved infrastructure, and financial stability.[1] The 'Monterrey Consensus', reached at the International Conference on Financing for Development of Monterrey (2002), recognizes the contribution of private international capital flows to long-term development and growth, especially of poorer countries, and calls for a favourable investment climate:

Private international capital flows, particularly foreign direct investment, along with international financial stability, are vital complements to national and international development efforts. Foreign direct investment contributes toward financing sustained economic growth over the long term. It is especially important for its potential to transfer knowledge and technology, create jobs, boost overall productivity, enhance competitiveness and entrepreneurship, and ultimately eradicate poverty through economic growth and development. A central challenge, therefore, is to create the necessary domestic and international conditions to facilitate direct investment flows, conducive to achieving national development priorities, to developing countries, particularly Africa, least developed countries, small island developing States, and landlocked developing countries, and also to countries with economies in transition.[2]

The adequate protection of foreign investments relates to economic growth and often contributes to the improvement of infrastructure and education.[3] Favourable conditions for foreign (and domestic) investments include a legal framework with reliable protection of property rights, an independent and effective judicial system,

---

[1] OECD, *Foreign Direct Investment for Development* (OECD Publications 2002); see L Colen, M Maertens, and J Swinnen, 'Foreign Direct Investment as an Engine for Economic Growth and Human Development: A Review of the Arguments and Empirical Relevance' (2009) 3 Hum Rts & Int'l Legal Discourse 177; E Neumayer and L Spess, 'Do Bilateral Investment Treaties Increase Foreign Direct Investment to Development Countries?' (2005) 33 World Development Report 1567; JW Salacuse, 'BIT by BIT: The Growth of Bilateral Investment Treaties and Their Impact on Foreign Investment in Developing Countries' (1990) 24 Int'l Law 655.

[2] 'Report of the International Conference on Financing for Development' (Monterrey, Mexico, 18–22 March 2002) UN Doc A/CONF.198/11 para 20.

[3] As the OECD points out in *Foreign Direct Investment for Development* (OECD Publications 2002) 5: 'FDI may help improve environmental and social conditions in the host country by, for example, transferring "cleaner" technologies and leading to more socially responsible corporate policies.'

legal certainty, and well-defined rules both for governmental interference and for entrepreneurial activities. In legal terms, a favourable investment climate is closely linked to the rule of law and 'good governance'. The regulatory balance between public interest (health, environmental protection, labour standards) and the legitimate interests of the investor is a lasting issue in international investment law. In July 2016 the G20 Ministerial Conference adopted the 'Guiding Principles for Global Investment Policymaking', which are based on preparatory work by UNCTAD.

2. Direct and Indirect Investment

Foreign investment is divided into direct investment and portfolio (indirect) investment. Various elements distinguish direct investment from other forms of investing capital: transfer of funds to an enterprise with a long-term perspective, some degree of control over the management, and the assumption of entrepreneurial risk.[4] The International Monetary Fund presented the standard definition of direct investment:

Direct investment is the category of international investment that reflects the objective of a resident entity in one economy obtaining a lasting interest in an enterprise resident in another economy (the resident entity is the direct investor and the enterprise is the direct investment enterprise). The lasting interest implies the existence of a long-term relationship between the direct investor and the enterprise and a significant degree of influence by the investor on the management of the enterprise. Direct investment comprises not only the initial transaction establishing the relationship between the investor and the enterprise but also all subsequent transactions between them and among affiliated enterprises, both incorporated and unincorporated.[5]

The World Bank defines foreign direct investment as follows:

Foreign direct investment are the net inflows of investment to acquire a lasting management interest (10 percent or more of voting stock) in an enterprise operating in an economy other than that of the investor. It is the sum of equity capital, reinvestment of earnings, other long-term capital, and short-term capital as shown in the balance of payments [...].[6]

By contrast, portfolio investment means the acquisition of shares, stocks, and bonds by foreign investors under terms which do not imply significant control over the respective business or other entrepreneurial functions of the investor. Portfolio investment does not focus on management interests or risks, but on an adequate return on capital.

The distinction between direct and portfolio investments gained relevance under the new powers of the European Union to conclude agreements relating to 'foreign

---

[4] R Dolzer and C Schreuer, *Principles of International Investment Law* (2nd edn, OUP 2012) 60; see also OECD, *Benchmark Definition of Foreign Direct Investment* (4th edn, OECD Publications 2008) 17.

[5] International Monetary Fund, *Balance of Payments Manual* (5th edn, 1993) para 359.

[6] World Bank Databank <http://data.worldbank.org/indicator/BX.KLT.DINV.WD.GD.ZS> (accessed 23 June 2016).

direct investment' (Article 207(1) TFEU). A strict understanding of the European Union's powers suggests that Member States retain competences for portfolio investments.[7]

The major part of foreign direct investments flows into industrialized economies like the United States, United Kingdom, the Netherlands, Australia, and Hong Kong as well as into certain emerging economies (such as China, India, Brazil, and Mexico). A large share of investments from China goes to Hong Kong. This indicates the importance of a good environment for investments with an open economy, a reliable legal system, and a stable financial sector. The low investment flows, often inferior even to development aid, to many less developed countries, especially of Sub-Saharan Africa, reflect serious deficiencies in the political system, the social and educational structure, the legal order and legal systems, often exacerbated by the lack of natural resources.

3. Investors

(a) Private and public investors

Most investors come from the private sector. However, many investors are corporations set up, owned, or controlled by the government of their home State. A number of internationally important investors are governmental agencies (eg entities of the central bank or the ministry of finance).

(b) Sovereign wealth funds

As a source of foreign direct investment from the public sector, sovereign wealth funds (SWFs) have gained enormous importance. The Generally Accepted Principles and Practices (GAPP or Santiago Principles) adopted by the International Working Group of Sovereign Wealth Funds in 2008 define sovereign wealth funds as

special purpose investment funds or arrangements, owned by the general government. Created by the general government for macroeconomic purposes, SWFs hold, manage, or administer assets to achieve financial objectives, and employ a set of investment strategies which include investing in foreign financial assets. The SWFs are commonly established out of balance of payments surpluses, official foreign currency operations, the proceeds of privatizations, fiscal surpluses, and/or receipts resulting from commodity exports.[8]

The European Central Bank qualifies sovereign investment funds 'as public investment agencies which manage part of the (foreign) assets of national states'.[9]

---

[7] See Ch XXXIV.1(b).

[8] International Working Group of *Sovereign Wealth Funds—Generally Accepted Principles and Practices—"Santiago Principles"* (October 2008) 27 <http://www.iwg-swf.org/pubs/eng/santiagoprinciples.pdf> (accessed 2 February 2016).

[9] R Beck and M Fidora, 'The Impact of Sovereign Wealth Funds on Global Financial Markets' (2008) 91 ECB Occasional Paper 6; see for a more precise overview, L Gramlich, 'An International Normative Framework for Sovereign Wealth Funds?' (2011) 2 EYIEL 45.

Sovereign wealth funds may be divided into five categories based on their objective: reserve investment corporations, pension reserve funds, fiscal stabilization funds, (long-term) fiscal saving, and development funds.[10] However, sovereign wealth funds may also pursue various objectives.

A number of countries have established sovereign wealth funds. Many of these funds owe their existence to revenues from the exploitation of natural resources. The United Arab Emirates, Singapore, Norway, Saudi Arabia, Kuwait, China, and Qatar own and operate the largest sovereign wealth funds (with fixed assets of more than USD 100 billion). The aggregated global value of sovereign wealth funds is estimated at about USD 10 trillion.[11]

The advocates of sovereign wealth funds argue that sovereign wealth funds are useful actors in the international monetary and economic system and that 'their investments have helped promote growth, prosperity, and economic development in capital-exporting and capital-receiving countries'.[12] Other voices point out that 'the growth of sovereign wealth funds reflects a dramatic redistribution of international wealth from traditional industrial countries like the United States to countries that historically have not been major players in the international financial system'.[13] Some strategic behaviour of sovereign wealth funds raises the suspicion that they serve as instruments of global competition between States for political and economic power.[14] High-technology industries, the raw material sector, and land rank high in the investment agenda of sovereign wealth funds.

The Generally Accepted Principles and Practices serve the objective

  i. [t]o help maintain a stable global financial system and free flow of capital and investment;
 ii. [t]o comply with all applicable regulatory and disclosure requirements in the countries in which they invest;
iii. [t]o invest on the basis of economic and financial risk and return-related considerations; and
 iv. [t]o have in place a transparent and sound governance structure that provides for adequate operational controls, risk management, and accountability.[15]

---

[10] L Gramlich, 'An International Framework for Sovereign Wealth Funds?' (2011) 2 EYIEL 43, 51.
[11] S Johnson, 'The Rise of Sovereign Wealth Funds' (2007) 44 Finance and Development 56; <http://www.imf.org/external/pubs/ft/fandd/2007/09/pdf/straight.pdf> (accessed 23 June 2016).
[12] Sovereign Wealth Funds—Generally Accepted Principles and Practices—Santiago Principles (October 2008) 3 <http://www.iwg-swf.org/pubs/eng/santiagoprinciples.pdf> (accessed 23 June 2016); see for a general analysis of the criticism and support of sovereign wealth funds, BJ Reed, 'Sovereign Wealth Funds: The New Barbarians at the Gate: An Analysis of the Legal and Business Implications of their Ascendancy' (2009) 4 Va L & Bus Rev 97.
[13] EM Truman, 'A Blueprint for Sovereign Wealth Fund Best Practices' (2008) No PB08–3 Peterson Institute Policy Brief 3.
[14] S Johnson, 'The Rise of Sovereign Wealth Funds' (2007) 44 Finance and Development 56 <http://www.imf.org/external/pubs/ft/fandd/2007/09/pdf/straight.pdf> (accessed 23 June 2016); H Schweitzer, 'Sovereign Wealth Funds: Market Investors or "Imperialist Capitalists"? The European Response to Direct Investment by Non-EU State-Controlled Entities' (2011) 2 EYIEL 79.
[15] International Working Group of Sovereign Wealth Funds, *Sovereign Wealth Funds—Generally Accepted Principles and Practices—"Santiago Principles"* (October 2008) 4 <http://www.iwg-swf.org/pubs/eng/santiagoprinciples.pdf> (accessed 23 June 2016).

Largest Sovereign Wealth Funds[16]		
Sovereign Wealth Fund Name	Country	Assets in USD Billion
Government Pension Fund—Global	Norway	847.6
Abu Dhabi Investment Authority	United Arab Emirates	792
China Investment Corporation	China	746.7
SAMA Foreign Holdings	Saudi Arabia	598.4
Kuwait Investment Authority	Kuwait	592
SAFE Investment Company	China	567.9

4. The Control of Foreign Investment

Under customary international law, a State's sovereignty allows it to freely condition and control the admission of foreign investors.[17] According to the 2016 UNCTAD World Investment Report, in 2015, no less than 46 countries worldwide adopted policy measures affecting foreign investment, mostly with the goal of liberalizing and stimulating foreign investment.[18] Many countries actually restrict foreign direct investments in 'strategic sectors' as, for example, the arms industry, commodity production, energy and water supply, telecommunication, and civil aviation. Regulations may entirely exclude strategic sectors from foreign investments or limit foreign direct investments (for example by setting a threshold of 49 per cent of equity capital). China, India, and Russia have very extensive restrictions in place (in general and in particular for strategic sectors). Some industrialized countries (for example France, Japan, and the United States) also subject foreign direct investments in some sectors to control and maintain restrictive measures.

In 1988, the US Congress enacted the Exon-Florio Amendment to review foreign direct investment which might affect national security.[19] The review lies with the Committee on Foreign Investments in the US (CFIUS), with the final decision on the restriction or interdiction of the investment being reserved to the President of the United States. In practice, US administrations have only blocked few foreign direct investments. The German Foreign Economic Relations Act allows restrictions on the purchase of companies or of shares by

---

[16] See for the overall ranking, <http://www.swfinstitute.org/sovereign-wealth-fund-rankings/> (accessed 23 June 2016).

[17] R Dolzer and C Schreuer, *Principles of International Investment Law* (2nd edn, OUP 2012) 227; A Joubin-Bret, 'Admission and Establishment in the Context of Investment Protection' in A Reinisch (ed), *Standards of Investment Protection* (OUP 2008) 9ff (10); OECD, *OECD's FDI Restrictiveness Index* (OECD Publications 2010).

[18] UNCTAD, *World Investment Report 2016* (United Nations Publications 2016) 90.

[19] 50 USC 2170.

non-EEA investors if the acquisition affects the public order or security of the Federal Republic of Germany.[20]

Select Bibliography

Ch Balding, *Sovereign Wealth Funds: The New Intersection of Money and Politics* (OUP 2012).

F Bassan, *The Law of Sovereign Wealth Funds* (Edward Elgar Publishing 2011).

AQ Curzio and V Miceli, *Sovereign Wealth Funds: A Complete Guide to State-owned Investment Funds* (Harriman House 2010).

R Dolzer and C Schreuer, *Principles of International Investment Law* (2nd edn, OUP 2012).

RJ Gilson and CJ Milhaupt, 'Sovereign Wealth Funds and Corporate Governance: A Minimalist Response to the New Mercantilism' (2008) 60 Stan L Rev 1345.

PJ Keenan and C Ochoa, 'The Human Rights Potential of Sovereign Wealth Funds' (2009) 40 GJIL L 1151.

L Loh, *Sovereign Wealth Funds: States Buying the World* (Global Professional Publishing 2010).

JJ Norton, 'The "Santiago Principles" and the International Forum of Sovereign Wealth Funds: Evolving Components of the New Bretton Woods II Post-Global Financial Crisis Architecture and Another Example of Ad Hoc Global Administrative Networking and Related "Soft" Rulemaking?' (2009–10) Rev Banking & Fin L 465.

A Persaud, *Sovereign Wealth Funds: The Long-Term Asset Management of National Savings* (John Wiley & Sons 2010).

R Sakar, 'Sovereign Wealth Funds: Furthering Development or Impeding It?' (2009) 40 GJIL L 1151.

KP Sauvant, LE Sachs, and WPF Schmit Jongbloed, *Sovereign Investment: Concerns and Policy Reactions* (OUP 2012).

H Schweitzer, 'Sovereign Wealth Funds: Market Investors or "Imperialist Capitalists"? The European Response to Direct Investment by Non-EU-State-Controlled Entities' (2011) 2 EYIEL 79.

EM Truman, *Sovereign Wealth Funds: Threat or Salvation?* (Peterson Institute for International Economics 2010).

---

[20] See § 47(12) no 46 of the German Foreign Economic Relations Act ('Deutsches Außenwirtschaftsgesetz') (as amended in 2015) and § 53 of the governmental regulation ('Verordnung zur Durchführung des Außenwirtschaftsgesetzes') implementing § 7(2) no 6 of the German Foreign Economic Relations Act; T Müller-Ibold, 'Foreign Investment in Germany: Restrictions Based on Public Security Concerns and their Compatibility with EU Law' (2010) 1 EYIEL 103ff.

XXXII

Customary International Law

1. Customary Standards and Foreign Investment

Rules relating to foreign international investments under customary law are rather rudimentary. Modern international investment law is clearly dominated by treaties, although treaty clauses are often meant to reflect or clarify customary standards. Under customary international law, States are free to decide whether or not they permit foreign investments within their territory. The freedom to exclude any form of foreign investment also implies that States may set their own conditions for the admission of foreign investments.[1] Once admitted and established, foreign investment enjoys some basic protection under the customary standard, especially in case of expropriation. In international law, any obligation of the host States as to admission, national treatment, or most-favoured-nation treatment derives from treaty law. Human rights, both under customary law and treaties, also provide some protection for foreign investors, for example in judicial proceedings. Among the customary rules on the treatment of foreigners (set out in greater detail above),[2] the most important is the so-called 'international minimum standard', which ensures treatment of foreign persons in terms of decency and grants them some degree of protection.[3] The international minimum standard overlaps with the standards of 'fair and equitable treatment' and of 'full protection and security' contained in modern investment treaties. The exact relationship between these two standards remains a controversial issue, unless it is clarified by the specific terms of a treaty or an interpretation by treaty bodies.[4]

Whilst some equate these treaty-based standards to the minimum standard, others understand them as distinct in scope. One of the areas in which customary law plays a major role pertains to the conditions for lawful expropriation.[5]

---

[1] See A Joubin-Bret, 'Admission and Establishment in the Context of Investment Protection' in A Reinisch (ed), *Standards of Investment Protection* (OUP 2008) 10.

[2] See Ch VI.4.   [3] See Ch VI.4(a).

[4] See Ch XXXIV.4(d).

[5] See SP Subedi, *International Investment Law* (2nd edn, Hart Publishing 2012) 73ff. For a detailed analysis of the relation between the FET standard and the international minimum standard see M Paparinskis, *The International Minimum Standard and Fair and Equitable Treatment* (OUP 2013) 83ff.

2. Expropriation and Compensation

(a) The conditions for lawful expropriation under customary international law

The taking of property by a State, like any other exercise of regulatory powers, requires a territorial or personal nexus with the expropriating State. In principle, every State may expropriate any property situated within its own borders.[6] The concept of 'expropriation' covers any deprivation of property rights.

The term 'property' in customary international law includes all alienable rights of private persons which have a market value, for example title to real and movable property, claims to payment, company shares, and intellectual property rights. Property in this sense also covers the 'goodwill' of a company, that is all business connections which affect the market value of the company and its market position.[7] The term 'property', however, does not cover purely volatile expectations and chances on the market.[8]

Expropriation may also be constituted by severe legal restrictions on the use which affect the core of property rights ('regulatory taking') or de facto interferences having a similar effect. The term 'nationalization' is often used to refer to expropriations of an entire sector (like the banking sector or the mining industry).[9] Expropriations without compensation are often referred to as 'confiscations'.[10]

As regards the expropriation of a State's own nationals, States, in principle, enjoy a broad margin of appreciation. Under constitutional law, expropriations must conform with fundamental rights to property including due ('just' or 'adequate') compensation; examples may be found in the Fifth Amendment to the US Constitution or Article 14 of the German Constitution. In addition, human rights treaties may also protect private property. Article 1 of the First Protocol to the European Convention on Human Rights provides:

Every natural or legal person is entitled to the peaceful enjoyment of his possessions. No one shall be deprived of his possessions except in the public interest and subject to the conditions provided for by law and by the general principles of international law.

The preceding provisions shall not, however, in any way impair the right of a State to enforce such laws as it deems necessary to control the use of property in accordance with the general interest or to secure the payment of taxes or other contributions or penalties.

The European Court of Human Rights interprets the reference to general principles of international law in Article 1(1) of the Protocol as referring only to the

---

[6] See Ch VI.4(a).

[7] For the opposite view in the early jurisprudence of the PCIJ, see *The Oscar Chinn Case (Britain v Belgium)* PCIJ Rep Series A/B No 63, 25. For an example of the consideration of the goodwill in case of an expropriation, see *American International Group, Inc v Islamic Republic of Iran* (1983 III) 4 Iran-USCTR 96 (106).

[8] PCIJ *The Oscar Chinn Case (Britain v Belgium)* PCIJ Rep Series A/B No 63, 25.

[9] See GM White, *Nationalisation of Foreign Property* (Stevens 1961).

[10] For a general outline of the protection of property in international law, see U Kriebaum and A Reinisch, 'Property, Right to, International Protection' in R Wolfrum (ed), *The Max Planck Encyclopedia of International Law* (OUP 2012) vol VIII, 522.

expropriation of foreigners. In the case of the expropriation of the State's own nationals, the Court derives the right to compensation from the principle of proportionality; an expropriation without due compensation amounts to an excessive sacrifice of the expropriated individual in the public interest.[11] The case-law of the Court accords a broad margin of appreciation to the Contracting States as to the terms of compensation, in particular in the case of nationalization of entire industry sectors.[12]

In EU law, the protection of property is part of the general principles of law which the European Court of Justice has developed on the basis of the European Convention on Human Rights and the different national constitutional traditions of EU Member States.[13] The Charter of Fundamental Rights of the European Union[14] guarantees the right to property and provides in Article 17 second sentence that

no one may be deprived of his or her possessions, except in the public interest and in the cases and under the conditions provided for by law, subject to fair compensation being paid in good time for their loss. The use of property may be regulated by law in so far as is necessary for the general interest.

According to Article 17(2) of the Charter 'intellectual property shall be protected'. The human right to property, as already recognized in the Universal Declaration of Human Rights (Article 17), is about to emerge as part of international customary law.

Under customary law, the 'international minimum standard' conditions the expropriation of foreigners. The reason for the special protection of non-nationals by international law lies in the fact that—in contrast to nationals—foreigners are usually excluded from the political process and from the political community which benefits from expropriations in the public interest; the payment of a due compensation re-establishes the proper balance of the private foreign interest and the interest of the public.[15]

According to the international minimum standard, the expropriation of foreigners must fulfil three conditions: it must serve a public purpose, it must be

---

[11] ECtHR *Lithgow v United Kingdom* (1986) Series A No 102 paras 112ff.

[12] ECtHR *Lithgow v United Kingdom* (1986) Series A No 102 para 122: 'A decision to enact nationalization legislation will commonly involve consideration of various issues on which opinions within a democratic society may reasonably differ widely. Because of their direct knowledge of their society and its needs and resources, the national authorities are in principle better placed than the international judge to appreciate what measures are appropriate in this area and consequently the margin of appreciation available to them should be a wide one. It would, in the Court's view, be artificial in this respect to divorce the decision as to the compensation terms from the actual decision to nationalise, since the factors influencing the latter will of necessity also influence the former.'

[13] ECJ Case C-44/79 *Liselotte Hauer v Land Rheinland-Pfalz* [1979] ECR I-3727 (3745).

[14] Charter of Fundamental Rights of the European Union [2000] OJ C364/1.

[15] See *Lithgow v United Kingdom* (1986) Series A No 102 para 116: 'Especially as regards a taking of property effected in the context of a social reform or an economic restructuring, there may well be good grounds for drawing a distinction between nationals and non-nationals as far as compensation is concerned. To begin with, non-nationals are more vulnerable to domestic legislation: unlike nationals, they will generally have played no part in the election of designation of its authors nor have been consulted on its adoption. Secondly, although a taking of property must always be effected in the public interest, different considerations may apply to nationals and non-nationals and there may well be legitimate reasons for requiring nationals to bear a greater burden in the public interest than non-nationals.'

non-discriminatory, and due compensation must be paid.[16] International case-law has mainly focused on the issue of proper compensation.

(b) Elements of expropriation

An expropriation, which calls for compensation, may take forms other than straight-forward deprivation of property. Severe restrictions on the use of the property may also amount to expropriation, if they essentially destroy the economic functions of the property or otherwise substantially affect its value. Examples are the cancella-tion of the permit to operate a power plant or a production site or the imposition of conditions which render an operation unprofitable. Common usage refers to these forms of interferences as 'de facto expropriation' or, if this process involves a gradual erosion of property rights over a long period of time, as 'creeping expropriation'. Another term used in this context is 'indirect expropriation' (a term which may also refer to the taking of company shares as opposed to direct expropriation of the company).[17] De facto expropriations are characterized by the erosion of the owner's legal or factual possibilities to derive reasonable economic benefit from the use of property (adequate in relation to the initial investment), leaving the right holder with the mere shell of a title.

The Iran–US Claims Tribunal assumed a de facto expropriation in a case in which a US company, in a joint venture with an Iranian company, operated a building project on real estate bought by the US company in Iran. The Iranian Government pushed the company out of the project management by nominating an administra-tor for the project.[18] In this context the arbitral tribunal stated:

[I]t is recognized in international law that measures taken by a State can interfere with property rights to such an extent that these rights are rendered so useless that they must be deemed to have been expropriated, even though the State does not purport to have expro-priated them and the legal title to the property formally remains with the original owner.[19]

Similarly, in *Tippets et al v TAMS-AFFA*, the Iran–US Claims Tribunal qualified the establishment of control by the Iranian government by appointing a manager who assumed administration without consulting the shareholders as an expropriation:

A deprivation or taking of property may occur under international law through interference by a state in the use of that property or with the enjoyment of its benefits, even where legal title to the property is not affected.

While assumption of control over property by a government does not automatically and immediately justify a conclusion that the property has been taken by the government, thus

---

[16] U Kriebaum and A Reinisch, 'Property, Right to, International Protection' in R Wolfrum (ed), *The Max Planck Encyclopedia of International Law* (OUP 2012) vol VIII, 522 (525ff).

[17] R Dolzer, 'Indirect Expropriation of Alien Property' (1986) 1 ICSID Rev 41; LY Fortier and SL Drymer, 'Indirect Expropriation in the Law of International Investment: I Know It When I See It, or Caveat Investor' (2004) 19 ICSID Rev 293.

[18] *Starrett Housing Corporation v Islamic Republic of Iran* (1983 III) 4 Iran-USCTR 122. See the arbitral award in the case *Biloune and Marine Drive Complex Ltd v Ghana Investments Centre and the Government of Ghana* (1994) 95 ILR 183 (207ff).

[19] *Starrett Housing Corporation v Islamic Republic of Iran* (1983 III) 4 Iran-USCTR 122 (154).

requiring compensation under international law, such a conclusion is warranted whenever events demonstrate that the owner was deprived of fundamental rights of ownership and it appears that this deprivation is now merely ephemeral. The intent of the government is less important than the effects of the measures on the owner, and the form of the measures of control or interference is less important than the reality of their impact.[20] ✕

Modern treaty practice addresses acts whose effects are similar to an expropriation. The North American Free Trade Agreement (NAFTA) in its Chapter 11 does not only cover expropriations in the traditional sense, but also measures 'tantamount to nationalization or expropriation' (Article 1110 of NAFTA).[21] In the case *Metalclad Corp v United Mexican States*, the arbitral tribunal, in order to determine whether an expropriation had taken place or not, focused on the detrimental effect of the governmental measures:

Thus, expropriation under NAFTA includes not only open, deliberate and acknowledged takings of property, such as outright seizure or formal or obligatory transfer of title in favour of the host State, but also covert or incidental interference with the use of property which has the effect of depriving the owner, in whole or in significant part, of the use or reasonably-to-be-expected economic benefit of property even if not necessarily to the obvious benefit of the host State.[22]

The modern broad understanding of expropriation also includes regulatory measures which deprive an investment of its value, minimize the return of profits, or which otherwise severely affect its economic substance ('regulatory taking').[23] According to this understanding, the host State may have to compensate for governmental measures destroying or shaking the legal or economic basis of an investment project.[24] The obligation of the host State to compensate for measures equivalent to expropriation does not only result from treaties on investment protection, but is actually part of customary international law.

When determining indirect or de facto expropriation, modern practice in investment arbitration tends to focus on the impact of regulatory and other measures on the operational capacity of the enterprise affected. In *LG&E Energy Corp. et al v Republic of Argentina* the arbitral tribunal held:

[I]n evaluating the degree of the measure's interference with the investor's right of ownership, one must analyze the measure's economic impact—its interference with the investor's reasonable expectations—and the measure's duration.

---

[20] *Tippets et al v TAMS-AFFA* (1984 II) 6 Iran-USCTR 219 (225f).

[21] See later at Ch XXXIV.4(g).

[22] *Metalclad Corporation v United Mexican States*, ICSID Case No ARB(AF)/97/1 (Award) (2001) 40 ILM 36 para 103. This arbitral award was subsequently annulled because it applied a standard of transparency which was not covered by Chapter 11 of NAFTA; see Supreme Court of British Columbia 2001 BCSC 664.

[23] See A Newcombe, 'The Boundaries of Regulatory Expropriation in International Law' (2005) 20 ICSID Rev 1; SR Ratner, 'Regulatory Takings in Institutional Context: Beyond the Fear of Fragmented International Law' (2008) 102 AJIL 475.

[24] For certain planning requirements as a condition for the construction of a project, see *MTD Equity Sdn Bhd and MTD Chile SA v Republic of Chile*, ICSID Case No ARB/01/7 (Award 2004) (2005) 44 ILM 91.

In considering the severity of the economic impact, the analysis focuses on whether the economic impact unleashed by the measure adopted by the host State was sufficiently severe as to generate the need for compensation due to expropriation. In many arbitral decisions, the compensation has been denied when it has not affected all or almost all the investment's economic value. Interference with the investment's ability to carry on its business is not satisfied where the investment continues to operate, even if profits are diminished. The impact must be substantial in order that compensation may be claimed for the expropriation.[25]

Under the BIT between China und Peru, in *Tza Jap Shum v. Republic of Peru*, the arbitral tribunal qualified (discriminatory) provisional measures of the Peruvian tax authority which imposed a tax lien blocking a company's access to bank account and deposits as expropriation because the measures 'not only reduced the profit generating capacity of the business but essentially eliminated or frustrated the operational capacity of the enterprise'.[26]

The concepts of de facto expropriation and of regulatory measures equivalent to expropriation are two of the central problems of the modern law of expropriation and investment protection. This holds particularly true for regulatory measures which do not necessarily confer an economic benefit on the host State. When the interference with property rights is not matched by a corresponding advantage for the State in economic terms, it is particularly difficult to determine whether an expropriation is given or not. Such regulatory interferences with the use of property may amount to an expropriation, but they may also be classified as general regulatory measures which do not trigger a duty to compensate. In particular, regulatory measures for the protection of the environment and of public health make it difficult to draw the line. Within the last decades, the problem of a reasonable differentiation has become more and more important.

In the *Tecmed v Mexico* case, the arbitral tribunal clarified that measures in the interest of environmental protection or other important public interests may, under certain circumstances, be classified as measures equivalent to expropriation.[27] Addressing the balance between essential public interests on the one hand and the economic rights and legitimate expectations of the rights holder on the other, the arbitral tribunal emphasized the aspect of proportionality, referring to the case-law of the European Court of Human Rights on the right to property (Article 1 of the First Protocol to the European Convention on Human Rights).[28] In *Tecmed v Mexico*, the arbitral tribunal held that the qualification of a measure as expropriatory essentially

---

[25] *LG&E Energy Corp., LG&E Capital Corp. and LG&E International Inc. v Argentine Republic*, ICSID Case No ARB/02/1 (Decision on Liability 2006) paras 190f.

[26] *Tza Yap Shum v Republic of Peru*, ICSID Case No ARB/07/6 (Award 2011) para 162. The Ad Hoc Committee rejected Peru's argument that the arbitral tribunal had engaged in a manifest excess of powers and failed to state reason in support to its approach to expropriation, see *Tza Yap Shum v Republic of Peru*, ICSID Case No ARB/07/6 (Decision on Annulment 2015) paras 73ff, 169ff.

[27] *Técnicas Medioambientales Tecmed SA v The United Mexican States*, ICSID Case No ARB(AF)/00/2 (Award) (2004) 43 ILM 133 para 121.

[28] *Técnicas Medioambientales Tecmed SA v The United Mexican States*, ICSID Case No ARB(AF)/00/2 (Award) (2004) 43 ILM 133 paras 122ff.

depends on its effect, that is on the degree in which the measure affects the economic value of the property right:

[I]t is understood that the measures adopted by a State, whether regulatory or not, are an indirect de facto expropriation if they are irreversible and permanent and if the assets or rights subject to such measure have been affected in such a way that [...] any form of exploitation thereof [...] has disappeared; i.e. the economic value of the use, enjoyment or disposition of the assets or rights affected by the administrative action or decision have been neutralized or destroyed. Under international law, the owner is also deprived of property where the use or enjoyment of benefits related thereto is exacted or interfered with a similar extent, even where legal ownership over the assets in question is not affected, and so long as the deprivation is not temporary. The government's intention is less important than the effects of the measures on the owner of the assets or on the benefits arising from such assets affected by the measures; and the form of the deprivation measure is less important than its actual effects.[29]

Additionally, the legitimate expectations of the owner as well as an appropriate balance between the conflicting interests of the host State and the owner are relevant.[30]

In *Ethyl Corp v Government of Canada*,[31] a US corporation which produced and marketed additives for unleaded fuel (MMT) in Canada through a Canadian subsidiary, challenged a Canadian federal law prohibiting trade in and import of MMT beyond the borders of the Canadian provinces. Canada tried to justify the prohibition by referring to the danger to health flowing from fuel emissions which involve MMT. Ethyl Corp initiated arbitral proceedings against Canada according to Chapter 11 of NAFTA and pleaded that the Canadian restriction on market access had an expropriatory effect. After the arbitral tribunal affirmed jurisdiction over the case, Canada withdrew the regulation and paid compensation.

Some critics fear that environmental protection may be seriously undermined by investment protection and the risk of compensation obligations.[32] Recent treaty practice responds to these concerns.[33]

The range of assets that may be expropriated is very broad and includes movable property, real property, bank accounts, shares of companies, and certain rights of use like concessions for the extraction of oil, gas, or metals. It is a controversial issue how far the infringement of commercial and similar contracts between the State and a foreign company may constitute an expropriation. The international rules

---

[29] *Técnicas Medioambientales Tecmed SA v The United Mexican States*, ICSID Case No ARB(AF)/00/2 (Award 2003) (2004) 43 ILM 133 para 116.

[30] See Ch XXXIV.4(d).

[31] *Ethyl Corporation v Government of Canada* (UNCITRAL Award on Jurisdiction 1998) (1999) 38 ILM 700ff; see AC Swan, 'Ethyl Corporation v Canada, Award on Jurisdiction' (2000) 94 AJIL 159.

[32] See P Sands, *Lawless World* (Penguin Books 2006) 117ff; K Tienhaara, *The Expropriation of Environmental Governance: Protecting Foreign Investors at the Expense of Public Policy* (CUP 2009).

[33] See Ch XXXIV.4(g).

on expropriation do not cover all kinds of contractual claims of a foreign investor against the host State. Otherwise, all infringements of contractual duties of the host State—for example a belated delivery of certain goods—would constitute an expropriation. According to a view developed in the United States, the breach of a contract by a sovereign act gives rise to State responsibility if the host State acted in a discriminatory or arbitrary manner.[34]

(c) Unlawful expropriation and restitution

Expropriations of foreign assets which as such (ie independent of the issue of compensation) violate international law, for example for being discriminatory, result in the duty to provide restitution. This duty means either to restore the state of affairs which existed before the infringement (natural restitution) or to pay full compensation.[35] Due financial restitution must redress any financial loss directly caused by the expropriation (*damnum emergens*) and, moreover, compensate for lost profit (*lucrum cessans*). This comprehensive compensation is particularly relevant if the taking of foreign property constitutes a breach of an investment treaty or a concession agreement with the foreign investor which is binding under international law.

(d) Due compensation

The amount of due compensation is one of the central issues of the international law of expropriation. The 'Calvo doctrine',[36] developed towards the end of the 19th century by the Argentinian international lawyer Carlos Calvo, subjects foreign persons to the same standard of protection as nationals, including due compensation.[37] This doctrine of national treatment was not adopted at the international level.[38] The prevailing doctrine of compensation has found its classic expression in the 'Hull formula', named after former US Secretary of State Cordell Hull. According to the Hull formula, compensation must be 'prompt, adequate and effective'. 'Effective' compensation means that it must be paid in a freely convertible currency.

In the 1960s and 1970s, the demand of developing countries for greater liberty to expropriate foreign property and to loosen the standard of full compensation became more and more important. This call for enlarged discretion to determine due compensation was closely associated with the push for a 'New Economic

---

[34] See American Law Institute, *Restatement (Third) of the Foreign Relations Law of the United States* (1987) vol 2, § 712(2).

[35] PCIJ *Case Concerning the Factory at Chorzów (Germany v Poland)* (Merits) PCIJ Rep Series A No 17, 47: 'The essential principle contained in the actual notion of an illegal act [...] is that reparation must, as far as possible, wipe out all the consequences of the illegal act and reestablish the situation which would, in all probability, have existed if that act had not been committed. Restitution in kind or, if this is not possible, payment of the sum corresponding to the value which restitution in kind could bear [must be made] [...]'.

[36] See earlier at Ch VI.4(b).

[37] See SP Subedi, *International Investment Law* (2nd edn, Hart Publishing 2012) 13ff, 186f.

[38] See Ch VI.4(b); BVerfGE 84, 90 (123).

Order'. It found an echo in the United Nations and is reflected, in particular, in the Charter of the Economic Rights and Duties of States of 1974. The Charter was adopted by the General Assembly of the United Nations with a large majority, while the important industrial States voted against or abstained.[39] Following the terms of Resolution 1803 (1962) of the UN General Assembly on the Permanent Sovereignty over Natural Resources, the 1974 Charter does not require 'full compensation' for expropriations of foreign property, but merely 'appropriate compensation' (Article 2(2)(c)). However, all the time, Western States maintained the classical standard of full compensation. This development with a divided international community brought about a considerable degree of legal uncertainty.[40]

In State practice, before and after the Second World War, a number of controversies over large-scale expropriations, especially by communist regimes, were settled in 'lump sum agreements'.[41] Under those agreements, the amount of compensation paid by the expropriating State varied between 20 and 80 per cent of the market value. In the past, the lump sum agreements served as a popular argument in support of the view that international law requires less than full compensation. Such bilateral agreements, however, are amicable settlements rather reflecting the will to compromise and other political considerations than a legal position on the standard of compensation.[42] Many of those agreements refer to expropriations which occurred many years ago or which were fruits of revolutionary processes driven by ideologies entirely hostile to the idea of compensation.

In the last decades, the issue of the level of due compensation under customary international law has lost much of its relevance. From the perspective of many developing countries, the quest for foreign investment and the efforts to create a favourable investment climate have dismissed expropriations as an unsuitable instrument of economic policy, at least as a matter of general policy. The collapse of socialist systems has resulted in a new balance of powers in favour of the classical position on expropriation in the international community. Many investment treaties follow the standard of full compensation or even refer to the market value as a basis for compensation. Finally, a great number of arbitral rulings have stressed that customary international law in principle demands full compensation for expropriations.[43] The case-law of the Iran–US Claims Tribunal in The Hague, as a rule, followed this line in connection with the expropriation of US assets after the revolution in Iran.[44] The *obiter dictum* in one decision of the Tribunal that in case of a nationalization of complete branches of industry less than full compensation may

[39] (1974) UNYB 402; see Ch II.2.
[40] See the arbitral award in the case *LIAMCO (Libyan American Oil Co v Libyan Arab Republic)* (1981) 20 ILM 53.
[41] See R Bank and F Foltz, 'Lump Sum Agreements' in R Wolfrum (ed), *The Max Planck Encyclopedia of Public International Law* (OUP 2012) vol VI, 950.
[42] See the arbitral award in the case *TOPCO/CALASIATIC v Libyan Arab Republic* (1978) 17 ILM 1 (24).
[43] See PM Norton, 'A Law of the Future or a Law of the Past? Modern Tribunals and the International Law of Expropriation' (1991) 85 AJIL 474.
[44] See eg *American International Group, Inc v Islamic Republic of Iran* (1983 III) 4 Iran-USCTR 96 (105ff).

be due, remains a singular and exceptional statement.[45] At the present time, the view that customary international law requires full compensation for the taking of foreign property is much more consolidated than two or three decades ago.[46]

Full compensation usually refers to the market value of the asset. When a company which actively participates in economic life is expropriated, modern arbitral practice tends not to focus on the net book value (the value of the investment net of amortizations), but on the current market value of the company including the goodwill (the fair market value).[47] According to the famous formula of the Iran–US Claims Tribunal's ruling in *Starrett Housing Corp v Islamic Republic of Iran*, the determination of the fair market value depends on what an interested and well informed buyer would be willing to pay for the asset:

[T]he price that a willing buyer would pay to a willing seller in circumstances in which each had good information, each desired to maximize his financial gain, and neither was under duress or threat.[48]

For the evaluation of a 'going concern', beyond the current value of the assets, future profits must be taken into account. On this basis, full compensation according to 'going concern value' comes very close to the compensation due in cases of illegal expropriations, which also covers lost profits. A widely recognized valuation method is the 'discounted cash flow method' referring to the future cash flow which will be generated by the investment, with a discount for costs and economic risks.[49]

3. The Extraterritorial Effects of Expropriations

If an asset is situated in the expropriating State, the territorial jurisdiction of the State covers any form of regulation as to this asset including the transfer of ownership. Within their own territory, States can regulate the transfer of property as well as effectively enforce it. The situation is different if the expropriated asset is later taken abroad.

Most problematic are expropriations of assets which are situated abroad at the time of taking. States may try to vest expropriation with an extraterritorial reach on

---

[45] *INA Corporation v Islamic Republic of Iran* (1985 I) 8 Iran-USCTR 373 (378); the later jurisprudence of the Tribunal did not join this idea and stressed the full compensation standard of customary international law, see *Sola Tiles Inc v Islamic Republic of Iran* (1987 I) 14 Iran-USCTR 223 (234ff); *Amoco International Finance Corporation v Islamic Republic of Iran* (1987 II) 15 Iran-USCTR 189 (223).

[46] See American Law Institute, *Restatement (Third) of the Foreign Relations Law of the United States* (1987) vol 2, § 712(1).

[47] *American International Group, Inc v Islamic Republic of Iran* (1983 III) 4 Iran-USCTR 96 (106); American Law Institute, *Restatement (Third) of the Foreign Relations Law of the United States* (1987) vol 2, § 712. The market value is also taken into account by the guidelines of the World Bank for the treatment of foreign direct investments (s III.3) (1992) 31 ILM 1379.

[48] *Starrett Housing Corporation v Islamic Republic of Iran* (1987 III) 16 Iran-USCTR 112 (201).

[49] *Starrett Housing Corporation v Islamic Republic of Iran* (1987 III) 16 Iran-USCTR 112 (126, 201ff).

the basis of personal jurisdiction, for example by expropriating a domestic company with assets located abroad. In this case, it is up to the foreign State where the assets are situated either to accord or to deny recognition to such exercise of personal jurisdiction and to its extraterritorial effects.

(a) The transfer of expropriated assets abroad

As a rule, States will recognize expropriations by foreign States if the expropriated assets are situated in the expropriating State ('positive territoriality principle'). The former owner of the asset can no longer claim the surrender value. The positive territoriality principle corresponds to the conflict of laws rule which, for the issue of ownership, refers to the law of the State where the expropriated asset is situated as the applicable law (*lex rei sitae*).

Complications arise if the expropriation violates standards of international law, for example because it was discriminatory or because due compensation was not paid. Under international law, other States are, in principle, free to recognize or not an expropriation which is contrary to international legal standards. Thus, a State may treat the taking of property as valid even though the expropriation fell short of the international standard of compensation. Only in exceptional cases of aggravated disrespect of international law, for example the violation of human rights by racial discrimination, recognition may amount to a 'perpetuation' of the violation and entail the recognizing State's responsibility for complicity.

The courts of many countries exercise the scrutiny discretion as the non-recognition of unlawful expropriations with restraint. The act of State doctrine[50] prevents courts from reviewing foreign sovereign acts as to their conformity with international law.[51] In *Luther v Sagor*, the English Court of Appeal applied the act of State doctrine to the confiscation of property in the Soviet Union and held that English courts will not question the validity of legislative acts of another State which affect the title to property within this State's territory.[52] In the United States, the Supreme Court followed the act of State doctrine in the case *Banco Nacional de Cuba v Sabbatino* and upheld the expropriation of a US national in Cuba as valid.[53] The US Congress, displeased with the judgment, enacted the (Second) Hickenlooper Amendment ('Sabbatino Amendment') to the Foreign Assistance Act[54] which directs courts not to apply the act of State doctrine in cases of expropriations unless the US President determines that application of the doctrine is required in a particular case by the foreign policy interests of the United States.

---

[50] See F de Quadros and JH Dingfelder Stone, 'Act of State Doctrine' in R Wolfrum (ed), *The Max Planck Encyclopedia of Public International Law* (OUP 2012) vol I, 62ff.

[51] See Ch VI.8(f).   [52] *Luther v Sagor* [1921] KB 532.

[53] *Banco Nacional de Cuba v Sabbatino* 376 US 398 (1964).

[54] 23 USC 2370(e)(2); see also American Law Institute, *Restatement (Third) of the Foreign Relations Law of the United States* (1987) vol 1, § 444.

German courts only review expropriations by other States with respect to their conformity with international law if there is a sufficient substantive nexus of the expropriation to Germany. Such a sufficient substantive nexus with Germany at the point of time of the expropriation ('domestic and temporal relation')[55] would be present if a German national is expropriated abroad. The review of foreign expropriations, triggered by the nexus to Germany, focuses on conformity with the German public order (*ordre public*), which refers to the fundamental principles of the German legal order (Article 6 of the Introductory Statute to the Civil Code). The German *ordre public* also includes the rules of customary international law and the general principles of international law incorporated by Article 25 of the German Constitution into domestic law. Once a sufficient connection with Germany can be established, German authorities and courts will not recognize foreign expropriations, if they are contrary to international law.

The *Chilean copper* dispute provides an illustrative example for the required connection. This dispute turned on the expropriation of Chilean copper mines owned by US companies. Copper from such a mine was shipped to a German company in Hamburg. The expropriated owner of the mine brought an action for restitution and invoked the unlawfulness of the expropriation, because the Chilean government had not paid due compensation. The District Court of Hamburg[56] confirmed the principle that an expropriation within the territory of the expropriating State will be recognized. The court did not question the expropriation, because it did not discern any sufficient nexus to Germany. The mere transport of the copper into German territory was not considered sufficient for creating such a nexus. The court quite openly explained that its view was also guided by the fear of political and economic frictions.[57]

In a similar case, the *Indonesian tobacco* dispute, the Court of Appeal of Bremen likewise deferred to concerns about economic interests.[58] In this case, a Dutch company, whose tobacco plantations had been nationalized in Indonesia, tried to recover a cargo of tobacco which had been shipped to Bremen, which hosts an important tobacco exchange. The Court of Appeal of Bremen displayed great reluctance to challenge foreign expropriation on the basis of international law:

[I]t is true that, if the courts of all States unanimously granted the former owner a right to reclaim of property due to the nullity of the nationalisation statutes, this could achieve the result that the confiscating State would be blocked and could not engage in trade with the expropriated goods any more. But at the same time the entire world trade would be affected and disturbed [...].[59]

This approach, apparently guided by concern for international trade, in the end served Bremen's position as a focal point of global tobacco trade.

---

[55] See BVerfGE 84, 90 (123).
[56] LG Hamburg (1973) 12 ILM 251; for the Chilean Copper Dispute see AF Lowenfeld, 'Chilean Copper, Nationalization, Review by Courts of Third States' in R Wolfrum (ed), *The Max Planck Encyclopedia of Public International Law* (OUP 2012) vol II, 145.
[57] LG Hamburg (1973) 12 ILM 251   [58] (1961/62) 9 AVR 318.
[59] (1961/62) 9 AVR 318 (352).

(b) The direct and the indirect expropriation of property situated abroad

An important property situated abroad issue of recognition relates to assets which were situated in a foreign State at the time of expropriation. This issue arises when a State, on the basis of its personal jurisdiction, extends the expropriation of a domestic company to corporate assets located abroad. Effectiveness of such an expropriation depends on whether the State, in which the property is situated, recognizes the expropriation. State practice follows the tendency that such expropriations of foreign assets are not recognized ('negative territoriality principle'). According to this widely applied principle, States will not recognize the transfer of title as to assets which are situated within their own territory. Thus, the attempt of a State to exercise sovereign powers over assets situated in another State and to directly expropriate extraterritorially will, as a rule, fail.

The case-law of the German Federal Court of Justice has extensively dealt with the issues of extraterritorial expropriation. According to the Federal Court of Justice, the expropriation of companies by a foreign State will not have any legal effects on the corporate assets situated in Germany.[60]

(c) The indirect expropriation of property situated abroad

More complex are the legal effects of the 'indirect expropriation' of a domestic company through expropriation of all or the principal shareholders. In this case, title to the company's assets formally remains unchanged. Still, in material terms, the company and the exercise of property rights are now controlled by the expropriating State. The expropriating State can, through the expropriation of the shareholders, achieve what it cannot attain through direct expropriation, that is control of the corporate property situated abroad.

Beyond implications under international law, the indirect expropriation of corporate property may raise constitutional issues in the country where assets are located, for many constitutions subject the expropriation of property to a legislative authorization and the payment of due compensation (see eg the Fifth Amendment of the US Constitution, Article 14(3) of the German Constitution). These constitutional standards, applied with the necessary modifications, may condition the recognition for foreign expropriations and their legal effects on corporate assets within domestic territory.

The German Federal Court of Justice approaches recognition of indirect expropriation of corporate assets through taking control of a company with great caution.[61] According to its view, a foreign State ought not to achieve control over assets situated in Germany just by evading the form of direct expropriation. The Federal Court of Justice follows the negative territoriality principle especially in cases in which the foreign State tried to gain control over the company's assets by expropriating

---

[60] BGHZ 25, 134 (143): 'Measures of expropriation of a State [...] only extend to the property which is subject to the territorial sovereignty of the country and may not reach beyond its frontiers'.
[61] BGHZ 25, 134 (144f); 62, 340 (343).

non-nationals in violation of international law, for example without compensation (confiscation):

The limits drawn by the territoriality principle [...] apply, if the assets of a legal person are expropriated. They also form the outer limits for the confiscation of shareholder rights at least when the shareholder rights are entirely or nearly entirely in foreign hands. According to general legal opinion, based on a natural perspective, in these cases the seizure of the shareholder rights has to be equated with the seizure of the assets of the legal person. It therefore cannot reach any further than a common confiscation of foreign assets. Otherwise, in those cases the territoriality principle would be disregarded and be replaced by an artificial legal manoeuvre which ultimately consists in the seizure of shareholder rights in a legal person which are entirely or nearly entirely in foreign hands instead of seizing the assets.[62]

In case of the expropriation of a company's shares by a foreign State, the German Federal Court of Justice developed the 'splitting doctrine' in order to eliminate extraterritorial effects on corporate assets which are situated in Germany. According to this doctrine, the corporate assets must be attributed to a new company split away from the expropriated company with the same circle of shareholders.[63] By creating such a 'split company', the Court tries to preserve the assets situated in Germany for the expropriated shareholders of the original company. The German 'splitting doctrine' has been the subject of a long controversy.[64] The fictional existence of a 'split company' destroys the economic and legal unity of the company and its property. The territoriality principle supports competing claims to jurisdiction. Shareholder rights are situated in the home State of the company (ie the State in which the company has its administrative seat or where it was founded). All these considerations rather suggest a model of balancing interests which is more flexible than the radical solution of the 'splitting doctrine'. This model would consider the amount of due compensation and the presence of nationals and non-nationals among the expropriated shareholders. As a rule, the interests of expropriated shareholders as relevant assets can be accommodated with an adequate pay-off. Within these parameters, the courts of one country should recognize the expropriation of shareholders in another country.

The issue of adequate compensation in terms of constitutional law emerged in connection with the French law of 1982 on the nationalization of certain industrial companies, banks, and financial companies and its effects on property situated in Germany. The nationalization extended to subsidiaries and holdings abroad. Compensation was based on the stock market price before expropriation and was to be paid in the form of long-term bonds with a very

---

[62] BGHZ 62, 340 (343).
[63] BGHZ 25, 134 (144ff); 62, 340 (343).
[64] See with further reference M Herdegen, 'Die extraterritoriale Wirkung der Enteignung von Mitgliedschaftsrechten an Gesellschaften in der Bundesrepublik Deutschland' (1991) 20 ZGR 547 (550ff).

moderate interest rate. Claims of expropriated shareholders with respect to corporate assets situated abroad failed before the Belgian and Swiss courts. In Germany, it was disputed whether or not the French expropriations of 1982 could be recognized with respect to the assets located in Germany. The principle underlying Article 14(3) of the German Constitution calls for compensation for the indirect expropriation of property in Germany as a precondition for recognition. However, the required standard of compensation must consider the localization of shareholder rights in the company's home State and is therefore lower than in cases of direct expropriation by the German State. Substantial compensation (higher than half of the asset's market value) must be sufficient for recognition.[65]

The decision of the British House of Lords in the case *Rumasa*[66] reflects a tendency to recognize the expropriation of shareholder rights with extraterritorial effect in case of converging interests of the States involved. In this case, a British subsidiary of Rumasa invoked certain industrial property rights with regard to a popular sherry brand before the English courts. The shareholders of the Spanish company Rumasa had been expropriated. Thus, in a way, the Spanish State stood behind the subsidiary's claim. The House of Lords rejected the respondent's argument that, through the claim, Spain in fact attempted to enforce the expropriation in the United Kingdom. Rather, the House of Lords assumed that the expropriation had already been completed in Spain. Referring to the then forthcoming accession of Spain to the European Union, the highest British court demonstrated a willingness to recognize the Spanish measures of expropriation with respect to British subsidiaries of indirectly nationalized Spanish companies:

[A]n English court will recognise the compulsory acquisition law of a foreign state and will recognise the change of title to property which has come under the control of the foreign state and will recognise the consequences of that change of title. The English court will decline to consider the merits of compulsory acquisition. In their pleadings the appellants seek to attack the motives of the Spanish legislators, to allege oppression on the part of the Spanish government and to question the good faith of the Spanish administration in connection with the enactment, terms and implementation of the law of the 29 June 1983. No English judge could properly entertain such an attack launched on a friendly state which will shortly become a fellow member of the European Economic Community.[67]

This judgment illustrates how policy considerations may determine the (non-) recognition of foreign expropriations affecting local assets.

---

[65] See M Herdegen, 'Die extraterritoriale Wirkung der Enteignung von Mitgliedschaftsrechten an Gesellschaften in der Bundesrepublik Deutschland' (1991) 20 ZGR 544(567f).

[66] *Williams & Humbert Ltd v W & H Trade Mark (Jersey) Ltd* [1986] 1 AC 368.

[67] *Williams & Humbert Ltd v W & H Trade Mark (Jersey) Ltd* [1986] 1 AC 431 per Lord Templeman. The Court assumed that there was a compensation mechanism for the shareholders without further reference.

Select Bibliography

EXPROPRIATION AND COMPENSATION

R Dolzer, 'Foundations of the Law of Expropriation of Alien Property' (1981) 75 AJIL 553.

R Dolzer, 'Indirect Expropriations: New Developments?' (2002) 11 NYU Envt'l LJ 64.

R Higgins, 'The Taking of Property by the State, Recent Developments in International Law' (1982 III) 176 RdC 259.

AK Hoffmann, 'Indirect Expropriation' in A Reinisch (ed), *Standards of Investment Protection* (OUP 2008) 151.

E Jiménez de Aréchaga, 'State Responsibility for the Nationalization of Foreign Owned Property' (1978) 11 NYU J Int'L L & Pol 179.

G Lagergren, *Five Important Cases on Nationalisation of Foreign Property* (Raoul Wallenberg Institute of Human Rights and Humanitarian Law 1988).

RB Lillich (ed), *The Valuation of Nationalized Property in International Law* (University Press of Virginia 1972) 4 vols.

S López Escarcena, *Indirect Expropriation in International Law* (Edward Elgar Publishing 2014).

I Marboe, *Calculation of Compensation and Damages in International Investment Law* (OUP 2009).

A Newcombe, 'The Boundaries of Regulatory Expropriation in International Law' (2005) 20 ICSID Rev 1.

PM Norton, 'A Law of the Future or a Law of the Past? Modern Tribunals and the International Law of Expropriation' (1991) 85 AJIL 474.

A Reinisch, 'Legality of Expropriations' in A Reinisch (ed), *Standards of Investment Protection* (OUP 2008) 171.

WM Reisman and RD Sloane, 'Indirect Expropriation and its Valuation in the BIT Generation' (2004) 74 BYIL 115.

M Sornarajah, *The International Law on Foreign Investment* (3rd edn, CUP 2010).

UNCTAD, *Taking of Property* (United Nations Publications 2000).

AS Weiner, 'Indirect Expropriations: The Need for a Taxonomy of "Legitimate" Regulatory Purposes' (2003) FORUM 166.

BH Weston, ' "Constructive Takings" under International Law: A Modest Foray into the Problem of "Creeping Expropriation" ' (1975) 16 Va J Int'l L 103.

THE EXTRATERRITORIAL EFFECTS OF EXPROPRIATIONS

F Mann, 'The Effect in England of the Compulsory Acquisition by a Foreign State of the Shares in a Foreign Company' (1986) 102 LQR 191.

N Sornarajah, *The Pursuit of Nationalized Property* (Springer 1986).

XXXIII

Concessions and Investment: Agreements between States and Foreign Companies

1. Stabilization and Internationalization

Companies investing abroad will strive for the best conditions for the operation and protection of their invested capital by and in the host State. The rules of customary international law on the protection of foreign property[1] are rather rudimentary in character and to some extent suffer from imprecision. Contractual arrangements have to cope with a structural problem flowing from the imbalance between a sovereign State and a foreign private enterprise: legal instability vis-à-vis all the regulatory powers of the host State. Regulations of the host State in favour of foreign investors are always subject to potential alterations in case of political change. In many developing countries and emerging economies reliability and stability are still not adequately supported by constitutional and political restraints of radical changes affecting investments. The same risk of change in legal regimes is inherent in agreements between the host State and the investor which are governed by the law of the host State. The contractual commitments of the host State are then just as reliable as the State's continuing willingness to abide by them. The alternative of subjecting the contractual relations to the law of a foreign State, as a rule, will be unacceptable for the host government. Exceptions are, for example, State bonds which are often subject to the law of the place of repayment (especially the law of New York or English law). If a State issues bonds governed by the law of another country, it cannot unilaterally modify its payment obligations through mandatory provisions. This limits a State's options to reschedule its public debt in a financial crisis.

Another option is the reference to 'transnational law' or 'general principles of contract law'. However, the contents of these transnational standards are often far from certain. A contract based on such principles is somehow floating between national and international law and cannot limit the powers of the host State under international law. Thus, the infringement of the contract by the host State does not establish its responsibility under international law.

Finally, a way to address the dilemma of reliable protection of the foreign investor is the adoption of a 'stabilization clause'[2] in the contract, which 'freezes' the

---

[1] See Ch VI.4.
[2] See M Sornarajah, *The International Law on Foreign Investment* (3rd edn, CUP 2010) 281ff.

relevant law as applicable at the time when the contract was concluded and thus precludes the unilateral alteration of contractual commitments by the host State. To be effective, such stabilization clauses must be anchored in international law and not in the law of the host State, thus constituting international commitments. Therefore, stabilization clauses are sometimes joined by special 'internationalization clauses' which explicitly lift the contract to the level of international law and thereby internationalize the relationship between the host State and the foreign company.[3] Often, a stabilization clause may be interpreted as also shifting the host State's commitments of non-interference on the plane of international law.

The effect of such stabilization and internationalization clauses is a matter of controversy. The different approaches are highlighted in a number of arbitral decisions rendered in context of the Libyan crude oil dispute.[4] This dispute was triggered by the repudiation of concession agreements for the exploration of crude oil which Libya had granted to several Western oil companies. In the 1970s, Libya nationalized its oil industry and thereby deprived the foreign oil companies of their rights granted under the concession agreements. The affected oil companies British Petroleum (BP), Texaco Overseas Petroleum Company (TOPCO), California Asiatic Oil Company (CALASIATIC), and the Libyan American Oil Company (LIAMCO) initiated arbitral proceedings under an arbitration clause in the agreements and tried to enforce their contractual rights. Libya argued that its national sovereignty could not be restricted by the concession agreements. The oil companies, in turn, relied on a stabilization clause, which prohibited the unilateral alteration of contractual rights. Another contractual clause provided that the concessions agreements should only be subject to Libyan law as far as Libyan law was in conformity with international law and referred to general principles of international law. This internationalization clause states:

This concession shall be governed by and interpreted in accordance with the principles of the law of Libya common to the principles of international law and in the absence of such common principles then by and in accordance with the general principles of law, including such of those principles as may have been applied by international tribunals.[5]

Libya unsuccessfully argued that as a sovereign State it had the power to dissolve the arbitral agreement with private companies. The three arbitral decisions concluded that the choice of law clause in the agreements was valid and that the standard of review, therefore, was independent from Libyan law. Nevertheless, the three decisions followed quite different approaches.

In the case *British Petroleum v Libyan Arab Republic*, arbitrator *Lagergren* rendered an arbitral award in Copenhagen[6] based on Danish law, which was the applicable law in the arbitral proceedings. The decision referred to the principle of

---

[3] E Paasivirta, 'Internationalisation and Stabilisation of Contracts versus State Sovereignty' (1989) 50 BYIL 315.

[4] R Dolzer, 'Libya-Oil Companies Arbitrations' in R Bernhardt (ed), *The Encyclopedia of Public International Law* (1997) vol III, 215.

[5] *Texas Overseas Petroleum Co & California Asiatic Oil Co v Libyan Arab Republic* (1978) 17 ILM 1 para 23.

[6] *British Petroleum Exploration Co v Libyan Arab Republic* (1979) 53 ILR 297.

autonomy of the parties, which is recognized in Danish law and permits the reference to international law. The award concluded that BP had been expropriated in an arbitrary and discriminatory manner. The award, however, rejected the claim to specific performance or full restitution (*restitutio in integrum*) and merely granted compensation for damages:

[W]hen by the exercise of sovereign power a State has committed a fundamental breach of a concession agreement by repudiating it through a nationalisation of the enterprise and its assets in a manner which implies finality, the concessionaire is not entitled to call for specific performance by the Government of the agreement and reinstatement of his contractual rights, but his sole remedy is an action for damages.[7]

The arbitral award in the case *LIAMCO v Libyan Arab Republic*[8] was based on the choice of law clause in the concession agreement and referred to general principles of private international law. Arbitrator Mahmassani granted the company compensation. The legal argument underlying the award is not entirely clear and the decision is essentially based on equity. The award denied the claim to specific performance as an infringement of the sovereignty of the host State.[9]

The arbitral award in the case *TOPCO/CALASIATIC v Libyan Arab Republic*[10] adopted a very different, innovative understanding of Libya's commitments under the concession agreement which broke new ground in the international law of concessions. Arbitrator Dupuy held that the concession agreement between US American oil companies and the Libyan State was rooted in international law and that the contractual position of the investors was therefore entrenched on the international level. According to the arbitral tribunal, the Libyan nationalization measures could not deprive the claimants of the rights granted in the concession agreements. As a legal consequence, the arbitrator concluded that Libya had to restitute the legal position of the oil companies (*restitutio in integrum*).[11]

The arbitral award in the case *TOPCO/CALASIATIC* set an important precedent supporting the view that a State may enter into an agreement with foreign investors on the basis of international law and that a private company thus holds what may be denominated as 'limited international subjectivity'. This doctrine that such agreements are subject to international law is quite controversial but has gained considerable support within the last years.

Agreements between a State and a foreign investor which are governed by international law, however, are subject to the rules on a fundamental and unforeseeable change of circumstances which may affect the validity of contractual commitments (*clausula rebus sic stantibus*).[12] In *The American Independent Oil Co v The Government of the State of Kuwait*, another oil concession dispute, an arbitral award

---

[7] *British Petroleum Exploration Co v Libyan Arab Republic* (1979) 53 ILR 354.

[8] *Libyan American Oil Co v Libyan Arab Republic* (1981) 20 ILM 1.

[9] *Libyan American Oil Co v Libyan Arab Republic* (1981) 20 ILM 1, 64f.

[10] *Texas Overseas Petroleum Co & California Asiatic Oil Co v Libyan Arab Republic* (1978) 17 ILM 1.

[11] *Texas Overseas Petroleum Co & California Asiatic Oil Co v Libyan Arab Republic* (1978) 17 ILM 1 paras 92ff.

[12] See Article 62 of the Vienna Convention on the Law of Treaties.

assumed that a stabilization clause, at least in long-term concession agreements, does not constitute a waiver by the host State which categorically excludes any expropriation.[13]

Apart from the classification of agreements between the investor and the host State, it is recognized that a State may not invoke its sovereignty in order to denounce an arbitral clause in the agreement with a foreign investor, unless the arbitral agreement itself, according to its terms, is clearly subject to the law of the host State. The possible interference of the host State with its substantive contractual commitments does not affect the validity of an arbitration clause. In this sense, arbitral agreements between the State and its foreign contract partner are implicitly stabilized under international law.[14] In the meantime, the issue of stabilization and internationalization of contractual relations between States and foreign investors has lost much of its practical relevance. The network of bilateral and multilateral treaties on investment[15] provides reliable mechanisms of protection and redress under international law.

2. Concessions

Concession agreements may refer to the extraction of raw materials (eg oil, gas, coal, and metals), the provision of water and energy, or the operation of infrastructures (eg roads, airports, and harbours). In the sectors of water, energy supply, and construction, concessions may establish the right to operate supply facilities or installations.

A model to develop large infrastructure projects are agreements which allow the investor to operate a supply system, construction, installation, or facility and charge for the use or supply. In the case of BOT (build, operate, transfer) projects, the object will be handed over to the host State after a certain period of time.[16]

The time span for the operation by the investor is significantly shorter than the period of time the object can be run economically. For BOT projects the agreement with the government of the State serves as the basis for a complicated network of contracts on the financing of the project and its technical operation.[17] The most prominent BOT project is the construction and operation of the tunnel under the Channel between France and Great Britain.[18]

Especially long-term concessions are susceptible to interferences by the host State into the established balance of rights and commitments. Concessions for oil, gas,

---

[13] *The American Independent Oil Co v The Government of the State of Kuwait* (1982) 21 ILM 976 paras 88ff, 95.

[14] See Ch XXI.   [15] See Ch XXXIV.1.

[16] See Ch XXVI.2.

[17] See F Nicklisch, 'The BOT Model—The Contractor's Role as Builder—Contract Structure Risk Allocation and Risk Management' (1992) 9 ICLR 425.

[18] See Ch XXVI.2.; see also R Goy, 'Le tunnel sous la Manche' (1986) 32 AFDI 741; see also M Herdegen, 'Der Konzessionsvertrag aus öffentlich-rechtlicher Sicht: das Beispiel des Kanaltunnelprojekts' in F Nicklisch (ed), *Rechtsfragen privatfinanzierter Projekte* (CF Müller 1994) 41.

or other materials may be denounced because the host government seeks to take control over natural resources (as in the Libyan oil disputes in the 1970s). Foreign investors may be expropriated as majority shareholders in national oil companies, because the host government wants to change the company's management and policy. In the case of energy or water supply or the operation of infrastructure (eg toll roads), interference with the agreed system of pricing[19] or the fixing of toll rates may amount to a de facto expropriation.

Select Bibliography

I Alvik, *State Contracts and International Arbitration* (Hart Publishing 2011).
C Ohler, 'Concessions' in R Wolfrum (ed), *The Max Planck Encyclopedia of Public International Law* (OUP 2012) vol II, 564.

---

[19] *CMS Gas Transmission Co v Argentine Republic*, ICSID Case No ARB/01/8 (Decision on Jurisdiction) (2003) 42 ILM 788, para 51.

XXXIV

Treaties on Investment Protection

1. Bilateral and Multilateral Agreements on the Protection of Investments

(a) Bilateral investment treaties and investment protection in preferential trade agreements

The traditional Treaties of Friendship, Commerce and Navigation (FCN treaties) which were concluded since the late 18th century until the middle of the 20th century by many Western States often contain provisions relating to the treatment of investments (admission and protection).[1] Up to now, the United States is party to over sixty FCN treaties.[2] Over the last decades, a new type of treaty on protection and promotion of investments has been established, the Bilateral Investment Treaties (BITs).[3] European States (led by Germany), the United States, Australia, Canada, China, Japan, and other industrialized countries have concluded a wide network of BITs with developing countries and other States.

In recent years, quite a number of BITs were concluded between developing countries. In 2015, about 3,000 BITs were in existence.[4]

In the last years, a number of bilateral or multilateral preferential trade agreements (or economic partnership agreements) extensively covered issues of investment protection. Especially in recent US practice, preferential trade agreements

---

[1] See for more information, AL Paulus, 'Treaties of Friendship, Commerce and Navigation' in R Wolfrum (ed), *The Max Planck Encyclopedia of Public International Law* (OUP 2012) vol IX, 1140; H Walker, 'Modern Treaties of Friendship, Commerce and Navigation' (1957–58) 42 Minn L Rev 805.

[2] AL Paulus, 'Treaties of Friendship, Commerce and Navigation' in R Wolfrum (ed), *The Max Planck Encyclopedia of Public International Law* (OUP 2012) vol IX, 1140 para 19; J Bonnitcha, *Substantive Protection under Investment Treaties* (CUP 2014).

[3] See generally on BITs, E Chalamish, 'The Future of Bilateral Investment Treaties: A De Facto Multilateral Agreement?' (2009) 34 Brooklyn J Int'l L 303; R Dolzer and C Schreuer, *Bilateral Investment Treaties* (OUP 1995); A Newcombe and L Paradell, *Law and Practice of Investment Treaties* (Kluwer Law International 2009); JW Salacuse, *The Law of Investment Treaties* (OUP 2010); JW Salacuse and NP Sullivan, 'Do BITs Really Work? An Evaluation of Bilateral Investment Treaties and their Grand Bargain' (2005) 46 Harv Int'l LJ 67; K Vandevelde, *Investment Treaties: History, Policy and Interpretation* (OUP 2010).

[4] UNCTAD, *World Investment Report 2016* (United Nations Publications 2016) 115.

assumed the role of BITs. With the new power in the area of investment agreements conferred by the Lisbon Treaty, the European Union currently negotiates trade agreements which include chapters on investment.

Several countries (eg the United States, Canada, China, Colombia, and Germany) negotiate bilateral investment treaties that are based on a model treaty.[5] As a rule, model treaties set forth the standards of national treatment,[6] most-favoured-nation treatment,[7] 'full protection and security'[8] and 'fair and equitable treatment'.[9] Other clauses address expropriation and compensation.[10]

Most BITs protect investments that have already been carried out and refer to the law of the host State for the admission of investments (post-establishment approach).[11] By contrast, the Model BITs of the United States, Canada, and Japan aim at a pre-establishment regime which guarantees market access in terms of national treatment and most-favoured-nation treatment (pre-entry approach).[12] However, even treaties which provide for a non-discriminatory admission of investments allow restrictions on entry either by enumerating the sectors open to foreign investments or by enumerating the closed sectors.

Dissatisfaction with certain arbitral awards on investors' claims or concerns about future conflicts between policy choices and treaty commitments have induced a number of States to withdraw from international agreements on investment protection, to consider their termination or to push for renegotiation. Some governments suspect that arbitral tribunals tend to display a bias in favour of foreign investors.

Under the influence of the Calvo doctrine,[13] opposition to investment treaties and the particular protection of foreign investors prevailed in Latin America for a considerable time. In more recent years, most Latin American countries have concluded a considerable number of agreements on investment protection. However, some Latin American States have recently returned to the traditional approach of the 19th century and the principle of national treatment.[14] Some countries (like Bolivia, Ecuador, and Venezuela) have cancelled BITs or the ICSID agreement and pursued the renegotiation of existing concession contracts with foreign investors.

---

[5] US Model Bilateral Investment Treaty (2012); Model Foreign Investment Protection and Promotion Agreement of Canada (2004); Chinese Model Bilateral Investment Treaty (2003); German Model Treaty concerning the Encouragement and Reciprocal Protection of Investments (2008); on the previous US Model BIT, see M Kantor, 'The New Draft Model BIT: Noteworthy Developments' (2004) 21 J Jnt'l Arbit 383; see also JA Rivas, 'Colombia' in Chester Brown (ed), *Commentaries on Selected Model Investment Treaties* (OUP 2013).

[6] See section 4(b) in this Chapter.   [7] See section 4(c) in this Chapter.
[8] See section 4(e) in this Chapter.   [9] See section 4(d) in this Chapter.
[10] See section 4(g) in this Chapter.

[11] For example Article 2(1) of the German Model BIT (2008) reads: 'Each Contracting State shall in its territory promote as far as possible investments by investors of the other Contracting State and admit such investments in accordance with its legislation.'

[12] See on 'establishment, acquisition, expansion' Articles 3 and 4 of the US Model BIT (2012).

[13] See Ch VI.4(b).

[14] See eg Article 301 of the Constitution of the Republic of Venezuela (1999) or the Supreme Decree No 28,701 which the government of Bolivia issued in 2006 to nationalize the country's oil and gas industry (2006) 45 ILM 1018 or Art 442 of the Constitution of the Republic of Ecuador.

434 Principles of International Economic Law

In Latin America, some disputes between US petroleum companies and Ecuador fuelled the controversy about investment protection and investment arbitration. In 2006, an arbitral tribunal ordered Ecuador to pay about USD 2 billion in compensation for discriminatory treatment in taxation to the US petroleum company Occidental (*Occidental Exploration and Production Co v The Republic of Ecuador*);[15] this amount is equivalent to the country's annual budget for education. In the famous *Lago Agrio* case, an Ecuadorian court, in 2011, ordered the US oil company Chevron to pay about USD 18 billion (later reduced to USD 9 billion by an appellate court) in damages for massive pollution of the environment in the Amazonian rainforest. In 2015, in *Chevron Corp v Yaiguaje*,[16] the Supreme Court of Canada held that the plaintiffs could enforce the Ecuadorian multi-billion judgment in Canada, where one of Chevron's subsidiaries was situated. Complaining about unfair treatment (including judicial impropriety), Chevron and Texaco (now a company owned by Chevron) then initiated arbitral proceedings against Ecuador under the bilateral investment treaty with the United States (*Chevron Corp and Texaco Co v Republic of Ecuador*). Chevron obtained an award on Ecuador's obligation to suspend enforcement of the Ecuadorian court's judgment and, subsequently, on its obligation to pay compensation.[17] The Chevron Corporation also brought an action against the Ecuadorian plaintiffs and their lawyers before a US court, contending that they had acted in a fraudulent way in the Ecuadorian proceedings.[18] As already indicated, several Latin American countries reverted to the Calvo doctrine and denounced their agreements on investment protection.

The Government of South Africa invoked the constitution-based agenda to redress inequalities of the apartheid regime and other injustices of the past (with co-ownership of historically disadvantaged persons in mining companies and other forms of 'black economic empowerment') as grounds to revoke the BITs with Germany, Spain, and other countries and to submit a legislative bill on a new domestic framework for investment protection.

Indonesia faces a billion US Dollar claim triggered by the revocation of a coal mining licence in *Churchill Mining PLC and Planet Mining Pty Ltd v Republic of Indonesia*.[19] After the ICSID arbitration tribunal had rejected Indonesia's objections to the tribunal's jurisdiction, Indonesia decided not to renew its BIT with the Netherlands and announced its intention to terminate more than 60 other agreements. Critics of this political trend warn of negative impacts on the investment climate in the countries concerned.

---

[15] *Occidental Exploration and Production Co v The Republic of Ecuador*, LCIA Case No UN 3467 (Final Award 2004); see also SD Franck, 'International Decisions: Occidental Exploration and Production Company v The Republic of Ecuador' (2005) 99 AJIL 675.

[16] *Chevron Corporation v Yaiguaje*, Supreme Court of Canada, Case No 35682, 2015 SCC 42 (2015).

[17] *Chevron Corporation and Texaco Company v Republic of Ecuador*, PCA Case No 2009-23 (Fourth Interim Award on Interim Measures 2013; First Partial Award on Track I 2013).

[18] *Chevron Corporation v Steven Donziger et al*, US District Court for the Southern District of New York, Case No 11-CIV-0691 (2014) (appeal pending).

[19] *Churchill Mining PLC and Planet Mining Pty Ltd v Republic of Indonesia*, ICSID Case No ARB/12/14 and 12/40 (Decisions on Jurisdiction 2014).

(b) The European Union as new actor in international investment law

The Treaty of Lisbon allows the European Union to play a new role in international investment law.[20] Article 207(1) first sentence of the TFEU establishes the European Union's exclusive competence to conclude agreements on foreign direct investment:

The common commercial policy shall be based on uniform principles, particularly with regard to changes in tariff rates, the conclusion of tariff and trade agreements relating to trade in goods and services, and the commercial aspects of intellectual property, foreign direct investment, the achievement of uniformity in measures of liberalisation, export policy and measures to protect trade such as those to be taken in the event of dumping or subsidies.

The exercise of new competence will have a considerable impact on the development of international investment law for the EU Member States, which, as a whole, rank first as exporters and as recipients of foreign direct investment.

The EU Member States are parties to about 1,300 bilateral agreements on investment with third countries. It is a matter of controversy whether the BITs concluded by the Member States of the European Union shall continue to apply. Under public international law, these agreements remain binding unless cancelled in accordance with their own terms. Regulation (EU) No 1219/2012, establishing transitional arrangements for bilateral investment agreements between Member States and third countries,[21] allows the continued existence of bilateral investment agreements between Member States and third countries. As the TFEU (including the provisions on free movement of capital) does not establish a comprehensive treaty-making power of the European Union as to indirect foreign investment, future agreements on foreign investment will have to be concluded as 'mixed agreements' with the European Union and its Member States.[22]

Accordingly, free trade agreements with a comprehensive regulation of foreign investment (like the free trade agreement with South Korea, the Comprehensive Economic and Trade Agreement with Canada (CETA) or, if successfully negotiated,

---

[20] See EU Commission, 'Towards a Comprehensive European International Investment Policy' (2010)COM343 final; JA Bischoff, 'Just a Little Bit of "Mixity"? The EU's Role in the Field of International Investment Protection Law' (2011) 48 CML Rev 1527; M Bungenberg, 'Going Global? The EU Common Commercial Policy after Lisbon' (2010) EYIEL 123; J Chaisse, 'Promises and Pitfalls of the European Union Policy on Foreign Investment—How Will the New EU Competence on FDI Affect the Emerging Global Regime?' (2012) 15 J Int'l Econ L 51; M Potestà, 'Bilateral Investment Treaties and the European Union: Recent Development in Arbitration and Before the ECJ' (2009) 8 Law & Prac. Int'l Cts & Tribunals 225; C-H Wu, 'Foreign Direct Investment as Common Commercial Policy: EU External Economic Competence After Lisbon' in PJ Cardwell (ed), *EU External Relations Law and Policy in the Post-Lisbon Era* (TMC Asser Press 2012) 375.

[21] Regulation (EU) No 1219/2012 of the European Parliament and of the Council of 12 December 2012 establishing transitional arrangements for bilateral investment agreements between Member States and third countries [2012] OJ L351/40.

[22] The European Court of Justice will issue an opinion on the EU–Singapore FTA, see ECJ Case A-2/15; see also the Commission's Proposal to conclude CETA as a mixed agreement, COM (2016) 443 final 4.

the future Trade and Investment Partnership Agreement with the United States (TTIP)) must take the form of a 'mixed agreement', which is to be ratified by the European Union and all its Member States.

In the European Parliament and in the Member States (especially in Germany), there is strong criticism of investment protection which might interfere with environmental, health, and social standards. There is also widespread resistance against investment arbitration which allows foreign investors to challenge legislative choices and to bypass national courts.

(c) Multilateral agreements covering foreign investment

i. *Multilateral agreements on trade and investment*

A number of trade agreements also include a chapter on investment protection.

The North American Free Trade Agreement (NAFTA)[23] does not only cover trade, but also investment protection (Chapter 11 of the Agreement). NAFTA also establishes a framework for settling investment disputes. It applies to the admission of investments (Articles 1102 and 1103 of NAFTA) as well as to post-establishment protection. The NAFTA Free Trade Commission's (FTC) Notes of Interpretation of 2001 clarified the scope and meaning of certain Chapter 11 provisions. These guidelines and arbitral case-law under Chapter 11 of NAFTA have influenced the interpretation of standard clauses in modern investment treaties in general.[24]

Recent mega-regional agreements, such as the CETA and the Trans-Pacific Partnership Agreement (TPP), also govern foreign investment and its protection. Substantive investment protection standards and dispute settlement clauses are particularly controversial issues in the negotiations between the EU and the United States on the TTIP.[25]

ii. *OECD Multilateral Agreement on Investment*

In 1995, the OECD initiated negotiations with all OECD countries on a Multilateral Agreement on Investment (MAI).[26] The MAI was understood to be a 'free standing international treaty, open to all OECD Members and the European Communities, and to accession by non-OECD Member Countries'.[27] The objective was to

---

[23] (1993) 32 ILM 289, 605, 1480, 1502, 1520; the Treaty entered into force on 1 January 1994.
[24] See M Kinnear and R Hansen, 'The Influence of NAFTA Chapter 11 in the BIT Landscape' (2005) 12 UC Davis J Int'l L & Pol'y 101 (110).
[25] See Ch XXIII. 10.
[26] See P Juillard, 'MAI: A European View' (1998) 31 Cornell Int'l LJ 477; PT Muchlinski, 'The Rise and Fall of the Multilateral Agreement in Investment: Where Now?' (2000) 34 Int'l Law 1033; G Rainer, 'Towards a Multilateral Agreement on Investment' (1998) 31 Cornell Int'l LJ 476.
[27] OECD, A Multilateral Agreement on Investment—Report by the Committee of International Investment and Multinational Enterprises (CIME) and the Committee on Capital Movements and Invisible Transactions (CMI) (1995) OCDE/GD(95)65, 5.

'provide a broad multilateral framework for international investment with high
standards for the liberalization of investment regimes and investment protection
and with effective dispute settlement procedures'.[28] Due to insuperable conflicts of
interest, for example with respect to different approaches to the national treatment
obligation, the MAI project failed in 1998.

iii. Energy Charter Treaty

Part III of the Energy Charter Treaty (ECT) of 1994[29] provides for a far-reaching
protection of investments in the energy sector. The general clause set forth in Article
10.1 reads as follows:

Each Contracting Party shall, in accordance with the provisions of this Treaty, encourage
and create stable, equitable, favourable and transparent conditions for Investors of other
Contracting Parties to make investments in its Area. Such conditions shall include a commitment to accord at all times to Investments of Investors of other Contracting Parties
fair and equitable treatment. Such Investments shall also enjoy the most constant protection and security and no Contracting Party shall in any way impair by unreasonable or
discriminatory measures their management, maintenance, use, enjoyment or disposal. In
no case shall such Investments be accorded treatment less favourable than that required by
international law, including treaty obligations. Each Contracting Party shall observe any
obligations it has entered into with an Investor or an Investment of an Investor of any other
Contracting Party.

Article 10.3 of the ECT requires most-favoured-nation treatment. The Energy
Charter Treaty covers the entry and stay of key personnel (Article 11), compensation for losses in case of emergencies or conflict (Article 12), conditions for expropriation including compensation (Article 13), and transfers related to investments
(Article 14). The Treaty accepts the contracting States' sovereignty with regard to
energy resources within the confines of international law. Thus, the States Parties
enjoy the right freely to determine access to energy resources and the system of
property (Article 18).

The dispute settlement regime refers to investor-State arbitration (Article 26) as
well as to State-to-State arbitration (Article 27). As to the law applicable to disputes,
Article 26.6 of the ECT refers entirely to the Treaty itself and other rules and other
standards of international law: 'A tribunal [...] shall decide the issues in dispute
in accordance with this Treaty and applicable rules and principles of international
law'. Arbitral awards issued are binding and final upon the parties (Article 26.8 of
the ECT).

It would be mistaken to confine the practical relevance of investment protection under the ECT to investments in the countries of the former Soviet Union.

[28] OECD, A Multilateral Agreement on Investment—Report by the Committee of International
Investment and Multinational Enterprises (CIME) and the Committee on Capital Movements and
Invisible Transactions (CMI) (1995) OCDE/GD(95)65, 5.
[29] (1995) 22 ILM 373; the Treaty entered into force on 16 April 1998.

The *Vattenfall* cases demonstrate the implications of the ECT for investments in EU Member States. On the basis of Article 26 of the ECT, in 2009 the Swedish energy supplier Vattenfall initiated arbitration proceedings against Germany, challenging environmental restrictions on a coal-fired power plant under construction in Hamburg after the claimant had invested considerable sums of money in the project.[30] Meanwhile, the dispute was settled amicably. In 2012, Vattenfall brought an arbitration claim against Germany, arguing that Germany's decision to close down two nuclear power plants after Germany's abrupt change of nuclear policy violated the ECT.[31]

As of 2016, almost 50 States (including the EU Member States, most successor States of the Soviet Union, Japan, and Turkey) and the European Union have ratified the ECT. Russia had signed the Treaty and applied it provisionally pursuant to Article 45.1 of the ECT. In 2009, Russia declared that it would not ratify the Treaty and terminated the provisional application.

In the landmark case *Yukos Universal Limited (Isle of Man) v The Russian Federation*[32] and two parallel proceedings, *Hulley Enterprises Limited (Cyprus) v The Russian Federation*[33] and *Veteran Petroleum Limited (Cyprus) v The Russian Federation,*[34] the arbitral tribunals held that Russia's commitment to provisionally apply the ECT also covered dispute settlement under the ECT.[35] In the *Yukos* case, Russian authorities had taken radical measures under tax law against the Russian oil company Yukos as well as against its officers, with the objective of destroying the company and liquidating its assets. Major shareholders (companies incorporated in other Member States of the ECT, that is the United Kingdom and, in the parallel proceedings, Cyprus) initiated arbitration proceedings under the ECT according to the UNCITRAL arbitration rules, administered by the Permanent Court of Arbitration (PCA) in The Hague. The arbitration tribunal ordered Russia to pay a total sum of USD 50 billion[36]—the largest sum ever awarded in investment arbitration. Russia argued that the arbitral tribunal lacked jurisdiction and invoked article 45 of the ECT, which subjects provisional application to conformity with the signing party's constitution and legislation. Finding inconsistency of the ECT with Russian laws, a Dutch court set aside the award.[37]

---

[30] *Vattenfall AB et al v Federal Republic of Germany,* ICSID Case No ARB/09/6 (Award 2011).

[31] *Vattenfall AB et al v Federal Republic of Germany* II, ICSID Case No ARB/12/12 (Pending).

[32] *Yukos Universal Limited (Isle of Man) v The Russian Federation*, PCA Case No AA 227 (Final Award 2014).

[33] *Hulley Enterprises Limited (Cyprus) v The Russian Federation*, PCA Case No AA 226 (Final Award 2014).

[34] *Veteran Petroleum Limited (Cyprus) v The Russian Federation*, PCA Case No AA 228 (Final Award 2014).

[35] See the arbitral award in the case *Yukos Universal Limited (Isle of Man)v The Russian Federation*, PCA Case No AA 227 (Interim Award on Jurisdiction and Admissibility 2009) paras 301ff.

[36] See *Yukos Universal Limited (Isle of Man)v The Russian Federation*, PCA Case No AA 227 (Final Award 2014) para 1827.

[37] Decision of the Court of The Hague of 20 April 2016, ECLI:NL:RBDHA:2016:4230, paras 5.95ff.An appeal is pending. On the annulment proceedings before Dutch courts see Section 1(c)(iii).

iv. *The Investment Agreement of the Organisation of Islamic Cooperation*

The Investment Agreement of the Organisation of Islamic Cooperation (OIC) of 1981[38] grants national treatment to foreign investors and subjects expropriation to prompt, adequate, and effective compensation 'in accordance with the laws of the host State' (Article 10). It gives investors access to the domestic courts of the host State and, alternatively, to conciliation and arbitration (Articles 16 and 17). The OIC Agreement has been ratified by 25 States including Oman, Pakistan, Saudi Arabia, and the United Arab Emirates. This Agreement allows both the investor and the host State to resort to arbitration and to bring a counterclaim (Article 17). Article 9 establishes obligations of the investor. Investors 'shall be bound by the laws and regulations in force in the host State and shall refrain from all acts that may disturb public order or morals or that may be prejudicial to the public interest'. They also shall 'refrain from exercising restrictive practices and from trying to achieve gains through unlawful means'. In *Hesham Talaat v Indonesia*, an arbitral tribunal held that the investor, by initiating arbitral proceedings against the host State also consented to the arbitral tribunal's jurisdiction over a counterclaim presented by the host State in conformity with Article 17 of the OIC Agreement.[39]

2. Personal Scope of Protection

International investment treaties, as a rule, cover any natural or legal person with the nationality of one of the contracting States, who makes an investment in the other contracting State. Thus, the German Model Treaty (2008), defines 'investor' with respect to Germany as

- any natural person who is a German within the meaning of the Basic Law of the Federal Republic of Germany or a national of a Member State of the European Union or of the European Economic Area who, within the context of freedom of establishment pursuant to Article 43 of the EC Treaty, is established in the Federal Republic of Germany;
- any juridical person and any commercial or other company or association with or without legal personality which is founded pursuant to the law of the Federal Republic of Germany or the law of a Member State of the European Union or the European Economic Area and is organized pursuant to the law of the Federal Republic of Germany, registered in a public register in the Federal Republic of Germany or enjoys freedom of establishment as an agency or permanent establishment in Germany pursuant to Articles 43 and 48 of the EC Treaty;
  which in the context of entrepreneurial activity is the owner, possessor or shareholder of an investment in the territory of the other Contracting State, irrespective of whether or not the activity is directed at profit; [...].[40]

---

[38] Agreement for Promotion, Protection and Guarantee of Investments among Member States of the Organisation of the Islamic Conference <http://www.oic-oci.org/english/convenion/Agreement%20 for%20Invest%20in%20OIC%20%20En.pdf> (accessed 23 June 2016).
[39] *Hesham Talaat Al-Warraq v Indonesia* (UNCITRAL Final Award 2014) para 663.
[40] See Article 1(3)(a) of the German Model BIT (2008).

Most investment treaties extend their scope of application to corporations owned or controlled by one of the contracting States. The US Model BIT (2012) explicitly includes a State Party in the definition of 'investor of a Party':

'[I]nvestor of a Party' means a Party or state enterprise thereof, or a national or an enterprise of a Party, that attempts to make, is making, or has made an investment in the territory of the other Party; provided, however, that a natural person who is a dual national shall be deemed to be exclusively a national of the State of his or her dominant and effective nationality.[41]

Many investment treaties extend their scope of application to investments made by persons from one contracting State by means of a subsidiary company founded under the law of the other contracting State or having its seat in the other State. This extended form of protection may be achieved either via the personal scope of application of the investment treaty (definition of protected 'investor'), that is by covering legal persons which are nationals of the host State, but are controlled by an investor from the other contracting State,[42] or via the substantive scope of application (definition of protected 'investment'), that is by covering the share of an investor from one contracting State in a company with the nationality of the other contracting State.[43]

Under Article 25(2)(b) of the ICSID Convention, a legal person with the nationality of the host State which is controlled by nationals of the other contracting State may be treated as national of the other contracting State, if the parties so agree:

'National of another contracting State' means:
(b) any juridical person which had the nationality of a contracting State other than the State party to the dispute on the date on which the parties consented to submit such dispute to conciliation or arbitration and any juridical person which had the nationality of the contracting State party to the dispute on that date and which, because of foreign control, the parties have agreed should be treated as a national of another contracting State for the purposes of this Convention.

As a rule, arbitral practice accepts incorporation of a company under the laws of a State party as a sufficient criterion for nationality even if the centre of management activities has been shifted to another country. In *Niko Resources (Bangladesh) Ltd v People's Republic of Bangladesh et al*,[44] the arbitral tribunal rejected the argument of the respondent State that there must be a real connection to the place of incorporation:

The Respondents have not presented any authorities to support their view that a requirement of a 'real connection', assuming it were applicable in diplomatic protection or in treaty claims, should apply to contract claims as in the present case. In the Tribunal's

---

[41] See Article 1 of the US Model BIT (2012).
[42] See *Aguas del Tunari SA v Republic of Bolivia*, ICSID Case No ARB/02/3 (Decision on Jurisdiction 2005), (2005) 20 ICSID Rev 450.
[43] See *Siemens AG v Argentine Republic*, ICSID Case No ARB/02/8 (Decision on Jurisdiction 2004), (2005) 44 ILM 138.
[44] *Niko Resources (Bangladesh) Ltd v People's Republic of Bangladesh et al*, ICSID Case No ARB/10/11 and ARB/10/18 (Decision on Jurisdiction 2013).

view such an additional requirement cannot be read into the text of the Convention; nor can the *travaux préparatoires* for the Convention justify the assumption that this had been intended. It is sufficient for a claimant to show that it has the nationality of another Contracting State by reference to one of the generally accepted criteria, in particular incorporation or seat.[45]

Unincorporated consortia of various companies do not qualify as a 'juridicial person' under the ICSID Convention.[46] Problems of the personal scope of protection may arise in the case of complex corporate structures which do not correspond to the typical investor–host State relation. In the case of 'multi-storey' corporations with interrelated companies of different nationality, companies at various levels of affiliation or control may be candidates for 'investor' or 'national'. If an investment treaty also protects investments which are indirectly controlled by a national of the other contracting State, the nationality of a parent company or even a grandparent company may trigger the application of the investment treaty. Investors from a non-contracting State or even from the host State itself may try to benefit from treaty protection by founding a company in a State which is a contracting party to an investment treaty with the host State. In this situation, the nationality of the company may serve as a key to the scope of investment protection. Thus, the choice of corporate structures may allow investors to engage in so-called 'treaty shopping'.[47]

The case *Aguas del Tunari SA v Republic of Bolivia* provides an interesting insight into the options available under complex corporate structures. In this case, the immediate investor—a Bolivian company—was indirectly (through an American and a Spanish company) controlled by a Dutch company. The Dutch company was owned by another Dutch company which was in turn controlled by the Dutch affiliate company of a US company and an Italian company. The Bolivian company relied on protection under the bilateral investment treaty between Bolivia and the Netherlands. According to this treaty, legal persons with nationality of the host State, which were under the direct or indirect control of nationals of another contracting State, were considered as nationals of the other contracting State. The arbitral tribunal considered the direct control of the Bolivian company by the Dutch company to be sufficient:

The Tribunal, by majority, concludes that the phrase 'controlled directly or indirectly' means that one entity may be said to control another entity (either directly, that is without an intermediary entity, or indirectly) if that entity possesses the legal capacity to control the other entity. Subject to evidence of particular restrictions on the exercise of voting rights, such legal capacity is to be ascertained with reference to the percentage of

---

[45] Ibid, para 203.

[46] *Consorzio Groupement LESI-DIPENTA v Algeria*, ICSID Case No ARB/03/08 (Award 2005) paras 37–41; *Impregilo v Pakistan*, ICSID Case No ARB/03/3 (Decision on Jurisdiction 2005) paras 132–139.

[47] See *Venezuela Holdings, B.V., et al v Bolivarian Republic of Venezuela*, ICSID Case No ARB/07/27 (Decision on Jurisdiction 2010) para 204; SP Subedi, *International Investment Law* (2nd edn, Hart Publishing 2012) 174ff.

shares held. In the case of a minority shareholder, the legal capacity to control an entity may exist by reason of the percentage of shares held, legal rights conveyed in instruments or agreements such as the articles of incorporation or shareholders' agreements, or a combination of these. In the tribunal's view, the BIT does not require actual day-to-day or ultimate control as part of the 'controlled directly or indirectly' requirement contained in Article 1(b)(iii). The tribunal observes that it is not charged with determining all forms which control might take. It is the Tribunal's conclusion, by majority, that, in the circumstances of this case, where an entity has both majority shareholdings and ownership of a majority voting rights, control as embodied in the operative phrase 'controlled directly or indirectly' exists.[48]

The German Model BIT (2008) limits the options to realise covered investments via a company owned or controlled by a national of the contracting States:

In the case of indirect investments, in principle only those indirect investments shall be covered which the investor realizes via a company situated in the other contracting State.[49]

When a company is embedded in a complex international corporate structure, financial transactions are not relevant for the purpose of determining the personal scope of protection as long as the State is not misled about the corporate structures.

In *Niko Resources (Bangladesh) Ltd v People's Republic of Bangladesh et al,* the arbitral tribunal emphasized the freedom of investors to organize their investment and corporate structure with respect to capital flows and other contributions:

177. The Tribunal considers that, in principle it is for the investor to decide how it wishes to structure its investment and what corporate organization it wishes to adopt for the investment, including the manner in which resources, activities and control are allocated between different corporate vehicles. The corporate structure of the investment is indeed part of the investor's prerogatives and responsibility. Depending on the structure adopted, the corporate vehicle used for the investment which becomes party to the investment contract may rely on the resources of the group to which it belongs to secure the investment, including funding, technology or other contributions.

178. Distinct corporate identities serve a legitimate function in the cross-border mobilization of investment. As long as the contracting parties are not mislead about the corporate structure and no laws and regulations are violated, there should be no objection to the choice made by the investor in this respect.[50]

Some investment treaties limit the personal scope of application through a so-called 'denial of benefits clause'.[51] Such a clause permits a contracting State, under certain

---

[48] See *Aguas del Tunari SA v Republic of Bolivia,* ICSID Case No ARB/02/3 (Decision on Jurisdiction 2005), (2005) 20 ICSID Rev 450 para 264.

[49] Article 1(1) of the German Model BIT (2008).

[50] *Niko Resources (Bangladesh) v People's Republic of Bangladesh et al,* ICSID Case No ARB/10/11 and ARB/10/18 (Decision on Jurisdiction 2013) para 177f.

[51] M Sornarajah, *The International Law on Foreign Investment* (3rd edn, CUP 2010) 329.

conditions, to deny investment protection to companies or other entities of another contracting State if they are owned or controlled by nationals of a non-party. Article 17 of the US Model BIT (2012) provides:

1. A Party may deny the benefits of this Treaty to an investor of the other Party that is an enterprise of such other Party and to investments of that investor if persons of a non-Party own or control the enterprise and the denying Party:
   (a) does not maintain diplomatic relations with the non-Party; or
   (b) adopts or maintains measures with respect to the non-Party or a person of the non-Party that prohibit transactions with the enterprise or that would be violated or circumvented if the benefits of this Treaty were accorded to the enterprise or to its investments.
2. A Party may deny the benefits of this Treaty to an investor of the other Party that is an enterprise of such other Party and to investments of that investor if the enterprise has no substantial business activities in the territory of the other Party and persons of a non-Party, or of the denying Party, own or control the enterprise.

An almost identical provision was included in the recent Trans-Pacific Partnership Agreement (Article 9.14 TPP).

Another issue is in how far companies which are controlled by citizens of the host State may claim benefits under an investment treaty. In the absence of clear treaty rules on a denial of benefits in such a case, arbitral practice has not been very receptive to the argument of abusive 'treaty shopping'.

In the *Yukos* case (*Yukos Universal Limited (Isle of Man) v The Russian Federation*),[52] two companies set up under the laws of Malta and Cyprus which were shareholders of the largest oil enterprise in Russia at the time (Yukos), initiated arbitral proceedings against Russia under the ECT. The companies complained about measures taken against Yukos, which ultimately resulted in the collapse of the enterprise. Russia challenged the jurisdiction of the arbitral tribunal on the grounds that the claimants, as mere 'shell companies', were controlled by Russian citizens. The ECT extends protected investments to company shares (Article 1(6)), without any further requirements. On this basis, the arbitral tribunal rejected Russia's argument and affirmed its jurisdiction over the claim.[53] This kind of ruling, though methodologically sound, may dampen enthusiasm for international investment protection in certain countries.

In the negotiations of the TTIP, the European Union seeks to avoid treaty shopping by limiting the personal scope of protection to investors who do substantial business in their home State.[54]

---

[52] See Section 1(c)(iii) in this chapter.
[53] See the arbitral award in the case *Yukos Universal Limited (Isle of Man) v The Russian Federation*, PCA Case No AA 227 (Interim Award on Jurisdiction and Admissibility 2009).
[54] See European Commission, *Concept Paper—Investment in TTIP and beyond—the path for reform* <http://trade.ec.europa.eu/doclib/html/153408.htm> (accessed 23 June 2016).

3. Protected 'Investments'

(a) Definition

Modern treaty practice tends to define 'investment' in very broad terms. For example, the US Model BIT (2012) and Article 9.1 of the Trans-Pacific Partnership Agreement (TPP) contain the following provision:

'[I]nvestment' means every asset that an investor owns or controls, directly or indirectly, that has the characteristics of an investment, including such characteristics as the commitment of capital or other resources, the expectation of gain or profit, or the assumption of risk. Forms that an investment may take include:
(a) an enterprise;
(b) shares, stock, and other forms of equity participation in an enterprise;
(c) bonds, debentures, other debt instruments, and loans;
(d) futures, options, and other derivatives;
(e) turnkey, construction, management, production, concession, revenue-sharing, and other similar contracts;
(f) intellectual property rights;
(g) licences, authorizations, permits, and similar rights conferred pursuant to domestic law; and
(h) other tangible or intangible, movable or immovable property, and related property rights, such as leases, mortgages, liens, and pledges.

Like the US Model BIT (2012) the German Model BIT (2008), by including 'shares of companies and other kinds of interest in companies' (Article 1(1)(b)), also covers portfolio investments. On the other side of the spectrum, some investment treaties limit their scope of application to direct investments.

In principle, the inclusion of company shares also protects minority shareholders. The arbitral award in the case *CMS Gas Transmission Co v Argentine Republic* illustrates that shareholding control is usually not the decisive element:

There is indeed no requirement that an investment, in order to qualify, must necessarily be made by shareholders controlling a company or owning the majority of its shares. It is well known incidentally that, depending on how shares are distributed, controlling shareholders can in fact own less than the majority of shares.[55]

The protection of shareholders is not limited to their legal rights under company law. Rather, the protection of shareholders extends to measures taken against the company as a whole, if they negatively affect the market value of the company (and indirectly the value of shares).[56]

---

[55] *CMS Gas Transmission Co v Argentine Republic*, ICSID Case No ARB/01/8 (Decision on Jurisdiction 2003), (2003) 42 ILM 788, para 51; see also the decision of the ad hoc Committee on annullment (2007) 46 ILM 1136 paras 69, 73.
[56] *CMS Gas Transmission Co v Argentine Republic*, ICSID Case No ARB/01/8 (Decision on Jurisdiction 2003), (2003) 42 ILM 788, paras 59, 66ff; *Siemens AG v Argentine Republic*, ICSID Case No ARB/02/8 (Decision on Jurisdiction 2004), (2005) 44 ILM 138, para 142; see also M Valasek and P Dumberry, 'Developments in the Legal Standing of Shareholders and Holding Corporations in Investor-State Disputes' (2011) ICSID Rev 34.

In *Poštová Banka v The Hellenic Republic*,[57] the arbitral tribunal held that a share-holder of a company cannot bring claims under an investment treaty against measures that affect the company's assets, unless such measures impair the value of his shares:

[…] [A] shareholder of a company incorporated in the host State may assert claims based on measures taken against such company's assets that impair the value of the claimant's shares. However, such claimant has no standing to pursue claims directly over the assets of the local company, as it has no legal right to such assets.[58]

Most recent international investment treaties apply to contractual rights and the payment of money or other claims which have economic value.[59] On this basis, State bonds are qualified as protected investments. In the case *Abaclat v The Argentine Republic*, the arbitral tribunal considered the purchase of Argentine State bonds as an investment in terms of the investment treaty between Argentina and Italy.[60] The arbitral tribunal referred to Article 1(1)(c) of the investment treaty, which includes 'obligations, private or public titles or any other right to performances or services having economic value, including capitalized revenues'.

The arbitral tribunal stressed the very broad scope of application of this provision:

It is true that the term 'obligations' is a broad term and can refer to any kind of contractual obligation, i.e., debt, and it is also true that the term 'title' is also very broad. However, put in the context of the further terms listed in lit. (c) such as 'economic value' or 'capitalized revenue', as well as considering that lit. (f) already deals with the more general concept of 'any right of economic nature', lit. (c) is to be read as referring to the financial meaning of these terms. Thus, the term 'obligation' may be understood as referring to an economic value incorporated into a credit title representing a loan. This kind of obligation would in the English language more commonly be called 'bond', rather than 'obligation'. Similarly, the term 'title' in Spanish and Italian would be more accurately translated into the English term of 'security', which means nothing more than a fungible, negotiable instrument representing financial value.[61]

By contrast, the arbitral award in *Poštová Banka v The Hellenic Republic*[62] ruled that Greek government bonds held by a Slovak bank and later affected by a 'hair-cut' (restructuring the Greek debt) under Greek legislation were not covered by the Slovakia–Greece BIT.[63] The arbitral tribunal found that the BIT's definition

---

[57] *Poštová Banka, AS and Istrokapital SE v The Hellenic Republic*, ICSID Case No ARB/13/8 (Award 2015).

[58] *Poštová Banka, AS and Istrokapital SE v The Hellenic Republic*, ICSID Case No ARB/13/8 (Award 2015) para 245.

[59] For the treatment of State bonds as an investment in terms of Article 25(1) of the ICSID Convention, see *FEDAX NV v Republic of Venezuela*, ICSID Case No ARB/96/3 (Decision on Jurisdiction 1997), (1998) 37 ILM 1378, para 29.

[60] *Abaclat and Others v The Argentine Republic*, ICSID Case No ARB/07/5 (Decision on Jurisdiction and Admissibility 2011).

[61] *Abaclat and Others v The Argentine Republic*, ICSID Case No ARB/07/5 (Decision on Jurisdiction and Admissibility 2011) para 355.

[62] *Poštová Banka, AS and Istrokapital SE v The Hellenic Republic*, ICSID Case No ARB/13/8 (Award 2015).

[63] Under Article 1(1) of the BIT protected investment 'means every kind of asset and in particular, though not exclusively includes […] c) loans, claims to money or to any performance under contract having a financial value'.

of protected 'investment', albeit framed broadly and clearly covering certain private bonds, remained silent as to public bonds. On this basis, the arbitral tribunal emphasized the differences between the definition in question and the one considered in the *Abaclat* case:

It is clear to the Tribunal that the list of investments contained in Article 1(1) of the Slovakia-Greece BIT does not include the language of the Italy-Argentina BIT from which the *Abaclat* tribunal derived its conclusions on admissibility and jurisdiction, and specifically, does not contain any reference to 'obligations' or to 'securities', much less to *public* titles or obligations.

Neither Article 1(1) of the Slovakia-Greece BIT nor other provisions of the treaty refer, in any way, to sovereign debt, public titles, public securities, public obligations or the like. The Slovakia-Greece BIT does not contain language that may suggest that the State parties considered, in the wide category of investments of the list of Article 1(1) of the BIT, public debt or public obligations, much less sovereign debt, as an investment under the treaty.[64]

Arbitral practice thus shows that the protection of bondholders depends on the structure and wording of investment treaties. Some agreements such as the CETA between Canada and the European Union and the TPP extend the protection of investments to 'bonds' and address specific issues of non-payment or restructuring of debt.[65]

(b) Conformity with the law of the host State

Some investment treaties limit the scope of application to investments which were made in accordance with the laws and regulations of the host State either in the definition of protected investments or through a special provision (so-called 'compliance with the law clause' or 'conformity clause').[66]

Such conformity standards may also result in the exclusion of claims based on corruption or other illegal actions.[67] In *Metal-Tech* the arbitral tribunal found that:

[T]he subject-matter scope of the legality requirement covers: (i) non-trivial violations of the host State's legal order [...], (ii) violations of the host State's foreign investment regime [...], and (iii) fraud—for instance, to secure the investment [...] or to secure profits. There is no doubt that corruption falls within one or more of these categories.[68]

According to the award in *World Duty Free v Kenya*, investors' rights tainted by corruption do not enjoy any form of protection, even in the absence of a

---

[64] *Poštová Banka, AS and Istrokapital SE v The Hellenic Republic*, ICSID Case No ARB/13/8 (Award 2015) paras 331f.
[65] Articles 8(1), 8(3) and Annex 8-B: Public Debt of CETA; Article 9.2.1, Annex 9-G On Public Debt of the TPP Agreement.
[66] See R Moloo and A Khachaturian, 'The Compliance with the Law Requirement in International Investment Law' (2011) 34 Fordham Intl LJ 1473.
[67] *Inceysa Vallisoletana SL v Republic of El Salvador*, ICSID Case No ARB/03/26 (Decision on Jurisdiction 2006).
[68] *Metal-Tech Ltd v The Republic of Uzbekistan*, ICSID Case No ARB/10/3 (Award 2013), (2015) 54 ILM 190, para 165.

conformity clause.[69] Other arbitral awards adopt a much more cautious approach to corruption.[70]

In *Niko Resources (Bangladesh) v People's Republic of Bangladesh et al*, the tribunal recognized that the host State may have a legitimate interest in maintaining a contract with a foreign investor, despite corruption of government officials, and concluded that the invalidity or annulment of such a contract depends upon a corresponding declaration of the host State.[71]

An important contribution to the understanding of conformity clauses was made by an ICSID tribunal in the case *Fraport AG Frankfurt Airport Services Worldwide v Republic of the Philippines.*[72]

In this case, the German company Fraport claimed compensation for the frustration of its investments in connection with the construction of an airport in the Philippines. The arbitral tribunal particularly referred to the conformity clause in the German–Philippine investment treaty. Fraport held shares in a Philippine company, which was granted a concession of the Philippine Government to build and manage an airport. According to the findings of the arbitral tribunal, Fraport had tried to circumvent legal thresholds for the permitted share of foreign enterprises in Philippine companies in the airport sector. The arbitral tribunal held that this violation of the Philippine law deprived Fraport's investments of protection under the Germany–Philippines BIT and affected the Philippines' consent to arbitration under the BIT. Consequently, the tribunal held that it had no jurisdiction over Fraport's claims:

Based on the foregoing analysis and after due and thorough consideration of the Parties' arguments and the evidence on the record, the Tribunal finds that Fraport violated the ADL when making its Initial Investment, the latter being consequently excluded as investment protected by the BIT because of its illegality. The illegality of the investment at the time it is made goes to the root of the host State's offer of arbitration under the treaty. As it has been held, '*States cannot be deemed to offer access to the ICSID dispute settlement mechanism to investments made in violation of their own law.*' [*Phoenix Action, Ltd v The Czech Republic*, ICSID Case No ARB/06/5 (Award 2009) para 101]. Lack of jurisdiction is founded in this case on the absence of consent to arbitration by the State for failure to satisfy an essential condition of its offer of this method of dispute settlement.[73]

[69] *World Duty Free Co Ltd v Republic of Kenya*, ICSID Case No ARB/00/7 (Award 2006), (2007) 46 ILM 339.
[70] See also AP Llamzon, *Transnational Corruption in International Investment Arbitration* (OUP 2014).
[71] *Niko Resources (Bangladesh) v People's Republic of Bangladesh et al*, ICSID Case No ARB/10/11 and ARB/10/18 (Decision on Jurisdiction 2013) paras 440ff.
[72] *Fraport AG Frankfurt Airport Services Worldwide v Republic of the Philippines*, ICSID Case No ARB/11/12 (Award 2014); the previous award in this case, ICSID Case No ARB/03/25 (Award 2007) was annulled for procedural reasons, see ICSID Case No ARB/03/25 (Annulment Proceeding 2010) paras 197ff.
[73] *Fraport AG Frankfurt Airport Services Worldwide v Republic of the Philippines*, ICSID Case No ARB/11/12 (Award 2014) para 467.

In the case *Alasdair Ross Anderson and Others v Republic of Costa Rica*, an ICSID tribunal denied treaty protection for an investment related to a snowball system.[74] Such a scheme, operating with fabulous expectations of profit, is usually based on fraud and a violation of criminal law. According to the award, under the conformity clause of the Canada–Costa Rica BIT, an investor, even if acting as a victim of a fraudulent scheme, has to use due diligence to assure that his investment is made in conformity with the laws of the host State.[75]

Minor infringements of a technical kind do not necessarily deprive an investor of protection under an investment treaty.[76] The host State cannot invoke violations of its laws by its own authorities in order to defeat claims of an investor.[77] It is still unclear whether a material violation of the laws of the host State affects the jurisdiction of the arbitral tribunal or whether it has to be reviewed as a question pertaining to the merits of the case. Modern arbitral practice tends to treat the issue as a matter of jurisdiction.[78]

4. Modern Standards of Investment Protection

(a) Admission and establishment of investments

Many investment treaties do not grant positive rights of entry and establishment to foreign investors and make the admission subject to the laws of the host State. This model still prevails, especially in BITs concluded by European countries and by developing countries. The 'pre-establishment-model' limits the host States' discretion as to admitting to foreign investments by the standards of national treatment and most-favoured-nation treatment (coupled with either a positive list or a negative list). Many countries, including the United States, Canada, and Japan, favour this model, which also governs most modern free trade agreements with an investment chapter.[79]

Some agreements grant admission of foreign investments even beyond national treatment and most-favoured-nation treatment. The Framework Agreement on the ASEAN Investment Area, in Article 7(1) determines that '[s]ubject to the provisions

[74] *Alasdair Ross Anderson and Others v Republic of Costa Rica*, ICSID Case No ARB(AF)/07/3 (Award 2010).
[75] *Alasdair Ross Anderson and Others v Republic of Costa Rica*, ICSID Case No ARB(AF)/07/3 (Award 2010) para 58.
[76] *Alpha Projektholding GmbH v Ukraine*, ICSID Case No ARB/07/16 (Award 2010) para 297; *Tokios Tokelés v Ukraine*, ICSID Case No ARB/02/18 (Decision on Jurisdiction 2004) para 183.
[77] *Ioannis Kardassopoulos v Georgia*, ICSID Case No ARB/05/18 (Decision on Jurisdiction 2007) para 182.
[78] *Alasdair Ross Anderson and Others v Republic of Costa Rica*, ICSID Case No ARB(AF)/07/3 (Award 2010) paras 47, 59; *Metal-Tech Ltd v The Republic of Uzbekistan*, ICSID Case No ARB/10/3 (Award 2013), (2015) 54 ILM 190, para 373.
[79] See for example 'Section B: Establishment of Investments' of CETA, in particular Article 8(4): Market Access.

of this Article, each Member State shall [...] open immediately all its industries for investments by ASEAN investors'.

The CETA provides market access in very liberal terms (Article 8(4)):

1. A Party shall not adopt or maintain with respect to market access through establishment by an investor of the other Party, on the basis of its entire territory or on the basis of the territory of a national, provincial, territorial, regional or local level of government, measures that:
   (a) impose limitations on:
      (i)   the number of enterprises that may carry out a specific economic activity whether in the form of numerical quotas, monopolies, exclusive suppliers or the requirement of an economic needs test;
      (ii) the total value of transactions or assets in the form of numerical quotas or the requirement of an economic needs test;
      (iii) the total number of operations or the total quantity of output expressed in terms of designated numerical units in the form of quotas or the requirement of an economic needs test;
      (iv) the participation of foreign capital in terms of maximum percentage limit on foreign shareholding or the total value of individual or aggregate foreign investment; or
      (v)   the total number of natural persons that may be employed in a particular sector or that an enterprise may employ and who are necessary for, and directly related to, the performance of economic activity in the form of numerical quotas or the requirement of an economic needs test; or
   (b) restricts or requires specific types of legal entity or joint venture through which an enterprise may carry out an economic activity.

   [...]

An important issue is the liberation of investments from performance requirements which govern business conduct. In WTO law, the Agreement on Trade-Related Investment Matters (TRIMs) eliminates a number of restrictive measures such as local content requirements.[80] Some agreements go beyond TRIMs in eliminating performance requirements. Thus, Article 8(5) of CETA provides:

1. A Party shall not impose, or enforce any of the following requirements, or enforce a commitment or undertaking, in connection with the establishment, acquisition, expansion, conduct, operation and management of any investments in its territory to:
   (a) export a given level or percentage of a good or service;
   (b) achieve a given level or percentage of domestic content;
   (c) purchase, use or accord a preference to a good produced or service provided in its territory, or to purchase a good or service from natural persons or enterprises in its territory;
   (d) relate the volume or value of imports to the volume or value of exports or to the amount of foreign exchange inflows associated with that investment;

---

[80] See Ch XIII.2.

(e) restrict sales of a good or service in its territory that the investment produces or provides by relating those sales to the volume or value of its exports or foreign exchange earnings;

(f) transfer technology, a production process or other proprietary knowledge to a natural person or enterprise in its territory; or

(g) supply exclusively from the territory of the Party a good produced or a service provided by the investment to a specific regional or world market.

[...]

This provision therefore illustrates the tendency of establishing TRIMs-plus standards on the regional level.

(b) National treatment

The principle of 'national treatment' requires equal treatment of foreign investors and national investors in like situations by a host State. In contrast to the minimum standard,[81] the principle of national treatment has no basis in customary international law but rests on international agreements.[82] National treatment is a common standard in investment treaties. Many national treatment clauses are only applicable once a business is established (post-establishment national treatment), whilst others also cover the establishment itself (pre-establishment national treatment). The US Model BIT (2012) follows a broad scope of application in Article 3(1):

Each Party shall accord to investors of the other Party treatment no less favourable than that it accords, in like circumstances, to its own investors with respect to the establishment, acquisition, expansion, management, conduct, operation, and sale or other disposition of investments in its territory.[83]

The obligation of national treatment also protects investors against de jure as well as de facto discriminations based on nationality. In practice, most of the discriminatory measures relate to a de facto discrimination. In any case, the decisive factor for a breach of the national treatment obligation is the practical impact of the measure rather than the host State's intention to discriminate against the foreign investor. In *Siemens v Argentine Republic*, the tribunal stated that 'intent is not decisive or essential for a finding of discrimination', further noting that the threshold issue for ascertaining whether a measure has resulted in discriminatory treatment is 'the impact of the measure on the investment'.[84]

---

[81] See Ch XXXII and Ch VI.4(a); see generally on the modern standards of investment protection, A Newcombe and L Paradell, *Law and Practice of Investment Treaties Standards of Treatment* (Aspen Publishers 2009); JW Salacuse, *The Law of Investment Treaties* (2nd end, OUP 2015); KJ Vandevelde, 'A Brief History of International Investment Agreements' (2005) 12 UC Davis J Int'lL & Pol'y 157.

[82] R Jennings and A Watts (eds), *Oppenheim's International Law* (9th edn, OUP 1996) 932f; C McLachlan, L Shore, and M Weiniger, *International Investment Arbitration: Substantive Principles* (OUP 2007) 212f.

[83] In the same terms, Article 3(2) of the US Model BIT (2012) refers to national treatment of investments.

[84] *Siemens AG v Argentine Republic*, ICSID Case No ARB/02/8 (Award 2007) para 321; other arbitral awards attach considerable importance to intent, see *Alex Genin, Eastern Credit Limited, Inc*

The scope of the required national treatment obligation depends on whether the foreign investor and domestic investors are placed in a 'like situation' or in 'like circumstances'.

In the case *Occidental Exploration and Production Co v The Republic of Ecuador*, the claimant, an oil company engaged in the exploration and production of oil under a contract with a State-owned oil company, was denied reimbursement of value added tax (VAT) for exports of oil, whilst national companies engaged in the export of other goods (eg flowers) received a VAT refund.[85] The refund, though under Ecuadorian legislation available to all exporters, was denied by the tax authorities to the claimant and to other oil companies.[86] Ecuador argued that taxation was already accounted for in the contractual arrangements of the claimant with the national oil company. Rejecting the GATT approach to 'like products', which bases the comparison on direct competition and substitutability, the arbitral tribunal did not follow a sector-by-sector analysis. The tribunal held that all exporters are situated in 'like' circumstances for purposes of tax refund.[87] Although the tribunal found that there had been no discriminatory intent in Ecuador's tax policy, it concluded that Ecuador had violated its national treatment obligation:

[...] OPEC has received treatment less favorable than that accorded to national companies. The Tribunal is convinced that this has not been done with the intent of discriminating against foreign-owned companies. [...] However, the result of the policy enacted and the interpretation followed by the SRI in fact has been a less favorable treatment of OPEC.[88]

In this case, the discrimination found by the tribunal by a cross-sector approach is far from obvious. The award in *Occidental Exploration and Production* hardly mitigated tendencies averse to the protection of foreign investments. Subsequently, in a deteriorated investment climate, Article 422(1) of the constitution of Ecuador (2008) prohibits the 'ceding of sovereign jurisdiction to international arbitration instances' in disputes between foreign companies or nationals and the Ecuadorian State. The Ecuadorian constitution, however, makes an exception for the settlement of disputes with other Latin American States or their nationals (Art. 422(2)). The Ecuadorian Government has

---

and *AS Baltoil v The Republic of Estonia*, ICSID Case No ARB/99/2 (Award 2001) (2002) 17 ICSID Rev 395, para 369.

[85] *Occidental Exploration and Production Co v The Republic of Ecuador*, LCIA Case No UN 3467 (Final Award 2004); see also SD Franck, 'International Decisions: Occidental Exploration and Production Company v The Republic of Ecuador' (2005) 99 AJIL 675.

[86] *Occidental Exploration and Production Co v The Republic of Ecuador*, LCIA Case No UN 3467 (Final Award 2004) paras 167ff.

[87] *Occidental Exploration and Production Co v The Republic of Ecuador*, LCIA Case No UN 3467 (Final Award 2004) para 173: the comparison 'cannot be done by addressing exclusively the sector in which that particular activity is undertaken'.

[88] *Occidental Exploration and Production Co v The Republic of Ecuador*, LCIA Case No UN 3467 (Final Award 2004) para 177.

withdrawn from several treaties on investment protection and settlement of investment disputes.

It is a controversial issue whether the principle of national treatment obliges the host State to treat the foreign investor no less favourably than the national investors in general or whether the national treatment standard requires the best treatment accorded to any national investor.

(c) Most-favoured-nation treatment

Modern bilateral investment treaties guarantee 'most-favoured-nation' (MFN) treatment.[89] The US Model BIT (2012) stipulates in Article 4(1):

Each Party shall accord to investors of the other Party treatment no less favorable than that it accords, in like circumstances, to investors of any non-Party with respect to the establishment, acquisition, expansion, management, conduct, operation, and sale or other disposition of investments in its territory.[90]

As national treatment, most-favoured-nation treatment is not a principle of customary international law.[91] The most-favoured-nation standard requires that an investor of a contracting State is treated at least as favourably as an investor of a third, non-contracting State.[92] Therefore, the most-favoured-nation principle constitutes a relative standard. As the ILC's Draft Articles on most-favoured-nation clauses define in Article 4:

A most-favoured-nation clause is a treaty provision whereby a state undertakes an obligation towards another state to accord most-favoured-nation treatment in an agreed sphere of relations.[93]

Some investment treaties exempt benefits resulting from customs unions or free trade agreements or certain tax privileges from the most-favoured-nation treatment. Most-favoured-nation clauses extend the scope of an agreement to benefits accorded between one of the contracting States and third countries. However, the application of a most-favoured-nation clause depends on similarity of the respective bilateral situations resulting from a comparable negotiating context (*ejusdem generis* rule).[94]

In the *Tecmed* case, the arbitral tribunal stated that the most-favoured-nation standard does not apply to agreements with third states which are inextricably

---

[89] See Article 3(2) of the German Model BIT (2008).

[90] In like terms, Article 4(2) of the US Model BIT refers to most-favoured-nation treatment of investments.

[91] See R Dolzer and C Schreuer, *Principles of International Investment Law* (2nd edn, OUP 2012) 206.

[92] UNCTAD, 'Most-Favoured-Nation Treatment', UNCTAD Series on Issues in International Investment Agreements II (2010).

[93] International Law Commission, *Draft Articles on Most-Favoured-Nation Clauses* (1978), text adopted by the International Law Commission at its 30th session.

[94] See Ch V.4(a).

linked to a specific bilateral negotiating situation with a particular set of rights and obligations. Benefits tied to such a specific context are not suitable for being applied to other investment treaties:

[M]atters relating to the application over time of the Agreement, which involve more the time dimension of application of its substantive provisions [...] go to the core of matters that must be deemed to be specifically negotiated by the Contracting Parties. [...] Their application cannot therefore be impaired by the principle contained in the most favored nation clause.[95]

As a rule, most-favoured-nation treatment covers the substantive rules contained in investment agreements between one contracting State and a third country which are more favourable than treatment under the basic BIT. Thus, the most-favoured-nation obligation may confer or at least clarify a claim to full compensation, in terms of fair market value, if a BIT between the host State and a third State establishes this compensation standard. In *CME Czech Republic BV (The Netherlands) v The Czech Republic*, the arbitral tribunal held:

The determination of compensation under the Treaty between the Netherlands and the Czech Republic on basis of the 'fair market value' finds further support in 'the most favored nation' provision of Article 3(5) of the Treaty. That paragraph specifies that if the obligations under national law of either party in addition to the present Treaty contain rules, whether general or specific, entitling investments by investors of the other party to a treatment more favourable than provided by the present Treaty, 'such rules to the extent that they are more favourable prevail over the present Agreement.' The bilateral investment treaty between the United States of America and the Czech Republic provides that compensation shall be equivalent to the fair market value of the expropriated investment immediately before the expropriatory action was taken.[96]

In *Hesham Talaat v Indonesia*, an arbitral tribunal applied the most-favoured-nation clause of the Agreement on Promotion, Protection and Guarantee of Investments among Member States of the Organisation of the Islamic Conference (OIC Investment Agreement) to the guarantee of fair and equitable treatment which was part of bilateral investment treaties ratified by Indonesia.[97]

A controversial issue is the application of a most-favoured-nation clause to dispute settlement provisions of BITs. The arbitral tribunal in *Salini Construttori SpA and Italstrade SpA v Jordan* rejected the claimant's submission that the most-favoured-nation clause contained in the BIT between Italy and Jordan extends to dispute settlement rules:

118. Article 3 of the BIT between Italy and Jordan does not include any provision extending its scope of application to dispute settlement. It does not envisage 'all rights or all matters covered by the agreement'. Furthermore, the Claimants have submitted nothing from

---

[95] *Técnicas Medioambientales Tecmed SA v The United Mexican States*, ICSID Case No ARB(AF)/00/2 (Award 2003), (2004) 43 ILM 133, para 69.

[96] *CME Czech Republic BV (The Netherlands) v The Czech Republic* (UNCITRAL Final Award 2004), 9 ICSID Reports 264, para 500.

[97] *Hesham Talaat M Al-Warraq v Indonesia* (UNCITRAL Final Award 2014) paras 540ff.

which it *might* be established that the common intention of the Parties was to have the most-favored nation clause apply to dispute settlement. Quite on the contrary, the intention as expressed in Article 9(2) of the BIT was to exclude from ICSID jurisdiction contractual disputes between an investor and *an* entity of a State Party in order that such disputes might be settled in accordance with the procedures set forth in the investment agreements. Lastly, the Claimants have not cited any practice in Jordan or Italy in support of their claims.

119. From this, the Tribunal concludes that Article 3 of the BIT does not apply insofar as dispute settlement clauses are concerned. Therefore the disputes foreseen in Article 9(1) of the BIT concluded between Jordan and Italy must be settled in accordance with the said Article. In the event that, as in this case, the dispute is between a foreign investor and an entity of the Jordanian State, the contractual disputes between them must, in accordance with Article 9(2), be settled under the procedure set forth in the investment agreement. The Tribunal has no jurisdiction to entertain them.[98]

In the case *Plama v Bulgaria*, the arbitral tribunal followed a similar line:

[A]n MFN provision in a basic treaty does not incorporate by reference dispute settlement provisions in whole or in part set forth in another treaty, unless the MFN provision in the basic treaty leaves no doubt that the contracting Parties intended to incorporate them.[99]

In exceptional cases, dispute settlement provisions may be covered by most-favoured-nation treatment if they merely remove procedural hurdles (eg a cooling off period or the submission of the dispute to national courts within a certain time period before initiating arbitral proceedings). In words of the arbitral tribunal in *Maffezini v Spain*:

[…] [T]he Tribunal is satisfied that the Claimant has convincingly demonstrated that the most favored nation clause included in the Argentine-Spain BIT embraces the dispute settlement provisions of this treaty. Therefore, relying on the more favourable arrangements contained in the Chile-Spain BIT and the legal policy adopted by Spain with regard to the treatment of its own investors abroad, the Tribunal concludes that Claimant had the right to submit the instant dispute to arbitration without first accessing the Spanish courts. In the Tribunal's view, the requirement for the prior resort to domestic courts spelled out in the Argentine-Spain BIT does not reflect a fundamental question of public policy considered in the context of the treaty, the negotiations relating to it, the other legal arrangements or the subsequent practice of the parties. Accordingly, the Tribunal affirms the jurisdiction of the Centre and its own competence in this case in respect of this aspect of the challenge made by the Kingdom of Spain.[100]

In any case, the extension of a specific dispute settlement mechanism (submission to a particular arbitration regime) provided in a treaty with a third State usually contradicts the intent of the parties to the basic treaty. As expressed by the arbitral tribunal in *Plama v Bulgaria*:

---

[98] *Salini Construttori SpA and Italstrade SpA v Jordan,* ICSID Case No ARB/02/13 (Decision on Jurisdiction 2004), (2005) 44 ILM 573, paras 118f.

[99] *Plama v Bulgaria,* ICSID Case No ARB/03/24 (Decision on Jurisdiction 2005), (2005) 44 ILM 721, para 223; see for an introductory note A Reinisch (2005) 44 ILM 717.

[100] *Maffezini v Spain,* ICSID Case No ARB/97/7 (Award 2000), (2001) 16 ICSID Rev 212, para 64.

[...] [A]n MFN provision in a basic treaty does not incorporate by reference dispute settlement provisions in whole or in part set forth in another treaty, unless the MFN provision in the basic treaty leaves no doubt that the contracting Parties intended to incorporate them.[101]

In line with this reasoning, dispute settlement provisions will be normally considered as the result of a specific negotiation situation, which in turn excludes the application of a MFN clause. Some recent treaties restrict the ambit of MFN clauses in particular by excluding their application to procedural matters. A prominent example is Article 8(7) of CETA:

For greater certainty, the 'treatment' referred to in paragraphs 1 and 2 [MFN] does not include procedures for the resolution of investment disputes between investors and states provided for in other international investment treaties and other trade agreements. Substantive obligations in other investment treaties and other trade agreements do not in themselves constitute 'treatment', and thus cannot give rise to a breach of this Article, absent measures adopted or maintained by a Party pursuant to those obligations.

(d) Fair and equitable treatment

The guarantee of 'fair and equitable treatment' has become one of the most important standards of international investment protection.[102] The interpretation of 'fair and equitable treatment' has been subject to much discussion. It is a matter of controversy, whether the fair and equitable treatment obligation merely reflects the minimum standard of customary international law[103] or whether it signifies a superior quality of treatment as an autonomous treaty standard. The interest of capital exporting countries in comprehensive protection of investors' reliance on legal stability, fair and predictable exercise of administrative powers, compliance with formal and informal commitments of the host State and all its entities, avoidance of undue delays, and procedural fairness, suggests a broad understanding of fair and equitable treatment, which adds a considerable value to customary standards. On the other hand, extensive interpretations in a number of arbitral decisions have fuelled concerns about undue restraints on regulatory freedom of host States and on new democratic choices. Especially enhanced environmental standards or changes of national policy, as in the case of Germany's radical turn in energy policy with the closure of nuclear power stations operated by foreign investors, may carry the risk of large compensation obligations. These implications have alarmed

---

[101] *Plama v Bulgaria*, ICSID Case No ARB/03/24 (Decision on Jurisdiction 2005), (2005) 44 ILM 721, para 223.
[102] See eg Article 2(2) of the German Model BIT; Article 1105(1) of NAFTA; Article 10(1) of the Energy Charter Treaty; see generally M Paparinskis. *The International Minimum Standard and Fair and Equitable Treatment* (OUP 2013); R Dolzer, 'Fair and Equitable Treatment: A Key Standard in Investment Treaties' (2005) 39 Int'l Law 87; OECD, 'Fair and Equitable Treatment Standard in International Investment Law' (2004/3) Working Paper on International Investment; R de Vietri, 'Fair and Equitable Treatment for Foreign Investment: What is the Current Standard at International Law' (2011) 14 Int'l Trade & Bus L Rev 414; I Tudor, *The Fair and Equitable Treatment Standard in the International Law of Foreign Investment* (OUP 2008).
[103] See Ch VI.4(a).

environmental activists and protagonists of regulatory freedom in politically sensitive areas in industrialized as well as in developing countries.

At least the core of fair and equitable treatment is consistent with the minimum
standard of customary international law:

[T]he minimum standard of treatment of fair and equitable treatment is infringed by conduct attributable to the State and harmful to the claimant if the conduct is arbitrary, grossly
unfair, unjust or idiosyncratic, is discriminatory and exposes the claimant to sectional or
racial prejudice, or involves a lack of due process leading to an outcome which offends
judicial propriety—as might be the case with a manifest failure of natural justice in judicial
proceedings or a complete lack of transparency and candour in an administrative process.[104]

In the *Neer* case (1926), the arbitral tribunal coined a classical formulation of the minimum standard.[105] For a violation of the minimum standard, the tribunal referred to
the host State and its authorities behaving 'in an outrageous way, in bad faith, in wilful
neglect of their duties, or in a pronounced degree of improper action'.[106]

Under Article 1105(1) of NAFTA, the relationship between the fair and equitable treatment obligation and the international minimum standard was a controversial issue.[107] Therefore, in 2001, the NAFTA Free Trade Commission adopted a
binding interpretation of the principle of fair and equitable treatment as reflecting
customary international law:

Article 1105(1) prescribes the customary international law minimum standard of treatment
of aliens as the minimum standard of treatment to be afforded to investments of investors
of another Party.

The concepts of 'fair and equitable treatment' and 'full protection and security' do not
require treatment in addition to or beyond that which is required by the customary international law minimum standard of treatment of aliens.

A determination that there has been a breach of another provision of the NAFTA, or
of a separate international agreement, does not establish that there has been a breach of
Article 1105(1).[108]

---

[104] *Waste Management Inc v United Mexican States*, ICSID Case No Arb(AF)/00/3 (Award 2004),
(2004) 43 ILM 967, para 98; see also *SD Myers Inc v Government of Canada* (UNCITRAL Partial
Award 2000), (2001) 40 ILM 1408, paras 262ff.

[105] *LFH Neer and Pauline Neer (USA) v United Mexican States* (Arbitral Award 1926) 4 RIIA 60.
According to a recent analysis of the *Neer* case, the findings of the United States – Mexico General Claims
Commission refer to the determination of a denial of justice rather than to the definition of the minimum
standard in general. See: J Paulsson and G Petrochilos, '*Neer*-ly Misled?' 22 ICSID Rev 242 (243ff).

[106] *LFH Neer and Pauline Neer (USA) v United Mexican States* (Arbitral Award 1926) 4 RIIA 60
para 5; a similar wording was used by the arbitral tribunal in the case of *Alex Genin et al v Republic of
Estonia,* ICSID Case No ARB/99/2 (Award 2001), (2002) 17 ICSID Rev 395, para 367.

[107] See on the discussion, CN Brower, Ch Brower, and JK Sharpe, 'The Coming Crisis in the
Global Adjudication System' (2003) 19 Arb Int'l 415 (428); P Dumberry, 'The Quest to Define "Fair
and Equitable Treatment" for Investors under International Law: The Case of the NAFTA Chapter 11
Pope & Talbot Awards' (2002) 3 JWI 657; PG Foy and RJC Deane, 'Foreign Investment Protection
under Investment Treaties: Recent Developments under Chapter 11 of the North American Free Trade
Agreement' (2001) 16 ICSID Rev 299; JC Thomas, 'Reflections on Article 1105 of NAFTA: History,
State Practice and the Influence of Commentators' (2002) 17 ICSID Rev 21.

[108] Free Trade Commission (FTC) Notes of Interpretation of Certain Chapter 11 Provisions (21
July 2001); see for a precise analysis: JC Thomas, 'Reflection on Article 1105 of NAFTA: History, State
Practice and the Influence of Commentators' (2002) 17 ICSID Rev 21.

Recent practices of Canada[109] and the United States follow this approach. The US Model BIT (2012) clarifies that the guarantee of fair and equitable treatment (as well as 'full protection and security') does not establish any obligation beyond the customary minimum standard. Article 5(1) and (2) of the US Model BIT states:

1. Each Party shall accord to covered investments treatment in accordance with customary international law, including fair and equitable treatment and full protection and security.
2. For greater certainty, paragraph 1 prescribes the customary international law minimum standard of treatment of aliens as the minimum standard of treatment to be afforded to covered investments. The concepts of 'fair and equitable treatment' and 'full protection and security' do not require treatment in addition to or beyond that which is required by that standard, and do not create additional substantive rights.

   The obligation in paragraph 1 to provide:
   (a) 'fair and equitable treatment' includes the obligation not to deny justice in criminal, civil, or administrative adjudicatory proceedings in accordance with the principle of due process embodied in the principal legal systems of the world; and
   (b) 'full protection and security' requires each Party to provide the level of police protection required under customary international law.

The same provision was included in Article 9(6) paras 1 and 2 of the TPP, which defines 'full protection and security' and 'fair and equitable treatment' by reference to the customary minimum standard.

The CETA defines the standard of 'fair and equitable treatment' in rather narrow terms, which come close to the established core of the customary minimum standard; however, CETA additionally provides for the protection of legitimate expectations. Article 8(10) of CETA states:

1. Each Party shall accord in its territory to covered investments of the other Party and to investors with respect to their covered investments fair and equitable treatment and full protection and security in accordance with paragraphs 2 to 6.
2. A Party breaches the obligation of fair and equitable treatment referenced in paragraph 1 if a measure or series of measures constitutes:
   (a) denial of justice in criminal, civil or administrative proceedings;
   (b) fundamental breach of due process, including a fundamental breach of transparency, in judicial and administrative proceedings;
   (c) manifest arbitrariness;
   (d) targeted discrimination on manifestly wrongful grounds, such as gender, race or religious belief;
   (e) abusive treatment of investors, such as coercion, duress and harassment; or
   (f) a breach of any further elements of the fair and equitable treatment obligation adopted by the Parties in accordance with paragraph 3 of this Article.
3. The Parties shall regularly, or upon request of a Party, review the content of the obligation to provide fair and equitable treatment. The Committee on Services and Investment [...] may develop recommendations in this regard and submit them to the CETA Joint Committee for decision.

---

[109] Article 5 of the Canadian Foreign Investment Promotion and Protection Agreements (FIPA).

4. When applying the above fair and equitable treatment obligation, a tribunal may take into account whether a Party made a specific representation to an investor to induce a covered investment, that created a legitimate expectation, and upon which the investor relied in deciding to make or maintain the covered investment, but that the Party subsequently frustrated. [...]

Other investment treaties are less explicit. In the absence of specific commitments or representations made by the host States, it is difficult to establish abstract guidelines for 'legitimate expectations', the frustration of which violates fair and equitable treatment. In general, the host State may rely on new material data (eg as to risk-assessment in environmental law as a basis for regulatory changes). A foreign investor must also conform to enhanced labour and social standards, which reflect rising standards of living or correspond to widespread international tendencies. On the other hand, abrupt turnarounds in political choices, which substantially modify the regulatory framework for businesses, may easily clash with legitimate expectations, especially if they are implemented without smooth transitions.

In any case, it is well acknowledged that the minimum standard as a part of customary international law has evolved over time. The interpretation of fair and equitable treatment in the rich arbitral case-law of the last decades has undoubtedly contributed to this development. In *Mondev International v United States of America*, the arbitral tribunal emphasized that 'the content of the minimum standard today cannot be limited to the content of customary international law as recognized in arbitral decisions in the 1920s'.[110]

The United States and Canada both declared in *ADF Group Inc v United States of America* that the interpretation of the international minimum standard is not static but rather in a constant process of development.[111] The arbitral tribunal sided with this view:

[W]hat customary international law projects is not a static photograph of the minimum standard of treatment of aliens as it stood in 1927 when the Award in the Neer case was rendered. For both customary international law and the minimum standard of treatment of aliens it incorporates, are constantly in a process of development.[112]

Equating fair and equitable treatment with the minimum standard (or a specific customary rule closely related to the minimum standard) works in two different ways. On the one hand, the equation means that 'fair and equitable treatment' is not more favourable than the customary standard and thus restrains the scope of the fair and equitable treatment. On the other hand, it also means that the minimum standard does not fall below 'fair and equitable treatment'. This understanding

---

[110] *Mondev International Ltd v United States of America*, ICSID Case No ARB(AF)/99/2 (Award 2002), (2003) 42 ILM 85, para 123.

[111] *ADF Group Inc v United States of America*, ICSID Case No ARB(AF)/00/1 (Award 2003), (2003) 6 ICSID Rep 470, paras 121, 179; see U Onwuamaegbu, 'ADF Group Inc. v United States of America (Case No ARB(AF)/00/1): Introductory Note' (2003) 18 ICSID Rev 193f.

[112] *ADF Group Inc v United States of America*, ICSID Case No ARB(AF)/00/1 (Award 2003), (2003) 6 ICSID Rep 470, para 179.

promotes a dynamic development of the minimum standard by assimilating it to modern investment protection standards. It is an open question whether the minimum standard, including the underlying parameters of 'decent' treatment (eg as to legal certainty or proportionality of State action), has developed dynamically or whether only the manner how traditional parameters (eg wilful neglect or arbitrariness) are applied has changed in the last decades. In *Mondev International v United States of America*, the arbitral tribunal acknowledged that the minimum standard has moved on and does not only protect from maltreatment in bad faith:

> To the modern eye, what is unfair or inequitable need not equate with the outrageous or the egregious. In particular, a State may treat foreign investment unfairly and inequitably without necessarily acting in bad faith.[113]

Adopting the evolutionary approach, the arbitral tribunal in *Waste Management II*,[114] after analysing arbitral case-law under Article 1105 of the NAFTA, held the minimum standard of treatment to include judicial propriety as well as transparency in an administrative process and the protection of the investor's reasonable expectations:

> [...] [T]he minimum standard of treatment of fair and equitable treatment is infringed by conduct attributable to the State and harmful to the claimant if the conduct is arbitrary, grossly unfair, unjust or idiosyncratic, is discriminatory and exposes the claimant to sectional or racial prejudice, or involves a lack of due process leading to an outcome which offends judicial propriety—as might be the case with a manifest failure of natural justice in judicial proceedings or a complete lack of transparency and candour in an administrative process. In applying this standard it is relevant that the treatment is in breach of representations made by the host State which were reasonably relied on by the claimant.[115]

The Dominican Republic–Central America Free Trade Agreement (DR–CAFTA) also links fair and equitable treatment as well as full protection and security to the minimum standard under customary international law (Article 10.5). In *Railroad Development Corporation*,[116] the arbitral tribunal followed the dynamic understanding of the customary standard as formulated in *Waste Management II*. In this case, the claimant, a US corporation, had won an international public bid pertaining to infrastructure and other railway assets for the provision of transport services in Guatemala. On the basis of a decree ratified by the Congress of Guatemala and a contract with the state-owned railway company the claimant restored commercial services on several railway lines through a domestic company in which it had a controlling share and made the agreed payments in return of the usufruct. After years of uncontroversial operation of the railway services, the Government

---

[113] *Mondev International Ltd v United States of America*, ICSID Case No ARB(AF)/99/2 (Award 2002), (2003) 42 ILM 85 para 116.
[114] *Waste Management, Inc v United Mexican States II*, ICSID Case No ARB(AF)/00/3 (Award 2004), (2004) 43 ILM 967.
[115] Ibid, para 98.
[116] *Railroad Development Corporation (RDC) v Republic of Guatemala*, ICSID Case No ARB/07/23 (Award 2012).

of Guatemala invoked the violation of formal requirements. After trying to intro-duce substantive modifications of the agreed conditions, which were unrelated to the alleged illegality, the Government formally declared the concession to be void (*lesivo* declaration).

In the circumstances of this case, the *lesivo* remedy has been used under a cloak of formal correctness allegedly in defense of the rule of law, in fact for exacting concessions unrelated to the finding of *lesivo*. […] [T]he Government should be precluded from raising violations of its own law as a defense when, for a substantial period of time it knowingly overlooked them, obtained benefits from them, and it had the power to correct them.

In the Tribunal's view, the manner in which and the grounds on which Respondent applied the *lesivo* remedy in the circumstances of this case constituted a breach of the mini-mum standard of treatment in Article 10.5 of CAFTA by being, in the words of *Waste Management II*, 'arbitrary, grossly unfair, [and] unjust'.[117]

The arbitral award found that the Guatemalan Government could not rely on vio-lations of domestic law which it had been aware of for considerable time and after receiving the benefit of the investor's operations.

By contrast, in *Glamis Gold Ltd v United States of America*, the arbitral tribunal followed a more static approach and assumed that the traditional standards, as developed in the *Neer* case, continue to apply today and only have to be concretized from a modern observer's view. However, the tribunal conceded that bad faith is not necessary to find a violation of fair and equitable treatment:

It therefore appears that, although situations may be more varied and complicated today than in the 1920s, the level of scrutiny is the same. The fundamentals of the Neer standard thus still apply today: to violate the customary international law minimum standard of treatment codified in Article 1105 of the NAFTA, an act must be sufficiently egregious and shocking—a gross denial of justice, manifest arbitrariness, blatant unfairness, a complete lack of due process, evident discrimination, or a manifest lack of reasons—so as to fall below accepted international standards and constitute a breach of Article 1105(1). The Tribunal notes that one aspect of evolution from Neer that is generally agreed upon is that bad faith is not required to find a violation of the fair and equitable treatment standard, but its presence is conclusive evidence of such. Thus, an act that is egregious or shocking may also evidence bad faith, but such bad faith is not necessary for the finding of a violation. The standard for finding a breach of the customary international law minimum standard of treatment therefore remains as stringent as it was under Neer; it is entirely possible, however, that as an international community, we may be shocked by State actions now that did not offend us previously.[118]

Outside the context of NAFTA, arbitral tribunals have frequently interpreted the standard of fair and equitable treatment in the respective BITs as an autonomous concept which does not necessarily coincide with the customary standard. In *Desert*

---

[117] Ibid, para 234f.
[118] *Glamis Gold Ltd v United States of America* (UNCITRAL Award 2009) para 616; see on this decision MC Ryan, '*Glamis Gold, Ltd v The United States* and The Fair and Equitable Treatment Standard' (2011) 56 McGill LJ 919; SW Schill, 'Case Note—*Glamis Gold Ltd v The United States of America*' (2010) 104 AJIL 253.

Line Projects LLC v Republic of Yemen, the arbitral tribunal found that exerting undue pressure on a foreign investor by physical or economic threat or duress, in order to reach a desired settlement, is inconsistent with the principle of fair and equitable treatment. The tribunal underlined that, to be valid, a settlement agreement must be concluded in conditions of fair and equitable negotiations:

The settlement agreement according to which the prevailing party in an arbitral proceeding renounces half of its rights without due consideration can only be valid if it is the result of an authentic, fair and equitable negotiation [...].[119]

Furthermore, the tribunal declared that a settlement agreement extracted by the government of Yemen by financial and physical duress violated the standard of fair and equitable treatment:

Considering and weighing all of the circumstances before it, the Arbitral Tribunal concludes that the Settlement Agreement was entered into by the Claimant under financial and physical duress and that the Respondent's objections in this regard should be dismissed. Moreover, the Arbitral Tribunal holds that the conclusion of the Settlement Agreement contravened the Respondent's obligations under Article 3 of the BIT. Therefore, the Arbitral Tribunal declares that the Settlement Agreement is not entitled to international effect.[120]

According to modern arbitral case-law, the standard of fair and equitable treatment protects the investor's legitimate expectations. Moreover, the principle obliges the host State to act in a transparent way and to take predictable decisions in accordance with international law. Arbitral rulings tend to interpret the standard of fair and equitable treatment, inter alia, as expression of the good faith principle and as protection of legitimate confidence in the consistency of the host State's actions. The award in *Tecmed v Mexico* affirmed this understanding in a persuasive way.[121]

In the *Tecmed* case, the Mexican Government replaced a previous licence of indefinite duration to operate a landfill by a new licence which had to be extended every year. Finally, the Government rejected Tecmed's request to renew the licence to operate the landfill more in response to political resistance than for legal considerations. Tecmed argued that the refusal of a renewed licence destroyed the economic basis of its investment and constituted a violation of its right to fair and equitable treatment.

In the view of the arbitral tribunal, the principle of good faith stands behind the obligation of fair and equitable treatment in the Spanish–Mexican BIT:

The Arbitral Tribunal finds that the commitment of fair and equitable treatment included in Article 4(1) of the Agreement is an expression and part of the bona fide principle

---

[119] *Desert Line Projects LLC v Republic of Yemen*, ICSID Case No ARB/05/17 (Award 2008), (2009) 48 ILM 82, para 179.

[120] *Desert Line Projects LLC v Republic of Yemen*, ICSID Case No ARB/05/17 (Award 2008), (2009) 48 ILM 82, para 194.

[121] *Técnicas Medioambientales Tecmed SA v The United Mexican States*, ICSID Case No ARB(AF)/00/2 (Award 2003), (2004) 43 ILM 133.

recognized in international law, although bad faith from the State is not required for its violation [...].[122]

In the *Tecmed* case, the tribunal held that the foreign investor may expect the host State to act consistently and transparently. From this perspective, the standard of fair and equitable treatment protects the foreign investor against unexpected modifications of the legal framework for the investment, if the host State established confidence in the stability and continuity of the legal conditions either by contractual agreements or by other commitments:

[Fair and equitable treatment] requires the contracting Parties to provide to international investments treatment that does not affect the basic expectations that were taken into account by the foreign investor to make the investment. The foreign investor expects the host State to act in a consistent manner, free from ambiguity and totally transparently in its relations with the foreign investor, so that it may know beforehand any and all rules and regulations that will govern its investments, as well as the goals of the relevant policies and administrative practices or directives, to be able to plan its investment and comply with such regulations. [...] The foreign investor also expects the host State to act consistently, i.e. without arbitrarily revoking any preexisting decisions or permits issued by the State that were relied upon by the investor to assume its commitments as well as to plan and launch its commercial and business activities. The investor also expects the State to use the legal instruments that govern the actions of the investor or the investment in conformity with the function usually assigned to such instruments, and not to deprive the investor of its investment without the required compensation. In fact, failure by the host State to comply with such pattern of conduct with respect to the foreign investor or its investments affects the investor's ability to measure the treatment and protection awarded by the host State and to determine whether the actions of the host State conform to the fair and equitable treatment principle. Therefore, compliance by the host State with such pattern of conduct is closely related to the above-mentioned principle, to the actual chances of enforcing such principle, and to excluding the possibility that state action be characterized as arbitrary [...].[123]

In *CMS Gas Transmission Co v Argentine Republic*, the arbitral tribunal followed this approach. In this case, a US investor had acquired a 30 per cent share in an Argentinean gas transportation company. This investment was based on a complex licence regime and statutory regulations under which the gas company had the right to calculate gas tariffs in US-Dollars and then convert them to Argentinean Pesos at the prevailing exchange rate. During Argentina's economic crisis, the Government of Argentina suspended this regime, which guaranteed stable returns of profit. As a result, the value of the investor's share dropped dramatically. The US investor claimed that Argentina had breached the fair and equitable treatment obligation 'as it has profoundly altered the stability and predictability of the investment environment, an assurance that was key to its decision to invest'.[124] The arbitral tribunal

---

[122] *Técnicas Medioambientales Tecmed SA v The United Mexican States,* ICSID Case No ARB(AF)/00/2 Award (2003), (2004) 43 ILM 133, para 153.
[123] *Técnicas Medioambientales Tecmed SA v The United Mexican States,* ICSID Case No ARB(AF)/00/2 (Award 2003), (2004) 43 ILM 133, para 154.
[124] *CMS Gas Transmission Co v Argentine Republic,* ICSID Case No ARB/01/8 (Award 2005), (2005) 44 ILM 1205, para 267.

supported this approach and found that '[...] a stable legal business is an essential element of fair and equitable treatment'.[125]

The protected expectations of the investor were specified in *LG & E v Argentine Republic*:

[T]he investor's fair expectations have the following characteristics: they are based on the conditions offered by the host State at the time of the investment; they may not be established unilaterally by one of the parties; they must exist and be enforceable by law; in the event of infringement by the host State, a duty to compensate the investor for damages arises except for those caused in the event of state of necessity; however, the investor's fair expectations cannot fail to consider parameters such as business risk or industry's regular patterns. [...]

[Thus] the fair and equitable standard consists of the host State's consistent and transparent behavior, free of ambiguity that involves the obligation to grant and maintain a stable and predictable legal framework necessary to fulfill the justified expectations of the foreign investor.[126]

However, in the case *National Grid PLC v Argentine Republic*, the arbitral tribunal adopted a more flexible interpretation of this standard in times of economic crisis:

What is fair and equitable is not an absolute parameter. What would be unfair and inequitable in normal circumstances may not be so in a situation of an economic and social crisis.[127]

This approach certainly does justice to the economic and social context of an investment. However, even in time of crisis, the foreign investor is not as committed to solidarity as nationals of the host State are. The adjustment of fair and equitable treatment to a strained situation of the host State may not go as far as pre-empting the application of the rules on necessity.

The CETA addresses the protection of legitimate expectations in a specific clause which refers to 'a specific representation to an investor to induce a covered investment'.[128]

In *MTD Equity Sdn Bhd and MTD Chile SA v Republic of Chile*, the arbitral tribunal deduced the host State's obligation to encourage and protect foreign investment proactively from the principle of fair and equitable treatment:[129]

[F]air and equitable treatment should be understood to be treatment in an even-handed and just manner, conducive to fostering the promotion of foreign investment. Its terms

---

[125] *CMS Gas Transmission Co v Argentine Republic*, ICSID Case No ARB/01/8 (Award 2005), (2005) 44 ILM 1205, para 274. In its decision partially annulling the award, the ad hoc Committee upheld the tribunal's approach to fair and equitable treatment, (2007) 46 ILM 1136 para 85.

[126] *LG & E Energy Corporation, LG & E Capital Corporation and LG & E International, Inc v Argentine Republic*, ICSID Case No ARB/02/1 (Decision on Liability 2006), (2006) 21 ICSID Rev 155, paras 130f.

[127] *National Grid PLC v Argentine Republic* (UNCITRAL Award 2008), (2009) 103 AJIL 722, para 180.

[128] Article 8(10)(4) CETA; cited above.

[129] On this issue, see T Wanjura, 'Azurix Corp. v. Argentine Republic: Tribunal Ruling in Favour of Foreign Investor Requires "Pro-Active Behaviour" by the Host State to Encourage and Protect Foreign Investment under the Fair and Equitable Treatment Standard of U.S.-Argentina BIT' (2007) 13 Law Bus Rev 983.

are framed as a pro-active statement—'to promote', 'to create', 'to stimulate'—rather than prescriptions for a passive behavior of the State or avoidance of prejudicial conduct to the investors.[130]

Recent practice tends to accord considerable weight to the host States' regulatory interests, recognizing a broad margin of discretion. In *Electrabel v Hungary*, an ECT arbitral tribunal held that 'the application of the ECT's FET standard allows for a balancing exercise by the host State in appropriate circumstances' and further noted that '[t]he host State is not required to elevate unconditionally the interests of the foreign investor above all other considerations in every circumstance'.[131]

The obligation of fair and equitable treatment has gained considerable relevance with regard to judicial proceedings. In *Mondev v United States of America*, the arbitral tribunal stated:

[...] In the end the question is whether, at an international level and having regard to generally accepted standards of the administration of justice, a tribunal can conclude in the light of all the available facts that the impugned decision was clearly improper and discreditable, with the result that the investment has been subjected to unfair and inequitable treatment.[132]

In connection with the discriminatory treatment of a Canadian investor before a Mississippi State court in *Loewen v United States of America*, the award specified the meaning of fair and equitable treatment and full protection and security, as enshrined in Article 1105(1) of NAFTA:

[W]e take it to be the responsibility of the State under international law and, consequently, of the courts of a State, to provide a fair trial of a case to which a foreign investor is a party. It is the responsibility of the courts of a State to ensure that litigation is free from discrimination against a foreign litigant and that the foreign litigant should not become the victim of sectional or local prejudice.[133]

After analysing the proceedings which showed racist and xenophobic elements tolerated by the judge, the arbitral tribunal concluded:

[T]he whole trial and its resultant verdict were clearly improper and discreditable and cannot be squared with minimum standards of international law and fair and equitable treatment.[134]

It is a controversial issue whether the investor may invoke a violation of the fair and equitable treatment obligation by judicial proceedings only after exhausting

---

[130] *MTD Equity Sdn Bhd and MTD Chile SA v Republic of Chile*, ICSID Case No ARB/01/7 (Award 2004), (2005) 44 ILM 91, para 113.

[131] *Electrabel S.A. v Hungary*, ICSID Case No ARB/07/19 (Award 2015) para 165. In *Philip Morris v Uruguay*, the arbitral tribunal recognized a broad 'margin of appreciation' of host governments, 'at least in contexts such as public health', *Philip Morris Brands Sàrl, Philip Morris Products S.A. and Abal Hermanos S.A. v Oriental Republic of Uruguay*, ICISD Case No ARB/10/7 (Award 2016) para 399.

[132] *Mondev International Ltd v United States of America*, ICSID Case No ARB(AF)/99/2 (Award 2002), (2003) 42 ILM 85, para 127.

[133] *Loewen Group, Inc and Raymond L Loewen v United States of America*, ICSID Case No ARB(AF)/98/3 (Award 2003), (2003) 42 ILM 811, para 123.

[134] Ibid, para 137.

domestic remedies (in the sense of the so-called 'finality rule'). Exhaustion of local remedies allows the judicial system of the host State to correct an unfair treatment by a lower court. Therefore, the award in *Loewen v United States of America* insisted in this requirement:

The purpose of the requirement that a decision of a lower court be challenged through the judicial process before the State is responsible for a breach of international law constituted by judicial decision is to afford the State the opportunity of redressing through its legal system the inchoate breach of international law occasioned by the lower court decision.[135]

Other arbitral awards have also acknowledged the existence of the aforesaid 'finality rule'.[136] However, the 'finality rule' does not apply in case of unfair treatment by the executive and legislative branches of the host State, even if effective judicial protection is available. In this case, the investor may directly initiate arbitral proceedings. It is therefore by no means obvious that judicial malfunction should always be privileged by a local remedies requirement. It seems arguable that a denial of justice may not only result from acts of the judiciary, but also from acts of executive or legislative organs. But even in this case the foreign investor is not deprived of direct access to arbitration without prior recourse to domestic remedies.

If the fair and equitable treatment standard is violated, the host State must pay compensation. Such claim to compensation may often overlap with possible compensation for expropriation. In practice, when measures diminish or even destroy the profitability of an investment without a straightforward taking of property, arbitral tribunals tend to base compensation on the principle of fair and equitable treatment rather than on expropriation, because the 'threshold of expropriation' is often difficult to establish.

Some treaties, especially US BITs and the European Energy Charter Treaty, contain an 'effective means' clause which primarily refers to the judicial protection of investors' rights. Thus, Article II(7) of the US–Ecuador Bilateral Investment Treaty provides:

Each Party shall provide effective means of asserting claims and enforcing rights with respect to investment, investment agreements, and investment authorizations.

Such a clause may be seen as a supplement to the standard of fair and equitable treatment in context of the judicial system of the host State, or as a protection against denial of justice.[137] The scope of 'effective means' clauses covers similar deficiencies in the administration of justice as the customary minimum standard or the principle of fair and equitable treatment in as much as these standards prohibit denial of

---

[135] *Loewen Group, Inc and Raymond L Loewen v United States of America*, ICSID Case No ARB(AF)/98/3 (Award 2003), (2003) 42 ILM 811, para 156.
[136] *Flughafen Zürich A.G. and Gestión e Ingeniería IDC S.A. v Venezuela*, ICSID Case No ARB 10/19 (Award 2014) paras 642f.
[137] See *Duke Energy v Ecuador*, ICSID Case No ARB/04/19 (Award 2008) paras 384–403.

justice. However, the 'effective means' clauses may establish stricter requirements as compared to the prohibition of denial of justice, which, in turn, does not usually go beyond measures inconsistent with common understandings of judicial propriety. In *Chevron Corporation (USA) and Texaco Petroleum Company (USA) v The Republic of Ecuador*, the arbitral tribunal found that endemic court congestion, which the host State allows to become a persistent feature of the domestic judicial system, violates the 'effective means' clause.[138]

(e) Full protection and security

Most investment treaties grant 'full (or "constant") protection and security' to covered investments.[139] The core meaning of this concept refers to measures taken by the host State to protect foreign investors and their investments against threats to the life and the property of the investor as well as other forms of harassment according to available means in terms of the diligence which can be reasonably expected. As a rule, 'full protection and security' refers to protection by the host State's authorities against physical violence and other threats, particularly from non-State actors. While the issue still remains somewhat controversial, some arbitral tribunals have expressly confined the scope of the 'full protection and security' standard to protection against private violence. For instance, in *Electrabel v Hungary*, the arbitrators concluded that, by assuring full protection and security, the host State assumes 'an obligation actively to create and maintain measures that promote security' and that these measures 'must be capable of protecting the covered investment against adverse action by private parties'.[140] However, this standard also applies to measures taken by the police or armed forces in response to riots, rebellion, or civil war.[141] As the arbitral tribunal in *Saluka Investments BV v The Czech Republic* states:

[T]he standard obliges the host State to adopt all reasonable measures to protect assets and property from threats or attacks which may target particularly foreigners or certain groups of foreigners.[142]

---

[138] *Chevron Corporation and Texaco Petroleum Company v Republic of Ecuador*, PCA Case No 2009-23 (Partial Award on the Merits 2010) paras 242ff.

[139] See Article 5 of the US Model BIT (2012); Article 4(1) of the German Model BIT (2008); Article 1105(1) of the NAFTA. See G Cordero Moss, 'Full Protection and Security' in A Reinisch (ed), *Standard of Investment Protection* (OUP 2008) 131; C Schreuer, 'Full Protection and Security' (2010) J Int'l Dispute Settlement 1; HE Zeitler, 'The Guarantee of "Full Protection and Security" in Investment Treaties Regarding Harm Caused by Private Actors' (2005) Stockholm Int'l Arb Rev 1.

[140] *Electrabel SA v Hungary*, ICSID Case No ARB/07/19 (Decision on Jurisdiction, Applicable Law and Liability 2012) paras 7.145f.

[141] *Asian Agricultural Products Ltd v Republic of Sri Lanka*, ICSID Case No ARB/87/3 (Final Award 1990), (1991) 6 ICSID Rev 533, para 48.

[142] *Saluka Investments BV v The Czech Republic*, PCA (Partial Award 2006), para 484. See also *Rumeli Telekom AS and Telsim Mobil Telekomunikasyon Hizmetleri AS v Republic of Kazakhstan*, ICSID Case No ARB/05/16 (Award 2008) para 668; *Eastern Sugar v Czech Republic*, SCC Case No 088/2004 (Partial Award 2007), (2007) IIC 310, para 203.

The relation of the full protection and security standard with the international minimum standard under customary law is a matter of interpretation of the relevant agreement. Under Article 1105(1) of NAFTA, the Free Trade Commission interpreted both standards as co-existent, with 'full protection and security' establishing particular obligations.[143] By contrast, the US Model BIT (2012) defines the concept of 'full protection and security' as referring to the treatment required under customary law and as not creating substantive rights in addition to the minimum standard (Article 5(2)). It adds that 'full protection and security' means that each party must 'provide the level of police protection required under customary law' (Article 5(2)(b)).

In the absence of such clarification, the argument in favour of full concordance with customary rules is much stronger for 'full protection and security' (given its connotation with physical security) than for 'fair and equitable treatment'. Several arbitral tribunals concluded that the minimum standard and the obligation to provide full protection and security have a similar meaning. In *Noble Ventures, Inc v Romania*, the arbitral tribunal appears to side with the view that 'full protection and security' has the same scope as the customary minimum standard:

[I]t seems doubtful whether that provision can be understood as being wider in scope than the general duty to provide for protection and security of foreign nationals found in the customary international law of aliens.[144]

Other tribunals infer a higher level of responsibility from specific 'full protection and security' clauses. The award in *Asian Agricultural Products Ltd v Republic of Sri Lanka* concluded:

In the opinion of the present Arbitral Tribunal, the addition of words like 'constant' or 'full' to strengthen the required standards of 'protection and security' could justifiably indicate the Parties' intention to require within their treaty relationship a standard of 'due diligence' higher than the 'minimum standard' of general international law. But, the nature of both the obligation and ensuing responsibility remain unchanged, since the added words 'constant' or 'full' are by themselves not sufficient to establish that the Parties intended to transform their mutual obligation into a 'strict liability'.[145]

As the later excerpt already suggests, States are not subject to strict liability for all acts of violence and disturbances. Arbitral practice understands 'full protection and security' not as an absolute guarantee but as an obligation to exercise due diligence.[146]

---

[143] Free Trade Commission, Interpretation of 21 July 2011; see JC Thomas, 'Reflection on Article 1105 of NAFTA: History, State Practice and the Influence of Commentators' (2002) 17 ICSID Rev 21.

[144] *Noble Ventures Inc v Romania*, ICSID Case No ARB/01/11 (Award 2005), (2005) IIC 179, para 164.

[145] *Asian Agricultural Products Ltd v Republic of Sri Lanka*, ICSID Case No ARB/87/3 (Final Award 1990), (1991) 6 ICSID Rev 533, para 50.

[146] *Noble Ventures, Inc v Romania*, ICSID Case No ARB/01/11 (Award 2005), (2005) IIC 179, para 164.

Consequently, the obligation of full protection and security cannot be construed as a guarantee of result. In this vein, the award in *Asian Agricultural Products Ltd v Republic of Sri Lanka* stated:

The Arbitral Tribunal is not aware of any case in which the obligation assumed by the host State to provide the nationals of the other contracting State with 'full protection and security' was construed as absolute obligation which guarantees that no damages will be suffered, in the sense that any violation thereof creates automatically a 'strict liability' on behalf of the host State.[147]

If violence and harassment do not stand in context with harassment by non-State actors and can be exclusively attributed to the host State, it incurs full responsibility already under the customary minimum standard.[148] If the host State's measures were provoked by public violence or even acts of rebellion, the host State must exercise due diligence to avoid or minimize damages to foreign investors.[149] Similarly, the host State has an obligation of due diligence to prevent damages resulting from private activities and to provide redress for violations already inflicted.[150] Sometimes, responsibility of the host State flows from activities which are neither covered by express governmental authority nor attributable to non-State actors. In the case of looting by soldiers, the arbitral tribunal in *American Manufacturing & Trading, Inc v Republic of Zaire* based the responsibility of the host State on its failure to prevent the damage inflicted on the foreign investor.[151] The excess of authority or contraventions of instructions by persons exercising governmental authority does not affect the attribution of their conduct to the State.[152] Such conduct *ultra vires* directly establishes responsibility of the host State independently from any obligations to protect.

Arbitral tribunals tend to assume a violation of the full protection and security standard if States have completely failed to respond to physical threats.[153] It is not relevant whether the State acted in bad faith.[154]

---

[147] *Asian Agricultural Products Ltd v Republic of Sri Lanka*, ICSID Case No ARB/87/3 (Final Award 1990), (1991) 6 ICSID Rev 533, para 48; see also *Técnicas Medioambientales Tecmed SA v The United Mexican States*, ICSID Case No ARB(AF)/00/2 (Award 2003), (2004) 43 ILM 133, para 177; *Saluka Investments BV v The Czech Republic*, PCA (Partial Award 2006) para 484.

[148] See *El Paso v Argentina*, ICSID Case No ARB/03/15 (Award 2011) paras 520–525.

[149] *Asian Agricultural Products Ltd v Republic of Sri Lanka*, ICSID Case No ARB/87/3 (Final Award 1990), (1991) 6 ICSID Rev 533, paras 43ff.

[150] See *Técnicas Medioambientales Tecmed SA v The United Mexican States*, ICSID Case No ARB(AF)/00/2 (Award 2003), (2004) 43 ILM 133, para 177; *Lauder v The Czech Republic* (UNCITRAL Final Award 2001) IIC 205 para 308; *Saluka Investments BV v The Czech Republic*, PCA (Partial Award 2006), para 484.

[151] *American Manufacturing and Trading, Inc. v Republic of Zaire*, ICSID Case No ARB/93/1 (Award 1997) para 6.05.

[152] See Article 7 of the International Law Commission's Articles on State Responsibility; J Crawford, *The International Law Commission's Articles on State Responsibility* (CUP 2002) 106ff.

[153] In *Wena Hotels Ltd v Arab Republic of Egypt*, ICSID Case No ARB/98/4 (Award 2000), (2002) 41 ILM 896, para 84, 134 the arbitral tribunal found a violation of the full protection and security standard, as the host State did not take any measures to prevent physical damage.

[154] *Asian Agricultural Products Ltd v Republic of Sri Lanka*, ICSID Case No ARB/87/3 (Final Award 1990), (1991) 6 ICSID Rev 533, para 77.

Some treaties expressly limit the scope of the 'full protection and security' standard to protection against physical harm. For instance, Article 8(10)(5) of CETA provides that 'full protection and security refers to the Party's obligations relating to the physical security of investors and covered investments'. Under many investment treaties, it is still an open question whether the principle of full protection and security, beyond physical protection, stretches to legal protection and security in terms of legal certainty and the stability of once acquired legal positions. This question is closely related to the equation of full protection and security with the international minimum standard. To the extent that full protection and security does not confer any more rights than customary law, it seems hardly arguable that the concept covers more than physical protection. In this line of argument, the arbitral tribunal in *Saluka Investment BV v The Czech Republic* expressed:

The practice of arbitral tribunals seems to indicate, however, that the 'full security and protection' clause is not meant to cover just any kind of impairment of an investor's investment, but to protect more specifically the physical integrity of an investment against interference by use of force.[155]

Other awards follow a more extensive understanding. In CME *Czech Republic BV (The Netherlands) v The Czech Republic*, the tribunal held:

The host State is obligated to ensure that neither by amendment of its laws nor by actions of its administrative bodies is the agreed and approved security and protection of the foreign investor's investment withdrawn or devalued.[156]

In *Compañía de Aguas del Aconquija SA and Vivendi Universal SA v Argentina Republic*, the arbitral tribunal rejected Argentina's argument that the full protection and security clause in the BIT between Argentina and France only applies to 'physical interferences':

If the parties to the BIT had intended to limit the obligation to 'physical interferences', they could have done so by including words to that effect in the section. In the absence of such words of limitation, the scope of the Article 5(1) protection should be interpreted to apply to reach any act or measure which deprives an investor's investment of protection and full security. [...] Such actions or measures need not threaten physical possession or the legally protected terms of operation of the investment.[157]

This broad understanding must be viewed with caution. The extension of full protection and security to legal certainty and the protection of acquired rights risks

---

[155] *Saluka Investments BV v The Czech Republic*, PCA (Partial Award 2006) para 484.

[156] *CME Czech Republic BV (The Netherlands) v The Czech Republic* (UNCITRAL Final Award 2004), para 613; see also *PSEG Global Inc et al v Republic of Turkey*, ICSID Case No ARB/02/5 (Decision on Jurisdiction 2004), (2005) 44 ILM 465, para 258; *Biwater Gauff (Tanzania) Ltd v United Republic of Tanzania*, ICSID Case No ARB/05/22 (Award 2008), (2008) 22 ICSID Rev 149, para 729.

[157] *Compañía de Aguas del Aconquija SA and Vivendi Universal v Argentine Republic*, ICSID Case No ARB/97/3 (Award 2007) para 7.4.15; a similar approach was taken by the arbitral tribunal in *Siemens AG v Argentine Republic*, ICSID Case No ARB/02/8 (Award 2007) para 303.

entirely blurring the distinction between this concept and the fair and equitable treatment standard.

(f) Umbrella clauses

Today, a considerable number of investment treaties contain an 'umbrella clause' which, in general terms, refers to compliance of contracting States with obligations they have assumed towards a foreign investor.[158] Thus, under Article 10(1), last sentence, of the Energy Charter Treaty,

[e]ach Contracting Party shall observe any obligations it has entered into with an Investor or an Investment of an Investor of any other Contracting Party.

The meaning of umbrella clauses is only straightforward if they are taken to state the obvious, that is that valid contractual or unilateral commitments must be observed. If this interpretation exhausts the significance of an umbrella clause, it would be little more than a pedagogic reminder.[159] However, it is far from clear whether the reference to the undertakings of the host State vis-à-vis the investor transforms obligations under domestic law, at least to some extent, into obligations under international law. In the absence of a clear wording, it cannot be presumed that an umbrella clause purports generally to shift any obligation of this kind onto the international plane. In the case *Noble Ventures, Inc v Romania*, the arbitral tribunal tried to give a meaningful understanding to the umbrella clause in the bilateral investment treaty between Romania and the United States:

Considering that Article II(2)(c) BIT uses the term 'shall' and that it forms part of the Article which provides for the major substantial obligations undertaken by the parties, there can be no doubt that the Article was intended to create obligations, and obviously obligations beyond those specified in other provisions of the BIT itself. Since States usually do not conclude, with reference to specific investments, special international agreements in addition to existing bilateral investment treaties, it is difficult to understand the notion 'obligation' as referring to obligations undertaken under other 'international' agreements. And given that such agreements, if concluded, would also be subject to the general principle of pacta sunt servanda, there would certainly be no need for a clause of that kind.[160]

---

[158] See eg Article 7(2) of the German Model BIT (2008); OECD, 'Interpretation of the Umbrella Clause in Investment Agreements' (2006/3) Working Papers on International Investment; AC Sinclair, 'The Origins of the Umbrella Clause in the International Law of Investment Protection' (2004) 20 Arb Int'l 411.

[159] See, however, the award in *SGS Société Générale de Surveillance, SA v Republic of Pakistan*, ICSID Case No ARB/01/13 (Decision on Jurisdiction 2003), (2003) 42 ILM 1290, para 172: '[W]e do not consider that confirmation in a treaty that a contracting Party is bound under and pursuant to a contract, or a statute or other municipal law issuance is devoid of appreciable normative value, either in the municipal or in the international legal sphere. That confirmation could, for instance, signal an implied affirmative commitment to enact implementing rules and regulations necessary or appropriate to give effect to a contractual or statutory undertaking in favour of investors of another contracting Party that would otherwise be a dead letter [...].'

[160] *Noble Ventures, Inc v Romania*, ICSID Case No ARB/01/11 (Award 2005), (2005) IIC 179, para 51.

In *SGS Société Générale de Surveillance, SA v Republic of the Philippines*, the tribunal held that a breach of a contractual obligation by the host State towards a foreign investor may violate an umbrella clause:

> To summarize, for the present purposes Article X(2) includes commitments or obligations arising under contracts entered into by the host State. The basic obligation on the State in this case is the obligation to pay what is due under the contract, which is an obligation assumed with regard to the specific investment (the performance of services under the CISS Agreement). But this obligation does not mean that the determination of how much money the Philippines is obliged to pay becomes a treaty matter. The extent of obligation is still governed by the contract, and it can only be determined by reference to the terms of the contract.[161]

Even then, the determination of the scope of an obligation of the host State under domestic law and a possible violation of this commitment may be subject to the jurisdiction of national courts.[162]

The scope of umbrella clauses is not limited to sovereign interferences with the legal position of investors under domestic law, but may also cover the mere violation of payment or other performance obligations. There is, however, no broad consensus on the conditions that bring obligations of the host State under national law within the scope of the umbrella clause.[163] In any case, the application of the clause should be confined to commitments of the host State which are fundamental for the realization of an investment and its economic value.

(g) Expropriation and compensation

A core element of bilateral or multilateral treaties on investment protection relates to expropriation and due compensation. Modern treaty practice covers direct expropriation (formal transfer of title or other form of overt taking) as well as indirect expropriation or 'measures tantamount to nationalization or expropriation'.[164] Article 1110(1) of NAFTA states that

1. No Party may directly or indirectly nationalise or expropriate an investment of an investor of another Party in its territory or take a measure tantamount to nationalisation or expropriation of such an investment, except:
   (a) for a public purpose;
   (b) on a non-discriminatory basis;
   (c) in accordance with due process of law and Article 1105(1) and
   (d) on payment of compensation in accordance with [subsequent paragraphs specifying valuation of expropriations and form and procedure of payment].

---

[161] *SGS Société Générale de Surveillance, SA v Republic of the Philippines*, ICSID Case No ARB/02/6 (Decision on Jurisdiction 2004), (2005) 8 ICSID Rep 518, para 127.

[162] *SGS Société Générale de Surveillance, SA v Republic of the Philippines*, ICSID Case No ARB/02/6 (Decision on Jurisdiction 2004), (2005) 8 ICSID Rep 518, para 128.

[163] See *CMS Gas Transmission Co v Argentine Republic*, ICSID Case No ARB/01/8 (Award 2005), (2005) 44 ILM 1205, para 299; decision of the ad hoc Committee on annulment (2007) 46 ILM 1136 paras 89ff.

[164] Article 4(2) of the German Model BIT (2008); Article 6(1) of the US Model BIT (2012); Article 13 of the Energy Charter Treaty.

As to the concept of indirect expropriation, no generally recognized definition has emerged yet. Unlike a direct expropriation, indirect expropriation does not affect title or amount to straightforward seizure. In this case, the investor is left with the more or less emptied shell of ownership. Modern arbitration practice focuses on the economic impact of a measure. The decisive criterion is the degree in which a measure affects the economic value in terms of profitability. Common formulas refer to the enjoyment of the property being 'neutralized'[165] or to 'substantial deprivation' of the economic uses and benefits.[166] Regulatory measures in the interest of environmental protection or public health may be qualified as indirect expropriation if they shorten the time span for operating an investment (eg a nuclear power station) or considerably reduce profitability. Determination of whether a measure crosses the threshold of expropriation is particularly difficult if the investor retains full control and ownership and if the investment still yields some profits. It is a controversial issue whether qualification of an action as indirect expropriation or measure tantamount to expropriation should only consider the adverse effect of a State measure on the investment ('sole effects doctrine') or also the aim and interests pursued by the host State. There is a strong tendency to focus on the balance between the inference with the investment and the public interest in terms of proportionality. An adequate balance may require compensation to establish proportionality.[167] Substantial deprivation of ownership, if uncompensated, will amount to full or partial expropriation. Even important public interests cannot justify massive ownership deprivation, as the foreign investor is not part of the political community which stands behind the public interests pursued. This point was made by the arbitral tribunal in *Tecmed v Mexico*:

There must be a reasonable relationship of proportionality between the charge or weight imposed to the foreign investor and the aim sought to be realized by any expropriatory measure. To value such charge or weight, it is very important to measure the size of the ownership deprivation caused by the actions of the state and whether such deprivation was compensated or not. On the basis of a number of legal and practical factors, it should be also considered that the foreign investor has a reduced or nil participation in the taking of the decisions that affect it, partly because the investors are not entitled to exercise political rights reserved to the nationals of the State, such as voting for the authorities that will issue the decisions that affect such investor.[168]

The US Model BIT (2012) lists a number of criteria which determine the qualification of an action as indirect expropriation. These criteria show some deference

---

[165] *Lauder v The Czech Republic* (UNCITRAL Final Award 2001) IIC 205 para 200.

[166] *CMS Gas Transmission Co v Argentine Republic*, ICSID Case No ARB/01/8 (Award 2005), (2005) 44 ILM 1205 para 262.

[167] *Técnicas Medioambientales Tecmed SA v The United Mexican States*, ICSID Case No ARB(AF)/00/2 (Award 2003), (2004) 43 ILM 133, para 122; see also G Bücheler, *Proportionality in Investor-State Arbitration* (OUP 2015).

[168] *Técnicas Medioambientales Tecmed SA v The United Mexican States*, ICSID Case No ARB(AF)/00/2 (Award 2003), (2004) 43 ILM 133, para 122.

to the exercise of regulatory power in the interest of legitimate public interests. Annex B paragraph 4 of the Model BIT provides:

(a) The determination of whether an action or series of actions by a Party, in a specific fact situation, constitutes an indirect expropriation, requires a case-by-case, fact-based inquiry that considers, among other factors:
   (i)   the economic impact of the government action, although the fact that an action or series of actions by a Party has an adverse effect on the economic value of an investment, standing alone, does not establish that an indirect expropriation has occurred;
   (ii) the extent to which the government action interferes with distinct, reasonable investment-backed expectations; and
   (iii) the character of the government action.
(b) Except in rare circumstances, non-discriminatory regulatory actions by a Party that are designed and applied to protect legitimate public welfare objectives, such as public health, safety, and the environment, do not constitute indirect expropriations.

In exceptional cases, judicial decisions may amount to indirect expropriation or be tantamount to expropriation if they arbitrarily invalidate an arbitral award or another title to payment.

In *SAIPEM SpA v The People's Republic of Bangladesh*, the arbitral tribunal qualified a judgment of the High Court Division of the Supreme Court of Bangladesh on the inexistence of an arbitral award as a measure equivalent to expropriation. An Italian investor had obtained an award against a State-owned enterprise under the rules of the International Chamber of Commerce (ICC) in a dispute over a gas pipeline project in the North East of Bangladesh. The Supreme Court had issued an injunction preventing Saipem from continuing the ICC arbitration proceedings. When the State-owned company applied to have the ICC award set aside, the Supreme Court of Bangladesh held that the ICC award was non-existent in the eyes of the law. In the following investment dispute, the arbitral tribunal ruled that the Supreme Court's decision, for the lack of sustainable reasons, violated the internationally accepted prohibition of abuse of rights as well as the obligations of recognition and enforcement of foreign arbitral awards under the New York Convention on the Recognition and Enforcement of Foreign Arbitral Awards (Article II(3)).[169]

Current treaty and arbitration practice set a high threshold for qualifying a measure as an expropriation, when the measure which interferes with property rights serves the public health, protection of the environment, and other legitimate public interests. NAFTA recognizes that contracting parties may take measures otherwise consistent with the chapter on investment (Chapter 11) to 'ensure that investment activity in its territory is undertaken in a manner sensitive to environmental concerns' (Article 1114(1)). Moreover, parties to NAFTA 'recognize that it is inappropriate to encourage investment by relaxing domestic health, safety or environmental measures' (Article 1114(2) first sentence).

---

[169] *SAIPEM SpA v The People's Republic of Bangladesh*, ICSID Case No ARB/05/7 (Award 2009), (2009) 48 ILM 996, paras 124ff.

The case *Philip Morris Asia Limited (Hong Kong) v The Commonwealth of Australia*[170] illustrates the potential of conflicts between very broadly framed investors' property claims and the interest in a stable legal framework, on the one hand, and the agenda of host States for enhanced health protection on the other. In the first investment arbitration case brought against Australia, Philip Morris Asia challenged the new Australian legislation concerning plain packaging of tobacco products under the BIT with Hong Kong. Australian law bans logos, designs, and trademarks other than the product's name and prescribes the same colour and typeface. The claimant qualified Australia's tobacco plain packaging rules as a violation of its intellectual property rights and, inter alia, as expropriation and as violation of the commitment to accord fair and equitable treatment. The arbitral tribunal found that, by changing its corporate structure with the purpose of benefiting from the applicable treaty, the investor had committed an abuse of right or of process and that, accordingly, the claim was inadmissible.[171] In a similar case brought by Philip Morris against Uruguay, the arbitral tribunal rejected the claim, paying deference to governmental policies for the protection of public health.[172]

In the *Yukos* cases (*Yukos Universal Limited (Isle of Man) v The Russian Federation, Hulley Enterprises Limited (Cyprus) v The Russian Federation, Veteran Petroleum Limited (Cyprus) v The Russian Federation,*[173] the arbitral tribunal held that Russia had breached its obligations under Article 13(1) Energy Charter Treaty (ECT) by expropriating the shareholders of the Russian oil company Yukos without the required compensation. The tribunal found that 'Yukos was the object of a series of politically-motivated attacks by the Russian authorities that eventually led to its destruction'[174] and that Russian authorities had mistreated Yukos, its officers (in particular its chief executive officer Mikhail Khodorkovsky) and employees with the primary objective to drive the company into bankruptcy and to appropriate its assets.[175] It further held that the measures of harassment leading to the company's demise had an effect equivalent to nationalization.[176] The tribunal concluded that the expropriation was not carried out 'under due process of law', as required by Article 13(1)(c) ECT, and referred to the arbitrary criminal persecution of Mikhail Khodorkovsky and other officers of Yukos.[177] The District Court of The Hague

---

[170] *Philip Morris Asia Limited (Hong Kong) v The Commonwealth of Australia,* PCA Case No 2012-12 (Award on Jurisdiction and Admissibility 2015).

[171] Ibid, paras 585, 588.

[172] *Philip Morris Brands Sàrl, Philip Morris Products S.A. and Abal Hermanos S.A. v Oriental Republic of Uruguay,* ICSID Case No ARB/10/7 (Award 2016) paras 306, 399.

[173] *Hulley Enterprises Limited (Cyprus) v The Russian Federation,* PCA Case No AA 226 (Final Award 2014); *Veteran Petroleum Limited (Cyprus) v The Russian Federation,* PCA Case No AA 228 (Final Award 2014); *Yukos Universal Limited (Isle of Man) v The Russian Federation,* PCA Case No AA 227 (Final Award 2014).

[174] *Yukos Universal Limited (Isle of Man) v The Russian Federation,* PCA Case No AA 227 (Final Award 2014) para 1253.

[175] Ibid, para 756.   [176] Ibid, para 1579.

[177] Ibid, para 1583: 'As to condition (c), Yukos was subjected to processes of law, but the Tribunal does not accept that the effective expropriation of Yukos was "carried out under due process of law" for multiple reasons set out above, notably in Chapter VIII.C.3. The harsh treatment accorded to Messrs. Khodorkovsky and Lebedev remotely jailed and caged in court, the mistreatment of counsel

annulled the interim award on jurisdiction and the final award on the merits.[178] The shareholders have announced their intention to appeal the District Court decision and have additionally commenced exequatur proceedings in several jurisdictions.

Modern investment treaties require that compensation shall be paid without delay, be equivalent to the fair market value of the expropriated investment immediately before the expropriation took place and shall be effective, that is fully realizable and freely transferable.[179]

There is controversy on whether and to what extent internationally recognized concerns as, for example, the protection of the environment and biodiversity may or must be considered in the calculation of compensation. In the case *Santa Elena v Costa Rica*, a US investor acquired property stretching over 30 kilometres along Costa Rica's Pacific coastline, for the development of a holiday resort. Later on, Costa Rica declared the zone as a nature reserve and expropriated the investor's land, thus frustrating the development project. Costa Rica argued that international treaties for environmental protection such as the Convention on Biological Diversity had to be taken into account in the determination of the amount of compensation. The arbitral tribunal rejected this approach:

While an expropriation or taking for environmental reasons may be classified as taking for a public purpose, and thus may be legitimate, the fact that the Property was taken for this reason does not affect either the nature or the measure of the compensation to be paid for the taking. That is, the purpose of protecting the environment for which the Property was taken does not alter the legal character of the taking for which adequate compensation must be paid. The international source of the obligation to protect the environment makes no difference.[180]

Despite vehement criticism[181] by environmental lawyers this approach seems persuasive. For privileging certain interests behind the taking of property over others for purposes of qualifying a measure as expropriation or for determining the amount of compensation would distort the balance between rights of the investors and the regulatory interests of the host State.

---

of Yukos and the difficulties counsel encountered in reading the record and conferring with Messrs. Khodorkovsky and Lebedev, the very pace of the legal proceedings, do not comport with the due process of law. Rather the Russian court proceedings, and most egregiously, the second trial and second sentencing of Messrs. Khodorkovsky and Lebedev on the creative legal theory of their theft of Yukos' oil production, indicate that Russian courts bent to the will of Russian executive authorities to bankrupt Yukos, assign its assets to a State-controlled company, and incarcerate a man who gave signs of becoming a political competitor.'

[178] See Section 1(c)(iii) in this chapter.

[179] See Article 4(2) of the German Model BIT (2008); Article 6(2) of the US Model BIT (2012); Article 1110 (2)–(6) of NAFTA; Article 13(1) of the Energy Charter Treaty.

[180] *Compañía del Desarrollo de Santa Elena, SA v The Republic of Costa Rica*, ICSID Case No ARB/96/1 (Award 2000), (2000) 39 ILM 1317, para 71.

[181] P Sands, *Lawless World* (Penguin Books 2006) 117–142.

(h) Necessity

In times of a severe economic crisis or peril to its security, a State may rely on necessity as a justification for temporary non-compliance with obligations. Customary law ties necessity to strict conditions and only allows suspension of obligations for the time in which these circumstances prevail. Under the International Law Commission's Draft Articles on State Responsibility,[182] a State can only invoke the exception of necessity to justify an act, if, inter alia, the act is the only means for the State to safeguard an essential interest against a grave and imminent peril and if the State has not (substantially) contributed to the situation of necessity (Article 25). Some investment treaties are far more generous than customary law and considerably expand the scope of necessity as a defence under international law. Article XI of the BIT between Argentina and the United States provides:

This Treaty shall not preclude the application by either Party of measures necessary for the maintenance of public order, the fulfillment of its obligations with respect to the maintenance or restoration of international peace or security, or the Protection of its own essential security interests.[183]

As the ad hoc Committee in *Sempra Energy International v Argentine Republic* justly emphasized, this clause is much broader than the exception of necessity under customary law.[184]

The Argentinean crisis (2001) gave rise to quite divergent assessments of the situation and its gravity with respect to necessity.[185] In the case *LG & E v Argentine Republic*, the tribunal held:

The Tribunal rejects the notion that Article XI is only applicable in circumstances amounting to military action and war. Certainly, the conditions in Argentina in December 2001 called for immediate, decisive action to restore civil order and stop the economic decline. To conclude that such a severe economic crisis could not constitute an essential security interest is to diminish the havoc that the economy can wreak on the lives of an entire population and the ability of the Government to lead. When a State's economic foundation is under siege, the severity of the problem can equal that of any military invasion.[186]

By contrast, in the case *CMS Gas Transmission Co v Argentine Republic*, the tribunal adopted a much stricter test, requiring 'catastrophic conditions' for a situation of necessity:

The Treaty in this case is clearly designed to protect investments at a time of economic difficulties or other circumstances leading to the adoption of adverse measures by the

---

[182] Official Records of the General Assembly, 56th session, supplement no 10 (A/56/10) 43ff.
[183] See SF Hill, 'The "Necessity Defense" and the Emerging Arbitral Conflict in Its Application to the U.S.-Argentina Bilateral Investment Treaty' (2007) 13 Law Bus Rev Am 547.
[184] *Sempra Energy International v Argentine Republic*, ICSID Case No ARB/02/16 (Decision on the Argentine Republic's Application for Annulment of the Award 2010) paras 192ff (198).
[185] See A Reinisch, 'Necessity in International Investment Arbitration—An Unnecessary Split of Opinions in Recent ICSID Cases? Comments on CMS v. Argentina and LG&E v. Argentina' (2007) 8 JWIT 191.
[186] *LG & E Energy Corporation, LG & E Capital Corporation and LG & E International, Inc v Argentina*, ICSID Case No ARB/02/1 (Decision on Liability 2006), (2006) 21 ICSID Rev 155, para 238.

Government. The question is, however, how grave these economic difficulties might be. A severe crisis cannot necessarily be equated with a situation of total collapse. And in the absence of such profoundly serious conditions it is plainly clear that the Treaty will prevail over any plea of necessity. However, if such difficulties, without being catastrophic in and of themselves, nevertheless invite catastrophic conditions in terms of disruption and disintegration of society, or are likely to lead to a total breakdown of the economy, emergency and necessity might acquire a different meaning.[187]

In *Continental Casualty Co v Argentine Republic*, the arbitral tribunal applied a more flexible understanding and referred to the 'necessity' qualification, as developed in connection with trade restrictive measures in international trade law:

[…] Since the text of Art. XI [of the US–Argentina BIT] derives from the parallel model clause of the U.S. FCN treaties and these treaties in turn reflect the formulation of Art. XX of GATT 1947, the Tribunal finds it more appropriate to refer to the GATT and WTO case law which has extensively dealt with the concept and requirements of necessity in the context of economic measures derogating to the obligations contained in GATT, rather than to refer to the requirement of necessity under customary international law. […] Within the WTO a measure is not necessary if another treaty consistent, or less inconsistent alternative measure, which the member State concerned could reasonably be expected to employ is available […].[188]

It seems, however, that the more lenient standard for 'necessary' trade measures does not provide an adequate reference for justifying non-compliance with obligations in investment law which is conditioned by the protection of essential, or even vital, interests of the host State.

5. Dispute Settlement

(a) Investor–host State arbitration and the new 'European model' of a permanent investment Tribunal

Modern investment treaties provide for the settlement of disputes between a party and a private investor through arbitration. Common arbitration mechanisms envisaged in investment treaties are arbitrations under the Convention of the International Centre for Settlement of Investment Disputes (ICSID),[189] under the ICSID Additional Facility Rules, under the UNCITRAL Arbitration Rules, and under the Arbitration Rules of the Stockholm Chamber of Commerce.[190]

In the European Union, discontent with the established patterns of investor-State arbitration (ironically designed by European States) broke the path for a new

---

[187] *CMS Gas Transmission Co v Argentine Republic*, ICSID Case No ARB/01/8 (Award 2005), (2005) 44 ILM 1205, para 354; see also the critical observations of the ad hoc Committee in the annulment proceeding (2007) 46 ILM 1136 paras 129ff.

[188] *Continental Casualty Co v Argentine Republic*, ICSID Case No ARB/03/9 (Award 2008) paras 192, 195. The application for annulment of Argentina and Continental Casualty were dismissed by an ICSID ad hoc Committee.

[189] See Ch XXXV.

[190] Article 10(2) of the German Model BIT (2008); Article 24(3) of the US Model BIT (2012); Article 26(4) of the Energy Charter Treaty; Article 1120(1) of NAFTA.

model for the settlement of investment disputes, the compentent organ being a tribunal with judges whose nomination is fully controlled by the contracting parties. In 2016, the European Union and Canada concluded the re-opened negotiations on the settlement of investment disputes under CETA and agreed on a permanent Investment Tribunal with judges nominated by both parties, including an Appellate Tribunal with the capacity to review such tribunal's decisions.[191] The free trade agreement with Vietnam adopts a similar model.[192] Initially, members of these dispute settlement bodies will serve on a case-by-case basis, with their availability assured through a retainer fee. Under both treaties, a decision by the competent bilateral committees may transform the judicial function into a full-time activity, thus turning the tribunals into truly permanent bodies. It remains to be seen whether the currently negotiated TTIP agreement will also follow this trend.

(b) The hybrid nature of investor-State arbitration

Investor-State arbitration on the basis of bilateral investment treaties or other international agreements combines elements of different legal regimes. Its jurisdictional basis (as to the State's consent to arbitration and the procedure) as well as the applicable substantive standards flow from an agreement between the host State and the investor's home State and, thus, root in public international law.

The establishment of a right of action for private investors against sovereign States by international agreement signifies a most important step in the protection of private actors under international economic law. Making reference to investor-State arbitration under Article 26 of the European Energy Charter Treaty, the arbitral tribunal in *Plama v Republic of Bulgaria* stated:

[...] Article 26 ECT provides to a covered investor an almost unprecedented remedy for its claim against a host state. The ECT has been described, together with NAFTA, as 'the major multilateral treaty pioneering the extensive use of legal methods characteristic of the fledging regulation of the global economy', of which 'perhaps the most important aspect of the ECT's investment regime is the provision for compulsory arbitration against governments at the option of foreign investors ...'; and these same distinguished commentators concluded: 'With a paradigm shift away from mere protection by the home state of investors and traders to the legal architecture of a liberal global economy, goes a coordinated use of trade and investment law methods to achieve the same objective: a global level playing field for activities in competitive markets'. By any standards, Article 26 is a very important feature of the ECT which is itself a very significant treaty for investors, marking another step in their transition from objects to subjects of international law.[193]

---

[191] See Articles 8(18)ff of CETA; the text of the agreement is available at <http://trade.ec.europa.eu/doclib/docs/2016/february/tradoc_154329.pdf> (accessed 23 June 2016).

[192] See chapter 8 of the EU–Vietnam Free Trade Agreement, section 3, sub-section 4, Articles 12ff; the text of chapter 8 is available at <http://trade.ec.europa.eu/doclib/docs/2016/february/tradoc_154210.pdf> (accessed 23 June 2016).

[193] *Plama v Republic of Bulgaria*, ICSID Case No ARB/03/24 (Decision on Jurisdiction 2005), (2005) ILM 44, 721ff para 141 referring to C Bamberger, J Linehan, and T Wälde, 'The Energy Charter Treaty in 2000', in M Roggenkamp (ed), *Energy Law in Europe* (OUP 2000), 11, 31f.

Investor-State arbitration finds some parallels in the rights of individuals to make complaints against human rights violations before international courts.[194]

Dispute settlement by means of arbitration, resting on consent between a State and a private party, places the investor on equal footing with the host State. It brings the dispute settlement in close structural affinity with commercial arbitration. Many arbitrators with an international commercial law background have contributed to shape international case-law on investment protection (whilst other arbitrators are drawn from the ranks of specialists in public international law). The world wide enforcement of awards by investors as well as counter-actions brought by host States are governed by international agreements like the New York Convention on the Recognition and Enforcement of Foreign Arbitral Awards, which were initially designed to cover commercial arbitration. Critics of the current regime for the settlement of investor-State disputes often refer to 'private arbitral tribunals', with an innuendo that this model of international arbitration lacks democratic legitimacy to rule upon sensitive public interests.[195] A closer analysis, however, does not support such a conclusion.

In addition to the different international law underpinnings, investment disputes have a public law dimension which flows from a balancing of private and public interests, as it is well known in constitutional and administrative law, in connection with 'regulatory taking' of property by environmental or other measures. Deferring to sovereign choices means according a broad discretion by host States when balancing conflicting interests. This flexibility obviously has a strong democratic component. The limitation of protected investments to investments made in accordance with the host State's laws also implies some deference to public law.

The public international law approach and the international commercial law perspective may inspire different readings of jurisdictional clauses and substantive rules on investment protection. On this ground, the 'hybrid nature' of investment arbitration has become the object of a lively academic and political discussion.[196] A public international approach and a comparative public law perspective tend to be more receptive to interests of the host State and to accord more regulatory freedom than a private (international) or 'contractual' approach, which leans more on distinct spheres of responsibility of the parties to an investment dispute, and which will be more strongly inspired by the autonomy of the parties for purposes of jurisdiction. The degree of deference to State sovereignty influences the more or less strict understanding of necessity clauses to expectations generated by the host State and its agents. 'Necessity' as an exonerating circumstance may be interpreted rather

---

[194] See eg Article 34 of the European Convention on Human Rights.

[195] See M Waibel et al (eds), *The Backlash Against Investment Arbitration: Perceptions and Reality* (Kluwer 2010).

[196] See S Montt, *State Liability and Investment Treaty Arbitration* (Hart 2009); SW Schill (ed), *International Investment Law and Comparative Public Law* (OUP 2010); A Roberts, 'Clash of Paradigms: Actors and Analogies Shaping the Investment Treaty Systems' (2013) 107 AJIL 45; Z Douglas, 'The Hybrid Foundations of Investment Treaty Arbitration', (2003) 74 BYIL 151; G Van Harten, *Investment Treaty Arbitration and Public Law* (OUP 2007).

strictly according to the principles of State responsibility[197] or in broader terms as they apply to 'necessary' measures in international trade law.[198]

In *Total SA v Argentine Republic*, an ICSID Tribunal defined the scope of 'legitimate expectations' (covered by the standard of 'fair and equitable treatment' and also relevant in context of expropriation) both on the basis of a comparative analysis of domestic public law, the European Convention on Human Rights and EU law and of public international law.[199]

The new 'European model' of dispute settlement by a permanent investment tribunal (as provided for in CETA and the free trade agreement between the European Union and Vietnam) reverts to the domain of public international law. It may become structurally similar to regional human right courts with jurisdiction over individual complaints.

(c) Jurisdiction of arbitral tribunals and recourse to domestic courts

An important procedural issue is how recourse to the courts of the host State affects the jurisdiction of arbitral tribunals and the admissibility of the claims. Some BITs contain a so-called 'fork in the road clause' under which investors must choose between taking a particular dispute to domestic courts and initiating arbitration proceedings. The investor's decision is binding and precludes recourse to other forms of dispute settlement. Sometimes, dispute settlement provisions in investment treaties compete with agreements between the host State and an investor which establish jurisdiction. These kinds of submission clauses may often be found in contracts between Latin American countries and investors. Modern international arbitration practice tends to interpret such contractual submission to the jurisdiction of national courts narrowly.

In *Lanco International Inc v The Argentine Republic*, Argentina challenged the jurisdiction of the ICSID arbitral tribunal on the grounds that according to an agreement with the claimant disputes had to be submitted to local courts. The arbitral tribunal rejected the submission and concluded that an arbitration clause in an international treaty trumped any agreement between the investor and the host State:

The Argentina-U.S. Treaty establishes the possibility of the investor choosing between the local courts [...] and other means of dispute settlement, such as arbitration, which requires

---

[197] *CMS Gas Transmission Co v Argentine Republic*, ICSID Case No ARB/01/8 (Award 2005), (2005) 44 ILM 1205, para 354; *Sempra Energy International v Argentine Republic*, ICSID Case No ARB/02/16 (Decision on the Argentine Republic's Application for Annulment of the Award 2010) paras 192ff; *Enron Corporation Ponderosa Assets, LP v Argentine Republic*, ICSID Case No ARB/01/3 (Award 2007) para 334. See also Section 4(h) in this Chapter and A Roberts, 'Clash of Paradigms: Actors and Analogies Shaping the Investment Treaty Systems', (2013) 107 AJIL 45 (47).

[198] *Continental Casualty Co v Argentine Republic*, ICSID Case No ARB/03/9 (Award 2008) para 192.

[199] *Total SA v Argentine Republic*, ICSID Case No ARB/04/01 (Decision on Liability 2010) paras 128–134. Argentina's application for annulment failed (Decision on Annulment 2016) para 325.

the previous agreement of the parties. In addition, the Argentina-U.S. Treaty, once certain requirements are met, allows the investor to submit the dispute to ICSID arbitration. The Argentina-U.S. Treaty therefore gives the investor the power to choose among several methods of dispute settlement; consequently, once the investor has expressed its consent in choosing ICSID arbitration, the only means of dispute settlement available is ICSID Arbitration.

[...] [T]his Argentina-U.S. Treaty is the first instance of the Argentina Republic having accepted submission to international arbitration without reservations. [...] Consequently, the Argentina-U.S. Treaty entails a definite change in the foreign investment regime in the Argentine Republic, allowing for recourse to international arbitration without intricate conditions and definitely discarding the exclusivity of territorial jurisdiction, as the foreign investor is not obligated to submit to the local courts.[200]

A similar conclusion was reached in *Compañía de Aguas del Aconquija SA and Vivendi Universal SA v Argentina Republic*. Confronted with a clause on the exclusive jurisdiction of the Argentinean administrative courts in a concession contract, the arbitral tribunal distinguished between claims based on the BIT and claims based on the concession contract. The tribunal concluded that the forum selection clause in the concession contract did not affect the claimant's right to submit the dispute to ICSID arbitration as to violations of the BIT:

Finally, the Tribunal holds that Article 16.4 of the Concession Contract does not divest this Tribunal of jurisdiction to hear this case because that provision did not and could not constitute a waiver by CGE of its rights under Article 8 of the BIT to file the pending claims against the Argentine Republic. [...] In this case the claims filed by CGE against Respondent are based on violation by the Argentine Republic of the BIT through acts or omissions of that government and acts of the Tucumán authorities that Claimants assert should be attributed to the central government. As formulated, these claims against the Argentine Republic are not subject to the jurisdiction of the contentious administrative tribunals of Tucumán, if only because, *ex hypothesi*, those claims are not based on the Concession Contract but allege a cause of action under the BIT.

Thus, Article 16.4 of the Concession Contract cannot be deemed to prevent the investor from proceeding under the ICSID Convention against the Argentine Republic on a claim charging the Argentine Republic with a violation of the Argentine-French BIT.[201]

(d) Exhaustion of local remedies

As a rule, investment treaties allow investors to initiate arbitral proceedings without seeking redress before domestic courts.[202] Some investment agreements, however,

---

[200] *Lanco International Inc v The Argentine Republic*, ICSID Case No ARB/97/6 (Decision on Jurisdiction 1998), (2001) 40 ILM 457, paras 31f.

[201] *Compañía de Aguas del Aconquija SA and Vivendi Universal SA v Argentina Republic*, ICSID Case No ARB/97/3 (Award 2001), (2001) 40 ILM 426, paras 53f; the ad hoc Committee confirmed this interpretation in the annulment proceedings, albeit the award was partially annulled on other grounds (2004) 19 ICSID Rev 89, paras 51ff, 119.

[202] See also Article 26 of the ICSID Convention: 'Consent of the parties to arbitration under this Convention shall, unless otherwise stated, be deemed consent to such arbitration to the exclusion of any other remedy. A Contracting State may require the exhaustion of local administrative or judicial remedies as a condition of its consent to arbitration under this Convention.'

require investors to have first recourse to local remedies, subject to certain exceptions. An example is Article 8 of the BIT between Argentina and the United
Kingdom, which contains a local litigation clause:

(1) Disputes with regard to an investment which arise within the terms of this Agreement
between an investor of one Contracting Party and the other Contracting Party, which
have not been amicably settled shall be submitted, at the request of one of the Parties to
the dispute, to the decision of the competent tribunal of the Contracting Party in whose
territory the investment was made.

(2) The aforementioned disputes shall be submitted to international arbitration in the
following cases:

   (a) if one of the Parties so requests, in any of the following circumstances:
      (i) where, after a period of eighteen months has elapsed from the moment when
          the dispute was submitted to the competent tribunal of the Contracting Party
          in whose territory the investment was made, the said tribunal has not given its
          final decision;
      (ii) where the final decision of the aforementioned tribunal has been made but the
           Parties are still in dispute;
   (b) where the Contracting Party and the investor of the other Contracting Party have so
       agreed. [...]

The case *BG Group v The Republic of Argentina* illustrates the difficulties associated
with the local litigation requirement under Article 8 of the BIT between Argentina
and the United Kingdom. BG belonged to a consortium which had acquired a
controlling interest in an Argentinean company holding an exclusive licence to
distribute natural gas. It initially operated under statutes which provided gas tariffs
calculated in US-Dollars and set at a level granting a reasonable profit. In its deep
economic crisis, Argentina radically changed this regime. Its legislation also curtailed judicial protection against the new economic measures and sanctioned firms
operating under public services contracts such as gas, distrusting companies which
litigated against the Argentinean State by excluding them from renegotiating the
terms of operation. Therefore, the arbitral tribunal held that BG Group was relieved
from compliance with the local litigation clause and accordingly assumed jurisdiction over BG Group's claims under the BIT.[203] It awarded BG Group considerable
damages for denial of 'fair and equitable treatment'.[204]

Direct access to dispute settlement by arbitration without the necessary
exhaustion of local remedies is a major advantage for the foreign investor. It
saves the investor from confrontation with the intricacies of local procedural
law, possible deficiencies of the judicial system including prejudice in favour
of the host State, and an often protracted and costly itinerary through several
stages until a final decision is adopted. On the other hand, the non-exhaustion

---

[203] *BG Group Plc v The Republic of Argentina* (UNCITRAL Final Award 2007) paras 104ff, 140ff,
216ff. See on the subsequent decision of the US Supreme Court in annulment proceedings below,
Section 5(f) in this Chapter.
[204] *BG Group Plc v The Republic of Argentina* (UNCITRAL Final Award 2007) paras 289ff,
413ff, 467.

of local remedies may submit legal disputes involving fundamental decisions of economic, environmental, or energy policy to international arbitration without involving the national courts which would otherwise, in a domestic legal context, address the issue.

In *Vattenfall v Federal Republic of Germany II*,[205] a Swedish energy company challenged measures (termination of operation permits for nuclear power stations) inextricably linked with a radical change in Germany's energy policy on the withdrawal from nuclear power before an ICSID tribunal under the ECT. No German court will rule upon the claim of the Swedish investor.

In recent times, direct access to arbitration 'circumventing' the involvement of local courts has caused criticism not only in developing countries but also in industrialized countries. Behind this criticism primarily stand concerns about the chilling effect of compensation claims flowing from enhanced environmental standards. For the investment agreements concluded by the European Union, a resolution of the European Parliament calls for the exhaustion of local remedies:

The European Parliament [...] [b]elieves that changes must be made to the present dispute settlement regime, in order to include greater transparency, the opportunity for parties to appeal, the obligation to exhaust local judicial remedies where they are reliable enough to guarantee due process, the possibility to use amicus curiae briefs and the obligation to select one single place of investor-state arbitration.[206]

(e) Transparency in investor-State arbitration

The Rules on Transparency in Treaty-based Investor-State Arbitration,[207] adopted by the United Nations Commission on International Trade Law (UNCITRAL) in 2013, provide for the publication of documents (Article 3), and permit third persons (eg NGOs) to file written submissions (*amicus curiae* briefs) (Article 4). The arbitral tribunal may invite a non-disputing party to the relevant treaty to make submissions on the interpretation of the treaty (Article 5). Exceptions to transparency refer to confidential and protected information (Article 7). The UN Convention on Transparency in Treaty-based Investor-State Arbitration[208] establishes that the UNCITRAL Rules shall apply to arbitration between a party and a claimant which is national of another party or which agrees to the application of the UNCITRAL Rules (Articles 1 and 2). A party may make reservations as to specific investment treaties or as to arbitration conducted under rules other than the UNCITRAL Arbitration Rules (Article 3(2)).

---

[205] *Vattenfall et al v Federal Republic of Germany II*, ICSID Case No ARB/12/12 (Pending).
[206] European Parliament Resolution of 6 April 2011 on the future European international investment policy 2010/2203(INI), para 31.
[207] See <http://www.uncitral.org/pdf/english/texts/arbitration/rules-on-transparency/Rules-on-Transparency-E.pdf> (accessed 23 June 2016).
[208] (2015) 54 ILM 747, see also<http://www.uncitral.org/pdf/english/texts/arbitration/transparency-convention/Transparency-Convention-e.pdf> (accessed 23 June 2016).

(f) The review control of arbitral awards by treaty bodies and national courts

Under the ICSID Convention, an arbitral award may be reviewed by ad hoc committees in annulment proceedings.[209] Although review is confined to narrow grounds, case-law lacks consistency and predictability. In the TTIP negotiations, the European Union considers the creation of an appellate mechanism, similar to the one envisaged in CETA and in the EU–Vietnam FTA.[210]

As for non-ICSID awards, an important mechanism of control of awards in investor-State arbitration are challenges by a party before the courts of the country in which the award was rendered or whose laws governed the arbitration proceedings. A prominent example is the decision of the District Court of The Hague which set aside the USD 50 billion award in the *Yukos* case.[211]

Recognition and enforcement of annulled awards may be denied under Article V(1)(e) of the New York Convention on the Recognition and Enforcement of Foreign Arbitral Awards, if

[...] the award has not yet become binding on the parties, or has been set aside or suspended by a competent authority of the country in which, or under the law of which, that award was made.

In *BG Group v Republic of Argentina*,[212] the BG Group sought to confirm and Argentina sought to vacate an arbitral award which had found that the claimant was relieved from compliance with the local litigation requirement of the US–Argentina BIT and that the arbitration tribunal had jurisdiction.[213] Argentina relied on US federal law under which a federal court may vacate an arbitral award if the arbitrators 'exceeded their powers'. The US Supreme Court confirmed the award. The split between the Court's opinion and the dissenting or partly concurring justices reflects fundamental differences in the interpretation of investment treaties. The majority, assimilating procedural provisions in an investment treaty with such clauses in 'an ordinary contract between private parties', assumed that interpretation lies primarily with arbitrators not courts. The dissenting opinion emphasizes the role of local litigation requirements in investments treaties as a condition to sovereign States' consent to arbitration and challenges the deferential approach to interpretation by arbitrators.[214]

---

[209] See Article 52 of the ICSID Convention.

[210] Council of the European Union Directives for the negotiation on the Transatlantic Trade and Investment Partnership between the European Union and the United States of America [17 June 2013] Doc 11103/13 DCL 1 (declassified 9 October 2014) para 23.

[211] See Section 1(c)(iii) in this Chapter.

[212] *BG Group v Republic of Argentina*, US Supreme Court 572 U.S. ___ (2014), 134 S.Ct. 1198 (2014), (2015) 54 ILM 133. See A Roberts and C Trahanas, 'Judicial Review of Investment Treaty Awards: *BG Group v. Argentina*' (2014) 108 AJIL 750ff.

[213] See Section 5(d) in this Chapter.

[214] CJ Roberts, dissenting, joined by J Kennedy, 572 U.S. ___ (2014); see also J Sotomayor, concurring in part.

Quite apart from these conceptual approaches,[215] the conclusion of the major-ity in *BG Group* is convincing. States, just like private parties to a dispute, must be deemed to have vested an international court or arbitral tribunal with full powers to decide on the scope of and the conditions for their own jurisdiction. With the pos-sible exception of awards which are manifestly *ultra vires*, the determination of the procedural limits of jurisdiction falls within the authority of arbitration tribunals and should not be subject to external control by the courts of third States.

6. The Call for Enhanced Respect for Regulatory Freedom of Host States

In recent years, strong criticism has emerged both in developing and industrial-ized countries against the restriction of policy choices of host States under invest-ment treaties as applied by arbitral tribunals. This criticism translates into a call for enhanced regulatory freedom of States, especially as to measures of health and environment protection as well as to social and labour standards which might affect foreign investors. In its resolution of 6 April 2011, the European Parliament under-lines the protection of 'the right to regulate' and

23. Stresses that future investment agreements concluded by the EU must respect the capacity for public intervention;
24. Expresses its deep concern regarding the level of discretion of international arbitrators to make a broad interpretation of investor protection clauses, thereby leading to the ruling out of legitimate public regulations; calls on the Commission to produce clear definitions of investor protection standards in order to avoid such problems in the new investment agreements;
25. Calls on the Commission to include in all future agreements specific clauses laying down the right of parties to the agreement to regulate, inter alia, in the areas of pro-tection of national security, the environment, public health, workers' and consumers' rights, industrial policy and cultural diversity;
26. Underlines that the Commission shall decide on a case-by-case basis on sectors not to be covered by future agreements, for example sensitive sectors such as culture, education, public health and those sectors which are strategically important for national defence, and asks the Commission to inform the European Parliament about the mandate it received in each case; notes that the EU should also be aware of the concerns of its devel-oping partners and should not call for more liberalisation if the latter deem it necessary for their development to protect certain sectors, particularly public services; [...].[216]

Recent treaty practice and arbitral case-law document a tendency to recalibrate the legal framework of investment protection. This recalibration aims at enhanced deference to regulatory discretion in the public interest.[217]

---

[215] See also Section 5(b) in this Chapter.
[216] European Parliament resolution of 6 April 2011 on the future European international invest-ment policy (2010/2203(INI)) paras 23ff.
[217] On changes in the investment protection policy of the United States J Alvarez, 'Why are We "Re-Calibrating" Our Investment Treaties?' (2010) 4 World Arbitration & Mediation Review 143. For

For example, Article 9.15 of the recent Trans-Pacific Partnership Agreement (2015) states:

Nothing in this Chapter shall be construed to prevent a Party from adopting, maintaining or enforcing any measure otherwise consistent with this Chapter that it considers appropriate to ensure that investment activity in its territory is undertaken in a manner sensitive to environmental, health or other regulatory objectives.

CETA emphasizes the 'right to regulate' in Article 8(9):

[T]he Parties reaffirm their right to regulate within their territories to achieve legitimate policy objectives, such as the protection of public health, safety, the environment or public morals, social or consumer protection or the promotion and the protection of cultural diversity.

Still, the negotiations on the Transatlantic Trade and Investment Partnership Agreement have nourished concern about the possible interference with existing European standards. In this context, the European Parliament calls for a new approach to investment protection and to the settlement of investment disputes:

The European Parliament [recommends] [...] to ensure that foreign investors are treated in a non-discriminatory fashion, while benefiting from no greater rights than domestic investors, and to replace the ISDS system with a new system for resolving disputes between investors and states which is subject to democratic principles and scrutiny, where potential cases are treated in a transparent manner by publicly appointed, independent professional judges in public hearings and which includes an appellate mechanism, where consistency of judicial decisions is ensured, the jurisdiction of courts of the EU and of the Member States is respected, and where private interests cannot undermine public policy objectives.[218]

This call for downgrading the protection of foreign investors to mere non-discrimination, deferring to domestic jurisdiction, for respecting domestic jurisdiction, and for deferring to public policy choices is somehow reminiscent of the Calvo doctrine with its rejection of special benefits and privileges for foreign investors.

For the settlement of investment disputes, the European Commission follows the same approach as the European Parliament and advocates an institutionalized investment court system with a Tribunal of First Instance and an Appeal Tribunal. The experience of dispute settlement systems with an appeal or revision mechanism in international economic law is mixed. Whilst the appeal mechanism in the dispute settlement of the World Trade Organization comes along with an enhanced legitimacy and authority, the annulment proceedings are sometimes associated with an unpredictable scope of review and considerable delay.

---

a more general assessment of recent trends in international investment treaty law, see SW Schill and M Jacob, 'Trends in International Investment Agreements, 2010–2011: The Increasing Complexity of International Investment Law' in KP Sauvant (ed), *Yearbook on International Investment Law & Policy 2011-2012* (OUP 2013) 141.

[218] European Parliament resolution of 8 July 2015 containing the European Parliament's recommendations to the European Commission on the negotiations for the Transatlantic Trade and Investment Partnership (TTIP) (2014/2228(INI)), S.2(d)(xv).

The model of an investment court system controlled by the State parties as advocated by the European Parliament found expression in CETA (on re-negotiation on the settlement of investment disputes) and the free trade agreement between the European Union and Vietnam. On the other side, the agreement on the TPP still follows the established model of investment arbitration.

Select Bibliography

BILATERAL AND MULTILATERAL AGREEMENTS ON THE PROTECTION OF INVESTMENTS

GA Alvarez, 'Investment Disputes under NAFTA' (2002) 18 Arb Int'l 309.

RD Bishop, J Crawford, and WM Reisman, *International Investment Disputes* (2nd edn, Kluwer 2014).

CN Brower and LA Steven, 'Who Then Should Judge: Developing the International Rule of Law under NAFTA Chapter 11' (2001) 2 Chi J Int'l L 193.

M Bungenberg, J Griebel, S Hobe, and A Reinisch (eds), *International Investment Law* (CH Beck, Hart Publishing, Nomos 2015).

G Coop and C Ribeiro, *Investment Protection and the Energy Charter Treaty* (JurisNet 2008).

J D'Agostino and O Jones, 'Energy Charter Treaty: A Step towards Consistency in International Investment Arbitration?' (2007) 25 J Energy Nat Resources L 225.

R Dolzer and C Schreuer, *Bilateral Investment Treaties* (2nd edn, OUP 2012).

Z Douglas, J Pauwelyn, and JE Viñuales (eds), *The Foundations of International Investment Law: Bringing Theory into Practice* (OUP 2014).

C Ribeiro (ed), *Investment Arbitration and the Energy Charter Treaty* (JurisNet 2006).

T Roe and M Happold, *Settlement of Investment Disputes under the Energy Charter Treaty* (CUP 2011).

JW Salacuse, *The Law of Investment Treaties* (2nd edn, OUP 2015).

SW Schill, *The Multilateralization of International Investment Law* (CUP 2014).

MODERN STANDARDS OF INVESTMENT PROTECTION

M Bungenberg, J Griebel, S Hobe, and A Reinisch (eds), *International Investment Law* (CH Beck, Hart Publishing, Nomos 2015)

R Dolzer, 'Fair and Equitable Treatment: A Key Standard in Investment Treaties' (2005) 39 Int'l Law 87.

R Kläger, *Fair and Equitable Treatment in International Investment Law* (CUP 2011).

A Reinisch (ed), *Standards of Investment Protection* (OUP 2008).

SW Schill, 'Multilateralizing Investment Treaties Through Most-Favoured-Nation Clauses' (2009) 27 Berk J Int'l L 496.

C Schreuer, 'Full Protection and Security' (2010) 1 J Int'l Dispute Settlement 1.

AC Sinclair, 'The Origins of the Umbrella Clause in the International Law of Investment Protection' (2004) 20 Arb Int'l 411.

I Tudor, *The Fair and Equitable Treatment Standard in the International Law of Foreign Investment* (OUP 2008).

M Valasek and P Dumberry, 'Developments in the Legal Standing of Shareholders and Holding Corporations in Investor-State Disputes' (2011) 26 ICSID Rev 34.

R de Vietri, 'Fair and Equitable Treatment for Foreign Investment: What is the Current Standard at International Law' (2011) 14 Int'l Trade & Bus L Rev 414.

HE Zeitler, 'The Guarantee of "Full Protection and Security" in Investment Treaties Regarding Harm Caused by Private Actors' (2005) 3 Stockholm Int'l Arb Rev 1.

DISPUTE SETTLEMENT

C Baltag, *The Energy Charter Treaty: The Notion of Investor* (Kluwer 2012).

RD Bishop, J Crawford, and WM Reisman, *Foreign Investment Disputes* (2nd edn, Kluwer 2014).

C Digan, ND Rubins, D Wallace, and B Sabahi, *Investor-State Arbitration* (OUP 2011).

G van Harten, *Investment Treaty Arbitration and Public Law* (OUP 2008).

HE Kjos, *Applicable Law in Investor-State Arbitration: The Interplay Between National and International Law* (OUP 2013).

C McLachlan, L Shore, and M Weiniger, *International Investment Arbitration* (2nd edn, OUP 2016).

SW Schill (ed), *International Investment Law and Comparative Public Law* (OUP 2010).

H Wehland, *The Coordination of Multiple Proceedings in Investment Treaty Arbitration* (OUP 2013).

XXXV

The International Centre for Settlement of Investment Disputes

The International Centre for Settlement of Investment Disputes (ICSID) was established under the Convention on the Settlement of Investment Disputes between States and Nationals of Other States of 1965[1] to provide a reliable and effective mechanism for the settlement of investment disputes between a contracting State to the Convention and a national of another contracting State through conciliation and arbitration (Article 1(2) of the ICSID Convention).[2] The ICSID is seated at the principal office of the World Bank in Washington, DC (Article 2). Over the last decade, the ICSID has become the main forum for the settlement of disputes between foreign investors and host States. After the withdrawal of Bolivia, Ecuador, and Venezuela, there are currently 161 signatory States with 153 States having ratified the ICSID Convention (as of mid-2016). The ICSID Convention governs the conciliation and arbitration procedures as well as the enforcement of arbitral awards.

The jurisdiction of the ICSID is established, if (1) the State Party to the dispute (ie the host State) and the home State of the investor are contracting States, and (2) the parties to the dispute (the host State and the investor) have consented in writing to arbitrate under the ICSID. Article 25(1) of the ICSID Convention provides:

The jurisdiction of the Centre shall extend to any legal dispute arising directly out of an investment, between a Contracting State (or any constituent subdivision or agency of a Contracting State designated to the Centre by that State) and a national of another Contracting State, which the parties to the dispute consent in writing to submit to the Centre. When the parties have given their consent, no party may withdraw its consent unilaterally.

Arbitration, according to the ICSID Convention rules, may be based on a dispute settlement clause in an investment treaty or on an ad hoc agreement concluded between the parties after the dispute has arisen. For the State which is party to an investment dispute, the ICSID clause in an investment treaty constitutes consent in writing, as required by Article 25(1) of the ICSID Convention. By submitting a request of arbitration, the private investor accepts the arbitration offer of the State.

By consenting to arbitrate under the ICSID Convention, the parties submit to the exclusive jurisdiction of the ICSID; a contracting State may make its consent

---

[1] (1965) 4 ILM 524.

[2] For a more detailed analysis, see L Reed, J Paulsson, and N Blackaby, Guide to ICSID Arbitration (Kluwer Law International 2004); C Schreuer, L Malintoppi, A Reinisch, and A Sinclair, The ICSID Convention—A Commentary (2nd edn, CUP 2009).

to arbitration dependent on the exhaustion of local remedies (Article 26). Article 27(1) prevents the home State of the foreign investor from exercising diplomatic protection in respect of another contracting State 'unless such other Contracting State shall have failed to abide by and comply with the award rendered in such dispute'.

Jurisdiction extends 'to any legal dispute arising directly out of an investment dispute' (Article 25(1) of the ICSID Convention). The ICSID Convention abstains from defining the term 'investment'. In *Salini v Kingdom of Morocco*, the arbitral tribunal read a number of criteria into the term 'investment' under the ICSID Convention:

The doctrine generally considers that investment infers: contributions, a certain duration of performance of the contract and a participation in the risks of the transaction [...] In reading the Convention's preamble, one may add the contribution to the economic development of the host state of the investment as an additional condition.[3]

The 'Salini' test implies that a protected investment must meet a double-barrelled standard, under the ICSID Convention and under the applicable investment treaty. The defect of the 'Salini test' is that it fails to respect the autonomy of States to define the scope of protected contributions also for the purposes of dispute settlement.

Recent practice sides with a more flexible standard, which simply requires a contribution of capital covered by the respective investment treaty.

In *Abaclat v The Argentine Republic*, the arbitral tribunal followed this approach and explained:

If it is obvious that the definition of Article 1(1) BIT and the criteria developed by a number of arbitral tribunals with regard to Article 25 ICSID Convention do not coincide, this is so because they can be said to focus each on a different aspect of the investment, i.e., they each look at the investment from a different perspective. The two perspectives can be viewed to be complementary, and to merely reflect a two-folded approach of the BIT and the ICSID Convention towards investment: At first, it is about encouraging investments, i.e., creating the frame conditions to encourage foreign investors to make certain contributions, and once such contributions are made, it is about protecting the fruits and value generated by these contributions.[4]

If there is a financial contribution which the contracting State qualifies as protected investment under the investment treaty, an investment is also established in terms of the ICSID Convention. The tribunal in *Abaclat v The Argentine Republic* tended to side with an approach which

[...] consists in verifying that Claimants made contributions, which led to the creation of the value that Argentina and Italy intended to protect under the BIT. Thus the only requirement regarding the contribution is that it be apt to create the value that is protected under the BIT.[5]

The ICSID Convention defers to the application of the rules of law chosen by the parties. In the absence of such agreement, 'the Tribunal shall apply the law of the

---

[3] *Salini Construttori SpA and Italstrade SpA v Kingdom of Morocco*, ICSID Case No. ARB/00/4 (Decision on Jurisdiction 2001), 6 ICSID Reports 400, para 52 (making reference to E. Gaillard, 'Centre International pour le Règlement des Différends relatifs aux Investissements (CIRDI)— Chroniques des sentences arbitrales' (1999) 126 J Droit Int'l 273 (278ff)).

[4] *Abaclat and Others v The Argentine Republic*, ICSID Case No ARB/07/5 (Decision on Jurisdiction and Admissibility 2011) para 349.

[5] *Abaclat and Others v The Argentine Republic*, ICSID Case No ARB/07/5 (Decision on Jurisdiction and Admissibility 2011) para 365.

Contracting State party to the dispute (including its rules on the conflict of laws) and such rules of international law as may be applicable' (Article 42(1)).

The ICSID Convention and the ICSID Arbitration Rules do not address the issue of a mass action or other collective proceedings. As the arbitral tribunal held in *Abaclat v The Argentine Republic*, this silence of the ICSID Convention cannot be interpreted as categorically prohibiting mass claims.[6]

Under the ICSID Convention each party may request interpretation of the award (Article 50), revision of the award in the light of the discovery of a new material fact (Article 51), and annulment of the award (Article 52). Under Article 52, grounds for annulment are limited to the incorrect formation of the arbitral tribunal (*lit* a), the manifest excess of powers of the arbitral tribunal (*lit* b), corruption on the part of a member of the arbitral tribunal (*lit* c), a serious deviation from a fundamental rule of procedure (*lit* d), and failure to state the reasons on which the award is based (*lit* e). Requests for annulment are decided by an ad hoc committee with three members (Article 52(3)). The annulment mechanism is very different from an appeal and is conceived to remedy very exceptionally serious deficiencies of the award or the underlying procedure. Still, in the past, some annulment decisions have interpreted the term 'manifest excess of powers' in a rather generous way, thus stirring considerable concerns about the stability of awards and the efficiency of the entire ICSID dispute settlement.[7] Some recent decisions suggest a more restrictive approach,[8] whilst other decisions follow a rather extensive understanding of grounds for annulment.

In *Sempra Energy International v Argentine Republic*, the ad hoc Committee distinguished between a failure to apply and a misapplication of the proper law:

So the question arises whether the error in law so identified constitutes an excess of powers. Excess of powers is normally invoked where it is claimed that the Tribunal has failed to apply the applicable law, and a line of decisions in ICSID practice confirms that failure to apply the applicable law may amount to an excess of powers, whereas erroneous application of the law does not constitute a basis for annulment.

It will therefore be necessary to determine whether the error in question amounts (i) to a failure to apply the law, in which event the award of The Tribunal may be annulled, or (ii) to a misapplication of the law, in which event the award, although to that extent defective, will not be annulled.[9]

The Committee found that the award under review ignored the distinction between the strict conditions for necessity under customary law and a broadly framed treaty exception for the preservation of the public order and national security.[10] It qualified this error in law as a failure to apply the proper law and not as a mere error in the application of the proper law.[11] The approach of the Committee is based on a

[6] *Abaclat and Others v The Argentine Republic*, ICSID Case No ARB/07/5 (Decision on Jurisdiction and Admissibility 2011) paras 515ff.

[7] See A Broches, 'Observations on the Finality of ICSID Awards' (1991) 6 ICSID Rev 321; MB Feldman, 'The Annulment Proceedings and the Finality of ICSID Arbitral Awards' (1987) 2 ICSID Rev 85.

[8] *CMS Gas Transmission Co v Argentine Republic*, ICSID Case No ARB/01/8 (Annulment Proceeding 2007), (2007) 46 ILM 1136, paras 136, 158.

[9] *Sempra Energy International v Argentine Republic*, ICSID Case No ARB/02/6 (Decision on the Argentine Republic's Application for Annulment of the Award 2010), paras 205f.

[10] Ibid, paras 195ff.   [11] Ibid, paras 207ff.

distinction between customary international law and treaty provisions and may be criticized for lack of receptivity to an integrative perspective of both sets of rules.[12]

According to Article 53

[t]he award shall be binding on the parties and shall not be subject to any appeal or to any other remedy except those provided for in this Convention. Each party shall abide by and comply with the terms of the award except to the extent that enforcement shall have been stayed pursuant to the relevant provisions of this Convention.

Each State party to the Convention 'shall recognize an award [...] as binding and enforce the pecuniary obligations imposed by that award within its territories as if it were a final judgement of a court in that State' (Article 54(1)).

This obligation does not derogate from the applicable rules on immunity from execution in order to avoid access to its capital (Article 55). However, respect for immunity from execution does not preclude national courts from recognizing an award and declaring it enforceable, as these acts do not constitute an enforcement measure.[13]

In investment disputes in which only one of the States involved, either the foreign investor's home State or the host State, is a party to the ICSID Convention, the dispute can be settled under the Additional Facility of the ICSID, which was created by the Administrative Council of the ICSID in 1978.[14] For investment disputes under NAFTA, the Additional Facility became relevant, as only the United States has ratified the ICSID Convention, whilst Canada (only signatory) and Mexico are not parties to it. Under Article 1120(1) of NAFTA, parties to an investment dispute may submit a claim to arbitration under the ICSID Convention, the Additional Facility under the ICSID, or under the UNCITRAL Arbitration Rules.

Select Bibliography

MI Egonu, 'Investor-State Arbitration under ICSID: A Case for Presumption against Confidentiality' (2007) 24 J Int'l Arb AR 479.
OE García-Bolívar, 'Protected Investments and Protected Investors: The Outer Limits of the ICSID's Reach' (2010) 2 Trade L & Dev 145.
A Parra, 'The Development of the Regulations and Rules of the International Centre for Settlement of Investment Disputes' (2007) 8 Stud Int'l Fin Econ & Tech L 226.
L Reed, J Paulsson, and N Blackaby, *Guide to ICSID Arbitration* (2nd edn, Kluwer Law International 2010).
C Schreuer, L Malintoppi, A Rheinisch, and A Sinclair, *The ICSID Convention: A Commentary* (2nd edn, CUP 2009).

---

[12] See Article 31(3)(c) of the Vienna Convention on the Law of Treaties.
[13] See French Court of Cassation *SOABI v Senegal* (1991) 30 ILM 1136; Cour d'Appell de Paris *SARL Benvenuti et Bonfant v Gouvernement de la République du Congo* (1981) 108 J Droit Int'l 843.
[14] Doc ICSID/11, Additional Facility for the Adminstration of Conciliation, Arbitration and Fact Finding (1979); generally on the Additional Facility, see A Broches, 'The "Additional Facility" of the International Centre For Settlement of Investment (CIRDI)' (1979) 4 YBCA 373.

XXXVI

Multilateral Investment Guarantee Agency

The Multilateral Investment Guarantee Agency (MIGA), a member of the World Bank Group, was established to encourage foreign investment in developing member countries by providing insurance for foreign investments against non-commercial risks.[1] According to the MIGA Convention of 1985[2] (amended in 2010), its objective is 'to encourage the flow of investments for productive purposes among member countries, and in particular to developing member countries [...]' (Article 2).

Under Article 11(a) of the MIGA Convention covered standard risks relate to currency transfer, expropriation, and similar measures (with the exception of non-discriminatory measures of general application which governments normally take to regulate economic activity in their territories), breach of contract, and war and civil disturbance. The MIGA offers insurance against the risk of breach of contract by the host government,

when (a) the holder of a guarantee does not have recourse to a judicial or arbitral forum to determine a claim of repudiation or breach, or (b) a decision by such forum is not rendered within such reasonable period of time as shall be prescribed in the contracts of guarantee pursuant to the Agency's regulations, or (c) such a decision cannot be enforced (Article 11 (a)(iii)).

Eligible investors are nationals of a Member State other than the host country and juridical persons which are incorporated and have their principal place of business in a Member State or are controlled through the majority of capital by a member or members or nationals thereof provided that such member is not the host country (Article 13 of the MIGA Convention). Investments shall only be guaranteed if they are to be realized in a developing country (Article 14 of the MIGA Convention).

Select Bibliography

SK Chatterjee, 'The Convention Establishing the Multilateral Investment Guarantee Agency' (1987) 36 ICLQ 76.

---

[1] See also SW Schill, 'Multilateral Investment Guarantee Agency (MIGA)' in R Wolfrum (ed), *The Max Planck Encyclopedia of Public International Law* (OUP 2012) vol VII, 410 para 1.
[2] (1985) 24 ILM 1598.

M Ikawa, 'The Multilateral Investment Guarantee Agency' (1999) 31 Stud Transnat'l Legal Pol'y 21.

G Ossman, 'Legal and Institutional Aspects of the Multilateral Investment Guarantee Agency as the Fifth Affiliate of the World Bank Group' (1996) 11 JIBL 359.

SW Schill, 'Multilateral Investment Guarantee Agency' in R Wolfrum (ed), *The Max Planck Encyclopedia of Public International Law* (OUP 2012) vol VII, 410.

JFI Shihata, *MIGA and Foreign Investment* (Martinus Nijhoff 1988).

JFI Shihata, 'The Multilateral Investment Guarantee Agency (MIGA) and the Legal Treatment of Foreign Investment' (1987) 203 RdC 95.

XXXVII

The Interplay of Investment Protection and Other Areas of International Law

Like other areas of international law, international investment law must not be read in isolation from other legal regimes. The international rules on investment stand in context with human rights, labour standards, and international environmental law.[1] In case the application of an investment treaty affects compliance with obligations under human rights or environmental law, the general principles of treaty interpretation require a 'systemic integration' of both obligations, which signifies that an investment treaty must be interpreted in the light of the other obligation (Article 31(3)(c) of the Vienna Convention on the Law of Treaties[2]).

Investment activities may often have human rights implications, especially with regard to the exploitation of natural resources.[3] Codes of conduct for investors, self-commitments and mechanisms of surveillance by the home State of investors are instruments to establish and to control corporate social responsibility.[4] Responsibility to ensure compliance with human rights standards essentially lies with the host State. Compliance with this responsibility often suffers from weak governmental structures and even deficient presence of the State within its own territory. Human rights standards under treaty and customary law, even if imperfectly observed, may be considered part of the laws of the host State which foreign investors must respect under conformity clauses or under specific commitments. Modern treaty practice has become more sensitive to labour and social standards including the prohibition of child labour, the right to collective bargaining, and occupational safety rules.[5]

In *Hesham Talaat v Indonesia*, an investment arbitration tribunal (set up under UNCITRAL rules) held that the standard of 'fair and equitable treatment' (applied through the most-favoured-nation clause of the Agreement on Promotion, Protection and Guarantee of Investments among Member States of

---

[1] For an outline of possible conflicts with an emphasis on human rights, environmental protection, and the pursuance of social and economic objectives, see SP Subedi, *International Investment Law* (2nd edn, Hart Publishing 2012) 149ff.

[2] See R Gardiner, *Treaty Interpretation* (OUP 2008) 250ff.   [3] See Ch VII.1.

[4] See Ch VII.3.   [5] See Article 13 of the US Model BIT (2012).

the Organisation of the Islamic Conference) must be interpreted in the light of customary law and the International Covenant on Civil and Political Rights (ICCPR) to which Indonesia is a party. In this case, the investor challenged its conviction for corruption and other crimes in a trial *in absentia*. The Tribunal held that fair and equitable treatment requires Indonesia to comply with the ICCPR under the customary principle of good faith.[6] It stated that it is 'the role of Civil Society—a role reflected and replicated in decisions of international arbitral tribunals—[...] to keep reminding the State party to adhere to the principle of good faith, and if and when the State has failed to do so, to so declare in its arbitral award'.[7]

The Tribunal emphasized that the rights enshrined in the ICCPR 'represent the basic minimum set of civil and political rights recognized by the world community'.[8] It found that the presumption of innocence (Article 14(2) of the ICCPR) and the guarantee of due process (Article 14(3) of the ICCPR) exclude a criminal trial *in absentia*. The award concluded that 'denial of justice constitutes a violation of the fair and equitable treatment standard'.[9]

In *Suez v Argentina*, Argentina argued, that it inferred with foreign investment to safeguard the human right to water of the inhabitants of the country, and claimed a broad margin of political discretion because of the fundamental importance of water for sustaining life and health. The arbitral tribunal found that the protection of human rights did not trump Argentina's obligations under an investment treaty and that Argentina simply had to respect both human rights obligations and obligations under an investment treaty.[10]

For some time, investment protection has drawn popular criticism for being insensitive to environmental issues or for having a chilling effect on environmental protection.[11] However, it must be recalled that it is the primary responsibility of the host State to consider implications for the environment when granting concessions or otherwise setting conditions for an investment. Pre-existing environmental standards under national and international law are apt to limit legitimate expectations of the investor which are protected by the treaty. It is true that changes of policy may trigger claims for compensation if they are inconsistent with previous assurances or commitments and if an investor could not reasonably foresee them. Then, the host State will have to balance political preferences with the financial consequences of its choice. Modern investment treaties do not defer to public interests in general terms. A number of treaties dedicate specific clauses to legitimate measures to protect the environment, human life, or health, and the life or health of animals and plants.[12]

---

[6] *Hesham Talaat M Al-Warraq v Indonesia* (UNCITRAL Final Award 2014) para 560.
[7] Ibid, para 560.   [8] Ibid, para 559.   [9] Ibid, para 621.
[10] *Suez Sociedad General de Aguas de Barcelona S.A. and Inter Agua Servicios Integrales des Agua, S.A. v The Argentine Republic*, ICSID Case No ARB/03/17 (Decision on Liability 2010).
[11] See P Sands, *Lawless World* (Penguin 2005) 136f; K Tienhaara, *The Expropriation of Environmental Governance: Protecting Foreign Investors at the Expense of Public Policy* (CUP 2009).
[12] Article 12 of the US Model BIT (2012); Article 1114 of NAFTA.

Select Bibliography

SF Puvimanasinghe, *Foreign Investment, Human Rights and the Environment* (Martinus Nijhoff 2007).

B Simma, 'Foreign Investment Arbitration: A Place for Human Rights?' (2011) 60 ICLQ 573.

KS Tienhaara, *The Expropriation of Environmental Governance: Protecting Foreign Investors at the Expense of Public Policy* (CUP 2009).

PART VI

INTERNATIONAL MONETARY LAW AND THE INTERNATIONAL FINANCIAL ARCHITECTURE

XXXVIII

International Monetary Law
and International Economic Relations

1. The Impact of Monetary Relations
on International Trade and Business

International monetary law constitutes a core sector of international economic law. International trade in goods and services and other international business transactions rest on cross-border payments and capital movements which, as a rule, affect two or more currency areas. Only monetary unions like the Eurozone (European Monetary Union) allow transboundary transactions to be realized within a single currency area.

The system established by the Conference of Bretton Woods (1944), with the Articles of Agreement of the International Monetary Fund (IMF), aims to create an international monetary order based on the free convertibility of currencies. It also aims to ensure free movement of capital and payments in conformity with the requirements of internal trade.

The Articles of Agreement of the IMF clearly reflect the understanding that a functional and open world trade order requires a stable international monetary system. According to Article IV, section 1 of the Agreement, the members of the Fund expressly recognize

that the essential purpose of the international monetary system is to provide a framework that facilitates the exchange of goods, services, and capital among countries, and that sustains sound economic growth, and that a principal objective is the continuing development of the orderly underlying conditions that are necessary for financial and economic stability.

The regulation of currency exchange vitally affects competitive conditions in international trade and business. Again and again, States resort to currency manipulation as an instrument to place their own economy in an advantageous position on the international markets. By means of an undervalued exchange rate, either by devaluation or by artificially keeping their own currency down (eg by massive purchase of foreign currencies), States may distort international competition in favour of their own export industry. The consequence may be serious trade and monetary conflicts as between the United States and China over the low exchange rate of the Chinese Yuan. Restrictions of payments and capital

movements hamper international business transactions and affect the repatria-
tion of profits by foreign investors. The ban on stabilization clauses related to the
value of money may affect the contractual balance in long-term business relations
under depreciating currencies.

Financial aid to countries with balance of payment problems, in particular heavily
indebted countries, provided by governments and international organizations such
as the International Monetary Fund (IMF) has become an important mechanism
to stabilize currencies. The financial assistance to some Euro countries granted by
the European Union, other members of the Eurozone and the IMF[1]demonstrates
the interrelation between financial sustainability and currency stability in a hitherto
unknown hard currency context.

Not only States but also private actors may influence the valuation of currencies
and exchange rates. Free movement of capital allows massive speculations with currencies. 'Carry trades' may distort capital flows. In this kind of deal, an investor sells
or borrows currency with a relatively low interest and uses the funds to purchase
a currency yielding higher interest, attempting to derive profit from the difference
between the rates (which may or may not correspond to his expectations). With the
assessment of the financial standing of States, rating agencies (US companies such
as Fitch, Moody's and Standard & Poor's) influence the interest rates for sovereign
borrowing as well as the exchange rates. Credit default swaps and other instruments
of insurance against the risk of sovereign default also affect the standing of States in
the capital markets.

2. The Bretton Woods System and the Development of Currency Exchange Arrangements

In the decades before the First World War, the major economic powers (France,
Germany, the United Kingdom, and the United States) tied their currencies to
gold. Under the 'gold standard' the parity of the Franc, the Mark, the Pound
Sterling and the US-Dollar remained stable. This system of rigid exchange rates
also extended to other States, which pegged their currency against one of the lead
currencies or to gold and kept reserves in this currency or in gold. The gold standard was based on an informal understanding among the governors of central banks
and disrupted with the outbreak of the First World War. In retrospect, despite its
inherent problems,[2] the gold standard is associated with an impressive increase of
international trade and international investment. The high degree of integration of
capital markets brought about a 'globalization' which, in this sector, was reached
again only decades after the Second World War.

---

[1] International Monetary Fund, *The IMF and Europe* (2014) <www.imf.org/external/np/exr/facts/
pdf/europe.pdf> (accessed 1 February 2016); C Walter, 'Debt Crisis' in R Wolfrum (ed), *The Max
Planck Encyclopedia of Public International Law* (OUP 2012) vol II, 1068.
[2] See KW Dam, *The Rules of the Game: Reform and Evolution in the International Monetary System*
(University of Chicago Press 1982).

The turbulence generated by changing exchange rate policies of the major powers after the First World War (especially in the 1930s), with manipulative devaluations and other protectionist strategies, inspired the negotiation of a legally entrenched universal regime designed to establish monetary relations with freely convertible currencies and stable exchange rates as a basis of economic growth towards the end of the Second World War.

The Conference of Bretton Woods (1944)[3] adopted the Articles of Agreement on the International Monetary Fund (IMF)[4] and shaped the international monetary system for decades. It also created the Agreement on the International Bank for Reconstruction of Development (the World Bank).

The main actors at the Conference were the chief negotiator for the United States, Harry Dexter White and, for the United Kingdom, Lord John Maynard Keynes. The IMF established a kind of 'currency pool' with the purpose to assist Member States with balance of payment problems and thus to ensure the liquidity on the international markets.

The Bretton Woods system rested on two pillars: the free convertibility of currencies and fixed exchange rates. The US-Dollar was pegged against gold and the United States guaranteed the convertibility of the US-Dollar into gold (0.88671 g gold per US-Dollar). For the other currencies, the fixed rates of exchange against the US-Dollar also established a fixed value against gold (par value). The IMF Agreement of 1944 allowed fluctuations of the exchange rates within a corridor of 1 per cent. To counter fluctuations beyond this margin, central banks of Member States were bound to intervene, buying or selling US-Dollars. With the US-Dollar being the lead currency with guaranteed convertibility into gold, the United States had no obligation to intervene. In the case of a 'fundamental disequilibrium' in the balance of payments, the exchange rates had to be adjusted. All these parameters constituted a system of fixed exchange rates with graded flexibility.

In the first decades of the post-Second World War era, the Bretton Woods system of fixed but adjustable exchange rates ensured considerable stability of monetary relations among the Member States. However, in the 1960s, increasing excessive government spending and inflation in the United States caused an expansion of the US-Dollar volume out of proportion with the US gold reserves. The gross overvaluation of the US-Dollar made the system of fixed exchange rates and the convertibility into gold unsustainable. In 1971, the US Government suspended the convertibility of the US-Dollar into gold, and the Bretton Woods system of fixed parities ultimately collapsed in March 1973, when major currencies started floating against each other. Floating exchange rates enabled economies to respond better to external shocks like the oil crisis of 1973.

---

[3] RN Gardner, *Sterling-Dollar Diplomacy in Current Perspective: The Origins and Prospects of Our International Economic Order* (3rd edn, Columbia University Press 1980); AF Lowenfeld, 'Bretton Woods Conference (1944)' in R Wolfrum (ed), *The Max Planck Encyclopedia of Public International Law* (OUP 2012) vol I, 1054.

[4] 726 UNTS 266.

The 1976 Amendment of the IMF Articles (in force since 1978) fundamentally reformed Article IV and allows Member States to choose exchange arrangements freely, except pegging their currency to gold. Article IV, section 2(b) of the IMF Agreement states:

Under an international monetary system of the kind prevailing on January 1, 1976, exchange arrangements may include (i) the maintenance by a member of a value for its currency in terms of the special drawing right or another denominator, other than gold, selected by the member, or (ii) cooperative arrangements by which members maintain the value of their currencies in relation to the value of the currency or currencies of other members, or (iii) other exchange arrangements of a member's choice.

3. Currency Exchange Regimes

Currency exchange may be subject to one of two different models: either the liberal system of free convertibility of currencies or the restrictive regime of currency exchange control. A system of freely convertible currencies allows the exchange of the domestic or other currencies for different currencies. There are varying degrees of freedom of convertibility, ranging from restrictions for certain transactions, for certain countries, or for certain persons to complete freedom for nationals and foreign persons alike.

Convertibility may be subject to various regimes. In accordance with an IMF categorization, three types of regimes can be distinguished:

- hard pegs, that is fixed exchange rates with a currency pegged to another currency ('anchor currency', eg the US-Dollar), to a currency basket or to gold ('gold standard');
- floating (flexible) exchange rates, determined by supply and demand on the markets;
- intermediary regimes ('soft pegs').

Among intermediary models are regimes with a currency tied to another currency or to a currency basket which allow for periodical, step-by-step adjustments responding to imbalances no longer reflected in the existing pegs ('adjustable' or 'crawling' pegs). Another intermediary regime of 'soft' pegs is a tight management of floating exchange rates with central bank intervention in the interest of predetermined targets ('managed' or 'dirty' floating). Often floating is confined to a certain managed margin ('crawling bands').

In 2009, the IMF adopted a Revised System for the Classification of Exchange Rate Arrangements with nine different regimes: exchange arrangements with no separate legal tender ('dollarization'), currency board arrangements (legal commitment to exchange domestic currency for a specified foreign currency at a fixed rate, coupled with legal instruments to ensure fulfilment of this obligation), conventional pegged arrangements, stabilized arrangements, pegged exchange rate within horizontal bands, crawling peg, crawl-like arrangements, floating, and free floating exchange rates.[5]

Floating exchange rates allow States to make autonomous decisions as to the supply of money, whilst in a system of fixed exchange rates monetary policies are intertwined. Adjustable pegs provide incentives for currency speculations whenever a currency comes under pressure. The risk of speculations is confined to transaction costs. Often, States react with drastic devaluation in order to avoid repeated devaluation within a short period of time. By contrast, flexible exchange rates immediately react to developments in the capital markets. It is, therefore, difficult for speculators to precisely prognosticate maximum lows.

Currently, 65 States (among them most industrialized Western States, including the United States, the members of the Eurozone and the other EU-States (with respect to third countries and Japan)) have floating exchange rates, 83 countries have soft pegs, and 25 States hard pegs.[6] China, having adhered to fixed exchange rates, officially introduced managed floating in 1994. In fact, China tied the Renminbi (Yuan) to the US-Dollar, with the People's Bank of China intervening to maintain a stable exchange rate ('soft peg'). Since 2005, the Chinese currency is pegged to a currency basket (rather than just the US-Dollar). Russia follows a regime of managed floating with a soft peg of the Rouble to a Euro/US-Dollar-basket.

Systems of currency exchange control tightly regulate currency exchange and the acquisition of foreign currencies. This kind of control was applied in the communist States of the former 'Eastern bloc'. It still prevails in countries with a State-trading monopoly regime. Exchange controls are a heavy barrier to international trade.

4. Monetary Unions

(a) Survey

Monetary unions (currency unions)[7] are the most advanced forms of economic integration. Monetary unions in a narrow sense rest upon an agreement between two or more States (or other territorial entities) to share a common currency and to pursue a common monetary policy. There must be a common central bank with the authority to issue the common currency and, thus, a transfer of monetary powers to be shared by all members. The main benefit lies in the elimination of transactions costs and the stabilization of exchange rates thanks to aggregated economic power. Monetary unions suppose a high or at least stable degree of economic convergence including fiscal policy, as there is no national exchange policy to address

---

[5] International Monetary Fund, 'Annual Report on Exchange Arrangements and Exchange Restrictions' (2009).

[6] International Monetary Fund, 'Annual Report on Exchange Arrangements and Exchange Restrictions' (2014).

[7] A Alesina and RJ Barro, 'Currency Unions' (2002) 117 QJ Econ 409.

gaps in economic growth rates between members, balance of payment problems, and other domestic or international disturbances. Members also renounce the possibility of creating their own money to pay off debts or to increase public spending (*seigneuriage*).

The most prominent monetary union is the Eurozone in the framework of the European Economic and Monetary Union. Another example is the Eastern Caribbean Currency Union with a regional central bank.

The former French colonies in West Africa and in Central Africa have preserved the legacy of a common currency ('CFA Franc'). The West African Financial Community (Communauté Financière d'Afrique) and the Central African Financial Cooperation (Coopération Financière Africaine) each constitute a monetary union with a common currency issued by a regional central bank. Their currencies (West African CFA Franc, Central African CFA Franc) are legal tender only in the respective monetary union, but are, in practice, fixed at par value and administered under the auspices of the French ministry of finances as elements of a single currency zone ('CFA zone'). Both CFA Francs are pegged to the Euro.

The acceptance of a national currency as non-exclusive legal tender in other countries is also termed a monetary union in the broader sense. In these cases of a currency union, some Member States issue a local currency that is pegged to the common currency, but is not accepted as legal tender outside of the issuing country.

When the currency of a foreign country is exclusively or predominantly accepted as legal tender ('anchor currency'), this does not constitute a monetary union. This applies to instances of 'dollarization' (eg Panama) or 'euroization' (eg Kosovo or Montenegro).

(b) The European Monetary Union

The rules on the European Economic and Monetary Union (EMU), as designed in the Treaty of Maastricht (1992), provided the framework for the establishment of the Euro in 1999, as the common currency for the participating States, that is the States entering in the third stage of the EMU (currently nineteen: Austria, Belgium, Cyprus, Estonia, Finland, France, Germany, Greece, Ireland, Italy, Latvia, Lithuania, Luxembourg, Malta, the Netherlands, Portugal, Slovakia, Slovenia, and Spain).

The issue of the common currency is managed by the European Central Bank (Article 128 of the TFEU).[8] Together with the central banks of the participating countries, the European Central Bank forms the European System of Central

---

[8] See J de Haan and H Berger, *The European Central Bank at Ten* (Springer 2010); DJ Howarth and P Loedel, *European Central Bank: The New European Leviathan?* (Palgrave Macmillan 2005); HK Scheller, *The European Central Bank: History, Role and Function* (2nd edn, European Central Bank 2006); R Smits, *The European Central Bank: Institutional Aspects* (Kluwer Law International 1997).

Banks which pursues the monetary policy of the European Union (Article 282(1) of the TFEU).

The guiding principles of the EMU[9] are:

- the maintenance of price stability as the 'primary objective of the European System of Central Banks' (Article 127(1) of the TFEU);
- the independence of the European Central Bank and the other banks of the ESCB (Article 130 of the TFEU);
- the principle of 'no bail-out', that is the exclusive liability of each Member State for its commitments (Article 125 of the TFEU);
- the prohibition of credit facilities for Member States and of the direct purchase of government debts by the European Central Bank (Article 126 of the TFEU);
- fiscal discipline with the avoidance of excessive public deficits (Article 126(1) of the TFEU);
- surveillance by the Commission and the Council of the European Union and possible sanctions for non-compliance (Article 126(2)–(13) of the TFEU); and
- the fulfilment of 'convergence criteria' as a condition for the accession to the Eurozone (Article 140 of the TFEU).

In addition, on the basis of the TFEU, the European Union adopted the 'Stability and Growth Pact' of 1997, a bundle of measures for monitoring, prevention, and surveillance of members' fiscal policy.[10] After the Council of the European Union softened the Pact in 2005 in terms of greater 'flexibility', the escalating debt crisis in the Eurozone drove the Council and members of the Eurozone towards tightening the rules ('six pack' of regulations in November 2011).

The critical parameters for fiscal discipline are limits for the annual budget deficit (3 per cent of GDP) and for the public debt (60 per cent of GDP), as laid down in Article 126(2) of the TFEU and the Protocol on the Procedure to Excessive Deficit. A sustainable financial position is also a crucial criterion of convergence (Article 140(1) of the TFEU, Protocol on the Convergence Criteria).

The so-called 'Fiscal Compact' (Treaty on Stability, Coordination and Governance in the Economic and Monetary Union) of 2012[11] limits the annual structural deficit to 0.5 per cent of the GDP ('debt brake'), calls for a continuous reduction of the public debt, and tightens monetary surveillance.

---

[9] See M Herdegen, 'Price Stability and Budgetary Restraints in the Economic and Monetary Union: The Law as Guardian of Economic Wisdom' (1998) 35 CML Rev 9; MW Klein, 'European Monetary Union' (1998) New England Econ Rev 3; FC Mayer and I Stanik, 'European Union, Historical Evolution' in R Wolfrum (ed), *The Max Planck Encyclopedia of Public International Law* (OUP 2012) vol III, 1000 paras 10ff; B Laffan and S Mazey 'European Integration: the European Union—Reaching an Equilibrium?' in J Richardson (ed), *European Union* (2nd edn, Routledge 2001) 31.

[10] See HJ Hahn, 'The Stability Pact for European Monetary Union: Compliance with Deficit Limit as a Constant Legal Duty' (1998) 35 CML Rev 77.

[11] Bundesgesetzblatt 2012 Teil II Nr. 28 vom 18 September 2012, 1006.

A central element in the original design of the EMU (system of the Treaty of Maastricht) is the 'no bail-out clause' (Article 125(1) of the TFEU):

The Union shall not be liable for or assume the commitments of central governments, regional, local or other public authorities, other bodies governed by public law, or public undertakings of any Member State, without prejudice to mutual financial guarantees for the joint execution of a specific project. A Member State shall not be liable for or assume the commitments of central governments, regional, local or other public authorities, other bodies governed by public law, or public undertakings of another Member State, without prejudice to mutual financial guarantees for the joint execution of a specific project.

The principle that each country should exclusively be responsible for its own debts is meant to sensitize capital markets and sharpen their vigilance for fiscal discipline. However, capital markets, by an all too benign assessment of this financial situation of indebted Euro countries and by relying on collective solidarity of others, were desensitized and provided continuous lending to heavily indebted countries at low interest rates before becoming alert to hardly sustainable public debt. At the end of this process, there was little 'convergence' in terms of budget deficit and public debt as well as interest rates for sovereign borrowing.

To stabilize the Euro and to ensure access to capital markets for indebted Euro countries, the European Union and the members of the Eurozone have established a 'rescue umbrella' with various mechanisms of financial assistance (European Financial Stabilization Mechanism, European Financial Stability Facility, European Stability Mechanism).[12]

In addition, the International Monetary Fund plays an important role in these rescue operations. Financial assistance to indebted Euro countries is subject to more or less rigorous adjustment programmes ('conditionality'), which are well known from the lending practice of the International Monetary Fund. Critics qualify these adjustment programmes as excessive austerity and a relapse into radical neoliberalism. In resolution 1884 (2012),[13] the Parliamentary Assembly of the Council of Europe joined the choir of critical voices:

The Parliamentary Assembly is worried about the impact of current austerity programmes on democratic and social rights standards. It is concerned that the restrictive approaches currently pursued, predominantly based on budgetary cuts in social expenditure, may not reach their objective of consolidating public budgets, but risk further deepening the crisis and undermining social rights as they mainly affect lower income classes and the most vulnerable categories of the population. [...] Facing the consequences of 'unbridled'

---

[12] On the compatibility of the European Stability Mechanism with the European treaties ECJ Case C-370/12, ECLI:EU:C:2012:756—*Pringle v Government of Ireland, Ireland and The Attorney General* (27 November 2012) para 137: 'However, Article 125 TFEU does not prohibit the granting of financial assistance by one or more Member States to a Member State which remains responsible for its commitments to its creditors provided that the conditions attached to such assistance are such as to prompt that Member State to implement a sound budgetary policy.' See also Article 136(3) TFEU: 'The Member States whose currency is the euro may establish a stability mechanism to be activated if indispensable to safeguard the stability of the euro area as a whole. The granting of any required financial assistance under the mechanism will be made subject to strict conditionality.'
[13] <http://assembly.coe.int/nw/xml/XRef/Xref-XML2HTML-en.asp?fileid=18916&lang=en> (accessed 23 June 2016).

economic liberalism, the European social model and its various national expressions should be protected as a common European vision, characterised by the general principles of a 'social market economy', and the welfare State should be further strengthened, including through new social partnerships placing the human being at the centre of concerns.

On the other hand it must be recalled that, in the Eurozone, only a certain degree of fiscal discipline in the less indebted States provided the basis for generous solidarity with and assistance to the Euro countries facing a financial crisis.

The European Central Bank is barred from purchasing government bonds directly from issuing EU States (Article 123(1) of the TFEU). It has, however, bought such government bonds in enormous quantities on secondary markets. National central banks (in particular the German Bundesbank) have indirectly financed deficits via the European interbank payment system TARGET2.[14] Additional instruments like the issue of common 'Euro-bonds' have been proposed. Apart from economic discussion, all these measures are matters of legal controversy, in particular in the light of the 'no bail-out clause' (Article 125 of the TFEU) and the prohibition for the European Central Bank to directly finance public debt.[15]

In particular, the announcement of the European Central Bank to buy, if necessary, bonds of Euro countries which are subject to adjustment programmes under the rules of the European Stability Mechanism on secondary markets without quantitative limits ('Outright Monetary Transactions'—OMT) has sparked controversies about the distinction between monetary policy (the European Central Bank's domain) on one hand and economic policy on the other. In a request for a preliminary ruling of the European Court of Justice, the German Constitutional Court had qualified this programme as monetary financing of public deficits which would no longer be covered by the European Central Bank's monetary mandate.[16]

The European Court of Justice recognizes that the objective of keeping a highly indebted Member State in the Eurozone would exceed the European Central Bank's monetary mandate.[17] However, the European Court of Justice concluded that the OMT programme is covered by the monetary powers of the European Central Bank, because it counteracts excessive spreads of interest rates of government bonds and thus supports the 'monetary transmission mechanism' of the European Central Bank's interventions. The Court linked this objective with the Bank's commitment to price stability (Article 127(1) of the TFEU).[18] This approach has drawn severe criticism, as the spread of interest rates simply reflects the assessment of the financial sustainability of a Euro country by the capital markets. It distinguishes between measures stabilizing the Euro (monetary policy) and the stabilization of the Euro zone by supporting indebted member countries (economic policy). The European

---

[14] Trans-European Automated Real-time Gross Settlement Express Transfer System; Deutsche Bank Research, 'Eurolands Hidden Balance-of-Payments Crisis' (2011) EU Monitor No 88.

[15] See M Ruffert, 'The European Debt Crisis and European Union Law' (2011) 48 CML Rev 1777.

[16] German Constitutional Court request for a preliminary ruling of the European Court of Justice, BVerfGE 134, 366 (398ff); see K Schneider, 'Yes, But ... One More Thing: Karlsruhe's Ruling on the European Stability Mechanism' (2013) 14 German Law Journal 53.

[17] ECJ Case C-62/14, ECLI:EU:C:2015:400—*Gauweiler and Others v Deutscher Bundestag* (16 June 2015).

[18] Ibid, paras 49ff.

Court of Justice, permitted the large-scale purchase of European government bonds subject to a number of conditions:[19]

- A minimum period must be observed between the issue of a security on the primary market and its purchase on the secondary market.
- There must be no prior announcement concerning either the decision to carry out such purchases or the volume of purchases envisaged.
- Purchases of government bonds must be confined to what is necessary for safeguarding the monetary policy transmission mechanism and the singleness of monetary policy and it must cease as soon as those objectives are achieved.
- The purchase programme may only cover bonds issued by those Member States which are undergoing a structural adjustment programme and which have access to the bond market again.
- Holding the bonds the ESCB has purchased until maturity depends on such action being necessary to achieve the objectives sought.

In deference to the European Court of Justice's ruling, the German Constitutional Court concluded that the European Central Bank, like other bodies of the European Union, enjoys a broad 'fault tolerance' and that therefore the German Bundesbank may participate in the OMT programme, as long as the conditions established by the European Court of Justice are met. Critical analysts blame both judgments for loosening control of the extensive exercise of the monetary powers of the European Central Bank and for allowing Germany to get caught in a collective liability for the debts of economically ailing Euro countries.

The OMT programme has so far not been put into practice. Yet, the mere announcement by the European Central Bank to initiate outright monetary transactions had significant influence on the development of interest rates. The European Central Bank and central banks of Euro countries have purchased enormous amounts of State bonds on the secondary markets. Critics qualify these purchases as coming close to monetary financing of public debt. In addition, the European Central Bank practises a policy of permanent low interest for credit institutions. These measures purport to support Euro countries with a large public debt to stabilize the banking sector and stimulate the economy. This policy of 'quantitative easing' follows the examples set by the Bank of Japan, the US Federal Reserve, and the Bank of England.

On 22 January 2015 the European Central Bank launched the Expanded Asset Purchase Programme (EAPP)[20] which creates new money by increasing the credit in its own account to purchase investment-grade securities from Euro area governments and European institutions as well as financial assets from banks, pension funds, insurance companies, and other private investors.[21]

[19] Ibid, paras 60ff, 106, 112, 116, and 118.
[20] The programme consists of the 'Third Covered Bond Purchase Programme (CBPP3)', the 'Asset-Backed Securities Purchase Programme (ABSPP)', and the 'Public Sector Purchase Programme (PSPP)'.
[21] European Parliament, 'The ECB's Expanded Asset Purchase Programme: Will Quantitative Easing Revive the Euro Area Economy?' (February 2015) <http://www.europarl.europa.eu/EPRS/EPRS-Briefing-548976-The-ECBs-EAPP-FINAL.pdf> (accessed 23 June 2016).

The debt crisis in the Eurozone, arising from the deficit of Greece, Ireland, Italy, Portugal, and Spain ('GIIPS'), documents the problems and pitfalls of a monetary union without common economic governance and with vast gaps in fiscal discipline, economic growth, and access to capital markets (reflected in spreads of interest rates). As members of the Eurozone, countries like Greece can neither devalue the currency to enhance international competitiveness nor generate fresh money to meet its outstanding obligations. Whether a country can unilaterally leave the Eurozone and revert to its own currency, is a matter of controversy.[22] From a practical perspective, any reasonable exit strategy can only be conceptualized in consensual terms. If an economically weak country leaves the common currency, it must pay its outstanding (international) obligations in Euros, which then becomes a hard foreign currency.

On the periphery of the EMU are the EU countries which do not (yet) participate in the common currency regime (Article 139 of the TFEU): Bulgaria, Croatia, the Czech Republic, Denmark, Hungary, Poland, Romania, Sweden, and the United Kingdom. Most of the non-participating States have joined the European Exchange Rate Mechanism II, in which exchange rates may fluctuate within a margin of 15 per cent.

5. 'Eurodollars' and other Eurocurrencies

The term 'Eurocurrencies' refers to deposits at a bank denominated in other than the local currency. Thus, US-Dollar deposits at a German or British bank are called 'Eurodollars'. Eurocurrencies and their trade are not a creation of governmental regulation or initiative, but the product of private initiative. In the late 1950s, merchant banks and other commercial companies located outside of the United States established the practice to denominate monetary claims in US-Dollars and to pay in this currency. During the Cold War, a subsidiary of the Soviet Central Bank, the Banque Commerciale pour l'Europe du Nord with the telex address 'Euro-Bank', accumulated deposits in US-Dollars outside of the United States with the purpose to evade a possible freezing of the US-Dollar accounts by the US Government. This is how the term 'Eurodollar' came into being.

The establishment of deposits in a certain currency at a bank located outside the State which issues the currency is a mechanism to evade the regulatory interference of the issuing State with the deposit. More important is the role of Eurocurrency accounts for transboundary payments. Eurocurrency deposits allow international businesses to take advantage of discrepancies in interest rates and to hedge the risk of fluctuating exchange rates. The central banks of the States issuing the currency can only interfere with the value of the deposits through the money supply and the interest rate.

---

[22] M Herdegen, 'Germany's Constitutional Court and Parliament: Factors of Uncertainty for the Monetary Union?' (1998) EMU Watch No 19.

Establishing a deposit in Eurocurrencies or making payments from a Eurocurrency account does not imply a transfer of currencies from one country to another. The bank of deposit does not necessarily dispose of the foreign currency in cash. The banks involved simply make and receive the payments in their local currency according to the applicable exchange rate (eg payment from Germany to the United States in Euros and in US-Dollars). Therefore, arrangements relating to Eurocurrencies do not qualify as 'exchange contracts' in terms of Article VIII, section 2(b) of the IMF Agreement and are not subject to exchange control regulations of the State issuing the foreign currency. Freezing orders of the State issuing the foreign currency (eg the United States) do not apply in the country where the deposit is held (eg the United Kingdom), even if the bank is a branch or subsidiary of the issuing State.[23]

On the other hand, the deposit holder may not claim that his bank only makes payments to foreign accounts in the foreign currency. As the English High Court held in *Libyan Arab Foreign Bank v Bankers Trust Co*, at the holder's behest, the bank must pay out the balance of the account in cash in the foreign currency.[24]

Select Bibliography

KC Butler, *Multinational Finance: Evaluating Opportunities, Costs, and Risks of Operations* (5th edn, Wiley-Blackwell 2012).
F Cesarano, *Monetary Theory and Bretton Woods: The Construction of an International Monetary Order* (CUP 2006).
T Cottier, JH Jackson, and RM Lasta (eds), *International Law in Financial Regulation and Monetary Affairs* (OUP 2012).
M Giovanoli, 'The Reform of the International Financial Architecture after the Global Crisis' (2009) 42 Int'l L & Pol 81.
M Giovanoli and D Devos, *International Monetary Law and Financial Law: The Global Crisis* (OUP 2010).
HJ Hahn and U Häde, *Währungsrecht* (2nd edn, CH Beck 2010).
R Lastra, *International Financial and Monetary Law* (2nd edn, OUP 2015).
AF Lowenfeld, 'International Monetary Law', in R Wolfrum (ed), *The Max Planck Encyclopedia of Public International Law* (OUP 2012) vol VII, 342.
C Proctor, *Mann on the Legal Aspect of Money* (7th edn, OUP 2012).
P Savona, *The New Architecture of the International Monetary System* (Springer 2000).
CD Zimmermann, *A Contemporary Concept of Monetary Sovereignty* (OUP 2013).

[23] *Libyan Arab Foreign Bank v Bankers Trust Co* (1987) 26 ILM 1600.
[24] *Libyan Arab Foreign Bank v Bankers Trust Co* (1987) 26 ILM 1600.

XXXIX

The International Monetary Fund: Objectives, Organization, and Functions

The Articles of Agreement of the International Monetary Fund (IMF Agreement)[1] were negotiated at the Conference of Bretton Woods (1944). The IMF was established to ensure a stable international monetary system as a basis of international trade and capital movements, to foster a sound economic growth and to contribute to a stable monetary regime of Member States (Article IV, section 1 first sentence of the IMF Agreement). Its main functions are twofold:

- coordination and surveillance of monetary relations, in particular of exchange rate policies; and
- assistance to members in economic difficulties.

Under the IMF Agreement, stable exchange currency arrangements and the free convertibility of currencies are cornerstones of international monetary relations.

1. Objectives

The IMF Agreement lays down the objectives of the Fund in Article I:

The purposes of the International Monetary Fund are:
  (i) To promote international monetary cooperation through a permanent institution which provides the machinery for consultation and collaboration on international monetary problems.
 (ii) To facilitate the expansion and balanced growth of international trade, and to contribute thereby to the promotion and maintenance of high levels of employment and real income and to the development of the productive resources of all members as primary objectives of economic policy.
(iii) To promote exchange stability, to maintain orderly exchange arrangements among members, and to avoid competitive exchange depreciation.

---

[1] 2 UNTS 39, 134; 606 UNTS 295; 726 UNTS 266.

514 off

(iv) To assist in the establishment of a multilateral system of payments in respect of current transactions between members and in the elimination of foreign exchange restrictions which hamper the growth of world trade.

(v) To give confidence to members by making the general resources of the Fund temporarily available to them under adequate safeguards, thus providing them with opportunity to correct maladjustments in their balance of payments without resorting to measures destructive of national or international prosperity.

(vi) In accordance with the above, to shorten the duration and lessen the degree of disequilibrium in the international balances of payments of members.

The Fund shall be guided in all its policies and decisions by the purposes set forth in this Article.

2. Membership

The IMF currently has 189 Member States. Each member is assigned a quota expressed in special drawing rights (Article III, section 1 of the IMF Agreement). The contributions of each member to the IMF's capital stock (subscription) are equal to its quota (Article III, section 1 second sentence). The largest share is allocated to the United States, the smallest to Tuvalu.

The quotas (Article III, sections 1 and 2 of the IMF Agreement) result from a number of weighted variables which reflect its relative position in the global economy: GDP with a weight of 50 per cent, openness to trade with a weight of 30 per cent, variability of current receipts (eg earnings from the export of goods and services) with a weight of 15 per cent, gold and international currency reserves with a weight of 5 per cent. Quotas are determined and adjusted by the Board of Governors. They cannot be changed without assent of the respective Member State. The quotas determine the voting power of each member, its representation in the Executive Board and its access to financing by the IMF.

The voting rights of members are weighted according to a complex system (Article XII, section 5 of the IMF Agreement). The total votes of each member shall be equal to the sum of its basic votes (equal for each member) and its variable, quota-based votes.

Recent reforms of the quota system have considerably enhanced the position of some industrialized States as well as dynamic emerging markets and developing countries such as Brazil, China, India, Mexico, Singapore, South Korea, and Turkey. It took until the beginning of 2016 for the 2010 reform to become effective.[2] Under the reform of the quota system, the largest quota shares are assigned to the United States (about 17.4 per cent), Japan (about 6.5 per cent), China (6.4 per cent), Germany (5.6 per cent), France (4.5 per cent), the United Kingdom (4.5 per cent), Italy (3.2 per cent), India (2.7 per cent), Russia (2.7 per cent), Canada

---

[2] International Monetary Fund, 'Historic Quota and Governance Reforms Become Effective', Press Release No 16/25 (27 January 2016).

(2.7 per cent), and Brazil (2.3 per cent).[3] An increase in the relative weight of basic votes shall strengthen the position of low-income countries. These reforms bring about higher representativeness of the decision-making mechanism and strengthen the overall legitimacy of the Fund's operations. The delay in the approval of the reform by the US Congress has created an impasse which provided an incentive for the BRICS (Brazil, Russia, India, China, and South Africa) to create their own development bank and financial crisis fund (Contingent Reserve Arrangement). In December 2015 the US Congress with a bipartisan agreement finally amended the Bretton Woods Agreements Act to empower the US Governor of the Fund to accept the IMF quota reform.[4] The US Congress's approval strengthens the IMF global position by according more influence in particular to the second largest economy in the world, China. This development might counteract the competitive role of the Contingent Reserve Arrangement.

3. Organization

The main organs of the Fund are the Board of Directors and the Executive Board chaired by the Managing Director.

The representative body and supreme organ of the IMF is the Board of Governors, with each member appointing a Governor (usually the minister of finance or the president of its central bank) and an Alternate (Article XII, section 2 of the IMF Agreement). The Executive Board with 24 executive directors conducts the business of the Fund (Article XII, section 3 of the IMF Agreement). The executive directors have the aggregated voting power of the group of countries which elected them (Article XII, section 3(i) of the IMF Agreement).

The 2010 reform abolished the category of five directors appointed by the five Member States with the largest quotas (hitherto the United States, Japan, Germany, France, and the United Kingdom) and reduced the representation of major European countries. The Executive Board elects the Managing Director of the Fund who heads the Fund's staff (Article XII, section 4 of the IMF Agreement). The International Monetary and Financial Committee provide policy guidance to the Board of Governors. The operations and transactions of the IMF are carried out either by the General Department or the Special Drawings Rights Department (Introductory Article, section 2, Article V, section 3, Article XVI, sections 1 and 2 of the IMF Agreement). Important decisions (eg the adjustments of quota under Article III, section 2(c)) require a majority of 85 per cent of the total voting power. This vests the United States (as the only member) with a veto power.

Questions of interpretation of the IMF Agreement arising between the Fund and a member or between members shall be decided by the Executive

---

[3] <www.imf.org/external/np/sec/pr/2011/pdfs/quota_tbl.pdf> (accessed 11 February 2016).
[4] US Consolidated Appropriations Act, 2016 Sec. 9002.

Board or, if required by a member, by the Board of Governors (as a rule deciding through its Committee on Interpretation; (Article XXIX (a) and (b) of the IMF Agreement)).

Amendments of the IMF Agreement, as a rule, must be approved by the Board of Governors and accepted by three-fifths of the members with 85 per cent of the total voting power, in certain cases by all members (Article XXVIII of the IMF Agreement).

4. Financing of the IMF

In the past, financing of the IMF had massively shifted from quota-dependent payments of subscriptions of each member to credits granted by a number of members on the basis of individual agreements. At times, the financing by credits was superior to regular payments of members according to individual quota. This development distorted the structural balance within the IMF, based on the correlation of voting power and financial contributions. The structural reform of 2010 should counteract this devolution, by doubling quota shares (subscriptions) to about USD 659 billion and by reducing financing via credits. The total volume of the Funds resources should remain at the current level.[5]

Payments in gold, made by members in the past (especially on subscriptions and subsequent quota increases), have endowed the IMF with considerable gold holdings (about 90,5 million ounces in September 2015).[6]

Another important source of financing are voluntary contributions of members to a trust fund for low-income countries (the Poverty Reduction and Growth Fund).

5. IMF Members' General Obligations and the Surveillance of Exchange Rate Policies: Stability and Fair Competitive Conditions

(a) General obligations of members and the 2013 Surveillance Decision

Article IV, section 1 of the IMF Agreement lays down the general obligations of members:

[E]ach member undertakes to collaborate with the Fund and other members to assure orderly exchange arrangements and to promote a stable system of exchange rates. In particular, each member shall:
  (i) endeavour to direct its economic and financial policies toward the objective of fostering orderly economic growth with reasonable price stability, with due regard to its circumstances;

---

[5] See <https://www.imf.org/external/np/exr/facts/finfac.htm> (accessed 23 June 2016).
[6] <https://www.imf.org/external/np/exr/facts/gold.htm> (accessed 23 June 2016).

(ii) seek to promote stability by fostering orderly underlying economic and financial conditions and a monetary system that does not tend to produce erratic disruptions;

(iii) avoid manipulating exchange rates or the international monetary system in order to prevent effective balance of payments adjustment or to gain an unfair competitive advantage over other members; and

(iv) follow exchange policies compatible with the undertakings under this Section.

Article IV, section 3 mandates the IMF with the surveillance over exchange rate policies of the Member States:

(a) The Fund shall oversee the international monetary system in order to ensure its effective operation, and shall oversee the compliance of each member with its obligations under Section 1 of this Article.

(b) In order to fulfil its functions under (a) above, the Fund shall exercise firm surveillance over the exchange rate policies of members, and shall adopt specific principles for the guidance of all members with respect to those policies. Each member shall provide the Fund with the information necessary for such surveillance, and, when requested by the Fund, shall consult with it on the member's exchange rate policies. The principles adopted by the Fund shall be consistent with cooperative arrangements by which members maintain the value of their currencies in relation to the value of the currency or currencies of other members, as well as with other exchange arrangements of a member's choice consistent with the purposes of the Fund and Section 1 of this Article. These principles shall respect the domestic social and political policies of members, and in applying these principles the Fund shall pay due regard to the circumstances of members.

A vital issue in international monetary law is the control of exchange rate misalignments, which may provide unfair advantages grossly distorting competition in international trade (Article IV, section 1(iii) of the IMF Agreement).[7] The IMF, however, does not dispose of effective sanctions against exchange currency manipulations. Therein lies an important weakness of the international monetary order and a heavy deficiency in the IMF's instruments.

The decision of the Executive Board on Bilateral and Multilateral Surveillance over Members' Policies (January 2013) elaborates members' obligations under Article IV, section 1 as well as the surveillance mechanism. The decision focuses on 'external stability' in terms of a balance of payments, which does not risk generating disruptive exchange rate movements:

Part I—Principles for the Guidance of the Fund in its Surveillance

A. The Scope of Surveillance [...]

(i) Bilateral Surveillance

5. The scope of bilateral surveillance is determined by members' obligations under Article IV, Section 1. Members undertake under Article IV, Section 1 to collaborate with the Fund and other members to assure orderly exchange arrangements and to promote a stable system of exchange rates (hereinafter 'systemic stability'). Systemic stability is most effectively achieved by each member adopting policies that promote

---

[7] CD Zimmermann, 'Exchange Rate Misalignment and International Law' (2011) 105 AJIL 423.

its own 'external stability'—that is, policies that are consistent with members' obligations under Article IV, Section 1 and, in particular, the specific obligations set forth in Article IV, Sections 1 (i) through (iv). 'External stability' refers to a balance of payments position that does not, and is not likely to, give rise to disruptive exchange rate movements. Except as provided in paragraph 7 below, external stability is assessed at the level of each member.

6. In its bilateral surveillance, the Fund will focus on those policies of members that can significantly influence present or prospective external stability. The Fund will assess whether these policies are promoting external stability and advise the member on policy adjustments necessary for this purpose. Accordingly, exchange rate policies will always be the subject of the Fund's bilateral surveillance with respect to each member, as will monetary, fiscal, and financial sector policies (both their macroeconomic aspects and macroeconomically relevant structural aspects). Other policies will be examined in the context of surveillance only to the extent that they significantly influence present or prospective external stability.

7. In the conduct of their domestic economic and financial policies, members are considered by the Fund to be promoting external stability when they are promoting domestic stability—that is, when they (i) endeavor to direct their domestic economic and financial policies toward the objective of fostering orderly economic growth with reasonable price stability, with due regard to their circumstances, and (ii) seek to promote stability by fostering orderly underlying economic and financial conditions and a monetary system that does not tend to produce erratic disruptions. The Fund in its surveillance will assess whether a member's domestic policies are directed toward the promotion of domestic stability. While the Fund will always examine whether a member's domestic policies are directed toward keeping the member's economy operating broadly at capacity, the Fund will examine whether domestic policies are directed toward fostering a high rate of potential growth only in those cases where such high potential growth significantly influences prospects for domestic, and thereby external, stability. However, the Fund will not require a member that is complying with Article IV, Sections 1(i) and (ii) to change its domestic policies in the interests of external stability [...].

Part II of the 2013 Surveillance Decision (Principles for the Guidance of Members' Policies) defines obligations of members under Article IV, section 1(iii) in Principle A:

A member shall avoid manipulating exchange rates or the international monetary system in order to prevent effective balance of payments adjustment or to gain an unfair competitive advantage over other members.

The IMF will qualify a member's policy as manipulation of exchange rates in violation of Article IV, section 1(iii) of the IMF Agreement only,

if the Fund determines both that: (A) the member is engaged in these policies for the purpose of securing fundamental exchange rate misalignment in the form of an undervalued exchange rate and (B) the purpose of securing such misalignment is to increase net exports (Annex para 2 *lit b*).

In many cases, it will be difficult to establish the necessary intent of unfairly distorting international trade by undervaluation of the member's currency.

In addition, the Surveillance Decision, in Principles for the Guidance of Members' Policies paragraph 21 Principle B through E, provides recommendation in terms of further guidance rather than obligations of members:

B. A member should intervene in the exchange market if necessary to counter disorderly conditions, which may be characterized inter alia by disruptive short-term movements in the exchange rate of its currency.
C. Members should take into account in their intervention policies the interests of other members, including those of the countries in whose currencies they intervene.
D. A member should avoid exchange rate policies that result in external instability.
E. A member should seek to avoid domestic economic and financial policies that give rise to domestic instability.

(b) Factors for alert

The 2013 Surveillance Decision, in paragraph 22, lists a broad range of factors which will alert the IMF:

In its surveillance of the observance by members of the Principles set forth above, the Fund shall consider the following developments as among those which would require thorough review and might indicate the need for discussion with a member:
   (i) protracted large-scale intervention in one direction in the exchange market;
  (ii) official or quasi-official borrowing that either is unsustainable or brings unduly high liquidity risks, or excessive and prolonged official or quasi-official accumulation of foreign assets, for balance of payments purposes;
 (iii) (a) the introduction, substantial intensification, or prolonged maintenance, for balance of payments purposes, of restrictions on, or incentives for, current transactions or payments, or
       (b) the introduction or substantial modification for balance of payments purposes of restrictions on, or incentives for, the inflow or outflow of capital;
  (iv) the pursuit, for balance of payments purposes, of monetary and other financial policies that provide abnormal encouragement or discouragement to capital flows;
   (v) fundamental exchange rate misalignment;
  (vi) large and prolonged current account deficits or surpluses; and
 (vii) large external sector vulnerabilities, including liquidity risks, arising from private capital flows […].

These factors indicate how difficult it may be to establish evidence of manipulative policies.

(c) Limits on the IMF's control and IMF consultations

For some time, the proper extent of Fund surveillance has been a matter of controversy. The IMF Agreement limits the scope of the Fund's surveillance in Article IV, section 3 last sentence, providing that the principles laid down by the Fund 'shall respect the domestic social and political policies of members, and in applying these principles the Fund shall pay due regard to the circumstances of members'.

This signifies that the IMF may and will analyse inflation and productivity growth, the overall revenue from taxes, possibly even the overall spending on pensions or social benefits, but should refrain from evaluating or recommending specific measures like the creation or increase of particular taxes or the reduction of minimum wages. In many instances, the line will be difficult to draw.

In the past, the IMF's scrutiny often extended to economic policies beyond the core of exchange rate policy and directly related areas. Under the 2007 Surveillance Decision, economic analysis and evaluation by the IMF shall focus on 'those policies of members that can significantly influence present or prospective external stability' (para 5 of the 2007 Surveillance Decision). The 2013 Surveillance Decision extends the scope of surveillance to policies of the members that can significantly affect 'domestic stability' (para 6 of the 2013 Surveillance Decision). A crucial element of surveillance are regular (annual) consultations with visits to members (ministry of finance, central bank, other government agencies, possibly non-governmental entities), which form the basis of published country reports.

6. Convertibility of Currencies and Restriction of Exchange Controls

National regulations on exchange control play an important role in international capital movements and transboundary payments. Such regulations may take the form of quantitative restrictions, necessary permits for the export of foreign currency, or even outright prohibitions to make payments in a foreign currency. In times of a financial crisis and a shortage of currency reserves, indebted States may be tempted to resort to exchange control regulations and to suspend payment in other (hard) currencies.

The principle of free convertibility of currencies is enshrined in Article VIII of the IMF Agreement which restrains exchange controls. The Agreement distinguishes between current transactions and the transfer of capital. Whilst restrictions on payments for current transactions are, in principle, prohibited, members enjoy ample freedom to control capital movements.

(a) Current transactions

Subject to narrow exceptions, no member shall, without approval of the IMF, impose 'restrictions on the making of payments and transfers for current transactions' (Article VIII, section 2(a) of the IMF Agreement) or engage in 'any discriminatory currency arrangements or multiple currency practices' (Article VIII, section 3).

Multiple currency practices, as a rule, are related to a member's action which generates unreasonable spreads (more than 2 per cent) between buying and selling rates for spot exchange transactions between the member's currency and another member's currency.[8] The restraint on exchange controls means that a State must ensure convertibility of its own currency.

Only a few countries still rely on the transitional provision of Article XIV, sections 1 and 2 of the IMF Agreement to maintain pre-accession restrictions on current transactions. All the other members may restrict current transactions only within the parameters laid down by the Fund (members with 'Article VIII status').

Payments for current transactions are defined in Article XXX(d) of the IMF Agreement:

(1) all payments due in connection with foreign trade, other current business, including services, and normal short-term banking and credit facilities;
(2) payments due as interest on loans and as net income from other investments;
(3) payments of moderate amount for amortization of loans or for depreciation of direct investments; and
(4) moderate remittances for family living expenses.

The prohibition of Article VIII, section 3 excludes discrimination against particular types of current transactions (such as imports of luxury goods) or discrimination against payment in a specific currency.

Article VIII, section 4(a) of the IMF Agreement provides the convertibility of foreign-held balances in context with current transactions:

Each member shall buy balances of its currency held by another member if the latter, in requesting the purchase, represents:
 (i) that the balances to be bought have been recently acquired as a result of current transactions; or
(ii) that their conversion is needed for making payments for current transactions.

In practice, members or their central banks need not rely on this option, wherever there is a functional market for trading the respective currencies.

(b) Capital transfers under the IMF Agreement

In the area of capital movements, the IMF Agreement places little restraint on exchange controls. Article VI, section 3 stipulates:

Section 3. Controls of capital transfers
Members may exercise such controls as are necessary to regulate international capital movements, but no member may exercise these controls in a manner which will restrict payments for current transactions or which will unduly delay transfers of funds in settlement of commitments, except as provided in Article VII, Section 3(b) and in Article XIV, Section 2.

The question, whether the prohibition of discriminatory restrictions (Article VIII, section 3 of the IMF Agreement) also extends to the transfer of capital, was

---

[8] See Decision No 6790-(81/43) as amended by Decision No 11728-(98/56).

resolved in 1956 by a controversial decision of the Executive Board in favour of members' discretion:

Members are free to adopt a policy of regulating capital movements for any reason, due regard being paid to the general purposes of the Fund. They may, for that purpose, exercise such controls [...] without approval of the Fund.[9]

However, full effectiveness of capital controls implies, to some extent, control of current transactions, which fall under the IMF's mandate of surveillance.[10]

(c) Freedom of payment and capital transfers under other universal or regional regimes

A number of universal or regional regimes further liberalize payments for current transactions and the movement of capital. Under WTO law, the General Agreement on Trade in Services (GATS) extends the liberalization of services under specific commitments to associated capital transfers and payments (Article XI:1). The exception of Article XII of the GATS allows restrictions in the case of balance of payment problems. However, these restrictions must conform to the IMF Agreement (Article XII:2 of the GATS).

Within the OECD, the Code of Liberalization of Capital Movements and the Code of Liberalization of Current Invisible Operations provide for the progressive abolition of restrictions on cross-border capital transactions and payments associated with an invisible operation (eg the import of services), in terms legally binding for OECD Member States.

Additionally, the freedom of capital movements under regional trade or integration arrangements and international investment agreements (guaranteeing the freedom to repatriate invested capital and earnings) have considerably curtailed the ambit of permitted capital controls. In a regional context, the European Union has established the most liberal and most comprehensive regime for free movements of capital and payments (Articles 63ff of the TFEU, Capital Movements Directive 88/361/EEC, Payment Service Directive 2007/64/EC).

As the ECJ held in the *Volkswagen* case[11] and in other cases related to 'golden shares', conferring special rights on the government, the freedom of capital movements prohibits even non-discriminating measures such as restrictions on the rights of major private shareholders of a company, if they may dissuade investors from other EU countries to acquire a substantial share in a company. EU Member States can, however, justify restrictions on capital movements with an overriding legitimate public interest in terms of strict proportionality.

---

[9] Executive Board Decision No 541-(56/39).
[10] See IMF (ed), *The IMF's Approach to Capital Account Liberalization Evaluation Report* prepared by S Tagaki et al (2005) 17–18.
[11] ECJ Case C-112/05 *Commission of the European Communities v Federal Republic of Germany* [2007] ECR I-8995.

7. Exchange Control Regulations and their Extraterritorial Effect

It is crucial for the parties to an international business transaction to know whether or not the exchange control regulations of a State are recognized or even enforced in other countries.

As a rule, States are free to give or to deny legal effect to exchange control regulations of other countries. These regulations pursue specific sovereign interests of the State concerned, which other countries need not share or even recognize. For this reason, national courts tend not to enforce or implement foreign exchange control regimes, unless there is a treaty obligation to give effect to such foreign restrictions.[12]

The IMF Agreement establishes the most important exception to this liberty of States not to acknowledge foreign exchange control regimes. Article VIII, section 2(b)[13] obliges the IMF members to give effect to the exchange control regulations of another member affecting 'exchange contracts':

Exchange contracts which involve the currency of any member and which are contrary to the exchange control regulations of that member maintained or imposed consistently with this Agreement shall be unenforceable in the territories of any member. In addition, members may, by mutual accord, cooperate in measures for the purpose of making the exchange control regulations of either member more effective, provided that such measures and regulations are consistent with this Agreement.

The rule of non-enforcement in Article VIII, section 2(b) of the IMF Agreement stands in close context with the surveillance of exchange control regulations by the IMF in terms of international solidarity in monetary relations. According to its title, Article VIII, section 2 relates to 'avoidance of restrictions on current payments'. Members, as far as—and only as far as—they submit their exchange control regime to the IMF's surveillance, may rely on other members respecting their control regulations. This interrelation of surveillance on the one hand and recognition on the other hand determines the ambit of the provision.

The understanding of the term 'exchange contract' is most controversial. A narrow interpretation only includes transactions which directly aim at the exchange

---

[12] BGHZ 31, 367 (372f); BGHZ 55, 334 (337f); French Court of Cassation (1998) 57 Rev Crit Dr Intern Priv 661 with note by J-P Eck; *United City Merchants (Investments) Ltd v Royal Bank of Canada* [1983] 1 AC 168, 188; Supreme Court of New York *Banco Francês e Brasileiro SA v John Doe No 1, et al* (1975) 14 ILM 1440; *Libra Bank Ltd v Banco Nacional de Costa Rica* 570 F. Supp 870 (896–902) (SDNY 1983); see American Law Institute, *Restatement (Third) of the Foreign Relations Law of the United States* (1987) vol 2, § 822 No 6.

[13] CT Ebenroth, *Banking on the Act of State* (Universitätsverlag Konstanz 1985); WF Ebke, *Internationales Devisenrecht* (Verlag Recht und Wissenschaft 1991); J Gold, ' "Exchange Contracts", Exchange Control, and the IMF Articles of Agreement: Some Animadversions on Wilson, Smithett & Cope Ltd. v. Terruzi' (1984) 33 ICLQ 777; FA Mann, 'Der Internationale Währungsfonds und das Internationale Privatrecht' (1981) 36 JZ 327.

of one currency for another.[14] This term relates to contractual relations, which, in some way, affect the currency balance or the balance of payments (ie the relation between the ingoing and outgoing flows of monetary transactions).[15] However, modern case-law, for example of the German Federal Court of Justice,[16] applies Article VIII, section 2(b) only to payments for current transactions as defined in Article XXX(d) of the IMF Agreement.[17]

This approach justly relies on the context of the rule of non-enforcement of Article VIII, section 2(b) of the IMF Agreement with the IMF's surveillance of 'restrictions of current payments' in terms of the title of section 2 and of subsection 2(a) of Article VIII. As explained in the precedent section, Member States may, by and large, manage restrictions of capital transfers without the IMF's surveillance. To extend the rule of non-enforcement to such restrictions of capital transfer would seriously affect the stability of capital transactions. There are, therefore, persuasive reasons to exclude non-current transactions like capital transfers.

The German Federal Court of Justice held that the payment obligation of a foreign partner in a German company under a resolution to increase the company's capital stock, as a transfer of capital, does not flow from an 'exchange contract'.[18] In this case, a Bulgarian bank as a partner of a German company could not rely on Bulgarian exchange control regulations to evade its obligation to pay in Deutsche Mark.

Government bonds do not classify as 'exchange contracts'.[19] This applies to the principal debt as well as to interest.

With respect to Argentinean bonds, the Court of Appeal of Frankfurt followed this line and stated:

> [T]he issue of Government bonds establishes long-term crediting obligations of economic importance (for the emittent State) and must, therefore, be considered as capital transfer. These are not subjected to the mentioned rule of the IMF Agreement (ie Article XXX (d)). This also applies to the interest promised in the bond conditions.[20]

Article VIII, section 2(b) first sentence of the IMF Agreement declares exchange contracts in contravention of exchange control regulations of a member to be 'unenforceable' in other Member States. It does not, however, qualify such contract as void. This suggests that the contractual obligation to pay, similar to natural obligations, maintains its legal effect, though courts and administrative authorities

---

[14] A Nussbaum, 'Exchange Control and the International Monetary Fund' (1949) 59 Yale LJ 421 (426).

[15] BGHZ 116, 77 (83).   [16] BGH NJW 1994, 390.

[17] (1) all payments due in connection with foreign trade, other current business, including services, and normal short-term banking and credit facilities; (2) payments due as interest on loans and as net income from other investments; (3) payments of moderate amount for amortization of loans or for depreciation of direct investments; and (4) moderate remittances for family living expenses.

[18] BGH NJW 1994, 390.

[19] See LG Frankfurt aM WM 2003, 783 (785); OLG Frankfurt aM NJW 2006, 2931.

[20] OLG Frankfurt aM NJW 2006, 2931.

may not assist the creditor in realising its outstanding claim against the debtor, as far—only as far—as foreign monetary interests are affected.

The German Federal Court of Justice closely analysed the effects of Article VIII, section 2(b) in a case in which a German bank had given a loan to a Greek company in German currency.[21] As the necessary permission of the Greek Central Bank only covered part of the interest to be paid by the debtor company, the company's chief executive assumed personal liability for the difference. When the creditor bank sued the chief executive, the court below held the entire exchange transaction to be unenforceable and the bank's action to be inadmissible. The Federal Court of Justice rejected this view:

Article VIII, section 2 (b) of the IMF Agreement purports to protect the foreign currency resources of a member State to the extent as this State resorts to this protection by its own exchange control regulations. For this purpose, it is not necessary to deprive the transaction of validity under private law. It suffices that courts and authorities of the member States do not assist the parties in enforcing a business prohibited by exchange control regulations [...].[22]

The recognition of exchange control regulations under the IMF Agreement does not warrant that the claims of the State concerned or other claims related to the control regime are enforced by other Member States.

Thus, in *Banco do Brasil, SA v AC Israel Commodity Co*, the Court of Appeals of New York rejected a claim for damages of the Central Bank of Brazil against a US company for being an accomplice in evading payment obligations in US-Dollars in connection with the export of Brazilian coffee into the United States.[23]

8. Special Drawing Rights

An important financial instrument is the 'special drawing right' which signifies an international reserve asset administered under the auspices of the IMF. The special drawing right (SDR) is not a currency, but rather an interest-bearing asset apt to be changed into freely usable currencies of IMF members. Its fungibility depends on the willingness of IMF members and certain international financial institutions such as the World Bank ('prescribed holders') to hold, recognize, and honour obligations denominated in SDRs. The value of an SDR (determined with 70 per cent of the total voting power, Article XV, section 1 of the IMF Agreement) is defined as a basket of weighted currencies (reviewed and adjusted every five years), until recently the US-Dollar, the Euro, the Japanese Yen, and the Pound Sterling. In 2015, the Executive Board of the IMF decided to include the Chinese Renminbi (Yuan) as a fifth currency, as of October 2016. The respective weight of these basket currencies then will be as follows: US-Dollar 41.73 per cent, Euro 30.93 per cent, Chinese Renminbi 10.92 per cent, Japanese Yen 8.33 per cent, and Pound

---

[21] BGHZ 116, 77.   [22] BGHZ 116, 77 (84f).
[23] *Banco do Brasil, SA v AC Israel Commodity Co* 190 NE 2d 235 (NY 1963).

Sterling 8.09 per cent. The currency value of the SDR is calculated daily (currently about USD 1.40).[24]

The IMF allocates SDRs to members in proportion to their quota (Article XV, section 2, Article XVIII of the IMF Agreement). If a member holds SDRs in excess of its quota, it earns interest. Conversely, in case of a shortfall it has to pay interest.

In economic terms, the allocation of SDRs allows a member to exchange its own national currency for other, 'freely usable currencies' as defined in Article XXX(f) of the IMF Agreement, that is currently the Euro, the Japanese Yen, the Pound Sterling, the US-Dollar, and the Chinese Renminbi.[25]

A member may avail itself of this instrument only in case of 'need' and not for the purpose of changing the composition of its reserves. The fulfilment of this criterion is, however, not subject to challenge (Article XIX, section 3 of the IMF Agreement) or to any conditionality imposed by the Fund.

With the IMF acting as an intermediary, there is a voluntary trade of SDRs between members acting as willing sellers and willing buyers (Article XIX, section 2(b) of the IMF Agreement). Over the years, this voluntary market became the dominant mechanism for changing SDRs into currencies. In addition, the IMF can fall back on a designation mechanism, designating members (with a strong balance of payments position) to buy SDRs with freely usable currencies from other members (Article XIX, section 2(a) of the IMF Agreement).

9. Use of the Fund's Financial Resources for Members in Economic Difficulties

(a) Assistance in case of balance of payment problems

A core function of the IMF is providing loans to member countries with a balance of payment deficit. Balance of payment deficits arise from a surplus of the outgoing payments and capital transfer over ingoing payments. Balance of payment problems can cause the country's currency to depreciate, even disrupt the whole economy. By assisting countries with difficulties to find financing at affordable conditions to meet their net international payments, the IMF operates as 'lender of the last resort'.

Article V, section 3 of the IMF Agreement governs the use of the Fund's general resources:

Section 3. *Conditions governing use of the Fund's general resources*
(a) The Fund shall adopt policies on the use of its general resources, including policies on stand-by or similar arrangements, and may adopt special policies for special balance of payments problems, that will assist members to solve their balance of payments

---

[24] Current value of SDR on <https://www.imf.org/external/np/fin/data/rms_five.aspx> (accessed 23 June 2016).
[25] Executive Board Decision of 30 November 2015.

problems in a manner consistent with the provisions of this Agreement and that will establish adequate safeguards for the temporary use of the general resources of the Fund.
(b) A member shall be entitled to purchase the currencies of other members from the Fund in exchange for an equivalent amount of its own currency subject to the following conditions:
   (i)   the member's use of the general resources of the Fund would be in accordance with the provisions of this Agreement and the policies adopted under them;
   (ii) the member represents that it has a need to make the purchase because of its balance of payments or its reserve position or developments in its reserves;
   (iii) the proposed purchase would be a reserve tranche purchase, or would not cause the Fund's holdings of the purchasing member's currency to exceed two hundred percent of its quota;
   (iv) the Fund has not previously declared under Section 5 of this Article, Article VI, Section 1, or Article XXVI, Section 2 (*a*) that the member desiring to purchase is ineligible to use the general resources of the Fund.
(c) The Fund shall examine a request for a purchase to determine whether the proposed purchase would be consistent with the provisions of this Agreement and the policies adopted under them, provided that requests for reserve tranche purchases shall not be subject to challenge [...].

Although Article V, section 3(b) of the IMF Agreement speaks in terms of a member 'purchasing' the currencies of other members, these transactions amount to lending, that is to foreign exchange credits. The credit is devolved with the member buying back its own currency in SDRs or freely usable currencies. Only purchases by members with a 'reserve tranche position' are not considered as borrowing from the Fund.

The oil shock of the 1970s, the debt crisis of the 1980s, and the crisis of some Latin American countries up to the early 2000s fuelled borrowing from the IMF. Afterwards, borrowing from the IMF and, consequently, the flow of interest paid to the Fund massively declined. Since 2008, the international financial crisis again made the Fund an important actor in rescue operations. In the meantime, with growing demand for loans and a massive increase in funds, the IMF's position in the global financial architecture has been considerably strengthened.

With loans to Hungary and Lithuania, the IMF, for the first time, provided assistance to Member States of the European Union. Greece became the first country of the Eurozone to borrow from the IMF.

(b) Drawing on reserve tranches

If the IMF's holdings of a member's currency (excluding the holdings that correspond to the member's use of the Fund's resources) are inferior to its quota, the member is in a 'reserve tranche position'. With its own currency, it may draw up the full amount of its reserve position, purchasing other currencies or SDRs (Article V, section 3(b) of the IMF Agreement). This transaction is not qualified as an IMF loan and is not subject to the obligation to repurchase.

(c) Credit facilities

The regular framework for IMF lending to members is related to the four credit tranches which each amount to 25 per cent of a member's quota. Whilst a member can relatively easily accede to loans in the first tranche, borrowing in the higher tranches is tied to adjustments in the economic policy (conditionality).

Regular loans available to all members are subject to non-concessional terms (market-related interest rate, so-called 'rate of charge') and are to be repaid in a relatively short time (usually 3¼–5 years). Most non-concessional assistance is provided on the basis of stand-by arrangements, designed to solve short-term balance of payment problems (Article XXX(b) of the IMF Agreement).[26] Other mechanisms for non-concessional lending are the Flexible Credit Line, the Precautionary and Liquidity Line, the Extended Fund Facility (for loans with an extended repayment period), and the Rapid Financing Instrument.

In addition, the Fund grants loans to low-income countries at concessionary (even zero) rates. For some time, this assistance made the IMF a major actor in development aid. The underlying reason for this controversial role of the Fund is the close connection between balance of payments problems and structural deficits in the economic and social system of low-income countries. The Poverty Reduction and Growth Trust established in 2010 in replacement of the Poverty Reduction and Growth Facility (1999) provides the umbrella for a number of concessionary facilities for low-income countries. The Extended Credit facility operates as the IMF's main instrument for medium-term assistance to poor countries with protracted balance of payment problems.

By providing concessional, long-term loans to developing countries, the IMF entered the field of the World Bank. Sometimes the programmes of adjustment required by both institutions were at variance. All this called for a stronger concertation between the IMF and the World Bank.[27] In 1974, both institutions established the Joint Development Committee. Under the criticism of the development financing of the IMF, the Fund has adjusted its policy in terms of a stronger focus on economic stability. In any case, the Fund is strongly committed to concessional assistance to low-income countries.

(d) Conditionality

A formal 'letter of intent' to the Executive Board, formulated after consultation between a borrowing country and the IMF, commits the country to implement specific economic and financial programmes which shall redress the balance of payments problems. Such commitments do not constitute a legal obligation, but rather

---

[26] See J Gold, 'The Legal Character of the Fund's Stand-By-Arrangements and Why it Matters' (1980) IMF Pamphlet Series No 35; S Schlemmer-Schulte, 'International Monetary Fund' in R Wolfrum (ed), *The Max Planck Encyclopedia of Public International Law* (OUP 2012) vol V, 1037.

[27] Referring to the relationship of World Bank and IMF, see JJ Polak and C Gwin, *The World Bank and the IMF: A Changing Relationship* (Brookings Institution Press 1994).

a condition for the IMF's (continued) lending.[28] This 'conditionality' has always been discussed controversially, in economic terms[29] as well as a restriction of sovereign options in economic and social policy. Conditionality became associated with the so-called 'Washington Consensus' which stands for a number of reform goals pursued by the IMF and other Washington-based financial institutions (in particular the World Bank), especially in context with financial assistance to Latin American countries. The term 'Washington Consensus', coined by the economist John Williamson, essentially refers to

- fiscal discipline;
- reordering of public expenditure priorities;
- tax reform;
- liberalizing exchange rates;
- competitive exchange rates;
- trade liberalization;
- liberalization of inward foreign direct investment;
- privatization;
- deregulation; and
- property rights.[30]

Critics challenged conditionality as causing unemployment or fostering other social problems and operating as a driving force behind the all too rash and short-lived economic reforms. In certain cases, this criticism certainly has substance. On the other hand, the supporters within and outside the Fund have always considered conditionality as a major contribution to better, efficient, and transparent governance and reduction of poverty. Experience in Latin America and elsewhere does not suggest that countries with governments following an entirely different economic strategy with financial unconditional assistance by foreign States fared better in reaching these goals. From the angle of international law, conditions for financial assistance do not amount to a violation of the principle of non-intervention in internal affairs.

The current IMF Guidelines on Conditionality and recent practice focus more on 'macro-critical' parameters (referring to macroeconomic goals or standards of the IMF Agreement), on social coherence (social safety nets) and on full identification

---

[28] See C Pinelli, 'Conditionality' in R Wolfrum (ed), *The Max Planck Encyclopedia of Public International Law* (OUP 2012) vol II, 591; EMG Denters, *Law and Policy of IMF Conditionality* (Springer 1996); A Dreher, 'The Development and Implementation of IMF and World Bank Conditionality' (2002) HWWA Discussion Paper No 165 <http://econstor.eu/bitstream/10419/19327/1/165.pdf> (accessed 23 June 2016); J Gold, 'Conditionality' (1979) IMF Pamphlet Series No 31.

[29] See WR Easterly, *The Elusive Quest for Growth: Economists' Adventures and Misadventures in the Tropics* (The MIT Press 2001).

[30] J Williamson, 'What Should the World Bank Think about the Washington Consensus?' (2000) 15 WBRO 251.

of governments with the proposed reform programmes ('national ownership') than conditionality did in the past.

Similar conditionality exists for financial assistance under EU law and under agreements between the Euro countries (European Financial Stability Facility, European Stability Mechanism) as well as for borrowing from the World Bank. When the IMF and European institutions provide loans to indebted Euro countries, conditionalities must be closely coordinated (under the IMF's lead).

Select Bibliography

W Bergthaler and W Bossu, 'Recent Legal Developments in the International Monetary Fund' (2010) 1 EYIEL 391.

MS Copelovitch, *The International Monetary Fund in the Global Economy: Banks, Bonds, and Bailouts* (CUP 2010).

RW Edwards, *International Monetary Collaboration* (2nd edn, Transnational Publishers 1997).

F Gianviti, 'The Reform of the International Monetary Fund (Conditionality and Surveillance)' (2000) 34 Int'l Law 107.

J Gold, *The Fund Agreement in the Courts* (International Monetary Fund, 3 vols 1962, 1982, 1986).

RM Lastra (ed), *The Reform of the International Financial Architecture* (Springer 2001).

R Leckow and M Strauss, 'Currency Control' in R Wolfrum (ed), *The Max Planck Encyclopedia of Public International Law* (OUP 2012) vol II, 930.

AF Lowenfeld, *International Economic Law* (2nd edn, OUP 2008) 593.

C Proctor, *Mann on the Legal Aspect of Money* (7th edn, OUP 2012).

HS Scott, *International Finance: Law and Regulation* (3rd edn, Sweet & Maxwell 2012).

CD Zimmermann, 'Exchange Rate Misalignment and International Law' (2011) 105 AJIL 423.

XL

The World Bank and Other International
Financial Institutions

1. The World Bank Group

(a) The World Bank (International Bank for Reconstruction and Development)

The International Bank for Reconstruction and Development (IBRD), commonly called the World Bank, together with the International Monetary Fund (IMF), forms the institutional backbone of the international monetary system and the international finance architecture designed at Bretton Woods. Together with its sister organizations and affiliates, the IBRD forms the World Bank Group, which comprises

- the IBRD;
- the International Development Association (IDA);
- the International Finance Corporation (IFC);
- the Multilateral Investment Guarantee Agency (MIGA), which provides insurance of private investments against non-commercial risks;[1] and
- the International Centre for the Settlement of Investment Disputes (ICSID).[2]

Unlike the IMF, the IBRD has a clear development mission. It was established to promote economic reconstruction after the Second World War, to assist less developed or war-afflicted countries and to promote international trade. Article I of the Articles of Agreement of the IBRD (IBRD Agreement)[3] provides:

The purposes of the Bank are:
(i) To assist in the reconstruction and development of territories of members by facilitating the investment of capital for productive purposes, including the restoration of economies destroyed or disrupted by war, the reconversion of productive facilities to peacetime needs and the encouragement of the development of productive facilities and resources in less developed countries.

---

[1] See Ch XXXVI.   [2] See Ch XXXV.
[3] Articles of Agreement of the International Bank for Reconstruction and Development (1945) 2 UNTS 134.

(ii) To promote private foreign investment by means of guarantees or participations in loans and other investments made by private investors; and when private capital is not available on reasonable terms, to supplement private investment by providing, on suitable conditions, finance for productive purposes out of its own capital, funds raised by it and its other resources.

(iii) To promote the long-range balanced growth of international trade and the maintenance of equilibrium in balances of payments by encouraging international investment for the development of the productive resources of members, thereby assisting in raising productivity, the standard of living and conditions of labor in their territories.

(iv) To arrange the loans made or guaranteed by it in relation to international loans through other channels so that the more useful and urgent projects, large and small alike, will be dealt with first.

(v) To conduct its operations with due regard to the effect of international investment on business conditions in the territories of members and, in the immediate postwar years, to assist in bringing about a smooth transition from a wartime to a peacetime economy.

The Bank shall be guided in all its decisions by the purposes set forth above.

The members of the IBRD are the same as the members of the IMF (Article II, section 1). They each hold a specific share in the capital stock of the Bank, with only a part of the subscribed capital actually paid in (Article II, section 3). This capital share, together with basic votes allocated to each member, determines the voting power of a member. Like the IMF, the IBRD has a Board of Governors as the supreme organ with a representative of each member (Article V, section 2) and a Board of Executive Directors (Article V, section 4). The Executive Directors conduct the general operations of the Bank and exercise the powers delegated to them by the Board of Governors. Five Executive Directors are nominated by the five members with the largest shares. The Executive Directors elect a Chairman, the President of the World Bank. The President manages the current affairs of the Bank under the direction of the Executive Directors and heads the independent staff (Article V, section 5). Up to now, the President of the World Bank has been nominated by the United States.

The World Bank operates as a kind of investment bank, borrowing from investors and lending to developing countries. It operates on the capital markets, mainly by issuing mid-term and long-term bonds. In addition, the Bank issues short-term notes and floating rate notes. Whilst the Bank initially had to rely essentially on the US market, in the last decades the European market and Japan became the most important sources of refinancing. As the outstanding obligations of the Bank are guaranteed by the callable capital of the Bank's members, the Bank enjoys an AAA rating. The Bank also borrows from central banks ('central bank facility'). In addition, the World Bank has tapped new sources of financing for special objectives by establishing trust funds such as the Global Environmental Facility,[4] the Trust Fund for Gaza and West Bank (TFGWB) or the Prototype Carbon Fund.

---

[4] R Dolzer, 'Global Environmental Issues: The Genuine Area of Globalization' (1998) 7 J Transnat'l L & Pol'y 157, 165.

The IBRD's operations focus on assisting economic and social development, especially by raising productivity. The IBRD instruments for financing are

- medium and long-term loans, with a concessional interest rate (for a term of usually up to 15 years, exceptionally up to 30 years);
- guarantees for loans provided by private lenders; and
- grants.[5]

Article III, section 4 of the IBRD Agreement governs the conditions on which the World Bank may guarantee or make loans:

The Bank may guarantee, participate in, or make loans to any member or any political subdivision thereof and any business, industrial, and agricultural enterprise in the territories of a member, subject to the following conditions:

(i) When the member in whose territories the project is located is not itself the borrower, the member or the central bank or some comparable agency of the member which is acceptable to the Bank, fully guarantees the repayment of the principal and the payment of interest and other charges on the loan.

(ii) The Bank is satisfied that in the prevailing market conditions the borrower would be unable otherwise to obtain the loan under conditions which in the opinion of the Bank are reasonable for the borrower.

(iii) A competent committee, as provided for in Article V, Section 7, has submitted a written report recommending the project after a careful study of the merits of the proposal.

(iv) In the opinion of the Bank the rate of interest and other charges are reasonable and such rate, charges and the schedule for repayment of principal are appropriate to the project.

(v) In making or guaranteeing a loan, the Bank shall pay due regard to the prospects that the borrower, and, if the borrower is not a member, that the guarantor, will be in position to meet its obligations under the loan; and the Bank shall act prudently in the interests both of the particular member in whose territories the project is located and of the members as a whole.

(vi) In guaranteeing a loan made by other investors, the Bank receives suitable compensation for its risk.

(vii) Loans made or guaranteed by the Bank shall, except in special circumstances, be for the purpose of specific projects of reconstruction or development.

According to Article III, section 5(b)

[t]he Bank shall make arrangements for the proper use of loans with due attention to considerations of economy and efficiency and without regard to political or other non-economic influences or considerations.

The World Bank also coordinates financial assistance for development projects by other international financial institutions or individual States and provides technical guidance.

After assisting the reconstruction of postwar Europe, in the 1950s and 1960s the World Bank essentially financed infrastructural, industrial, and agricultural

---

[5] P Benoit, 'The World Bank Group's Financial Instruments for Infrastructure' (1997) <http://siteresources.worldbank.org/EXTFINANCIALSECTOR/Resources/282884-1303327122200/101benoit.pdf> (accessed 23 June 2016). ·

projects (eg roads, power stations, harbours) in developing countries. Later, it also became engaged in social projects. For some decades, non-project lending has ranked prominently in the Bank's agenda. Thus, in recent years, loans in general or sectoral structural adjustment programmes (development policy programmes) have accounted for about a half of the Bank's lending volume.

The World Bank uses two different legal arrangements for loans.[6] The 'investment loan' instrument applies to loans for infrastructural, industrial, agricultural, or social projects in terms of an agreement under public international law.[7] The terms for 'development policy loans' are structurally similar to the IMF concept of concessional lending to low-income countries. In a 'letter of development policy' the country soliciting another country a loan lays down the measures for economic reforms. The World Bank's conditionalities still reflect the essence of the 'Washington Consensus' and its neo-liberal parameters,[8] however, with an additional emphasis on social and environmental standards.

The principal objective of the World Bank is sustainable poverty reduction.[9] When financing development projects, the World Bank is guided by the 'Comprehensive Development Framework' (CDF). Adopted in 1998, the CDF responds to frequent criticisms of previous development strategies as primarily emphasizing short-term macro-economic stabilization and balance of payment corrections.[10]

The CDF gives new weight to long-term social and environmental implications. Thus, the comprehensive approach addresses the improvement of education, health care, and other social standards as well as conditions for a good investment climate and for economic growth. Within the CDF, each country should design its own development agenda, with citizen participation and on the basis of a dialogue involving donors, the private sector, and civil society. The World Bank's so-called 'policy dialogue' includes issues like fighting corruption, increasing the level of education, access to water and energy, social security, and urban development.

The IBRD Agreement (Article IV, section 10) subjects the Bank and its staff to political neutrality:

The Bank and its officers shall not interfere in the political affairs of any member; nor shall they be influenced in their decisions by the political character of the member or members concerned. Only economic considerations shall be relevant to their decisions, and these considerations shall be weighed impartially in order to achieve the purposes stated in Article I.

The World Bank has always been one of the driving forces behind pushing for 'good governance'.[11] Since the late 1980s, World Bank Studies corroborated the

---

[6] See IBRD, *General Conditions for Loans* (World Bank 2005).
[7] A Broches, 'International Legal Aspects of the World Bank' (1959-III) 98 RdC 297; JW Head, 'Evolution of the Governing Law for Loans Agreements of the World Bank and Other Multilateral Development Banks' (1996) 90 AJIL 214.
[8] See Ch IX.2.
[9] See World Bank's Operational Manual, 'Poverty Reduction' (2004) 1 Operational Policies No 1.
[10] See the forceful presentation of this criticism by former World Bank vice-president and chief economist JE Stiglitz, *Globalization and its Discontents* (WW Norton & Co 2002).
[11] See S Schlemmer-Schulte, 'The World Bank's Role in the Promotion of the Rule of Law in Developing Countries' in J Wolfensohn, S Schlemmer-Schulte, and K-Y Tung (eds), *Liber Amoricum*

need for a sound institutional framework under the rule of law, committed to accountability and transparency of the public administration as the basis for economic development and reduction of poverty.[12] For some time, the World Bank has financed institutional reforms directed at good governance and the rule of law. Nowadays, the Bank extends the concept of good governance to a pluralist structure, respect for human rights, and democratic participation of citizens in democratic political processes.[13]

The World Bank's statute prohibits interference into the political affairs of a member (Article IV, section 10). This prohibition does not, however, prevent the World Bank's commitment to good governance as long as it serves the objective of economic development.

In context with assistance for legal and judicial reforms, the World Bank formulated standards for the rule of law as preconditions for stable economic development:

- legal norms binding on all branches of the State;
- equal treatment of every person under the law;
- recognition and protection of human dignity of each individual;
- a system of justice accessible to all;
- transparent legislation;
- fair laws;
- predictable enforcement; and
- accountable governance.[14]

Some ill-considered decisions (in particular the financing of a project in India, implying a most controversial resettlement of the local population) gave rise to sharp criticism. The Bank reacted by establishing the World Bank Inspection Panel,[15] which became a model for other bodies ensuring accountability.

As an independent body of experts, the Inspection Panel investigates possible violations of the Bank's own standards and makes recommendations to the Executive Board. Investigations by the Panel may be triggered by an Executive Director or by individual complaints of affected persons from the recipient countries.

Ibrahim F.I. Shihata: International Finance and Development Law (Brill Academic Publishers 2001) 677.

[12] World Bank, *Sub-Saharan Africa: From Crisis to Sustainable Growth* (World Bank Publications 1989).

[13] World Bank, *World Development Report* (World Bank Publications 2000/01) 113.

[14] World Bank, *Initiatives in Legal and Judicial Reform* (World Bank Publications 2004) 2–3.

[15] See DD Bradlow and S Schlemmer-Schulte, 'The World Bank's New Inspection Panel: A Constructive Step in the Transformation of the International Legal Order' (1994) 54 ZaöRV 392; S Schlemmer-Schulte, 'The World Bank's Experience with its Inspection Panel' (1998) 58 ZaöRV 353.

(b) The International Finance Corporation

The International Finance Corporation (IFC)[16] was established as the private sector arm of the World Bank group to integrate private business into international development assistance. The IFC, though legally a separate organization, is closely linked to the World Bank. The IFC invests in 'productive private enterprises' in developing countries by granting loans at market rates or by investing in the capital stock (Article III of the IFC Agreement). As a rule, the IFC will finance up to 25 per cent of the total cost of a project. In 2012, the IFC adopted new 'Performance Standards on Social and Environmental Sustainability' for private enterprises, which aim to minimize and mitigate environmental and social risks associated with projects financed by the IFC. These standards are an important document of reference in the current discussion on corporate social responsibility.[17]

(c) The International Development Association

The International Development Association (IDA)[18] gives 'soft loans' to 'eligible' low-income development countries on particularly favourable conditions (a term of usually 35–40 years with very low interest rates; see Articles I and V of the IDA Agreement). The IDA finances itself by subscriptions of members, by new contributions ('replenishments') from the industrial donor countries and by income flowing from the World Bank's profits.

2. Regional Development Banks and Other Regional Financial Institutions

A number of international institutions finance development projects in a regional context.[19] The Inter-American Development Bank (established in 1959, seated in Washington, DC), the African Development Bank (established in 1964, seated in Abidjan), the Asian Development Bank (established in 1966, seated in Manila), the Caribbean Development Bank (established in 1969, seated in Bridgetown), and the European Bank for Reconstruction and Development (EBRD; established in 1969, seated in London) have Member States from the respective regions as well as non-regional members.

---

[16] International Finance Corporation Act (1955) 264 UNTS 117; 439 UNTS 318; 563 UNTS 362; see S Asrani and P Dann, 'International Finance Corporation' in R Wolfrum (ed), *The Max Planck Encyclopedia of Public International Law* (OUP 2012) vol V, 793.

[17] See Ch VII.3.

[18] International Development Association Act (1960) 439 UNTS 249; see L Gruder, 'International Development Association' in R Wolfrum (ed), *The Max Planck Encyclopedia of Public International Law* (OUP 2012) vol V, 768.

[19] JR Knop, 'Regional Development Banks' (1969) 4 JL & Econ Dev 93; SD Krasner, 'Power and Structure of Regional Development Banks' (1981) 35 Int'l Org 303.

Unlike most other regional development banks, the EBRD has a clear 'political' mandate: to promote transition to open market-oriented economies in countries of Central and Eastern Europe committed to multiparty democracy and pluralism (Article 1 of the EBRD Agreement).

The European Investment Bank (Articles 308–309 of the TFEU) does not only finance projects within the European Union, but has become a pillar of the EU development and cooperation policies with partner countries. The Islamic Development Bank (established in 1973, seated in Jeddah) finances development in the member countries and in other Muslim communities in accordance with the Sharia.

China initiated the establishment of the Asian Infrastructure Investment Bank (AIIB).[20] The creation of this powerful development bank illustrates China's ambition to extend its influence in the international financial architecture and accordingly met with considerable and essentially unsuccessful opposition from the US Government. Parties to the Articles of Agreement include a number of Asian States, Russia, Australia, France, Germany, Italy, the United Kingdom, and several other West European States. Its purpose is to

(i) foster sustainable economic development, create wealth and improve infrastructure connectivity in Asia by investing in infrastructure and other productive sectors; and (ii) promote regional cooperation and partnership in addressing development challenges by working in close collaboration with other multilateral and bilateral development institutions (Article 1(1) of the Articles of Agreement).

In order to strengthen their financial and monetary independence from the World Bank and the International Monetary Fund based in Washington, DC, the BRICS States created a development bank and a development fund.

In 2014, the Member States of the African Union agreed on the Protocol on the Establishment of the African Monetary Fund which includes the Statute of the African Monetary Fund.[21] 'The purpose of the Fund shall be to foster macroeconomic stability, sustainable shared economic growth and balanced development in the Continent, so as to facilitate the effective and predictable integration of African economies' (Article 3(1) of the Protocol). The Protocol and the Statute have not yet entered into force.

3. The Bank for International Settlements

The Bank for International Settlements (BIS)[22] was established with the objective to promote cooperation among central banks, to administer resources for

---

[20] The Articles of Agreement of the Asian Infrastructure Investment Bank (AIIB) are available at <http://www.aiib.org/html/aboutus/basicdocuments/AOA/> (accessed 23 June 2016).
[21] (2015) 54 ILM 511.
[22] M Jacobs, 'Bank for International Settlements' in R Wolfrum (ed), *The Max Planck Encyclopedia of Public International Law* (OUP 2012) vol I, 821.

loans to members and for other financial operations and to manage, as trustee or agent, international financial transactions (initially in context with the payment of German reparations arising from the First World War). The Bank's head office is in Basel. The BIS is based on an international treaty (the Convention Respecting the Bank for International Settlements of 1930), the Constituent Charter, and the Statutes of the BIS recognized by Switzerland.

The BIS has hybrid functions reflected in its status. The Bank is a company limited by shares organized under Swiss company law, in terms of the Constituent Charter and its Statutes of the BIS (Articles 1 and 2 of the BIS Statutes). At the same time, it constitutes an international organization and operates beyond the reach of Swiss law. Its shareholders are the central banks of the Member States (currently numbering about 60). Deposits are made by central banks and a few intergovernmental organizations (eg the IMF). By granting (short-term) credits to the central banks of its members, the BIS acts as the 'bank of central banks'. The BIS operates in the capital markets like a private bank.

As an international organization, the BIS provides a forum for regulators of financial markets and other authorities responsible for financial stability. In 1974, the central bank governors of the 'Basel Club' (ie the Group of 10 (G10) plus Switzerland) established the Basel Committee on Banking Supervision (as it is named today). In the Basel Committee, central bank governors and heads of supervisory authorities discuss and formulate standards for the banking sector (the 'Basel Accords').[23] In 1996, the Basel Committee, the International Organization of Securities Commissions and the Association of Insurance Supervisors established a Joint Forum on Financial Conglomerates.

Select Bibliography

AO Adede, 'Legal Trends in International Lending and Investment in the Developing Countries' (1983 II) 180 RdC 9.

R Daniño, 'The Legal Aspects of the World Bank's Work on Human Rights' (2007) 41 Int'l Law 21.

CL Gilbert and D Vines, *The World Bank: Structure and Policies* (CUP 2000).

JW Head, 'Evolution of the Governing Law for Loan Agreements of the World Bank and Other Multilateral Development Banks' (1996) 90 AJIL 214.

M Megliani, *Sovereign Debt: Genesis—Restructuring—Litigation* (Springer 2014).

NH Moller, 'The World Bank: Human Rights, Democracy and Governance' (1997) 15 NQHR 21.

SR Roos, 'Die Weltbank als Implementierungsgarant menschenrechtsschützender Völkerrechtsnormen' (2003) 63 ZaöRV 1035.

---

[23] See Ch XLII.3.

S Schlemmer-Schulte, 'International Bank for Reconstruction and Development' in R Wolfrum (ed), *The Max Planck Encyclopedia of Public International Law* (OUP 2012) vol V, 363.

IFI Shihata, *The World Bank and the IMF Relationship—Quo Vadis?* (London Institute of International Banking, Finance and Development Law 2002).

World Bank, *A Guide to the World Bank* (3rd edn, World Bank Publications 2011).

XLI

Debt Crises and State Insolvency

1. The International Management of Debt Crises

The power of taxation and the usually ample State property nourish the far-spread concept of the State as a reliable debtor. However, from a historical perspective, State insolvency is by no means a rare phenomenon. It is usually triggered by an unsustainable burden of foreign debt. Whilst countries can meet outstanding debts in their own currency by speeding up the money press (fostering inflation), this mechanism is no answer to debts in foreign currencies. The last two centuries witnessed about ninety cases of State insolvency, moratorium, and default on foreign debt, which include European States such as Denmark, Germany, Greece, and Russia.

In the 1970s, favourable conditions created incentives for developing and emerging market countries to borrow extensively from international financial institutions like the World Bank and its affiliates, from industrialized donor countries and also from private banks. Later, economic conditions deteriorated for many countries (eg by declining competitiveness, falling prices for commodities, rising interest rates, and the withdrawal of private lenders). For these and other reasons, numerous debtor countries did not manage to use these credits for lasting economic stabilization and their debt burden increased. In the last two decades of the 20th century, a number of developing and emerging market countries, especially in Latin America (eg Mexico, Brazil, Argentina), in Sub-Saharan Africa and in South-East Asia, as well as Russia entered into a severe debt crisis. The last decades witnessed restructuring or collection of sovereign debt on a very large scale.[1] Response by the IMF played a vital role in managing these crises.[2] The debt crisis of Russia in the late 1990s and the Argentine crisis (1995–2005) tell ambivalent lessons about the IMF's policy with tightening and relaxing conditionalities in volatile political conditions, in the face of sincere and cooperative willingness of governments, subsequent defiance, default on payments, and new appeals for rescue.[3] More recently,

---

[1] LF Guder, *The Administration of Debt Relief by the International Financial Institutions* (Springer 2009); L Rieffel, *Restructuring Sovereign Debt: The Case for Ad Hoc Machinery* (Brookings Institution Press 2003).

[2] See AF Lowenfeld, *International Economic Law* (2nd edn, OUP 2008) 667ff.

[3] See AF Lowenfeld, *International Economic Law* (2nd edn, OUP 2008) 699ff (on Russia), 719ff (on Argentina).

Hungary, Greece and other heavily indebted members of the Eurozone had to rely on the European Union and the European Central Bank, on multilateral assistance from other EU members and on the IMF for financial rescue.

In the meantime, many of the highly indebted developing countries (most from Africa) have been released from debt to a considerable extent. In 1996, the IMF and the World Bank group launched the Heavily Indebted Poor Countries (HIPC) Initiative for debt relief. This initiative provides massive reduction of debt for eligible countries (about 40) under certain conditions, for example if they have established a track record of reform and sound policies (like the fight against corruption) and have designed a strategy for poverty reduction. In 2005, the G8 summit of Gleneagles started the Multilateral Debt Relief Initiative (MDRI) that supplemented the HIPC providing that the World Bank, the African Development Fund, and the International Development Association help economically weak states facing an unmanageable debt burden by a 100 per cent relief under HIPC conditions. As there have been no more such debts, the process of liquidating the Fund started in the beginning of 2015.

A number of mechanisms have been developed to ease the debt burden of poor countries vis-à-vis private creditors.[4] The valuation of debt from a market perspective (rather than valuation at its nominal value) plays an important role in rescheduling processes. In 1989, as a response to the Mexican crisis, the so-called 'Brady initiative' of the US Government laid the ground for an agreement with the Mexican Government which left creditor banks to opt, inter alia, for converting existing 30-year debt instruments into debt reduction bonds (with a reduced nominal value and the existing interest rates) or for debt service reduction bonds (with existing nominal value and a reduced interest rate). The principal of these bonds ('Brady bonds') was secured by 30-year zero bonds (which paid no interest) sold by the US treasury to Mexico (which in turn could finance the purchase with loans from the World Bank and other international lenders). This model was also adopted in context with the restructuring of debts of other countries.

A vehicle to reduce the debt and stimulate investment is the conversion of debt into equity to be invested in the debtor country through 'debt-equity swaps'.[5] In this process, to be approved beforehand by the debtor country's authorities, a private investor purchases a developing country's debt instrument denominated in foreign currency (usually from a foreign bank) at a market price inferior to its nominal value (reflecting the market's expectation of the debt to be honoured), presents the debt instrument for redemption at a superior price in local currency to the debtor's central bank and invests the proceeds in the debtor country according to the approved scheme. The success of such conversion programmes essentially depends on the investment climate prevailing in the debtor country.

[4] EC Buljevich, *Cross Border Debt Restructuring: Innovative Approaches for Creditors, Corporate and Sovereigns* (Euromoney Institutional Investor PLC 2005).
[5] M Bowe and JW Dean, 'Debt Equity Swaps: Investment Incentive Effect and Secondary Market Prices' (1993) 45 Oxford Economy Papers 130; DH Cole, 'Debt-Equity Conversions, Debt-for-Nature Swaps, and the Continuing World Debt Crisis' (1992) 30 Colum J Transnat'l L 57.

2. Restructuring Sovereign Debt: The 'Paris Club' and the 'London Club'

There are two important processes of rescheduling sovereign debt, the 'Paris Club' and the 'London Club'. Since the early 1950s, the 'Paris Club', set up by creditor countries, operates as an intergovernmental forum, under the auspices of the French Ministry of Finance, for addressing problems arising from possible or actual default of debtor countries and for negotiations on relief between debtor and creditor countries. As a rule, the IMF, the World Bank, the OECD, and the UNCTAD also participate in the meetings. The objective of restructuring sovereign debt is the establishment of a new schedule for payment with a postponement and reduction of the debt (principal or interest rate). As a rule, restructuring of debt is tied to a stand-by arrangement with the IMF and a programme of economic adjustment according to IMF conditionality.

The 'London Club' (Bank Advisory Committee) is the framework set up by commercial banks for rescheduling sovereign debts to private creditors ('haircut'). In recent years, bondholders and suppliers joined the creditors' ranks in the negotiations with debtor countries. In 2004, the Institute of International Finance, a global association of commercial and investment banks and other financial corporations, adopted the Principles for Stable Capital Flows and Fair Debt Restructuring in Emerging Markets,[6] which met with the approval of the Group of 24 (G24).[7]

3. State Insolvency and International Law

(a) General aspects

Beyond the statutes of international lenders like the IMF or the World Bank, international law offers little conceptual guidance for relief from the perspective of heavily indebted countries. The 'gun-boat diplomacy', practised by great powers in the late 19th century and early 20th century, included military intervention to ensure military enforcement of sovereign debt to private creditors (most prominently in the Venezuelan debt crisis of 1902 with a naval blockade by the United Kingdom, Germany, and Italy). In the Drago-Porter Convention (1907),[8] Contracting States, in principle, renounced military enforcement as the primary means of settling

---

[6] Institute of International Finance, Principles for Stable Capital Flows and Fair Debt Restructuring in Emerging Markets (2005) 10–14 <http://www.iif.com/download.php?id=4fyB5BGIKzU=> (accessed 23 June 2016).

[7] Communiqué of the Inter-Governmental Group of Twenty-Four on International Monetary Affairs and Development (15 April 2005) para 6 <https://www.imf.org/external/np/cm/2005/041505.htm> (accessed 23 June 2016).

[8] Hague Convention II Respecting the Limitation of the Employment of Force for the Recovery of Contract Debts (1907) Treaty Series 537.

claims of their own nationals, long before the comprehensive prohibition of the use of force under the UN Charter (Article 2(4)).

Under existing customary law, the right to development (acclaimed in principle, controversial in substance)[9] or the emerging principle of solidarity towards developing countries[10] may establish an obligation of creditor countries to enter, *bona fide*, into negotiations on clearly sustainable debt. However, neither the right to development nor the principle of solidarity gives rise to any tangible claims to debt relief or to fresh money.

Under conditions for borrowing from the IMF, default will put at risk the release of further tranches under a stand-by arrangement and the IMF's willingness to grant credits in the future. This explains why States have hardly ever defaulted on IMF loans (Argentina did, however, in September 2003, before clearing its arrears a few days later, after a new arrangement had been negotiated).[11] Under cross-default clauses used by banks, a country's default on debt may trigger a domino effect: default on one debt constitutes default on other loans covered by the clause and makes these loans immediately due and payable.

The former UN Commission on Human Rights (now the UN Human Rights Council) took a very critical stance towards economic adjustment programmes in conflict with the insurance of human rights standards:

[T]he exercise of the basic rights of the people of debtor countries to food, housing, clothing, employment, education, health services and a healthy environment cannot be subordinated to the implementation of structural adjustment policies and economic reforms arising from the debt.[12]

This approach may be an over-simplification. It ignores the long-term impact of unsustainable debt and insufficient productivity on social standards and on the capacity of the State adequately to ensure the rights under the International Covenant on Economic, Social and Cultural Rights. Still, the possible tensions between economic adjustment and human rights from a short or medium-term perspective call for serious consideration.

In the case of State insolvency, international law only provides some rather rudimentary rules which govern relations between the debtor country and its sovereign or private creditors.[13] On the one hand, the principle of sovereign equality of States

---

[9] A Marong, 'Development, Right to, International Protection' in R Wolfrum (ed), *The Max Planck Encyclopedia of Public International Law* (OUP 2012) vol III, 85; N Roht-Arriaza and SC Aminzadeh, 'Solidarity Rights (Development, Peace, Environment, Humanitarian Assistance)' in R Wolfrum (ed), *The Max Planck Encyclopedia of Public International Law* (OUP 2012) vol IX, 278ff paras 6ff.

[10] R Wolfrum and C Kojima (eds), *Solidarity: A Structural Principle of International Law* (Springer 2010); R Lastra and L Buchheit (eds), *Sovereign Debt Management* (OUP 2014).

[11] See AF Lowenfeld, *International Economic Law* (2nd edn, OUP 2008) 729ff.

[12] UNHCR Res 82 (6 January 2000) UN Doc E/CN.4/2000/82.

[13] See R Dolzer, 'Staatliche Zahlungsunfähigkeit: Zum Begriff und zu den Rechtsfolgen im Völkerrecht' in J Jekewitz (ed), *Festschrift für Karl Josef Partsch zum 75. Geburtstag* (Duncker & Humblot 1989) 531; M Herdegen, 'Der Staatsbankrott: Probleme eines Insolvenzverfahrens und der Umschuldung bei Staatsanleihen' (2011) 65 WM 913; JA Kämmerer, 'Der Staatsbankrott aus völkerrechtlicher Sicht' (2005) 65 ZaöRV 651; K von Lewinski, *Öffentlichrechtliche Insolvenz und Staatsbankrott* (Mohr Siebeck 2011); C Ohler, 'Der Staatsbankrott' (2005) 60 JZ 590; C Paulus,

(Article 2(1) of the UN Charter) leaves no room for any procedure of liquidating sovereign debtor's assets, as in bankruptcy under national law. On the other hand, the debtor State's jurisdiction to regulate debt towards foreign creditors and to restructure or suspend its own payment obligations denominated in foreign currencies is rather limited.

Internationally operating banks and other private creditors are sensitive to the law governing sovereign debt instruments. Debt instruments denominated in US-Dollar or another foreign currency and issued by countries without an impeccable record of compliance are usually payable in one of the big financial centres of the world (eg London or New York) or are explicitly governed by US, British, German, or other foreign law. In the United States, the Federal Court of Appeals for the Second Circuit established in *Allied Bank International v Banco Credito Agricola de Cartago*[14] that bonds or other debt instruments payable in the United States are obligations situated in the United States. Therefore, legislation or executive acts of the debtor country suspending payment or unilaterally reducing obligations amount to extraterritorial taking of property, which the United States will not recognize under the act of State doctrine. All this protects bondholders against unilateral interference with their claim by the debtor State. Moreover, unilateral measures of the debtor State ordering a moratorium on or the restructuring of loans which are subject to foreign law need (and, in practice, will) not be respected by other States under Article VIII, section 2(b) of the IMF Agreement.[15]

Capital markets are sensitive to these legal implications. In the Eurozone, heavily indebted countries like Greece or Portugal had issued different types of bonds, most being subject to domestic law of the issuing country (Greek or Portuguese law), some governed by English law. When the Euro crisis became aggravated, interest rates for the two types of bonds spread considerably, with a premium on the English law-governed, possibly safer asset class. Sovereign debt which is payable in New York is also subject to US jurisdiction. This explains why the litigious aspects arising from Argentina's default in 2001 (actions for payment and for attachment of assets) were essentially handled by one federal judge of the US District Court for the Southern District of New York.

(b) Necessity

Under the rules of State responsibility, it is a most controversial issue when and to what extent a State may refuse or suspend payment on its debt. Although the rules on necessity immediately apply only to obligations under international law

---

'A Standing Arbitral Tribunal as a Procedural Solution for Sovereign Debt Restructurings' in CA Primo Braga and GA Vincelette (eds), *Sovereign Debt and the Financial Crisis: Will This Time Be Different?* (World Bank Publications 2011) 317; C Paulus, 'Überlegungen zu einem Insolvenzverfahren für Staaten' (2002) 56 WM 725.

[14] *Allied Bank International v Banco Credito Agricola de Cartago* 757 F.2d 526 (2d Cir 1985).
[15] See Ch XXXIX.7.

(ie loans granted by sovereign creditors or international organizations like the IMF or the World Bank), they have implications on foreign debt to private creditors and on the adjudication of private payment claims by national courts.

According to public international law, problems of solvency, in principle, neither destroy the legal basis for payment obligations nor release the State from its debt. The citizenship of the debtor State, as a kind of solidary community, must share their State's responsibility for mismanagement of its own government. This calls for an analysis that differs from the cases of corruption. Addressing corruption induced by government, modern international law, in terms of responsibility and redress, looks behind the shell of the State at the interest of the population which, ultimately, is the victim of intransparent public administration and bad governance.[16] In contrast, contracting debt, unlike corruption, is not per se directed against the interests of the population at large. However, public international law must and will be sensitive to an economic and financial situation, in which the unmitigated compliance of payment obligations seriously affects the debtor State's responsibility for human rights standards, internal peace, and national security. The international order is committed to the existence of the individual member of the community of States and to the values behind elementary human rights. Thus, public international law would jeopardize its own legitimacy, if it allowed compliance of payment obligations to trump the fulfilment of the core functions of the debtor State or economic and social human rights standards. In practice, debtor States and creditors do not insist on maximizing possible legal positions (full compliance on the one hand and complete release from or suspension of payment obligations on the other hand), but try to reach a balanced agreement in times of severe crises.

International tribunals and arbitral bodies have taken the broader implications of a State's inability to pay its debts into account. In its award in the *French Company of Venezuelan Railroads* case (1905), a mixed claims commission set up by France and Venezuela, conserved Venezuela's argument of insolvency:

[The government] can not be charged with responsibility for the conditions which existed in 1899, prostrating business, paralyzing trade and commerce, and annihilating the products of agriculture; nor for the exhaustion and paralysis which followed: nor for its inability to pay its just debts; nor for the inability of the company to obtain money otherwise and elsewhere. All these are misfortune incidents to government, to business, and to human life. They do not beget claims for damages.[17]

In the famous *Socobel* case, Belgium had taken up the claim of a Belgian corporation which had obtained an arbitral award for payment of a considerable sum in gold against Greece. Before the Permanent Court of International Justice, the Greek Government pleaded that its economic situation prevented Greece from immediately complying with the award. The Permanent Court of International Justice held that it had no jurisdiction to decide whether the Greek Government could rely on

---

[16] See Ch IX.
[17] *French Company of Venezuelan Railroads Case, France v Venezuela* (1905) vol X RIAA 285, 353 (mixed commission of arbitrators).

the alleged financial crisis as *force majeure* and allowed the Belgium demand.[18] Both parties recognized that a case of *force majeure* (disputed in the actual case) could allow a debtor State to suspend payments in a financial crisis.

Under the modern law of State responsibility, a State may rely on necessity as a justification for suspending compliance with an international obligation.[19] In addition, natural catastrophes and similar external interferences with the State's capacity to act may also qualify as *force majeure*. The Draft Articles of the International Law Commission on State Responsibility contain rather strict conditions for justification by necessity (Article 25):

Necessity

1. Necessity may not be invoked by a State as a ground for precluding the wrongfulness of an act not in conformity with an international obligation of that State unless the act:
   (a) is the only way for the State to safeguard an essential interest against a grave and imminent peril; and
   (b) does not seriously impair an essential interest of the State or States towards which the obligation exists, or of the international community as a whole.
2. In any case, necessity may not be invoked by a State as a ground for precluding wrongfulness if:
   (a) the international obligation in question excludes the possibility of invoking necessity; or
   (b) the State has contributed to the situation of necessity.

It is a most controversial issue, whether a debtor State can invoke justification even if its own government, by economic or financial mismanagement, contributed to the situation of necessity. As a rule, a substantial contribution of an affected State precludes reliance on necessity.[20] However, at least in the case of State insolvency, a more lenient standard seems appropriate. In virtually all cases of State insolvency, the government of the debtor country has at least substantially contributed to the situation. Therefore, balancing the interests of the debtor State and its population on the one hand and the interests of the creditors on the other hand, it seems appropriate to allow the reliance on necessity if exogenous factors beyond the responsibility of the debtor State played an essential role in generating insolvency.[21]

Several ICSID awards addressed the argument of necessity in context with the Argentine crisis in the beginning of 2000. In the case *CMS Gas Transmission Co v Argentina*, the arbitration tribunal held that the Argentine crisis was rooted in

---

[18] PCIJ *The 'Société Commerciale de Belgique' (Belgium v Greece)* [1939] PCIJ Rep Series A/B No 78 paras 160–79.

[19] J Crawford, *The International Law Commission's Articles on State Responsibility: Introduction, Text Commentaries* (CUP 2002) Article 25, 2.

[20] See ICJ *Case Concerning the Gabčíkovo-Nagymaros Project (Hungary v Slovakia)* [1997] ICJ Rep 7 paras 51–2; J Crawford, *The International Law Commission's Articles on State Responsibility: Introduction, Text Commentaries* (CUP 2002) Articles 25, 20.

[21] See R Dolzer, 'Staatliche Zahlungsunfähigkeit—Zum Begriff und zu den Rechtsfolgen im Völkerrecht' in J Jekewitz (ed), *Das Recht des Menschen zwischen Freiheit und Verantwortung—Festschrift für Karl Josef Partsch* (Duncker & Humblot 2002) 551.

the policies of successive administrations, and that the 'government policies and their shortcomings significantly contributed to the crisis and the emergency'.[22] In *Enron v Argentina*[23] and *Sempra Energy International v Argentina*,[24] the arbitral tribunals rejected Argentina's argument that exogenous factors had mainly contributed to the financial crisis. In any case, necessity does not permanently release a State from its debt burden, but only allows the State to suspend pending payments as long as a situation of necessity lasts.[25] In addition, the debtor State must pay compensation for specific damages arising from temporary non-compliance.[26] The due compensation does not, however, include interest on the arrears.[27]

Modern arbitral decisions on investment law do not lightly assume a situation of necessity. In the case *LG & E v Argentine Republic*,[28] an ICSID arbitral tribunal based the justification by necessity on an existential threat to Argentina at the end of 2001:

It faced an extremely serious threat to its existence, its political and economic survival, to the possibility of maintaining its essential services in operation, and to the preservation of its internal peace.[29]

A situation of necessity justifies only measures necessary to safeguard a State's essential interests. However, arbitral decisions sometimes take different views on this issue, even when they evaluate the same economic crisis.[30]

A number of investment treaties have special necessity and safeguard clauses which allow the host State to take measures to counter an economic crisis or

---

[22] *CMS Gas Transmission Co v Argentine Republic*, ICSID Case No ARB/01/8 (Award) (2005) 44 ILM 1205 para 329; See AK Bjorklund, 'Emergency Exceptions: State of Necessity and *Force Majeure*' in P Muchlinski (ed), *The Oxford Handbook of International Investment Law* (OUP 2008) 490.

[23] *Enron Corporation Ponderosa Assets, L.P. v Argentine Republic*, ICSID Case No ARB/01/3 (Award 2007).

[24] *Sempra Energy International v Argentine Republic*, ICSID Case No ARB/02/16 (Annulment Proceeding) (2010) 49 ILM 1445 paras 186ff.

[25] See ICJ *Case Concerning the Gabčíkovo-Nagymaros Project (Hungary v Slovakia)* [1997] ICJ Rep 7 paras 47, 63, 101; *CMS Gas Transmission Co v Argentine Republic*, ICSID Case No ARB/01/8 (Award) (2005) 44 ILM 1205 paras 379ff; Article 27 *lit* c of the Draft Articles on Responsibility of States for Internationally Wrongful Acts.

[26] See Article 27 *lit* b of the Draft Articles on the Responsibility of States of Internationally Wrongful Acts; *CMS Gas Transmission Co v Argentine Republic*, ICSID Case No ARB/01/8 (Award) (2005) 44 ILM 1205 paras 390ff.

[27] J Crawford, *The International Law Commission's Articles on State Responsibility: Introduction, Text Commentaries* (CUP 2002) Article 27, 4.

[28] *LG & E v Argentine Republic*, ICSID Case No ARB/02/1 (Decision on Liability) (2007) 46 ILM 36 para 257.

[29] For a different assessment of the Argentine crisis, see *CMS Gas Transmission Co v Argentine Republic*, ICSID Case No ARB/01/8 (Award) (2005) 44 ILM 1205 paras 318ff (denying circumstances of necessity). See also the decision of the ICSID (Ad hoc Committee) in the case *CMS Gas Transmission Co v Argentine Republic*, ICSID Case No ARB/01/8 (Annulment Proceeding) (2007) 46 ILM 1136 paras 101ff.

[30] See on the Argentine crisis *CMS Gas Transmission Co v Argentine Republic*, ICSID Case No ARB/01/8 (Award) (2005) 44 ILM 1205 paras 318ff (denying situation of necessity); *LG & E v Argentine Republic*, ICSID Case No ARB/02/1 (Decision on Liability) (2007) 46 ILM 36 paras 256ff (assuming a situation of necessity).

internal disturbances.[31] The investment treaty between Argentina and the United States provides in Article XI:

This Treaty shall not preclude the application by either Party of measures necessary for the maintenance of public order, the fulfilment of its obligations with respect to the maintenance or restoration of international peace or security, or the Protection of its own essential security interests.[32]

For host States, such clauses are far more favourable than the rules on necessity under customary law.[33] In particular, they vest the host State with considerable margins of appreciation and discretion. This has far-reaching implications for claims of foreign creditors under public debt instruments (bonds, promissory notes). To the extent that investment treaties cover these claims, necessity clauses in investment treaties broaden the scope for suspending payments and other measures taken by debtor States. Thus, the extension of covered investments to debt instruments under investment treaties, apparently strengthening the position of bondholders, may, in the end, weaken their protection.

In a landmark decision, an ICSID arbitral tribunal held in the case *Abaclat v Argentina* that the BIT at stake covered claims of bond holders and assumed jurisdiction of thousands of claims against Argentina.[34] The reasoning of the arbitral tribunal as to the treatment of bonds and other similar instruments as protected can be applied to many other investment treaties.

Some investment treaties, however, contain clauses on necessity which are much narrower than Article XI of the BIT between Argentina and the United States.[35] To the extent that these narrower clauses only refer to losses of investments 'in the territory' of the host State, they do not affect bonds and other debts payable abroad.

It is a matter of controversy, whether a State can rely on necessity also towards private creditors. Clauses on necessity in investment treaties directly refer to private claims. The situation under customary law is not entirely clear. After Argentina defaulted on its foreign debt in 2001, the Government pleaded necessity in a number of litigations. In *Lightwater Corp Ltd v Argentina*, the Court brushed the argument of necessity aside.[36] The Constitutional Court of Germany held that the customary rules on necessity only apply to claims under international law and not

---

[31] W Burke-White and A von Staden, 'Investment Protection in Extraordinary Times: The Interpretation and Application of Non-Precluded Measure Provisions in Bilateral Investment Treaties' (2008) 48 Va J Int'l L 307.

[32] See SF Hill, 'The "Necessity Defense" and the Emerging Arbitral Conflict in Its Application to the U.S.-Argentina Bilateral Investment Treaty' (2007) 13 Law Bus Rev Am 547.

[33] (Ad hoc Committee) *CMS Gas Transmission Co v Argentine Republic*, ICSID Case No ARB/01/8 (Annulment Proceeding) (2007) 46 ILM 1136 paras 101ff; (Ad hoc Committee) *Sempra Energy International v Argentine Republic*, ICSID Case No ARB/02/16 (Annulment Proceeding) (2010) 49 ILM 1445 paras 186ff.

[34] *Abaclat and Others v The Argentine Republic*, ICSID Case No ARB/07/5 (Decision on Jurisdiction and Admissibility 2011) paras 353ff.

[35] See Art 4(3) and (4) of the German Model BIT (2008); Art 5(5)(b) of the US Model BIT (2012).

[36] *Lightwater Corp Ltd v Republic of Argentina* 2003 Dist Lexis 6156 (SDNY 2003).

to claims by creditors.[37] This ruling can hardly stand up to scrutiny. The Court distinguished the arbitral cases decided under bilateral investment treaties on the ground that, even though the claimants were private individuals, like those private energy suppliers CMS Energy or LG&E, the law governing the disputes was international law.[38] It contradicts a whole array of arbitral decisions, which applied the rules on necessity to relations with private investors, under customary law and investment treaties.[39] Moreover, the rules on necessity protect essential functions of the debtor State vis-à-vis the international community at large and must, therefore, be respected by other States and foreign courts adjudicating claims of foreign creditors. It would be inconsistent if States had to respect a situation of necessity in relation to their own claims, but could entirely ignore this defence in the enforcement of private claims through their own machinery of justice. The sovereign interests shielded by the rules on necessity, which also have a human rights dimension, do not simply give way to private interests. Finally, the principle of non-intervention in the internal affairs of other States prohibits States from jeopardizing the fulfilment of basic functions of other States by enforcing private claims in a crisis threatening the very survival of a debtor State.

A German district court held that a situation of necessity does not bar an action for payment because only subsequent measures of execution could possibly interfere with the sovereign function of the debtor.[40] This view ignores that the rules on necessity affect the payment obligation as such and not only execution measures.

(c) Collective restructuring of debts and objecting minority lenders

In a severe financial crisis, the debtor State will negotiate with private creditors to reach an agreement on restructuring debts. Often, some creditors will be opposed to a restructuring of debt accepted by the majority of creditors. In the absence of specific contractual clauses, the legal position of non-consenting creditors is a difficult issue. Creditors rejecting a restructuring of the debts may try to pursue their claims before the courts of the country where the bonds are payable. These problems are exacerbated when institutional investors with a speculative and aggressive strategy ('vulture funds') purchase debt instruments of States in a financial crisis at

---

[37] BVerfGE 118, 124 (dissenting opinion at 146ff); SW Schill, 'German Constitutional Court Rules on Necessity in Argentine Bondholder Case' (2007) 11 ASIL Insights Issue 20 <http://www.asil.org/insights/volume/11/issue/20/german-constitutional-court-rules-necessity-argentine-bondholder-case> (accessed 23 June 2016); AK Bjorklund, 'Emergency Exceptions: State of Necessity and *Force Majeure*' in P Muchlinski (ed), *The Oxford Handbook of International Investment Law* (OUP 2008) 516.

[38] AK Bjorklund, 'Emergency Exceptions: State of Necessity and *Force Majeure*' in P Muchlinski (ed), *The Oxford Handbook of International Investment Law* (OUP 2008) 517.

[39] *LG & E v Argentine Republic*, ICSID Case No ARB/02/1 (Decision on Liability) (2007) 46 ILM 36 paras 245ff; (Ad hoc Committee) *CMS Gas Transmission Co v Argentine Republic*, ICSID Case No ARB/01/8 (Annulment Proceeding) (2007) 46 ILM 1136 paras 101ff; (Ad hoc Committee) *Sempra Energy International v Argentine Republic*, ICSID Case No ARB/02/16 (Annulment Proceedings) (2010) 49 ILM 1445 paras 186ff.

[40] LG Frankfurt a.M. JZ 2003, 1010 with note by A Reinisch; see also OLG Frankfurt a.M. NJW 2003, 2688.

a considerable discount with the intention of bringing an action for payment at the full nominal value.

The case-law of US courts does not always follow a clear line. Solidarity among lenders and equal treatment of creditors is a recurring theme. In *Crédit français Int'l, SA v Sociedad Financiera de Comercio, CA*,[41] the Supreme Court of New York relied on the terms of a syndicated loan to reject the claim of a minority lender which opposed the arrangements accepted by the majority.

In this case, the plaintiff was a member of a consortium of banks which had given a loan to a State-owned financial institution of Venezuela. In order to cope with a financial crisis, the Venezuelan Government had decided not to pay the debt principal in US-Dollars, whilst allowing continuing payments of interest. Unlike the plaintiff, the majority of the consortium had agreed to accept this situation rather than driving their Venezuelan debtor into insolvency. The Supreme Court of New York held that, under the underlying contractual arrangement, the syndicated loan constituted a joint venture and that the plaintiff, as a minority lender, could not enforce its individual claim in conflict with the agreement among the majority of lenders.

The broader implications of enforcement of minority claims were highlighted by the *Elliott* litigation against Peru.[42] On the secondary market, Elliott, a hedge-fund, had purchased defaulted bonds issued by the central bank of Peru and guaranteed by the Republic of Peru, with the intention of collecting the full debt through litigation before US courts. After a restructuring of the Peruvian debt in accordance with the Brady Plan, accepted by most creditors, Elliott sued for the full amount of the debt including accrued interest. In *Elliott Associates, LP v Banco de la Nación and the Republic of Peru*,[43] the Court of Appeals of the Second Circuit, reversing the judgment of the court below, held for the plaintiff and emphasized the voluntary nature of a restructuring agreement and the interest (also of debtor countries) in maintaining a functional secondary market for defaulted sovereign debt.

After obtaining the judgment against Peru and its central bank, Elliott sought assets of Peru to execute the judgment. When Peru moved funds to New York for payment of other creditors under the restructuring agreement, Elliott claimed that it should be paid like the other (consenting) under a *pari passu* clause[44] contained in the Peruvian bonds (in accordance with international bond practice) and tried to intercept the funds. A US District Court held that this clause entitled Elliott to equal treatment, that is to payment from the funds on the same basis as the other creditors.[45] After Peru had redirected the funds to Belgium for paying creditors in Europe, the Brussels Court of Appeal, also impressed by the *pari passu* argument, granted Elliott a restraining order.[46] Peru then paid Elliott in full and the

[41] *Crédit français Int'l, SA v Sociedad Financiera de Comercio, CA* 490 NYS 2d 670 (Sup Ct 1985).
[42] See AF Lowenfeld, *International Economic Law* (2nd edn, OUP 2008) 737f.
[43] *Elliott Associates, LP v Banco de la Nación and the Republic of Peru* 194 F.3d 363 (2d Cir 1999) para 71.
[44] See Section 3.(f) in this Chapter.
[45] *Elliott Associates, LP v Republic of Peru* US LEXIS 14169 (SDNY 2000).
[46] Court of Appeal of Brussels *Elliott Associates, LP v Republic of Peru* General Docket No 2000/QR/92 (2000).

restraining order was lifted. Other courts were less sympathetic to similar claims under the *pari passu* clause. In *Kensington International Ltd v Congo*, the English Court of Appeal confirmed the exercise of judicial discretion denying a restraining order sought by an affiliate of Elliott's.[47]

More recently, in *EM Ltd v Argentina*, the US Court of Appeals for the Second Circuit confirmed a decision of the court below which had placed the interest in a collective restructuring backed by a vast majority of creditors above the claims of non-consenting buyers of defaulted Argentine debt. After 76 per cent of creditors had accepted a restructuring scheme, providing the exchange of old bonds for instruments, plaintiffs sought to attach the old bonds deposited with US banks and to restrain disposition of these bonds. The District Court for the Southern District of New York had exercised its judicial discretion to vacate the orders of attachment and restraint.[48] The Court of Appeals affirmed this ruling and held:

[T]he District Court acted well within its authority to vacate the remedies in order to avoid a substantial risk to the successful conclusion of the debt restructuring. That restructuring is obviously of critical importance to the economic health of a nation.

The UNCTAD Consolidated Principles on Responsible Sovereign Financing (2012)[49] proclaim a duty of lenders to respond to a financial crisis of sovereign debtors in terms of a consensual debt restructuring:

In circumstances where a sovereign is manifestly unable to service its debts, all lenders have a duty to behave in good faith and with cooperative spirit to reach a consensual rearrangement of those obligations. Creditors should seek a speedy and orderly resolution to the problem (Principle 7).

As the German Federal Court of Justice held in a case brought against Argentina, customary international law does not establish an obligation on lenders to cooperate in terms of such a restructuring of sovereign debts.[50]

In September 2014, the UN General Assembly adopted Resolution 68/304 'Towards the establishment of a multilateral legal framework for sovereign debt restructuring processes'.[51] This resolution, sponsored by Bolivia, can be understood as a direct reaction to the successful actions of hedge funds before US courts. In the resolution, the General Assembly recognized that

the efforts of a State to restructure its sovereign debt should not be frustrated or impeded by commercial creditors, including specialized investor funds such as hedge funds, which seek to undertake speculative purchases of its distressed debt at deeply discounted rates on secondary markets in order to pursue full payment via litigation.

---

[47] *Kensington International Ltd v Republic of the Congo* [2003] All ER (D) 159.
[48] *EM Ltd v the Republic of Argentina* F.Appx. 131 (2d Cir 2005).
[49] UNCTAD Principles on Promoting Responsible Sovereign Lending and Borrowing (Amended and Restated as of 10 January 2012).
[50] BGH NJW 2015, 2328, 2330ff paras 28ff.
[51] UNGA Res 68/304 (17 September 2014) UN Doc A/RES/68/304. This resolution was adopted with 124 votes in favour, 11 votes against, and 41 abstentions.

The General Assembly, inter alia, decided

[…] to elaborate and adopt through a process of intergovernmental negotiations, as a matter of priority during its sixty-ninth session, a multilateral legal framework for the sovereign debt restructuring processes with a view, inter alia, to increasing the efficiency, stability and predictability of the international financial system and achieving sustained, inclusive and equitable economic growth and sustainable development, in accordance with national circumstances and priorities.

In 2015, the UN General Assembly adopted Resolution 69/319 on 'Basic Principles on Sovereign Debt Restructuring Processes'.[52] The resolution calls for debt restructuring to be guided by the principles of sovereignty, good faith, transparency, impartiality, equitable treatment, sovereign immunity, legitimacy (including the rule of law), sustainability, and majority restructuring.

Reacting to the public outcry in the United Kingdom at vulture fund litigation against poor African countries, the UK Parliament adopted the Debt Relief (Developing Countries) Act 2010. The Act protects poor countries, with about 40 States qualifying for reduction in their foreign debt under the HIPC Initiative of the IMF and the World Bank and against claims of creditors claiming the full amount of debt. The Act limits claims to the rate of reduction set under the HIPC for each eligible country's debt.

(d) Statutory mechanisms for restructuring sovereign debt

The experiences with the debt crises of the last decade and controversial litigation initiated by 'vulture funds' (eg in the *Elliott* case) set off a number of proposals for a statutory mechanism to cope with the insolvency of States and to reach a restructuring of sovereign debt, which is internationally recognized.[53] The challenge lies in devising a reliable legal framework which joins all creditors together, provides for a procedure managed by a neutral body, bars the enforcement of individual claims, and lays the foundation of re-establishing long-term solvency of the debtor State (rehabilitation). Analogies to national laws on bankruptcy call for caution. Thus, liquidation of sovereign debtors' assets lies absolutely outside of the possible functions of a restructuring mechanism. On the other hand, the US Bankruptcy Code has inspired many proposals. This applies, in particular, to chapter 11 of the Bankruptcy Code which allows a debtor to restructure its business and to continue operations under protection of the bankruptcy court.

The Proposal of a Sovereign Debt Restructuring Mechanism (SDRM), designed within the IMF,[54] aims at a leading role of the IMF on the basis of an amendment of the IMF Agreement. Key elements of this concept are:

- majority restructuring, with restructuring accepted by a qualified majority of creditors to be binding on the non-consenting minority;

---

[52] UNGA Res 69/319 (29 September 2015) UN Doc A/RES/69/319.
[53] AO Krueger, *A New Approach to Sovereign Debt Restructuring* (International Monetary Fund 2002); CG Paulus, 'Rechtliche Handhaben zur Bewältigung der Überschuldung von Staaten' (2009) 55 RIW 11.
[54] The proposal is closely associated with the then deputy managing director of the IMF Anne Krueger, see AO Krueger, *A New Approach to Sovereign Debt Restructuring* (International Monetary Fund 2002).

- a stay on creditor litigation after commencement of reorganization proceedings;
- protection of creditor interests, with the debtor country being precluded from making payments to non-priority creditors and with assurances for preserving the values of public assets as well as commitments to economic rehabilitation;
- priority financing, with privileges for private creditors providing fresh money; and
- a statutory framework based on a universal treaty, preferably an amendment to the IMF agreement.

The reformed structure of the IMF, with enhanced influence of countries like China, India and many developing countries, might vest the Fund with new legitimacy for administering a sovereign debt restructuring mechanism. Another option is a treaty for a new restructuring body administering private claims, modelled after the ICSID Convention. In any case, only a treaty reliably ensures international recognition for restructuring measures.

(e) Collective action clauses

A contractual solution to the problem of the non-consenting creditor are collective action clauses (CACs),[55] which have become a widely accepted element of bonds and other debt instruments issued by States. Collective action clauses provide a contractual basis for the restructuring of sovereign obligations with the consent of a qualified majority of creditors. Majority restructuring provisions allow the debtor country and the majority of creditors to reach an agreement binding upon all bondholders including the non-consenting minority. Majority enforcement provisions bar minority creditors from enforcing claims through litigation. For a long time, collective action clauses were contained in sovereign bond contracts governed by English law. In the last decade, countries like Mexico, Brazil, Italy, South Africa, and even the United States have included collective action clauses in their bonds governed by the law of New York.[56] Under the Agreement on the European Stability Mechanism (Article 12(3)), the countries of the Euro group committed themselves to include standardized and identical collective action clauses in the terms of new bonds from June 2013. As the German Federal Court of Justice rightly concluded, the acceptance of a restructuring of sovereign debts by a majority of creditors can be opposed to the claims of holdout creditors only if the terms under which a government bond was issued provide such a majority decision.[57]

---

[55] R Gray, 'Collective Action Clauses: Theory and Practice' (2004) 35 GJIL 693.

[56] SJ Galvis and AL Saad, 'Collective Action Clauses: Recent Progress and Challenges Ahead' (2004) 35 GJIL 713; M Gugiatti and A Richards, 'The Use of Collective Action Clauses in New York Law Bonds of Sovereign Borrowers' (2004) 35 GJIL 815.

[57] BGH NJW 2015, 2328, 2331ff paras 33ff.

(f) *pari passu* clauses

A standard clause in government bonds grants equal treatment of bondholders and other creditors of the State (*pari passu* clause). As previously mentioned, such a clause typically means that the debtor state may not discriminate between bondholders who accepted an agreement on restructuration on the one hand and non-consenting bondholders on the other hand. In *Argentina v NML Capital*, the US Court of Appeals for the Second Circuit held that the creditor State, under a *pari passu* clause, must pay out the same quota to non-consenting bondholders which it is willing to pay to consenting creditors. In this context, the Court of Appeals underlined the interest in maintaining the integrity of the New York marketplace for borrowers and lenders and, by implication, the attractiveness of New York as an international centre of capital transactions:

We do not believe the outcome of this case threatens to steer bond issuers away from the New York marketplace. On the contrary, our decision affirms a proposition essential to the integrity of the capital markets: borrowers and lenders may, under New York law, negotiate mutually agreeable terms for their transactions, but they will be held to those terms. We believe that the interest—one widely shared in the financial community—in maintaining New York's status as one of the foremost commercial centers is advanced by requiring debtors, including foreign debtors, to pay their debts.[58]

This judgment not only serves national and local interests. It rightly insists in non-discrimination of bondholders according to the issuing of a State's own terms.

Select Bibliography

D Asiedu-Akrofi, 'Sustaining Lender Commitment to Sovereign Debtors' (1990) 30 Colum J of Transn'l L 1.

D Carreau and NN Shaw, *La Dette extérieure/The External Debt* (Martinus Nijhoff 1995).

DH Cole, 'Debt-Equity Conversions, Debt-for-Nature Swaps, and the Continuing World Debt Crisis' (1992) 30 Colum J Transnat'l L 57.

R Dolzer, 'Staatliche Zahlungsunfähigkeit: Zum Begriff und zu den Rechtsfolgen im Völkerrecht' in J Jekewitz (ed), *Festschrift für Karl Josef Partsch zum 75. Geburtstag* (Duncker & Humblot 1989) 531.

FP Feliciano and R Dolzer, 'The International Law of External Debt Management—Some Current Aspects (Report of the Committee for International Monetary Law)' in International Law Association, *Report of the Sixty-Third Conference (Warsaw)* (1988) 472.

M Herdegen, 'Europäische Bankenunion: Wege zu einer einheitlichen Bankenaufsicht' (2012) 40 WM 1889.

R Lastra and L Buchheit (eds), *Sovereign Debt Management* (OUP 2014).

RG MacLean, 'Legal Aspects of the External Debt' (1989 II) 214 RdC 31.

RSJ Martha, 'Inability to Pay under International Law and under the Fund Agreement' (1994) 41 NILR 85.

---

[58] US Court of Appeals for the Second Circuit, *NML Capital, Ltd. et al v Republic of Argentina* (2013).

J Morgan-Foster, 'The Relationship of IMF Structural Adjustment Programs to Economic, Social, and Cultural Rights: The Argentine Case Revisited' (2003) 24 Mich J Int'l L 577.

CG Paulus, *A Debt Restructuring Mechanism for Sovereigns* (Hart Publishing 2014).

SL Schwarcz, 'Sovereign Debt Restructuring: A Bankruptcy Reorganization Approach' (2000) 85 Cornell L Rev 956.

RD Sloane, 'On the Use and Abuse of Necessity in the Law of State Responsibility' (2012) 106 AJIL 447.

F Vischer, 'Zur Stellung der Anleihegläubiger bei Zahlungsunfähigkeit des Schuldnerstaates' (2011) 21 Schw Z Int & Eu R 243.

M Waibel, *Sovereign Defaults before International Courts and Tribunals* (CUP 2011).

XLII

International Regulation of the Banking Sector

1. The Need for Enhanced Cooperation of Supervisory Authorities and for Harmonized Standards

The banking sector has always been extensively engaged in cross-border transactions. Over the last decades, the international business of banks and their international presence through affiliates or branches in other countries have continuously increased. The difference between States in standards for licensing and supervision of banks as well as in the implementation of existing standards gives rise to strategic behaviour (regulatory arbitrage). The risks associated with certain more or less transparent products have become highly contagious, as the crisis triggered by international trade with products on securitized bundled mortgages from the US subprime sector (and with their derivatives) shows. The collapse of a major bank may not only affect the stability of the banking sector in the respective country, but also generate an international domino effect, especially if the bank is a part or even head of an international financial conglomerate.

The case of the Bank for Credit and Commerce International (BCCI), which was established in 1972 and later became one of the largest banks worldwide, told a lesson on how a hardly penetrable network of holdings, subsidiaries, and branches in various corners of the globe may escape the effective supervision by national authorities. A reliable view of the entire group's operations only emerged after several national authorities had established a multinational 'college' of supervisor bodies and the Bank of England had conducted an investigation of possible fraud. In 1991, a concerted action of supervisory authorities closed the BCCI and its affiliates.[1]

Even more, the global financial crisis in the late 2000s highlighted the urgent need to strengthen international cooperation and to further harmonize standards for supervision.

The Basel Committee on Banking Supervision based at the Bank for International Settlements,[2] adopted a number of standards and principles for banking supervision and capital adequacy.

The Financial Stability Board (FSB), the successor of the Financial Stability Forum, was established in 2009 at the London Summit of the Group of Twenty (G20)

---

[1] R Dale, 'Banking Regulation after BCCI' (1993) 8 JIBL 8.   [2] See Ch XL.3.

to coordinate at the international level the work of national financial authorities and international standard setting bodies (SSBs) in order to develop and promote the implementation of effective regulatory, supervisory and other financial sector policies. In collaboration with the international financial institutions, the FSB will address vulnerabilities affecting financial systems in the interest of global financial stability (Article 1 of the FSB Charter).

The FSB secretariat is located at the Bank for International Settlements in Basel. According to Article 2(1) of the FSB Charter, the FSB shall

(a) assess vulnerabilities affecting the global financial system and identify and review on a timely and ongoing basis the regulatory, supervisory, and related actions needed to address them, and their outcomes;
(b) promote coordination and information exchange among authorities responsible for financial stability;
(c) monitor and advise on market developments and their implications for regulatory policy;
(d) advise on and monitor best practice in meeting regulatory standards;
(e) undertake joint strategic reviews of the policy development work of the international standard setting bodies to ensure their work is timely, coordinated, focused on priorities, and addressing gaps;
(f) set guidelines for and support the establishment of supervisory colleges;
(g) support contingency planning for cross-border crisis management, particularly with regard to systemically important firms;
(h) collaborate with the International Monetary Fund (IMF) to conduct Early Warning Exercises; and
(i) undertake any other tasks agreed by its Members in the course of its activities and within the framework of this Charter.

Among the FSB members are the members of the G20, for the European Union the European Central Bank and the European Commission, international financial institutions (the Bank for International Settlements, the IMF, the OECD, and the World Bank), and International Standard-Setting, Regulatory, Supervisory and Central Bank Bodies (such as the Basel Committee on Banking Supervision).

2. Supervisory Authorities and Macro-prudential Oversight of the Financial System

The Basel Concordat of 1975 (revised in 1983)[3] is a report of the Basel Committee on Banking Supervision on 'Principles for Supervision of Banks' Foreign Establishments' with recommendations of best practice as to the allocation of supervisory powers over banks with transnational activities. It distinguishes between supervision of solvency (measured by the capital, ie assets minus liabilities) and liquidity (ie a bank's financial ability to meet its obligations as they come due, with its readily available resources). According to the revised Basel Concordat,

---

[3] Committee on Banking Regulations and Supervisory Practices (1983) 22 ILM 901.

the supervisor of the parent corporation shall be primarily responsible for controlling the solvency of foreign branches, whilst subsidiaries shall be under joint supervision of parental authorities (consolidated supervision) and host authorities. Responsibility for supervising liquidity primarily lies with the supervisory authority of the host State, for legally separate subsidiaries as well as for branches. However, in supervising the liquidity of foreign establishments of a bank, host and parental authorities shall closely cooperate.

In the European Union, the so-called 'CRD IV package', which includes Directive 2013/36/EU[4] and Regulation (EU) No 575/2013[5], governs the cross-border activities of credit institutions and investment firms, prudential supervision, and implements the prudential standards of Basel III. The objective is a 'single-rule book' with a single set of harmonized prudential rules. Under Directive 2013/36/EU, the territorial allocation of prudential supervision of the foreign establishments of EU credit institutions follows authorization (Articles 33, 34, 49, and 155 of the Directive). Thus, prudential supervision by the home State (home or parental supervision) applies to foreign branches operating within the freedom of establishment in other Member States. However, host States retain supervision of the liquidity in cooperation with the home State (Article 156(1) of the Directive) and may implement monetary policies also against branches of foreign banks (Article 156(2) of the Directive). Subsidiaries are, as a rule, subject to supervision of the country in which they are established (host or local supervision). Thus, the organization of foreign establishments, either as a legally separate corporation or as a mere branch, becomes a crucial factor for supervisory powers. However, prudential supervision of credit institutions, which belong to a banking group, as to risk evaluation and risk management, shall be exercised on a consolidated basis by the home State of the parent company, in cooperation with the local authorities (Articles 111ff of the Directive).

In 2010, the European Union created a supranational supervisory structure, with three European supervisory authorities cooperating with their national counterparts in the supervision of the financial sectors (banking, insurance, and securities):

- the European Banking Authority (EBA);
- the European Insurance and Occupational Pensions Authority (EIOPA); and
- the European Securities and Markets Authority (ESA).[6]

---

[4] Directive 2013/36/EU of the European Parliament and of the Council of 26 June 2013 on access to the activity of credit institutions and the prudential supervision of credit institutions and investment firms, amending Directive 2002/87/EC and repealing Directives 2006/48/EC and 2006/49/EC of the European Parliament and of the Council [2013] OJ L176/338.
[5] Regulation (EU) No 575/2013 of the European Parliament and of the Council of 26 June 2013 on prudential requirements for credit institutions and investment firms and amending Regulation (EU) No 648/2012 of the European Parliament and of the Council of 4 July 2012 [2013] OJ L176/1.
[6] On the new EU supervisory system, see N Moloney, 'EU Financial Market Regulation after the Global Financial Crisis: "More Europe" or More Risk?' (2010) 47 CML Rev 1317; on the various models for banking supervision in the European Union, see M Herdegen, *Bankenaufsicht im Europäischen Verbund/Banking Supervision within the European Union* (De Gruyter 2010).

The European supervisory authorities shall contribute to common regulatory and supervisory standards and practices as well as to a consistent application of EU law, thus preventing regulatory arbitrage. The European Banking Authority has executive powers (eg settling disagreements between national authorities in cross-border situations, emergency measures), develops draft regulatory technical standards and implementing standards (to be endorsed by the Commission), and issues guidelines and recommendations.[7]

In context with the 'European Banking Union' the Single Supervisory Mechanism (SSM) was created. Regulation (EU) No 1024/2013[8] vests the European Central Bank with extensive powers of supervision over credit institutions within the Euro zone and other participating EU Member States. In particular, the European Central Bank exercises comprehensive control over major banks with systemic relevance whilst supervision of other banks, as a rule, remains with national banking authorities.

In addition, Directive 2014/59/EU[9] provides a framework for the recovery and resolution of credit institutions and certain investment firms. Regulation (EU) No 806/2014[10] creates a Single Resolution Mechanism (SRM) for institutions established in one of the Member States which participate in the SSM (Article 4). The Single Resolution Board (SRB), an Agency of the European Union, shall ensure that credit institutions which face a crisis and cannot be stabilized shall be resolved effectively and with minimal burdens for the taxpayer and the economy (Articles 2 and 42). The SRB adopts resolution plans for banks supervised by the European Central Bank and supervises implementation by national authorities (Articles 7, 8ff, 28ff). The SRB administers the Single Resolution Fund (SRF) which replaces the national resolution funds of participating States and shall be financed by contributions from the banking sector (Article 67ff).

Furthermore, Directive 2014/49/EU[11] establishes new standards for deposit guarantee schemes in the European Union.

---

[7] Articles 8ff of the Regulation (EU) No 1093/2010 establishing a European Supervisory Authority (European Banking Authority) [2010] OJ L331/12.

[8] Council Regulation (EU) No 1024/2013 of 15 October 2013 conferring specific tasks on the European Central Bank concerning policies relating to the prudential supervision of credit institutions [2013] OJ L287/63; it remains highly doubtful whether Article 127(6) TFEU provides a sufficient basis for this regulation.

[9] Directive 2014/59/EU of the European Parliament and of the Council of 15 May 2014 establishing a framework for the recovery and resolution of credit institutions and investment firms and amending Council Directive 82/891/EEC, and Directives 2001/24/EC, 2002/47/EC, 2004/25/EC, 2005/56/EC, 2007/36/EC, 2011/35/EU, 2012/30/EU, and 2013/36/EU, and Regulations (EU) No 1093/2010 and (EU) No 648/2012, of the European Parliament and of the Council [2014] OJ L173/190.

[10] Regulation (EU) No 806/2014 of the European Parliament and the Council of 15 July 2014 establishing uniform rules and a uniform procedure for the resolution of credit institutions and certain investment firms in the framework of a Single Resolution Mechanism and a Single Resolution Fund and amending Regulation (EU) No 1093/2010 [2014] OJ L225/1.

[11] Directive 2014/49/EU of the European Parliament and of the Council of 16 April 2014 on deposit guarantee schemes [2014] OJ L173/149.

For the macro-prudential oversight of the financial system of the European Union, the European Systemic Risk Board (ESRB) was established.[12] Members of its general board include the President and Vice-President of the European Central Bank, the governors of the national central banks, a member of the European Commission, the chairpersons of the three European Supervisory Authorities, and one representative per Member State of its competent supervisory authorities. Together with the three European Supervisory Authorities, their Joint Committee, and the supervisory authorities of the Member States, the ESRB forms the European System of Financial Supervisors (ESFS). In context with the financial crisis in the Eurozone, governments of Euro countries have agreed to establish a European Banking Union with a new architecture of banking supervision. According to different models under discussion, a unitary European banking supervision shall either lie with the European Central Bank, the European Banking Authority, or the European Stabilization Mechanism.

3. Global Regulatory Standards for Adequate Bank Capital and Risk Management: the Basel Accords

The Basel Committee on Banking Supervision formulated standards for an adequate capital base of banks and risk management, the so-called 'Basel Accords' (Basel I of 1988,[13] Basel II of 2004,[14] Basel III of 2011/12).[15] The Basel Accords reflect regulatory standards which are recognized worldwide. Although not legally binding, the Basel I Accord has been implemented by most countries. The ambitious and complex framework governs the domestic regulation in many States and is considered as a reference standard for a level playing field in international competition. This global recognition, de facto, vests the Basel Committee with a kind of supranational regulatory power.

Since Basel I, the Basel Accords are based on the widely shared assumption that the financial stability of a bank is very closely linked to its capital base. Experience with the break-down of the Herstatt Bank (Germany), the Banco Ambrosiano (Italy), or Continental Illinois (United States) corroborated this nexus. Subsequent Accords have further developed the standards of capital adequacy. Basel II and Basel III address other factors that have a bearing on a bank's stability.

---

[12] Regulation (EU) No 1092/2010 of the European Parliament and of the Council of 24 November 2010 on European Union macro-prudential oversight of the financial system and establishing a European Systemic Risk Board [2010] OJ L331/1.

[13] Basel Committee on Banking Supervision, *International Convergence of Capital Measurement and Capital Standards* (1988) <www.bis.org/publ/bcbs04a.pdf> (accessed 23 June 2016).

[14] Basel Committee on Banking Supervision, *International Convergence of Capital Measurement and Capital Standards, A Revised Framework* (Comprehensive Version 2006) <www.bis.org/publ/bcbs128.pdf> (accessed 23 June 2016).

[15] Basel Committee on Banking Supervision, *Basel III: The Liquidity Coverage Ratio and Liquidity risk Monitoring Tools* (2013) <www.bis.org/publ/bcbs238.pdf> (accessed 23 June 2016); Basel Committee on Banking Supervision, *Basel III: A global regulatory framework for more resilient banks and banking systems* (2010, revised 2011) <www.bis.org/publ/bcbs189.pdf> (accessed 23 June 2016).

Under Basel I (and Basel II), credit institutions must have a minimum capital base of 8 per cent of the risk-weighted assets (overall lending volume). Basel I distinguishes between different classes of capital covering market risk: Tier 1, that is primary or core capital (shareholders' equity in common stock of the bank or bank holding company and retained earnings), Tier 2, that is supplementary capital, and finally Tier 3 (short-term subordinated debt covering market risk). Claims against OECD countries were assigned a risk weight of 0 per cent.

The Basel II Accord provides a more nuanced risk assessment, according to the different degrees of credit exposure and the individual risk profile of borrowers. Banks may opt between different methodologies for calculating the credit risk for the purposes of capital requirements, the standardized approach relying on external ratings, or an internal ratings-based approach (with two variations). Under the standardized risk weighting, for example of claims against sovereign borrowers, the determinations of rating agencies are crucial. The regulatory system of Basel II[16] rests on three 'pillars':

- minimum capital requirements according to the quality of the borrower;
- a supervisory review process with internal and external mechanisms; and
- market discipline, relying on a number of disclosure requirements enabling market participants to assess the adequacy of the capital base.

The European Union and most States with an important banking sector have fully or essentially implemented Basel II. In the United States, the adjustment of the regulatory framework to Basel II has been a protracted and contentious process. In contrast to the European Union, US implementation of Basel II is binding only upon large and internationally active 'core banks'.

The international financial crisis of 2007–08, fuelled by a misleading rating of certain borrowers and of instruments with a high credit risk (such as securitized subprime mortgages), revealed some structural defects in the architecture of Basel II and made the management of liquidity risk a salient issue of bank resilience in a deteriorating environment. Despite an adequate capital base, a number of banks had entered into problems of liquidity.

The rules of Basel III[17] are based on the three pillars of Basel II. They tighten the standards for the quality of the capital base. The predominant form of Tier 1 capital ('core tier') shall be common shares issued by the bank and retained earnings. The Tier 1 capital must be at least 6 per cent of risk-weighted assets at all times. Tier 3 capital shall be abolished. New mechanisms shall ensure that all counterparty credit risks are reflected in the capital framework. A leverage ratio shall supplement the

---

[16] Basel Committee on Banking Supervision, *International Convergence of Capital Measurement and Capital Standards, A Revised Framework*; Bernd Engelmann and Robert Rauhmeier (eds), *The Basel II Risk Parameters: Estimation, Validation, Stress Testing—with Applications to Loan Risk Management* (2nd edn, Springer 2011).

[17] Basel Committee on Banking Supervision, *Basel III*; Simon Gleeson, *International Regulation of Banking* (2nd edn, OUP 2012).

risk-based framework and constrain the build-up of leverage in the banking sector. Counter-cyclical buffers, built up in periods of growth, shall stabilize banks in a downturn. Important innovations relate to short-term and medium-term resilience to liquidity shocks. The 'liquidity coverage ratio' shall ensure that banks have sufficient high quality assets to cope with a stress scenario of 30 days. The 'net stable funding ratio' shall provide a sustainable maturity of assets and liabilities. The process of gradual implementation of the rules of Basel III shall be concluded in 2019.

Select Bibliography

M Giovanoli and D Devos (eds), *International and Financial Law. The Global Crisis* (OUP 2010).

M Herdegen, *Bankenaufsicht im Europäischen Verbund/Banking Supervision within the European Union* (De Gruyter 2010).

R Lastra, *International Financial and Monetary Law* (2nd edn, OUP 2015).

A McKnight, *The Law of International Finance* (OUP 2008).

N Moloney, E Ferran, and J Payne (eds), *The Oxford Handbook of Financial Regulation* (OUP 2015).

L Quaglia, *The European Union and Global Financial Regulation* (OUP 2014).

HS Scott and A Gelpern, *International Finance: Law and Regulation* (3rd edn, Sweet & Maxwell 2012).

Index